Prof. A. B. Gardner
from ...

Nov. 12. 1876

Engᵈ by A H Ritchie

*Yours True,*
*Marshall Lefferts*

# HISTORY

OF THE

# Seventh Regiment, National Guard,

STATE OF NEW YORK,

## DURING THE WAR OF THE REBELLION:

WITH

A PRELIMINARY CHAPTER ON THE ORIGIN AND EARLY HISTORY OF THE REGIMENT, A SUMMARY OF ITS HISTORY SINCE THE WAR,

AND A

## ROLL OF HONOR,

COMPRISING BRIEF SKETCHES OF THE SERVICES RENDERED BY MEMBERS OF THE REGIMENT IN THE ARMY AND NAVY OF THE UNITED STATES.

By WILLIAM SWINTON, A. M.,
AUTHOR OF "CAMPAIGNS OF THE ARMY OF THE POTOMAC," ETC.

*ILLUSTRATED BY THOMAS NAST.*

New York and Boston:
FIELDS, OSGOOD, & CO.
1870.

University Press: Welch, Bigelow, & Co.,
Cambridge.

# CONTENTS.

# HISTORY OF THE SEVENTH REGIMENT.

## CHAPTER I.

### ORIGIN OF THE SEVENTH REGIMENT.

IN the southerly corner of Fulton and Nassau Streets, in the city of New York, there stood, half a century ago, the famous Stoneall's "Shakespeare Tavern." To that favorite hostelry, as a birthplace, can be traced more than one of the institutions and societies now flourishing in the New York of our day; and thither we must go back some twoscore years for the origin of the "Seventh Regiment New York State National Guard."

In one view, we should resort to a still earlier period in the history of the State and of the Republic to find the fountain-head of the Seventh Regiment. For, since this corps was fashioned, not out of new material, but out of a militia organization already existing, — to wit, the "Eleventh Regiment of Artillery," — it would be necessary, in like manner, to trace this "Eleventh" to the year of its creation, namely, the year 1812; while, pursuing the pedigree of the "Eleventh" itself, we should, erelong, find ourselves among the military antiquities of the bygone century and the wȧr of the Revolution.

Such genealogic researches are aside from our present purpose. Suffice it to say that, in the year 1824, there existed a so-called "Eleventh Regiment of New York State Artillery," and that this regiment consisted, as did most of the militia regiments of that day, of two battalions; whereof one was artillery proper, the other infantry. Of the four infantry companies, the First was commanded by Captain Irad Hawley, the Second by Captain John Telfair, the Third by Captain William B. Curtis, and the Fourth by Captain Howard A. Simons.

Now, on the evening of the 25th of August, 1824, the officers of the four companies of the Infantry Battalion of the old Eleventh Regiment, at a meeting held at the Shakespeare Tavern, adopted a resolution to the effect that the said battalion "be hereafter known and distinguished by the name of National Guards." The origin of this name, for so many years the worthy designation of the Seventh Regiment, and of that organization *exclusively*, is associated with a historic event of singular interest. A few days previous to the above-mentioned meeting (namely, the 16th of August, 1824), there had occurred a parade of the New York militia for the reception of La Fayette on his last visit to this country. On this occasion the illustrious soldier and patriot reviewed the forces at the Battery. While the troops were awaiting the arrival of La Fayette, a number of the officers of the Eleventh had gathered together, and the conversation chanced to turn on a project which had long engaged their attention, to wit, the independent organization of the Infantry Battalion. It happened that a good deal of difficulty had been experienced regarding the choice of a suitable name. On this occasion reference was made, by some one present, to La Fayette's connection with the Paris National Guard, when immediately Major John D. Wilson asked why "National Guards" would not be a good name for the proposed corps? This electric utterance at once crystallized their desires in a fixed purpose and on a clear ideal; and when, therefore, a few days later, the gathering at the Shakespeare occurred, the resolution to adopt the designation of "National Guards" was enthusiastically passed. Its promulgation was received by the members of the corps with general favor.

It remained to secure the permission and co-operation of the governor, *ex officio* commander of the State militia. The official documents requisite to the perfect organization of the corps, and its recognition as an independent unit in the militia force of the State, did not arrive until the year following the adoption of the name of the National Guards. But, meanwhile, its members were not idle, and the drills were kept up with marked regularity. Moreover, the first great step towards the completion of the battalion was taken in the adoption, on the 30th of August, of the famous gray uniform. Its design was taken from the neatly fitting, single-breasted gray office-coat of Philetus H. Holt (then a private in the Fourth Company), which attracted the attention of Captain Prosper M. Wetmore, Acting Brigade-Major, and Major John D. Wilson, as a suitable model for the new uniform. It was proposed, and a pattern suit complete was exhibited by Major Wilson to the four companies, separately assembled at the Shakespeare, and was agreed to by the members with great unanimity. A coat of arms and motto were designed by Corporal Asher Taylor, of the Fourth Company, who has ever since held honored connection with the regiment, and whose *esprit de corps* and enthusiasm in all that concerns the Seventh and its welfare five-and-forty years have not been able to quench. The coat of arms and motto were approved by the board of officers and adopted as the heraldic insignia of the corps. It was Asher Taylor, also, who first wore in public the gray uniform.

More important still, to the original four companies of the battalion were presently added two more, under Captains Lownds and Stevens. The interest taken by these gentlemen in the new organization began with the inspiring incident of the La Fayette review, already detailed. On that occasion the group of officers was joined by Oliver M. Lownds, Esq., a popular and influential citizen, and it was proposed to him that he should raise a company to add to the others in forming the National Guard. The proposition was made by Linus W. Stevens, who then commanded a company in the first or artillery battalion of the Eleventh, and who, "being dissatisfied with the treatment of officials, who had neglected to provide his company with guns for artillery practice," had purposed retiring from the militia service, but was now resolved to accept a commission in the new organization. With the spirit of generous rivalry that characterized the founders of the corps, Captain Stevens agreed to waive the right of his own company to the number "5" in the regiment, and to come in as number "6," leaving "5" to the company to be raised by Mr. Lownds.

Such was the personal popularity of the latter gentleman that he soon succeeded in enrolling the required number; and, on the 25th of December of the same year, he presented his company as a Christmas gift to the National Guards. It was admitted as the Fifth Company, and, being composed of picked men, was a valuable and welcome addition to the corps. Captain Stevens was allowed to select twenty-four of the best men and one officer (Lieutenant J. H. Williams) from his old company of the artillery battalion. Two days after the admission of Captain Lownds's company, they came in as the Sixth Company.

At length, on the 27th of June, 1825, an order was issued by the Commander-in-Chief, Governor De Witt Clinton, instituting the battalion of the National Guards. This liberated the corps from the heterogeneous association with the artillery battalion, but the change actually made did not prove satisfactory. The order separating the battalion from the Eleventh Regiment of Artillery directed its consolidation with the infantry companies of the Second Regiment. This arrangement was not a happy one. Difficulties very soon arose, and such ill-feeling was engendered on both sides that the National Guard determined to part company with its associates. Accordingly, representations of so forcible a character were made at head-quarters, that, in the following October (1825), a general order was issued detaching the corps and organizing it into a separate battalion. Having now legal existence as a battalion, it was entitled to a Lieutenant-Colonel and a Major. On the 18th of October a meeting was held for the election of these officers, which resulted in the unanimous choice of Prosper M. Wetmore as Lieutenant-Colonel and Linus W. Stevens as Major. To the six companies already mentioned had been added, in October, another, — the Seventh, — under Captain Van Buren. It now required but one more company to raise the battalion to the dignity of a regiment, — a consummation devoutly wished by all its members. Accordingly, on the 10th of April following, the Commandant detailed the following gentlemen to organize the new company: Lieutenant Andrew Warner, of Seventh Company, to be Captain; William H. Insley, First Lieutenant; and William P. Millard, Second Lieutenant. With such spirit and energy did these officers enter into this duty, that, on the 4th of May, the requisite number was enrolled and the new company admitted to the battalion as the Eighth Company of the National Guard. Being informed of this, Governor De Witt Clinton, two days later, — namely, the 6th of May, 1826, — issued an order organizing the battalion into a regiment, to be named the "Twenty-Seventh Regiment of Artillery."

So much of mere dry chronology it has been necessary here to group together, that we may the better grasp the successive steps through which the National Guard became a regiment, and laid the broad basis of its historic fame.

If, now, we hold firmly by the noble appellation National Guard, it will prevent our becoming confused in the varying technical designations of the corps. We have seen the memorable circumstances under which the name was chosen. Well, it was the National Guard while still incorporated with the old Eleventh Artillery; it was the National Guard while consolidated with the Second Regiment; and it was still the National Guard now that it became independent, and was dubbed the "Twenty-Seventh Regiment." When, years later, it had become the "Seventh," it still held its proud blazon of National Guard. Nor was it ever till the Legislature, in 1862, filching from the corps its "good name," gave this designation to all the militia of the State, that the Seventh ceased to be *the* National Guard. Nevertheless, if we shall succeed in at all fitly setting forth the history of this regiment in the late war, it may appear by what new and multiplied titles it has acquired the right of retaining the baptismal name which hallowed its birth two-score years and more ago.

The regiment having now attained separate identity, it remained to choose its officers. To this end the Commandant, on the 16th of May, 1826, issued the first "Regimental Order," appointing the 23d of the same month for the election. Pursuant to this order the officers met at the Shakespeare; and the result was the choice of Prosper M. Wetmore as Colonel, Linus W. Stevens as Lieutenant-Colonel, and John Telfair as Major.

The selection of these officers gave general satisfaction,

and their promotion was designed as a tribute of respect and appreciation on the part of the regiment. Colonel Prosper M. Wetmore had formerly been Captain of the Fourth Company, and at the time our history opens he was Brigade-Major of Brigadier-General Benedict's staff. He had entered very warmly into the project for the organization of the National Guard, and was indefatigable in promoting the growth and welfare of the corps. He retained his position as Colonel for about a year, and resigned in April, 1827. Lieutenant-Colonel Stevens was, as has already appeared, one of the National Guard's early and most steadfast friends ; and we shall presently have occasion to refer to the relations of that able and accomplished officer with the regiment he loved and adorned. Major Telfair is equally entitled to the honor of being one of the founders of the Seventh Regiment. He had passed through all the grades of the service; was a sergeant during the war of 1812, a lieutenant of the Second Company of the old Eleventh Regiment in 1820, and its captain in 1823. He had declined the majority at the previous election in 1825, and only accepted it now at the urgent solicitation of Colonel Wetmore. As it was, he did not hold his commission long, for he resigned on the 20th of June following, and Howard A. Simons was elected in his stead. He was greatly beloved by the Second Company, and in 1833 he was induced to resume its captaincy, from which he finally retired in 1836. Telfair is one of the noblest names in the bead-roll of the regiment, on which he lavished his affections and his fortune.

The National Guard paraded for the first time as a regiment on the 31st of May, 1826, to receive an elegant stand of colors from the Mayor of New York. Asher Taylor, in his interesting "Notes on the Colors of the National Guard," gives the following agreeable account of the origin of these colors: "When the corps was detached as a separate command, the subject of providing suitable colors for it had engaged the early attention of the board of officers; and Captain John Telfair, Captain James T. Flinn, Lieutenant Charles B. Spicer, Adjutant Andrew Warner, and Surgeon Edward P. Marcellin were appointed a committee to procure a standard which should be the banner of the National Guard. The committee spent some time in bowing around and flirting and coquetting among their fair friends, in the hope of eliciting an offer from some of them to embroider and present a standard; and Young Moustache will be amazed to learn that all their efforts were in vain, as they reported (March 29, 1826) that '*the expectations hitherto entertained on that subject had not been realized*,' — a humiliating admission that would wellnigh 'burst the kids' of half the gallant and irresistible fellows of the regiment in the present day. Subscription papers for the requisite funds were circulated through the ranks of the corps, and promptly filled up; and the committee adopted designs for the colors, devised and prepared by Sergeant Asher Taylor. They consisted of, first, a regimental standard, 'the banner of the National Guard,' of red silk, bearing the arms of the corps on a shield, supported by wreaths of oak and laurel, with the crest, an eagle, and the motto, '*Pro Patria et Gloria*'; second, a State standard of blue silk. The designs were traced on silk by Sergeant Taylor, and embroidered very beautifully, in natural colors, under his supervision, by Mrs. Windsor."

It was upon the occasion of the presentation of the first of these, the regimental standard, that the regiment made its maiden parade. The Hon. Philip Hone, Mayor of the city, in presence of a brilliant assemblage, delivered the standard with an eloquent address. The State standard was presented on the 4th of July following, on which occasion the semi-centennial anniversary of American Independence was celebrated with immense pomp and circumstance. The presentation took place in Castle Garden, where "a large collection of distinguished officers had assembled around the illustrious De Witt Clinton, the Governor of the State," who delivered the standard to Colonel Wetmore, accompanied by a glowing eulogy, to which the Commandant replied in fitting terms. On the conclusion of the military ceremonies, the Governor and Mayor, with their suites, and the officers of the division, repaired to Washington Parade-Ground, where a public feast had been prepared by the city corporation. "Immense awnings," says the annalist, "were erected, beneath which two tables, each four hundred and fifty feet long, groaned under vast quantities of substantial viands"; and we catch the vision of a quite Homeric banquet, at which were "two oxen, roasted whole, two hundred hams, immense piles of bread, innumerable barrels of beer," and the like hearty provant.

Meanwhile, amid these festivities, the weightier matters of drill and discipline were not neglected. Hitherto, it is said, too little attention had been devoted to military instruction; and the want of proficiency in the manual of arms is illustrated by the fact that at a *feu de joie* in the Park, the previous year, a member of the Second Company discharged the rammer from his musket, to the great terror and consternation of the numerous spectators. During the winter of 1825-26, Congress adopted a new system of tactics, known as "Scott's Tactics." The United States Army having been ordered to drill in the new system, it was immediately adopted by the more intelligent and ambitious militia organizations; and the National Guard promptly commenced its study and practice. To complete our chronology of the year 1826, we may add, that on the 18th of October the annual inspection and review of the National Guard took place at the Battery, — present, 277; total, present and absent, 437. On the 13th of November, there was a brigade field-day at Brooklyn Heights, and the annual parade took place on the 25th of November.

It has already been mentioned that the resignation of Colonel Wetmore took place in 1827. Lieutenant-Colonel Linus W. Stevens was then promoted to the colonelcy. In this gentleman the National Guard gained a Commandant of superior merit, and one who infused into it a rare activity and spirit; but, unfortunately, the regiment, a year later, lost this able officer by his resignation in July, 1828. On the retirement of Colonel Stevens, Lieutenant-Colonel Manning was promoted to the colonelcy, and Captain Levi Hart was elected Lieutenant-Colonel. The regiment never paraded under Colonel Manning, as he resigned his commission in September, 1828. Ex-Colonel Stevens was unanimously elected Colonel, but positively declined the office, and Lieutenant-Colonel Hart was then promoted to the colonelcy. In January, 1830, Colonel Hart resigned his commission, and ex-Colonel Stevens, at the unanimous and urgent request of the line officers of the regiment, accepted the colonelcy. Upon his recommendation, Morgan L. Smith was elected Lieutenant-Colonel, and John M. Catlin, Major. The return of Colonel Stevens to the command of the regiment revived its fortunes at once.

In perusing the annals of the regiment during the year 1830, we note that the usual number of drills and parades took place and were well attended. One of the parades (November 26th) was in honor of the French Revolution of that year, which resulted in the elevation of Louis Philippe to the throne. The annual inspection and review took place on the 26th of October at the Battery. Total present, 360; present and absent, 472. The following year, 1831, the regiment was active and prosperous, and performed an unusual amount of military duty.

It was during this latter year that the regiment made its first encampment. This took place at Poughkeepsie, and the camp was named Camp Clinton. The members, to the number of two hundred and fifty-six, were conveyed by boat, under the management of Quartermaster Sniffen, and remained at Poughkeepsie from the 2d to the 5th of July, amid varied duties and festivities. The experiment was so complete a success that it was repeated the following year (Camp Putnam), and often in the subsequent history of the regiment.

In 1834 the regiment was called upon for the first time to quell a riot in the city, — a duty which on many memorable after-occasions fell to its lot. The trouble in this case grew out of the bitter hostilities existing between the Whigs and Democrats at the election in the spring of 1834. The civil authorities attempted to stop the disturbance, but were powerless. Finally the Whigs took possession of the Arsenal, and the Mayor, having learned this fact, ordered out the National Guard. The regiment assembled promptly, and within two hours after the order was issued three hundred of its members were guarding the Arsenal and patrolling the adjoining streets. The regiment continued on duty until the next morning, when, the canvass having been completed and the excitement having subsided, it was dismissed with the thanks of the Mayor. In July of this same year a similar duty devolved upon the National Guard, it being called upon to quell the "Abolition riots," in which a number of buildings, including three churches, were sacked by the mob. The regiment on this trying occasion behaved with an admirable mingling of firmness and forbearance, that won for it the warmest praise from all good citizens. The riots began on the 9th, and culminated on the 11th. On the evening of the latter day, the Twenty-Seventh Regiment was called upon by the Mayor to march to Spring Street, where the churches of Drs. Ludlow and Cox had been sacked by the mob, who were intrenched in great force behind barricades, and had already dispersed a body of cavalry. It lacked but an hour of midnight when the Guard, under Colonel Stevens, took up its march from the City Hall, where it had been stationed by the authorities. A great mob followed it; and at the corner of Spring and Sullivan Streets it received a galling fire of stones and other missiles, hurled from windows and housetops, which wounded many of the troops. Clearing a path through the barricades, the regiment moved forward in column by division, at half distance, and drove the rioters to the intersection of Spring and Varick Streets, where, halting, it formed square, dividing the mob suddenly in all directions, and so ending the affair. "The National Guard was charged," said Mayor Lawrence, in his message to the Common Council, "with the duty of removing the rioters from a section of the city where the most violent outrages had been committed, and, in the performance of this service, while assailed by the missiles of the mob, evinced a forbearance commendable in the citizen, united with a determination which belongs to the character of the soldier."

In December, 1834, Colonel Stevens resigned his commission. Lieutenant-Colonel Smith was elected Colonel; Major Catlin, Lieutenant-Colonel; and Captain Roome, Major. The retirement of that able and accomplished officer was a matter of general regret. Many years later he was familiarly known as "the Father of the National Guard," — a title which he had fairly earned by constant devotion to its best interests. We shall in the sequel see that affection for the corps never ceased to animate the breast of Colonel Stevens, and that even during the war, as a member of the Veterans, he was active in its welfare. This estimable gentleman died in 1863.

The memories of the veteran members will go back to these years in many pleasing recollections. There were target excursions to Ponson's, and competitive drills, and a general spirit of joyous activity. In the year 1835 the Order of Merit was established, and competitive drills for its honors were instituted. In the first drill which took place the contest was chiefly between the Seventh Company, Captain Cairns, and the Eighth Company, under Lieutenant Shumway. The honors were carried off by the former. In the following year the contest was renewed, and again the leading rivals were the Seventh and Eighth Companies. But this time the judges awarded the palm to Shumway's company, — a result which so chagrined Captain Cairns that he withdrew from the regiment, taking with him a large part of his company. This led to such bitterness of feeling, that, finally, the Order of Merit was abolished altogether.

In the summer of 1837, Colonel Smith and Major Roome resigned their commissions. Lieutenant-Colonel Catlin was elected Colonel; Captain Jones, Lieutenant-Colonel; and Captain Burt, Major. In March, 1838, a troop of horse was organized and attached to the regiment.

It is worthy of note that at this period a movement was set on foot by the National Guard to obtain drill-rooms from the city corporation. This movement was finally successful in 1839, when the rooms over Centre Market were granted to the militia of New York for military purposes.

In March, 1839, Major Burt resigned his commission, and E. T. Backhouse was elected his successor. In the latter part of the year, Colonel Catlin resigned, and Lieutenant-Colonel Jones was elected Colonel; Major Backhouse, Lieutenant-Colonel; and Captain W. R. Vermilye, Major. In May, 1843, Lieutenant-Colonel Backhouse resigned, and Major Vermilye was elected Lieutenant-Colonel, and Captain George G. Waters, Major. In April, 1844, Lieutenant-Colonel Vermilye was elected Colonel; Major Waters, Lieutenant-Colonel; and Captain Andrew A. Bremner was promoted to the majority. In May, 1845, Lieutenant-Colonel Waters resigned, and, in June, Major Bremner was promoted to the lieutenant-colonelcy; in September, Captain Duryee, of the Second Company, was elected Major. Colonel Vermilye resigned in August; and, in November, Lieutenant-Colonel Bremner was elected Colonel; Major Duryee, Lieutenant-Colonel; and Adjutant Divver, Major."

And now we come to another great historic epoch in the annals of the regiment. On the 27th of July, 1847, Governor Young ordered the "Twenty-Seventh Regiment of Artillery (National Guard), under the command of Colonel Bremner, to be hereafter called and known as the *Seventh* Regiment New York State Militia."

In May, 1847, Major Divver resigned his commission, to serve as an officer in the United States Army in Mexico. Captain A. B. Brinckerhoff took his place. In October, 1848, Colonel Bremner, an energetic, accomplished, and popular officer, resigned his commission. Lieutenant-Colonel Duryee was, in January, 1849, elected Colonel; Major Brinckerhoff, Lieutenant-Colonel; and Captain Morton, Major. Soon after, an engineer corps was organized, which subsequently formed the nucleus of a howitzer company, and, still later, of the Tenth (K) Company.

With this bald chronology let us take leave of the five-and-twenty years preceding 1849; for, though the annals of the regiment contain many interesting records of this period, we must forbear even the briefest mention of them. Dismissing these, therefore, we are brought at length to that important chapter in the history of the National Guard, — the Astor Place riots.

It does not come within the scope of the present work to enter with any fulness of detail into the story of this notable affair; and, indeed, the general facts are too familiar to render this necessary. It is well known that the trouble originated chiefly with some friends of Mr. Forrest, the American tragedian, whose unfavorable reception in

England was partly attributed by them to the intrigue of Mr. Macready. In the winter of 1848–49, Mr. Macready made his farewell visit to the United States, and the friends of Mr. Forrest determined to seize on that occasion to avenge him. Macready's first engagement was tranquil enough; but on the evening of the 7th of May, his first appearance in his second engagement at the Astor Place Opera House, he was driven from the stage by a mob. On the 10th another attempt was made to secure him a hearing, and it was this that precipitated the famous riot. On the evening in question, fully twenty thousand men and boys, the dregs of the city, gathered, by previous concert, around the theatre, armed with stones, sticks, and pistols. It so chanced that the pavement in Broadway had been raised for the purpose of repairing the sewers, and the round paving-stones furnished to the mob an arsenal of terrible ammunition. Three hundred police were driven back, after a gallant struggle to disperse them; and at length Colonel Duryee, who had, in pursuance of General Sandford's orders, held the Seventh Regiment ready at Centre Market, was ordered up. At 9 P. M. the regiment arrived at Astor Place, preceded by the National Guard Troop and a company of cavalry. The mounted men, ten abreast, charged through the place from Broadway; but their horses, galled by the fire of the mob, became unmanageable, and they reached Third Avenue, having accomplished nothing. The Seventh Regiment then followed, in column of platoons, headed by Colonel Duryee, clearing a way to Third Avenue; thence, in column of companies, clearing Eighth Street, and, finally, again moving through Broadway into Astor Place, and forming line in front of the theatre. The volleys of stones from the mob there became very severe; but the regiment preserved its magnificent discipline under the trying ordeal.

General Sandford, the division commander, gave orders

to wheel half the regiment to the right and the other half to the left, in order to divide and drive the mob; but the attempt was unsuccessful, and many officers and men, including Generals Sandford and Hall, Colonel Duryee, and Captains Shumway and Pond, were wounded. An effort to use the bayonet was also unsuccessful, the mob crowding so as not to allow free formation or use of the pieces. At length the authority to fire, which General Hall had long been unsuccessfully begging of the Mayor, was given by Sheriff Westervelt, after a final warning to the mob by Recorder Tallmadge. The first volley was purposely aimed high; the second was point-blank, and was delivered with terrible effect; and, pressing hard on the flying mob, the troops soon cleared Astor Place of rioters. In La Fayette Place and Eighth Street the leaders rallied the rabble once more, and returned to the attack; but a third volley scattered them completely, and ended the Astor Place riot.

The next day the city was very disorderly, but a large military and police force kept down all dangerous disturbance. The Seventh was on duty the three days following, but the lesson it had already given the mob proved effectual. Twenty of the rioters were thought to be killed or mortally wounded, and fifty or sixty were more or less severely wounded; of the regiment, over one hundred and fifty officers and men were seriously injured, of whom seventy were carried to their homes. All, however, recovered, and to this day many show the honorable wounds of Astor Place.

From that eventful night dates, perhaps, the civic popularity and national prestige of the Seventh Regiment. Its courage, promptness, discipline, and steadiness were long the theme of conversation, and no honors of city or citizens were thought too high to be paid to these trustworthy guardians of law and order. The Arsenal riots in 1834, the Abolition riots in the same year, the stevedore riots of

1836 and 1852, the flour riots of 1837, the Croton Works riots in 1840, the Astor Place riots in 1849, the Mayor Wood, Mackerelville, and Sixth Ward riots of 1857, the quarantine riot in 1859, and the draft riots of 1863, bear witness that this public confidence has not been misplaced.

In 1850 Colonel Duryee, always untiring in his efforts to improve the regiment, established evening battalion drills, and the next year "drills by wing." In February, 1851, Marshall Lefferts, who had the year before entered the regiment as a private, but who had for three years previous been a member of General Hall's brigade staff, was elected Major. In June, 1852, Major Lefferts was chosen Lieutenant-Colonel of the regiment. In December, 1854, the board of officers began the movement which resulted in giving the regiment the Tompkins Market Armory. On May 1, 1856, Edgar M. Crawford was elected Major.

In June, 1857, the regiment acceded to a request to visit Boston and participate in the Bunker Hill Monument celebration of that year. Nothing can well describe the astonishment and admiration which its appearance on that occasion created.

In July, 1858, the regiment was selected to escort the remains of President Monroe from New York to Virginia. Colonel August, who officially welcomed the regiment to Virginia, said: "The fame of your gallant corps is coextensive with the broad limits of this Union, and the name of National Guard is the synonyme of model citizen soldier." Colonel Carey pronounced it "the first corps of the nation, — always known to the country, and to-day endeared to Virginia." Many pages of such eulogy could be cited, but Mr. Udolpho Wolfe's volume on the Richmond excursion leaves nothing to be added.

The 9th of May, 1859, is also an historic day in the annals of the regiment. It was then that the famous association of the exempt members of the Seventh Regiment was organized, called the "Veterans of the National Guard," subsequently incorporated by the Legislature of New York. Its objects are, "1st, To institute a bond of fellowship and union between former and present companions in arms; 2d, To institute and perpetuate an official record and registry of the origin, acts, and members of the Seventh Regiment; and 3d, To create a fund for useful and benevolent purposes."

In July, 1859, Colonel Duryee, one of the ablest, most earnest, and most valuable commanders that had ever graced the head of the regiment, and in all respects a consummate soldier, after twenty-one years' service resigned his commission. Under his care the regiment had reached an unprecedented degree of perfection and celebrity, and his name will always be spoken of with gratitude and respect by the National Guard. In August, Lieutenant-Colonel Lefferts was elected Colonel; Major Edgar M. Crawford, Lieutenant-Colonel; and Adjutant William A. Pond, Major.

On the 29th of March, 1860, a new company was organized on the basis of the Engineer Corps. E. L. Viele was designated as Captain, G. L. Farrar as First Lieutenant, and E. M. Le Moyne as Second Lieutenant. The order from head-quarters prescribed that "this company will serve with prairie howitzers when so ordered," and also that "it will be designated by the letter K." In December following, Major Pond was elected Lieutenant-Colonel, and Captain Shaler was elected Major.

To other hands must be left the task of following in detail the regimental annals of the six-and-thirty years that preceded the Rebellion, — its regular civic parades, inspections, drills, and reviews, division, brigade, and regimental; its famous camps, Clinton, Putnam, Hamilton, Schuyler, Trumbull, Scott; its grand excursions to Boston, Bunker Hill, Mount Vernon, Newport, Richmond, West Point,

Washington; its return courtesies to military corps visiting the city, and to distinguished visitors in whose honor the city authorities have always exhibited the Seventh with so much pride; its receptions of such famous civic guests as Jackson, Tyler, Polk, Scott, and as La Fayette, Kossuth, and, later, the Japanese ambassadors, the Russian officers, and the Prince of Wales; its celebrations of public events, like the completion of the Erie Canal, of the Croton Water Works, of the Crystal Palace, and of the Atlantic Cable; its part in public obsequies, like those of Presidents Adams, Jefferson, Monroe, J. Q. Adams, Jackson, Harrison, Taylor, and those of La Fayette, Clay, Webster, Worth; or its regimental benefactions, charities, and subscriptions to private or public enterprises, to be reckoned by hundreds of thousands of dollars.

When the Clark Mills equestrian statue of Washington was unveiled at the National Capitol in 1860, the presence of the Seventh was asked for by Congress and accorded. The President of the United States, Mr. Buchanan, thanked the regiment in a very earnest and elaborate speech, of which one memorable paragraph was: "The military precision in your march, the admirable manner in which you go through your exercise, and the stout, hardy, noble, and defiant look which you exhibit, show that in the day and hour of battle you would not be mere parade soldiers, but that you would be in its very front." At the Prince of Wales celebration, in October, 1860, the Prince said to General Sandford, regarding the Seventh: "It is the finest regiment I have ever seen in any country." Lord Lyons and General Bruce used similar expressions then and afterwards. An able article in the "London United Service Magazine," the same month, devoted entirely to a discussion of the "world-renowned Seventh Regiment of New York," says: "The Seventh Regiment has unceasingly devoted itself to the attainment of military excellence, and I will venture to say that the civilized world does not possess a finer corps, in every sense of the term. Judging from the opportunities of comparison which a life spent among European and Asiatic armies has given me, I should say that no troops in the world can march, fire, and go through the ordinary operations of a field-day with more precision than the National Guard." The Toronto "Globe" declared, at the same time: "In return for the hospitality extended to the Prince of Wales, the Seventh Regiment — the crack corps of the Union — should visit Great Britain. There is no infantry regiment in the world whose drill is more perfect, or which presents a more splendid appearance."

When Camp Scott was founded, in 1860, the Colonel of the regiment received the following letter from Lieutenant-General Scott: —

West Point, July 7, 1860.

Dear Sir, — Being temporarily lame, I pray you to pardon me for declining the invitation to visit your regiment on Staten Island, which has done me the honor to call its camp of instruction by my name, and I have long honored the noble corps. It has well earned the title of the National Guard at Richmond, at Boston, and at Washington, as on frequent occasions at home, where I do not think it too much to say that law and order, the life and property of every citizen, depend, in the last resort, on the high moral tone, the steady valor and discipline, of the Seventh Regiment of New York Volunteers.

With high respect I remain, my dear Colonel,

Yours truly,

Winfield Scott.

To Colonel Lefferts, *National Guard.*

The same year, Stephen A. Douglas, then candidate for the Presidency, pithily described the Seventh, in a public letter, as "that unrivalled regiment of citizen soldiers."

The Seventh Regiment was often invited to other cities for the purpose of stirring up local ambition in volunteer troops. The regimental letter-books show that in all parts of the country regiments took it as a model. Some called themselves its "namesakes," using the famous title "National Guard"; very many copied its "bill of dress," the familiar "gray with black trimmings"; scores of regiments, new and old, adopted the various company by-laws and by-laws of council; questions of drill, discipline, and organization were sent from all parts of the country to its commanding officer as umpire; even the insignia and coat of arms were in some cases copied; and these tributes came not only from the seaboard States, but even from as far west as Illinois and Iowa. Ellsworth, in speaking at a public dinner of his alert and excellent company of Zouaves, said: "When my comrades here did me the honor to call upon me to take command of them, I set before myself and them the Seventh Regiment as our model. This is the secret of our success."

On the 5th of September, 1860, Robert Ould, United States Attorney for the District of Columbia (afterwards a well-known Confederate officer), presented to the regiment from the corporation of the city of Washington a splendid stand of colors, the most elegant and costly ever given to the Seventh Regiment. Mr. Ould's eloquent address was full of good Union sentiments, and the flag he handed to Colonel Lefferts was carried by the regiment, a few months later, to the rescue of the city that gave it. The same day was made illustrious by another grand presentation, made by the corporation of another famous city, — the formal transfer to the regiment of the Tompkins Market Armory, the most splendid building for this purpose in the world. "It is doubtful," said Mayor Wood, in his address on that occasion, "whether this elegant structure, so creditable to the city, would ever have been erected, but for the regiment's hold upon public esteem. Your claims to its occupancy are based upon grounds of substantial service." It was indeed a magnificent armory, worthy of the name and fame of the Seventh Regiment.

But now our rapid historic survey has brought us down to the most stirring year of the regimental history, and to the beginning of the story to whose record this volume is mainly devoted. On the 1st day of January, 1861, the active strength of the regiment was 895 men, making a gain over the previous year of 97 men. The field and staff contained 22; the first company, 85; the second, 127; the third, 91; the fourth, 100; the fifth, 85; the sixth, 100; the seventh, 96; the eighth, 100; the Engineer and Artillery, 50; the troop, 39. This body meant something more, however, as we have seen, than mere numbers; it meant soldierly port, discipline, tried steadiness, and national prestige. The question at this time asked on all hands was, Would the Seventh Regiment, in the stormy days near at hand, show itself worthy of its great name and fame?

# CHAPTER II.

## THE SUMMONS TO THE FIELD.

ON Saturday, the 13th of April, 1861, the cannon of Beauregard echoed from Charleston Harbor across the continent. On Monday thereafter a Proclamation of the President summoned the militia of the Republic, to the number of 75,000, to assemble and execute its insulted laws.

This call found the Seventh Regiment of New York ready. Three months before, on the 14th of January, its board of officers had privately passed the following resolution, presented by Major Shaler: —

"*Resolved*, That, should the exigency arise, we feel confident in having the commandant express to the Governor of the State the desire of this regiment to perform such duty as he may prescribe." *

* This notably early action on the part of the Seventh was forthwith communicated to Lieutenant-General Scott, then at Washington; and his estimate of the regiment is expressed in the following extract from his reply to General Sandford, dated January 19, 1861: "Perhaps no regiment or company can be brought here from a distance without producing hurtful jealousies in this vicinity. If there be an exception, it is the Seventh Infantry of the city of New York, which has become somewhat national, and is held deservedly in the highest respect."

The "exigency" had come, — that exigency darkly outlined in the terse, significant vote, — an exigency even then too menacing to ignore or neglect. The national capital was in danger, and the cry was for help.

Armed with this authority, Colonel Lefferts now put his regiment at the disposal of Governor Morgan, and, while waiting a reply, called a meeting of his officers next day, whereat, there being forty present, this resolve was unanimously passed: —

"That the Colonel be requested to notify the Major-General that this regiment responds to the call of the country as made by the President through the Governor of the State, and that the regiment is *ready to march forthwith.*"

Through the city and the State, through other cities and States, the tidings went that the Seventh would march in the van. As its name had long been familiar to the people, its prompt devotion was hailed as a token that whatever was best and dearest in the North would be laid on the altar of patriotism. As the Guards, Queen Victoria's household troops, were among the first to spring forward for the Crimean War, so the flower of the citizen soldiery of the Union was pledged in the march of the Seventh to the relief and defence of the national capital.

The day following, April 17th, the merchants of New York met in their Chamber of Commerce, where thirty-one gentlemen gave $100 each "for the equipment of the Seventh Regiment for active service." The list of subscribers was then doubled, the total sum put down being $6,140. The following are the names of the subscribers on this occasion: —

| | | | |
|---|---|---|---|
| Moses H. Grinnell, | $100.00 | S. Wetmore, | $100.00 |
| George B. De Forrest, | 100.00 | R. M. Blatchford, | 100 00 |
| L. G. Cannon, | 100.00 | Thomas Addis Emmet, | 100.00 |
| C. R. Robert, | 100.00 | A. C. Gray, | 100.00 |
| Royal Phelps, | 100.00 | W. B. Duncan, | 100.00 |

| | | | |
|---|---|---|---|
| Phelps, Dodge, & Co., | $100.00 | Stewart Brown, | $100.00 |
| Charles H. Russell, | 100.00 | Andrew Foster, | 100.00 |
| Edwin Bartlett, | 100.00 | Joseph W. Alsop, | 100.00 |
| Charles Christmas, | 100.00 | Joseph Gaillard, Jr., | 100.00 |
| Edward Minturn, | 100.00 | Henry Chauncey, | 100.00 |
| S. B. Chittenden, | 100.00 | James S. Wadsworth, | 100.00 |
| Moses Taylor, | 100.00 | August Belmont, | 100.00 |
| Theodore Dehon, | 100.00 | John Bridge, | 100.00 |
| Ogden Haggerty, | 100.00 | Clark & Mosely, | 100.00 |
| William M. Evarts, | 100.00 | Benj. F. Breeden, | 100.00 |
| G. S. Robbins, | 100.00 | Benj. Nathan, | 100.00 |
| George Griswold, | 100.00 | P. S. Forbes, | 100.00 |
| John A. Stevens, | 100.00 | W. W. De Forest, | 100.00 |
| James Gallatin, | 100.00 | Charles Davis, | 100.00 |
| E. Walker & Son, | 100.00 | Isaac Bell, | 100.00 |
| H. R. Dunham, | 100.00 | Frederick Bronson, | 100.00 |
| Hamilton Fish, | 100.00 | Howell L. Williams, | 100.00 |
| Robert B. Minturn, | 100.00 | B. H. Hutton, | 100.00 |
| D. F. Manice, | 100.00 | Almon W. Griswold, | 100.00 |
| George W. Blunt, | 50.00 | New York Stock Ex. | 1,000.00 |
| James H. Titus, | 100.00 | Rufus Prime, | 20.00 |
| William Curtis Noyes, | 100.00 | Washington Coster, | 20.00 |
| Shepherd Knapp, | 50.00 | Aymar & Co., | 100.00 |
| Charles H. Marshall, | 100.00 | Bleecker Outhout, | 100.00 |
| A. V. Stout, | 100.00 | Levi E. Morton, | 100.00 |
| W. Whitewright, Jr., | 100.00 | C. B. Loomis, | 25.00 |
| John L. Aspinwall, | 100.00 | R. Alsop, | 100.00 |
| J. F. D. Lanier, | 100.00 | G. C. Ward, | 50.00 |
| Henry Chauncey, Jr., | 50.00 | Benj. L. Swan, | 100.00 |

Major-General Sandford, notified by Colonel Lefferts of the action of the officers, both telegraphed and wrote at once to General Scott that "the Seventh Regiment was ready and waiting orders to proceed to Washington." During the 17th, Colonel Lefferts addressed the same officer, informing him that the Seventh had a full set of camp equipage, and could go into camp without delay outside of Washington. The following is the text of the despatch:—

NEW YORK, 17th April, 1861.

LIEUTENANT-GENERAL WINFIELD SCOTT, U. S. A.

SIR, — Major-General Sandford has already telegraphed and written, informing you that the Seventh Regiment New York State Militia are ready, and waiting orders, to proceed to Washington as per order of the Governor. I fear that he may have failed to inform you that we have a full set of camp equipage, and can and should prefer to go into camp within the vicinity of the city of Washington; but of course have no preference over your orders.

I have the honor to remain,
Your obedient servant,
MARSHALL LEFFERTS,
*Colonel Commanding.*

Anticipating the orders for march, the men were preparing their knapsacks and settling their affairs, while, through the day, many exempt members, repairing to Colonel Lefferts's office, begged the privilege of enrolment. After nightfall, also, Colonel Lefferts's residence was besieged by persons desirous of sharing the fortunes of the corps. Among those at this time accepted as a recruit was Captain Schuyler Hamilton, formerly of the staff of General Scott. Of course the commandant had in most cases to say nay to these solicitations; and as he was jealously watchful lest the quality of the regiment should be impaired, he could only take such as had been well drilled.

The left-wing drill (which had been ordered previous to the events just related) was witnessed at night by an overflowing audience of ladies and gentlemen; and already the scenes at the armory, thronged with devoted friends of the regiment, showed how deep and tender emotion the prospect of its departure stirred. During the drill, General Sandford, having received the hoped-for order from General Scott, communicated the news to Colonel Lefferts, who subsequently informed the officers. It was wellnigh midnight when these orders reached the regiment; but early next morning Colonel Lefferts had arranged for transportation. General Scott had instructed the regiment to proceed by rail to Washington. The Quartermaster-General, however, declared himself unable to furnish transportation for an earlier hour than 5 P. M. of the following day, the 19th. Three o'clock of the afternoon of the 19th was accordingly fixed as the hour of march from the armory.

The publication of the orders in the newspapers of the 18th caused a spontaneous rush to the armory. The regiment was already filled to its maximum, and hundreds of recruits were turned away. It would have been easy to recruit a brigade in a day. When it set out on its unknown path, it marched 991 strong.

The following were the orders for the march: —

GENERAL HEAD-QUARTERS, STATE OF NEW YORK,
ADJUTANT-GENERAL'S OFFICE, ALBANY, April 17, 1861.

In pursuance of a requisition from the President of the United States, Major-General Sandford is hereby directed to detail one regiment of eight hundred men, or two regiments amounting to the same number, for immediate service, to be reported forthwith to the President of the United States, and to serve until relieved by other regiments, or by a regiment or regiments of the volunteer militia, to be organized under an act of the Legislature of this State, passed April 16, 1861.

By order of the Commander-in-Chief,

J. MEREDITH READ, JR.,
*Adjutant-General.*

HEAD-QUARTERS, FIRST DIVISION N. Y. S. M.,
NEW YORK, April 17, 1861.

In pursuance of the foregoing general orders No. 43, from General Head-quarters, the Seventh Regiment N. Y. S. M., under the command of Colonel Lefferts, is hereby detailed for immediate service at the national capital.

Colonel Lefferts will direct his Quartermaster to report, at noon to-morrow, to the Major-General, for orders for the transportation of the regiment, its camp equipage and baggage, and for a requisition for a sufficient quantity of ammunition to furnish each man with twenty-four rounds.

Colonel Lefferts will order his regiment to assemble at their armory on Friday next, at 3 o'clock, P. M., armed and equipped for embarkation, each man supplied with provisions for twenty-four hours.

Colonel Lefferts, upon his arrival at Washington, will report for orders to Lieutenant-General Scott.

The Major-General congratulates the Seventh Regiment upon being the first corps detailed from this State, in response to the call of the constituted authorities of our country, to support the Union and the Constitution, and to vindicate the honor of that glorious flag which was consecrated by the blood of our fathers.

Brigadier-General Hall will promulgate this order immediately.

By order of

CHARLES W. SANDFORD,
*Major-General Commanding.*
GEORGE W. MORELL,
*Div. Eng., Acting Div. Inspector.*

HEAD-QUARTERS SEVENTH REGIMENT N. Y. S. M.,
NATIONAL GUARD, NEW YORK, April 18, 1861.

In compliance with orders from his Excellency the Governor, and division orders of this date, this regiment will assemble at Head-quarters on Friday, 19th instant, at three o'clock, P. M., in full fatigue and overcoat, with knapsack, to embark for Washington City.

The men will each take one blanket, to be rolled on top of knapsack, suitable underclothing, an extra pair of boots (shoes are better), knife, fork, spoon, tin cup, plate, body-belt, and cap-pouch, to be carried in the knapsack. The men will provide themselves with one day's rations.

There will be allowed three servants to each company, who must report to the Quartermaster at twelve o'clock, M., and receive their "pass." Each officer will be allowed one small trunk, which must be distinctly marked and left at the armory before twelve M., 19th instant.

All uniformed men, whether recruits or not, will report for duty. Recruits who have just joined will also report, and will be assigned a post in column.

Commissary Patten will receive instructions from the Colonel, and leave for Washington this P. M.

Appointments. — J. C. Dalton, Jr., M. D., Surgeon's Mate, vice Cameron, resigned. By order of

MARSHALL LEFFERTS, *Colonel.*
J. H. LIEBENAU, *Adjutant.*

The honorary members, and members of this regiment who from circumstances are prevented from accompanying the regiment to Washington, are requested to send overcoats and knapsacks to the armory, care of Sergeant Scott, armorer, before twelve o'clock to-day.

At night, pursuant to a printed call issued and signed by Asher Taylor, Adjutant of the Veterans of the National Guard, the latter assembled at the armory to take measures for protecting it during the absence of the regiment. Not only the building, but the streets adjoining, were crowded by the excited admirers of the corps, who, till late at night, made the building ring with their hearty cheers. Inside, everywhere there was hurry of eager youth, "buckling on the harness of war," while the Veterans convened in the room of the board of officers. Colonel M. L. Smith took the chair, with Major J. B. Wilson as Vice-President. Colonel Lefferts, amid great cheering, made a short speech, commending the armory to the Veterans. Colonel Vermilye, Jackson S. Schultz, Esq., and Captains Cyrus H. Loutrel, Meigs, and Roome responded, accepting the trust, and the Veteran roll was signed by large numbers of ex-members.

That memorable April week, which began with the clamor of guns against Fort Sumter, and ended with the march of the Seventh Regiment in New York and the bloodshed in Baltimore, is still fresh in memory. As the largest city of the Republic, New York witnessed the most fervid exhibitions of that master-passion of war, which, for the moment, seemed, throughout the land, to have fused and consumed all others. Trade stopped in its channels; counting-room and workshop alike were deserted; people seemed to live in the streets, the better to see, hear, and tell what alone was worth sight, speech, or thought; the national flag crowned all house-tops, alike the church and the factory, and floated from all the shipping, while the very children wore the tricolored ribbons and sang war songs; all public bodies discussed first the country's needs and afterwards their own; clergymen preached, not peace, but a sword; men grouped everywhere to talk about the terrible days in store;

and as the Seventh Regiment was the special pride of the city, its prompt devotion was the constant theme of gratitude and praise.

It would be impossible to repeat all the words of cheer that came to the regiment at this moment. A letter sent by Mr. Peter Naylor at this time to Colonel Lefferts said: "I most deeply sympathize in the cause which you and your noble command are about to defend, perhaps in bloody conflict, to maintain the supremacy of our good old flag, now floating over our national capital. . . . . Please find enclosed my check for one hundred dollars, to increase the fund appropriated for your regiment. . . . . A gentleman, arrived in this city yesterday directly from Mississippi, has laid a wager that the capital would be in possession of the secessionists by Monday morning next."

Another letter, from Dr. J. P. Batchelder, under date of April 19, says: "In the box accompanying this is a bullet which, discharged from a musket in the hands of a Tory traitor, penetrated the side of my father, Lieutenant Archelaus Batchelder, at the battle of Bennington, on the 17th August, 1777. Has not the time arrived when its mission may be reversed with propriety, i. e. from a musket in the hands of a patriot to the side of a secession traitor?"

# CHAPTER III.

## THE MARCH TO THE WAR.

THE day of departure dawned auspicious. It was noted as a happy omen that it was the anniversary of an historic day,— of that 19th of April, made illustrious by the "embattled farmers" of an earlier generation of heroes: but not till later was it known in how pregnant a sense had this day brought the Lexington of a new war.

The time of the march being noised abroad throughout the city and the neighborhood, long before noon the people assembled to bid the regiment God speed. A million spectators crowded and jostled along the line of march. Offices and stores were shut, and the myriad cares and duties of ordinary life were put off to another day. Old and young, all ranks and classes, joined in the throng, which was pervaded by an electric sympathy, breaking all bonds of custom. Other militia regiments, stimulated by the example of the Seventh, had already followed its initiative, and, while preparing their own march for a later day, eagerly cheered that of the corps whose prerogative it was to lead the column.

The region of the armory, then as now over Tompkins Market, was especially thronged; and as carriages drove up now and again with members of the regiment and their families, who had come to say farewell, each soldier lad was hailed with cheers and blessings. Within, there was fitting of uniforms, buckling of belts, rolling of blankets, packing and strapping of knapsacks, the ring of the rammer, the calling of orders, the scuffle of busy feet hurrying to and fro, the cheery laugh and joke, the hasty messages to friends, joined in confused sound. Here and there a member, struck with sudden contrition for past delinquencies "in peace times," was hard at work on the manual of arms, under a sergeant's tutoring. Veterans were protesting they could don the uniform as of yore, and march with the best of the "boys." Recruits were turned sorrowfully away. There were tender farewells too, hearty grasps of the hand from fathers who trembled a little as battle rumors fell on the ear; tears and kisses of mothers, sisters, sweethearts, wives, who came with cordials and comforts for the march, and with sadder gifts of lint and bandages, prepared by quivering hands at home.

The officers, consulting anxiously apart, or moving from room to room, giving the necessary orders, found themselves overwhelmed with generous offers of aid for the regiment. Among these voluntary offers was the sum of $1,000 presented to Colonel Lefferts, forming a part of the fund already referred to, to "do what he pleased with for the comfort of the regiment." He first bought revolvers for all his officers, and, after a small expenditure in addition, turned over the balance to the regimental fund. Clerks, both in public offices and mercantile houses, had received leave of absence, with wages continued. To some, advances on salaries had been given; to others, presents of money, clothing, equipments. Fathers and friends had been profuse with dirks and revolvers, for service in that "march through Baltimore" which the Seventh was planning. The few who left young families behind received word of honor that no harm or want should come to them, whatever might betide in war. The Stock Exchange, the Merchants' Exchange, the Corn Exchange, and similar public bodies, most of which had representatives in the regiment, were liberal with money and kindly attentions. Before the start, a fine national flag was given to the regiment by E. H. Simon, Esq., of the Seventy-First Militia, with kindly wishes from the donor, and a fit response from Colonel Lefferts. To a member of the 5th Company, a director in an insurance company pledged an annuity of $1,000, to be settled on his wife, in case he should fall in battle; the letter was read before the company. Mr. Edward Minturn, a public-spirited citizen, was especially active in providing funds for the immediate requirements of the regiment.

And there were sacrifices made by men of the regiment, too, for the sake of marching. To many the prospect of adventure was exhilarating; but the apparent certainty of speedy battle, and the thoughts of dear ones left behind, banished frivolity. One soldier was to have been joined in wedlock the Monday coming, and the guests were invited; the nuptials of some were recent, those of others had been arranged for May; but it was no time for marriage or giving in marriage.

The newspapers of the day of the march and the day after are filled with descriptions of its details. One of them, depicting the scenes in and around the armory, records for us the ejaculations of the hour in language which, if it seems overstrained now, vividly tells the excitement of that day: "You could hear the advice, 'Take care of yourself, old fellow, and I 'll see to things at home'; the promise, 'I 'll come back promoted, father, or I won't come at all'; and then, in a woman's voice, 'God bless you. I shall think of you and pray for you all the time. It 's very hard to, but —' and then a few tears, low whisperings, and a kiss. . . . . 'By George,' laughed another, adjusting his sword-belt, 'I came up here to bid you good by, but I could n't stand it, so I jumped into these things, and am going along.' 'What do you think the Governor said to me?' asked a young recruit; 'why, he said, "Remember Sumter," and vowed he 'd like to go too.' 'That 's like Fanny!' shouted another, 'she said she 'd go if she were a man. Do you think I 'd back out after that?' Another: 'Here 's a bouquet Mollie sent me. Look at the label: "May peace bring you back to me!"' 'Mother gave me this little flag, God bless her. I 'll never disgrace it.' 'What do you think of that for a badge' (displaying a beautifully worked rosette); 'that goes over my heart.' Breaking up these conversations there came, once in a while, cheers upon cheers for the Seventh and the Union, and snatches of national songs, shouted with hearty, untremulous voices."

Just before the start the people and the regiment were thrilled by the news of the bloody attack on the Massachusetts regiment in Baltimore; and when it was known that the Seventh would "go through Baltimore at all hazards," the excitement became intense.

At 3 P. M., the rapid roll of the drum, beating the assembly, put an end to the stowing of cartridges and the filling of canteens, to the cramming of knapsacks, to the leave-takings of friends. Agreeably to orders, Quartermaster-General Tompkins had, the day before, arranged for the transportation of the regiment to Washington by the New Jersey Railroad, so as to leave the foot of Courtlandt Street at five o'clock on Friday afternoon. Informed of the need of despatch, Mr. Felton, the president of the road, had sent from Philadelphia a telegram urging haste. It was as follows: "Don't let this by any means get into the newspapers. Make your arrangements to leave New York as many hours earlier than five o'clock as you possibly can." The preparations were accordingly hastened. A mammoth van carried off the officers' baggage, its eight horses gayly caparisoned with flags; and the people cheered the banner furnished by one of them to the driver, on which was written, "Our glorious Seventh knows no North, no South, no East, no West, but only the whole Union!" The two light howitzers (twelve-pounder brass pieces) were taken down the stairways to the rear of the building. Nine cheers were given as it was announced that every gun was taken from the racks, that every uniform had a man in it, and that the march would be through Baltimore.

The orderlies were now calling their rolls in the company rooms, and the men, the last good-by said, rapidly fell into line. The captains said a few words each to their companies, then marched them into position in the large hall and drill-room. The eight companies were overflowing, and, adding the men who joined at Jersey City, being delayed from sooner reporting for duty, the regiment was 991 strong, — a number never known on any mere show parade. The whole body, too, was perfectly armed, uniformed, and equipped, even the band carrying revolvers wherewith to defend themselves in the expected street brawls. It was thus that the Seventh, in the full pomp and circumstance of war, carrying not only the physical strength of a thousand men, but all that inestimable *morale* which attends fully caparisoned and equipped soldiery, led the van in the march of New York to the war.

At four o'clock a great shout went up from the crowd, as the regiment, filing out of the armory, marched into Lafayette Place, forming line between Fourth and Eighth Streets. There was incessant cheering and singing of national airs during the half-hour while the regiment was forming. The sergeants having reported, and assignments having been made to equalize the companies, platoons of police, sixty strong, now opened the way, the band burst out with martial music, the howitzers rattled forward, drawn by the men assigned to them, the companies wheeled into column, and, amid a fresh outburst of cheers and songs and fresh tears and farewell gestures from the overlooking windows, the regiment moved along Lafayette Place, bowered in flags and streamers, turned into Great Jones Street, and thence into Broadway.

Broadway, the great aorta of the metropolis, was pulsing with an intensity unexampled in the city's history. For hours the people had swarmed upon every standing-place along the two-mile route, climbing, like the Roman populace at Pompey's triumphs, "to towers and battlements, yea, to chimney-tops." The transit of the Eighth Massachusetts Regiment, earlier in the day, had only whetted expectancy to keener edge for the pageant that remained. Struggling to betoken in some visible symbol the feeling within them, all the people had, with common instinct, resorted to the display of that sacred emblem of patriotism, the flag of the country. Everywhere, accordingly, the national colors floated, making Broadway a carnival scene. Splendid banners flapped in the wind from every larger house-top, or curled from fresh flag-staffs; pennants streamed from ropes athwart all the streets of the city, and from all mast-heads in the harbor; façades were swathed with broad bands of red, white, and blue; flags were thrust out from the windows. As if ever mindful of the shame of Sumter, men and women bore the tricolor on their breasts, wore it in their hats, fastened it to their horses' heads, and caused the very children to wave their tiny bunting along the streets.

In such garb was Broadway decked to hail the regiment. Zouaves heading the column, in a spontaneous escort, with red shirts, blue flowing trousers, gay fez caps, and hairy knapsacks trussed up behind; the motley costumes of work-

## ERRATUM.

The name Charles J. Ingersoll, printed at the foot of the Illustration entitled "The March down Broadway," should read James H. Ingersoll.

THE MARCH DOWN BROADWAY.

*From the Original Painting by* NAST, *owned by* MR. CHARLES J. INGERSOLL.

men in paper caps and leather aprons; the handsome attire of the regiment itself, and their flashing bayonets, — made the pavements below as picturesque as the bannered parapets above, and the windows dressed with the gay garments of ladies. Over the whole the sun poured the glory of his parting rays.

It was less a march than a triumphal procession. Many thousands joined the moving column, preceding the march in escort, or following in rear. Street, sidewalks, areas, fences, stoops, balconies, windows, roofs, nay, trees, lamp-posts, awnings, every foot of available space, held spectators, and for long distances on the side streets the compact throngs struggled for a glance. So soon as, at any point, the people caught sight of the familiar gray, black-trimmed uniform and caps, set off by the blue overcoat, or even at the shimmer of the distant bayonets, they took up the cheering, which never for a moment ceased. At every point tradesmen and others were assembled to give concerted cheers, and the firemen had run their engines up the side streets, where they jangled the bells as the regiment passed. "Was there ever such an ovation?" wrote gallant Fitz James O'Brien, who carried a gun that memorable day. "When Trajan returned conqueror, dragging barbaric kings at his chariot-wheels, Rome vomited its people into the streets, and that glorious column that will ever be immortal was raised. But what greeted the Emperor at his outset? The marble walls of Broadway were never before rent with such cheers as greeted us when we passed. The faces of the buildings were so thick with people, that it seemed as if an army of black ants were marching, after their resistless fashion, through the city, and had scaled the houses. Handkerchiefs fluttered in the air like myriads of white butterflies. An avenue of brave, honest faces smiled upon us as we passed, and sent a sunshine into our hearts that lives there still."

Thus, through the multitudes parting for a moment to let the regiment pass, surging in upon the column at every step, and closing in dense masses behind it, the regiment marched along Broadway. At one point, such was the press that the crowd got in between the band and the regiment, and threatened to fatally disrupt the order of march. The police were quite useless; but Colonel Lefferts, halting the column, caused the street to be cleared at the point of the bayonet, and then marched on. Prompt to do it honor, Major Anderson, of Sumter, appeared on the balcony of the store of Ball, Black, & Co., and the companies of the regiment, successively pausing, joined in the thunders of applause with which the people greeted the foremost American of that day. Then onward again, under the canopy of flags and amid the deafening cheers, pressed the regiment, threading lower Broadway. As they marched, presents of all sorts were handed the soldier lads from the jostling bystanders, or came hurtling from roof and casement, "It was worth a life, that march," writes Winthrop. "Only one who passed, as we did, through that tempest of cheers, two miles long, can know the terrible enthusiasm of the occasion. I could hardly hear the rattle of our own gun-carriages, and only once or twice the music of our band came to me, muffled and quelled by the uproar. We knew now, if we had not before divined it, that our great city was with us as one man, utterly united in the great cause we were marching to sustain. This grand fact I learned by two senses. If hundreds of thousands roared it into my ears, thousands slapped it into my back. My fellow-citizens smote me on the knapsack, as I went by at the gun-rope, and encouraged me each in his own dialect. 'Bully for you!' alternated with benedictions, in the proportion of two 'bullies' to one blessing. I was not so fortunate as to receive more substantial tokens of sympathy. But there were parting gifts showered on the regiment, enough to establish a variety shop. Handkerchiefs, of course, came floating down upon us from the windows, like a snow. Pretty little gloves pelted us with love-taps. The sterner sex forced upon us pocket-knives new and jagged, combs, soap, slippers, boxes of matches, cigars by the dozen and the hundred, pipes to smoke shag and pipes to smoke Latakia, fruit, eggs, and sandwiches. One fellow got a new purse with ten bright quarter-eagles. At the corner of Grand Street or thereabouts, a 'b'hoy' in red flannel shirt and black dress pantaloons, leaning back against the crowd with herculean shoulders, called me: 'Sa-ay, bully! take my dorg! he 's one of the kind that holds till he draps.' This gentleman, with his animal, was instantly shoved back by the police, and the Seventh lost the 'dorg.' These were the comic incidents of the march, but underlying all was the tragic sentiment that we might have tragic work presently to do."

There were mottoes and inscriptions flung out in the path, of which some said expressively, "1775—1861"; others, "Remember Lexington and Concord"; others, "Trust in God and keep your powder dry," or, "The National Guard is for the Union." People recalled the recent parade of the regiment in honor of the Prince of Wales, when its soldierly appearance was warmly praised by the royal guest; but contrasted with that holiday show the present was grander from the reflected glory of its great purpose. But one of the writers of that day, carefully noticing, saw that "there were many handkerchiefs that did not wave, but were pressed convulsively to hide the starting tears"; while on the side streets, along the margin of the hurrying throng, close carriages were drawn up to the curbstones, "at whose back windows were the pale faces of mothers, their eyes raining tears as they strained for one more look at sons marching away."

Swinging at length, about half past five, out of Broadway

into Courtlandt Street, the head of column found the latter more lavishly decorated than any other part of the route, — a bewildering bower of flags, banners festooned and clustered on every hand, and bands and streamers crossing the street in profusion. Here the merchants, from the business quarters of the island, had been waiting for hours, and now took up the chorus of cheers. The wharves, the buildings on the dock, the ferry-houses, the vessels in the harbor, were also gayly decked with flags, and crowded with sympathetic spectators, who showered blessings on the Seventh as it entered the ferry-boat, while the tugs and steamers on the river rang their bells and sounded their whistles. So dense was the jam in the square fronting the ferry, that it became impossible to march the regiment through in order, and the men escaped as best they could from the caresses of the crowd to the boat on the river.

Jersey City was not a whit behind New York in the fervor of its greeting and the splendor of its holiday attire. Here, also, men and women had since morning awaited the regiment, filling the region around the ferry landing and the railroad depot. Banners everywhere decorated the façade of the latter building, and hung from the galleries, roof, and cross-ties. The great galleries were filled with ladies, and, at the entrance of the regiment, the band playing the "Star-spangled Banner," the building echoed with applause. "The whole city," say the papers of the day, "turned out for only that momentary sight of the Seventh, and, as if to make up for the shortness of the time by an intensity of enthusiasm, the ladies tossed their handkerchiefs, and stripped off their ornaments to throw to the soldiers, as they passed along." The troops, the baggage, and the artillery being on board, the long train, at twenty minutes of seven, rumbled out of the depot, and, amid a torrent of farewell cheers and blessings, gayly responded to by the soldiers, the Seventh moved away to its unknown mission.

But the "march down Broadway" was not the end of the triumphal progress of the Seventh Regiment. As they hurried across New Jersey, the people flocked all night to see them and cheer them, — at every town and hamlet men building bonfires on the route, and women and children bringing flowers. "Everybody has heard," writes Theodore Winthrop, "how the State of New Jersey, along the railroad line, stood through the evening and the night to shout their quota of good wishes. . . . . I think I did not see a rod of ground without its man, from dusk till dawn, from the Hudson to the Delaware." In a similar strain, Fitz James O'Brien says: "All along the track shouting crowds, hoarse and valorous, sent to us, as we passed, their hopes and wishes. When we stopped at the different stations, rough hands came in through the windows, apparently unconnected with any one in particular, until you shook them, and then the subtle magnetic thrill told that there were bold hearts beating at the end." Telegrams were sent forward to Philadelphia and back to New York to record the rate of progress of the train. From New Brunswick, N. J., the news was sent by telegraph to New York: "The route has been one continual ovation, and at every station they have been greeted with the booming of cannon and the shouts of thousands of the patriotic citizens of New Jersey, who have almost lined the road; and houses at a distance of half a mile from the road were seen illuminated." Two hours later, at eleven o'clock, came the telegram from Philadelphia: "The Seventh not arrived yet, though expected more than an hour. The streets are thronged to witness them march. They were at New Brunswick at nine o'clock, but it will be twelve ere they reach here."

It is only by thus recalling minute details that we can now appreciate the intense interest surrounding every step of this regiment, and the reliance everywhere placed upon it in that hour of national peril. "New York," said the leading article of one of the chief daily newspapers of that city, on the morning of the day just described,—"New York loves the Seventh. It has distilled its best blood into it. While the regiment is away from the city, the heart of New York, as if connected with it by some telegraphic fibre, will thrill with its success or choke at its disaster." Some days later, the wife of one of the officers of the regiment wrote to him thus: "The enthusiasm here about the Seventh exceeds everything. I think, if a member of it is injured in any way, the excitement will pass all bounds. The name of the regiment is in every one's mouth; every one seems to look on each member of it as a near relative." Indeed, the very day after the departure, a rumor that the regiment had been attacked and had suffered severely threw the whole city into tumult, till a denial came in the evening extras, issued for that purpose.

It was a night of light-hearted enjoyment, however, for the younger members of the regiment, with a great deal of singing and very little sleeping. Once seated in the cars, they had taken the precaution to secure a good meal from the delicacies with which their friends had loaded them. Then came a moment's pause in the excitement, during which they looked squarely in the face the stern mission on which they were speeding. The evening papers were examined, and their great news, the fighting in Baltimore, was discussed. The feeling it aroused was one of resolution and of vengeance. On all hands the hope and the expectation were expressed of "going through Baltimore" on the following day. These earnest discussions, as we have said, were in turn succeeded by songs and pleasant talk, and interrupted also by the enthusiasm of the Jerseymen along the route, whose demonstrations prevented sleep, even if the cheery talk and laughter and song had allowed it. "Those fine old songs," writes Fitz James O'Brien, "the choruses of which were familiar to all, were sung with sweet voice. We were assured many times, in melodious accents, that 'the whiskey bottle lay empty on the shelf,' and several individuals of that prominent, but not respectable, class known as 'bummers' were invited to 'meet us' on 'Canaan's happy shore.' The brave old Harvard song of 'Upidee' was started, and, shameful to say, Mr. Longfellow's 'Excelsior' seemed naturally to adapt itself to the tune. I do not think the 'pious monks of St. Bernard' would have been edified had they heard themselves alluded to in that profane music."

The "Notes on the Colors of the National Guard" says that "oranges and other fruit, pies, cakes, bouquets, bottles of wine, pipes, tobacco, sandwiches, boxes of segars, and lots of other things were, in great abundance, at every halt, thrust in through the car windows to the men; at one place, Burlington, I believe, a party of ladies were found waiting in the street and at the depot, long after midnight, with pails of iced water and tin cups."

At length, towards two in the morning, the train rolled into the Broad Street Depot. A messenger came into the car, lantern in hand, and, asking if Colonel Lefferts were there, announced to him that Superintendent Felton was anxiously awaiting him for consultation.

Here for the present let us leave the regiment. The greater part made their way to the hotels, — the Lapierre, Continental, and Girard, — while others, at six o'clock, received a good impromptu breakfast at the Deaf and Dumb Asylum, finding the superintendent "a man for the emergency." The hospitality * of the people of Philadelphia, as

* A letter signed A. A. Curtis, in the New York Herald of April 30, 1861, says: "The people of Philadelphia treated us very well; some of the citizens invited us to their houses to dinner. One poor widow woman opened her house, and gave us bread and coffee, hot."

Theodore Winthrop writes: "A mountain of bread was already piled up in the station. I stuck my bayonet through a stout loaf, and, with a dozen comrades armed in the same way, went about foraging for other *vivres*. It is a poor part of Philadelphia; but whatever they had in the shops or the houses seemed to be at soon as the city was awake, made up all deficiencies in supplies.

Such were the outward circumstances that attended the march of the Seventh Regiment to the war; but that which gave this event its deep significance, and rendered it national and historical, was not on the surface.

It was the fortune of the National Guard to make the first marked declaration of opinion which committed, definitively and absolutely, to the war the representative city of the Union. In that early period of darkness and distress, when doubts and fears possessed men's minds, and hesitancy and difference of sentiment paralyzed action, the Seventh Regiment boldly declared itself; and in so doing pledged New York, whose foremost families, whose wealth, and whose influence it represented in its very composition, to the cause of the Union. Its instant demonstration was the one *act*, which, in crystallizing opinion, fused and fixed New York in allegiance to the flag. The effect upon other militia regiments of the city was immediate and decisive. The same enthusiasm spread through the city, and the splendid uprising which, on the 20th of April, assembled a hundred thousand men in Union Square, was the electric response to the challenge of the National Guard, when, at its meeting three nights before, it pledged itself to the flag and the Union.

our disposition. I stopped at a corner shop to ask for pork, and was amiably assailed by an earnest dame, — Irish, I am pleased to say. She thrust her last loaf upon me, and sighed that it was not baked that morning for my 'honor's service.' A little farther on, two kindly Quaker ladies compelled me to step in. 'What could they do?' they asked eagerly. 'They had no meat in the house, but could we eat eggs? They had in the house a dozen and a half, new laid.' So the pot to the fire, and the eggs boiled."

The "History of the Second Company" preserves the fame of a rubicund Falstaff of the "City Troop," who visited the company, whiskey bottle in hand, while it was seated in the train expecting to start for Baltimore. Circulating his friendly bottle, he explained that he was a *horn-swoggler*, i. e. a devotee of good Bourbon; and his "Go in, boys, we 're after you," became a favorite byword in the campaign.

At this mighty "mass meeting" the name of the Seventh Regiment was on every lip. The gallant and eloquent Senator Baker, of Oregon, who, a few months later, fell at Ball's Bluff, cried, "The Seventh Regiment has gone, let seventy-and-seven follow." General Dix read a despatch which said, "The Seventh Regiment had reached Philadelphia in safety, were on their way to Annapolis, and would thence march to Washington." Governor Raymond said, as the papers report: "I understand that General Scott has sent word to this city that *the capital is in danger*. . . . . I trust in Heaven that before three days, ay, before two days, at least fifty thousand men will be concentrated at the capital of the country to protect it from the hands of traitors. (Cries of 'What about the Seventh Regiment?') They were in Philadelphia this morning, and it was determined that they would be sent on by water, but I believe the Seventh kicked against it, and were anxious to go through Baltimore. (Great cheering.) The Seventh Regiment, they would recollect, paid a visit to Baltimore, at which time they received the courtesies and hospitalities of their fellow-soldiers there, and they were anxious to see whether these same men had become their enemies and the enemies of their country at the same time. The Seventh was the pet regiment of New York, and well it deserved to be. (Three cheers were given for the Seventh Regiment, during which Mr. Raymond sat down.)" Mr. Halleck "called upon all young men to enroll as volunteers, and to proceed to Washington to strengthen the Seventh Regiment." Mr. Hull "made allusion," says the report, "to the events at Baltimore, and the rumor that the gallant Seventh Regiment had forced their way through the mob. (Cheers.) The news was not precise as yet, but he would say that if the Baltimoreans had spilt one drop of blood of that New York regiment, the resentment to follow would be terrible."

William Curtis Noyes's reference to "the thousand men, the flower of the city of New York," was received with like applause. "What man, by words," said Mr. W. J. A. Fuller, in his speech, "could inspire such military enthusiasm and ardent patriotism as did the roll of the drum and the tread of the New York 'Imperial Guard,' the gallant Seventh, as it marched through our streets yesterday?" In fine, alluding to the same great march, the gallant O. M. Mitchell, who, like Baker, was an eloquent speaker at this grandest of American mass meetings, and, like Baker, soon sealed that day's pledge with his life, said, according to the report: "I for one will lay my life down. It is not mine any longer. Lead me to the conflict. Place me where I can do my duty. There I am ready to go, I care not where it leads me. My friends, that is the spirit that was in this city on yesterday. I am told of an incident that occurred which drew the tears to my eyes, and I am not much used to the melting mood at all. And yet I am told of a man in your city who had a beloved wife and two children depending upon his personal labor day by day for their support. He went home and said, 'Wife, I feel it is my duty to enlist and fight for my country.' 'That 's just what I 've been thinking of too,' said she. 'God bless you, and may you come back without harm; but if you die in defence of the country, the God of the widow and the fatherless will take care of me and my children." That same wife came to your city. She knew precisely where her husband was to pass as he marched away. She took her position on the pavement, and, finding a flag, she begged leave just to stand beneath those sacred folds and take a last fond look on him whom she, by possibility, might never see again. The husband marched down the street, their eyes met, a sympathetic flash went from heart to heart; she gave one shout and fell senseless upon the pavement, and there she lay for not less than thirty minutes in a swoon. It seemed to be the departing of her life. But all the sensibility was sealed up. It was all sacrifice. She was ready to meet this tremendous sacrifice upon which we have entered, and I trust you are all ready. I am ready. God help me to do my duty. I am ready to fight in the ranks or out of the ranks. Having been educated in the Academy, having been in the army seven years, having served as commander of a volunteer company for ten years, and having served as an adjutant-general, I feel I am ready for something. I only ask to be permitted to act, and in God's name give me something to do."

Easily may we imagine that, as the report goes on to say, "the scene that followed the close of Professor Mitchell's eloquent and patriotic remarks baffles description. Both men and women were melted to tears, and voices from all parts of the vast multitude re-echoed the sentiments of the speaker, and every one seemed anxious to respond to the appeal to rush to the defence of the country."

# CHAPTER IV.

## THE NEW PATH.

WHEN the Seventh Regiment left New York, it fully expected to march through Baltimore to Washington. The news of the fighting in Baltimore had fired it with the ambition of forcing its way instantly through that city; and the press telegram of the morning from Philadelphia told the country: "The Seventh has arrived here. The members generally express a desire to go through Baltimore."

That desire was doomed to disappointment, as I shall now proceed to recount.

Immediately on reaching Philadelphia, Colonel Lefferts, who had expected to go to Washington by rail, was informed by Mr. Felton, president of the Philadelphia, Wilmington, and Baltimore Railroad, that the passage of troops through Baltimore had been forbidden by Governor Hicks, of Maryland, and by Mr. Brown, Mayor of the city, who had telegraphed Mr. Felton to that effect.

To Colonel Lefferts's response that, if not allowed to go

peaceably through Baltimore, he must force a path through, Mr. Felton answered that Baltimore could not be reached by the train, as the bridges between that city and Havre de Grace had been destroyed by the mob, the rails torn up, and the track made impassable. This latter objection Colonel Lefferts saw at once to be fatal to his plan. Mr. Felton expressed his ability to take the train through to Havre de Grace, if that were desired. But the real difficulty, namely, in getting from Havre de Grace to Washington — a distance of eighty miles — would still be unsurmounted. To attempt to march his men that distance, unused as they were to campaigning, unprovided with trains, supplies, or even sufficient ammunition, was not for an instant to be thought of. As to the prohibitions of Governor Hicks, Mayor Brown, and the Baltimore people, who had sent on their menaces, Colonel Lefferts freely declared they would not weigh a straw with the regiment. But he saw that it was a physical impossibility for his unprovided force to march through to Washington without being fatally delayed on the route, even if it got through at all.

As for waiting in Philadelphia till trains, supplies, and ammunition could be accumulated, that, too, would be a fatal delay. The sole aim of Colonel Lefferts — that which absorbed all his thoughts and enlisted all his energies — was to push through to Washington at the earliest practicable moment, whatever the route. If he waited in Philadelphia, or if he marched on the railroad through Baltimore, the object of his mission, the relief of Washington, would certainly be foiled. Promptly, therefore, Colonel Lefferts fixed his attention on *other* possible routes to Washington.

Before proceeding, however, to detail the interesting series of events that grew out of this new and unexpected turn of affairs, it will be in place to glance at some historic surroundings which are necessary to a complete comprehension of the situation.

It has been noted that the revolt of the Marylanders had interposed a bar to the march of troops to Washington. It is now a matter of history that the insurrection in Baltimore was even more serious, that the destruction of the adjoining railroad was more thorough, and that the orders not to march through the city were from higher authority, than the Seventh Regiment was aware of in Philadelphia. The mob that fought the Sixth Massachusetts ruled Baltimore for many days; they pillaged the gun-shops for arms, and the bakeries and dram-shops for supplies. While the Seventh was traversing New Jersey, an armed force from Baltimore captured the train coming from Philadelphia, and burned that night three railroad bridges, — the Canton Bridge, Gunpowder Bridge, and Bush River Bridge. It was ten days before, by great energy, the railroad could be rebuilt; it was twenty-five days before Baltimore was occupied by Union troops; it was months before soldiers from the North "marched through Baltimore to Washington."

A letter published in a New York paper of that period, says: —

"I left New York half an hour after the Seventh Regiment; passed them at Elizabeth; arrived at Canton, an outskirt of Baltimore, at four o'clock on Saturday morning. Found the bridge at that place in flames. The only citizen present beside myself was a friend originally from Baltimore. The firing was in charge of a hook and ladder company, a steam fire company, and a company of axemen, the latter numbering about forty men. As soon as the bridge fell, they marched in good order up the railroad to destroy the main bridges. At this time the Seventh Regiment was supposed to be about two hours behind us. The women, children, and passengers were deserted wholly by all connected with the train, and left to find the best of their way to Baltimore. My friend and myself walked around the creek; and on our way to the city found the artillery regiment, with ten brass pieces, assembled, even at this unusual hour, four o'clock in the morning, their horses all harnessed, their guns run out into the street, waiting, ready at a moment's call, the object being to attack the Seventh Regiment. The barricades across Pratt Street, composed of carts, timber, anchors, and other objects, then presented themselves, with bullet-holes and other marks of violence plainly discernible. Went immediately to the capital. Washington is quiet, though there are many who are dissimulate. All other parts of Maryland seemed to be as one man for secession. Returned to Baltimore on Saturday night. Found the city in the greatest state of excitement. On Sunday, all the churches were dismissed without service. The streets were crowded with cavalry and troops all day Sunday."

Reference has been made to the "prohibition" of Governor Hicks and Mayor Brown, and to the authority on which they claim to have acted. The following telegrams, not before published, will give some idea of the state of Baltimore at that time. The first from Mr. Garrett, President of the Baltimore and Ohio Railroad, to Hon. G. W. Brown, Mayor of Baltimore (who at that time was in Washington, arguing with President Lincoln), runs thus: —

"Three thousand Northern troops are reported to be at Cockeysville. Intense excitement prevails. Churches have been dismissed, and the people are arming in mass. To prevent terrific bloodshed, the results of your interview and arrangements with President Lincoln are awaited."

In two hours came this response from Washington: —

"Your telegram received on our return from our interview with the President and Cabinet, and General Scott. Be calm, and do nothing. I return to see the President at once, and will telegraph again. Wallis, Bruce, and Dobbin are with me."

Two hours later Mayor Brown telegraphed: —

"We have again seen the President, General Scott, Secretary of War, and other members of the Cabinet, and the troops are ordered to return forthwith to Harrisburg. A messenger goes with me from General Scott."

In fact, the President had already written to Governor Hicks and Mayor Brown, on the 20th of April, in answer to the letter they sent by Messrs. Bond, Dobbin, and Bruce, as follows: —

"Troops *must* be brought here, but I make no point of bringing them *through* Baltimore. Without any military knowledge myself, of course I must leave details to General Scott. He hastily said in presence of these gentlemen [the three messengers], 'March them *around* Baltimore, and not through it.' I sincerely hope the General, on fuller reflection, will consider this practical and proper, and that you will not object to it. By this a collision of the people of Baltimore with the troops will be avoided, unless they go out of the way to seek it."

To such complexion had the national authority come at the hour when the Seventh marched to the relief of Washington! It was not, however, as we have seen, the compact privily struck betwixt the rulers of the Republic and the officials at Baltimore which had determined Colonel Lefferts, at Philadelphia, to the course he actually took. Ignorant of that compact, he at once, on receiving from Mr. Felton positive proof of the enemy's destruction of the railroad, sent the following despatch: —

PHILADELPHIA, 5 o'clock, A. M., April 20, 1861.

HON. S. CAMERON, *Secretary of War, Washington.*

SIR, — Having arrived at Philadelphia, we are informed by the President of the Philadelphia and Baltimore Railroad that Governor Hicks states that no more troops can pass. In fact, the Baltimore and Ohio Road refuses to transport. We will wait for instructions.

MARSHALL LEFFERTS.

This despatch was handed to Mr. Felton for transmission upon a wire from his office, and to be put in cipher, which Mr. Felton said he was then using.

Time passed, and again the Colonel telegraphed. No answer came to these messages. Conjecturing (as indeed it proved true) that telegraphic communication had been destroyed by the enemy, Colonel Lefferts then took the responsibility of deciding his own route. Two ways only of reaching Washington were open to him. One of these was by the Potomac River, the other by way of Annapolis. Both routes had advantages, both disadvantages; the absolute mystery in which the movements of the enemy were then shrouded, and the severance of communication between himself and Washington, made the choice a difficult one. He judged it probable, however, that if so far north as Baltimore secession was running riotous and rampant, in Virginia affairs would be worse. He judged it probable, also, that the earliest act of the enemy would be to plant batteries along the Potomac, to prevent the passage of transports with troops on board. Moreover, he foresaw the importance of opening, and keeping open, the route from Annapolis to Washington, in any event, for that gathering militia column from the loyal States, whereof his own regiment was the van.

Accordingly, Colonel Lefferts chose the route to Annapolis. At quarter past eight o'clock of the same morning he sent the following despatch to New York. The message was sent in a cipher which the Colonel had had the foresight to arrange with his brother-in-law, Mr. Allen.

PHILADELPHIA, Saturday morning, 8.15 o'clock,
April 20, 1861.

W. H. ALLEN, 92 *Beekman Street.*

We cannot go by way of Baltimore. Will go to Annapolis. Require a good vessel and provisions to be sent there immediately. Go with this to William H. Aspinwall and General Sandford.

M. LEFFERTS.

This point settled, but one other remained, — *how best to reach Annapolis.* The more obvious way was to take steamer at once at Philadelphia, and proceed thither. Yet it was *possible*, as Mr. Felton said, to continue on the railroad as far as Havre de Grace, and thence embark for Annapolis. On inquiry, however, it was found that the only possibly available vessel at Havre de Grace was the ferry-boat Maryland. But as the Rebels had already got so far towards Havre de Grace in their work of destruction, it was probable that, foreseeing this move, they would reach this single ferry-boat, burn or disable it, and so ruin all hopes of reaching Washington in that way. To guard against this contingency, Colonel Lefferts resolved to secure his steamer at Philadelphia, and go by the Chesapeake Bay to Annapolis. In this way he would make success sure, while the time lost would be trifling compared with the peril of depending on the safety of this single boat at Havre de Grace. Besides, to go by sea gave a chance of opening communication with government vessels near Fort Monroe, and learning from them the situation of affairs at Washington. If the Potomac was still free, or if a convoy could be had in case it were closed by batteries, the regiment could be hurried rapidly up the river to the capital; otherwise, the Annapolis project remained open.

Having decided upon this course, Colonel Lefferts chartered the steamer Boston, and hastily fitted her up. Three days' rations of beef and bread, and some extra ammunition, were bought and put on board, and two o'clock the same afternoon was fixed as the hour of departure. This vessel Colonel Lefferts chartered and provisioned entirely on his own responsibility, drawing drafts on his firm in New York for the money. The result he was able to announce, as early as eleven o'clock that morning, in the following cipher message to New York: —

PHILADELPHIA, 11 o'clock, April 20, 1861.

W. H. ALLEN.

We have chartered the steamer Boston, and shall try to go up to Washington. May return to Annapolis. Show this to same parties. For three hours, messages will reach me at steamer Boston, foot Spruce Street.

M. LEFFERTS.

It is proper here to mention that the course of the commandant met the warm approval of his officers. When Colonel Lefferts had determined that a change of route was necessary, he assembled the captains of companies in council, and, on presenting to them Mr. Felton, the latter again showed his telegraph despatches from the Maryland officials and the agents of the road, and restated the situation. The officers were all of the same mind with their Colonel; and it was manifest that a common sentiment animated the whole command.

It will be remembered that the Eighth Regiment of Massachusetts militia left New York some hours before the National Guard. That regiment reached Philadelphia on Friday evening. The obstacles in the path of the Seventh now lay equally in that of the Eighth; and during Saturday morning the men of the two regiments, encountering each other at the railroad depot and in the streets, exchanged rumors and speculations upon their future course. Different in composition and in experience, the two regiments yet had a great-hearted sympathy of loyalty and honor, which infinitely overlapped the narrow distinctions of accidental circumstance, and at sight they were friends. The difference of temperament in the men — grim in the one case, gay in the other — served afterwards to cement their *cameraderie*.

With the Eighth Massachusetts had come Brigadier-General B. F. Butler, who, as a Brigadier-General of the Massachusetts militia, had been put in command of the various regiments already sent by Governor Andrew from that State. In connection with this officer, and his presence in Philadelphia contemporaneous with that of the National Guard, it is necessary here to interpose a commentary upon a certain historical topic which to the Seventh Regiment must ever be of the highest importance. The want of harmony between the officers of the Seventh and Brigadier-General Butler, and the mortification experienced by the latter on finding that Colonel Lefferts declined to put the regiment under his control, in the absence of authority for such a procedure, induced him, under the prickings of wounded vanity, to put forth some gross misrepresentations, and subsequently led some unwise friends of the Massachusetts General to falsify the historic facts of the period whereof we now write. More especially, a very silly effort has been made in some quarters to rob the Seventh Regiment of a part of its well-won laurels, in order to grace with a stolen chaplet the brow of General Butler. That portion of this effort which relates to the credit of "opening the route from Annapolis" (the undivided credit of which Butler's friends modestly claim for him), it is now necessary to pass in review.

The first relations of Colonel Lefferts and General Butler happened as follows. Early on the morning of the 20th April, an aid came to Colonel Lefferts in the depot, saying that "General Butler would like to see him at the Lapierre House." Never having heard of that officer, Colonel Lefferts inquired, in passing, who he was, and observed that he himself was now awaiting despatches from Washington, but would be happy to wait on him at a later hour. About seven o'clock Butler himself came down to the depot, and asked Colonel Lefferts "what he proposed to do." The Colonel answered that he had not decided, but was awaiting replies from Washington to his messages. There the interview terminated, and General Butler left the depot.

Here we may pause to note how matters stood with the Massachusetts Brigadier. He had reached Philadelphia the evening before the arrival of the Seventh, at which time, so far as was known, communication remained open to Washington. Yet he had not only done nothing,* but seemingly had formed no plan of procedure. On the contrary, as has

* At eleven o'clock, P. M., of the 19th, Governor Andrew, at Boston, received word from Butler at Philadelphia: "We shall go through at once." At midnight another despatch was received from Butler: "I will telegraph again, but shall not be able to get ready as soon as I had hoped."

A letter sent from Philadelphia by a member of the Eighth Massachusetts on the night of the 19th, and published in the Eastern papers a few days later, says: "We have got to push our way through Baltimore, in the morning, at the point of the bayonet. But our boys are determined, and in for it. Our bayonet exercise has got to put the whole regiment through. To tell you the truth, our boys expect to be split to pieces. But we have all made up our minds to die at our post. We have one great consolation before us: the famous Seventh Regiment of New York will join us to-night, and at three o'clock in the morning we expect to take up our line of march. There is an unheard-of hot time before us. We are furnished with no ammunition as yet, and are to rely on our bayonets and revolvers solely."

been noted above, his frame of mind was that of an inquirer, and his whole interview with Colonel Lefferts consisted in asking what *he* proposed to do. It puzzles one to know why Butler had not pushed through to Washington when the road was apparently open. Why did not some of that irrepressible energy which broke out later in the day manifest itself in some determinate action? Was he waiting for the Seventh, which he knew to be on the way? Whatever may be the explanation of this incomprehensible inactivity, certain it is that the General cuts a very different figure from the doughty dare-all he appeared, when, several hours later, he had become acquainted with the plan of Colonel Lefferts.

For when, about 10 A. M., Butler again repaired to the depot, he was informed by Colonel Lefferts (who, as has been seen, having received definite information of the state of the road to Baltimore, had already, in a despatch to New York, dated 8.15 A. M., announced his decision) that the Seventh Regiment was to proceed by transport to Annapolis.

This information had a remarkable effect upon General Butler, who, seeing that the Seventh was already on the point of departure, now eagerly attempted to induce Colonel Lefferts to fall in with a plan which he then for the first time revealed. This was that Colonel Lefferts should join his regiment to the Massachusetts force, and that the whole command should go forward to Havre de Grace by rail, and there take a boat — the ferry-boat Maryland — to Annapolis.

After hearing all the arguments which General Butler urged for his plan, General Lefferts was compelled to inform him that he regarded his own route, previously chosen, as the wiser, under all the circumstances. But, while the consultation went on, rumor came that the ferry-boat had been seized and barricaded. General Butler then admitted that it would not be practicable to carry out his first plan, and that the advance by rail must be made in force.

If Colonel Lefferts had before been at all disposed to vacate his own judgment to make room for General Butler's, this last intelligence would have recalled him from such a purpose. The truth was, however, as we have seen, that he had already gone over the geographical question thoroughly, and, having considered the very plan which General Butler embraced, had deliberately rejected it. Anxious, nevertheless, to reach Washington at the earliest moment, he listened attentively to General Butler's project; but he could not help pointing out to that officer that the very intelligence just received regarding the Maryland forbade the idea of a conjoined march to Havre de Grace. General Butler was acting on the supposition that the ferry-boat had already fallen into the hands of the enemy.* To imagine that the ferry-boat was already "seized and barricaded" by the Rebels, and yet that its machinery would be left intact, and the boat unharmed for service, on the approach of a large hostile force, did not seem quite rational to Colonel Lefferts. Yet this was the ground taken by Butler, who proposed to recapture the boat from the enemy.

Chagrined by the refusal of Colonel Lefferts to abandon his projected route, Butler went about his own business; but he did not fail to vent his spleen in a despatch transmitted to Governor Andrew, and in which the following words occur: —

"Eleven A. M. *Colonel Lefferts has refused to march with me.* I go at three o'clock to execute this imperfectly written plan.† If I fail, purity of intention will excuse want of judgment or rashness."

It would be difficult to conceive a more barefaced piece of *suppressio veri* than is wrapped up in this assertion.

* This is acknowledged by Parton. "The plan was a little changed in the morning, when the rumor prevailed that the ferry-boat at Havre de Grace had been seized and barricaded by a large force of Rebels. The two companies were not sent forward. It was determined that the regiment should go in a body, seize the boat, and use it for transporting the troops to Annapolis." ("General Butler in New Orleans," p. 18.)

† "Imperfectly written," indeed, since it must have been formed since the interview with Colonel Lefferts, less than an hour previous.

That Colonel Lefferts "refused to march with" Butler is true, as this narrative has already shown; but it has been seen *in what sense* it is true: it has been made manifest that this refusal on the part of the commander of the National Guards resulted from a careful consideration of the situation, which dictated the rejection of Butler's plan as quixotic and unsure; and that this plan was cast aside for a line of action previously and independently chosen, and better fitted to realize the one paramount object of the march, to wit, the relief of Washington. We might indeed feel disposed to pass by this despatch as the hasty utterance of a splenetic brigadier; but we are debarred from such a course by the fact that in the sketch of his life drawn up by Mr. Parton, under Butler's own supervision, the biographer has reiterated this calumny in a narrative replete with palpable injustice to the Seventh Regiment. It behooves us, therefore, to invite the renewed attention of the reader to the actual facts as detailed in this history.

So far as concerns the implication contained in the despatches and the book, that to General Butler belongs the sole credit of discovering the military importance of occupying Annapolis, and of reaching that point by way of Havre de Grace, this narrative has already set that matter right. The idea occurred to Colonel Lefferts before its announcement by General Butler. So far as concerns the wisdom of proceeding by rail from Philadelphia to Havre de Grace, or by boat at once to Annapolis, we have also set forth the considerations that governed the officers of the Seventh Regiment.

If any further proof, however, be wanted on this latter point, General Butler's biographer is the witness to be called. Mr. Parton tells us, as we have seen, that the ferry-boat had been reported as "seized and barricaded by a large force of Rebels." If this were so, these Rebels could unquestionably fire or sink the steamer, or ruin her machinery, or even carry her away intact, provided they were not strong enough to check Butler's movement to capture it. As this was the only boat at Havre de Grace, General Butler would have had, at best, to return to Philadelphia, or to wait in that little town till another boat could be sent him. In either case, the delay in reaching Washington would be unpardonable. And General Butler not only risked the destruction of the single transport by the Rebels supposed to hold it, but its destruction by our own forces. Mr. Parton writes thus: —

> "'I may have to sink or burn your boat,' said the General to Mr. Felton.
>
> "'Do so,' replied the President, and immediately wrote an order authorizing its destruction if necessary."

What General Butler had *proposed to do* with the Eighth Massachusetts, in case either he or the enemy had sunk or burned the ferry-boat, we shall never know. But it is clear that the position of that regiment in neither case would have been enviable.*

It may be suggested that General Butler discredited the report of the seizure of the ferry-boat. This, however, is disproved by his total change of plan of advance, predicated on a belief in that intelligence; and it must be owned that the news was at that time probable enough. His biographer also puts the fact beyond doubt by detailing the plan of an attack on the ferry-boat. "General Butler," he says, "went through each car, explaining the plan of attack, and giving the requisite orders. His design was to halt the train one mile from Havre de Grace, advance his two best drilled companies as skirmishers, follow quickly with the regiment, rush upon the barricades and carry them at the point of the

* Captain Clark, in the "History of the Second Company," suggests that "it is more than probable that General Butler would not have adopted so uncertain and unreliable a route, if he had had the same unlimited credit which the Seventh Regiment possessed in Philadelphia, and which secured for it a steamer and the necessary supplies."

bayonet, pour headlong into the ferry-boat, drive out the Rebels, get up steam, and start for Annapolis." This was the strategic plan in which the Seventh Regiment respectfully declined to participate. Mr. Parton "keenly regrets the refusal of officers of the favorite New York regiment to join General Butler in his bold and wise movements," but charitably adds that "they doubtless thought that their first duty was to hasten to the protection of Washington, and avoid the risk of detention by the way."

The fact is, that the Seventh went to Annapolis in the way it originally proposed to go. It had started for Washington, and its first duty was to reach that city at the earliest hour: were there any work to do, it would be quite as likely to come *there* as at any more northerly point. The railroad being hopelessly broken, but two possible routes remained, the one up the Potomac, the other by way of Annapolis. Of these the former, if practicable, would be really the shorter, in point of actual hours on the way. Yet, as it was probably blockaded by hostile batteries, the start from Philadelphia was made with the expressed resolve to turn to Annapolis, unless positive official news was received that Washington could be reached sooner by way of the Potomac. To go by rail to Havre de Grace was a mere experiment in an hour which did not admit of doubts. To steam from Philadelphia gave a choice of the Annapolis route or the Potomac, with a certainty of success. The route of the Seventh, and not that of General Butler, was adopted by all succeeding regiments from the North for many and many a day.

But let us now resume the thread of our narrative. The steamer Boston could not be made ready till four o'clock. She was wont to ply betwixt Philadelphia and New York, and on the day of her sudden chartering was ready to start for the latter port with a full cargo. But in five hours' time the cargo was out, and the regimental stores and baggage in. Between two and three o'clock, the sergeants called, "Fall in." Soon after, the regiment was tramping down Jefferson Avenue to the wharf where the Boston lay, and embarked. It was surmised at once that the boat was a "snug fit," with no room to spare; at 4.20 the hawsers were cast off from the wharf.

It was an inexpressibly lovely April afternoon, worthy of latter May or June. As the boat left the dock and steamed down the Delaware, the multitude of spectators broke out into hearty cheers, and the men-of-war at the Navy-Yard manned their yards and dipped their colors. The regiment sent back responsive cheers, for the thought of a forward movement filled all faces with smiles and all hearts with joy. Though yet uninformed of their route, an inkling of it had been gained by the troops, and, at all events, they were Southward bound. As the rays of parting day streamed over the boat, lighting up the picturesque groups, and brightening their gay uniforms, arms, and equipments, a memorable scene was presented. "Fellows fumbling in haversacks for rations," writes O'Brien in his spirited, sketchy way, "guards pacing up and down, with drawn bayonets; knapsacks piled in corners; bristling heaps of muskets, with sharp, shining teeth, crowded into every available nook; picturesque groups of men lolling on deck, pipe or cigar in mouth, unbuttoned jackets, crossed legs, heads leaning on knapsacks; blue uniforms everywhere, with here and there a glint of officers' red lighting up the foreground."

Daybreak of Sunday found the regiment on the ocean. Another delicious day had dawned, — mild, clear, and bright, the air soft but inspiring, and the sky befitting the latitude the regiment had reached. Very fortunate it was for the regiment that the weather was so propitious. Transports, from time immemorial, have been the special horror of the soldier. With all provision for comfort, he

ON BOARD THE BOSTON.

usually has a hard lot on shipboard, and much more when the voyage is sudden and without preparation. Lovely as was the starry night, — and such indeed were all the days and nights on the Boston, — when the members of the Seventh came to compare notes, at five o'clock on Sunday morning, regarding their experiences, they found them by no means *couleur de rose*.

The thousand and more men filled the craft to overflowing, from the upper cabin to the dark and damp hold. The men slept in their overcoats wherever they could, — some on bags of coal, some on the open deck, some in the close hold, — "dovetailed," writes one soldier, "only that there was very little of the dove about it." * However, what was lost in sleep was made up in singing, laughing, and chatting; reveille at five stirred up all the sleepers, and, crowding out, they shook themselves, and indulged in the luxury of a wash in the fire-buckets. Guard-mounting and drill came regularly on the transport, and served, in keeping up the discipline, to remind the gay campaigners that it was no holiday task they had in hand.

As usual on transports, especially with raw troops, the commissary department was difficult to manage, and the regiment fell far short, both in quantity and quality, of ordinary army rations. A biscuit or two, and a small bit of

* Another letter says: "About nine o'clock, after we had had supper (which consisted of a piece of meat and a hard cracker, served up in pails, each man taking a chunk of meat on his tin plate), we rolled ourselves up in our blankets, used our knapsacks for pillows, and laid ourselves on the soft, downy planks of the Boston, in regular style, the first man putting himself in position, and each man closing in with him. When we wanted to take a turn, we would all have to wake up and turn together."

The Chaplain of the regiment, the Rev. Dr. S. H. Weston, in his devout and eloquent sermon delivered in St. John's Chapel, after the return to New York, says: "The boat was old and small, and even in smooth water careened so that the men had to be moved from side to side to keep her on an even keel. How so many could be crowded into such narrow quarters is still to me a mystery. What would have been the result, in the event of a heavy storm, it is fearful to contemplate. The lower hold, filled with men, was almost unendurable; with the hatches on, it would have been a 'Black Hole.'"

beef, comprised the short allowance, to be moistened with "a vision of coffee"; but the dandies and epicures, tin cup and tin plate in hand, filed up one by one at the order, "Fall in for rations!" and made up for lack of victuals by surplus of good-humor. In guard duty, in discussing the grim battle-work believed to be impending, in lounging on the decks, watching the dim line of shore on the horizon and the wheeling ducks and loons, while the slanting sun browned and hardened the pale faces of the city youth, the long day wore away. At eleven o'clock, the Episcopal service was read by the Chaplain, Dr. Weston, to such of the men as could get within hearing, and fitting remarks were made thereon. About noon, the capes of Chesapeake Bay were reached.

Evening drew on apace, and as the boat sped easily along, it appproached to where it became needful to decide, once for all, whether to continue in Chesapeake Bay to Annapolis, or to deflect therefrom up the Potomac. Accordingly, as Colonel Lefferts had designed, the passing boats were hailed, with intent to find out whether the Potomac was yet blockaded by the enemy; for, before leaving Philadelphia, Colonel Lefferts had telegraphed to the Secretary of War his departure, and had asked to be met off Fortress Monroe or at the mouth of the Potomac by a despatch-boat with orders as to the route to Washington. This telegram, the wires being cut by the enemy, never reached Washington; and accordingly, neither from the light-ship, which was passed and hailed at five o'clock, nor from the other vessels in the neighborhood, was any official news, nor any favorable news whatever, to be had.

The orders now given to the captain of the boat were "to head for Annapolis" till otherwise instructed; and as to attempt the Potomac with an unarmed, overcrowded transport might be only losing time, on being driven back by batteries, to Annapolis the boat went on.

Before nightfall there was no longer any doubt of the proper course. The only news derived during the day had been the story (and perfectly true it proved) of a Yankee skipper, homeward-bound, who related that the enemy (under General Taliaferro) had occupied Norfolk and Portsmouth in force, and that Gosport Navy-yard, with all its immense stores and munitions of war, had been abandoned and burned by our forces, while the very fleet itself had been scuttled and was that moment in flames! Such a narrative, falling short though it did of the actual truth, portended sweeping triumphs of the enemy, who, with the national fleet destroyed, could hardly fail, not only to blockade the Potomac, but to keep it blockaded. In the councils of the officers on this point, Colonel S. R. Curtis, a West Point officer of sound judgment and of large experience in the Regular Army, joined cordially. At this time he was a member of Congress from Iowa; but he immediately re-entered the service as Brigadier-General of volunteers, and very soon as Major-General fought the famous battle of Pea Ridge. He accompanied the regiment from Philadelphia to Washington, and thence wrote to the New York papers a eulogium of its conduct during the expedition, to which we shall duly refer.

As the sun went down, some scores of the finest singers in the regiment sang, grouped together on the deck, melodious religious hymns. As the softened flood of harmony floated out upon the solemn stillness of the air, the scene, the measureless sea, and the hour, — that of parting day, — added effect to the chant. The moon rose with matchless beauty to complete the scene; and the rugged mate of the steamer, glancing toward it, saw three distinct and beautiful circles surrounding it, — red, white, and blue! "There!" he cried, "is our flag in the sky! God never will let it be struck down under foot!" A thrill ran through the men as all, looking into the heavens, recognized the phenomenon, clear and unmistakable. Cheers and songs greeted the felicitous omen. This event, related in many private letters, found its way also into print, and was celebrated by some of the poets of the day.

Soon after midnight the steamer reached the mouth of the Severn. The engines were slowed, and she crept onward at a snail's pace, waiting for the day. Dawn found the steamer at the mouth of the harbor of Annapolis; and when the morning fog lifted, it disclosed directly ahead a frigate, with sails unbent, and the stars and stripes flying to the morning breeze. Hearty cheers burst from the crowded decks of the Boston at the sight of the dear emblem. As the steamer came up, the man-of-war hailed, "Let go your anchor!" This order was repeated many times before it was understood, and meanwhile motions were made from the frigate to back; at length her ports were opened, her guns run out, and the gunners took their places. Then the Boston slowed, and was again hailed. "Are you the Seventh Regiment of New York?" "Yes!" "Let go your anchor, and send an officer on board." Already the anchor was let go and a boat lowered, when a naval officer put off from the frigate, reached the Boston, and quickly returned to his own ship, accompanied by Colonel Lefferts. It was the renowned frigate Constitution, the school-ship of the Naval Academy, saved, as history has recorded, from falling in her old age into the hands of the enemy watching to seize her.

The greeting received by the Boston showed that her arrival had been expected. Yonder, half a mile farther on, was the steamer Maryland, hard and fast on a mud-bank; and her decks were crowded with the Eighth Massachusetts, their bayonets glittering in the sun. And in the distance, farther up the beautiful bay, girt with its verdure-clad banks, rich in Maryland farms and plantations, rose the roofs and spires of Annapolis.

## CHAPTER V.

### THE SEVENTH AT ANNAPOLIS.

WHEN, on the morning of April 22d, the steamer Boston dropped anchor in front of the little capital of Maryland, the National Guard discovered that their comrades of the Eighth Massachusetts had reached the harbor of Annapolis before them. The Maryland, however, was aground, and the sorry plight in which the Seventh found their gallant friends removed all disposition to banter them. Whether from the crowded freight of men, or the negligence of the pilot, the Maryland, after waiting in the harbor from early dawn of Sunday to that of Monday without landing her troops, was, in the captain's manœuvres, stuck fast in the mud. However, a good service had been rendered in the interim by General Butler, who, at the request of Captain Blake, commanding the Constitution, had towed Old Ironsides away from the shore to a safe distance from the hostile militia, who menaced each moment to seize her. Besides this, General But ler had had a day's wrangling with Maryland authorities, who wished to prevent him from landing.*

Colonel Lefferts now promptly addressed himself to the task of landing and occupying Annapolis in force. He had already, in a letter written the previous day, informed General Sandford of the movements of the regiment, and now appended thereto a hasty postscript. The following is the letter, with its postscript; they verify what has already been said regarding the Annapolis route: —

ON BOARD STEAMER BOSTON,
Sunday, 3 o'clock, P. M., April 21, 1861.

GENERAL SANDFORD.

I sent a cipher despatch yesterday to W. H. Allen, 92 Beekman Street, the translation of which I requested might be handed to you, and also to William H. Aspinwall. I fear, however, that some trouble may have been experienced in making it out. I therefore repeat the substance of it.

We arrived in Philadelphia about daylight on Saturday morning. I was informed by the president of the railroad between Philadelphia and Baltimore that we could not go by way of Baltimore; that Governor Hicks, the Mayor, etc., had telegraphed that no more troops must come that way. I should still have forced my way, but was informed by the same authority that the Baltimore and Ohio Road refused to transport, and that bridges had been burnt, etc. I then turned my attention to some other route. Later in the day I was informed by the Quartermaster-General of Philadelphia that he had a despatch from Government stating that communication was cut off between Baltimore and Washington. I then chartered the steamer on which we now are, and, at the time of writing this, am entering Chesapeake Bay. I telegraphed to the Secretary of War, immediately on our arrival at Philadelphia, that we could not go through, and were waiting for instructions. I received no answer to this up to the time of my departure, so that I was compelled to act upon my own responsibility. Upon leaving, I again telegraphed him through the only channel open (the president of the Philadelphia and Baltimore Road), that we would leave that P. M. by steamer for Washington. I expected, therefore, on reaching this point (off Fort

* Here was a second instance of masterly inactivity on General Butler's part. He had passed an entire day and night in exchanging missives with the Annapolis authorities about landing his troops. On the other hand, as we shall presently see, Colonel Lefferts, though arriving with his regiment so much later, was the first to land his troops and take possession of the town.

Monroe) some kind of instruction, but see no Government vessels in sight. I have decided to go on as far as the mouth of the Potomac, and, should there be no Government vessel there, shall proceed to Annapolis to keep open that line of communication, — an indispensable necessity in future operations. Upon arriving at Annapolis, I shall of course be guided by circumstances. We may have to march from thence to Washington, without Government controls the railroad. Of course I am placed in a very embarrassing position, but must do the best I can, keeping in view the object we had when we started. I forgot to say that, in the cipher despatch to W. H. Allen, I requested that you would immediately cause a vessel with supplies to be sent to Annapolis, as it is only a town of some eight hundred inhabitants, and those not friendly; and, should we be compelled to intrench ourselves at that place, we might have difficulty in provisioning.

Monday morning, 8.30 o'clock.

We have arrived at Annapolis, and find some of the Massachusetts troops here. We shall land, and endeavor to make our way to Washington. We should have reinforcements and provisions sent here at once. I can give no further information. There is considerable excitement.

M. Lefferts, *Colonel.*

He also prepared the following telegram, to be sent through General Butler. It is dated at 1 p. m., "on board steamer Boston," and is addressed to Secretary Cameron: —

"My command, about one thousand strong, arrived and ready for duty. All well Provisions short. Colonel Curtis, who is with me, volunteers in any capacity."

The luckless Maryland was, as we have seen, aground; and the Seventh Regiment asked themselves what the condition of things would have been had they been on Butler's transport, fixed on the bar. However, instead of hurrying to gain for his own regiment the glory of first occupying Annapolis, Colonel Lefferts, when informed by Captain Blake, on his visit to the Constitution, of the sorry plight of the Massachusetts regiment, expressed his desire to use the Boston at once for towing her consort off from the shoal where she had stuck hard and fast. Accordingly, when the tide rose, the Boston steamed up to the Maryland to assist her. The persevering Massachusetts lads had for hours been resorting to all sorts of devices to get clear, and had put forth herculean efforts; they threw over baggage-trucks, coal, crates, shifted themselves forward and aft, and ran suddenly from side to side, but all in vain. Now the Boston gave them a hawser, and tugged for hours at the top of her engine-power; all, too, in vain.

Meanwhile, Colonel Lefferts and a few of his officers had gone ashore to consult with the officers of the Naval School, and to learn from them the situation. Communication was opened in this way, also, with General Butler, who had, as we shall presently see, requested Colonel Lefferts's advice and co-operation in endeavoring to land his troops. Colonel Lefferts was met by the Mayor of Annapolis, who formally protested against his landing. He replied that he should be obliged not only to land, but to force his way through to Washington, and that, for the "bloodshed" they predicted, those must be responsible who should oppose. The naval officers, being then appealed to by the Mayor to testify upon the sentiment of the people of Maryland, confessed that it was so impregnated with "States' rights" that they seemed disposed to resist any "invasion" of their soil by any forces. Colonel Lefferts again responded that his regiment had been ordered to go to Washington, and would go, — peaceably if they could, forcibly if they must.

Returning, soon after noon, to the steamer, Colonel Lefferts determined to land his regiment. But first he caused the effort to relieve the Maryland to be continued some hours longer. This labor, however, for the sake of the main enterprise and of the comfort of both regiments, had at length to be ended. Crowded and half famished, debarred so long from sleep and from exercise, the Seventh were anxious to get ashore and to be on their way. As for the Massachusetts men, they had suffered still more from fatigue, famine, and want of sleep; for General Butler's movement — having taken little thought of failure or delay, had been conducted without sufficient rations. Mr. Parton tells us the hapless men of the Eighth were "packed as close as negroes in the steerage of a slave-ship"; that "the General trod upon many a growling sleeper"; that the ration served out was "the allowance of a biscuit, an inch of salt pork, and a tin cup half full of water"; that the men were "tired and hungry, black with coal-dust, and tormented with thirst, — the General himself not tasting a drop of liquid for twelve hours"; and that "his men were almost fainting for water." The Chaplain of the Seventh adds: "Some in their agony drank salt-water, and became delirious." Grimy and haggard, their faces black with the coal-dust in which they had been living, their stomachs empty, their muscles tired with tugging, the gallant fellows were hardly less glad than the Seventh, when the latter, heading towards the government dock, called out that they would send back the steamer to relieve and debark them.

At five o'clock the Boston touched the wharf, and the regiment marched to the green slope stretching down from the Academy to the Severn, and so encamped at Annapolis, — the pioneers of the war in occupying that city.

The route of the regiment had now been vindicated in practice, as it had before been sanctioned by theory. The voyage from Philadelphia was a rough initiation into service, but not to be compared, as we have seen, with the experience of the Eighth under General Butler. These hardships would have been intensified by the more than double pressure proposed to be put upon the single transport and its supplies. The Eighth was 724 strong; the Seventh, 991. Of course it would have required three trips and three return trips for the Maryland to have taken them all, "packed as close as negroes in a slave-ship" at that. These six trips, and the time of embarkation and disembarkation, would have brought the whole force into Annapolis many hours later than by the Seventh Regiment's route. A part of the Seventh, if not the whole, would have been left behind at Havre de Grace, unless it had countermarched to Philadelphia, nor would there have been any Boston at hand to help the stranded Maryland. Such was the union of discomfort, delay, and mishap which the Seventh had declined.

A large detail was at once put on guard, at the dock, over the baggage and stores, and around the temporary encampment and its stacked arms; another detail was made for fatigue duty in unloading the steamer, so giving a broad hint to the new campaigners that a good soldier must occasionally be something of a porter; and there was soon, too, a busy attendance on the company messes, with "buckets of cooked meat and crackers." Then the men bade good by to their transport Boston,* which Colonel Lefferts sent back to the aid of the Massachusetts men, all of whom were landed before dawn.

The batch of Maryland protests against the Seventh's invasion was not all unladen. The Mayor and a delegation of the citizens met Colonel Lefferts in the town and disbursed the balance. To hint, menace, entreaty, argument, that officer only replied that they must talk about those things at Washington, whither he was bound at all speed. His Honor Mr. Mayor of Annapolis then modestly requested that Colonel Lefferts would take his regiment outside of the city, adding that its presence "was a great outrage, would lead to trouble," etc. "That rests with yourselves," rejoined the Colonel: "if let alone, we shall disturb nobody;

* "Good by to her, dear old, close, dirty, slow coach!" cries Winthrop. "She served her country well in a moment of trial. Who knows but she saved it? It was a race to see who should first get to Washington; and we and the Virginia mob, in alliance with the District mob, were perhaps nip and tuck for the goal."

but you must keep hands off." In order, however, to show that he had no other than the most peaceable designs, Colonel Lefferts offered to leave immediately for Washington, provided the Annapolis authorities would supply the regiment with provisions and wagons for the sick and wounded, adding that the full price would be paid. The Mayor made answer that wagons could not be furnished; and so these high diplomacies came to an end.

Colonel Lefferts next called his officers together, and laid before them the facts reported to him by the United States officers and others with regard to the condition of Maryland. All communication with Washington had been cut; Baltimore as long ago as Friday was in arms; Annapolis was hostile; Norfolk, Portsmouth, and Gosport Navy-yard had fallen; the railroad had been torn up by the enemy between Annapolis and Washington; the Seventh Regiment was in the van (save for the heroic Sixth Massachusetts) of the armed and equipped militia, marching to relieve the menaced capital, — and what delays it had met! It seemed probable that Washington must have already fallen. It was therefore resolved to press forward early in the morning by forced marches to Washington. Aware of the importance of reopening the railroad thither, the regiment would gladly have undertaken that task; but the unknown fate of Washington, which might be sealed by a single hour's delay, forced it to choose the bolder alternative of marching at once by the turnpikes. Preparations were therefore made for an early march on the following (Tuesday) morning; and as the regiment had only ten rounds of ammunition, and no provisions beyond the morning's ration, means were promptly taken to procure supplies.

Already the regiment had been drawn from the greensward into the old fort, whose scanty quarters were soon occupied with the tired troops, rolled up in their blankets, with knapsacks for pillows, and enjoying the unwonted lux ury of sleeping at full length on the floor or the ground. Maugre the closeness, it was a paradise to the Boston, and the hospitable midshipmen kindly took as many as possible of their new friends into their own rooms in the navy buildings. The cooks, who had supplied hot coffee wherewith to moisten the Seventh's rations of salt pork and beef, promised greater favors for the morning; in short, the whole Academy, from commandant to servant, treated the Seventh with great kindness. Save the strong detail for guard, who now, in the white moonlight, for the first time paced their beats in a hostile country, the regiment was overcome with refreshing sleep.

Before sunrise the regiment was astir, and more new sensations were enjoyed, — a wash at the pump and a breakfast on the grass. It was a queer, ancient, somnolent city on whose outskirts the regiment was now posted, "looking very much," said O'Brien, in marching through it, "as if some celestial school-boy, with a box of toys under his arm, had dropped a few houses and men as he was going home from school, and the accidental settlement was called Annapolis." The ancient structures along its narrow and winding streets were interspersed with some finer mansions, and towering above them was the old State House, where Washington resigned the command of the first Union army. The fort, half a century old, and shabby enough for purposes of defence, was set off by the fine Academy buildings and the pretty grounds, and even by its grimly protruding muzzles, over which waved the national ensign. The uniforms of the cadets (pleasant and well-bred fellows), and those of their new comrades, the Seventh, decorated the scene. The long, slender piers stretched into the picturesque bay, where lay the Constitution, Maryland, and Boston. The day was very warm, but charming.*

* Theodore Winthrop humorously notes the general hair-cutting, or, as we might say, the shaving of heads, according to the inevitable rite of the priesthood

Officers and men were making ready for instant march, hastily writing a few words home, knowing not what a day might bring forth. Some of these letters, or extracts from them, written that morning, found their way into the papers of New York. One, from an officer, says: —

"We shall shortly march for Washington. Cannot get horses, and shall have to leave our baggage and any unable to march. We are in an enemy's country, and cannot buy even an egg. Very many of us slept on the ground last night, but the weather was warm and pleasant. We expect to have fighting by the way to Washington. Men in good spirits."

Another, dated "Annapolis, April 22, 9 o'clock," and signed J. H. A., says: —

"We expect to march from here to Washington to-day. . . . . The boys talk of nothing but war, and are true to the Union to a man."

A third closes spiritedly in these words: —

"We are all resolved to do our duty, and die, if need be, marching under the flag and keeping time to the music of the Union. The conviction is that, even if we are all killed, such a feeling will be excited throughout the country, that all the Union men of all the States will rally to the call of the drums, and put down rebellion and treason.

"George."

A fourth says: —

"I stand it much better than some of the poor devils around me, who faint from privation and fatigue. We are now on shore, in one of the finest countries I have ever seen, with plenty of good water. Rumors fly thick that we are surrounded by enemies on every side, and will have a bloody march of it. We went at the call of duty to do service for our country, and not only am I prepared to suffer fatigue, but to spill my blood in her cause. The war feeling predominates, and we are to march."

A fifth soldier writes to the Evening Post: —

"We were finally quartered for the night in the old fort built during

who sacrifice at the altars of Bellona, and without which no recruit would believe himself a soldier. "It was the day we had our heads cropped. By evening there was hardly one poll in the Seventh tenable by anybody's grip."

the war of 1812. Never did men enjoy sleep more than we did, as we rolled ourselves up in our blankets and stretched out at full length, with a knapsack for a pillow. This was a luxury not before enjoyed by many of us since we had left New York; for our boat was so excessively crowded that only a favored few could so indulge. The Massachusetts troops, whom we found here on our arrival, disembarked this morning from the ferry-boat.

"H. E. T."

A sixth writes home: —

"The war seems to have begun, and I have got into the sport; but I am determined to stand by the stars and stripes to the bitter end. I shall do my duty at every hazard. We will show these traitors, before we are through with them, that we are as brave as they; I believe that God and the right are on our side, and we must succeed.

"E. C."

A seventh, W. E. C., says: —

"DEAR FATHER, — We arrived here last night. We have taken entire possession of this town. If we had not, the Rebels would, so we are very comfortable now. The Rebels have all the rails up from here to Washington."

An eighth, from on board the Boston, writes: —

"All are well and in good spirits, and we will give a good account of ourselves. The secession men have everything on the Potomac, and it is reported to us that Washington is in their hands. We are going there, at all events, or we will be heard of no more.

"Tell the *Union boys* to come along in strength; there is work to do, and it must be done at once.

"Thank God, this regiment is a unit, and will do its duty."

A ninth, from the same place, says: —

"We are about to land and march to Washington, — by force, if necessary. We expect to fight."

A tenth, C. R. S., says: —

"The supposition is that we shall fight all the way through, as it is reported that there are 15,000 soldiers ready to oppose."

But these examples will doubtless suffice to show the tone and spirit of the Seventh at Annapolis. These letters were *avant-couriers* in that mighty host of "soldiers' letters" which for four years thereafter continually went North from "the front," to straining eyes and beating hearts at home.

All, it is seen, were alert for the expected start; but checks, unlooked for and vexatious, interposed. Early in the morning the quartermaster and his party began to hunt after transportation suitable for the baggage, supplies, ammunition, and sick, on the road to Washington. But serviceable animals and wagons could not be procured at any price, — the very few secured, after much exertion, being unfit for the exigencies expected. Provisions, too, were only with the greatest difficulty obtained. Cash down was demanded and paid for everything, especially as the city still claimed to be loyal.

At this juncture Colonel Lander and one other messenger came in from Washington. General Scott, troubled at the delay of the regiment, had sent forward no less than eight messengers with despatches to Annapolis. Of these eight messengers two only got through; the rest were stopped by falling into the hands of the enemy, or from other causes.* Colonel Lander also had been captured by scouts, but by a *ruse de guerre* escaped. His news was that the "situation of affairs at Washington was extremely critical, and that the Government was intensely anxious that the Seventh Regiment should hasten to its relief." This intelligence strengthened Colonel Lefferts in his purpose to push through by the wagon-road, rather than to delay at all in repairing the railroad track. Efforts were redoubled to secure rations, ammunition, and a makeshift of a train. But soon after another messenger came in, direct from Washington, with later despatches from head-quarters to the commanding

* Commissary Patten, who had been sent through to Washington by Colonel Lefferts before communication was destroyed, was twice made prisoner by the Marylanders.

officer of the Seventh Regiment. These despatches announced the safety of the city thus far, and suggested to Colonel Lefferts that while he should push through rapidly, yet it would be also desirable for him to endeavor, as he marched, to reopen railroad communication with the North.

All entered heartily into the execution of this plan. Two companies of the Eighth Massachusetts had already occupied the depot, and had begun the work of mending the track. The story of their exploits is immortal. Finding an old locomotive, damaged and useless, in a locked-up storehouse, they set to work to repair it. Charles Homans, of Company E, found the engine an old acquaintance, — "Our shop made her," — and he and his associates soon had it in running order. Before nightfall the machine was ready, and the track, for about three miles, repaired.

To divert, meanwhile, the forebodings of delay among his own men, and to keep them well in hand, Colonel Lefferts, in the forenoon, had held a parade and drill, with a review by Captain Blake. Prominent citizens and their families were admitted to the ground, and carried away wondrous stories of the prowess of the Seventh. On the other hand, the courtesy and liberality of the men told, in their way. The petty traders and negro boys swarmed around the school, to exchange for "fips" fruits and cakes which had cost pennies. The officers paid generously for such scanty provisions as could be had. So, what with generosity and soldierly bearing, the Seventh, before it left Annapolis, had half vanquished its undecided population. Nevertheless, there were many threats of violence, ominous gatherings of militia, and reckless adventurers around the town, and menaces of attacking the Academy.

By sunset, Colonel Lefferts's preparations were made for the march. He therefore wrote and forwarded the following to Governor Morgan of New York: —

"SIR, — Upon the arrival of my command at Philadelphia, I found it impracticable to reach Washington via Baltimore, and, after waiting eight hours for answer from the Secretary of War, I made up my mind, from all the information I could gather, that Annapolis would of necessity become a most important point or military base. I immediately chartered a steamer and embarked for this place, and was the first to land, and feel I have done already some little service to the government.

"The Massachusetts troops, or, at least, a portion of them, passed from Philadelphia via Havre de Grace. To-morrow morning at daylight I leave for Washington via Annapolis and Baltimore Railroad, and may have to march forty miles, as the people have torn the rails, bridges, etc. We shall also have fighting. I have yesterday and to-day had couriers from Washington, and I am directed to press on.

"I have been detained twenty-four hours for want of sufficient funds to provision the men for a three days' march. I hear to-day of fresh troops to arrive, and, in my judgment, they are needed here to replace us as soon as we leave, so as to keep the communication open."

While Colonel Lefferts was sending this report to his superior officer, the Governor of New York, General Butler was sending a report on his part to *his* superior officer, the Governor of Massachusetts. The word which General Butler sent was that he was waiting to be reinforced from the North before going to Washington; and the proof thereof is contained in the official "Abstract of the Operations of the Massachusetts Troops, under the Command of Brigadier-General Butler," published from the Executive Department of that State, on the 24th, and in which it was announced that "General Butler and his forces on Tuesday evening were eagerly awaiting the arrival of the Fifth (Massachusetts) Regiment, with its accompanying artillery, battery, and rifle battalion, *upon the arrival of which, together with the New York regiments which departed for Annapolis on Sunday and Monday*, they would be fully able to open and maintain communication between Annapolis and Washington." In New York, the following day the same news was announced by the editor of the Times, on authority of a special messenger just from Annapolis, who declared that as it was "believed that the Rebels were collected in the vicinity of the road, to the number of 12,000 or 15,000, General Butler did not deem it prudent to move forward until he had been reinforced."

These facts are here mentioned, because they show that General Butler was again waiting for reinforcements here as at Philadelphia; and as he has taken occasion to offensively charge the Seventh Regiment with doing this, and to imply that he did *not* so wait, it is necessary to put the official fact on the record. The messages sent to the respective governors tell the whole story. Colonel Lefferts deemed reinforcements a necessity, and had written to have them pushed forward; but it clearly appears that he had ordered his march without reference to their previous arrival. Their approach at midnight, after the march had been arranged the previous evening for daylight, was simply a happy circumstance.

For, in fact, at sunset, the arrangements for the march were substantially made. The provisions of pork and crackers had been bought, and during the night these were packed. Orders were issued for the Second Company (Captain Clark), the Sixth (Captain Nevers), and a detachment of the Tenth, under Lieutenant Bunting, to start at four o'clock, A. M., along the railroad towards Annapolis Junction. A messenger (Mortimer Thompson) crossed the bay in an open boat to carry to New York tidings of the proposed march, with directions to forward supplies to Washington.

The Seventh Regiment's march from Annapolis to Washington presents *now*, with the mighty events of a four years' war intervening, a very different appearance from that of April, 1861. Maryland was then mainly in hostile possession. Lander,—a dashing officer, whose heroic life was soon afterwards thrown away in an heroic exploit,—

on reaching the Naval Academy, on the 23d, and consulting with the officers of the Seventh Regiment, said, according to Colonel Clark, who, as Captain, was present at the interview, that, "in his opinion, derived from personal observation, the regiment would meet with serious resistance upon the road to Washington, and could not expect to reach that point without a loss of 200 or 300 men. The party by whom he had been arrested numbered 400 men, and all the roads were infested with troopers and bushwhackers. Yet so perilous was the situation of affairs at Washington, that he advised a forward movement at any cost; and as it was impossible to make suitable provision for the conveyance of sick or wounded men, that they be left upon the road, to the mercy and humanity of the Marylanders."

Captain Blake and Lieutenant Matthews were equally impressed with the hostile sentiment of Eastern Maryland, and expressed their opinion that the Seventh Regiment's march to Washington would be sharply contested. "Five minutes after we had landed," says Chaplain Weston, "the officer in command of the Naval School informed me that, if we made a forced march, we might possibly carry two thirds of our number through. . . . . All declared we would meet with a warm reception." Governor Hicks and Quartermaster Miller held the same opinion. They informed General Butler and Colonel Lefferts of the set purpose of the Marylanders to resist the passage of troops over their soil. "Large parties of secessionists," the officers of the Constitution declared, had been round that ship every day, "noting her assailable points. The militia of the county were drilled in sight of the ship during the daytime; during the night, signals were exchanged along the banks and across the river." Bodies of infantry and cavalry were observed by scouts around the town, and the militia paraded in Annapolis.

General Butler was also much impressed by the gravity of the situation. At Philadelphia he bought intrenching tools, on the theory that "all Maryland was supposed to be in arms"; and in that city, when he assembled his officers for consultation on his proposition to go forward, he declared that, "as some might consider it rash and reckless, he was resolved to take the sole responsibility himself." He therefore caused thirteen revolvers to be put on his table at the Girard House, and, says his biographer, "taking up one of the revolvers, he invited every officer who was willing to accompany him to signify it by accepting a pistol. The pistols were all instantly appropriated." In the same conviction, he marched upon Havre de Grace with skirmishers deployed so as to "rush upon the barricades, and carry them at the point of the bayonet." Arrived at Annapolis at midnight, he found the whole town, says his biographer, "awake and astir. Rockets shot up into the sky. Swiftly moving lights were seen on shore, and all the houses in sight were lighted up. Noting these signs of disturbance, he cast anchor, and determined to delay his landing till daylight." He found the frigate Constitution "surrounded by a population stolidly hostile to the United States," with the local militia drilling in sight of her, and throwing up signals such as he had seen on arriving. He rescued the Constitution, while "groups of sulky secesh stood scowling around and muttering execrations," and in his official order on that subject, he declared the frigate to have been "substantially at the mercy of the armed mob, which sometimes paralyzes the otherwise loyal State of Maryland." Accordingly, General Butler sent word, as we have seen, that he was awaiting reinforcements before proceeding to Washington; and meanwhile, with a view to conciliating a popular sentiment which he found so threatening, on this same Tuesday, the 23d, he offered the Massachusetts men to the task of protecting the slave property of the neighborhood of Annapolis, and, addressing Governor Hicks by letter, begged him "to announce publicly that any portion of the forces under my command is at your Excellency's disposal" to quell a negro insurrection which he imagined to be impending. Such was General Butler's view of the situation.*

While preparing for his march, on Tuesday, Colonel Lefferts, that he might have the regiment instantly ready for any service, allowed no straggling into the city, and required the camp guard-duty to be performed with the utmost care and precision. The regiment took pride, in turn, in showing themselves true soldiers, who understood discipline and were prompt at duty; and when, late on Tuesday night, rockets from the Constitution were thrown

* Mr. Parton, in his biography of General Butler, from which the preceding facts and citations are collected, meets at this point a difficulty. As the New York Seventh and the Eighth Massachusetts were at Annapolis together, the glory of the "march through Maryland" is one which they must share in common. This, however, is not, apparently, what General Butler's biographer desires. His purpose seems to be to get all the laurels for his own hero. Hence he paints the difficulties and dangers which surrounded General Butler in the highest colors; but the *same* difficulties and dangers, when speaking of the Seventh, he draws in caricature. But, in the latter case, he obviously renders Butler's revolver scene, strategic advance on Havre de Grace, and historic "capture of the Constitution," by which latter, as Butler's thrasonical order said, "the blood of our friends shed by the Baltimore mob is in so far avenged," all a travesty and farce. The truth is that Butler's actual view of the situation is that already given in the text,—the one taken not only by the Mayor and citizens of Annapolis, who talked with him and with Colonel Lefferts, but also by officers of such experience and attested courage as Colonels Lander and Curtis, and Captain Blake and his lieutenants. General Butler was at that time an obscure militia officer, whose martial exploits were in their infancy, and whose professional military judgment was not valuable. That he was annoyed at the slight attention which the officers of the Seventh Regiment gave to his suggestions is natural, but there was no reason then for their doing otherwise. His course hitherto had been extravagant, his notions of military authority were crude, he refused to understand why a march could not be undertaken without food, and told Captain Blake, "I have got no orders, I am making war on my own hook," which indeed seemed to be the case. Of course the Seventh Regiment could hardly pay much attention to that sort of thing, and, in fact, declined to be led by him at all, whereby he sagely concluded that they had "resolved to remain at Annapolis!" But I am trenching now upon a dispute which is treated of in the following chapter.

up (the preconcerted signal for the approach of an unknown force), and the "long roll" beat at the Academy grounds, in *seven minutes*, by the watch, from the first drum-tap, the whole regiment, sick and well, was in line, all armed and equipped, and with the howitzers manned. The midshipmen had started from their sleep with equal celerity, and, forming a hundred strong, had hurried down the slope with their howitzers.

But it was a friend that approached,—the Baltic, loaded with the troops that left New York after the Seventh. The Baltic's lights had been discovered, for she and her consorts were expected; but they had instantly been shut out of sight by a thick haze. It was this disappearance which caused the suspicion of foul play. When the fog lifted, the moon glittered on rows of motionless bayonets upon the shore. The glass now told the character of the coming vessel, and ranks were broken, and blankets sought again, save by the detail who prepared the rations for the morning's march. The midshipmen separated, too, heartily eulogizing the celerity and discipline of the National Guard.

# CHAPTER VI.

## A DISPUTED COMMAND.

FROM the moment General Butler set eye on the Seventh Regiment, he seemed possessed with the desire to command it,—a desire which was not reciprocated. The wish being father to the thought, that officer at length, by persistent fancying, appears to have fallen into the delusion that he actually *did* command the regiment. On no other ground, at any rate, can we account for his conduct at Annapolis. It has been seen how at Philadelphia he was anxious to order the regiment to Havre de Grace, and how he was amazed that the regiment did not go thither. But, having reached Annapolis, where he awaited the Seventh, he was seized by the same frenzy, and exhibited it in orders addressed to Colonel Lefferts, based on the wild supposition that the New York National Guard was a part of the "Third Brigade, Second Division, Massachusetts Volunteer Militia," over which he professed to have command. This conclusion, however, he reached only by degrees; for an early communication to the Seventh Regiment, on its arrival off the mouth of the Severn, politely ran, in the form of a request, as follows: —

STEAMER MAYFLOWER,* April 22, 1861.

Will Colonel Lefferts, Honorable Mr. Curtis, and Captain Hamilton do me the favor to accompany me and my detachment in our landing at Annapolis, and give me the benefit of their advice and assistance.

Most respectfully,
Your friend and servant,
B. F. BUTLER, *Brigadier-General.*

Thus we perceive that while the Mayflower was firmly taking root, as if contemplating being transplanted, General Butler felt hardly equal to adopting the tone of authority which doubtless he felt to be his due as commander of "the brigade." However, during the day, Colonel Lefferts was favored with an official copy (from the same brigade head-quarters) of "Special Brigade Orders, Nos. 36 and 37," — for to such figures had the special orders already ascended without Colonel Lefferts's knowledge. The latter order, "No. 37," on opening, he found to consist of four full pages, dated April 22, 1861, prescribing company drills (from five to seven, A. M.) upon General Butler's command; also describing the danger of improperly stacking loaded arms, and narrating that one accident had already occurred from this cause; also asserting that "deeds of daring, successful contests, and glorious victories had rendered Old Ironsides" a "fitly chosen school-ship," and that for the Eighth Massachusetts to have saved her from capture was "a sufficient triumph of right, and a sufficient triumph for us. By this the blood of our friends shed by the Baltimore mob is in so far avenged. The Eighth Regiment may hereafter cheer lustily on all proper occasions, but *never without orders.*"

* "Mayflower" doubtless means "Maryland"; the biographer of General Butler, however, employs the latter name, in place of the one wherewith the General's patriotism had christened the craft.

The order proceeded to announce also that "we have been joined by the Seventh Regiment of New York," that there must be no "unauthorized interference with private property" in the State, and so forth. At length Colonel Lefferts came, just at the end, to the paragraph clearing up the mystery: —

Colonel Lefferts's command not having been originally included in this order, he will be furnished with a copy for his *instruction.*

By order of

B. F. BUTLER, *Brigadier-General.*

WM. H. CLEMENCE, *Brigade-Major.*

Although Colonel Lefferts felt "instructed" on a variety of points by this comprehensive special order, yet the distinction therein drawn between the "we" and the "Seventh Regiment" prevented him, perhaps, from conning it so carefully as he might otherwise have done. However, if the Seventh did not perform the precise drills therein ordered, (for it did not contemplate a sufficiently long stay at Annapolis for "daily company drills"), at least its members witnessed with pleasure those of their comrades of the Eighth; as to the prohibited "outrages on private property," on which the General was characteristically sensitive, they *did* refrain from them, as the citizens of Annapolis could testify.

The next "brigade order," whereof the original lies before us, is unique in having no date, — a matter, however, of less importance, as no attention was paid to it. It runs as follows: —

HEAD-QUARTERS BRIGADE UNITED MILITIA, 1861.

SPECIAL BRIGADE ORDER, No. 38.

Colonel Lefferts's command will report themselves ready for such duty as shall be assigned them at half past eight o'clock this morning.

By command of

B. F. BUTLER, *Brigadier-General.*

W. H. CLEMENCE, *Brigade-Major.*

While No. 38 had thus the merit of brevity over its

predecessor, No. 37, yet its uncertainty in point of time, and the lack of historic data to determine how the Seventh Regiment N. Y. S. M. and the Eighth Regiment M. V. M. became welded into a "Brigade United Militia," befog alike the chronicler and the reader.

A hiatus of six special brigade orders now occurs in the records of the Seventh Regiment, nor can any memory or fancy of its officers fill the gap. On the next morning the special brigade orders had reached in number forty-five, and the United Militia had become the United States Militia, as the following copy shows: —

HEAD-QUARTERS BRIGADE U. S. MILITIA,
ANNAPOLIS, MD., April 23, 1861.

SPECIAL BRIGADE ORDER, No. 45.

The General commanding the 3d Brigade orders that *no officer or private belonging to his command suffer himself to leave the grounds belonging to the United States government,* without a special requisition from him. Colonel Munroe of the Eighth and Lefferts of the Seventh Regiments will see that the execution of this order is strictly complied with in their respective commands.

By order of

B. F. BUTLER,
*Brigadier-General of 3d Brigade.*

W. H. CLEMENCE, *Brigade-Major.*

But here we must break off in our documentary record, enough having been cited, doubtless, to show that there was a "disputed command" respecting the Seventh Regiment. Already had that body unconsciously been converted from New York State Militia to "United Militia" and "United States Militia," and from the "First Division" of New York, under General Sandford, to the "Second Division, Third Brigade," of Massachusetts, under General Butler. What other transformations the many special orders from 1 to 36, and from 39 to 45, might reveal, the members of the Seventh will never know; most of them learn now for the first time in what varying capacities they served at Annapolis.

It should here be added that, on the evening of the 22d of April, when the Seventh Regiment had landed at Annapolis, and stacked arms on the Academy Green, General Butler came upon the ground, and, after exchanging a few words with Colonel Lefferts, commenced a speech to the officers of the Seventh, who were grouped together discussing a variety of topics. Colonel Lefferts, meanwhile, was listening as patiently as possible to the thousand reports, requests, and suggestions made to him on landing, and was issuing orders for the disposition of the regiment for the night and for unloading the Boston for the use of the Eighth Massachusetts, who were suffering great hardships on board the Maryland, still aground in the harbor. Thus engaged, Colonel Lefferts had no time to hear General Butler's remarks, nor did he know their object, until, when his immediate duties had been finished, he learned through his officers, whom he assembled for consultation, that Butler's aim had evidently been to try to get such ascendency over the regiment as to bring them under his own control, — the thing he had been aiming at ever since leaving Philadelphia. On hearing this, Colonel Lefferts stated to his officers that he had received from General Butler the extraordinary "orders" already quoted, but had given them no attention whatever, on account of the intrinsic absurdity of an officer in the militia of one State claiming authority over the militia of another, neither being yet in the United States service. He added that as this theory seemed to be now revived by General Butler, it was necessary to formally refuse to place the regiment at his disposal, the more especially as his pretensions had not yet been substantiated by any show of etiquette, discretion, or military knowledge.

This view the officers unanimously supported; and it was also agreed to by common consent that, unless official assurance should previously be received of the safety of Washington (regarding which nothing whatever was known), Butler's proposition to march by railroad, laying the track, was not to be thought of; that, on the contrary, the turnpike must be taken, in order to reach Washington at the earliest practicable hour. These ideas — namely, that the regiment could not, under General Butler's assumptions, co-operate with him in a plan which they did not approve — the officers unanimously desired Colonel Lefferts to embody in a letter to General Butler, as being their own views. This he did; and the following letter, hastily written and despatched, though more courteous and conciliatory in tone than the facts demanded, yet had the desired effect, namely, to disabuse General Butler of any ungrounded expectations he may have entertained as to the effect of his recent eloquence on any of the officers of the Seventh Regiment.

ANNAPOLIS ACADEMY, Monday night, April 22.

GENERAL B. F. BUTLER, *Commanding Mass. Volunteers.*

SIR, — Upon consultation with my officers, I do not deem it proper, under the circumstances, to co-operate in the proposed march by railroad, making track as we go along, particularly in view of a large force hourly expected, and with so little ammunition * as we possess. I must be governed by my officers in a matter of so much importance. I have directed this to be handed to you immediately upon your return from the transport ship.

I am, sir, yours respectfully,

M. LEFFERTS, *Colonel.*

From this polite but expressive note, General Butler learned, first, that he was treated, despite his pretensions, as simply "commanding the *Massachusetts* volunteers"; secondly, that the Seventh Regiment would not co-operate in *any plan involving its being put under his command;* thirdly, that these conclusions were not those simply of Colonel Lefferts, who was naturally jealous of outside influence of the sort Butler aimed at, but those of his

* Ten rounds per man.

officers, by whose opinion in the matter, after consultation, the Colonel was governed.

And indeed, when, the next day, the regiment, after having been unexpectedly delayed in its contemplated march on the dirt-road direct to Washington (as official and unofficial documents and letters have already explained), learned that the capital was still in our hands, so that *then* the railroad route had become the more advantageous, it took the latter without any consultation with Butler and entirely independent of him. The dispositions were made and orders for the march issued, so far as is known by the regiment, without Butler's being aware of them; the main body of his troops were left in the town when the Seventh had entirely quitted it; nor, but for a long halt in repairing a bridge, many hours later, would Colonel Lefferts have been made aware that Butler's force had followed on.

The Seventh Regiment has never sought to detract one iota from the glory of their gallant brethren of the Eighth, their comrades in this famous campaign; nor, on the other hand, have the Eighth ever claimed for themselves that exclusiveness of credit which General Butler has claimed for them — and him.

One other incident relating to this same period may here be appropriately introduced. As Butler, after his speech on Monday evening, was about to return to the transport, he suggested to Colonel Lefferts to seize and occupy the railroad depot. On conferring with Captain Blake on this matter, the latter sent up two or three of his young men, who found everything quiet at the depot, under charge of the watchman; so that it appeared wholly unnecessary to make any other occupation. Next morning Butler, who, finding that his suggestion had not been followed, had meanwhile moved upon the depot in grand force, fumed and blustered a good deal on meeting Colonel Lefferts.

"I thought," said he, "you told me you would take the depot: when my people got there, they found nothing but one man and a black-and-tan dog." As Colonel Lefferts was aware of this fact, he contented himself with saying that for that very reason he "had not seen the necessity of using a whole regiment for its capture."

The rebuff, and the pithy note sent him by Colonel Lefferts the night before, opened his eyes to the true character of his relations with the Seventh. It showed him that the two regiments in Annapolis were independent commands, and that while the Seventh would gladly co-operate with its comrade where its judgment approved, it could not be ordered about by pretended authority. The ground assumed by General Butler, that he had the *right* to command Colonel Lefferts, the latter would not admit. He had been ordered by the Governor of New York to report to General Scott at Washington, not to General Butler by the way. He had neither the right nor the disposition to put his own State militia under the command of a militia officer from another State. The fiction of "United States Militia" created by General Butler in this dilemma was ridiculous, nor had that officer even the shadow of authority from the War Office to extemporize such a fiction, being himself under command of Governor Andrew of Massachusetts. As to General Butler's military qualifications, nothing whatever was at that time known of them, nor was it clear that his experience was greater than that of the commanding officer of the historic National Guards; while, in fact, the lapse of a few weeks showed that General Butler, apt as he might be for the profession of arms, had considerable yet to learn.

The upshot of this quarrel greatly chagrined General Butler, and colored his after-memory of the facts relating to the whole expedition. However, it settled his pretensions to control the Seventh Regiment; he promptly accepted the situation, and there was never after any question of "disputed command." *

So much for this interesting episode: and now — to resume the thread of our narrative, broken at that point where, messengers to the Seventh from Washington having brought tidings from Washington, it had become as desirable to proceed by railroad, repairing on the way, as before it had been needful to advance without delay along the turnpike.

* Captain Clark's History says: "The selfish ambition of General Butler was deeply outraged at this reply, and his indignation and anger at the refusal of the Seventh Regiment to obey his orders knew no bounds. He threatened arrests and court-martials, and to report the case to the War Department, and he made himself generally ridiculous; and at that time and since, by misrepresentations of the facts, and ungenerous inferences and reflections, he has spared no effort to injure the reputation of Colonel Lefferts, and indirectly stigmatize the Seventh Regiment."

## CHAPTER VII.

### THE MARCH TO WASHINGTON.

AT three o'clock, A. M., of Wednesday, the 24th of April, the Second Company (Captain Clark) and Sixth Company (Captain Nevers) were astir for the march, and with them the detachment of the Tenth under Lieutenant Bunting. Details had been occupied from twelve o'clock till three in getting ready rations and ammunition. At four o'clock the whole detachment reported, under command of Captain Nevers as senior officer, and soon after were off on the road to Annapolis Junction.

It will be obvious, without further comment, what had been achieved, and what was now proposed for accomplishment. The purposes of the enemy were still unknown. A despatch from private sources, in the Philadelphia papers of the preceding day, said: "The troops intended to march immediately for Annapolis Junction. The citizens of the town and neighborhood were prepared to give them a guerrilla fight in their march." Captain Blake, anxious to pioneer the Seventh's way through Annapolis, sent a letter for that purpose to Colonel Lefferts: —

COLONEL, — I feel so sure that if the service suggested is performed by one of our youths it would lead to disastrous consequences, that I am extremely reluctant to order one of them upon it. I sketch another route which is perfectly direct and as little exposed as any one you can take.

Very respectfully,

G. S. BLAKE.

P. S. — You can leave the Academy grounds by another gate. The upper one would perhaps be best. I direct the officer in charge to report to you, to show you out of the grounds and point out the route to the depot.

On the reverse page of the original letter we find the "route" alluded to sketched with precision. But no opposition was encountered at the start. Captain Nevers's advance-guard, with the Second Company leading, passed through the city just before daylight, and up the hill to the depot, where the Eighth Massachusetts greeted them heartily. Their Yankee ingenuity had, the day before, repaired the dislocated engine "J. H. Nicholson" (which ought on the spot to have been rebaptized the "Charles Homans"), and had got the torn-up tracks relaid for three miles, under a guard of two companies. The train now moved forward.

It was a novel column in the Seventh's experience. First came two open platform-cars, formed by sawing off the tops of two old cattle-cars. On the first was the howitzer, loaded with grape, with eight of Lieutenant's Bunting's men on each side as guard. That officer was at the forward end, acting as conductor to the train, and giving the engineer (a Massachusetts lad) his signals; beside him stood a man detailed to watch for breaks in the road. On the second open car were the ammunition for the howitzer, and a guard of six picked riflemen, three on each side. Then came the wheezy locomotive. After that, two small cars, the first containing the Second and the other the

Sixth Company. This was all that could be mustered of the "rolling-stock," the railroad company having gathered up all their good cars and engines and sent them back to Baltimore.

Off the train started, amid the applause of the Massachusetts Eighth, and the "passengers" all in good spirits, though in rather close quarters for comfort. The train ran slowly along on the track laid down the day before by the Massachusetts men, and, two miles out, found the picket-guard of the Eighth Massachusetts, consisting of two companies, about one hundred and fifty strong, under Lieutenant-Colonel Hinks. The poor fellows were in deplorable straits, having had nothing to eat for twenty-four hours, and bitter were their complaints against General Butler's repeated experiments in campaigning without supplies. Off came the knapsacks and haversacks of the Seventh, out came their rations; each man found a half-starved comrade with whom to share his beef and bread; and thus, from the dole of provisions packed at Annapolis for the exigencies of march and battle, the Seventh supplied their less fortunate brother-soldiers with a hearty meal. The latter could hardly express their gratitude. Fitz James O'Brien, who marched with the body of the regiment, writes: "These brave boys, I say, were starving while they were doing all this good work. What their Colonel was doing I can't say. As we marched along the track that they had laid, they greeted us with ranks of smiling but hungry faces. One boy told me, with a laugh on his young lips, that he had not ate anything for thirty hours. There was not, thank God, a haversack in our regiment that was not emptied into the hands of these ill-treated heroes, nor a flask that was not at their disposal. I am glad to pay them tribute here, and mentally doff my cap." The previous conduct of the Seventh in delaying, hour after hour, to haul off the stranded Maryland, and their haste to

OPENING THE ROAD TO WASHINGTON.

share provisions with the famished Eighth on their landing at Annapolis, were capped by this last instance of soldierly hospitality, and thenceforth the men of the two regiments were enthusiastic friends. This detachment of the Eighth Massachusetts now accompanied the train.

As the train moved on, a small body of men were discovered ahead, busily destroying the track. Skirmishers were immediately sent out to capture them, but the party took the alarm and ran to the woods. Three miles out, the road was broken up so badly that it required regular repairs. The orders of Colonel Lefferts, however, had been for the advance to push on a mile farther, and there halt until the remainder of the regiment should come up. Accordingly the engine and the two rear cars were abandoned, and drag-ropes were fastened to the two front platform-cars, carrying the howitzer, with its ammunition and the knapsacks. A body of skirmishers was thrown out from each company on either flank of the railroad, — those of the Second Company under Lieutenant Farnham, and those of the Sixth under Lieutenant Halstead, — and continued to act as such during the entire march. The remainder of Captain Nevers's command manned the drag-ropes, and pulled along the two cars, stopping now and again to put back some rail thrown out of its place.

By nine o'clock, however, the distance prescribed by Colonel Lefferts had been passed, and Captain Nevers accordingly halted his men and stacked arms, and under the shade of the woods the troops ate the now scanty ration set aside for breakfast. A reconnoitring party was pushed ahead, but found nothing but mounted citizens flying from the path of the column, and apparently unarmed. The single farm-house, a log structure, on the hill which formed the temporary camp, was deserted; but presently the lord of the manor crept from his hiding-place in the woods, fear for his property at length overcoming fear for his person. The pleasant jingle of silver, and the flavor of wine from Captain Clark's flask (which latter he cautiously required Colonel Hinks and Lieutenant Bunting to taste before partaking), put his fears to flight, and he came out quite strong for "the Union as it was."*

Meanwhile, at dawn, the reveille had roused the main body of the regiment. Blankets and overcoats were rolled up and strapped upon knapsacks; canteens were filled with water tinged with vinegar; three days' rations, consisting of six navy biscuit and pieces of raw salt pork or beef, were served to each man; cartridges were distributed, and guns loaded, for the start. It was a delicious April morning, and the fragrance of the apple-blossoms and the fresh green grass filled the air. No word coming from the advance, the regiment left the Naval Academy soon after seven, and threaded the queer, old-fashioned little city of Annapolis. The town was all alive, and many an eye looked askance at the "invaders," but the on-lookers wisely held their hands from blows and their tongues from taunts. In truth, the Annapolitans were already gained over; for while the imposing array of the famous Seventh had disheartened the hostile, their courtesy and liberality had pro-

* A letter of Lieutenant Bunting gives some details of this "raid." He says: "Having nothing to eat, I took twelve men and went to a house on the top of the hill, where we could see all around the country for some distance. Saw nothing of the enemy, so we knocked at the door. No answer. Opened the door, and went in. Found the house empty. Looked in the cupboard and found some preserves. We ate them in short order. Looked under the bed, and found a basket of eggs (hens', ducks', and turkeys'), which we sucked. Then we found a second cupboard, and in it some fat bacon. This we sent after the eggs and preserves, and were ready for either a fight or a march. As we were getting ready to leave, a man came rushing in, in great haste and much scared. We extended the hospitalities of the house to him, and he took a seat. We soon ascertained that he was the proprietor, and that his family had got scared and run into the swamp. Sent him after them, when they returned. We recounted the damage we had done, and told the old fellow to fix his price. He said we were heartily welcome, — we knew he lied, — and that the things were worth probably $3. We gave him $10, and he was the happiest man in the State."

voked admiration and even a certain sympathy.* Thus, before the regiment set out from Annapolis, its conquest was half achieved.

Colonel Lefferts left Annapolis in good hands. The transports in the Severn were loaded with four regiments of militia, following in the wake of his own, and two more were daily expected, so that Annapolis and its neighborhood were henceforth safe. His own men were as well provisioned as possible under the circumstances, and had started fresh and in good spirits on their march. When in Philadelphia, as we have seen, Colonel Lefferts had sent word to New York that Annapolis was the point to which recruits and supplies were to be sent forward. Nine of his men came in the Baltic, and provisions were on the way to the same point. Before dawn, Colonel Lefferts had despatched a message to the Baltic, to endeavor to obtain additional supplies, and immediately received from Colonel (now Major-General) Butterfield the following answer: —

"I have the honor of acknowledging receipt of your communication of this date, and, in compliance with your request, I now send you herewith a detachment of nine men of your regiment, brought on by me from New York. The troops under my command will receive marching orders from Lieutenant-Colonel Keyes.

"We are all ready to support you, each eager to be first.

"The strength of my command is nine hundred and over. I will lay your communication before Colonel Keyes immediately upon his return to the ship. The rations on board are property of the United States government, and are uncooked provisions. You will please send a requisition for what you want, and I will endeavor to procure them for you. The transport R. R. Cuyler has on board the Seventy-First Regiment N. Y. S. M.; the Columbia, the Sixth Regiment N. Y. S. M.; the Coatsacoalcos, the First Regiment R. I. troops, led by Governor Sprague in person. The Eighth and Sixty-Ninth Regiments were to have followed us the next day from New York."

* A letter to the New York Times, from the Sixth New York Militia, which landed at Annapolis just after the Seventh left, says: "The Seventh have won golden opinions here. When they started, they found the farmers terrified, but the name of the Seventh National Guard seemed to act like magic."

Leaving the officers' baggage and camp equipage at the Naval Academy, Colonel Lefferts pushed through Annapolis to the depot, and thence out along the track to overtake the advance. It was about eight o'clock when he left the station, and the troops marched briskly. The morning breeze had died away, and soon the sun poured down upon the heads of the men, as one of the sufferers expressed it, "like hot lava." The railroad runs for miles through a gorge, which, in concentrating the sun's heat, excludes any breath of fresh air, and the country around is arid and sandy. The men had had a scanty breakfast, little rest the preceding night (on account of the alarm and the early start), and, indeed, little to boast of in rest or rations for many days; but they clung manfully to the march, and fell headlong under the sun's rays only to hurry on again and reach the ever-advancing column. About ten, the shanty or farm-house where Captain Nevers's advance was posted was reached.

The main march and the main difficulty and danger were now before the regiment. The only serious opposition was expected near the Junction; and the few citizens encountered on the road confirmed the report that a concentration of the enemy had been intended there, it being not only a strategic point important to hold, but also at a considerable distance from the Union force in reserve at Annapolis. The only information, however, was that resistance there had been *planned;* whether the prompt march of the Seventh might not foil the intent was still conjectural. The regiment, having been rested, was now moved forward along the track. The Second and Sixth Companies, having had the longest rest, pushed on in advance. At the head of the main column was Lieutenant Bunting's platform-car with its howitzer; some distance behind, another platform-car fitted up for the sick and wounded and for medical stores; while a third, containing the remaining howitzer (also loaded with grape) and its ammunition, which had been brought on by the main body, brought up the rear. Skirmishers were again thrown out on each flank to the distance of half a mile to scour the country and guard against sudden assault from mounted guerilla parties.

Three miles more, under the noonday sun, the regiment pursued its exhausting march. The scouting-parties plunged into forest and fen on either side, sweeping the country in a swath a mile broad. The main force on the track toiled wearily along upon a railroad laid on sleepers but little sunk in the sandy or clayey soil, now in an arid open country, and now plunging through a cut where no breeze ruffled the stifling atmosphere. The engine and passenger cars had been left behind for the use of the Eighth Massachusetts, now also on the march from Annapolis; but the platform-cars afforded a chance to give a lift to the sun-struck and the exhausted, whom their gallant comrades at the drag-ropes pulled along. Despite the fatigue, heat, and lack of water, the labor of scouting to the outlying companies, and that of repairing the track to the main column, the troops all behaved gallantly,* and the regiment marched more solidly than is customary with recruits. The skirmishers, threading woods and swamps, reported stray mounted men hovering about, but no force whatever on either flank. The saying of the people of Annapolis, that the regiment "could not march ten miles without fighting their way," had been happily falsified.

About 3 P. M., a water-station on the railroad, dignified by the name of Millersville (though local habitation there

* Instances of the plucky conduct of individuals on this march were published in the newspapers of the time, but need not be repeated. One of these, for example, gives the name of a private who, "while marching from Annapolis to the Junction, was sun-struck, and lay insensible for two hours. On recovering his senses, he was told by the Colonel and surgeons that he must go back to New York, but begged to be permitted to join his company, and, watching his chance, escaped and caught them, and performed his duty as a scout all that night. On arriving at Washington he had a relapse, and lay for two days unconscious."

was none), had been reached, but the labor of repairing the track had been such that, even with very brisk work during the last three hours, but three miles had been accomplished. "The Engineer Corps," says O'Brien, "had, of course, to do the forwarding work, — New York dandies, sir, — but they built bridges, laid rails, and headed the regiment through that terrible march." Sometimes the missing rails were found in the bushes near the road, and sometimes they had been dragged several rods distant, and plunged into thicket or marsh. Accordingly, the scouts were directed to keep an eye for rails as well as Rebels, and woods were searched and ditches dragged till nearly all were replaced. Some rails and sleepers, however, had been hidden beyond discovery; their places were supplied by substitutes taken up from "turn-outs" and from the Annapolis switches. The spare timber and rails, with the spikes and hammers, were piled on a car and pushed on by the men. In these labors the Massachusetts men, some of whom had continued on with the Seventh, lent their hearty and valuable aid. Such was the noontide work of a day on which the thermometer ranged from 85° to 90°, and whose full rations were two biscuits and a bit of raw pork.

But an unexpected rest was now at hand. The railroad bridge crossing the stream just beyond Millersville station had been burned by the enemy. As the bridge was twenty feet high and sixteen feet long, to rebuild it, even though some of the old timbers could be used, was an affair of two hours. While the regiment was halting for this purpose, the engine and train came up, thus proving the success of the day's track-laying. It brought up, too, the men who had fallen out from exhaustion; and, these having been disembarked, Colonel Lefferts sent it back for the use of the Eighth Regiment. Only two men of the Seventh, despite the fatigues of the day, went back on this train, — one, a man sun-struck; the other, private De Van Postley, of the Second Company, wounded in the knee by the discharge of his own pistol. The rest of the stragglers and exhausted got recruited during the halt.

Just as preparation was making to rebuild the bridge, a storm came up. Refuge was taken in the forest, and blankets were stretched as tents; but the storm burst on the camp with great fury, and soaked, not only the blankets, but the men under them. It was a refreshing shower-bath for the moment, but it made clothing and blankets poor protection against the ensuing night.

When the storm was nearly spent, the heavy regimental detail for the working party went briskly to work, under Sergeant Scott, of the non-commissioned staff, and armorer. The Engineer Corps guided operations, and the men worked heartily. Trees were selected, felled, cut down, and hewed into timber, the joists laid, the rails cut with rough chisel and sledge to the proper length, and then spiked to the wood. By hearty and sharp work, in two or three hours the Millersville Bridge — the first and last bridge the Seventh had ever been called upon to construct — was finished.* When the work was done, and the last stroke of the axe and clang of the sledge were heard, the sun had sunk below the horizon.

During the long halt at Millersville, the main body of the Eighth Regiment, which had left the Annapolis depot in the forenoon, came up to the Seventh's camp. The main body of the Seventh was halted at the watering-station, a quarter of a mile or less from the bridge, while the latter

* Major Winthrop writes pleasantly of the Seventh's exploits in track laying and bridge-building: "Scott called for a working party. There were plenty of handy fellows among our engineers and in the line. Tools were plenty in the engineers' chest. We pushed the platform-car upon which howitzer No. 1 was mounted down to the gap, and began operations. Scott and his party made a good and quick job of it. Our friends of the Massachusetts Eighth had now come up. They lent a ready hand, as usual."

was under repair by the working party detailed for the purpose. The Eighth halted at the bridge, being thus interposed between the advance and the main body of the Seventh; and, interested in the work of bridge-building and track-laying going on in the stream, some of them were prompt to "bear a hand" and help the work along. The bridge was soon after finished, and Colonel Monroe of the Eighth, at the request of Colonel Lefferts, drew his men aside, whereupon the main body of the Seventh closed up to the advance. With the column thus formed, and the bridge complete, the Seventh started on once more to pioneer the way, exchanging hearty adieus with their Massachusetts friends. "By twilight," says Winthrop, "there was a practicable bridge. The engine was despatched back to keep the road open. The two platform-cars, freighted with our howitzers, were rigged with the gun-ropes for dragging along the rail. We passed through the files of the Massachusetts men resting by the way, and eating by the fires of the evening the suppers we had in great part provided them; and so begins our night-march."

Night had indeed come. Colonel Lefferts would have been fully justified, after the hard day's work, in making a halt until daylight, and perhaps it would have been more prudent to do so. But he pushed on, and in the same order of march. Of the three platform-cars which the regiment dragged with them, one contained the two howitzers and their ammunition; a second, the spikes, sledges, rails, chairs, and timbers; while the third, deftly arranged with knapsacks and blankets, served as an ambulance for those who fell disabled from the ranks.

It was a delicious night, with the moon at full orb. The bright rifle-barrels glinted in the sombre forests, as the long column plunged into and anon emerged from the narrow defiles through which the railroad runs. Overcome by the heat and burden of the day, and by want of rest and food, the regiment had little thought of the matchless beauty of the scene. The march under the burning sun had been succeeded by a march more trying, in which "every railroad tie was a wearying stumbling-block," and the rough road-bed was slippery from the rain. The clothing of the men was drenched, and chill, cutting blasts swept out from the swamps and through the dark ravines. The work of laying the track was laborious in the darkness, and the dragging of the cars was tiresome. The skirmishers of the Second and Sixth Companies in advance had no pleasant quest in brake and fen on either hand.

Had Colonel Lefferts's present plan embraced only the pioneering of the way to Washington, he could have accomplished that by a forced march, dropping all encumbrances, and pushing through "by daylight" to the Junction. But he had proposed to lay a track for other regiments, and so, through the night-hours, whenever a rail was missing, a halt was cried. The scouting-parties scoured field and ford for it; sometimes the search was a long one, sometimes the rail was sunk in the gloom of the woods, sometimes it was but a few rods distant in the hollow of a neighboring field. But, far or near, it was ferreted out, and the chairs, too, on which it rested, unless, as often happened, the latter, with the spikes themselves, had been left on the roadside by the stupid guerillas. To be prepared for more successful hidings, the side-tracks at turn-outs were torn up and dragged along on the cars, with whatever other material might be turned to account.* In one place about twenty feet of track, rails, chairs, and ties,

* "So, 'Out crowbars!' was the word. We tore up and bagged half a dozen rails, with chairs and spikes complete. Here, too, some of the engineers found a keg of spikes. This was also bagged and loaded on our cars." (Winthrop's "Our March to Washington.") Again the same gay campaigner writes: "Three rails were up. Two of them were easily found. The third was discovered by beating the bush thoroughly. Bonnell and I ran back for tools, and returned at full trot with crowbar and sledge. . . . . Not a half-mile passed without a rail up. Bonnell was always at the front, laying track, and I am proud to say that he ac-

had been lifted up, and pitched to the bottom of the steep embankment. The howitzer ropes were fastened upon this section, and it was hauled up into place.

What with bushwhacking, and tugging at rails, and laying of track, the march seemed intolerably slow. The officers, kept up by a sense of responsibility, were, like the men detailed for scouting and blacksmithery, happier in their labors than the unoccupied majority, to whom halting and marching were alike wearisome. At first the ground seemed so damp that the men hesitated to throw themselves upon it, at a pause, in their wet clothing; but at length, overcome by exhaustion, at the cry of "Halt!" they tumbled on the earth, there dozing till the word "Attention!" broke their brief dreams. "In several instances," says one account, "sleeping men rolled down the railroad embankment, to the imminent danger of life and limb; and when on the march they trudged along half conscious, half dreaming, many exhibiting the symptoms which are ascribed to those who perish from hunger, cold, and exhaustion. It was not uncommon to notice men marching forward upon the uneven railroad track with their eyes completely closed, their heads falling forward or from side to side." Fitz James O'Brien says: —

"I know not if I can describe that night's march. I have dim recollections of deep cuts through which we passed, gloomy and treacherous

cepted me as aide-de-camp. Other fellows, unknown to me in the dark, gave hearty help. The Seventh showed that it could do something else than drill."

A despatch to the New York Tribune, from Washington, says: "The track was torn up at intervals for a long distance. To mend this was a slow and tedious work. The rails and sleepers had been dragged from their places and flung away. These must be found, fitted, and fastened. This too, by men used to Wall Street, Park Place, the Fifth Avenue, and the Bloomingdale Road, but not hitherto counted expert as builders of railroads. Nevertheless, they succeeded. . . . . This experience has been a good one. It has shown the North of what stuff their most cherished sons are made. The race of the present day is not effeminate, nor indolent, nor dried up, nor burnt out. Vigorous and full of the manliest manhood, it will show to the whole country that it is equal to the charge committed to it in these trying days."

looking, with the moon shining full on our muskets, while the banks were wrapped in shade, and each moment expecting to see the flash and hear the crack of the rifle of the Southern guerilla. The tree-frogs and lizards made a mournful music as we passed. The soil on which we travelled was soft and heavy. The sleepers lying at intervals across the track made the marching terribly fatiguing. On all sides dark, lonely pine-woods stretched away; and high over the hooting of owls or the plaintive petition of the whippoorwill rose the bass commands of 'Halt!' 'Forward, march!' and when we came to any ticklish spot the word would run from the head of the column along the line, 'Holes,' 'Bridge, pass it along,' &c.

"As the night wore on, the monotony of the march became oppressive. Owing to our having to explore every inch of the way, we did not make more than a mile or a mile and a half an hour. We ran out of stimulants, and almost out of water. Most of us had not slept for four nights, and as the night advanced our march was almost a stagger. This was not so much fatigue as want of excitement. Our fellows were spoiling for a fight; and when a dropping shot was heard in the distance, it was wonderful to see how the languid legs straightened, and the column braced itself for action. If we had had even the smallest kind of a skirmish, the men would have been able to walk to Washington. As it was, we went sleepily on. I myself fell asleep walking in the ranks. Numbers, I find, followed my example."

In the same strain, Winthrop says: "Hardly any one had had any full or substantial sleep or meal since we started from New York. They napped off, standing, leaning on their guns, dropping down in their tracks, on the wet ground, at every halt. They were sleepy, but plucky." Still another published account says: "The boys were so tired that, when we stopped, they fell down to sleep as if they were dead."

There were calls for the advance to "scare up the Rebs"; but the guerillas kept out of harm's way.* As the

* C. S. H. writes: "I was one of the skirmishers, and did not sleep a wink from two and a half o'clock on Wednesday morning until four on Thursday morning. There were thirty-five of our company that went ahead of the rest to look for the Secessionists. One of the party saw four men tearing up the track a little distance off. The order was given: 'Throw away your blankets, double-quick, march.' On we went on the run, and then the order was given: 'Ready, right oblique, aim.' But the rascals were already in the woods."

regiment threaded the gloomy forest aisles, or plunged into the dismal and deceitful defiles of the road, it would have been an easy prey to an equal force lying in ambush and sure of the ground. However, the enemy, alarmed by the absurdly extravagant reports of the numbers and prowess of the Seventh, did not collect, had not, indeed, sufficient time for organization. The only alarm in the night was a trivial one, produced by the accidental discharge of a gun, which alarmed the skirmishers in advance, who thereupon fired several muskets and pistols to announce their own position.

So the night wore on, without a respite in the toilsome march. One of Colonel Lefferts's officers, coming to the head of the column, declared to the Colonel that it was "inhuman" to continue the march. But the Colonel, who had not slept a moment for two nights and a day, and rightly judged that the spirit of his men was one with his own, pressed on. Some of the officers of the Eighth Massachusetts also came up from their own regiment in the rear, and urged the commander of the Seventh to abandon the platform-cars on which the howitzers were transported. He replied that he should abandon nothing, and marched steadily on.

At length, between three and four o'clock, just as day was dawning, the regiment debouched from the woods and swamp. It was hard by Annapolis Junction, at which point opposition had been looked for. The Colonel halted the regiment in an open ground, and taking a detachment of about one hundred and fifty skirmishers, proceeded with them to reconnoitre. He found the Junction deserted.

Returning to the regiment, resting in a wheat-field, he allowed fires to be built of the neighboring fence-rails, for which, as for anything else seized during the campaign, liberal payment was made at once. Most of the men lay down directly to sleep, while others started in pursuit of provisions. The people of the village and of the farm-houses were aroused by the foraging-parties of the hungry troops; and bread, eggs, milk, fowls, and other edibles, were gladly brought out for sale.

It was found that the railroad between Washington and the Junction had been kept from the hands of the insurgents, and that the government, anxious for the arrival of the regiment, had already, the day before, sent a train of cars to the latter point to receive it. For a few hours, therefore, and until the train should arrive, the regiment took rest and sleep, — the advance in the village, and the main body around their camp-fires in the wheat-field. At length the train came, in charge of the "National Rifles," Captain Smead. The whole regiment was soon on board the cars, which were crowded to overflowing, and, leaving the Junction at ten o'clock of April 25th, arrived at noon, without further incident of importance, in the city of Washington.

# CHAPTER VIII.

## RESULTS OF THE MARCH.

TIRED as they were, when Colonel Lefferts saw, on arriving at Washington, its state of anxiety and alarm, he did not hesitate to march his men from the depot to the President's mansion; and it was only after passing in review before the President, who stood, all smiles, ready to greet the reinforcement he had so long looked for, that the men were allowed to break ranks and go in search of rations and rest.

The arrival of this splendid array of reinforcements produced a happy effect upon the people of Washington, and not less upon the national authorities. "The effect of this movement," said the Adjutant-General of the United States, "no one can estimate so well as those of us present in our capital. At this time we were surrounded by enemies, with traitors in our midst, and, worst of all, those of my own profession, on whom the government had a right to look for support. Then it was that you came forward, with bayonets far more in number than you ever paraded on a gala-day. And when, after great difficulties and delays, you reached the capital, what a thrill of delight pervaded our loyal population! In every direction you could hear, 'THE SEVENTH HAVE COME!' The anxious week, and especially the dark Sunday, had passed, and we felt secure."

It was doubtless a delicious mingling of the feelings of joy and pride, — joy to find the capital still in the hands of the nation, and pride at the consciousness of having come through trials to its rescue, — that inspired the regiment, and made its march through Pennsylvania Avenue that day, despite the week's weariness, a superb exhibition of soldierly precision.* But there was enough in the circumstances of that day to give the regiment spirit. "Until we actually saw the train awaiting us [at Annapolis Junction]," says Winthrop, "and the Washington companies who had come down to escort us drawn up, we did not know whether our Uncle Sam was still a resident of the capital." When, therefore, the flag of the Union was descried floating over

* A Washington letter to the New York Herald, sent via Perrysville and Havre de Grace, says: "The five days of isolation from the remainder of the world, which to Washington seemed a month, have ended. The Seventh Regiment, reported now to have been cut to pieces; now to be coming up the Potomac in the old Constitution, towed by steam-tugs; now to be marching across the country, and now to be aground in a vessel off Annapolis, — reached the railroad station here about noon yesterday. The whistle, not heard for many hours in our isolated position, brought an excited crowd to welcome them to the city; and the welcome extended along Pennsylvania Avenue to the White House, where they were reviewed by the President and Secretaries Seward and Cameron.

"As you will see, when I tell you the history of the previous thirty-six hours, it required no little spirit to march that hot, dusty two miles, over heated pavements. One of the most stalwart men in the regiment, a man who weighs one hundred and eighty pounds, and has always been a leader in gymnastics and boating, told me this morning that his feet felt at every step as though knives were running through them. A sergeant's feet were a mass of blisters, and many others were in a bad plight. Yet, with true Seventh Regiment pluck, after such a march as Regular troops seldom make, — a march worse, says one of the band, who served in the Mexican War, and at other times in the Regular Army, than any forced march within his experience, — every man, except three cr four who were sun-struck on the previous day and had not then entirely recovered, was in the ranks. All are well now, and present their usual fine appearance."

the dome of the Capitol, the regiment burst into hearty cheers. No wonder that, as a correspondent wrote to the New York papers, "they were hailed everywhere as saviours, and when they had marched up Pennsylvania Avenue, the people, in their overwrought feelings, broke the ranks, and grasped the hands of New York's National Guard with tears of joy; the Clay Battalion, the Lane Guard, the President, his Cabinet, and General Scott, repeatedly expressed indebtedness." *

The news flashed through the city, and thence across the country, wherever the wires had not been cut by the enemy. It is only by noting the universal expressions of satisfaction and relief in the public press of the North everywhere, on learning the news, that the true measure of the reliance placed upon the Seventh in this darkest hour of national exigency can be fixed. A despatch to the New York Tribune, from Washington, on the day of arrival, April 25th, gives a more vivid account of the feeling existing in that city than any later historic description could furnish. It runs thus: —

"The Seventh Regiment has arrived amid the wildest enthusiasm. As they approached the station, the Sixth Massachusetts Regiment were outside the Capitol, and a mighty cheer went up from the mass, which was distinctly heard far off in the town. At once the city, before so dull, was alive, and running toward the station. One would have thought the invasion was of a foe, and that a panic had seized the population.

"At one o'clock the regiment was on the Avenue, marching in splendid style toward the White House. They looked worn and weary, as well they might, after their rough work. Nevertheless, they were all in good spirits, and they walked almost with springing steps. As they

* Another correspondent says: "They marched up Pennsylvania Avenue about one o'clock, in soldier-like style, with knapsacks, canteens, great-coats, etc., weather-bronzed, and looking like veterans. Cheers greeted them; and as they passed in review before President Lincoln at the White House, he evidently felt that he was well supported in his determination to preserve the Union and to enforce the laws. Mrs. Lincoln presented the regiment with a magnificent bouquet from the conservatory at the White House."

passed along, they were received with frequent cheers, and the ladies continually waved their handkerchiefs, while smiles were on every face. No body of men could ever meet a more enthusiastic or hearty greeting than they, to whom every bosom seemed to warm. When in place of the drums and fifes, the full band struck up, the whole city danced with delight. A greater change never passed over a town, than that wrought in the space of half an hour by the coming of the long-looked-for Seventh.

"The regiment marched to the White House, paid a salute to the President, before whom they passed in review, then went directly to their quarters at Willard's, Brown's, and the National Hotels. At the former place they at once gathered about the fountain in the enclosed yard to wash. While thus engaged, they were addressed by Cassius M. Clay and General Lane, to whose remarks they responded with their peculiar cheer. Then came dinner, which was partaken of with a relish known only to the hungry.

"The few Secessionists in town have wilted quite away. Few can be found, and those few are anxiously looking toward Virginia, to whose bosom they hasten. They can be spared. There is no news in town, and there is no need of any. Three hours ago we were the dullest, most tired people in the world. Now every man is on the alert. The infusion of Massachusetts and New York, who, shoulder to shoulder, came through the enemy's country to the relief of the national capital, has acted like a cordial, and even the most sluggish are now enthusiastic. We feel that we have a right to be proud of New York and her sister, and we propose to maintain our rights, in this respect at least.

"Mr. Lincoln was the happiest-looking man in town as the regiment was marching by him. As an Illinois man remarked, 'He smiled all over,' and he certainly gave in his countenance clear expression to the feeling of relief born in all by this wished-for arrival."

In a similar spirit, on the day following, the Washington correspondent of the New York Commercial Advertiser wrote: —

"The New York Seventh, your own National Guard, first insured the safety of the city, which had been held prior to their arrival by a force of Regulars and Volunteers, entirely inadequate to the defence of so large an area. Had the Secessionists been able to concentrate four or five thousand men, and to erect batteries on Arlington Heights, commanding the President's house and the departments around it, they might have taken possession of the greater portion of the city by a *coup de main.*

"The Massachusetts Sixth could have held the Capitol, which was well provisioned, and in a state of defence, and the other public buildings might have been defended, but the troops garrisoning them could not have prevented 'raids' through the extended city. The Secessionists hoped for this attack, and their organs at Baltimore and Richmond invited it.

"But when the New York Seventh marched up Pennsylvania Avenue, traitors hung their heads, and the doubters became strong Union men at once."

While the regiment indulged in baths and clean linen, in hearty meals and in sleep, in sight-seeing or in letter-writing, Colonel Lefferts, who had been at once sent for by President Lincoln, remained in consultation with him for two hours. The President asked a great many questions regarding the condition of Maryland, whose status on the great subject of the hour was still doubtful, and regarding also the march of the regiment. Colonel Lefferts was able to announce that he had brought his command through to Washington without the loss of a man, having marched twenty miles the day before, repairing the railroad as he went. The President then complimented the regiment, and said that he thanked its members from the bottom of his heart.

Thence Colonel Lefferts proceeded to head-quarters, and reported to Lieutenant-General Scott for duty. On expressing his regret at the unexpected delay which had occurred at Annapolis, he was stopped by General Scott, who said in his most emphatic tone, "You have made a fine march, sir; you have done all that could be done, and you have my thanks." The Lieutenant-General then asked Colonel Lefferts what his regiment required. To this Colonel Lefferts replied: "Nothing but rations; our camp equipage will soon be up from Annapolis." With this answer the commanding general seemed pleased, and the Colonel thereupon withdrew.

Perhaps no more terse or just view of the situation of

Washington at this time can be given than that contained in the report made a few weeks later to the famous Union Defence Committee * of New York, by its chairman, Simeon Draper, Esq., one of whose sons marched with the Seventh, and read by the secretary, Prosper M. Wetmore, Esq., the first colonel of the same regiment. It said: —

"At the moment of their appointment, the committee found a civil war raging; portions of the army and navy seriously demoralized; treason working its will upon the property and flag of the country; and the capital of the nation, with all its treasures of archives and history, lying almost at the mercy of an unscrupulous assailant. Arsenals had been pillaged; public vessels had been surrendered without a shot fired in their defence; bodies of troops had laid down their arms in dishonor; and in the judgment of the world, serious apprehensions were entertained that an unjustifiable rebellion might become a successful revolution. . . . . With a generous frankness, which confers honor upon the stations which they fill, the chief executive officers of the national government and the distinguished commanding general of the army have been pleased to say, that the safety of the national capital and the preservation of the archives of the government, at a moment when both were seriously menaced, may fairly be attributed to the prompt and efficient action of the State and city of New York,

* This Committee was organized originally as follows: —

| | |
|---|---|
| John A. Dix, *Chairman*, | Charles H. Marshall, |
| Simeon Draper, *Vice-Chairman*, | Robert H. McCurdy, |
| William M. Evarts, *Secretary*, | Moses H. Grinnell, |
| Theodore Dehon, *Treasurer*, | Royal Phelps, |
| Moses Taylor, | William E. Dodge, |
| Richard M. Blatchford, | Greene C. Bronson, |
| Edwards Pierrepont, | Hamilton Fish, |
| Alex. T. Stewart, | William F. Havemeyer, |
| Samuel Sloan, | Charles H. Russell, |
| John Jacob Astor, Jr., | James T. Brady, |
| John J. Cisco, | Rudolph A. Witthaus, |
| James S. Wadsworth, | Abiel A. Low, |
| Isaac Bell, | Prosper M. Wetmore, |
| James Boorman, | A. C. Richards, |

The Mayor of the city of New York,
The Comptroller of the city of New York,
The President of the Board of Aldermen,
The President of the Board of Councilmen.

united with the vigorous efforts of the noble Commonwealth of Massachusetts, devoted to the same patriotic objects."

A United States Senator publicly declared, on the morning of April 14th: "Unless the people of the free States fill up this city with their troops, it will be seized by the Secessionists." The Washington correspondent of the New York Evening Post asserted, the same day, from what he claimed to be high authority, in reference to "the panic that exists among a portion of our citizens," that an "arranged attack" of the Secessionists was already under way, and that "there are to-day five thousand armed Rebels who meet nightly for military drill within a few miles of Washington," and "nearly one thousand within the District, enrolled and armed, and ready at the command of their officers to lead an attack upon the government."

The ten days that followed at Washington, before the arrival of the Seventh, were distressing. The city was less like the proud capital of a powerful nation than a beleaguered citadel in fear of capture. The breaking up of rail, mail, and wire communication with the North prevented the government from knowing how the people were rallying to its support; officers of the army and navy dropped daily, one after another, into the enemy's column; the latter was believed to be menacing Washington, while, in the rear, Maryland threw itself up as a barrier against the approach of troops across its soil to defend the capital. So sorely pressed, so sore distressed, was the government at this juncture, that it stooped to parley with Maryland, whose Governor had "felt it his duty to advise the President of the United States to order elsewhere the troops off Annapolis, and also that no more be sent through Maryland, and that Lord Lyons be requested to act as mediator between the parties, to avoid the effusion of blood." The government instructed Secretary Seward to assure Governor Hicks that "the force now sought to be brought through Maryland is intended for nothing but the defence of this capital"; and furthermore that "the national highway thus selected by the Lieutenant-General has been chosen by him, upon consultation with prominent magistrates and citizens of Maryland, as the one which, while a route is absolutely necessary, is further removed from the populous cities of the State, and with the expectation that it would therefore be the least objectionable one." These significant diplomacies show how necessary it was felt to be, at whatever concessions, to get "the troops off Annapolis" into the capital; and meanwhile, with the handful of Regulars and militia, and the pioneer Massachusetts Sixth at disposal, the citizens themselves, including the government officials, organized for its defence, and, under such leaders as Clay of Kentucky and Lane of Kansas, patrolled the streets by night, and stood on guard at the bridges, the President's house, the Capitol, the Navy-yard, and the departments. As for Baltimore, it was in the hands of a mob which tore down Union flags and proclaimed itself for secession; and the interior of Maryland was hardly more hopeful, it would seem, since troops from Harrisburg, that reached Ashland, Maryland, while the Seventh was approaching Annapolis, were ordered back by the War Department, and made to pass by way of Philadelphia and Chesapeake Bay.

On the day the Seventh Regiment arrived at Washington, the New York papers contained the news brought through from Washington the previous Tuesday by special messenger. This news said that "in Washington there was great alarm felt in consequence of the immense difficulties of getting in reinforcements, and the apprehension that the city would be attacked while it was comparatively undefended. There were not more than from four to five thousand men under arms for the defence of the capital, and of these there were only a few hundred Regulars. There was no confidence in the fidelity of the District militia. The arrival of the Seventh Regiment was anxiously prayed for, but no reinforcements had arrived from any quarter after Friday evening, when the Massachusetts regiment arrived from Baltimore. The fear of famine is superadded to the dangers of war. All who could remove their families to places of greater safety were doing so, and were it not for the almost impossibility of getting away, all the women, children, and non-combatants would desert the city.

"No means of defence are neglected. The public buildings are all barricaded, as if General Scott looked to the probability of having to dispute the possession of the city point by point.

"There was nothing positive known of the movements of the hostile forces. It had been reported that Arlington Heights, on the opposite shore of the Potomac, were held by four or five thousand men, under command of Colonel Lee, and also that General Beauregard had reached that position and was reconnoitring. The Heights are probably two miles, as the bird flies, from the White House and Treasury building, so that cannon of long range might from there destroy the city. Another statement was that the Virginians were concentrated below Alexandria. If so, they would probably cross the Potomac down there, and march up to the Heights commanding the Navy-yard, which could easily be destroyed from there. At all events, an attack on Washington was at any moment imminent."

The next day, one of the same leading papers declared: —

"The capital on Tuesday afternoon was in peril of capture, owing to the fact that the expected reinforcements had not arrived from the North in consequence of the interruption of the passage through Maryland, and there is an earnest, urgent appeal from Washington for more troops and for field-pieces. There is not a moment to be lost. It appears, that, in addition to the Virginia troops in the vicinity of Washington, Jefferson Davis and Beauregard are at Richmond with twenty-seven thousand men, and for all we know to the contrary may now be in possession of the Federal capital.

"The motive of the obstruction of the Northern troops at Baltimore and other points in Maryland is now fully developed. It is evident that the design was to cause such delay as would enable the invaders to be present in force at Washington before the Federal troops could reach the scene of action from the North. It is all a question of time. The city has no natural or artificial strength to enable it to hold out against superior odds, and it has so many approaches that a small body of troops cannot effectually protect it long. We learn that the long bridge is well secured by General Scott, and that he has broken down the bridge at Georgetown; but by means of boats or rafts it is possible for troops to cross the Potomac higher up, and, perhaps, even below Washington.

"So apprehensive of danger was the Commander-in-Chief, that barricades were constructed before the windows of the public buildings, earthworks were thrown up, women and children, and even men, were fleeing. All things indicated an approaching conflict. But if the Southern troops did not succeed in effecting a capture yesterday, they will be met to-day by a force large enough to keep them at bay till fresh troops arrive from the North; and there is a consolation in the case of Washington, that, even if it should be taken, it is not such a stronghold as can be retained against superior numbers, and the ability of the North to speedily retake it cannot be doubted."

Such were the circumstances under which the Seventh reached Washington. If some of the dangers to the capital were, in that hour of panic, exaggerated, enough remained that were real. But, on the day after the Seventh's arrival, President Lincoln sent word to Philadelphia that "the Seventh Regiment and the Massachusetts regiment were now in Washington. There was great need of reinforcements, but Washington might be considered safe for the country and the Constitution."

As with the ultimate safety of Washington, so with the march of the Seventh to its rescue, the happy issue from peril must not deceive us as to the peril that actually existed. "I saw in Washington," writes the Chaplain of the regiment, Dr. Weston, "and there heard read, a mass of captured telegraphic despatches, in which was disclosed the plan for cutting off the Seventh by destroying the bridges, removing the rails, and charging with cavalry through every cross-road they were to pass. The plan was admirably conceived, and I afterwards learned in Washington why it was abandoned. It seems the colonel of the body of the enemy's horse (some five hundred strong) had been sent in disguise to Annapolis, to watch our movements. He was there on the eve of our march, and saw the rapid formation of the troops in order of battle, when the alarm was given to which I have before alluded. He returned and reported it was inexpedient to attack. This information I had direct from a Union man, who had fled from Maryland, and who received it from a friend, a member of the enemy's cavalry; so the information was sufficiently authentic and direct. Hence the reported destruction of the Seventh, from the Charleston papers. They reported as done what was so well planned and confidently anticipated. The Rebels may have been deterred, too, by the knowledge of masses of troops in the rear, which had just arrived by the Baltic and other transports."

The rumors of the slaughter of the Seventh, near the Junction, came from three or four sources. In a Charleston paper of the time in question appears, with display heads, and a great flourish of trumpets, this ferocious despatch: —

"By Telegraph! — Glorious News! — Three times Three for Maryland! — The crack regiment of New York, the Seventh, met and entirely defeated between Annapolis and Marlboro'. Just as we were going to press last night, a despatch was received by General Gwynn that the Seventh Regiment of New York, in their attempt to proceed from Annapolis to Washington, were met and cut to pieces by the Marylanders, between that city and Marlboro', Maryland."

And in a Baltimore paper may be found the following memorable paragraph: —

> "THE SEVENTH REGIMENT. — The great question of interest now is, whether or not the New York Seventh Regiment was 'cut to pieces' on the route from Annapolis to Washington, as alleged. We publish all we have been able to gather on the subject; and as accounts from three or four various sources all agree, it seems there should be truth in the report. And yet it is hardly reasonable. The regiment is near a thousand strong, the best drilled and disciplined troops in all the North, and entered Maryland with a prospect that their passage would be disputed. It is hardly to be supposed that they were unprepared for the onset, and still more improbable that they should be defeated and 'cut to pieces' by an undisciplined and indifferently armed body of civilians. And then again, the engagement probably occurred on Sunday or Monday last, and it is strange that we have no details up to this late day. We hope, however, that it is true, and that every Northern soldier who desecrates the soil of a Southern State will meet with a similar fate."

Into what stress of anxiety and grief these rumors, reaching to New York, plunged the friends and kin of the Seventh Regiment, may easily be imagined. An officer's wife wrote to him from New York, on the morning of April 26th: "We were all awakened with a start, at four o'clock this morning, by that ominous sound, the ringing of the door-bell. . . . . There was a terrible report about here, on Saturday last, the day after you started, that there had been a fight somewhere, and a large number of the regiment killed. . . . . The ladies of New York are doing their part nobly; meetings are held all over the city to form societies for preparing lint, bandages, clothing, and everything that may be needed in case of war. The enthusiasm here about the Seventh Regiment exceeds everything. I think, if a member is injured, the excitement will surpass all bounds. Its name is in every mouth, and every one, even those who have not the slightest personal connection with it, seems to look upon each member as a near relative."

On the day after the Seventh's arrival, the remainder of Gunpowder Bridge, near Baltimore, was destroyed, and the report of the destruction of the Bush River Bridge was confirmed. Three days after its arrival, telegraphic communication was opened for the first time in nine days direct to New York; and on the same day arrived the Seventy-First New York and Sixth Pennsylvania Regiments, and the Fifth and the remainder of the Eighth Massachusetts. The telegram from Washington which announced these welcome reinforcements added: —

"All report a hard journey from Annapolis, the greater part on foot, with a scanty stock of provisions.

"The Seventy-First marched over the turnpike, for the most part, near the railroad, to the Junction, where they arrived at four o'clock on Friday morning. They waited there for the cars until four in the afternoon, and were just seated when they were called to arms and formed in line of battle. Yells and shouts were heard on all sides, and it was apprehended that they had been surrounded. After three hours' delay they returned to the cars, but were ordered to be ready during the night. Fires were seen in all directions."

Major-General S. R. Curtis, who, as has been seen, accompanied the regiment from Annapolis, soon after wrote to a friend a letter which was given to the papers, and in which he said: —

"I have, as you know, seen many troops, and commanded some of the best in our army; but I confess I never saw the peer of the Seventh Regiment. The *material* is here to make honorable competition, but they have not yet become successful rivals.

"The Massachusetts Eighth deserve great credit for the endurance, intelligence, and courage they manifested; and General Butler is a man of great zeal, energy, and intelligence; but the Seventh New York is made up of educated, intelligent gentlemen, all raised in ease and luxury, but perfectly resigned to the exposures, fatigues, and privations incident to the hardest service I ever witnessed.

"I know this regiment gets many compliments, but I declare no men ever more deserved them. The good order and great strength they evinced, united with the zeal and mechanical skill of the Massachusetts regiment, seemed a triumphant march to our besieged capital, settled the question of its safety, and stifled the insurrection in Maryland. I was urged to remain in Annapolis to assist in organizing that post, but at the urgent request of Colonel Lefferts, who is a most gallant officer and amiable gentleman, I came on with him, and am still recognized and continue to do some service as a member of his staff.

"I, of course, reported myself also to General Scott for duty, and in my various positions have found constant employment since my arrival; sometimes in one department and sometimes in another."

High praise though this be, it is not overstrained, when we consider that the regiment was a body of militia, not of veterans, — city youth trained to civil life, unused to such hardships as the march furnished.

We have seen how the march of the Seventh thrilled the North; it only remains to note the effect the same event produced at the South, where the regiment was hardly less known and honored.

At first the news of its promptness in leading New York to the front was received with incredulity, and next the cry was raised that "the Seventh would not invade." For example, a Baltimore letter to a New York paper said: —

"The Baltimoreans have almost as great a pride in our Seventh Regiment as New-Yorkers have, and feel assured that the Seventh will never fight against them. It was currently reported there yesterday, that the officers of the Seventh had said that they volunteered only to defend Washington, and would never march into either Virginia or Maryland to invade these States. This report was very generally believed, though it does not coincide with the desires expressed both at New York and Philadelphia by members of the Seventh, to march through Baltimore at every hazard, and to avenge the Massachusetts troops."

A telegram from Washington carried the same report, whereupon the New York News said: —

"THE NOBLE SEVENTH GOD BLESS THEM! — A telegraphic despatch has said: 'The New York Seventh Regiment declare *they will not* INVADE; consequently they are looked upon with suspicion by the administration.'

"This statement has been strengthened by assurances to the same effect, given in public and private correspondence from Washington. Whatever the administration may suspect or design is not the point to be considered in adverting to the favorite regiment of this city, always regarded with enthusiastic and just pride by our whole population. The intelligence, refinement, true nationality, and honor of this splendid body of citizen soldiery cannot encourage any step tending to national disgrace. The defence of the Federal capital was demanded, and they freely and promptly responded to the call. That service they have nobly performed thus far, and it will be continued without a murmur. Should the hostile invasion of Virginia be decided upon, we cannot expect that they will advance against their countrymen with whom a few months ago they were on terms of social friendliness, partaking of bounteous and earnest hospitalities. Against the homes and hearths of their recent hosts they cannot turn the reckless and indiscriminate fire that is the characteristic of relentless and devastating war. For the hastening of those peace measures which every good man must desire, the general feeling of the Seventh Regiment is a glorious harbinger. It may yet be chronicled that our brilliant regiment has turned the tide of war, not by the force and shock of arms, but by the moral power of their unquestioned patriotism, expressing itself within the domain of humanity and reason."

This article being widely copied, Colonel Lefferts received a letter from a citizen of Hartford, saying: "What we see in the public prints this evening of the course and intentions of your regiment has produced a *glorious thrill* in our city. . . . . Can brother go to war with brother, father against son, over the negro question? I hope not. Then, Colonel, do all you can to stop such an unholy war as now stares us in the face." This delusion, however, was soon dispelled, and was succeeded by an intensity of hate which was compliment enough to the regiment, by showing that its action was as annoying to the enemies of the Union as it had been inspiring to its friends. The Montgomery (Alabama) Mail, after alluding to the fact that many of the members of the regiment had "travelled through the South on missions of business or pleasure, and been received as brothers and treated with princely hospitality by our citizens," while the organization had been "the guests of Richmond, Baltimore, and Washington," broke into this strain of rage and passion: —

"After all the favors and honors lavished on these first-class gentlemen and merchant soldiers of New York City, they were the first to respond to the call of a perjured President and his perfidious Secretary of War, and to march in 'hot haste' as the vanguard of Lincoln's army of mercenary marauders in an infamous raid upon the integrity and the peace of the South. We feel no hesitancy in denouncing the conduct of the Seventh Regiment in this voluntary invasion of the South, with arms in their hands and oaths upon their consciences to slay our people and burn our property, in obedience to the secret orders of a malignant and perfidious Cabinet, as base, mean, and dishonorable, not only as a regiment, but as individuals. Let the South remember the Seventh New York Regiment, and if the base stuff it is made of can stand long enough in the field, let it be annihilated by the avengers of an invaded country. . . . . Henceforth and forever let the Seventh New York Regiment and the merchants and the city it represents be remembered by every man, woman, and child in all the South. Let the finger of scorn and the hisses and bitter execrations of all honest men follow each and every member of this disgraced regiment to an unhonored grave. Had they arose to defend their section, their State, or their city, we might have honored them as patriots. The day of reckoning will come. In that day New York will be remembered, and the voice of the South shall be 'Come out of her, my people.'"

Another Southern paper discoursed as follows: —

"The pleasing illusions which have been indulged concerning the existence of some lingering traits of gratitude and delicacy in the hearts of the Seventh Regiment were all dispelled by the paragraph published yesterday. A general feeling of satisfaction, however, is expressed that, now we know them in their true colors, they will form part of the force which is to invade Virginia. They will receive, beyond a doubt, such attentions as such men deserve. Probably the Seventh Regiment is the best-drilled regiment in the Northern Army; but its qualities are more adapted to show than use."

A Virginia paper of the same date announces that

"All the souvenirs from the New York Seventh Regiment, which are now in Richmond, have been draped in mourning. Mayor Mayo of

Richmond has returned his certificate of membership given him by the regiment, and requesting them to destroy any mementos of friendship they may have from him."

In allusion to this action, and to the general braggadocio that preceded the shock of arms, the New York Times rather mockingly said: —

"'O that we only had gentlemen to fight,' was the lament of Dixie's land. 'Give us foemen worthy of our steel,' was their constant petition. Quite a shout of delight went up, we remember, from the press of Mobile, when it was published that 'the New York Seventh' had gone to the war; for it was generally known that it was rich and — respectable. And yet so strange and contradictory are notions among the chivalry, Virginia, the first land for first families, did not share in this gratified emotion. Virginia 'gentlemen' were indignant when they learned that the Seventh had marched forth under the stars and stripes. It was considered an offence not to be forgiven, that gentlemen should 'take up arms against the South.' And aristocratic Richmond returned all the souvenirs it held of our gallant 'Seventh!'"

Another slip from the Baltimore American will perhaps amuse the reader of to-day, and serve as well to show the importance attached to the march of the Seventh Regiment: —

"A 'CRACK' REGIMENT. — Colonel Pettigrew of Charleston is raising a regiment of mounted riflemen for service in Virginia. It is composed wholly of picked men, each member being required to furnish his own horse and accoutrements. The regiment will be specially pitted, it is said, against the Seventh of New York.

But now we must forbear from further citations of this nature, and return to the narrative proper, which left the Seventh Regiment encamped in the national capital.

# CHAPTER IX.

## THE SEVENTH IN THE CAPITOL.

IT was a strange scene, and typical of the historic epoch, — soldiery sat in the seats of the law-givers, — *inter arma silent leges.* When the tramp of the Seventh Regiment resounded through the Capitol, and its muskets rang on the marble floor, when the neat gray uniforms, with spotless belts and glittering bayonets, swarmed into the halls of debate, the significance of this new drama struck every actor. Henceforth not the ballot, but the bullet.

Colonel Lefferts established his head-quarters in the Speaker's room; his staff occupied the committee-rooms; the companies were assigned to the floor, the galleries, and the lobbies. Each desk below and sofa above found its occupant. The Capitol became very cheerful and lively, but withal martial and orderly. Strong guards were mounted at the doors within and without, and drill, discipline, and soldierly deportment were strictly enforced. Sentries guarded all the approaches, while on either side of the broad steps at the rear of the building, which was the entrance in chief use, a howitzer was mounted. Strict rules and "strict construction" were now in force in these legislative halls.* The square east of the building formed a convenient drill-ground, and the drilling was constant; and "in the rests between our drills," wrote Winthrop, picturesquely, "we lay under the young shade on the sweet young grass, with the odors of snowballs and horse-chestnut blooms drifting to us with every whiff of breeze."

On the afternoon of the 26th of April, 1861, the regiment was mustered into the service of the United States for the term of thirty days, unless sooner discharged. In one sense, the main purpose of the regiment had already been accomplished. Its mission was to save the national capital in its first great hour of peril. That had been done, and, in addition, a route had been opened, over which regiment after regiment, following in the wake of the Seventh, poured into Washington. But the capital was still in more or less danger of attack by the enemy, and the Seventh accordingly pledged itself freely to an additional month's service. At 3 P. M., the regiment having assembled by companies in the Capitol Square, Major (afterwards Major-General) McDowell, the mustering officer, appeared in full uniform, accompanied by President Lincoln, the Secretary of State, the Secretary of War, and many distinguished officials. Line was formed, and the regiment was then broken into column by companies. As Major Mc-

* A private letter from a member of the Fifth Company says: "Last evening our party were on duty at the outer gate, where two aids of Major McDowell approached and attempted to pass the guard after tattoo. We challenged them, when they approached and said they were of the United States Army and aids of Major McDowell. We told them we neither knew them nor Major McDowell, and that they could not pass. They said they were entitled to pass the guard at all times. A call was made for the sergeant, who took them to the guard-room, where the officer of the day released them, complimenting us for our strict adherence to duty. Several incidents of the same kind have occurred."

Dowell, in his soldierly voice, called the roll, and each man answering "Here!" brought his piece successively to the "carry," the "order," and the "parade rest," he was struck by their intelligent and soldierly appearance. "Sir," he said to one of the captains, "you have a company of officers instead of soldiers." Square being formed, Major McDowell said: "In accordance with a special arrangement made in your case with the Governor of New York, you are now mustered into the service of the United States for thirty days, unless sooner discharged. The magistrate will administer the oath." Hereupon, to use Winthrop's language, "a gentleman *en mufti*, but wearing a military cap, with an oil-skin cover, was revealed. Until now he had seemed an impassive supernumerary. But he was biding his time, and, with due respect be it said, saving his wind, and now in a stentorian voice he ejaculated, '*The following is the oath!*'

"*Per se* this remark was not comic. But there was something in the dignitary's manner which tickled the regiment. As one man the thousand smiled, and immediately adopted this new epigram among its private countersigns.

"But the good-natured smile passed away as we listened to the impressive oath, following its title. We raised our right hands, and, clause by clause, repeated the solemn obligation, in the name of God, to be faithful soldiers of our country. . . . .

"We were thrilled and solemnized by the stately ceremony of the oath. This again was most dramatic; a grand public recognition of a duty; a reavowal of the fundamental belief that our system was worthy of the support, and our government of the confidence, of all loyal men. And there was danger in the middle distance of our view into the future, — danger of attack, or dangerous duty of advance, just enough to keep any trifler from feeling that his pledge was mere holiday business.

"So, under the cloudless blue sky, we echoed in unison the sentences of the oath. A little low murmur of rattling arms, shaken with the hearty utterance, made itself heard in the pauses. Then the band crashed in magnificently.

"We were now miserable mercenaries, serving for low pay and rough rations."

The crowd thronging the enclosure set up a great shout as the Seventh Regiment became United States soldiers.* The muster-roll will be found on page 140.

The Eighth Massachusetts arrived at Washington soon after the National Guard, and was also quartered within the Capitol, under the dome; while the Sixth Massachusetts was already in the Senate Chamber, — twenty-five hundred men there in all, glowing with "the brotherhood of ardent fellows first in the field and earnest in the cause." On the 27th of April, the day after the muster in, the Seventh Regiment invited the Eighth to the best collation they could give, in token of the friendship of comrades who had divided the perils and sufferings of the great march. As the Seventh had, during this march, earned the esteem and gratitude of the Eighth by "sharing the crust," this more leisurely entertainment increased their kindly feelings; † and as it

* A newspaper correspondent says: "This afternoon the Seventh paraded in grounds before the eastern portico of the Capitol, where they were 'mustered in.' Some of the chivalry had hopes that they would not take the oath of allegiance, but when, after Major McDowell had read it twice, that all might understand it, he called on those ready to enlist to raise their right hands and to repeat the pledge, every right arm was raised, and every man reverentially swore to protect and defend the United States. It was a solemn sight, and one which bore glorious testimony that the Republic is safe. Colonel Lefferts then requested that any man who had not taken the oath would leave the ranks. Not a man moved."

† A letter from the Seventh says: "Just now, as I passed through the Rotunda, there was a non-commissioned officer mounted on the staircase to the dome, explaining to the Massachusetts men, who were drawn up in order around the Rotunda, what our men had done. In the centre were piled fifteen kegs of lager-beer, two thousand boiled eggs, piles of cheese, boxes of lemons and oranges, smoked beef, pipes and tobacco, bread, &c., and a squad of men of the Seventh had begun to draw and pass around the provender. It was hard to say which party looked the more delighted, the donors or the recipients."

so happened about this time that one of the Massachusetts line officers was accidentally wounded, his foot being crushed, the Seventh quietly and at once contributed five hundred dollars by subscription, and gave it to the sufferer. A town meeting was held in Beverly on the 15th of May, 1861, where the following resolution was unanimously passed, and forwarded to the Seventh Regiment: —

"*Resolved*, That we tender to the far-famed SEVENTH REGIMENT OF NEW YORK our heartfelt thanks for their many kindnesses to our Eighth Massachusetts Regiment, and especially for their liberality towards our wounded fellow-citizen, Lieutenant Moses S. Herrick."

The Eighth Regiment, at their meeting, passed the following resolutions on the same subject, of which a neat copy was sent to Colonel Lefferts: —

HEAD-QUARTERS COMMANDERS OF COMPANIES,
EIGHTH REGIMENT M. V. M., WASHINGTON, April 29, 1861.

TO COLONEL LEFFERTS, OFFICERS AND MEMBERS OF THE NEW YORK SEVENTH REGIMENT.

At a meeting of this regiment, held this morning, the following Preamble and Resolutions were unanimously adopted: —

*Whereas*, The trials and the fortunes of war have brought us into close intimacy and companionship with the New York Seventh Regiment [National Guard], therefore

*Resolved*, That we feel it a duty owing not only to them, but to our own hearts, to express, so far as may be in our power, our grateful obligations to them for their many favors.

*Resolved*, That we deeply appreciate the hearty welcome extended to us on landing at Annapolis, and their kind attention after the fatigues of transportation and hazardous though successful service.

*Resolved*, That they have done all in their power to lessen the just feelings of dissatisfaction which have prevailed throughout the regiment by sharing with us their rations and their little conveniences, and by ever being the first to offer assistance.

*Resolved*, That especially are our thanks due to the noble Seventh for the generous entertainment furnished on the afternoon of Saturday, April 27th, — an entertainment so spontaneous, so bounteous, so heartily appreciative of our condition, that no words can do it justice or do justice to our gratitude.

*Resolved*, That in one other and *very* especial particular does their generosity and benevolence touch our hearts. We refer to the voluntary subscriptions raised among them for the benefit of one of our officers accidentally wounded.

*Resolved*, That the term of aspersion so often used in connection with the volunteer militia, "holiday soldiery," has been, in all the conduct of the regiment to which we are so much indebted, triumphantly refuted, and that it will hereafter be worthy of the highest fame, — fame that will ever attach to the name of the "*Generous, Gallant, Glorious Seventh.*"

*Resolved*, That wherever the Seventh may go we would go, where they lodge we would lodge, and, if ever their colors go down before the hosts of the enemy, the Eighth of Massachusetts would be the first to avenge their fall with the heart's blood of every man.

KNOTT V. MARTIN, *Chairman.*

GEO. T. NEWHALL, *Secretary.*

A fortnight later, the following letter was forwarded to the regiment by order of Lieutenant-General Scott, commanding the army: —

HEAD-QUARTERS OF THE ARMY, WASHINGTON, D. C.,
May 13, 1861.

COLONEL LEFFERTS, *Commanding Seventh Regiment N. G. of N. Y. M.*

General Scott desires the following extract of a letter from his Excellency Governor Andrew of Massachusetts may be communicated to you and your regiment: "A contribution of stores for *free* issue to the troops has been forwarded. Ice contributed by Messrs. Addison Gage & Co., and the provisions by the proprietors of the Faneuil Hall Market." After indicating the distribution to be made of stores, occurs the following: "With the wish of the contributors that the New York Seventh should be remembered, as they did not forget the Massachusetts Eighth."

Very respectfully,

SCHUYLER HAMILTON,
*Lieutenant-Colonel and Military Secretary.*

Not the least unwonted scene at the national Capitol was presented on the Sunday the Seventh spent there. The regiment held service morning and evening. The pulpit was the Speaker's desk, covered with the national flag, and with the Bible resting on the flag. The regiment (except the two hundred on guard) occupied the floor and galleries, the band the reporters' gallery, the choir of twenty admirable voices, picked from a thousand, the Clerk's circle below.

"Fellow-citizens and soldiers," the Chaplain said, "you are engaged in making material for future historians, perhaps in fulfilling the very prophecies read to you this morning. The capital is echoing to the tread of armed legions; but yesterday, on this classic hill, your thousand hands were raised to Heaven, and your thousand voices joined in swearing fidelity to the Constitution of your land. . . . . Our duty is to defend our human rights, our country and firesides, and to leave the rest with God. To this contest you have solemnly pledged yourselves. The eyes of the whole nation are upon you. Your country expects you to do your duty both as warriors and heroic endurers. In the quality of bravery you are above suspicion, but those rare virtues, fortitude under disease and privation, and exact obedience to command, are those you are especially called upon to exercise. He who cannot obey cannot command. You have already done well, with the gallant aid of our companions, those brave foremost offerings of Massachusetts, whose sons once saved our Constitution, and have been the first to bleed for it again. Let the Seventh Regiment so demean itself that hereafter it shall be a glory to have been with it in this campaign. Napoleon told his men that their greatest reward should be to have it said, 'There goes one of the army of Italy.' You may be equally proud to hear the words: 'There goes one of the National Guard.' And let the title be no misnomer. Guard well the Republic; see that it suffers no harm from the unnatural children who have turned against it."

A published letter, referring to the morning service, says: —

"The Seventh is fortunate in its Chaplain, — the Rev. Dr. Weston, formerly rector of St. John's Church, New York, a man of talents, refinement, and piety. . . . . For once the magnificently elaborate decorations of the interior — the gilding, painting, enamel, oak, marble, and velvet — blended together to the eye in the dim, religious light that falls softly from the translucent ceiling, produced a half-appropriate effect. . . . . That wonderful Episcopal service! Who, of whatever sect or creed, has not acknowledged its beauty and power? Who has not felt its marvellous comprehensiveness, through which it adapts itself to the expression of every human want? Thus, to-day, the words of the collect — 'Defend us, thy humble servants, in all assaults of our enemies; that we, surely trusting in thy defence, may not fear the power of any adversaries' — had a meaning never felt before. The prayer 'for the President, and all others in authority,' seemed to be uttered with a reserved intention to sternly assist in the fulfilment of the boon it asked. But the following passage of the litany was impressive above all the rest: 'From all sedition, privy conspiracy, and rebellion, good Lord, deliver us!'"

The same afternoon, the President of the United States, the Secretary of State, and other distinguished gentlemen, visited the quarters of the regiment, and were enthusiastically greeted. President Lincoln "complimented the soldiers on their fine appearance and gentlemanly bearing, and thanked them for the promptness with which they had answered the call of the country." Secretary Seward followed in a similar strain.

When the Seventh arrived in Washington, Assistant Adjutant-General Irvin McDowell had command of the capital, and from his Order No. 1 an idea may be formed of the general run of duties required of the regiment: —

HEAD-QUARTERS, CAPITOL, WASHINGTON, D. C.,
April 27, 1861.

ORDERS No. 1.

I. Roll-calls will be as follows: —

| | |
|---|---|
| Reveille, . . . . . . . | 5 o'clock, A. M. |
| Retreat, . . . . . . . | At sunset. |
| Tattoo, . . . . . . . | 10 o'clock, P. M. |

All must be present or accounted for at each of these calls. Absentees without authority will be reported to Head-quarters.

II. Guard-mounting, conducted as far as possible according to regulations, will be at half past seven o'clock, A. M.

There will be two police guards of a company, each stationed at the east entrance of the wings of the Capitol. During the tour of duty, the members of the guard not on post as sentinels, or absent for some necessary purpose and with the permission of the officer of the guard, will remain in or near the guard-room. They will not remove their equipments, but hold themselves ready at all times, night or day, to take their arms instantly.

An officer of the day will be detailed from the field officers or from the senior captains, when there are not enough of the former to afford sufficient relief.

Lieutenant Collins, Topographical Engineers, will turn off the guard.

III. Police call will be sounded immediately after reveille, and half an hour before retreat.

Commanders of regiments and companies will see that the quarters occupied by their men are thoroughly cleaned at the times above named. In addition to this, a detail, to consist of the guard of the day before, will be made for the general police of the Capitol, under the general direction of the officer of the day, who will give such directions to the officers of the police as will insure the cleanliness of the halls, passages, &c. of the entire building. Brooms, mops, &c. will be furnished the police, and will be receipted for by the officer of the police.

IV. Loud talking, whistling, singing, scuffling, or running will not be permitted within the building.

At tattoo, all must retire to their quarters; and at taps, which will be at a quarter of an hour after tattoo, the gas must be lowered in all the quarters and halls, and quiet must prevail throughout the building.

Those of the District of Columbia Volunteers allowed to work during the day will not be required to attend "retreat," but must be present at "tattoo." Those other than the District of Columbia Militia who are allowed to mess outside of the building will be marched to and from meals. The officer in charge will be responsible for them during their absence, that they remain away not more than a reasonable time for their meals, and that they are quiet and orderly.

Passes in writing may be given by commanders of companies to their men, a few at a time, to be absent when not on duty, between reveille and retreat; and in very special cases, when countersigned by the commanders of regiments, they may be extended to tattoo. These passes must be exhibited to the guards.

No civilian not belonging to the Capitol will be allowed within it or within the grounds without a written pass from Head-quarters, unless he be on a visit to one of the regimental commanders within the building. In the latter case he will be conducted to such commander by one of the guard. Officers in uniform will be allowed to pass freely. Hucksters and newsboys will be allowed a place near the entrance to the grounds, which they must not go beyond.

So far as neatness or soldierly decorum went, there was never, of course, any complaint found with the Seventh during the time it did duty at the Capitol. For the rest, Colonel Lefferts's Order No. 1 gives a clew to the routine of daily work, privilege, and restraint. This is the order: —

HEAD-QUARTERS SEVENTH REGIMENT N. Y. S. M.,
CAPITOL, WASHINGTON, D. C., April 28, 1861.

STANDING ORDER No. 1.

For the government of the regiment so long as quartered in the Capitol, this order will be enforeed.

Commandants of companies may give an order to pass the guard any time between réveille and six o'clock, P. M., after which hour the pass must be countersigned by a field officer. Such leave of absence will not extend beyond two hours, without express permission from the commandant, and not exceeding ten men from each company absent at one time.

The men must be marched to their meals by companies, in charge of a commissioned officer, the files counted before leaving quarters, and verified on return of the company. Those absenting themselves without permission must be reported at Head-quarters. Companies will be allowed one hour and a quarter for meals, except those which go to Willard's Hotel; they will be allowed one hour and a half.

A guard of one file from each company, under a commissioned officer, will be detailed each twelve hours (irrespective of the regular police guard of the building), and posted to control the various passages to our quarters, and no persons excepting members of the regiment allowed to enter without a pass from a field officer.

Commandants are particularly instructed to see their men collect their accoutrements and muskets, and so arrange them that they can be used upon immediate call, without confusion.

There will be morning drills and afternoon parades, to be specified in daily orders.

The recruits of each company must be drilled morning and afternoon by one of their company officers, and when in fit condition will be admitted to the ranks.

The commandant is disposed to allow the largest liberty of action to the men consistent with duty and discipline, but all orders will be rigidly enforced, and delinquents punished.

All orders will be posted upon the wall behind the Speaker's desk, in the Hall of Representatives, to which reference must be made.

MARSHALL LEFFERTS,
*Colonel Commanding.*

From the necessity of the case, meals were taken at the Washington hotels. The companies marched punctually, and with precision, thrice a day for this purpose, and thus became aware of the presence of brother-soldiers who had now come to reinforce them from all parts of the North. The Washington people invariably greeted these appearances with enthusiasm.*

Thus, in fine quarters, with hotel fare and an easy routine of duties, the regiment passed its time with pleasure. Each morning, after the "baths and basins" so much prized, after the squad drill for recruits, and the breakfast, "all turn out to witness guard-mounting, and to listen to the splendid music of the band; and, having secured available positions, quietly smoke their pipes, and criticise the movements of the old guard and the new. At nine o'clock a company drill completes the military duties of the morning. Passes to visit the town are now in great demand. They who do not seek or obtain them sleep upon the sofas, or dream in the shade of the fine trees of Capitol Square, or occupy Congressional chairs, and write long epistles to friends at home," which last item was so important, that it seems Mr. Van Wyck and two other Congressmen were kept busy all day franking. Afternoon drill and evening parade must come in to fill up the picture. Theodore Winthrop writes: —

"All our life in the Capitol was most dramatic and sensational. Before it was fairly light in the dim interior of the Representatives'

* A letter-writer says: "Washington, since we arrived here, has become a different place, and people think that the Secessionists in this city will soon be played out,' as the boys say. Our appearance has inspired the people with military ardor. Companies of Union volunteers are being organized, the stars and stripes wave in every direction. The city has a very martial appearance. The people here think that we are immortal, and nothing is too good for us. When we march to a hotel for our meals, which is three times a day, in fatigue dress, body-belts only, and no muskets, the streets, for the mile we march, are crowded with men, women, and children, cheering and waving handkerchiefs. . . . . I occupy the Honorable John A. Stevens's seat, and my colleague is the Honorable Charley Howe. We sleep in the chairs, and put our knapsacks under the desk. There is the roll to fall in."

Chamber, the reveilles of the different regiments came rattling through the corridors. Every snorer's trumpet suddenly paused. The impressive sound of the hushed breathing of a thousand sleepers, marking off the fleet moments of the night, gave way to a most vociferous uproar. The boy element is large in the Seventh Regiment. Its slang dictionary is peculiar and unabridged. As soon as we woke, the pit began to chaff the galleries, and the galleries the pit. We joked, we shouted, we sang, we mounted the Speaker's desk and made speeches, always to the point; for if any but a wit ventured to give tongue, he was coughed down without ceremony. With all our jollity we preserved very tolerable decorum. The regiment is *assez bien composé.* Many of its privates are distinctly gentlemen of breeding and character. The tone is mainly good, and the *esprit de corps* high. If the Colonel should say, 'Up, boys, and at 'em!' I know that the Seventh would do brilliantly in the field. I speak now of its behavior in-doors. This certainly did it credit. Our thousand did the Capitol little harm that a corporal's guard of Biddies, with mops and tubs, could not repair in a forenoon's campaign. What crypts and dens, caves and cellars, there are under that great structure! And barrels of flour in every one of them this month of May, 1861. It was infinitely picturesque in these dim vaults by night. Sentries were posted at every turn. Their guns gleamed in the gaslight. Sleepers were lying in their blankets wherever the stones were softest. Then in the guard-room the guard were waiting their turn."

Reinforcements soon reached the regiment to the number of one hundred and seventy-five men, under command of Captain Viele. They consisted of members of the regiment who from sickness, absence, or other cause, did not make the "pioneer march" the week before, together with recruits. It will be remembered that, immediately on arriving in Philadelphia, and finding the direct road blocked to Washington, Colonel Lefferts telegraphed in cipher to Mr. W. H. Allen of New York: "We cannot go by way of Baltimore. Will go to Annapolis. Require a good vessel and provisions to be sent there immediately. Go with this to William H. Aspinwall and General Sandford." A similar request was sent by Colonel Lefferts, as we have also seen, to General Sandford, from on board the steamer Boston at Annapolis. Although there was doubt about the position of the regiment, its friends promptly chartered a vessel and filled it with supplies.* Recruits

* The following letters relating to this matter will be read with interest: —

I.

NEW YORK, April 22, 1861.

DEAR COLONEL, — Since the reception of your telegram on Saturday, 2 P. M., to Mr. Allen, saying, "Require a good vessel and provisions *there*" (Annapolis), General Sandford construed your telegram to mean thus: "We are bound to Annapolis, and doubtless will require a good vessel and provisions to go there." When your second despatch came, saying "We have chartered the Boston, and try to go to Washington," General Sandford said, "This is an evident countermand of the first telegram." I do not understand it so. Your brother, Mr. Allen, has, like me, felt very worried, and this morning (Saturday afternoon nothing could be done, the stores being all closed) I went to see Colonel Hincken. He agreed with me that you wanted provisions and a vessel. . . . . From the Quartermaster's I went to the Chamber of Commerce, where a committee happened to be in session. I showed them your despatch, and they all agreed it meant you wanted a boat and provisions at Annapolis, and gave me a check for $ 2,500 towards the cause. We are in darkness here, the wires north of Washington being all down since Saturday. We are intensely anxious about you. . . . .

Respectfully, A. KEMP, *Paymaster.*

II.

NEW YORK, April 25, 1861.

DEAR SIR, — Your letter per special messenger reached me at the house at half past four this morning. Your first necessity seems to be for provisions. I am happy to say that the steamer Daylight left here at two o'clock yesterday afternoon with ample supplies (for a time at least) for the special use of the regiment. She should be at Annapolis by to-morrow morning, when, if not resisted on the way, you will doubtless be in Washington. But I suppose when troops have once passed over the road, arrangements will be made for holding it, and the stores can be forwarded with little delay. Mr. Kemp has worked in this matter most energetically, and taken responsibilities upon himself to any extent required. We feel convinced, however, that the supplies must have reached you shortly after date of your despatch. . . . . Just as the Daylight was ready to sail yesterday, an aid of General Sandford came down to order her to haul out in the stream and wait until the Parkersburg could accompany her, — a delay of some hours at least. Mr. Kemp returned his compliments to the General, saying he meant no disrespect, that this was a private affair, every hour counted, that he took the responsibility, and the steamer should sail in twenty minutes; and she *did* sail in twenty minutes. . . . . The Daylight also took out about one hundred and seventy-five recruits for the regiment. . . . . You can imagine the intense anxiety for news, about the safety and whereabouts of the Seventh particularly. We have about two dozen false rumors to one authentic one. One of the worst was on Saturday last, to the effect that there had been a fight somewhere (a very loose despatch), and fifty to one hundred were killed.

Yours truly, WM. H. ALLEN.

and reinforcements were only too abundant. Eighteen members sailed with the Eighth Regiment, and on the morning of the 24th the main detachment, one hundred and seventy-five strong, well armed and equipped, under command of Captain Viele, was drawn up in the armory, and marched with three days' rations and twenty rounds of ammunition per man. Opportunity being given by Captain Viele for any one to withdraw who felt incompetent to perform the most arduous service, no foot stirred, and the throng of spectators applauded. Their line of march was crowded, and the old scenes of the waving of flags and hats and handkerchiefs, the cheers, the multitude of volunteer escorts, and the dense crowds on the wharf, were repeated. At half past two, P. M., the little propeller Daylight started from her dock with these reinforcements. She carried also about six hundred barrels of preserved meats, bread, vegetables, and stoves and supplies of all kinds for the regiment, the donations of kinsmen, friends, and countrymen, who had chartered the vessel, and now despatched it to the Seventh at Washington. The journey was performed without remarkable incident, and at 6, P. M., of the 27th, the detachment arrived at Washington and reported. The Daylight then went to Annapolis for the baggage and camp and garrison equipage.

The Daylight was the first unarmed vessel from the North to run the risk of the batteries which, it was reported, the Secessionists were preparing along the Potomac. The Union Defence Committee of New York, alluding to this achievement in their Report of June 29, 1861, says: "A detachment of two hundred men of this (Seventh) regiment, led by Captain E. C. Viele of Colonel Lefferts's staff, was the first military body which opened the passage and passed to the city of Washington by the Potomac River. Much credit was justly accorded to that officer for the skill, spirit, and perseverance evinced by him." On the

30th of April, accordingly, the regiment was assembled for evening parade at half past four o'clock, P. M., and the detachments which had reported for duty since the previous muster were, at five o'clock, mustered into the service of the United States, and their names were added to the muster-roll.

I append now, therefore, the whole roll of the regiment for the campaign of 1861, adding, for the sake of convenience, the subsequent musters of April 30th and May 14th to the rolls of the 26th of April. While in most cases the appearance of names at either of the two later dates indicates reporting to the regiment after the preceding muster, it does not in all cases, — sickness or absence on duty operating, in some instances, to postpone the muster in. All those members or recruits who joined it on or after the 1st of May were mustered under the date of the 14th.

## MUSTER-IN ROLL

OF THE

## SEVENTH REGIMENT (NATIONAL GUARD) N. Y. S. M.

Called into the service of the United States by the President thereof, from the nineteenth day of April, 1861, for the term of thirty days, unless sooner discharged. Mustered in at Washington, on the twenty-sixth day of April, 1861, by Major Irvin McDowell, U. S. A.

*Colonel.*
MARSHALL LEFFERTS.

*Lieutenant-Colonel.**

*Major.*
ALEXANDER SHALER.

*Staff.*
J. H. Liebenau, *Adjutant.*
Egbert L. Viele,† *Capt. of Engineers.*
Locke W. Winchester, *Quartermaster.*
Timothy M. Cheeseman. *Surgeon.*
John C. Dalton, *Surgeon's Mate.*

* Lieutenant Colonel W. A. Pond, an able and accomplished officer, was prevented by sickness from marching with the regiment, and from the same cause was forced, soon after its return, to resign, to the great regret of his brother officers.

† Mustered, April 30, with the Daylight detachment, as elsewhere recorded.

Sullivan H. Weston, *Chaplain.*
Meredith Howland, *Asst. Paymaster.*
William Patten, *Commissary.*
John A. Baker, *Ordnance Officer.*
George W. Brainerd, *Asst. Quartermaster.*
Charles J. McClenachan, *Military Secy.*

*Non-commissioned Staff.*

Robert C. Rathbone, *Sergt. Major.*
John H. Draper, *Ordnance Sergt.*
Simon C. Scott, *Color-Bearer.*
Thomas H. Pierce, " "
L. L. S. Clearman, *Com. Sergt.*
Oscar Ryder, *R. G. Guide.*
James J. Morrison, *L. G. Guide.*
Isaac W. Dean, *Sergt. Guard.*
Robert M. Weed,* *Quartermaster Sergt.*

*Band.*

Graham, David, *Drum Major.*
Graffula, Claudius, *Band Master.*
Common, George, *Sergeant.*
Barrett B. George, *Corporal.*
Anderson, John.
Bader, Frederick.
Bader, Henry.
Capper, Carlo.
Connor, Henry.
Curley, Thomas.
Dubuy, Oliver.
Ferrier, Charles.
Fohs, Joseph.
Fohs, Peter.
Frieberg, Frederick.
Fritze, Edward.
Gebhart, William.
Gessner, Joseph.
Haas, Frederick.
Kendall, George.
Koswick, William.
Lindner, Carl.
Origbi, Joseph.
Plass, Carl.
Quintana, Luciano.
Rumpler, Adelbert.
Salomons, Mitchell.
Spendler, Otto.
Spraidler, Henry.
Strobe, Henry.
Strobe, John.
Tette, Louis.
Underhill, John.
Werring, John.
Worm, Louis.

---

## FIRST COMPANY (A).

*Captain* (see below).

1*st Lieutenant*, C. H. Meday.
2*d Lieutenant*, J. L. Harway.

*Sergeants.*
Hume, W. H.
Robe, H. C.
Bogert, P. I.
Funston, H. M.

*Corporals.*
Wilson, C. S.
Kitchen, G. H.
Pierce, F. O.

*Drummers.*
Roland, James.
Statter, John.

* Reported for duty, May 21.

*Privates.*

Allen, J. H.
Archer, A. J.
Aston, F. S.
Barr, S. E.
Belknap, Augustus.
Bensel, J. Warner.
Bogert, Henry.
Boyce, G. W. G.
Brinckerhoff, W. E.
Brown, W. H.
Buchanan, D. D.
Cable, John H.
Clark, Nathan.
Cook, G. T.
Cooper, T. W.
Cooper, W. H.
Davidge, R. C.
Davis, B. F.
Denslow, W. J. W.
Dieffendorff, C. P.
Digges, T. M.
Donaldson, W. J.
Evans, R. D.
Grout, T. J.
Hamilton, Robert.
Hart, F. H.
Hart, O. H.
Haslasher, George.
Hays, D. L.
Heubeser, C. E.
Hewlett, A. C.
Howe, C. H.
Hyde, E. J.
Imuren, J. H., Jr.
Kingsland, D. C.
Kirkland, T. S.
LeFort, George.
Leggett, S.
Lindeman, H.
McIlvaine, F. E.
McKervan, J. P.
Merkle, Augustus.
Meday, G. K.
Miller, J. H.
Mott, J. W.
Murray, James.
Orpen, C. N.
Patterson, Duke.
Perry, D. A.
Rawson, E. B.
Reynolds, C. L.
Saunders, George F.
Seaver, T. A.
Shields, W. H.
Sibell, J. W.
Simonson, J. H.
Slocomb, F. D.
Smith, F. A.
Snyder, Edward L.
Spelman, W. B.
Spofford, C. H.
Stagg, H. P.
Sumner, A. C.
Thwait, S. C.
Todd, R. S.
Trenor, E.
Trenor, H. H.
Trenor, J. J.
Trenor, J. W.
Trenor, T. F.
Welcker, John.
Wilbur, E. R.
Van Ness, George.
Villiers, Thomas.
Waldron, R. S.

*Mustered in April* 30, 1869.

*Corporals.*

Sheppard, J. K.
Davidson, William.

*Privates.*

Apellas, Frederick.
Bang, Fred. J.
Banomin, Charles.
Barnum, Henry C.

Briggs, Charles A.
Clark, John R.
Cowperthwaite, F. H.
Darling, John E.
Eckel, Edward H.
Forbes, Edward.
Gompertz, G. S.
Griffith, Wm. N.
Hurnd, G. W.
Kahler, Frank.
Kelley, Joseph G.
Kurz, William.
Muarquaretz, Charles.
Rogers, Joel L.
Sharp, William A.
Spring, Edward A.
Steinway, Albert.
Swartz, John H.
Villiplait, Alfred B.
Villiplait, D'Hulesse.
Wheeler, W. P.
Yort, Henry.

*Mustered in May* 14, 1869.

*Captain*, W. P. Bensel.

*Privates.*

Bell, S. M.
Clough, Henry.
Ellis, Henry.
Humphreys, W. S.
Lober, J. H.
Lyon, C. H.
Plass, R. H.
Ring, G. W.
Tugman, C. A.
Wetmore, Aug. J.
Whitman, Fred.

## SECOND COMPANY (B).

*Captain*, Emmons Clark.

1*st Lieutenant*, Noah L. Farnham. 2*d Lieutenant*, Edward Bernard.

*Sergeants.*

Palmer, Peter (*Orderly*).
Dyer, Henry B.
Macfarland, Joseph E.
Miller, David.
Van Norden, Charles S.

*Corporals.*

Ware, Richard F.
Fonda, Richard D.
Bernard, George A.
Janes, Charles H.

*Drummer*, Norwood, Richard.

*Privates.*

Alden, Henry H.
Alden, James M.
Allison, Richard.
Allison, William G.
Amerman, Jacob B.
Baker, Edgar.
Bedford, Evert E.
Bird, John H.
Bloomfield, John C.
Boardman, Daniel F.
Booth, Orrin F.
Bristow, Henry.
Brower, Bloomfield.
Buchan, Robert C.
Bucken, William T.
Burnett, Gilbert J.
Burtis, A. M.
Chapman, William O.
Chase, Amos M., Jr.
Codey, Stephen W.

Codey, William H.
Colton, Walter.
Comstock, J. J., Jr.
Curtis, Albert A.
Darling, William Lee.
Debenham, George.
Du Barré, James.
Eadie, William R.
Edwards, William.
Evans, George M.
Eveleth, Henry P., Jr.
Farnham, William T.
Florence, Sylvester.
Garrison, Abraham.
Gordon, Henry.
Gould, Robert S., Jr.
Gregory, Benjamin.
Gregory, Frank.
Haddock, W. M.
Hall, Oscar.
Halsey, Norwood A.
Hatfield, Abram, Jr.
Hatfield, Robert F.
Harter, Frederick A.
Havens, Jonathan N.
Hayes, Henry.
Hill, Charles S.
Holder, Thomas W. K.
King, James S.
Lane, Henry R.
Lawrence, John.
Kelty, Eugene.
Leonard, Robert W.
Mather, S. Talmadge.
Mather, Thomas D.
McDonald, Wm. A.
McGuire, Charles H.
McKinley, Robert.
McManus, Edward.
Miller, James W.
Miller, Levi.
Mix, Eugene.
Mix, James B.
Mix, William H.
Molineux, Edward L.
Nodine, William.
Oakey, John.
Overton, Charles P.
Phalon, Henry L.
Phipps, Gurdon S.
Peixotto, Moses L. M.
Porter, Henry M.
Postley, De Van.
Powell, James W.
Putnam, Glenn.
Quilliard, Gulian V.
Roome, James W.
Roome, John.
Russell, James F.
Salisbury, Richard L.
Savage, Henry F.
Scoville, William H.
See, William B.
Selover, George W.
Smith, Granville B.
Smith, James A.
Sterling, Charles R.
Stevenson, John.
Struthers, Stephen R
Tay, Charles H.
Taylor, Archibald.
Taylor, John H.
Thayer, Lucius M.
Tuttle, David H.
Tybring, George F. E.
Vanderbilt, Isaac S.
Vandewater, John W.
Vanduzer, William A.
Ward, Egbert.
Ward, Rodney C.
Way, David T.
Webster, Edward B.
Weir, Julian V.
Whitfield, Edwin.
Wight, George J. L.
Williams, Edgar.
Williams, Reginald H.
Williamson, John, Jr.
Wilson, James.

*Mustered in April* 30, 1861.

Agens, F. G.
Backus, F.
Beardsley, De Witt.
Cohen, H.
Cooley, J. C.
Dudley, Lewis G.
Findlay, A.
Foster, Frederick.
Halsey, H. P.
Hatfield, Townsend L.
Healy, H. G.
Milu, D. L.
Morrison, F. S., Jr.
Nichols, L.
Perkins, H. H.
Phyfe, W. S.
Rusher, C. J.
Shelley, Charles C.
Sturgis, Edward.
Torrey, James.
Vandervoort, J. V. W.
Vroom, A. F.
Weir, J. F.

*Mustered in May* 14, 1861.

Ames, James B., Jr.
Bulkley, George L.
Burtis, W. A., Jr.
Gittens, John K., Jr.
Gregory, Henry S.
Jones, M. L.
Moulton, Sylvester T.
Smith, George M.
Sniffen, Francis A.
Stratton, E. W.

## THIRD COMPANY (C).

*Captain*, JAMES PRICE.

1st *Lieutenant*, John Wickstead, Jr.
2d *Lieutenant*, George T. Haws.

*Sergeants.*

Murray, John W. (*Orderly*).
Stephens, Theo. B.
Leggett, Richard L.
Fitzgerald, Louis.
Dore, Joseph.

*Corporals.*

Tracy, George Douglass.
Baily, Wm. P.
Crane, Cyrus R.
Clinton, De Witt.

*Drummer*, Van Raden, Augustus.

*Privates.*

Abbott, Charles A.
Allen, Henry.
Bacon, George.
Banks, Joseph E.
Barker, Charles, Jr.
Barrett, John.
Bend, Wm. B.
Bogert, Charles L.
Broderick, Wm. E.
Burdett, Jacob, Jr.
Butler, Geo. B., Jr.
Chapman, Joseph H.
Chesebrough, Robt. A.
Chesebrough, Wm. H.
Clinton, Chas. W.
Collins, Geo. S.
Conroy, Thos. L.
Conroy, Wm. F.
Cook, Vincent L.
Crane, Lorin P.

Elliott, Theodore.
Ferry, Darius, Jr.
Fish, Latham A.
Foster, Clinton.
Graham, Joseph F.
Hale, Wm. D.
Hickox, Thomas N.
Holt, Edmund O.
Hughes, Charles.
Hurst, Fred. K.
Irving, Thos. R.
Kennedy, Charles.
Lewis, Curtis.
Marshall, Geo.
McKibben, Gilbert H.
Merle, Chas. F.
Milligan, Samuel G.
Mott, Henry H.
Oakley, Alfred.
Oakley, Nelson H.
Peterson, Christian G. W.
Platt, William C.
Pollard, Don Alonzo.
Portington, Robert C.
Radcliffe, Herman G.
Reeve, Isaac T.
Robinson, William G.
Sebert, John.
Sexton, Samuel J. M.
Simonson, Joseph, Jr.
Smith, Alexander M. C.
Smith, Eugene B.
Spooner, Henry T.
St. John, Wm. M.
Tremaine, Henry E.
Van Houten, Isaac.
Van Riper, James.
Van Wyck, Wm. E.
Warren, James R.
Warren, Joseph C.
Wellman, Wm. P.
White, Oliver G.
Whitney, Wm. M.
Wicks, George, Jr.
Wilson, James W.
Wolfe, Hudson G.
Wright, David F.
Wright, John G.
Yard, Wesley S.

*Mustered in April* 30, 1861.

Beers, W. H.
Benedict, Eugene F.
Browne, Charles L.
Burton, William C.
Clowes, Theodore F.
Colgate, Clinton G.
Doolittle, James K.
Eastman, Wm. H.
Gendar, Thomas V.
Gulager, Philip D.
Hoxie, Wm. E.
Jordan, Conrad N.
Lawrence, George P.
Marshall, Alexander.
Owens, Charles B.
Pollock, William J.
Smith, Wm. H. H.
Tremaine, Walter R.
Tuthill, Samuel B.
Verplanck, Wm. A.
Watkins, William L.

*Mustered in May* 14, 1861.

Bomford, George N.
Bunce, Theo. D.
Colline, Wm. S.
Rader, Louis B.
Regna, George W.

## FOURTH COMPANY (D).

*Captain,* William H. Riblet.

1st *Lieutenant,* William Gurney.

2d *Lieutenant,* John W. Bogert.

*Sergeants.*

Peter M. Myers (*Orderly*).
Edward H. Little.
Jeremiah V. Meserole.
Alfred B. Chapman.
Henry Everdell.

*Corporals.*

Charles E. Bogert.
Robert H. Eddy.
Edward R. Young.
James Farnam.

*Drummer,* Henry Eidman.

*Privates.*

Aymore, J. S.
Belden, Henry C.
Blauvelt, J. Harmon.
Bruden, Abner H.
Bruden, Charles E.
Brundage, Minthorne T.
Bunting, Robert S.
Burns, Thomas.
Canfield, Jesse W.
Carpenter, Silas S.
Carter, Herman G.
Chesebrough, State.
Crary, Charles H.
Crocker, George A.
Cust, Stephen B.
Daugherty, Horace F.
Davenport, Charles F.
Dickerson, George A.
Earle, Edward.
Everdell, Francis.
Ewen, Austen D.
Ewen, Edward D.
Ewen, Norman
Fairbanks, Charles M.
Fay, Logan.
Ferry, Edwin N.
Fielding, William T.
Fiske, William E.
Gaston, William.
Gautier, Samuel.
Hall, Henry M.
Halsted, Robert.
Harrison, Edmund A.
Haywood, Melville.
Hennessey, John F., Jr.
Hickox, Charles R.
Hollingshead, William M.
Holly, Henry S.
Honeywell, Charles R.
Huntington, Chas. P.
Husted, Theodore I.
Hyde, Melancthon W.
Jarvis, John.
Karr, Frank D.
Kipp, William H.
Lambert, William.
Lawrence, Edward L.
Lawrence, George A.
Lefferts, John C.*
Little, John L.
Mallon, James E.
Manning, Geo. F.
Marshall, Alexander S.
Miller, William M.
Mills, James.
Moies, John E.
Morse, L. W.
Nichols, William L.
Nugent, Henry.
Olssen, Edward J.

* On detail duty at Annapolis till after musters.

Osborne, Elisha R.
Outcalt, Cornelius B.
Peacock, Thomas R.
Ridden, John C.
Sanford, Geo. H.
Sangster, George.
Smith, Ernest L.
Smith, Frank K.
Smith, Milton.
Smith, Samuel J.
Smith, William H.
Snodgrass, Archibald A.
Spaulding, Zeph. S.
Starr, Samuel H.
Steele, William S.
Swords, Charles H.
Taylor, Joseph D.
Weyman, Edmund H., Jr.
Wood, William W.
Wright, William C.

*Mustered in April* 30, 1861.

Aikman, Augustus H.
Balen, Peter, Jr.
Burdick, Charles.
Callamore, Gilman.
Farmington, Adam.
Fay, Patrick H.
Jarvis, Edward A.
Lefferts, Marshall, Jr.
Roome, William H.
Ryan, James E.
Sharpe, Samuel C.
Sinclair, Hyatt.
Steele, Peter B.
Woodhouse, Lorenzo G.

*Mustered in May* 14, 1861.

Baggs, John W.
Dubois, John S. L.
Edwin, William A.
Merritt, Abraham.
Owen, Mortimer B.
Walz, Ernest L.

## FIFTH COMPANY (E).

*Captain,* Wm. A. Speaight.

1st *Lieutenant,* Christopher Corley.

2d *Lieutenant,* James Gaylor.

*Sergeants.*

Halsted, Wm. P. (*Orderly*).
Sprole, Wm. T.
Eckel, Frederick.
Earle, Justus D.
Miller, John P.

*Corporals.*

Seward, Wm. J.
Braisted, Peter D.
Wall, William, Jr.
Barnes, Seth S.

*Privates.*

Baker, Thos. E.
Barrett, Geo. P.
Benedict, Chas. A.
Bissell, Geo. W.
Bogardus, Abraham.
Brusle, Wm. A.
Burlew, Henry.
Cowles, Wm.
Eckel, J. Lewis.
Filley, F. C.
Fisher, Philip J.
Fleet, Augustine.
Foot, Alfred.
Franklin, J. B.
Frothingham, Chas. L.
Fuller, Benj. F.
Gardner, Etienne V.
Genin, Erastus.

Gumbling, Wm. M.
Halsted, Elbert K.
Hardenberg, Isaiah D.
Harward, Wm. E.
Haynes, Charles O.
Husted, Gilbert M.
Hutchings, Edward W.
Hyde, Albert W.
Jauncey, Joseph.
Kappner, Ignave G.
Keefler, Billopp R.
Kellinger, Samuel M.
Kingsland, Edward A.
Kingsland, William H.
Lester, David.
Lewis, Geo. T., Jr.
Magarr, W. W.
Marten, Benjamin T.
McDonald, Joseph.
Mezzetti, Geo. Washington.
Moore, Wm. A.
Nixon, Charles L.
Pangburn, W. H.
Reed, Robert.
Rink, Peter.
Romaine, Wm. H.
Sadler, Thomas.
Sargeant, James A.
Scott, William A.
Seligman, S.
Silva, John.
Stokeley, Noah B.
Stuart, Wm.
Sullivan, Timothy J.
Thomas, George M.
Timolatt, Hippolytt N.
Tucker, George.
Vanderbilt, De Witt C.
Webb, James A.
Wood, John Wardell.
Wyckoff, Albert T.
Yeaton, Samuel C.

*Mustered in April* 30, 1861.

Benedict, Erastus C.
Bennett, Warren C.
Corrie, Frederick H.
Hawkins, John U.
Hawley, Frank E.
Hayden, A. L.
Mapes, Daniel S.
Mitchell, Samuel E. L.
Noe, A. A.
Noe, J. Augustus.
Prentiss, Wm. A.
Price, George A.
Stern, Louis.
Sutherland, James.
Waldron, Frederick E.
Waterbury, W. H.

*Mustered in May* 14, 1861.

Banks, S. A.
Berlin, Henry.
Fox, John W.
Gaddis, Theo. F.
Holbrook, Judson W.
Perkins, Frederick W.
Reynolds, James E.
Richards, Daniel W.
Rockfeller, Charles M.
Stugers, Edmund N.

## SIXTH COMPANY (F).

*Captain*, BENJAMIN M. NEVERS, JR.

1*st Lieutenant*, Richard F. Halsted. 2*d Lieutenant*, Joseph B. Young.

*Sergeants.*

Ford, George W. (*Orderly*).
Bartlett, Charles G.
Brady, Abner S.
Ruggles, James F.

*Corporals.*

Freeman, William B.
Kemble, Gouverneur, Jr.
Walke, Charles.

*Drummer,* Hugh McCormack.

*Privates.*

Annan, Alexander.
Bassett, Frederick B.
Benkard, James, Jr.
Bird, Edward O.
Birmingham, Erskine.
Boyden, George.
Brinckerhoff, Guidon G.
Browing, Geo. Leslie.
Brown, Charles E.
Brown, Clarence F.
Cambreling, Churchill J.
Carey, Samuel.
Carnes, Louis M.
Chadwick, Philip R.
Clarkson, Floyd.
Cogswell, Andrew K.
Comstock, George S.
Congdon, Henry M.
Congdon, Walter.
Cooper, Poinsett.
Cowdrey, Edward A.
Cowdrey, Frank H.
Cozzens, Edward.
Cutting, James D. W.
Cuvillier, Louis L.
Dick, William B.
Dock, Ritner.
Douglas, Archibald.
Duryee, Jacob.
Ebaugh, Theo. O.
Elsworth, Arthur M.
Erving, John.
Falls, DeWitt C.
Ferris, Garwood C.
Foster, John A.
Foster, John E.
French, John W.
Frost, William C.
Gardner, Charles C.
Halsted, Edward L.
Hawes, J. H. Hobart.
Jaudon, Peyton.
Jenkins, Elisha J.
Kimball, Charles A.
King, Rufus.
Lamb, Anthony J.
Laraque, Edward.
Lawrence, Samuel B.
Marrinner, David.
McLaren, John J.
McLaren, Jos.
Middlebrook, George L.
Miller, Lindley H.
Palmer, Geo.
Rankin, Samuel H. L.
Raymond, James P.
Robbins, Samuel H.
Rowe, Thomas P.
Ryder, Mitchell.
Schuyler, Philip, Jr.
Shaw, Robert G.
Sheldon, Alexander E.
Smedbury, Charles G.
Still, H. A.
Stoutenburgh, W. A.
Sturgis, Edward C.
Sutton, Charles T.
Taylor, Henry.
Teer, Henry T.
Thomas, Charles W.
Thomas, George F.
Thorpe, Gould H.
Tirripson, John W.
Tomes, Charles H.
Tucker, Fang. C.
Ulshoeffer, W. Gracci.
Van Benschoten, Edward W.
Vance, William H.

Van Duzer, Charles F.
Vermilye, Washn. R., Jr.
Vernon, George R.
Walduck, David M.
Watts, George B.
Weely, James.
West, Edward W.
Weston, Roswell.
Whiting, William T.
Wilson, George W.
Winston, F. M.
Winthrop, William W.

*Mustered in April* 30, 1861.

Bartow, Wm. J.
Coggeshall, George H.
Ford, Charles E.
Harrison, Francis.
Hayes, James E.
Lawrence, W. Hudson.
Roome, William P.
Ryckman, John W.
Shaw, William G.
Wheeler, F. A.
White, George H.
Young, George W.

*Mustered in May* 14, 1861.

*Sergeant,* Catlin W. W. Stuyvesant.

*Privates.*

Arnold, Henry.
Bissell, Aug. H.
Edgar, Geo. P.
Erhardt, Joel B.
Tracy, Frederick A. T.
Tracy, William W.
Stillwell, Richard H.
Wood, W. Stanard.

## SEVENTH COMPANY (G).

*Captain* (see below).

1*st Lieutenant,* John D. Moriarty.

*Sergeants.*

Winans, Chas. N. (*Orderly*).
Henry, E. S.
Cameron, John L.
Hobbs, Charles, Jr.
Ely, George W.

*Corporals.*

Bidwell, H. S.
Delano, T. E.
Bowerman, R. N.
Coper, John J.

*Privates.*

Alcoke, R. S.
Annable, T. H.
Barker, L. E.
Barnett, John L.
Beech, C. J.
Bennett, A. C. W.
Bennett, C. F.
Bogert, A. S.
Bootman, R. W.
Britton, A. N.
Britton, F.
Callender, W. E.
Chatfield, H. S.
Collins, W. N.
Cortelyou, J. H.
Crane, E. S.
Crary, B. N.
De La Mater, Charles H.
Delano, Jesse.
Donaldson, E.
Dunscomb, J. H.
Easton, B. C.

Fitch, George R.
Fowler, D. H.
Geisse, W. F.
Gibson, W. H.
Gibson, R. O.
Hall, Charles.
Hathaway, T. E.
Holderge, D. M.
Holmes, G. F., Jr.
Howell, A. J.
Hughes, J. B.
Ingersoll, J. H.
Klanbey, A.
Lauderback, D., Jr.
Law, R. H.
Lent, L. H.
Matthews, H. E.
McKesson, J., Jr.
Montange, W. H.
Moon, W. S., Jr.
Moore, Geo. G.
O'Brien, Fitz James.
Oliver, Richard.
Palmer, J. H.
Phipps, John M.
Pinckney, F. H.
Pomroy, E. H.
Pontin, H. C.
Putnam, E. T.
Risily, L. S.
Robinson, J. J.
Sherman, S. J.
Shortland, Thomas.
Skilleen, G. W.
Smith, R. B.
Steers, F. J.
Stewart, R. K.
St. John, W.
Tallman, Geo. N.
Thompson, S. W.
Tiffany, Lyman.
Trotter, F. E.
Turnbull, G. P.
Turner, W. M.
Van Ness, E.
Vanderwird, H.
Vidal, T. C.
Wheelwright, W. G.
Williamson, C.
Winters, H. J.

*Mustered in April* 30, 1861.

*Captain*, John Monroe.

*Privates.*

Avery, John, Jr.
Chevalier, George.
Coyne, John H.
Eddy, Edward, Jr.
Hayden, James.
Lent, William H.
Maury, Geo. A.
McDonough, Lewis.
McJimsey, Eugene.
Oldershaw, John.
Oliver, Frank W.
Olmstead, Wm. N.
Reddy, James I.
Schermerhorn, Louis.
Schermerhorn, Wm. H.
Schram, James.
Shaffer, N. D.
Spencer, William P.
Steers, A.
Stone, William H.
Talmadge, G. Clinton.
Tiffany, Henry D.
Thorp, Richard A.
Van Loan, Benj. F.

*Mustered in May* 14, 1861.

Anderson, Smith W.
Clegg, Walter O.
Hartwell Charles.
Howe, Oscar.
Hutchins, Robert A.
Tufts, Wm. Fuller.

## EIGHTH COMPANY (H).

*Captain,* Henry C. Shumway.

*1st Lieutenant,* Chas. B. Bostwick.

*2d Lieutenant,* Chas. B. Babcock.

*Sergeants.*

Spurr, John (*Orderly*).
Sears, Samuel W.
Kittle, Edward C.
Green, Henry D.
Burger, Wm. L. M.

*Corporals.*

Hidenberg, Gould B.
Mears, Charles E.
Loder, Benjamin, Jr.

*Drummers.*

Hackenfort, Jerry.
Susdorf, Charles Fred'k.

*Privates.*

Abrams, James.
Allen, Charles D.
Allen, William B.
Austen, David E.
Baker, John M.
Barbey, Adolphus H.
Bassett, William H.
Bearnes, Joseph H.
Beaumont, Charles L.
Beecher, Henry C.
Brooks, George W.
Brown, Edward S.
Brown, William H.
Brownell, Silas B.
Burdett, George F.
Burkhalter, John H.
Burkhalter, Stephen, Jr.
Burrage, Robert P.
Casey, James S.
Cozzens, Thos. N.
Coles, William H., Jr.
Denison, Lyman.
Eager, Peter.
Easton, Alfred H.
Field, Robert M., Jr.
Field, Samuel B.
Ford, Robert O. N.
Foster, Samuel L.
Gouge, Edward H.
Grant, Frank H.
Grant, James B.
Hall, Robert L. S.
Herrick, Elias J.
Hertzel, George W.
Hillman, John S.
Howell, William P.
Hubbell, Henry W., Jr.
Hull, John H.
Johnson, Ebenezer R.
Lamb, Joseph.
Lane, I. Remsen.
Leveridge, Albert D. W.
Lewis, Thompson.
Mabee, Foster N.
Macy, Theodore E.
Marvine, William H.
Mather, Dewitt Clinton.
McMillan, Alexander.
Meeks, Albert V.
Moller, William H.
Moran, Edward.
Morgan, John W.
Morrison, James, Jr.
Morrison, William A.
Muller, Adrian H., Jr.
Murfey, George W.
Murfey, John H.
Neilson, Edward N.
Newville, Clarence M.
Owen, William H., Jr.

Parmelee, Lewis C.
Peet, Frederick T., Jr.
Phillips, Henry J.
Polhamus, Henry A.
Pomeroy, George H.
Robinson, James E.
Rogers, Edmund P.
Rollinson, Samuel O.
Ryder, Alfred V.
Smith, Edwin A.
Smith, George W.
Spear, Adrian.
Spear, Percival B.
Stephenson, Lewis W.
Trowbridge, Joseph A.
Williams, George B.
Willis, John O.
Wood, Alexander.
Wood, Thomas H.

*Mustered in April* 30, 1861.

Arms, Charles E.
Arrowsmith, Gilbert L.
Blake, Clarence A.
Buckley, William W.
Davidson, Albert.
Flagg, Montague.
Gansvoort, H. S.
Gifford, Sanford R.
Green, Frank W.
Half, Edward P.
Hansman, Charles H.
Hastings, Eastburn.
Hay, Sidney.
Jandon, Frank.
Jung, Charles T.
Keese, J. Larry.
Levick, James N. J.
Mason, Albert.
McKee, Charles.
Patterson, Wm. G.
Peet, Charles B.
Rankin, Benjamin.
Reeve, Charles.
Rushton, John C.
Smith, L. Bayard.
Spencer, Pierre F.
Talcott, E. N. Kirk.
Van Pelt, Samuel K.
Webber, John T.
Welch, Edward A.
Whitehouse, Edward U.
Wilson, Henry S.

*Mustered in May* 14, 1861.

Baker, James T.
Cargill, Frank.
Champion, Charles S.
Crochett, John A.
Daskam, James W.
Ellis, William J.
Farrell, William R
Grant, T C.
Harris, James D.
Holden, Edward B.
Hollister, Henry H.
Hurlburt, William H.
Jacobson, William C.
Keene, John P.
Lapsley, Howard.
Mansfield, William D.
Moss, Charles D.
Murray, G. W.
Murray, Henry S.
Oley, John H.
Pease, Walter D.
Pierce, Charles E.
Richardson, George P.
Rogers, Philip C.

## NINTH COMPANY (I).

*Captain*, —— ——.

1st *Lieut.* (*commanding*), Henry A. Cragin. 2d *Lieut.*, Charles C. White.

*Sergeants.*

McBride, Irwin H. (*Orderly*).
Fuller, Andrew J.
Keeler, Edwin, Jr.
Moore, Lawrence, Jr.

*Privates.*

Barrie, John.
Bonnell, Henry.
Childs, Henry A.
Concklin, James R.
Concklin, John P., Jr.
Corey, Robert P.
Dean, William L.
Edgar, Samuel P.
Fitzpatrick, Thomas A.
Mack, Valentine.
MacLane, Archibald.
Merriman, Elijah R.
Mingay, Elwood B.
O'Beirne, James R.
Osborne, Charles H.
Swezey, Joseph H. S.
Sweet, Milton B.
Warren, Charles J.
White, Charles D.
White, George W.
Winthrop, Theodore.
Van Iderstein, Peter, Jr.
Young, David A.

*Mustered in May* 14, 1861.

Andrews, G. D.
Arthur, H. E.
Avery, H. N.
Ball, C. J. C.
Barker, Joshua.
Barney, N. C.
Barrett, A. R.
Brainard, L. W., Jr.
Bramhall, W. L.
Bugle, Benedict.
Bush, Theodore H.
Carman, Richard.
Church, E. D.
Coan, W. B.
Coombs, Philip.
Cumming, A. M., Jr.
Davis, G. D., Jr.
Dayton, G. E.
Dayton, W. C., Jr.
Doughty, G. R.
Durbin, J. P., Jr.
Durfee, Fenton.
Durnnell, G. H.
Eddy, Clinton.
Ellis, Franklin.
Farmer, George E.
Fisher, W. H.
Fordred, Drayson.
Franklin, Daniel R.
Giberson, Samuel.
Goodrich, L. O.
Graves, E. C.
Harmsted, R. M.
Howell, I. R.
King, C. E.
Knapp, E. S.
Law, R. J.
Lockwood, F. A.
Lord, J. R.
Manning, John.
Marlor, George.
Martin, P. H.
Matthews, James.
McCrea, J. E.

McCrosson, T. A.
McDonald, Alexander, Jr.
McSpedon, W. A.
Merchant, A. T.
Mitchell, R. C.
Moore, J. C.
Nandaine, G. D.
O'Brien, Oswin.
Olney, J. E.
Potter, W. S.
Rockwell, Fenton.
Rutherford, J. H.
Ryan, W. H.
Seaman, J. C
Seaman, Wm.
Spaulding, F. S.
Speir, A. B.
Stout, T. P.
Taylor, H. B.
Tufts, J. M.
Tyloff, Ivan.
Tyng, T. M.
Van Nest, W. L.
Wagner, Charles F.
Welles, M. G.
Wheeler, William.
White, D. W.
White, James G.

## TENTH COMPANY (K).

*Captain* (see below).

1st *Lieutenant*, E. M. Lemoyne. 2d *Lieutenant*, T. B. Bunting.

*Sergeants.*

Robinson, John E. (*Ordnance*).
Lord, Thomas, Jr. (*Orderly*).
Lawrence, Jon.
Schmidt, Leopold

*Corporals.*

Dana, Samuel.
Lentilhon, Jos.
Leland, Francis L.

*Privates.*

Delafield, Edward.
DeRuyter, Charles.
D'Hervilly, Edward.
Drake, David.
Drake, Lawrence.
Dubois, C.
Edey, Henry.
Hall, R. B.
Harper, John T.
Holbrook, H. H.
Hollister, E. P.
Lacombe, Jas. P.
Leggett, F. W.
Leland, Charles H.
Livingston, Charles.
Ludovici, Julius.
Luqueer, F. T., Jr.
Osborn, C. H.
Oakley, W. H.
Pearsall, T. W., Jr.
Peterson, Oscar L., Jr.
Pierson, Henry, Jr.
Plume, J. Henry.
Prentice, C. K.
Ray, James.
Richardson, L. R.
Sands, Henry.
Schenck, C. A.
Seabury, Robert S.
Slasson, Wm.
Slossan, J. Lawrence.
Slossan, J. Stewart.
Spies, Francis.
Staples, Wright.
Wotherspoon, H. H.
White, John C.
Wallace, W. S.
Welles, E. B.
Wright, Edward.
Winslow, John.

*Mustered in April* 30, 1861.

*Sergeant*, Van Renssalaer, S. *Corporal*, Bleecker, James.

*Drummer*, Burlinghoff, Charles T.

*Privates.*

Beebe, Edward.
Bibby, Alfred.
Bleecker, T. B.
Boell, Charles B.
Brown, Lewis M.
Gadsden, Charles A.
Gawtry, H. E.
Guion, George.
Grant, Wm. E.
Hargons, P. A.
Harman, Edward.
Hecksher, John E.
Jones, T. F.
Niel, J. Delany.
Taylor, James B.
Tompkins, W. W.
Tucker, John A.
Voorhies, Charles H.

*Mustered in May* 14, 1861.

*Captain*, George C. Farrar.

*Privates.*

Chanler, J. W.
Chauncey, C. W.
Costar, Charles.
Costar, John.
Coster, Jeremiah.
Cumming, R. L.
Curtis, Samuel B.
Foote, Edward.
Frieborn, Thomas.
Fuller, H. W.
Hart, Lucius, Jr.
Lafarge, A.
Macy, C. A., Jr.
Manning, J. C.
McAllister, John.
McJimsey, Robert M.
Milhan, Edward L.
Miller, Henry W.
Morris, R. L.
Morris, Robert.
Morse, N. B., Jr.
Moss, Nathan F.

Though the Daylight was chartered by friends of the regiment in New York, Colonel Lefferts made efforts to have the government assume the expense. It has already been noted that he wrote to this effect to Governor Morgan, at Annapolis, on the 23d of April. On the 1st of May he received the following reply: —

"I hasten to reply to your letter of the 23d instant, written, at Annapolis, Md., this moment at hand, requesting me to write to you at Washington.

"Approving as I do of the course adopted by you in making your way to Washington with the gallant regiment under your command, I have, in relation to the question of funds expended on your journey to Washington, to ask you to represent the case to the Secretary of War, who, I do not doubt, will give directions for the immediate reimbursement of the sum thus expended.

"You will without delay advise me of the result of such application to the Secretary of War.

"I am, &c., &c.,

"E. D. MORGAN."

To this letter, on the same day, Colonel Lefferts replied as follows: —

"I made application at the proper department to have the charter-party of a vessel just arrived with stores for us assumed by them, which I urged upon the ground that she also brought troops. They informed me that no doubt, at a future day, we would be refunded the outlay, but they would not pay just now. This vessel and stores were sent by my directions when I expected to be hemmed in, perhaps for weeks. This vessel and cargo cost us $4,000 charter-party, and $8,000 for stores; there was so much confusion consequent upon the hurried manner in which troops have been sent forward, that it was absolutely necessary to make outlays upon my own responsibility, or lie idly waiting for others to move. In order to save the government from all trouble for us, and when others actually required more attention, I said I would commute for my rations, and take care of ourselves. This costs us fifty cents per man, over and above the amount received for rations; it seems hard that I must call upon my men for money in such a case.

"I now leave the matter to be disposed of as you may deem best."

But the Union Defence Committee promptly came forward and assumed the entire outlay; and the following characteristic letter on the subject will give some idea of the general fervor of enthusiasm which existed regarding the regiment: —

"MY DEAR COLONEL, — Ere this reaches you, I presume you will have received my telegram saying the Union Defence Committee had given me a check for the full amount of the charter and the entire invoice of goods sent you. I think old Kemp deserves well of his regiment. He has worked night and day to bring the result of his expedition to a successful issue, and to-day his exertions are crowned with success; he has his money, and the Daylight is home, safe and sound. I won't annoy you with the detail of how I have been bamboozled about from one committee and sub-committee to another. These committees have been perfectly overwhelmed with work themselves, often till one and two in the morning; but I started to succeed and have. God bless my dear boys! If they only knew how, for days and days without news, the true, full heart of New York has beat for them, they and yourself would be proud of that magic figure *seven*. It pained me greatly to see in the papers that the Richmond Grays, Captain Elliot, were at Norfolk. When he was here, and we all swore devotedness to the Union, I presumed the flag borne in his command represented the flag of the Union. I little dreamed he would feel it his duty to fight under any other. . . . .

"A. KEMP, *Paymaster Seventh Regiment.*"

The time had now come for the Seventh Regiment to take another step. As soon as the camp equipage left at Annapolis had been brought on, Colonel Lefferts prepared to go into camp. The regiment received the intelligence with joy. Neither their "barracks" nor their fare suited them as would the soldier's ration and the soldier's shelter. Their round of duty, too, had become monotonous. The following is a specimen of it, chosen at random from a mass of regimental orders. It is General Order No. 9, dated April 28, 1861: —

"Company C, Captain Price, and Company E, Captain Speaight, are detailed for guard duty for the 29th inst. Guard-mounting at half past seven o'clock, A. M. Adjutants' call at twenty minutes past seven, A. M.

"The guard for the protection of our own quarters will report in the hall by the Colonel's quarters at seven, A. M. Lieutenant Harvey is hereby detailed as officer of this guard, and a sergeant of the First Company, together with a corporal, as non-commissioned officers of the guard.

"Commandants will drill their companies as well as recruits during the forenoon. Evening parade at half past four o'clock, P. M., full uniform, with knapsacks.

"The Park fronting the Capitol is hereby designated as Regimental Parade-Ground until further notice. First sergeants' call for consolidated report at six o'clock, A. M."

Troops were now pouring into Washington as the Seventh marched out from the thick of the population again in the van, as it were, to the picket-lines. It gladly surrendered its luxurious quarters to later comers.

Major Irvin McDowell was in command of the Capitol building when the Seventh appeared for the relief of Washington. But soon after, — namely, April 28, — Colonel (afterwards Major-General) Mansfield, U. S. A., was assigned to the command of the Department of Washington, and it was to him, accordingly, that Colonel Lefferts addressed his proposition to go into camp. The *terrain* selected, or rather desired, is one of the finest for camp purposes around the city, and was then known as Dr. Stone's farm. Its site was on Meridian Hill, two miles due north from Willard's, on the Harper's Ferry Road, — a farm of forty acres, with its fine old mansion on an elevated, undulating terrace, commanding the plain of Washington, and having a full view of the city and the Potomac broadening beyond. Its position and its fine grounds, covered with grand old ivy-circled oaks, had made it the favorite residence of several Presidents from the time of Madison, who built the villa. A broad parade-ground was available on the spot most suitable for the camp.

But this desirable ground, though offered to the regiment by the proprietors, was not secured without difficulty. On the 30th, Colonel Lefferts informed Colonel Mansfield that the regimental camp equipage had just been received, adding: "I visited in person the grounds of Mr. Stone, suggested by Lieutenant-General Scott, as the place designated for an encampment, and am prepared to proceed and occupy the ground upon receipt of an order from you to that effect." This letter was promptly returned, with the following indorsement in Colonel Mansfield's hand: "The General-in-Chief prefers that this regiment be camped at Fletcher's Kalorama, in rear of his house, represented to be a fine camping-ground. It is out on West 20th Street. Go and examine the premises, and, if suitable, go into camp there." There was no comparison between the two places, and resort was had to the representations and influence of good judges. These were successful, and Colonel Lefferts received from Colonel Mansfield authority "to encamp his regiment on Meridian Hill."

On May day (suggesting many a witticism regarding "May moving") the regiment assembled at evening parade at 4 P. M., with knapsacks and overcoats rolled thereon, and received the expected order, which ran as follows: —

"By directions from head-quarters, the regiment will go into camp to-morrow at the farm of Mr. Stone, Meridian Hill. The hour of march will be stated in orders to-morrow morning.

"Quartermaster Winchester is directed to have the camp equipage transported immediately to the place herein designated.

"Lieutenant E. M. Le Moyne, commanding, will have his command ready for marching orders, with one day's rations, at three o'clock this P. M.

"Captain Viele will accompany the command, and superintend the laying out of the camp.

"Commissary Patten will cause the necessary stores to be transported from the Navy-yard."

The Ninth and Tenth Companies, under Captain Viele, marched the same afternoon to Meridian Hill, and began to lay out the camp. Colonel Lefferts meanwhile informed Major McDowell of the movement in these words: —

"In compliance with orders from head-quarters, I shall move my main body of troops to-morrow afternoon at half past three o'clock for encampment on Meridian Hill. I have detailed two of my companies for guard duty to-morrow, but have to ask whether you will give other directions or make arrangements to relieve my companies from duty during the day, that they may go with the main body to camp.

"Allow me at this opportunity to thank you most heartily for your many kind attentions, and express my regret at moving away from the building which has brought us into such close and pleasant contact."

Major McDowell, on the same day, answered as follows: —

HEAD-QUARTERS OF THE CAPITOL,
May 1, 1861.

COLONEL MARSHALL LEFFERTS, *Seventh Regiment N. Y. S. M.*

COLONEL, — Agreeably to the request contained in your note of this date, I have given directions that the companies of your regiment be relieved from the detail for guard for to-morrow.

It is with sincere regret I find the hour for your departure at hand. It is a positive pleasure to have your regiment here, for I do not exaggerate when I say a finer body of a thousand men are not on the face of this globe.

With the kindest wishes for you all, I have the honor to be, Colonel,

Very respectfully, your most obedient servant,

IRVIN MCDOWELL,
*Assistant Adjutant-General.*

On the 2d of May, at four o'clock, P. M., the regiment, with full ranks, marched out of the Capitol, down Pennsylvania Avenue, "exchanging enthusiastic adieus," say the newspapers of the day, "with the Massachusetts regiment, and cheered all along the route. In front of the National Hotel, Governor Sprague's (the Rhode Island) regiment presented arms. The Seventh Regiment presented a fine appearance, and was followed by a long train of baggage-wagons." And so ended the regiment's occupation of the national Capitol.

## CHAPTER X.

### CAMP CAMERON.

THE new camp had been christened, by Colonel Lefferts, "Camp Cameron," in honor of the Secretary of War, and by that name it has passed into history. Situated on Meridian Hill, a mile out on Fourteenth Street, and opposite Columbia College, the camp was both healthy and beautiful. The head-quarters commanded a view of the Potomac, as well as of the capital, and of Arlington Heights beyond. The camp was in a fine clover-field, enveloped by woods, where was neatly disposed the camp equipage, consisting of two hundred and twenty wall-tents, supplied with "those straw bags we kindly call our mattresses." The wagons brought on the delicacies and substantials which poured in daily from friends in New York.

The initiation into camp-life was, however, a severe one. The first night was unusually cold, and covered the field with a heavy frost. The next morning a violent north-cast storm set in, lasting till the afternoon of the following day. The unfloored tents did not keep out the rain; the men lay in their blankets in the wet clover. The details for guard duty were thoroughly drenched, and their beats were through mire. The kitchens were not yet up, and those at head-quarters were forced to do duty for all the companies. "Jasper" writes to the New York Times, under date of May 3d:—

"During the day we have been getting ready for housekeeping, and cooking our own meals. Scouts are ransacking the city on foot and in hacks, making extensive purchases of tin pans, kettles, pots, basins, &c. We have selected cooks, and are going into camp-life in earnest. The rain pours in torrents, and we are not able to floor our tents, so we turn in on the straw, and sleep warm by indulging in the classic Dutch style of bundling. Several of us have been engaged in boiling potatoes in a huge kettle for the noon meal. Somehow the vast kettle keeled over and upset the pot, the water put out the fire, and we were effectually dished. We essayed the boiling of some rice; the rice was tip-top, but it would burn. After a while we shall learn the ropes, and those of us who are not married will learn all the secrets of housekeeping before our thirty days has expired. There are about two hundred and fifty tents on the ground, six men being allowed to each tent, with the exception of the officers, who have a tent to themselves. The Second Company, the advance guard on the march from Annapolis, are a mighty jolly set, and have among them several fine singers. One of the tents was christened Canterbury Hall last evening, but this morning the frost lay deep on the ground, and the name was changed to the Winter Garden. The scene at the noonday meal to-day was ludicrous in the extreme. Each man was to take his turn with tin plate and cup, and as each company has full a hundred men, the last ones had a pretty hard time of it dodging the pouring rain. In a few days everything will be in apple-pie order, the streets and avenues will be laid out, and the Seventh will be happy to receive their lady friends; but at present everything is in a most heterogeneous jumble, save and except the discipline, which is always perfect. In pleasant weather the spot selected is a beautiful one, overlooking Fort Washington away down the Potomac, but just now the mud is nearly a foot deep. The solitary sentries, stern as Roman soldiers, will have a hard time of it to-night.

"As I write, the camp-fires are being lighted to cook the evening meal, and the red glare of the torches throws a picturesque light over the white canvas that holds so many of the flower of our city. Young men who were never in a kitchen are now deeply engaged in the mysteries of the *cuisine* ; while others are preparing their coffee in alcoholic arrangements, which are warranted not to burn the aromatic beverage. Others, again, by the light of their chandeliers, which swing from the roof of their tents, are busily engaged in reading loved missives from home, or writing laconic notes on the back of their knapsacks. A general cheerfulness pervades the entire regiment; and what would be thought terrible hardships at home are here turned into merry jests."

The Chaplain says: "Our encampment was called Mount Pleasant, but, for a time, this was a palpable misnomer. It rained incessantly, the weather cold, the tents were without floors; the men, without beds, were compelled to lie down (many of them drenched to the skin from being on guard) in the wet, rank clover. The hospital was soon filled with invalids, and I can only attribute their rapid recovery to their youth, spirits, temperate habits, and the skill of our excellent medical staff." *

But, on the 4th, the floods ceased, fair weather came, tent-floors were constructed, and, during three days thereafter, the camp was busily set in order.

The regiment was glad to be out of the city, where now had arrived six regiments from New York, three more from Massachusetts, two from Pennsylvania, and one from Rhode Island, — a total, with the Regulars and city militia, of perhaps fifteen thousand men. The position it had occupied was on the road to Harper's Ferry, and was one of more responsibility than the men themselves were aware of. Colonel Lefferts was instructed to post strong guards,

* A letter of May 3d from the regiment says: "The straw mattresses furnished were very small and poor, and only enough to supply three or four to a tent, and each tent occupied by six men, so that our sleeping arrangements were not the most comfortable. There was a stack of hay in the field which the boys soon demolished, and carried to their quarters, — that is, those who were fortunate enough to get any, — and then, to improve matters, we had no supper. About nine o'clock the sergeant obtained from the commissary a hard biscuit and a small piece of cheese for each man."

and, on the very day the camp was occupied, he received the following order, in General Mansfield's own hand: —

HEAD-QUARTERS, DEPARTMENT WASHINGTON, May 2, 1861.

COLONEL LEFFERTS, *Commanding Seventh Regiment.*

SIR, — Lieutenant-General Scott desires me to say to you, that, in case of an alarm of attack at night, you will march your regiment directly to the President's house.

Please put out your pickets from your camp on the highway, far enough for you to rally before attacked.

I apprehend, however, no attack at this time.

Very truly,

JOS. K. F. MANSFIELD,
*Colonel Commanding.*

On the same day, at a later hour, he received a hurried note from the same officer, in these words: —

HEAD-QUARTERS, DEPARTMENT WASHINGTON, May 2.

COLONEL M. LEFFERTS, *Seventh New York Regiment.*

Please have your command furnished with full supply of ball cartridges before dark, and hold them ready at any moment to take the field.

JOS. K. F. MANSFIELD,
*Colonel Commanding.*

(*Confidential.*)

Labor and taste soon made the new camp a soldiers' village, and every tent a cottage filled with congenial and happy inmates. Eight companies were established on the broad elevated plateau, covered with high and rich clover (which, however, the perpetual tramp of so many men soon wore to the ground), in regular rows of wall tents, without the fly, arranged in broad and neat streets. The Ninth and Tenth, or howitzer companies, were quartered in outbuildings; the former, however, soon after occupying a large *marquee.* In front of the tents, and sloping gently down, was the broad and handsome parade-ground and drilling-field. A broad avenue, shaded by oaks, willows, and poplars, some of whose branches interlaced, conducted by an easy ascent from Fourteenth Street to the

Stone mansion; and on this, a few rods from the gate (the latter under the charge of two sentinels), was established the guard-tent. A chain of sentinels prescribed by their beats the limit of the camp. Partly concealed by the splendid oaks so thick around it, but rising above them, was the villa, with its carriage-porch of four granite pillars in front, forming a commodious head-quarters, with the Colonel's quarters in the large, neat parlor, and those of his staff and of the Engineer Corps in various other rooms around and above. The cellars, outbuildings, and green-house contained the commissary stores, and the enormous quantity of "barrels, boxes, cans, and bottles" of food and condiments continually sent on by friends of the regiment. The guns were put in battery, a flag-staff raised, and all the appointments of a camp scene — since so familiar to Americans — were complete. The tents of the company officers were, of course, on a line at right angles to those of the men. Each "street" had its amusing name, sometimes connected with that of an officer; and each tent a droller one, with the list of its occupants on a placard at the door. The following sketch of the camp is given with but few condensations from the original, which, in a letter dated Washington, May 16, 1861, appeared in the columns of a New York daily paper: —

"How the jolly Seventh enjoy life in Camp Cameron is something the people of Washington will remember when this war is a thing of the past. About a mile and a half north of Washington, and on the high-road to Harper's Ferry, you begin to ascend Meridian Hill, flanked right and left by green fields and picturesque clumps of foliage, now in full leaf and flower. . . . . You now leave the shaded avenue, the road to the camp leading north, over a plain, open field, and a gradual ascent of some twenty rods, which, when you have reached, you find yourself on the crown of Meridian Hill. The camp is pitched on ground sloping to the north, the drill-ground facing to the south, and extending the whole length of the tents. The camp, of square tents, is laid out in streets with great regularity, and presents a picturesque appearance. Many of the streets, and even the tents, are named after some familiar avenue or place of resort in New York; and the neatness and precision with which everything appertaining to the soldier is arranged, denotes the character of the men forming the corps. The camp was all astir just then, for it was near dinner-time, and many were the invitations to stop and share their 'rations.' Little furnaces were erected here and there between the tents, and the imp-like figures of little black boys were busy over stew and fry pans. It was instructive to see how men reared in tenderness, and accustomed to all the luxuries of New York life, adapted themselves thus readily to all the hardships of camp-life. But they have improved in health under it, and seem to enjoy it heartily.

"The tents are all nicely floored, and provided with good blankets and mattresses. In one, members might be seen stretched, some sleeping, some reading, some singing, — all in dark gray undress. Others were furbishing up their muskets, whitening their belts, or polishing their own boots. At times you fell upon a young gentleman reading letters from home. It is curious to see what a variety of things are sent here by friends of the regiment in New York, as well as relatives of the members. Barrels of ale, cider, and apples, boxes of oranges and lemons, jars of pickles and preserved meats, cans of various kinds of sweet meats, cases marked 'hardware,' which means brandy and whiskey (called by some 'fighting mixture'), and crackers and sardines. All these are denominated 'medical stores.' New York takes good care of the Seventh, and I may have added that many of the donors of these presents are unknown to the recipients.

"After strolling through the camp for some time, I shaped my course for the tent in which Gifford the artist was located. Here I met with a warm welcome from an old friend and companion. All was neatness and order in this tent, just what you might expect of such an occupant. The mattresses, covered with blankets, were carefully stowed on one side; there was a place for and a row of polished boots in their places; the knapsacks, bright and clean, were all in their places at one end; the accoutrements hung in their places; the 'medical stores,' of which there was a bountiful supply, stood in one corner; and the little table and the pewter looked as bright as if it had just come from the hands of a skilful kitchen-maid. A rack at the head of the camp held the arms. A very small edition of a darkey was cooking the noonday meal over a fire at the door."

Of the head-quarters the same visitor writes: —

"On the right are the Colonel's and Quartermaster's quarters, plainly furnished, but comfortable. These are the best parlors, where Madison and Adams used to entertain their guests. On the left are the quarters of the Lieutenant-Colonel, Adjutant, and Major, their swords and other weapons hanging on the walls; tables covered with papers, a few chairs, and camp-stools making up the furniture. An intricate passage leads you into the rear, and, passing down a few steps, you find yourself in store-rooms of various kinds, the bakery, the Quartermaster's department, and various oval departments, where the members of the Engineer Corps have taken up their quarters, some stretched on mattresses, others busy with their arms and uniforms. Returning to the first floor, you ascend bridge-shaped stairs, and are on the second floor, where the officers and non-commissioned officers of engineers have their quarters. The rooms are small, but high of ceiling and airy, and were formerly used for bedrooms. Each room is occupied by six or eight men, according to size, and called by some familiar name. One was 'Bleak House,' another 'Snug Home,' and a third, I think, 'Muggins.'

The day after the camp was occupied, the following order was issued: —

HEAD-QUARTERS SEVENTH REGIMENT, "CAMP CAMERON,"
MOUNT PLEASANT, WASHINGTON, May 3, 1861.

STANDING ORDER NO. 1.

This Camp shall be called "Camp Cameron," in honor of the Secretary of War.

The Chain of Sentinels shall be the limit of the Camp.

No member of the regiment shall pass outside of the limits of the Camp without express permission of the Officer of the Day, and then only by way of the guard tent, where he shall report himself going and returning. Not more than ten men of any one company shall be absent at one time.

The Officer of the Guard shall keep a list of men so leaving Camp, with the time of their reporting to him, and submit the same with his Guard Report in the morning.

Every man must be present at morning and afternoon drill, unless he is on the sick report or has a written excuse from his commandant.

"REVEILLE" at sunrise, when the morning gun will be fired by the guard; immediately after roll-call the tents will be put in order and the streets cleaned of all straw, &c., which must be removed from the Camp-Ground.

Half an hour after "Reveille," the signal for *Recruit squad drill*, which will last one hour.

"Surgeon's Call" at half past six, A. M., when the sick in camp, of each company, who are able, will be marched to the Dispensary, in charge of a non-commissioned officer.

"Peas on a Trencher," call for breakfast, at seven o'clock, A. M., when the companies will be formed and receive their rations in turn.

Call for details for guard duty at twenty minutes before eight, A. M.

Call for details to repair to Regimental Parade at ten minutes before eight, A. M.

"Troop" for guard-mounting at eight, A. M., — immediately after which the First Sergeant, with a detail of men, will draw their RATIONS for the day.

The "Assembly" for company drill, at half past nine, A. M. This drill will last one hour. The Troop will be drilled with the Howitzers; the Regimental Engineer will select some place in the immediate neighborhood, where the Engineer Corps will be practised in the construction of Gabions and Fascines.

"Roast Beef" will be sounded for dinner at twelve, M.

The "Assembly" for Companies to form for Battalion Drill will be at five, P. M.

First Sergeant's call fifteen minutes after.

To the Color to form by Battalion at half past five, P. M.

Evening gun to be fired at sunset.

"Tattoo" at ten, P. M. Taps at half past ten, P. M.

There will be roll-calls on the company parades, at Reveille, and evening parades superintended by a commissioned officer.

The recruits will be exercised at least twice a day by an officer or non-commissioned officer.

All drills will be attended in full fatigue dress, officers and non-commissioned officers omitting the sash.

Company and squad drills will be supervised by Major Shaler, who is hereby directed to attend in person, and direct a programme of exercises.

When off duty, in the public streets, all officers, non-commissioned officers, and privates will wear the body-belt alone, the coat buttoned. On dress parades, the officers and sergeants will wear the sash.

The cap-cover will be worn in wet weather only.

Pistols will not be carried by officers or men except in actual conflict, or when on the march.

All fancy articles of dress are prohibited at all times.

By order of

MARSHALL LEFFERTS, *Colonel Commanding.*

One modification of this order was made next day, in consequence of the issue of General Orders No. 17 from Department Head-quarters, which prescribes that

"Tattoo will take place throughout the city of Washington and its vicinity at half past nine o'clock, P. M.; after which all troops, both officers and soldiers, will remain in camp or quarters until reveille, unless out under orders, or with special permits from their commanders. A patrol will pass through the city under the orders of the Provost-Marshal, and all irregularities will be promptly corrected."

Ten days later (May 14) General Mansfield issued the following General Order No. 21: —

"I. On an alarm of fire, the troops at their respective camps and quarters will not leave their limits unless ordered out.

"II. There will be no serenading by bands after tattoo (half past nine, P. M.), except by written permit from these head-quarters.

"III. Field officers of the day will be detailed, who will receive their orders direct from these head-quarters.

"IV. In case of an attack and consequent alarm, which will be made known by the firing of three minute-guns and the tolling of the church bells, the troops will assemble for battle on their respective parade-grounds, and wait orders."

Major Shaler was directed to arrange a Manual of Arms, substantially like Hardee's, taken from the French, and to instruct the commissioned officers therein, and superintend the drills of the men.

From the "Standing Order No. 1," and the various orders for drill, target practice, and so forth, which followed, a good idea may be drawn of life at Camp Cameron. First came the inevitable and startling sunrise gun, and thereupon the instantaneous clatter of drums and fifes, beating and playing the reveille; then the ringing orderly's cry, "Fall in for roll-call!" followed by the roll-call itself; then the morning wash at the spring in the oak-grove, at the rear of the camp; then an hour's drill for recruits before breakfast; then breakfast, welcomed with keen appetites; next, the always interesting ceremony of guard-mounting, followed by an hour's company drill, and two hours' battalion drill, which, with a little rest, fill up the time till dinner. Appetites whetted by exercise and out-door life would have found little to complain of in the government rations, even with beef and coffee sometimes ques-

CAMP CAMERON.

tionable in quality; but the farmers also bring in the produce of their dairies and gardens from all the country around, and delicacies come from home in great wagon-loads daily. Idling, smoking, writing letters, reading, playing at games, cleaning muskets, equipments, or quarters, leaving camp upon passes, now suggest their claims to attention. Target practice or skirmish drill and more recruit drill follow, and afterwards the daily inspection of quarters by the officer of the day, conducted with great formality, while the band plays its best. Then comes dress parade, when "all Washington appears." The camp is full of guests, men, women, and children, high government officials and army officers often, and many ladies; all testify their admiration. Gymnastic sports succeed the parade. The sunset gun tells that evening has come, and, as the tent-fires light up, the moon sails serene into the heavens, and looks down on Camp Cameron, — on the manly youth singing patriotic songs, and talking over the events of an era in which each day is a lifetime, or out yonder on the Harper's Ferry Road, watching in the silent night, with eye and ear and hand alert against the enemy.

The letters published by camp correspondents of the New York papers, at this period, are full of interesting and often amusing details. One in the New York Post says: —

"The 'sensation' of each day at Camp Cameron is the arrival of a black covered wagon, inscribed 'Seventh Regiment, United States Mail and Express,' which brings more mail matter every afternoon than passes through the post-offices of a German principality in a week. . . . . Evening dress parade at Camp Cameron is becoming a fashionable resort, and even the belles of Georgetown, who have been more or less carried away by the secession mania, are extending their afternoon strolls to the college grounds, to witness the imposing lines of glistening gun-barrels moving at the Colonel's word, and to hear Grafulla's fine band perform national airs."

Another letter says: —

"One tent has its kitten, another its dog, another two crows, — anything, in short, to pet. And it is curious to see how these pets, except the crows, are borrowed and jealously watched. In front of some of the tents, imitations of court-yards are made, with sods and small evergreens."

A third says: —

"Government furnishes us, among our rations, small droves of cattle; the guards, with long poles and staves, and pants turned up, and slouched in their appearance, may be seen taking charge of them, driving them daily through Pennsylvania Avenue to water, and then back to pasture, and, as called for, preparing them for cooking, and then for the table. . . . . We have four mountain howitzers here, and two rifled cannon on their way, we hope, and have so understood. We certainly will have a fine battery when it is complete, viz. four howitzers and four rifled cannon."

Not only letters but "supplies" came daily from New York in such abundance, that, on the 10th of May, Quartermaster Winchester sent this telegram to the Adams Express Company in New York: "Do advise our friends to stop sending things to us. We have no means of keeping them; besides, we are surfeited. Hereafter, demand prepayment on anything sent to us, except letters and articles of dress, which please send free." Yet, a fortnight later, a Philadelphia paper announces that, "on the 22d, the regiment received between eight and nine hundred boxes, bales, and packages from New York, containing supplies, donations, gifts, &c., and embracing all the luxuries the market could afford."

On Sunday, May 5th, took place the first inspection and the first dress parade at the camp. At 10 A. M. the articles of war were read to the regiment, formed in hollow square, by the Chaplain; at half past one, P. M., divine service was held under the shade of the oaks fronting head-quarters. On the afternoon of the 7th, the regiment was reviewed by General Mansfield, many other distinguished persons being present; and afterwards the various companies were visited by Major Anderson, who was everywhere greeted with hearty cheers. The next day the troops were reviewed and the camp was inspected by the Secretary of War, who was received with a salute of thirteen guns. On the 11th the dress parade was witnessed by the Secretaries of State and of the Navy, Senator Wilson, Mr. Thurlow Weed, and others; on the 12th, by the President, the Secretaries of State and of the Treasury, and the French and Brazilian Ministers; on the 13th, by the President and Secretary Seward. On the 15th, the President, Secretary Seward, and Mr. Astor, Mr. M. H. Blatchford, Mr. Simeon Draper, and Mr. C. H. Russell of the Union Defence Committee, were among the guests; on the 21st, Senators Foote, Sumner, and Clemens. No fair day passed without its throng of distinguished visitors, and the drills and parade were a constant theme of admiration. Secretary Seward paid the regiment the compliment of inviting each field officer and company commander to his levee of Tuesday, May 21st.

On the 9th of May, Private J. Larrie Keese of the Eighth Company was killed by the accidental discharge of a musket. As this was the first death in the regiment, and Keese was a young man of excellent business, social, and literary abilities, and a general favorite, gloom was cast over the camp. Appropriate resolutions were passed by his comrades, and a sergeant and six men were detailed by the Colonel to accompany the remains, in their metallic coffin, to Brooklyn. In the latter city, imposing and impressive funeral ceremonies were held at Christ Church by Rev. Dr. Canfield, and a throng of five thousand citizens came to pay the last rites of respect to the first of the long list of hero martyrs that the Seventh Regiment was destined to furnish to the country. The cortege, preceded by an escort of the National Guard Reserve Corps, and two platoons of the Ninth Regiment, and many military guests, proceeded to Greenwood Cemetery, where Keese was buried with military honors. The following is the official correspondence on this event: —

To the Telegraph Operator.

To the Chief Operator of the Telegraph Office.

I do not wish the death of one of our men communicated by telegraph, as I have sent forward a courier to announce it, for which I will be responsible. Suppress any message announcing the fact.

Respectfully,

M. Lefferts, *Colonel.*

Colonel Lefferts to Mrs. Keese.

Camp Cameron, Washington, May 9, 1861.

Mrs. Keese, *Brooklyn.*

My dear Madam, — It is with feelings of the deepest sympathy that I am compelled to inform you of the death of your son, J. Lawrence Keese, this morning, by the accidental discharge of a musket. He has fallen none the less in defence of his country's altar and his home. His brother soldiers will mourn his loss, while they profess their profound sorrow at his untimely end.

Believe me truly your friend,

Marshall Lefferts,
*Colonel Seventh Regiment.*

This letter will be delivered by a special courier, Mr. McJimsey.

Second Letter from Colonel Lefferts.

Washington, Camp Cameron, May 10, 1861.

Mrs. Keese.

My dear Madam, — I addressed you a few lines yesterday by special messenger, with the sad news of the death of your son. I will not, at this time, trespass upon your sorrowful moments further than to express my heartfelt sympathy with your loss. I enclose a few locks of his hair and his shirt-studs and sleeve-buttons. The rest of his effects are in charge of his cousin, Mr. McJimsey.

May the blessings of Him who doeth all things well cause this blow to fall lightly.

Yours truly,

Marshall Lefferts,
*Colonel Seventh Regiment.*

One of the daily papers adds: —

"It is said that young Keese, when summoned to go to the war, expressed an opinion that he should never return alive, and at his suggestion the marriage ceremony between himself and Miss Maria Tucker —

to whom he had been engaged for some time — was performed. The newly wedded pair were together for one short half-hour immediately after the ceremony, when he took his leave. That night he passed with the regiment in quarters, and the only time his wife saw him alive after the interview spoken of was in the ranks next day, when the regiment marched down Broadway."

Target-firing was practised daily, in accordance with a general order from the department. Commandants of companies were directed to divide their commands into three squads, designated target squads, each under the command of a commissioned officer and one sergeant, and every morning (when not raining) between the hours of seven o'clock, A. M. and twelve, M., the squads were to be marched to the target-ground, and each man allowed two cartridges for practice.

On the day after the arrival at Camp Cameron, the following was the strength of the regiment: —

*Consolidated Morning Report of the Seventh Regiment N. Y. S. M., May* 3, 1861.

| | Present. | | | | | | Absent. | | | | |
|---|---|---|---|---|---|---|---|---|---|---|---|
| | Effective. | | | Sick. | | | | | | | |
| Company. | Field and Staff. | Comm'd Officers. | Privates. | Field and Staff. | Comm'd Officers. | Privates. | Field and Staff. | Comm'd Officers. | Privates. | Total Privates. | Aggregate. |
| | 14 | | | | | | | | | | 14 |
| 1 | | 2 | 107 | | | 1 | | 1 | 6 | 115 | 117 |
| 2 | | 3 | 141 | | | 2 | | | 3 | 146 | 149 |
| 3 | | 2 | 96 | | | 2 | | 1 | 2 | 101 | 103 |
| 4 | | 3 | 102 | | | 1 | | | 3 | 106 | 109 |
| 5 | | 3 | 83 | | | 3 | | | 3 | 89 | 92 |
| 6 | | 2 | 100 | | | 4 | | 1 | 3 | 108 | 110 |
| 7 | | 2 | 105 | | | | | | 3 | 108 | 110 |
| 8 | | 3 | 113 | | | 1 | | | 6 | 120 | 123 |
| 9 | | 2 | 29 | | | | | | 1 | 30 | 32 |
| 10 | | 2 | 70 | | | 1 | | | 2 | 73 | 75 |
| 10 | 14 | 24 | 946 | | | 15 | | 3 | 32 | 996 | 1,034 |

J. HENRY LIEBENAU, *Adjutant.*

The regiment, as the campaign progressed, was greatly swelled by recruits. It marched, as we have said, with nine hundred and ninety-one men. Its first accession consisted of the detachment which followed in the Baltic, under Colonel Butterfield; its next of the one hundred and seventy-five men who came on the first trip of the Daylight. From these were subtracted some who returned to New York sick, having broken down during the Annapolis march or later.

For several days this strength remained about the same. On the 13th of May the regiment showed an aggregate of 1,156, and this was increased by additions of various sorts. The consolidated report of May 20th showed 1,231 men, with only two in hospital and twenty-seven on furlough. The highest aggregate ever reached at any one time was 1,270; but the total number of men, including band, &c., connected with the regiment during the campaign, was considerably greater. So early as the 29th of April, Colonel Lefferts wrote to New York that he could receive no more recruits, except forty or fifty for the Second Company of artillery. However, many came to the camp unbidden. On the 13th of May a detachment of sixty-eight recruits for the Ninth (howitzer) Company arrived at Washington in the Matanzas, under command of Sergeant Tyng of the Sixth Company. They were all enlisted within two days, and had been drilled three times a day during the week before their departure. They marched from the armory to the pier, on the 9th, amid great enthusiasm, escorted by Company E, 9th Regiment (Lieutenant Meeks), and Company A, 55th Regiment (Captain Tissot) of the New York Militia, and were greeted on board the boat by a large assembly of the friends of the regiment.

In speaking of recruits and supplies, it becomes necessary to refer once more to the Veterans and "National Guard Reserve," who at this time took the liveliest interest in the regiment proper, and supported it with a zeal and enthusiasm which only the most perfect *esprit de corps* could inspire. It has heretofore been noted how, on the evening before the regiment marched to the war, the Vet eran Association met at the armory to organize a "home guard." Two days later (Sunday, April 21), Paymaster Thomas M. Adriance of the Veterans wrote to Colonel Lefferts: "The armory is constantly thronged with applicants to join the Seventh Regiment at Washington. Some are going on at all events, and trust to prove fit for admission. The Veteran Guard and ex-members, and the members of the Seventh who cannot leave the city, are organized into eight companies to take the place of the regiment while absent." On the 25th, Adjutant Asher Taylor wrote: "We are still pressed with applications for admission to the regiment, and give the same answer, i. e. they may go forward on their chances of being acceptable to you or any of the companies of the regiment. It looks as if we would have two hundred more to send forward in four or five days. . . . . The organization of the 'National Guard Reserve' was completed on Tuesday evening, the stay-at-homes and exempts of the several companies forming companies, electing officers, &c. Colonel Stevens was elected Colonel; Vermilye, Lieutenant-Colonel; and Holt, Major." They are all going into drill in earnest."

On the 27th, there were enrolled 429 men in the "National Guard Reserve." On the 28th, Colonel Stevens reported to Colonel Lefferts, that recruits for the regiment were drilled daily by competent men from eight to eleven, A. M., and from three to six, P. M., — six hours. In the evenings the large drill-room at the armory was used by the National Guard Reserve, "Which," adds Colonel Stevens, "numbers about five hundred men, and is constantly increasing. We can send you one hundred recruits per week for some weeks to come, and such men as any company, even of the Seventh Regiment, will be glad to enlist." In fine, on the 30th, Colonel Stevens officially reported to General Sandford that "the ex-members of the National Guard have organized eight companies, averaging fifty-six men to each company, for home service, — the corps to be denominated 'National Guard Reserve.' The company and field officers have been duly elected, and the staff officers appointed."

After this explanatory preface, the following correspondence regarding recruits in 1861 will be read with interest: —

ADJUTANT TAYLOR TO COLONEL LEFFERTS.

NEW YORK, May 2, 1861.

COLONEL LEFFERTS.

SIR, — Before receiving your letter, one hundred recruits had been selected, and arrangements made with General Sandford for their transportation, and Colonel Stevens concluded that it would be impossible to disturb the arrangement without creating a dissatisfaction that it would be better to avoid; they have been under drill by Lieutenant Vermilye, Captain Farrar, Mr. Easton, and Mr. Tyng, and are considerably advanced in "war's dread art." Four gentlemen of the Engineer Corps stated that you needed fifty men at once for the Second Company of Engineers, and we concluded that you could dispose of the one hundred now going forward without difficulty.

The organization of the National Guard Reserve is very satisfactory. There are now something like six hundred enrolled, and the drilling of the companies is carried on regularly.

With respect, yours truly,

ASHER TAYLOR, *Adjutant of N. G.*

COLONEL LEFFERTS TO COLONEL STEVENS.

CAMP CAMERON, WASHINGTON, May 5, 1861.

MY DEAR COLONEL, — I have written twice to you. In one of my letters I said we would not receive any more recruits, except some forty or fifty to complete the Second Company of artillery. One of my members has a telegraph to-day, saying that fifty men are waiting for transportation, to join the corps referred to. I have no letter from you in reference to this matter, but I have telegraphed and written to General Sandford, requesting him to furnish transportation, which I hope he will do; if not, I think Paymaster Kemp will arrange it. . . . .

I am sorry to see, by the papers, that the President has requested our

Governor to stop any more troops coming forward. My own idea is that we want fifty thousand men here. . . . .

Yours truly,

MARSHALL LEFFERTS, *Colonel.*

ADJUTANT TAYLOR TO COLONEL LEFFERTS.

NATIONAL GUARD RESERVE, NEW YORK, May 7, 1861.

COLONEL LEFFERTS,

DEAR SIR, — Since mine of 2d instant, General Sandford has declared peremptorily that no more men shall receive transportation to the regiment, except furlough men, returning. Some few of our recruits, we have reason to believe, have shipped through, and are, or soon will be, with you.

There are about fifty who have applied for permission to enter the artillery companies, some of them have straggled along with Sergeant Law, and the remainder await report from him of their admission as members of the company, when they will be pushed forward by any way that may offer, leaving sixty others awaiting your further order. They are so impatient for service that we cannot hold them, and it is very probable that some of them have already found their way to your colony. The selection of the fifty has been made by Lieutenant Delamater of the Troop. . . . .

Respectfully yours,

ASHER TAYLOR, *Mil. Sec. N. G. R.*

COLONEL L. W. STEVENS TO COLONEL LEFFERTS.

NEW YORK, May 9, 1861.

DEAR COLONEL, — This will be handed to you by Mr. Tyng of the Eighth Company, who goes out in charge of the artillery company for whom he has acted as drill sergeant during their detention here, and a most valuable man he has proved himself.

General Sandford had promised to forward forty men, but flatly refused to send any more. Upon the whole, we found so much red-tapeism, that, finding this steamer ready to leave with stores and an empty cabin, we arranged to send them by her at $12 each, of which the men have paid $5 each, and we shall raise the balance "by hook or by crook."

We have twenty or thirty more first-rate men on hand, ready and anxious to go forward as soon as you say the word; we have not and shall not recruit any more until you direct us to do so.

I am writing in haste, but have time to say, success and prosperity to you and the corps.

Yours very truly,

L. W. STEVENS, *Colonel elect N. G. R.*

LIEUTENANT KEMP TO COLONEL LEFFERTS.

NEW YORK, May 10, 1861

DEAR COLONEL,— Your letter ordering forward sixty artillerists I received, and yesterday sent you a telegram saying they would sail per steamer Matanzas at 5 P. M. On the minute they were on board. Colonel Stevens has been very efficient in this matter, so has Friend Schultz. We divided up the work and it went ahead. It has again been my misfortune to find my movements under your orders opposed by General Sandford. He would only give a pass for forty men, and those he made arrangements for on board Empire City, as per enclosed order, which please retain. I showed him your letter: he replied he could send but forty. The sixty men were all ready waiting at armory. . . . . I hunted around the docks, found the steamer Matanzas had been chartered by government (except cabin). She had provisions the day before for one hundred passengers from Matanzas, but the government took her in a hurry. So her provisions, poultry in ice, &c., &c., were all on board. The owners agreed to take my party, cabin fare, good state-rooms, &c., for $ 12 a man. I went back to the armory, told my story, and suggested to the men if they wanted to go speedily, comfortably, and be well cared for, if they would pay $ 5 per man I would see to paying the balance. The vote was taken, and every man voted yes. We hope to be able to pay the balance without calling on regimental funds. I cannot speak in too high terms of Mr. Tyng, who has worked day and night to get these men into shape. At the moment of departure I found *sixty-eight* on board. I understand the surplus are approved by companies, and are going to run the risk of being wanted and elected. . . . .

Yours truly,

A. KEMP.

On the 11th of May, Surgeon Cheesman suggested in writing to Colonel Lefferts that "a guard be kept over all the wells from which the camp is supplied with water." This recommendation was carried into effect, and, in addition, all hucksters and petty traders were forbidden to enter the camp without a pass given by the Colonel.

While at Camp Cameron, the regiment received from Mr. Rutherford Stuyvesant, a member of the corps, two twelve-pounder howitzers, with equipment and ammunition complete. Accompanying the gift was the following letter: —

175 SECOND AVENUE, NEW YORK, May 3, 1861.

MARSHALL LEFFERTS, *Colonel Seventh Regiment, N. Y. S. M.*

SIR, — Being deprived, by ill health, of the great pleasure of sharing in the dangers and fatigues so well endured, and in the credit, so well merited, of the Seventh, I desire to testify my admiration for them as soldiers, and my affection for them as comrades, as well as my devotion to the sacred cause for which they are armed. With this intent, I have procured and forwarded to your address a pair of mounted howitzers, with their equipment and ammunition, which I desire to present to the regiment, with my best wishes.

I am, very respectfully, yours, &c.,

RUTHERFORD STUYVESANT.

These howitzers had some difficulty in reaching their destination, but were finally received and put in battery with the pieces originally brought forward. Under date of New York, May 9, 1861, General Sandford wrote to Colonel Lefferts on this subject as follows: —

"I sent the two howitzers presented to your regiment under the care of Brigade-Major Smith (1st Brigade) to Annapolis.

"I have just seen a letter from Major Smith to General Spicer, asking him to inform me that Colonel Abel Smith, commanding the Thirteenth Regiment, had taken possession of these howitzers and declined to forward them, saying he needed them at Annapolis.

"I have written to Colonel Smith to-day to say that he must send them to you at once. If there is any delay in so doing, please inform me.

"I have a general order not to forward recruits, but I have taken the responsibility of sending forty for these howitzers to-day by the Empire City."

About the same time (May) Colonel Lefferts telegraphed to New York to obtain four more pieces of artillery for the use of the regiment. Through the efforts of Mr. J. J. Astor, Jr., who took the liveliest interest in the regiment, an appropriation for two rifled twelve-pounders was made by the Union Defence Committee; and the pieces were forwarded, together with 400 rounds of shot, 400 of shell, 800 cartridges, 1,200 caps.

Many other donations for the campaign came to the regiment at Camp Cameron. From the "New York Medical Association for the Supply of Lint, Bandages, &c. to the Army," located in the Spingler Institute building, came a box of lint and bandages, "prepared," said the note of Dr. G. M. Smith, who forwarded it, "by a few young ladies, for the Hospital Department of your regiment." At the same time (May 11) the first contribution from one of the "Ladies' Havelock Associations" of New York reached the regiment, — a thousand and more white linen cap-covers of the British pattern, so famous in India and the Crimea, worn also by the French at Solferino. Colonel Lefferts promptly wrote to the "Ladies of the Havelock Association, Mrs. George T. Stevens, Mrs. John C. Peters, and others," in acknowledgment: "On behalf of the Seventh Regiment, I thank you for the beautiful and serviceable present of one thousand 'Havelocks.' They add so materially to the comfort of the men to whom you have sent them, that, could you see how eagerly they have been sought and worn, you would feel, I doubt not, well repaid for the labor they have cost."

In the Daylight's rich cargo was a supply of loose, dark gray, knit worsted jackets, the gift of Mr. W. H. Aspinwall to the regiment. These excellent presents were distributed amongst the men after reaching Camp Cameron, and proved exceedingly comfortable. The jackets were instantly christened "Aspinwalls" by the regiment. "They came to hand," wrote Colonel Lefferts, "at the very time when I was considering the propriety of ordering a quantity of flannel blouses. You have thus anticipated our wants. They all arrived safely, and will be distributed to-morrow, when we get into camp." The "Aspinwall" and the "Havelock" made a remarkable change in the appearance and comfort of the troops, and the experiences of campaign taught other practical devices and variations in uniform. In their new costume, stalwart, hearty, and sun-browned, the regiment would hardly have been recognized by those accustomed only to the casual parades of the city, to untanned faces, and stiff gray uniform. "No more tight-bodied dress-coats," writes one member, luxuriating in the cosey freedom of his fatigue suit; "no more pretty white cross-belts to hamper us down; no more heavy, stiff caps; no more fashionable pantaloons. Give us a little time after we get home, — i. e. if we do get there, — and we will show you a serviceable, neat, and inexpensive uniform."

Besides material gifts and supplies, the regiment received abundance of kindly messages, — grateful letters from societies and individuals, from other regiments, from towns, from patriotic citizens and admiring friends. Before the writer many such documents are on file, which it would hardly be tasteful (even were there space) to insert. A dozen odes and sonnets, of various lengths, dedicated to the regiment, commemorating one or another feature of its achievements or adventures, show that the bards of the country were as busy as the press in crowning it with laurels. Music also was composed in honor of its march. A terrible struggle soon gave occasion to patriots and poets and historians to bring their best words to commemorate the deeds of thousands upon thousands of patriot heroes, and, among them, many a gallant soldier of the Seventh, —

"To deck their hearse
Who in warm life-blood wrote their nobler verse."

But, meanwhile, attention was largely concentrated on the regiments that pioneered the path to Washington, and first sprang to save the capital from dishonor.

Before the regiment had been many days at Camp Cameron, its members began to devote themselves to the country "for the war"; and as soon as the President called for three years' volunteers, one gallant soldier after another gave himself wholly to the good cause. The first officer to leave the regiment was the brave and accomplished Farnham, First Lieutenant of Company B., who, having been elected to the lieutenant-colonelcy of Ellsworth's famous regiment, resigned his lieutenancy on the 7th of May. Two days later, Captain Schuyler Hamilton was appointed military secretary, with the rank of lieutenant-colonel, upon the staff of the Lieutenant-General. "I shall always," wrote Colonel Hamilton to Colonel Lefferts, in asking to be discharged by promotion, "esteem it an honor to have marched with the Seventh, and trust that I may still consider myself an honorary member of the corps whose uniform I shall continue to wear." The official order from General Scott's head-quarters ran as follows: —

"Captain Schuyler Hamilton, Aide-de-Camp to the General-in-Chief during the Mexican War, and now a member of the Seventh Regiment of New York Volunteers, is hereby again appointed to the staff of the General-in-Chief, as a military secretary with the rank of lieutenant-colonel, under Section 16 of the act approved March 3, 1857. He will be obeyed and respected accordingly."

These depletions gradually took away from the regiment, even at the outbreak of the war, many of its best-drilled and most capable men; and in a double sense General McDowell's word was fast proving true, — "it is a regiment of officers." The talk of commissions was one of the leading subjects of conversation, and a letter dated May 21st says: "Five men from a single company, only one above the position of private, and he a sergeant, have received commissions in one regiment alone, — three of the rank of captain. One brigadier commandant wants twelve captains from the Seventh."

Mention has already been made of the valuable services rendered to the regiment by Colonel (later Major-General) Samuel R. Curtis, a volunteer aid on Colonel Lefferts's staff. On the 4th of May, that officer wrote to Colonel Lefferts: "I shall take great pleasure in reporting myself to you to-morrow morning. I have been on the 'sick-list' for forty-six hours, but now I am myself again." Colonel Lefferts responded by informing him of his election as an honorary member of the Eighth Company (Brevet-Colonel Shumway commanding), the senior company of the regiment. "It is done," he wrote, "from the great respect in which you are held, and the love they bear you, while I personally desire to express my thanks for your valuable aid and counsel since you joined us at Philadelphia. As a member of our corps, our doors will always be open to you, and a hand of welcome extended." Colonel Curtis wrote in reply: "Please make my acceptance known to the Eighth Company, with my grateful acknowledgments for the distinguished honor; and be assured also of my hearty thanks to you personally, and to the officers and men of your regiment universally, for the courtesy and kindness shown me during the march and since we arrived in this city. It will be a great pleasure to me hereafter to cherish the recollection of our acquaintance, and to remain associated as an honorary member of your distinguished corps."

But the regiment, after a few weeks at Camp Cameron, began to be eager for more active work. A letter in the New York Tribune, dated from the camp, May 21st, very well expresses this anxiety in saying: —

"It is a curious fact, but none the less true on that account, that we have to look for news almost exclusively to the New York papers, and that, too, not only in relation to items of general interest, but actually in reference to our own movements.

"The rumors about the camp would, I judge, average about fifty *per diem.* One man, who has been all night on guard, will rush into his tent at about 5 A. M., and surprise his half-awakened tent-mates by an oracular announcement: 'Well, boys, we are going to march to Harper's Ferry.' 'When?' asks one. 'Who says so?' inquires a less sanguine man. 'Are you joking?' asks a third; and a hasty but emphatic 'Don't know,' answers all three at once. And then follow speculations, surmises, doubts, expressions of anxious, eager delight at the prospect of getting *something to do*, instead of lying idle here, growing fat.

It is useless to attempt to conceal the fact that the regiment is absolutely aching for some work. I never saw in my life a happier, more contented set of men than those who left Annapolis as advance detachment, for then they really had good reason to believe, I may almost say to *know*, that there was actual work, serious work, before them. But now for the want of excitement, — I do not say of work in the way of constant drills, — the men are going into all sorts of quiet deviltry, and some of it not so very quiet either. . . . .

"There is the inevitable question of being sent home. 'Orders will be out to-morrow'; 'No, they won't'; 'I heard that we were to go home next week.' 'Two months longer,' sings out another man. 'What, and do nothing?' Then to while away spare minutes, I cannot say hours, come bayonet fencing, gymnastic exercises, games of ball, mock parades, funerals of salt junk, etc."

The time for the "forward movement" was nearer at hand than this writer anticipated. When and how it was made we shall now proceed to narrate. But first, however, we must record an interesting event which immediately preceded it.

Many ladies of New York, the kindred of its members, had joined in making the regiment a beautiful silk flag, — a national flag, perfectly simple, the staff of lance-wood, with a silver spear-head. The colors were sent to the regiment through Mr. Frederick Prime of Edgewood, Westchester County, New York, at whose suggestion Adjutant-General Thomas was requested to make the formal presentation. On the day originally appointed for the ceremony the colors did not arrive; but on the 23d of May the presentation took place at twilight of a beautiful day, after dress parade, in presence of the President and his family, and five thousand enthusiastic spectators.

A salute of thirteen guns announced the arrival of the President, who, accompanied by General Thomas and Colonel Lefferts, inspected the regimental line, and then returned to his barouche. The regiment then formed square, and General Thomas, advancing, banner in hand, said: —

"SOLDIERS OF THE GALLANT SEVENTH, — I stand before you this day as the representative of a large number of the ladies of New York, to present to you this beautiful banner, prepared by them. I hold in my hand a book, with lines of dedication, containing the autographs of one hundred and seventeen ladies. Why this honor has fallen on me, when others in higher station and more competent to perform the pleasing duty could readily have been chosen, I know not, except that, having for the last few years been stationed in their city, I thus became known to them, and they considered me almost a New-Yorker. This crowning act of theirs, however, makes me almost altogether a New-Yorker. It seems quite superfluous for me to speak of the Seventh, for its fame as an excelsior regiment is known far and wide; yet still there are some incidents which I cannot overlook. That revered chieftain, the greatest captain of the age, near whose person it has been my happiness to serve, has repeatedly said, 'The Seventh is a national regiment.' Its organization is complete, its drill perfect, its *personnel* the flower of our New York youth. But to show its title to being considered a national regiment. When the State of Virginia desired to receive the remains of one of her sons, a departed President, this regiment came forward and escorted the honored remains to the capital of that State. And when honor was to be done in the dedication of a statue of the Father of his Country here in the city bearing his name, and which he founded, the Seventh was the regiment sent for that duty. And when the government of our beloved country was in danger of overthrow, and its capital likely to be seized by traitors, the Seventh, on the first note of alarm, sprung to arms, and hastened to the place of danger to help to defend everything most sacred to a true loyal American. The effect of this movement no one can estimate so well as those of us present in our capital. Our General-in-Chief, with the approval of the administration, had hastily assembled such a body of Regulars as were within reach, and enrolled several companies of local militia, inadequate in numbers, but ready to do their best. At this time we were surrounded by enemies, with traitors in our midst, and, worst of all, those of my own profession, on whom the government had a right to look for support. Men taken in their youth, educated, fostered, sustained, in this time of our need began to fall on every hand, until we knew not whom to trust. Our war-chief rose in sublimity, and made preparations for defence. Then came that great upheaving of the North and West which satisfied us that the government would be sustained, and every loyal heart throbbed with gratitude to the God of battles who had provided us deliverance, — that Supreme Being who 'ruleth in the heavens and on the earth, and doeth all things well.' Then it was that you came forward, with bayonets far more in number than you ever paraded on any gala-day. And when, after great difficulties and delays, you reached the capital, what a thrill pervaded our loyal population. In every direction you could hear, 'The Seventh have come.' The anxious week, and especially the dark Sunday, had passed, and we felt secure. This beautiful emblem which I now present is the work of many loved ones of your home. They have devoted the work of their hands to you, and many prayers for God's protecting favor have been breathed over its folds, and many that God give you and them his Holy Spirit for the dear Redeemer's sake. I am especially charged to tell you, that if your country calls you to action, it is their earnest wish that their flag should be carried in your ranks, for, with these colors in your midst, they will feel almost as if they, too, were defending the sacred cause of liberty and right. This great war-cloud coming down from the North and West will soon burst, and burst it must, over the South, and you may soon be called to unfurl this very banner. And if so, recollect that, though you number twelve hundred and fifty, there is a particular stitch dedicated by fair hands to each one of you; and I charge you most solemnly never to let that stitch be dishonored by a traitorous foe, nor suffer it to be trailed in the dust. I will now read the lines of dedication, and place the banner in your hands."

These were the lines of dedication: —

"The flag of our country! What deeper assurance
Of sympathy, honor, and trust could we send?
The crown of our fathers' unflinching endurance,
'T is the emblem of all you have sworn to defend, —
Of freedom and Union, with honor intwined, —
The cause of the nation, of God and mankind."

The bearer of the flag then handed it to Colonel Lefferts, who unfolded it, and held it while the band played the "Star-Spangled Banner." The Colonel then gave it to the ensign of the regiment, and replied as follows: —

"General, — The history of all heroic ages bears testimony to the devotion with which the regimental colors are always regarded. The true soldier turns to them in more than Eastern devotion. They are his rallying-point of battle; and where the clashing of steel tells of the deadliest struggle, its honored folds float proudly in the breeze. To it the straining eye of the soldier ever turns when it is obscured for a moment by the smoke of the conflict, and he gathers new courage from the light of his advancing standard, and where that leads he will follow.

And if this emblem of his country's glory wavers or is stricken down, he rushes to the rescue, as though with its fall would be cloven down his country's honor and renown. To-day, in this hour of peril and great events, where the destinies of centuries are crowded into the narrow space of days and hours, the fair daughters of our honored State present through you, General, an ensign destined, we hope, to be not only the rallying-point of my command, but the symbol of our country's permanence and glory. In this our hour of danger an effulgence rays out from its stripes like the halo of glory that encircles the sainted head, while the stars from their field of azure blue reflect the light of harmony and peace to those who recognize its supremacy and power. But to the contemner and the traitor they blaze with wrath, and, as of old, 'the stars will fight against Sisera.' Most gratefully then do we tender our sincere thanks to the fair donors of New York; and, while we accept the beautiful and appropriate gift, we pledge ourselves that with our consent it shall never falter or fall before any foe, foreign or domestic, that shall assail the

'Land of the free and the home of the brave.'

"For your kind presentation, and the manner in which you have alluded to my command, you have our joint and sincere thanks."

Nine hearty cheers were given by the regiment, as the color-bearer took the colors, and passed to his post in the ranks.

The following letters relate to the flag: —

I.

Colonel Lefferts.

My dear Sir, — Some threescore young ladies, relatives of the young men of your command, have with their own hands prepared a silk flag, which they very much desire should be presented to the regiment during its absence from our city on its present sacred mission. I am requested to ask your permission that it may be sent to you (it is a national flag, and perfectly simple, the staff made of lance-wood, with a silver spear-head), in the hope that it may be used on all proper occasions, and not kept merely for parade. The contributions made by the young ladies exceed the cost of the silk and mounting of the flag, and they request you to receive and dispose of this money for such useful ends as to your individual judgment may deem advisable.

I remain, with respect, yours, &c.,

Frederick Prime.

Pelham Post-Office, Westchester Co., N. Y.,
Edgewood, May 5, 1861.

II.

EDGEWOOD, May 10, 1861.

COLONEL LEFFERTS.

MY DEAR SIR, . . . . Your suggestion as to a record of the names of the donors will be met by a small volume containing the autographs of the contributors, and opening with a few lines of presentation. Many of the names subscribed are peculiarly associated with the Revolutionary history of our city. The first signatures are those of the grand-daughters of John Jay, Alexander Hamilton, and General Clarkson, aid to General Washington, and of the daughter of Comfort Sands, who was the last surviving member of the Committee of Safety of the city. The intention was to send the flag to you, but if you prefer that some other person should act for the donors, I would suggest Adjutant-General Thomas of the United States Army, unless you deem it inexpedient to make the request. I enclose a note from my daughter to General Thomas, which you will please read and use at your discretion. . . . .

Yours, &c.,

FREDERICK PRIME.

## CHAPTER XI.

### THE SEVENTH IN VIRGINIA.

WITH the record of this last charming and impressive scene, let us gather together and break the thread of our story of Camp Cameron life, passing by numberless details of its commingled duties and pastimes.

One feeling alone marred the delight of camp experience, — impatience for more strenuous action. It was an impatience shared, however, by every patriot in the land, — a fatal impatience, resulting in the repulse at Manassas. The daily departure of comrades as officers of new regiments created a feverish anxiety in others to follow their example. Everywhere the wish was for one more tour of service in the field as a regiment, one expedition into the enemy's country, before the thirty days should expire, and then a quick return to New York, a sight of friends and families so suddenly left, of business so suddenly dropped, and then and there deliberate preparation for the future. As for the immediate object of the march, the safety of Washington, that had been accomplished, since twenty regiments had already followed the Seventh over the road from Annapolis to Washington. "You went to Washington," wrote Paymaster Kemp from New York to one of the officers, as early as May 13, "with the positive understanding (and this position is proven by General Sandford's order) that you were to hurry on to the capital, to be relieved as soon as a sufficient body of troops should be there to take your place. You have, or will have in a day or two, *more* than enough. Thousands are here quarrelling because they are not sent forward; our city requires you back. In these exciting times, a spark may set the city in a blaze. We here are without arms, without a nucleus to rally around in case of riot. We all suppose our wars are to be sustained either by volunteers or by draft. Should our country need you again hereafter, I do not question that our boys would be ready, as they always are, to answer any demand upon their services."

Nevertheless, the fact that their term of service was soon to expire, and that the object of their march had been accomplished, did not diminish the feverish impatience, even of the hundreds who were preparing to return to the war, for one more "forward movement" as a regiment before the muster out.

This desire was, happily, to be gratified. To a few of the throng that witnessed the flag presentation just described the ceremony had a deep significance. On that day, Colonel Lefferts had received the following order: —

HEAD-QUARTERS, DEPARTMENT WASHINGTON, May 23, 1861.

COLONEL LEFFERTS, *New York Seventh Infantry.*

SIR, — Please have your regiment at the head of Long Bridge by two o'clock to-night, and let them march without music or noise, and report to Colonel Heintzelman, United States Army.

MANSFIELD, *B. G. & Com'd'g.*

I shall be glad to see you at my office immediately.

Such was the initial order, so far as concerns the Seventh Regiment, of General Scott's famous occupation of Arlington Heights, — a movement without which Washington would have fallen a prey to any hostile force able to seize and hold these important positions. It is famous in history also as the first reconnoissance in force of the war, the first forward movement, the first "invasion" of the soil of Virginia. From that night there was war *à l'outrance.*

When the companies had been marched to their quarters after the flag presentation, the captains announced the orders they had received for the march. The tumultuous and long-continued cheers, the joy that beamed in every face, the fire that flashed in every eye, told how eagerly the news had been watched for, and how sweet was the prospect of duty and danger. "The instant," says the Tribune correspondence, "the ranks were broken in the company streets, cheers upon cheers arose from right to left at the joyful intelligence." The Times correspondent from the camp says: "The prayers and hopes, the substance of all our songs, have now a prospect of a speedy fruition. At 7 P. M., last night, when the captains of the different companies told their men the orders they had just received from Colonel Lefferts, the enthusiasm and joy defied description. It was not hushed at 'tattoo' or at 'taps,' but continued until each man stepped forward on our beautiful lawn, at twenty minutes after one this morning. . . . . Last night will never be forgotten by our National Guard; nor will Washington, or the entire country, forget an event which marks an epoch in the great struggle which was really commenced when the ten thousand left Washington, each eager for the fray, and all and every man of them true as steel to his God, his country, and his starry flag." No one knew what was in store, whether a march or a battle, a movement with the support of few troops or many. It was enough to know that the march was towards the enemy, that every report and rumor declared the first great blow of the war was to be struck, and that the Seventh was to engage in the conflict.

Two companies, however, the Ninth and Tenth, did not share the general exhilaration, but walked about with rueful faces. They were to remain in charge of the camp, while the eight infantry companies marched, and "their disappointment and disgust," says one letter, "were immense. A few members were accepted as volunteers in other companies, and were in high feather till their captains sent a sergeant through the camp to bring in all stragglers." "It is said we are to follow," writes one of the Ninth Company, "in charge of the baggage. I hope so." "What a happy thousand were the line companies!" writes Winthrop. "How their suppressed ardor stirred! No want of fight in those lads! Every man was merry, except two hundred, who were grim. These were the two artillery companies." The following were Colonel Lefferts's instructions to Captain Farrar, Company K, dated 11 P. M., May 23d: —

"SIR, — You will immediately parade your company, and relieve from further duty the present camp-guard. As soon as the regiment leaves the ground, all persons except those in uniform must be excluded from the camp-ground. Any friends wishing to see members of the regiment can do so at the Colonel's head-quarters. There is a large amount of property in camp, and you must exercise the utmost vigilance and care. You will have one prisoner in the camp-ground. He is to be held until further notice."

The orders were to march without knapsacks, in light marching order, with one day's rations in haversacks, and forty rounds per man in the cartridge-boxes. The evening was spent, therefore, in distributing rations and ammunition, in filling canteens and haversacks, in looking to muskets and equipments, in stowing away property in the tents, in packing knapsacks to be sent on, perhaps, afterwards, and in writing final letters home. One of these letters, from a member of the Sixth Company, says: "The rumors are various and conflicting. The most reliable seems to be, that several thousand men are to be landed at Alexandria to-night. We may march by ten or twelve o'clock. This may very probably precipitate a hostile movement and open the fighting. The men are sending off hurried letters and completing necessary arrangements. All are very busy. We only know and feel that we are doing our duty, and that the country is with us."

At one o'clock, A. M., the companies formed line, and the column noiselessly filed down the Avenue. Was it for Harper's Ferry or Alexandria? The drummers turned up the road to the former point, but Colonel Lefferts hurried forward and moved them in the opposite direction. "Alexandria!" said some of the men; "Hurrah for Richmond!" said others. "None cared where," says one letter, "so long as we had at last a chance for active duty." Each carried his full canteen and haversack, and his stout army blanket rolled and thrown over the left shoulder, with the ends tied at the right thigh.

It was a magnificent summer's night, the full moon gleaming as lustrous as when, a month before, she shone on the same gallant column, forcing its way through the woody defiles beyond Annapolis, in its pioneer march to Washington. "Full moon at its fullest, — a night more perfect than all perfection, mild, dewy, refulgent," says Winthrop. The glimmer of the moonlight on the polished gun-barrels and the bright faces in the column threw into broader contrast the dim objects around, half veiled by the shade of the trees. The tramp of a thousand men moving as one echoed through Fourteenth Street, and some citizens threw up their windows. "A hag in a nightcap reviewed us from an upper window of Willard's Hotel as we tramped by," says Winthrop. "Opposite Willard's," says a letter, "we witnessed curious and unique apparitions of femininity and masculinity. . . . . All along the street the same spectacle presented itself, and, as we neared the Long Bridge, crowds began to assemble." When near the Washington Monument, the regiment was ordered to halt, to allow the New Jersey brigade, which was behind time, to pass to its place in the column. An hour slipped away, — an hour which seemed a moment to such as had dropped asleep on the cobble-stones, and whom the Colonel's call, "Attention, battalion!" started from pacific dreams. "Five of us, tent-fellows when in camp, clustered in a knot on the pavement and slept," says a soldier's letter.

Half a mile more, and the Potomac appeared, a broad and beautiful river of molten silver in the reflected moonlight; and hither and thither in the tranquil, delicious night, bayonets flashed on both shores. The secrecy with which the movement had been planned demanded silence in its execution. But when the head of column turned upon Long Bridge, a low murmur of delight ran throughout the ranks. Then the regiment passed the guard stationed to prevent civilians crossing, stretched across the mile of rickety and rotten planks and trembling girders, defended at intervals by earthworks, and at 4, A. M., at the first faint gleam of dawn, stood on Virginia soil.*

Half a mile farther on the Alexandria Road came orders to halt and stack arms, — the Seventh's first bivouac in Virginia. A picturesque bivouac it was. The sleepy dropped on the railway track and slept soundly. The active organized into impromptu forage parties, laid hold on neighboring fence-rails (all the fences in Virginia have since been

* It may be worth while here to state the precise nature of Colonel Lefferts's instructions from General Mansfield. In his personal interview with that officer, he had received private instructions to cross the bridge, and if he should not already have seen Colonel Heintzelman, to whom he was to report, then to halt not far beyond the bridge, and, holding his command well in hand, to cover the bridge.

ACROSS LONG BRIDGE TO VIRGINIA.

burned), and soon had fires flaming in the air, and raw pork and ham sizzling and frying in better or worse cookery. The camp-fires glowing in the gray of morning; the stacks of arms with canteens, haversacks, and red blankets pendent; the groups in gay soldiers' costume gathered about the embers; the prone and slumberous figures, with track ties for couches, their blankets for bedding, the iron rail, covered by the coat-cape, for a pillow; recumbent men scattered on the road and in the grass; the dim and distant clusters and fires of other regiments around and ahead, the sun climbing to outshine the paling moon, — it was all a memorable picture.

Broad day came. The troops in advance were seen to be busily intrenching. Mounted orderlies and couriers dashed forth and back, clattered across Long Bridge;, and one aide-de-camp, as he galloped breathlessly by, towards Washington, hoarsely called, "Alexandria taken this morning by the Fire Zouaves, — Ellsworth killed." The words thrilled like those tidings on the former march of the baptismal blood poured by Massachusetts on the pavements of guilty Baltimore.

And now the mystery of the movement began to clear, reports of its success being fuller and fuller. The story as it has passed into history may be briefly told. Resolving to take permanent possession, without further delay, both of Alexandria and Arlington Heights, — which latter commanded Washington, and whence a single hostile battery could have fired the city with its shells, — Lieutenant-General Scott directed General Mansfield to select a suitable force for this twofold purpose and to accomplish it. With great secrecy the plan was formed and executed. Thirteen thousand troops, chiefly volunteers, divided into two columns, simultaneously, at two o'clock on the morning of the 24th of May, assembled from a dozen different camps and crossed the Potomac. Ten days previous a steamer had dropped anchor off Alexandria, seven miles below Washington, and held the city under its guns. The left column descended the Potomac in steamers from the Navy-yard, landed at Alexandria in the gray dawn, seized the telegraph and the railroad, and occupied the town. The gallant young Ellsworth was in immediate command with his Fire Zouaves in advance, and there fell at the outset of the conflict, the Warren of his generation. Lieutenant-Colonel Farnham, but lately of the National Guard, succeeded to his command.

Meanwhile the right column crossed Long Bridge and Chain Bridge, and while a detachment took Alexandria in reverse, capturing several small bodies of infantry and cavalry which were on picket duty at Alexandria, Arlington Heights, &c., and afterwards extending reconnoissances in various directions, especially towards Fairfax Court-House, the main body, in which the Seventh Regiment found itself, busily went to work intrenching. Such was the move, in fine, which gave to the Union Army the right bank of the Potomac, and its defences, prolonged to thirty or forty miles, and hence virtually the possession of Washington, which its guns commanded.

Now the sun blazes hotter and hotter as he rises in the heavens. The Jerseymen are bravely at work intrenching on the ridge ahead. Soon the road becomes uncomfortable under the sun, and, scaling the fence, the regiment changes its bivouac to the race-course, and constructs fantastic tents and booths, some of blankets thrown over musket-stacks, or stretched in long lines with bayonets for tent-poles, some of branches of trees, some of rails, — anything to keep out the broiling sun. From the race-course is visible the white mansion of General Lee on Arlington Heights. Through clouds of stifling dust, wagons loaded with picks and spades come forward, and everywhere engineers are drawing lines for intrenchments.

The Seventh occupied a point, as we have seen, between Long Bridge and Columbia Spring, on the line of the Washington and Alexandria Railroad, which, with the turnpike, was along the Potomac, and not far from it. The works thrown up by the Jersey brigade were located at the point where the road, after running westerly from the bridge, bends southerly, and aims directly for Alexandria. It was an important position. The task assigned to the Seventh was that of covering Long Bridge, and also of holding itself in readiness, in reserve, for any emergency on any part of the field, — an important duty, as might have been expected from the opinions already expressed regarding it by the three officers mainly concerned in the expedition, — Generals Scott, Mansfield, and McDowell.

At 6, P. M., of the 24th, the regiment was ordered forward to a cedar-grove near Columbia Spring, hard by the redoubt constructing on the Heights, that it might be ready at hand in case of a night alarm. This open wood furnished a fine place also for a bivouac. Within is an excellent spring. "Every one," says a letter written that evening, "is as happy and jolly as possible." The grounds belonged to the Arlington estate, and were sodded and neatly kept. The lawns were deliciously shaded by beautiful trees of all the local varieties; and these yielded not only boughs for bivouac tents, but wood for fuel.

The next morning (Saturday, May 25th), Colonel Lefferts, at daylight, sent Captain Viele to the trenches, with a request to the engineer officer in command there that he would allow the Seventh to go to work and relieve the New Jersey regiment, which was constructing the southeastern angle of the redoubt. The latter officer did not relieve the New Jersey regiment, but he accepted the proposal of Colonel Lefferts in marking out more definitely the southwestern angle redoubt, and allowing the men of the Seventh to construct it. At once a strong working party was detailed from the regiment and went to work. A part, armed with axes, felled a large peach-orchard of several acres, with a few cedars, about three hundred trees in all, which covered the glacis of the work and obstructed it. The rest, with pick and shovel, dug in the trenches. This detail was relieved by others after two hours, and so, with good spirits and cheerfulness, the work went briskly on all day long.* The rain fell in torrents during the morning; but the sun came out hot afterwards, and dried the men who had been drenched. The noon meal and night meal of crackers and pork were well earned by the hungry and wet diggers; some country people helped to eke out the rations also, by bringing in for sale a little butter, milk, and bread. At night, sleep was sweet to the tired men, who lay flat on the ground, in the woods, with cartridge-boxes for pillows, and feet to the camp-fires.

During the evening, Colonel Farnham, of the Fire Zouaves, Ellsworth's successor, visited the camp of the Seventh, and was received with great enthusiasm by the comrades with whom he had made the march from Annapolis to Washington. It was his farewell visit. He fell at Bull Run.

It should have been mentioned, that, the day before the order for the expedition was issued (namely, the 22d),

* One letter of Saturday speaks of the jokes and *badinage* of the work: "'Arrah! ye worked betther nor that whin ye was on the Erie Canal.' 'Don't be ashamed o' your trade, man.' 'Some of these gentlemen who have been wanting furloughs to go home and attend to their business will have no occasion to go now.' And so on until we left the trenches, each relief bringing with their fresh strength new and brilliant supplies of jokes and fun. Still, they did work, and heartily too. Many an arm is sore, many a back is lame to-day. I have not bled for my country exactly, but I can say, with solemn, heartfelt pride, that I have raised blisters for her."

Another letter, dated Saturday, 4 P. M., says: "The great majority of our men are now digging in the trenches. You should see them at this moment, in the broiling sun, with their red and blue and check flannel shirts, working away like beavers, with pickaxe and spade. The intrenchments are all staked out, with wooden framework in place. The trenches are fairly under way. The New Jersey regiment are at work on the extreme end, and our boys about the centre."

General Sandford, having made his appearance in Washington and reported at head-quarters for duty, was ordered to assume command of all the New York regiments within the District of Columbia. On the morning after the occupation of Virginia, — that is, on the 24th, — he established his divisional head-quarters at the Arlington House, and issued next day the following Proclamation: —

PROCLAMATION FROM GENERAL SANDFORD.

HEAD-QUARTERS, DEPARTMENT OF FAIRFAX, VA.,
ARLINGTON HOUSE, May 25, 1861.

Fairfax County being occupied by the troops under my command, I deem it proper to repeat publicly the assurances I have personally given to many of the good citizens about me, that all of its inhabitants may return to or remain in their homes and usual pacific occupations, in peace and confidence, and with assured protection to their persons and property, as the United States forces in Virginia will be employed for no other purpose than that of suppressing unlawful combinations against the constituted authorities of the Union, and of causing the laws thereof to be duly respected and executed.

By order of

MAJOR-GENERAL CHAS. W. SANDFORD.

GEORGE W. MORELL, *Division Inspector*.

On the same (Saturday) morning he sent the following order to Colonel Lefferts, who received it at ten o'clock, A. M: —

"Colonel Lefferts will detail a working party from his regiment for duty in the trenches this morning. His regiment will be relieved this afternoon by one of the Massachusetts regiments detailed by General Mansfield, upon the arrival of which the Seventh will return to the camp in Washington City, and wait further orders."

General Sandford's order, however, having been anticipated, Colonel Lefferts addressed to that officer the following reply: —

IN CAMP, VIRGINIA, May 25, 1861, Ten o'clock, A. M.

SIR, — Special order of this date just received. I sent Captain Viele at daylight this morning to the trenches, asking of the engineer in command, as a special favor, that he would allow my men to go to work and relieve the New Jersey regiment. He consented for us to throw up a new line marked out, and they are now at work, thus anticipating so much of your order. . . . .

Respectfully,

MARSHALL LEFFERTS, *Colonel Commanding.*

Sunday, the 26th, was a day of hard work. Nearly the whole regiment was detailed for digging, felling trees, burning brush, &c. The working parties were made about two hundred strong, and each relief was on from two to three hours. Divine service was held in the morning by the Chaplain, who, at the conclusion, laid down the Scriptures and took up the shovel, and, heading his congregation of young soldiers, went to work in the trenches, practising as vigorously as he had preached, and illustrating Luther's maxim, *Ora et labora.*

Till evening the Seventh worked untiringly, manning a space of four hundred yards in the trenches. On the other faces of the redoubt the New Jersey Second, Third, and Fourth were engaged. The burning sun would have been almost intolerable but for the havelocks, never so grateful a present as on that oppressive day; and bathing in the Potomac was doubly refreshing. A Washington telegram says: —

"The heat was oppressive all day, but the plucky men of the Seventh vied, nevertheless, with the hardy yeomen of New Jersey in handling picks, shovels, and wheelbarrows. Only two defensive works are erecting, — one near the end of the Long Bridge, constructed by the New York Seventh and the New Jersey regiments; and the other directly opposite Georgetown. Both are going up on commanding elevations."

A letter to a New York paper says: —

"The New York Seventh are highly praised for their pluck and good digging in ditches and trenches in Virginia. Some of them have their hands badly blistered."

An editorial article in the New York Express says: —

"The correspondents note the gallant Seventh and brave Sixty-Ninth,

IN THE TRENCHES.

both at work in the trenches together, night and day, sun and rain, and the former, though more delicately trained, as only second to the latter in the hard work of digging the earth. The sword and musket, for a season, have given way to the shovel and the pick."

A private letter says: —

"Our fellows stripped to their shirts and pants, and, with neck and bosoms open, picked and shovelled until red-hot and dripping. We astonished the United States engineers in charge of the work."

A Tribune correspondent says: —

"Red shirts and blue, pink and brown, white havelocks and bare heads, were in one jolly confusion. Long shovels and short, picks and wheelbarrows, were flying in every direction."

Each detachment, when relieved, was allowed an hour for bathing; and it took the opportunity to gather strawberries, which were abundant.

It was pleasant for them to see the work rise shapely and strong under their hands, obviously commanding, from its elevation, the railway, road, canal, and river for miles around, and forming a strong advanced *tête de pont* for Long Bridge, the main road to Washington. It is pleasant now to recall, that, while but two defensive earthworks of magnitude were erected at this period for the protection of the capital, — this and the one directly opposite Georgetown, — the Seventh Regiment left its handiwork on the larger one, that stout work known in the history of the war as Fort Runyon.

But its work, and the object of the whole expedition, had now been successfully accomplished. The District of Columbia forces had already returned to their habitual stations. On the evening of the 26th, Colonel Lefferts received the following flattering acknowledgment and order: —

HEAD-QUARTERS, DEPARTMENT WASHINGTON, 26th May, 1861.

COLONEL LEFFERTS, *Commanding New York Seventh Regiment.*

SIR, — Your regiment has accomplished all that was intended, in crossing over to Arlington to take possession of the Heights, having labored in the intrenchments manfully also.

The security of this city makes it imperative you should resume your encampment on this side, and you will, this afternoon, march over accordingly, and hold your regiment here ready to turn out when called upon.

I would recommend that you afford your command an opportunity to bathe in the canal, if desirable, before you march.

Very respectfully, &c.,

JOSEPH K. F. MANSFIELD,
*Brigadier-General and Commanding.*

About sundown the regiment was put *en route* for its old position as outpost on the Harper's Ferry Road. It left Virginia with the feeling that it had taken a worthy share in a movement which had made Washington secure. The occupation of Arlington Heights was the key to the defence of Washington; from the works thrown up beyond Long Bridge extended afterwards a famous defensive line of enormous proportions, such as no Confederate column, even in the height of victory, ever ventured to assail. Even the army wrecked at Manassas there stranded and was safe.

The regiment did not wait for a wash in the canal; however, it took an abundant shower-bath, on the way to camp, in the shape of a drenching rain. At 9, P. M., the camp was reached, and the two companies left behind received their worn, wet, and tired comrades with a hearty welcome. "One hand," says a letter, "holding pieces at 'present arms,' the other waving caps, shaking hands, or welcoming by a slap on the shoulders the men as they passed the guard-tent; the band on the right of the guard playing 'Home Again,' while to this music was added the ringing cheers of the glad fellows who had so reluctantly remained at home while we 'went to the wars.'"

While the Seventh were in Virginia on Saturday, an alarm of attack had been started in Washington. Sherman's Battery dashed across Long Bridge, infantry regiments followed, and the whole country was aroused by the news of a great battle. Some of the friends of the Seventh in New York will remember to this day the anxiety of the 25th of May.*

* Here is a specimen of the despatches which came to the New York papers of that day: —

"ATTACK ON THE TWELFTH AND SEVENTH NEW YORK REGIMENTS.

"WASHINGTON, May 25, 1861.

"About eleven o'clock this forenoon the picket guard of the Twelfth New York regiment was attacked, half a mile beyond Arlington Heights, by about seven hundred and fifty infantry of the Rebels. Only a few shots were fired by the Rebels. The guard returned the fire, and hastened to the main body to give the alarm, when the Twelfth Regiment was called to arms. The Seventh New York Regiment, being near the Twelfth, was also soon in marching order, having been fired upon by a body of cavalry without doing harm. The two regiments — the Twelfth and Seventh — were soon in line of battle. As soon as the Rebels discovered they were about to be attacked by the Federal forces, they fled.

"The greatest excitement prevailed in the city. The house-tops were covered with people, anxious to get a glimpse at the expected battle. The Massachusetts Fifth was ready to march in five minutes after receiving the order. The President's mounted guard, consisting of Georgetown volunteers, formed part of Colonel Ellsworth's funeral cortege, and had hardly reached the depot when the alarm was communicated to them. They immediately started at a full gallop across the bridge, although service cannot be required of them outside.

"The President, while in the processsion to-day, accompanying the remains of Colonel Ellsworth to the cars, was informed by a courier of stirring hostilities on the Virginia side; General Mansfield was similarly advised, and this was the foundation of the military movements here to-day. A dense smoke was meanwhile seen on the line of Arlington Heights, and cannonading heard. The latter, however, were funeral minute-guns, and the former probably from camp-fires. The troops now here have been ordered to hold themselves in readiness to march at a moment's notice."

# CHAPTER XII.

## A MISSION ACCOMPLISHED.

THE National Guard, in hastily abandoning everything to rush to the defence of the capital, enlisted for thirty days. That period had now expired; but the War Department specially requested the Seventh, on which so much reliance had been placed, to remain a few days beyond their time, until some dispositions of troops connected with the late movement should be completed.

This was an appeal which could meet with but one response from the National Guard. Accordingly, when, at the battalion drill of Tuesday, May 28th, Colonel Lefferts, as Captain Clark states in the "History of the Second Company," "alluded to this subject eloquently and patriotically," the regiment, as one man, expressed a willingness and a desire to remain in the field and faithfully perform every duty, so long as the government required its services. Returning cheerfully to the routine of camp duty, it observed all drills and other requirements with customary strictness. The Washington despatch of that morning to the New York Herald thus reports the appeal of Colonel Lefferts to his men: —

"At the regular parade of the Seventh this morning, Colonel Lefferts ordered his men to form square, and, addressing them, said that the thirty days for which the regiment had enlisted had now expired, but that *the government was still in want of their services*, and that hence *he hoped the regiment would consent to stay as long as it was wanted.* If it did, those members whose presence was indispensably necessary at home would be granted leave of absence. The question was then put, when the men, with a unanimous shout, expressed their willingness to serve as long as the country wanted them."

The New York Times correspondent, in the same spirit, says: —

"Early this morning, Colonel Lefferts, at battalion drill, took the sentiment of the Seventh about remaining until ordered home by government, their time having expired. Furloughs were offered to all who wished, but only five out of twelve hundred and twenty-five asked for them. I can inform you officially that the government wish the Seventh here for a few days. When feeling perfectly secure, they will be ordered to return home."

While such was the conduct of the Seventh, it is due to mention that the sentiment of a majority of the regiment, as reported by the company officers to Colonel Lefferts, favored a temporary return to New York whenever the government should signify its desire to release the organization from service. That it could have been otherwise will hardly be imagined by any one who for a moment considers the circumstances under which the National Guard so suddenly started to Washington. Families had been left unprovided for; extensive businesses had been dropped, and, in the general derangement of finance, were going to ruin; commercial positions had been sacrificed, and the call of the country had alone been heard.

Colonel Lefferts had announced, by authority of the government, that only a few days' additional service was desired, and, as has already been seen, there was enthusiastic unanimity in the response to his earnest appeal; but a few hours later, on the same day, Colonel Lefferts received from one of his company officers the following note, whose terms were direct and decisive: —

"I have had a personal interview with every member of our company now in camp. There is perfect unanimity of sentiment, and that is to stay two or three days longer.

"The sentiment is equally unanimous not to stay beyond Saturday at the latest. The members of this company are unanimous in saying that they will be obliged to go on that day, if not before relieved. I hope you will be able to make arrangements so that this company, which has so nobly responded to your request, may go home at that time with honor, and before that time if possible. I wish you distinctly to understand, that this unanimity has been obtained upon your assurance that we are to go home by Saturday next, at the latest."

Of course there were no two interpretations to be put upon this missive, and Colonel Lefferts promptly exerted himself to see that the desires of the government and the regiment, which seemed to agree, were carried out. At first, however, some question was raised in New York as to whether any troops who had once gone to the front should ever return, even when mustered out, "till the war was over." But this feeling, which chiefly arose from a popular misapprehension that "the affair would be ended in sixty days," was dispelled, when it became known that hundreds of those who were desirous to return purposed, as soon as possible, to hurry back "to the front" in the higher stations which were now every day pressed upon them. This generous response of the regiment to his appeal relieved from anxiety Colonel Lefferts, who, their lawful time having expired, was forced to rely greatly upon the voluntary action of his officers and men; and, on the other hand, the unanimity reported to him as existing among his own men, showed that the present campaign could not be prolonged beyond the time already specified. Among the many letters received at this time, in New York, from the regiment, and now placed at the service of the writer, is one from Colonel Lefferts, from which I extract a few lines: —

"The time for which we were mustered into the service expired on Sunday, and I found the largest part of my regiment desirous to return. Their sacrifices have been very great, and I know they should return; but much depends on the next few days, during which the government is desirous that we should remain. At the drill, this morning, I addressed the men, pointed out our position, and received a most encouraging response: they would all willingly stay a few days longer. Some, to whom I had granted furloughs, returned them to me, and said they would stand by me, come what would."

With reference to the unanimity of sentiment reported to him by his officers, he wrote:—

"The regiment are not divided. They will move, as they always have done, *together*."

In a thoughtful and appreciative article, the New York Tribune at this time said: —

"Our Seventh Regiment is coming home at the expiration of the thirty days for which it was mustered into service. This is well. A war such as that before us requires soldiers enlisted for its duration. Of such there will be no lack, and they are in rapid process of organization. To this end our means and arms should be addressed, leaving our uniformed militia at home as a body always ready and always to be relied on in any sudden peril. Such was that which menaced Washington when the Seventh marched forth so instantaneously to its rescue, and it is not too much to say that the arrival of the Seventh New York and Eighth Massachusetts Regiments did save Washington from attack. For this the regiment went. The peril was great, and they knew it, and were anxious to encounter it. That peril is now past; and we speak advisedly when we say that it was the wish and decision of the General-in-Chief that this fine regiment should be restored to its home, available in twelve hours from this city for any future call, and ready as they are available.

"Let us then welcome back our gallant Seventh, proud of what they have done, and confident that no call can be made upon them in moments of danger that they will not answer with a will and with like good result."

On the evening of the 30th of May, in presence of a large number of distinguished officers, the regiment, having been formed in square, was formally addressed in a farewell speech, in behalf of the government, by the Secretary of War, General Cameron. " He began," says the report, " by paying a graceful compliment to the regiment for the earnest promptness with which they had responded to the President's call for volunteers to come forward to Washington for the defence of the capital, so fraught with hallowed national associations. They had come ready to sacrifice their lives, if necessary, for the cause of the Union, and on their route had passed through dangers which had tried their courage and fortitude to the fullest extent. They had come as defenders of their country, offering themselves at a moment when the government and the nation at large were burdened with gloom and apprehension; and the joyous welcome accorded them was never more worthily bestowed. In the name of the government, he thanked not only them, but the liberal city which had sent them, and the devoted families which had spared them to undergo any perils that might ensue in behalf of the land of their love. They had remained until now the imminent danger had passed away. But the struggle was not over, and he knew that when they were wanted again they would come as swiftly and manfully, and with the same self-sacrificing devotion, as before. The contest was one in which a free people were determined to exhibit before the world their capacity for self-government, and to confirm their power to preserve and perfect the free institutions which had given its chief glory to this land. As he had before said, there might be a necessity for those whom he addressed to rejoin this patriot army. ' Yes,' he said, ' we may meet again. The same feeling which prompted you, when you first heard that your country was in danger, will once more, if need be, rally you in her defence. It is not for me to determine when this struggle will end. But I may say how it shall end. Sooner or later it can have but one conclusion, and that will be when the disturbing cause which gave rise to it is utterly obliterated. Again I thank you. You will return to meet that cordial welcome always tendered to the brave, — that honorable recognition won by those who have passed with manful fidelity through the labors and perils allotted therein.' "

As probably no volunteer or militia regiment was ever dismissed from national service with such distinguished attention from the War Office, so none surely ever received a more complimentary mustering-out order than that which General Thomas, Adjutant-General of the army, now handed to Colonel Lefferts. It read as follows : —

SPECIAL ORDER, No. 146.

WAR DEPARTMENT, ADJUTANT GENERAL'S OFFICE,
WASHINGTON, D. C., May 30, 1861.

The commanding officer of the Seventh Regiment of New York Volunteers will proceed with his regiment to the city of New York, where it will be mustered out of the service of the United States by Lieutenant M. Coggswell, Eighth Infantry.

It is the desire of the War Department, in relinquishing the services of this gallant regiment, to make known the satisfaction that is felt at the prompt and patriotic manner in which it responded to the call for men to defend this capital, when it was believed to have been in peril, and to acknowledge the important service which it rendered by appearing here in an hour of dark and trying necessity.

The time for which it had engaged to serve has now expired, the service which it was expected to perform has been handsomely accomplished, and its members may return to their native city with the assurance that its services are gratefully appreciated by all good and loyal citizens, whilst the government is equally confident, that, when the country again calls upon them, their appeal will not be made in vain to the young men of New York.

By order,
L. THOMAS, *Adjutant-General.*

In compliance with this order, Colonel Lefferts directed the regiment to parade at half past three o'clock of the following afternoon, in overcoats, armed and equipped for the march ; each soldier carrying his canteen, haversack, two days' rations, and his blankets rolled and strapped upon his knapsack.

Soon Camp Cameron was a wreck of its former self. Near midnight a serenading party, composed of the regimental band and five files of men, bearing torches, under command of Lieutenant Bostwick, drew up in front of the President's mansion, and performed patriotic airs. Mr. Lincoln and his family sat at the open window. Thence the party went to the residence of Secretary Seward, who addressed them as follows: —

"I see in my visitors to-night my friends and neighbors of the State of New York. I have ever thought, I have always known, that the Union would not be worth much without the State of New York; and by the events that are now progressing, New York believes that she would not be much without the Union. We live in stirring times. People are trying to abolish Yankee Doodle, Hail Columbia, and the Star-Spangled Banner. And they are also trying that other and greater impossibility, to abolish the Fourth of July. Congress will meet on the Fourth of July, with the country in the midst of a civil war. Let us hope that when it meets again, on the next Fourth of July, we may have peace, harmony, and a restored Union. Gentlemen, will you do me the favor to walk into the house and take a glass of wine with me."

From Secretary Seward's the detachment proceeded to Willard's, and serenaded General McDowell, Major Slemmer, and General Mansfield, the latter of whom made a short speech, as did his adjutant, Drake de Kay.

After the orders had been issued for departure, an alarm came from the Virginia shore, and Colonel Lefferts received from General Mansfield instructions to "*be careful against a surprise to-night from Harper's Ferry.*" The night passed, however, without disturbance; and, the rumor of hostile movement proving baseless, Colonel Lefferts, who had again proposed to retain the regiment, resumed, on the 31st, arrangements for departure. The camp equipage was sold to the government, and the camp furniture, fixtures, utensils, provisions, &c. were sent as a gift to the Ninth

New York Volunteers, — "the generous donations filling," says a daily paper, "ten large army-wagons." A considerable sum of money was also given by members of the regiment to the Washington Monument Society.

Just before the regiment was ready to march, General Sandford sent in haste to Colonel Lefferts the following letter: —

WASHINGTON, May 31, 1861.

COLONEL, — I have just received intelligence, through the highest military sources, that there was a collision yesterday on Federal Hill, Baltimore, between the pickets of our troops and some of the Baltimore rowdies, in which three of the latter were shot. A great excitement prevails there, and I am advised that it is imprudent to let the Seventh go through Baltimore *at night*. This opinion is from the highest sources. I deem it my duty, therefore (whilst I omit to issue an order), to advise you to defer your departure until an early hour to-morrow morning.

I am, very truly, your obedient servant,

CHAS. W. SANDFORD.

Besides this letter from Sandford, Colonel Lefferts received word to the same effect from General Scott.

It seemed a perplexing question; but it was at once decided to march through Baltimore at night, not from any idle desire to precipitate a contest, but because this seemed the path of duty. If Baltimore was still in condition to resist the passage of Union troops, the Seventh, which had opened the way to Washington, could not do better service than in opening the way back. The Colonel therefore declined to accept the advice of General Sandford, but ordered the regiment to proceed with fixed bayonets and muskets loaded.

At half past three, P. M., of May 31st, the regiment broke camp, and marched to the depot over the dusty highway. Here a new difficulty presented itself. The railroad authorities had been advised by "the railway officers of the War Department" to transfer the regiment to Locust Point station, there to be ferried across, in order to avoid a march through the city. The following telegram was received by Colonel Lefferts, on the morning of the 31st, from Baltimore, from W. Prescott Smith, of the Baltimore and Ohio Railroad: —

"Our agent at Washington telegraphs me that you stated you would march your regiment through Baltimore. Permit me to advise you, that, by direction of the Railway Officers of the War Department to-day, we have arranged with Bay steamers and Philadelphia road to transfer you at the harbor from our Locust Point station to Canton. This will obviate any march here, and greatly facilitate your movements."

This telegram verified inferentially the rumor spoken of by Generals Scott and Sandford regarding the opposition preparing in Baltimore, and in addition appeared to show, as General Sandford had said, that the War Department held the same view as himself in the matter. However, it did not offer any additional reason why the Seventh should not march through the city in spite of the reported mob. Instead, therefore, of accepting this change of railroad arrangements under the suggestion of the War Department, it was resolved not to do so unless a peremptory order should come from the Department which could not be disobeyed. Accordingly the Colonel, at quarter past six, P. M., marched his regiment, and despatched the following message to Superintendent Smith: —

"ON THE TRAIN, May 31, 1861.

"Your despatch received. Was it the *order* of the War Department to go to Locust Point? Does any cause exist why we should not march from depot to depot? I of course wish to obey instructions. Answer at Relay House."

At the Relay House, Colonel Lefferts received the following telegram from Superintendent Smith: —

"We were directed specifically from Washington, by the General Railway Managers for War Department, to arrange for your transfer at Locust Point. We have to do so, and to change it at this late hour would make delay and confusion. But for this, no cause would exist why you should not march from depot to depot as you prefer. The plan arranged is more expensive and troublesome to us, but will facilitate yours. We will take you to Locust Point accordingly."

It now only remained to appeal to Washington, and this Colonel Lefferts did at once, and was gratified at receiving permission to "use his own judgment," with assurance that his wishes should be conformed to. Accordingly he sent word to Superintendent Smith at Baltimore: "We prefer to march from depot to depot, as no reason seems to exist why we should not." And such, in fine, was the arrangement consummated. Arriving at Baltimore, Colonel Lefferts carefully formed his regiment in line, broke it into column, and, placing himself at the head, started for the Camden Station through the city, mainly over the route taken by the Sixth Massachusetts. The regiment, 1,250 strong, with its battery and baggage, made an imposing appearance. It arrived unchallenged at the other depot, and thence, starting about midnight, reached Philadelphia at ten o'clock on the morning of June 1st. Proceeding forthwith down Prime Street to the wharf, it took the steamboats Fashion and Washington for Camden, thence to move on to New York.

What reception was in store from the great city that had so shouted and wept when, six weeks before, taking their lives in their hands, they had set out to hew a path to Washington? Strange as it now reads, this question the regiment asked itself with some misgiving; for at that frenzied epoch, a few fickle people, forgetting their recent worship of the regiment, had clamored that it ought to keep its colors at the front "till the end of the war," on the ground that "the Rebellion would be crushed in ninety days." They ungraciously contrasted its return with the conduct of the three months' and other regiments from the same State, forgetting the fundamental difference that these latter had taken time to prepare themselves for a long stay, and had taken not only time, but *measures*, to so prepare themselves, by carrying a majority of *recruits* to the war, who had joined for that very purpose, while the Seventh had gone at once, and first, and had carried wholly its own members, for the instant rescue and safety of Washington.

However, this ungracious criticism was temporary in duration, and limited even then to few people. The great heart of the city went out in warm welcome. All the press was cordial in its greeting. It was recalled that the order from Albany, in accordance with which the Seventh marched, was one detailing them "for immediate service, to be reported forthwith to the President of the United States, to serve until relieved by other regiments, or by a regiment or regiments of volunteer militia"; and that the Seventh had already done a great deal more voluntarily than this order contemplated. "The suddenness of the call upon them," said a leader in the Evening Post, "and their promptitude in responding to it, placed them in circumstances very different from those of the New York regiments which followed them. They necessarily left their business affairs in an unsettled condition. They did not allow *any* considerations to interfere with their patriotism and sense of duty. All personal matters were put in abeyance. They did not fill up their ranks with recruits, but went in a body just as they were. Other regiments waited for recruits, and, while waiting, had time to arrange their private affairs, while those who could not make satisfactory arrangements stayed at home. In fact the Seventh, being the most perfectly drilled and equipped regiment, hurried off to hold the ground until the others could get ready to relieve them; and it is only fair and right that they should now come home to arrange *their* affairs, as others did *before they went*. No one can doubt, that, should the government hereafter require their services for any period, or for the war, they will promptly give them." The Herald's leader, in the same spirit, said: "We believe the administration and General Scott, in pursuance of the voluntary engagement entered into with the Seventh Regiment of New York Militia, when they requested it to come temporarily to Washington in the hour of need, have given orders for its return at the end of its month of service; and unless stirring events or the public exigencies should require their detention, this gallant corps will probably be home in a day or two. It gave the first impetus to the rising of the North. The regiment started upon a notice of thirty-six hours, with full ranks, consisting of its active and exempt members (three fourths of the whole), and no recruits. Its marching numbers exceeded by one hundred and fifty its muster on any gala-day in its history. No other city regiment had more than three hundred of its real members on starting. The rest are all recruits. Many of the members of the Seventh left families behind unprovided for, and, from its sudden departure, others had no time to arrange their business matters, which have been neglected ever since. Several of them are bankers and merchants, and have suffered severely. One of the principal officers is said to have failed from that cause, and others are on the brink of ruin. This regiment has rendered good service. It proceeded to the capital when danger stared it in the face, and when it might have had to stand the first shock of the enemy, and when it was expected that it must fight its way through to Washington."

The "Veterans," on their part, had long before expressed their desire to give a hearty greeting to their younger brethren, and Adjutant Asher Taylor had expressed this desire in the following communication to Colonel Lefferts: —

"I arrived at home last evening, very much gratified at all I saw and heard of our regiment at Washington, especially at its splendid condition, and am deeply moved by the solicitude expressed by all I meet for its safe return, and the welfare of its members. It is the heart's blood of New York. I am directed by Colonel Stevens to ask if it would be agreeable to you to have a reception by the National Guard Reserve, of which he is the commander. He had a very satisfactory battalion drill of his command last evening, mustering some three or four hundred, all that arms could be provided for. Please command us in anything we can do for you or for the regiment."

On the 31st of May it was determined that the reserve should assemble at nine o'clock, A. M., of the following day, leave the armory by companies, form regimental line at Lafayette Place, and march to Cortlandt Street Ferry, in season to escort the returned volunteers to the armory. It was further resolved that only veteran or exempt members of the regiment should be allowed to parade. On the same day the Executive Committee of the Union Defence Committee held a meeting, and passed the following resolutions:—

*Resolved*, That this committee desire to express their cordial recognition of the efficient services rendered to the cause of the country, at a critical emergency of its public affairs, by the Seventh Regiment of New York State Militia, commanded by Colonel Marshall Lefferts; and sharing fully in the general feeling of gratification which pervades the community at learning that the Commanding General of the United States Army, under the sanction of the President of the United States, has acknowledged, in special general orders, "the important service rendered by that regiment in an hour of dark and trying necessity," the committee desire to unite their congratulations with those of their fellow-citizens in extending a welcome hand to cheer the return of a body of soldiers who have conferred such high honor on the city of New York.

*Resolved*, That this committee will take pleasure in attending the reception to be given to the Seventh Regiment on its arrival in this city to-morrow.

*Resolved*, That these proceedings be published, and a copy furnished to Colonel Lefferts.

J. J. ASTOR, JR.,
*Chairman pro tem. Executive Committee.*

PROSPER M. WETMORE,
*Secretary Executive Committee*

At ten o'clock, on the morning of June 1st, ladies bearing

baskets heaped with exquisite flowers began to decorate the front of the armory, the main entrance, the stairways, and the facings of the Seventh Street entrance. Soon the words "WELCOME HOME" appeared over the arch in evergreen letters, beautifully bordered with white and red roses. At one o'clock the Reserve, three hundred strong, under the command of Colonel Stevens, marched to Jersey Ferry, and stacked arms. At two o'clock a large detachment from the Sickles Brigade, and very many of the officers of that brigade, preceded by one of their bands, joined the escort. Knots of officers from other corps, a body of juvenile "Zouaves," and the Union Defence Committee, all proceeded in the same direction; and a multitude of citizens, including many ladies, thronged the line of march, crowded around the ferry, and filled the railway depot in Jersey City. It was absolutely the pageant of the 19th of April repeated, with the godspeed turned to hearty congratulation.

At half past four, P. M., the regiment reached Jersey City, and was greeted by the throngs in the great flag-crowned galleries, and all the neighborhood of the depot, with tumultuous cheers and waving of handkerchiefs. The welcoming crowd was even larger and more enthusiastic here than that which six weeks before had bidden it adieu; and when the regiment took the ferry-boat, a final shout rent the air, the artillery boomed from the docks, and, as before, the various craft on the river showed their flags, and cheered heartily as the boat steamed across. As for the enthusiasm amid which the men again set foot in New York, those who survive the war still hold it in memory.

When brief greetings had been exchanged between those who, six weeks before, feared they had parted forever, and when Mr. Astor had presented the Resolutions of the Defence Committee, the Seventh and its escort took up the line of march through Cortlandt Street, Broadway, Union

Square, and Fourth Avenue, to its armory. With the streaming flags and bunting and inscriptions of welcome, the streets thronged with men heartily cheering, every building bright with women waving handkerchiefs, the booming of cannon, and the merry peal of the bells of Trinity, with its familiar chimes, the Seventh knew that it had not lost its old place in the love and respect of the Empire City.

The hotels and public buildings all along the route were covered with flags, and bore scores of such inscriptions as these: —

WELCOME.

BRAVE GUARDS, YOU HAVE PERFORMED YOUR DUTY.

ALWAYS READY.

DEFENDERS OF OUR FLAG, WELCOME.

GOD BLESS YOU.

Every on-looker noted some change which six weeks' service had wrought, — the bronzed and hardy look of the men; or their uniforms, neat, but worn and travel-stained; or such little fantastic emblems of campaigning as the black and battered pipes worn in the caps. At the armory the enthusiasm was very great. Mr. Astor, the members of the Union Defence Committee, and other distinguished citizens, had already gathered in the balcony, and it was the purpose of Colonel Lefferts that they should say a word to the men in behalf of the citizens of New York. But the spontaneous greetings of the multitude, and the wild excitement and cheering, made any formal welcome impossible. No one could be heard; and Colonel Lefferts, simply raising and waving the flag amid torrents of applause, abruptly concluded all ceremonies. The companies marched to their rooms, singing and cheering, and a hearty shake of the hand was then ready for friends and kin. Nor was the ovation ended there; for any soldier who passed from the armory was cheered again, and cheered as he passed through the streets to his home.

The same day Colonel Lefferts issued the following order: —

"The regiment will assemble at Head-quarters, on Monday, 3d instant, at half past one o'clock, P. M., fully equipped, for the purpose of being mustered out of the service of the United States by Lieutenant M. Coggswell, Eighth Infantry U. S. A., who has been assigned that duty.

"The Colonel takes this opportunity to express to the officers and soldiers his deep sense of the manly virtues and patriotism which have actuated all in their discharge of duty, from the time we received our marching orders for the protection of the Federal capital to the present time; how far the objects of the mission have been accomplished, and how well the duty has been performed, must be left to the impartial judgment of the future. I congratulate you, brother soldiers, that it was our good fortune to lead the strong and noble army of our good and loyal State, which stands with poised arm to strike down all who may defy the power of the national ensign, which it has planted in the face of those who would trail its sacred folds in the dust.

"Let it be understood that we are ready, at a moment's warning, to march at the call of the constituted authorities in defence of our flag and country."

On Monday, the 3d of June, 1861, five-and-forty days after its march on the 19th of April, the regiment was mustered out of service. The same evening the Board of Councilmen unanimously adopted the following Preamble and Resolutions, offered by Mr. Lent: —

"*Whereas*, The officers and men of the gallant Seventh Regiment New York State Militia, noted for the alacrity with which they always respond to the call of duty, after having nobly and successfully aided in accomplishing the task of opening the way to and protecting the capital of the nation, whilst in imminent danger, from armed traitors, who beleaguered it on every side, have just returned to our city, where, both as a military organization and as distinguished and patriotic citizens, they have enjoyed a wide-spread reputation, which their soldierly demeanor, united vigilance, and unflagging energy in discharging the arduous duties from which they have just returned prove them to have so well merited; Be it therefore

"*Resolved*, That we, the Common Council of the city of New York, welcome them back with feelings of joy and gratitude to our city, which feels a just pride in them both as citizens and soldiers, and to their families and homes, which they have honored by their noble demeanor, and now make happy by their presence.

"*Resolved*, That the clerk of the Common Council have the foregoing Resolutions suitably engrossed, and forward the same to the regiment."

These Resolutions, being duly passed by the aldermen and approved by the Mayor, were presented, handsomely engrossed, to the regiment. Soon after, the Union Defence Committee made a report of their services, in which they said : —

"Massachusetts may justly claim the merit of having placed the first regiment of citizen defenders of the Constitution in the field, but her patriotic soldiers were promptly followed and speedily outnumbered by those of New York. The Seventh Regiment, commanded by Colonel Marshall Lefferts, so long the pride of the city of New York, abandoned the ties of home and business, and with an alacrity that has scarcely a parallel in military history, marched its thousand disciplined men steadily to the capital, where it performed, efficiently and faithfully, all its duties, and whence it has returned, at the close of its full term of service, distinguished by the grateful commendation of the President, and the Commanding General of the Army."

# CHAPTER XIII.

## OFFERS OF SERVICE.

SO ended, as I have written, the first campaign of the Seventh Regiment as an organization during the Rebellion.

As soon as the regiment was mustered out, its members began to return to the front, "for three years or the war." That date of muster-out was June 3d. Less than ten days thereafter a list was published of members of the Seventh who had already accepted commissions in the United States service, many before the regimental campaign was ended. This list comprised four colonels, two lieutenant-colonels, two majors, twenty-one captains, seven adjutants, and forty-one lieutenants, several of the latter being in the Regular Army,—a total of seventy officers up to that date, in a list announced to be "by no means complete." Very truly had General Scott and General McDowell pronounced this "a regiment of officers."* Before winter the blood of the Seventh had

* "During the recent stay of the Seventh Regiment in Washington, General Scott,

crimsoned nearly every battle-field in Virginia. The high-souled and brilliant Winthrop, on the 10th of June lay dead on the field of Big Bethel, in the uniform of the Seventh Regiment. Farnham, the born soldier and worthy successor of Ellsworth, brave, patriotic, and full of promise, received his death-wound soon after at Manassas. The gallant Alden was buried a little later on the disastrous field of Ball's Bluff.

Early in autumn, Colonel Lefferts, who had already sent five officers, at his request, to Colonel Lander, then commanding a brigade in Western Virginia, desiring to open a new avenue of service, despatched the following letter to General James S. Wheat, Adjutant-General of the Virginia Militia, at Wheeling: —

> "Sir, — Several of the gentlemen in my command have received appointments in Western Virginia, either in regiments as line officers, or attached to regiments as instructors, which personally has given me much satisfaction.
>
> "My object in writing is to ask whether you can find places for any more, for I have a number who wish to enter the service, and who are competent and reliable, — if the matter is placed in my hands, I shall send none others; while I have a pride that *all* who go from my regiment shall do it credit, I have a deep interest in the cause in which they enlist, and wish none but worthy and capable ones to represent it."

While attending to these duties, Colonel Lefferts was busily engaged, also, in endeavoring to keep up the unprecedented condition of soldierly discipline and efficiency to which the regiment had arrived by reason of its experience in actual service, — a matter of some difficulty, owing to con stant depletions. Ten days after the return of the regiment, Major Shaler, an exceedingly able and accomplished officer, was commissioned as Lieutenant-Colonel of the Six ty-Fifth Regiment New York Volunteers (United States

in reply to the offer of Colonel Lefferts to keep the regiment in active service, said: 'Why, Colonel, you do not want your regiment here, — you have a regiment ot officers.'" — *New York Times*, June 12.

Chasseurs), and Lieutenant-Colonel Pond was forced to resign his commission from ill health, thus leaving Colonel Lefferts for a time without field officers. However, in September, Captain James Price, of the Third Company, was chosen Lieutenant-Colonel; and, in December, Captain Benjamin M. Nevers, of the Sixth Company, was chosen Major. Both these officers had accompanied the regiment on the march to Washington. As an organization, meanwhile, the regiment, besides parading as funeral escort to General Lyon and Colonel Montieul, and to its own Winthrop, Farnham, and Alden, paraded also for the reception of several regiments returning from the seat of war, and with the greatest pleasure, on the 31st of July, to welcome its gallant comrades in campaign, the Eighth Massachusetts.

In giving the order for muster-out, on the return of his regiment, Colonel Lefferts had closed with these words: "Let it be understood that *we are ready at a moment's warning to march at the call of the constituted authorities in defence of our flag and country.*" This promise he made good by allowing no opportunity to pass without tendering the services of the regiment, both in fort and field.

Immediately on receiving the startling and unexpected news that the army had been defeated at Manassas, on the 21st of July, 1861, and that the capital itself was menaced, Colonel Lefferts telegraphed to the Secretary of War that his regiment was "*ready to march forthwith*" to Washington. But the peril proved to be less imminent than at first reported, and as three years' troops were then pouring in in great numbers, the offer was not accepted.

To Governor Morgan he proposed that the regiment should learn to use the heavy guns in the harbor forts, so that in case of need the garrisons could be reinforced instantly by efficient troops, — a practice afterwards adopted by militia regiments in other coastwise cities. In the middle of December, notwithstanding the severity of the season,

Colonel Lefferts renewed and urged that suggestion, this time in a letter to the Governor, saying: —

"Upon the return of the regiment under my command from Washington, I expressed to the Union Defence Committee, and to certain gentlemen who promised to communicate with you, the desire of the regiment to continue prepared for active service in case of being called upon, and suggested that we might be ordered to one of the forts in our harbor, for the purpose of instruction and practice in heavy sea-coast artillery. Subsequent events have only confirmed my previous views of the importance of the great State of New York having within itself a sufficient number of practised artillerists, who could, at an hour's notice, occupy our forts and man the guns, the great safeguards of the city of New-York and her vast commercial interests. . . . .

"The regiment can be put on duty by detachments, and I can safely say that within a very short period the Executive can rely upon eight hundred to one thousand competent gunners, each capable of commanding as 'the chief of piece.'

"The subject of our coast defences has been of late so elaborately and scientifically discussed, that I have nothing further to urge in reference to the matter, beyond the necessity of giving to the whole *a practical turn.* If, to effect this, the services of myself and my command can be made available, I can only assure your Excellency that we shall be found ready and willing to obey your orders."

In reply the Governor sent his thanks, with assurances, that, "when circumstances should make it necessary" to take the course indicated, "the prompt and patriotic offer of the Seventh would not be forgotten."

From August to February the great army lay, organizing and drilling, "quiet on the Potomac." But winter wore away, and the first fortnight in February was thick with rumor of advance. As soon, therefore, as authentic tidings came that General McClellan purposed to fight "the great, decisive battle of the war," Colonel Lefferts hastened to ask for the Seventh a share in that struggle, proposing that the Seventh should "take the field" for a short period, to "meet the sudden emergency" of the "battle on the line of the Potomac now near at hand." The following is the letter: —

NEW YORK, February 21, 1862.

MAJOR-GENERAL GEORGE B. MCCLELLAN, *Commander-in-Chief United States Army, Washington.*

SIR, — I have been led to the opinion, from circumstances transpiring within the last week or two, that you may need more men to fully carry out your military plans, and that a battle on the line of the Potomac is near at hand. If this is so, I feel confident that the members of my regiment will respond promptly and heartily to any demand from you, and that you can rely upon eight hundred to one thousand well-drilled and effective men. You are probably aware that the regiment is entirely composed of business men, clerks, etc.; and while, therefore, they cannot take the field for a long period, with their present organization, yet they can, as they did in the early part of this struggle, meet a sudden emergency, and are now ready for that purpose.

I am, sir, with great respect, your obedient servant,

M. LEFFERTS,
*Colonel Commanding Seventh Regiment N. Y. S. M.*

Lest, through the absorbing cares of the coming campaign, the General should overlook his proposal, Colonel Lefferts took the precaution to send a similar message to the Secretary of War. From the latter the response was first heard in the following telegram: —

WASHINGTON, February 26.

COLONEL M. LEFFERTS, *New York.*

The Secretary of War was duly notified by me of the desire and readiness of the Seventh Regiment to be called to Washington in case of any emergency which would render their services valuable to the government. The Secretary expressed his gratification at the tender of service, and desired me to express his thanks to you, and say, that, should any emergency arise, he would unhesitatingly call upon you and your regiment. Respectfully,

E. S. SANFORD.

This received, Colonel Lefferts, while awaiting the response to his letter from head-quarters, got his command in readiness for service. The answer came, at length, as follows: —

HEAD-QUARTERS OF THE ARMY, March 7, 1862.

COLONEL MARSHALL LEFFERTS, *Command'g Seventh Reg't. N. Y. S. M.*

COLONEL, — I am directed by the Commander-in-Chief to acknowledge the receipt of your letter of the 21st ultimo, offering the services of your regiment to the government, and to reply that the General commanding will in all probability be glad to avail himself of services of the Seventh Regiment within ten days or a fortnight.

I am, Colonel, very respectfully, your obedient servant,

EDW. McK. HUDSON,
*Lieutenant-Colonel and A. D. C.*

From this reply it was concluded, not only that the forward movement would take place "within ten days or a fortnight," but that the Seventh Regiment would have some share in it. Accordingly, Colonel Lefferts directed his commanders of companies, "without giving unnecessary publicity to the matter, to notify their commands at once of the strong probability of their being called upon at short notice for active service, so that their arrangements could be made to hold themselves in readiness." * He then ordered the Quartermaster to make forthwith a personal inspection of the camp equipage and stores, and to report in writing to him upon their condition.

* *Extract from the Regimental Minutes.*

"NATIONAL GUARD ARMORY, Saturday evening, March 8, 1862.

"On the adjournment of the meeting of the Dress Committee, Colonel Lefferts requested the field officers and commandants of companies to remain, — being present Lieutenant-Colonel Price, Major Nevers, Brevet-Colonel Shumway, Captain Clark, Lieutenant-Commanding Schermerhorn, and the Military Secretary.

"The Colonel then mentioned the fact of his having received a letter from the Commander-in-Chief, in reply to his of 21st February, in which General McClellan states, through his aide-de-camp, that in all probability the services of the regiment would be required in ten days or a fortnight. This letter was dated 7th instant, by mistake, being postmarked 6th. The Colonel requested the captains present, without giving unnecessary publicity to the matter, to notify, without delay, their commands of the strong probability of their being again called upon, at short notice, for active service, that they might make necessary arrangements, and hold themselves in readiness. He said that he should rely upon the captains to carry out these instructions.

"The meeting then adjourned, the Colonel stating that he should call a meeting of commandants of companies not present this evening for Monday evening, to explain the matter to them and give them similar instructions.

"Monday, March 10th. — The following notice was sent to Captains Bensel, Speight, Young, Farrar, Haws, and Easton. Captain Riblet was verbally notified to the same effect by the Military Secretary.

"DEAR SIR, — The Colonel requests that you will attend a meeting of the com-

But the second campaign of the Seventh was not yet to begin. A few days after General McClellan's notification to the regiment, the enemy evacuated his position at Manassas. Three weeks later the Army of the Potomac had been gathered from its winter bivouacs and deployed on the peninsula formed by the York and James Rivers. There was to be no "battle on the line of the Potomac." It is, however, none the less pleasant and proud a record in the regimental annals, that, at this seeming crisis of the war, the battalion was offered both to the general commanding and to the War Bureau for any duty that might be assigned to it. All the services and all the offers of service of the Seventh Regiment were at the hour of peril or the pivotal point of decision. It pioneered the path to Washington when the road was most thickly beset with dangers. It remained on duty in Washington until the capital was safe. In the doubtful hour that succeeded Bull Run it again volunteered to go to the front. When a great battle was expected in the spring, it volunteered again. In the summer of 1862 and in the summer of 1863, when the enemy assumed the offensive and menaced the North, it marched at a few hours' notice. Let us now describe in course these latter events.

mandants of companies, to be held at the armory this evening at eight o'clock, on business of importance.

"Yours respectfully,

"WM. H. ALLEN, *Military Secretary.*

"In compliance with the above, at quarter before nine, P. M., were present in the council-room Colonel Lefferts, Captains Easton, Haws, Farrar, Young, Riblet, and Speight, and Lieutenant Meday. The Colonel explained the purpose of the meeting, and read his letter to General McClellan, and the reply, stating, as on Saturday evening, that he wished the men quietly notified to hold themselves in readiness, and should rely upon the commandants to see that everything necessary was done. The subject was then discussed, and the feeling expressed that the members of the regiment would respond promptly to the call; and the meeting adjourned."

# CHAPTER XIV.

## THE BALTIMORE CAMPAIGN.

DURING an anxious month in the spring of 1862, the gaze of the country had been fixed upon two great armies, which, like a pair of wrestlers, cautiously advancing and retreating on the York and James "Peninsula," now feinting, now parrying, now striking, seemed ever ready, yet ever reluctant, to hazard the decisive clutch, when suddenly, towards the end of May, a startling apparition diverted all eyes to the Valley of the Shenandoah. Stonewall Jackson, with a compact column of fifteen thousand men, in part withdrawn from McClellan's front, before Richmond, suddenly burst from the head of the valley upon Fremont, who was stationed as warder of its passes, dealt him a single furious blow, and, swerving without a pause to repeat it, swept down through the valley in an avalanche, and fell full upon Banks, whose smaller corps drifted helplessly before him, and only paused, spent and broken, within the borders of Maryland.

The strategic purpose of this division is now a matter of undisputed history, as it soon became one of bitter experience. With great fatuity, the campaign had been opened by a division of the Union forces into four armies, there being, besides the Army of the Potomac proper, an aggregate of sixty thousand men embraced in the commands of Generals McDowell, Fremont, and Banks, none of which were in supporting distance of each other or of General McClellan. But when the latter reached the Chickahominy, McDowell was ordered forward to join him; and, to avert this reinforcement of forty thousand fresh troops, General J. E. Johnston, who commanded the Confederate forces, ordered General Jackson to gather in hand the troops left with him in the valley, now largely reinforced from Richmond, and to march them swiftly northward, so as to menace the national capital.

History has recorded, too, how successfully this purpose was accomplished. McDowell's forty thousand men were halted and turned aside to "bag Jackson"; who, meanwhile, adroitly slipping by his converging pursuers, rejoined Johnston. Then, with the Union forces weakened and the Confederate force strengthened, there succeeded the seven days' battles, which left the former on the banks of the James.

But, for the moment, what fate might befall the Chickahominy campaign was not thought of in Washington or at the North. The only cry was that of April, 1861, "The capital is in danger!" The news ran that a powerful army, stealing from McClellan's front, had swept away everything in its course, and menaced the North with invasion and the capital with capture. If Washington was wild with excitement, the North was stricken with alarm. "Save the capital!" was all it could coherently utter.

The Seventh Regiment heard, as it heard in April, 1861, and marched.

The afternoon of Saturday, the 24th of May, that day on which Banks commenced his retreat from Strasburg, Colonel Lefferts received the following news of the stirring events in Virginia: —

To COLONEL LEFFERTS, 12 *Albion Street.*

General Wool reports Rebels moving north from Richmond, and Sec'y State telegraphs to governors, "Hold all military in readiness for moving." Will keep you posted.

C. SUMNER.

The general despatch thus alluded to as having been sent to the governors is now historic and famous. But the telegram sent by the War Bureau to Governor Morgan was special and significant. It ran as follows: —

WASHINGTON, May 24.

MAJOR-GENERAL MORGAN, *Albany.*

The operations of the enemy on the Shenandoah may require speedy reinforcements. Please organize one regiment as speedily as possible. *The Seventh New York* should also be in readiness to move if called for.

EDWIN M. STANTON, *Sec'y War.*

To meet this request, Governor Morgan caused the following telegram to be sent to Colonel Lefferts: —

ALBANY, May 24, 1862, 3.16, P. M.

COLONEL M. LEFFERTS.

The Governor desires the Seventh Regiment should be in readiness to meet any call of the government. Please inform me by telegraph its present strength.

THOS. HILLHOUSE.

To this telegram Colonel Lefferts replied, a quarter of an hour later, as follows: —

"Your telegraph despatch this moment, three o'clock thirty minutes, received, and am ready for service. Our rolls show about nine hundred. A fair proportion can be relied upon."

On Sunday night, news having reached the government that Banks, harassed by the exultant enemy, had retreated fifty-three miles since Saturday morning, and had been driven to the Potomac itself, President Lincoln called upon

Governor Morgan to send him the militia of the city of New York, to help check the enemy and defend Washington. An hour before midnight, Colonel Lefferts received by telegraph from the Governor an order to proceed as soon as possible to the seat of war, and hurriedly wrote and despatched to the morning papers a notice to the Seventh Regiment to assemble at nine o'clock of the same (Monday) morning. Before this hour, he telegraphed the Governor, "I have a meeting of my regiment at nine o'clock this morning. What can I say to them about length of time we shall probably be absent?" At half past ten, A. M., the answer came: "The Governor directs me to reply, that the Seventh will be mustered for three months' service. THOMAS HILLHOUSE."

Meanwhile, at 9, A. M., a large body of the regiment, having seen the notice in the morning papers, assembled at the armory, and were ordered to prepare to march the same day for three months' service. Six, P. M., was fixed for the hour of departure, and the nine hours' interim was devoted to notifying other members and preparing for the campaign.

At the appointed hour the regiment marched, six hundred strong, despite depletions, brevity of notice, and the absence of members in the country for the summer; large accessions were soon after made to its ranks. Of the enthusiasm of the city upon the departure, it need only be said that it was almost a repetition of that of thirteen months before, even as the excitement and anxiety of the North fell little short of those of the 19th of April, 1861. As before, the regiment did not wait for the formality of a muster into the service. "The influence of their example," wrote Adjutant-General Hillhouse, next day, to Secretary Stanton, "on other regiments and volunteers, was most beneficial." The only militia regiment that marched that night was the Seventh; but on the same day the Governor ordered the

Eighth, Eleventh, Seventy-First, and Thirty-Seventh Regiments to get themselves in readiness to follow, and, in fact, within the next four days, ten regiments were off. The Seventh, as in 1861, led the column.

A New York journal, in describing the meeting of the Seventh on Monday morning, says: "Shortly before nine o'clock Colonel Lefferts arrived at the armory, and was received with loud demonstrations of applause. The despatch from Secretary Stanton to Governor Morgan, calling for one regiment of militia from this State, accompanied by a special request for the Seventh, was then read to the men, together with the subsequent requisition for the other regiments. The reading was received with the most enthusiastic demonstrations of applause, the men clapping their hands and cheering vociferously. The Colonel then informed them that they would be required to be ready that evening, as he wished them to be first on the war-path. This announcement electrified the troops, and cheer after cheer resounded through the building. The regiment was then dismissed, the men proceeding to their respective meeting-rooms, and such an overhauling of lockers as ensued was never witnessed there before." Another paper of the same city describes the scene with similar spirit. "As early as eight o'clock," it says, "the spacious drill-room at the armory was crowded by the members, anxious to be the first to answer to the call of Secretary Stanton. Shortly after, Colonel Lefferts arrived, and his appearance was hailed with every manifestation of delight by his command.

"'This is what I have been wishing for.'

"'Ain't this jolly?'

"'But how can you leave your business?' inquired one.

"'This, and this only, is my business now,' was the response.

"'Never was there so much enthusiasm shown; the

whole of the men seemed to hail their departure from the city as a positive pleasure. Colonel Lefferts then read the despatches from Secretary Stanton, calling for more troops, which was received with the most vociferous cheering. He then made a short and spirited address, asking the men if they were willing to answer the call. A most unanimous 'Yes!' was the answer."

Colonel Lefferts thereupon hastily drew up his orders for march, and issued them forthwith. They were substantially the same as those of the year before, and read as follows: —

HEAD-QUARTERS SEVENTH REGIMENT (NATIONAL GUARD),
NEW YORK, May 26, 1862.

In compliance with orders from his Excellency the Governor of this State to proceed to Washington, the regiment will assemble at Headquarters at a quarter before seven o'clock, P. M., this 26th instant, in full fatigue dress, with knapsack, haversack, and canteen, overcoats rolled and strapped upon the knapsack, and blankets suspended from it. Officers will sling their overcoats. Regimental line will be formed at seven o'clock. Each man will provide himself with one day's rations, and carry in his knapsack suitable underclothing, an extra pair of boots (shoes are much better), knife, fork, spoon, tin plate, and cup, an extra pair of pants, and those that have retained their "Aspinwalls" had better take them. Each officer will be allowed a small trunk, which must be distinctly marked, and left at the armory before six o'clock, P. M. Recruits who may not have procured their uniforms will, however, report for duty, and be assigned a post in the column. Each company will be allowed to take one servant, who must have a pass signed by the commandant of the company.

MARSHALL LEFFERTS, *Colonel.*

GEO. W. SMITH, *Acting Adjutant.*

A member, taking a copy, and mounting a caisson, read the orders aloud to his comrades.

Promptly at seven o'clock the line was formed in Lafayette Place, with a great crowd of on-lookers. "Many a fervent 'God bless you!' was uttered," says a journal already quoted, "and many a bright eye was dimmed at parting. The march down Broadway was a complete triumph; the sidewalks were crowded with an enthusiastic people, who cheered themselves hoarse in honor of the brave fellows as they passed. Flags were streaming from the principal buildings, fireworks were let off, and each man endeavored to surpass his neighbor in giving vent to his delight at seeing the Seventh once more on its way to the war."

About 9, P. M., of May 26th, the regiment embarked on the steamer Red Jacket, at Pier No. 2, North River, and, just before ten, moved out, with the band playing a lively air, and the men giving responsive cheers to the shouts of the great multitude gathered at the wharf and on the wharves adjoining. Elizabethport was reached after eleven, and at midnight the train started for Baltimore. On arriving at Elizabeth, the Seventh found the depot filled with people waiting to cheer them as the year before, and the "Star-Spangled Banner" was sung enthusiastically when the train moved on. Harrisburg was reached by noon of the next day. At Easton, Reading, and other places along the route, the citizens were assembled to cheer the Seventh, while ladies threw bouquets into the cars. At half past five, P. M., Baltimore was reached; and at 6, P. M., Colonel Lefferts marched the regiment across the city, the band playing, to take the train for Washington. Just as it was about to enter the cars, an order came to Colonel Lefferts directing him to report to General Dix, commanding the Middle Department, with head-quarters at Baltimore. This order was received with universal vexation and chagrin; but a rumor prevailing that it really signified the transfer of the regiment directly to Banks's corps at Harper's Ferry, it was discussed with more complacency. Arms were stacked and knapsacks piled in the depot, which was set apart for the bivouac. But leave being given to seek the comforts of the Eutaw and other hotels, it was speedily made use of by most of the regiment.

Baltimore was, however, destined to be the scene of the Seventh Regiment's second campaign. For, as it turned out, Jackson, having accomplished his object in thwarting the projected junction of McDowell with McClellan, made good his retreat up the valley to his mountain eyrie, and soon after, at the summons of Lee, crossed over to the left flank of the main Confederate Army. It being, therefore, no longer now a question of the safety of Washington, but of the pursuit of Jackson, the Seventh was retained at Baltimore, there to await the shifting fortunes of the grand Virginia campaign, which on any day might demand its presence at the front. Thither, also, other New York militia regiments duly followed.

General Dix designated Stewart's Grove, in the outskirts of the city, two miles from the Eutaw House, as the camp-ground. The camp was laid out on a plateau, amongst the grand old oaks crowning Stewart's Hill, adjacent to the family mansion of the Confederate General Stewart. It commanded a fine view of Baltimore, with its harbor and the bay beyond, and of the beautiful woods and fields around the city. Its only lack was a good parade-ground. At ten o'clock on the morning of May 28th, the regiment marched to Stewart's Hill, and there pitched its tents. A long storm inaugurated this camp, like Camp Cameron, and seasoned the troops to rough service at the start. In a few days the tents were floored, the streets cleared, the cook-houses put in order, and a beautiful camp was established. Campaign devices, taught by experience, aided by open purses, made the quarters comfortable. A published letter of May 30th says: "The Seventh is now comfortably quartered on Stewart's Hill, new tents having been furnished them, and all floored over. To-day quite a number were allowed the freedom of the city, and they paid visits about town, viewing the monuments and public buildings. The men are very anxious to be in active service, and it is understood that Colonel Lefferts made application to the Secretary of War to allow his regiment to join General Banks's column, as it is momentarily anticipated that an attack will be made at Williamsport. Every man in the regiment seems anxious to have the opportunity for active field service. They are exceedingly opposed to being kept at Baltimore. The Eighth Regiment is expected here this evening. They will, no doubt, meet with a similar reception to the New York Seventh."

As soon as the camp was established, Colonel Lefferts issued the following

STANDING ORDER, No. 1.

The Chain of Sentinels shall be the limit of the Camp.

No member of the regiment shall pass outside of the limits of the Camp without permission of his Commanding Officer, and then only by way of the guard-tent, where he shall report himself going and returning.

The Officer of the Guard shall keep a list of men so leaving the camp, with the time of their reporting to him, and submit the same with his Guard Report in the morning.

Every man must be present at morning and afternoon drill, unless he is on the sick-report, or has a written excuse from his commandant.

"Reveille" at sunrise.

Immediately after the roll-call the tents will be put in order, and the streets cleaned, and all rubbish must be removed from the Camp-Ground.

Half an hour after "Reveille," the signal for Recruit Squad Drill, which will last one hour.

"Peas on the Trencher" at seven o'clock, A. M.

Call for details for guard duty at twenty minutes before eight, A. M.

Call for details to repair the Regimental Parade at ten minutes before eight, A. M.

Troop for guard-mounting at eight, A. M. Immediately after which, the first sergeant, with a detail of men, will draw their rations for the day.

Surgeon's call at nine o'clock, A. M, when the sick in camp of each company will be marched to the dispensary, in charge of a non-commissioned officer.

The assembly for company drill at half past nine, A. M., unless otherwise ordered.

"Roast Beef" will be sounded for dinner at twelve, M.

First sergeant's call, quarter after five o'clock, P. M.

To the color to form by Battalion, at half past five, P. M.

"Evening gun" to be fired at sunset.

Tattoo at ten, P. M. Taps at half past ten, P. M.

There will be roll calls on the company parades, at Reveille, and evening parades, superintended by a commissioned officer.

The recruits will be exercised at least twice a day by an officer or a non-commissioned officer.

All drills will be attended in full fatigue dress, officers and non-commissioned officers omitting the sash.

When off duty in the public streets, all officers, non-commissioned officers, and privates will wear the waist-belt alone and the coat buttoned. On dress parades, the officers and sergeants will wear the sash.

The cap-cover will be worn in wet weather only.

Pistols will not be carried by officers or men, except in actual conflict, or when on the march.

All fancy articles of dress are prohibited at all times.

From this order the daily routine of the camp may be gathered. It did not differ essentially from that of Camp Cameron. There were recruit drills before breakfast and at various times through the day; company drills in the morning; battalion drills in the afternoon; dress parade in the evening. The severe rains of the first ten days of camp-life made its duties very disagreeable; and among the extra nuisances, it would appear, were the musical performances of two young buglers, who sounded all day long the calls of a battery of the Third Artillery, encamped near by.

Hardly had the regiment gone into camp before daily details were made, by orders from head-quarters, for escort duty at the funerals of soldiers who had died at the United States Hospital in Camden. On May 29th an escort of a corporal and eight privates of the Seventh Company attended the funerals of Privates A. C. Keym, Eleventh Maine Volunteers, D. Crawford, Seventy-Second New York Volunteers, and D. K. Sturgis, Eighty-Fifth Pennsylvania Volunteers ; on May 31st a similar escort of the Eighth Company, those of Privates H. Delgart, One Hundred and Fourth Pennsylvania Volunteers, and J. Galligan, One Hundred and Fourth New York Volunteers; on June 2d an escort of a sergeant and fourteen privates of the Ninth Company attended the funerals of Sergeant A. W. Gains, Seventy-Seventh New York Volunteers, and Private Wesley Robinson, Sixth New Jersey Volunteers ; on June 3d an escort of a corporal and eight privates of the Third Company, those of James Atchinson, Eleventh Maine Volunteers, David Vail, Sixth New Jersey Volunteers, and V. Sfefferman, Purnell Legion; on June 4th a similar escort of the Second Company, that of Private Thomas Leland, Eleventh Maine Volunteers ; on June 13th, a similar escort, that of Private Hartz, Eighty-Fifth Pennsylvania Volunteers.

On the 30th of May the following order was received from headquarters: —

SPECIAL ORDERS, No. 143.

HEAD-QUARTERS MIDDLE DEPARTMENT,
BALTIMORE, May 30, 1862.

. . . . .

II. The commanding officer of the Seventh New York State Militia will detail from his command one company to act as guard at the Mount Clare Depot, for the work-shops, buildings, and public property, relieving the detail from the Third New York Volunteers now there.

The detail so made will report at once to the agent of the B. and O. R. R, at the depot.

By command of Major-General Dix,
D. T. VAN BUREN, *Assistant Adjutant-General.*

Each company by turns was detailed for this duty, marched to tho station, and took up its quarters in some passenger cars, a "paymaster's car" being the head-quarters, and another car the kitchen. The post had been created by General Dix in consequence of a serious political riot which had happened there, endangering the use of the road for government purposes. Mount Clare station contained the machine-shops, car-works, and one of the chief freight depots of the railroad, — it occupying ten acres and employing a thousand men. The duty here was light. The Second Company was first detailed, and, on the day after its arrival, General Dix visited the station, and expressed his satisfaction at the appearance of the guard. The following afternoon, being Sunday, Chaplain Weston, who had preached a sermon in the morning at Camp Dix, preached another at Mount Clare. On the 2d day of June this detail was relieved by the Eighth Company, Captain Shumway, which in turn, on the 5th of June, was relieved by thirty-five men of the Ninth Company, Captain Easton.

General Dix having received orders, on the 1st of June, to repair to Fort Monroe and assume command at that point, Major-General Wool was assigned to command the Middle Department; but, during the interim before his arrival, the command devolved upon Brigadier-General W. R. Montgomery, United States Volunteers. In his general order announcing his departure, General Dix said: "It is a source of deep regret to the Major-General commanding that he is compelled to leave without being able to review the regiments of New York Militia, — the Seventh, Eighth, Thirteenth, Twenty-Second, Thirty-Seventh, and Forty-Seventh, — which, under a second appeal from the Chief Magistrate of the Union, have laid aside their various occupations on the briefest notice, at great personal sacrifice, and, hurrying to the field, are now occupying positions in and around Baltimore. In their patriotism and their devotion to the government of their country, the Union feeling of the city will meet with a cordial sympathy. It is a great alleviation of the regret with which the Major-General commanding parts with them, that he is soon to be succeeded by a distinguished general officer of the Regular Army, from their own State."

The camp of the Seventh Regiment, previously known as Camp Dix, was commonly called thereafter Camp Wool, in honor of the new commander. On the 5th of June, in compliance with General Montgomery's order of the previous day, a daily guard of four men was detailed for the General Hospital at Camp Andrew, reporting to Brigade-Surgeon Ira Russell, in charge of the hospital.

In marching from New York, at a few hours' notice, many members of the Seventh Regiment had made considerable sacrifices. Such as could go to the war for three years had already gone, and were scattered by scores through the armies of the Union. Those now at Baltimore, business needs, or family duties, or ill health, or similar cause, had prevented from absenting themselves through so long a war. They were all prepared for short campaigns, but even these were made at a sacrifice. If it be true that the wealth and pecuniary independence of a few left them free to act, the responsible business positions of most others were sources of anxiety. Some members gave up these positions; others were peremptorily recalled by employers who could not or would not allow them to finish the campaign, except on penalty of being thrown out of their places. To those salaried men whose families had been accustomed to good social positions, the withdrawal from business and the stopping of their incomes were particularly trying. To consider and act upon all these cases, giving temporary or permanent furloughs as circumstances might demand, was the hard task imposed upon Colonel Lefferts, who was always extremely anxious that the effective strength of the regiment should be as great as possible.

There were members of the regiment also who lagged behind, and urgent means were employed to bring these forward. Still, despite these causes, and despite the numbers now in the volunteer army and the suddenness of the present call, the regiment, as we have seen, marched six hundred strong; it was joined at Camp Dix by others who were detained for a day or two in New York. On the 4th of June,

Adjutant George William Smith made the following report of the strength of the regiment: —

*Abstract of Consolidated Morning Report*, June 4, 1862.

| COMPANY. | PRESENT AND ABSENT. | ABSENT. |
|---|---|---|
| A (First) | 55 | 7 |
| B (Second) | 91 | 5 |
| C (Third) | 75 | 6 |
| D (Fourth) | 66 | 1 |
| E (Fifth) | 51 | 2 |
| F (Sixth) | 85 | 5 |
| G (Seventh) | 80 | 5 |
| H (Eighth) | 78 | 4 |
| I (Ninth) | 75 | 2 |
| K (Tenth) | 57 | 6 |
| | 713 | 43 |
| Field and staff, and non-commissioned do. | 11 | |
| Band and field music | 54 | |
| Total, present and absent | 778 | |
| Deduct | 43 | |
| Total, present | 735 | |

To keep up this effective strength, and to add to it by bringing forward every officer and man delaying without sufficient reason in New York, was now the task. Recruits offered themselves, ten from Schenectady, others from Philadelphia and elsewhere. These were declined, but it was suggested to the Veteran Reserve Corps that something might be done in recruiting in New York. The following letter was received in reply from Colonel Schultz: —

NEW YORK, June 4, 1862.

COLONEL MARSHALL LEFFERTS.

MY DEAR SIR, — Yesterday I received your telegram, and at once wrote a note to Colonels Stevens and Vermilye to meet me in the evening; also, Lieutenant-Colonel Pond. All concurred in saying that your wishes should be attended to at once.

We all thought best not to say, or allow any one else to say, anything about recruiting in the papers. This course may cause a little delay in spreading the information that, under certain limitations, you are willing to receive recruits, but we thought for the present this will be the best course. It will give us an opportunity to select better men.

The conditions which will be imposed are: —

*First.* The recruit to pass, as to character, etc., the officer in attendance.

*Second.* He must serve for seven years in the regiment, if elected.

*Third.* To be assigned to such company as you may direct.

*Fourth.* To take his chances of an election on his return.

*Fifth.* To equip himself at his own expense, except musket.

You shall hear further from us as we progress.

Very truly,

J. S. SCHULTZ.

The duties of Camp Wool were soon ended. On the 5th of June, Colonel Lefferts received an order from General Montgomery to have his command in readiness to move to Fort Federal Hill by eleven o'clock, A. M., of the 6th of June, to relieve the Third New York Volunteers at that place. This order was disagreeable to the regiment, not merely because the camp had now been put into admirable condition, and in the "perfect days" of June it was hard to think of exchanging tents for barracks, but also because it was feared that this transfer portended a long stay at Baltimore, and a farewell to hopes of active participation in the stirring events going on at the front. The importance of the new post was the main consolation.

# CHAPTER XV.

## FORT FEDERAL HILL.

FEDERAL HILL, rising bluff and imposing from the Patapsco, is the strategic key to the city of Baltimore, with the river and harbor, as well as to Fort McHenry and the other defensive works, and to all the subjacent country. Seized and fortified by General Butler, in May, 1861, its possession became synonymous with the possession of Baltimore. But the great earthwork reaching nearly to the river bank, called Fort Federal Hill, was thrown up in the autumn of 1861, by Duryee's Zouaves (Fifth New York Volunteers), commanded by Colonel Duryee, formerly Colonel of the Seventh Regiment. In March, 1862, this regiment was succeeded by the Third New York Volunteers, Colonel Alvord. In now relieving the latter, the Seventh took pride in knowing that at least it had added an admirable regiment to the Virginia battle-fields. The high reputation of these two preceding garrisons of Federal Hill sufficiently guaranteed the importance of the post.

The fort itself was described at this time as "an immense square fortification, with three large bastions, the guns of which command the river above and below, and every part of the city beyond. A lunette commands the approaches from the land side. The fort is entered upon its southwest face by a bridge and a huge gate, and the entrance is protected by a ditch. Large two-story buildings occupy three sides of the quadrilateral, within the high embankments, and upon the fourth are situated a neat cottage, commonly called the colonel's quarters, a guard-house, and an unimposing building which affords ample accommodation for the commissary and quartermaster's departments. Three large magazines, conveniently situated, and an imposing signal station, complete the necessary structures within the fort. The buildings enclose a large parade-ground, sufficient in extent for ordinary military purposes; and the square is ornamented with native trees, which please the eye and afford an agreeable shade. The barracks are of wood, two stories high, with double verandas, supported by slight pillars, and facing inwards towards the square. One building is occupied by the officers, and the others are divided into rooms ninety feet in length, each division furnishing ample accommodation for a company of a hundred men. Three tiers of bunks occupy each side of the company quarters, and are arranged in the most convenient and approved manner. Company kitchens also occupy the ends of the large centre building, and there are rooms in the same building for the band and the sutler. With its ample supply of excellent water, complete drainage, airy situation, and comfortable quarters, Fort Federal Hill is one of the most healthy and agreeable military posts in the country."

At this time the armament and ammunition of the fort were as follows: —

FORT FEDERAL HILL.

*Armament.*

Six 8-inch columbiads.
Two 10-inch mortars.
Two 8-inch S. C. howitzers
Twenty-three 32-pounder guns.
Five 24-pounder howitzers (Flank Defence).
One 6-pounder gun (brass).

*Ammunition.*

1,200 8-inch Columbiad shell; 100 8 inch Columbiad grape; 1,100 10-inch mortar shell; 400 32-pounder shell; 150 32-pounder canister; 150 32-pounder grape; 920 32-pounder solid shot; 126 24-pounder howitzer, F. D., shell (fixed); 64 24-pounder howitzer, F. D., grape (fixed); 60 24-pounder howitzer, F. D., canister (fixed); 28 6-pounder gun (brass), solid shot (fixed); 42 6-pounder gun (brass), canister, (fixed); 1,000 hand grenades, 1, 3, and 5 pounds; 9,200 pounds cannon powder; fuses, cartridge-bags, and implements, complete.

On the afternoon of the 6th of June, the Third Regiment marched out and the Seventh marched in; after a thorough scrubbing, the quarters were occupied. Three days later, Major-General John E. Wool assumed command of the Middle Department, with head-quarters at Baltimore. On the 19th the regiment was mustered into the United States service for three months, to date from May 25th, by Colonel B. L. Beall, United States Army. That officer, on the 21st, wrote to Colonel Lefferts, requesting him to direct that four muster-rolls be made out instead of three; the fourth, he added, " I am directed to send to the Commission of the Land Office in Washington City, as it is contemplated to grant land to the volunteers." This record may be worthy of preservation, to note the furthest point to which the regiment ever went on the road to land bounties.

I have already said that the regiment took the oath of service for three months, but the incidents connected with this act form a story by themselves. It will be remembered that, on leaving New York, it was distinctly stated by the authorities that the regiment should be mustered in for not less than thirty days nor more than ninety days, and that the muster-in for more than thirty days should be at its own option. Soon after its departure, therefore, the Adjutant-General of New York addressed the War Office, saying: "The Seventh Regiment, National Guard, left for Washington last night. They left without being mustered into the United States service, as the demand seemed to be pressing, and the influence of their example on other regiments and volunteers was most beneficial. The period for which they are to serve is left to be arranged after their arrival in Washington; but they left with the understanding that it should not be less than thirty days, nor more than three months, *nor are they to be under any obligation to remain longer than the former period, unless they consent to after their arrival.*"

On receiving this letter, Secretary Stanton sent to Colonel Lefferts, then at Baltimore, a request that he would come on at once to Washington, to settle with him personally the term of service. The Colonel, on arriving at the War Office, found that the Secretary was very desirous to have the regiment mustered for three months.

"Well, Mr. Stanton," said Colonel Lefferts, "the term of service we set out for was thirty days, and it is fair that the regiment itself should be first consulted, if it is to be sworn in for ninety."

"Do just as you please about it," answered Mr. Stanton, shortly, and with a displeased air.

"Mr. Secretary, don't misunderstand me," replied the Colonel. "I am perfectly willing, as you have seen, to muster in for three months, but must keep faith with my men. I think I can set your mind at rest, that, after a fair statement of the facts, they will at once respond to your wishes."

On that, Mr. Stanton became calmer, and rejoined: "It is *very* important, Colonel, that you should muster in for three months; the other regiments will be sure to follow your example. However, probably your term of service will not last over thirty days, for in ten days we expect McClellan will be in Richmond."

On his return to Baltimore, Colonel Lefferts called the regiment together and told the men what had taken place, what the government desired, and how the present action of the regiment would go into its history, not as compulsory, but as voluntary, and undertaken in behalf of the country. What the response was we have already seen. But even to the present day, some of those who were at Baltimore in 1862 are wont, on meeting the Colonel, to joke him on the affair, laughingly accusing him of "coaxing sixty days' extra" service out of the regiment.

I now append the muster-roll of the Baltimore campaign of 1862. It should be noted that the members marked "not mustered" in some cases joined the regiment after the 25th day of May, and in some cases were merely absent on leave or on detailed service on that day.

## MUSTER-IN ROLL

OF THE

## SEVENTH REGIMENT (NATIONAL GUARD) N. Y. S. M.

Called into the service of the United States, by the President thereof, from the twenty-fifth day of May, 1862, for the term of three months, unless sooner discharged. Mustered in at Baltimore, on the twenty-fifth day of May, 1862, by Colonel B. L. Beall, U. S. A.

*Colonel.*

MARSHALL LEFFERTS.

| *Lieutenant-Colonel.* | *Major.* |
|---|---|
| James Price. | Benjamin M. Nevers. |

*Staff.*

Geo. Wm. Smith, *Adjutant.*
Stephen Rogers, *Surgeon.*
James H. Rogers, *Assistant Surgeon.*
Rev. S. H. Weston, *Chaplain.*
Chas. T. McClenachan, *Quartermaster.*
Wm. H. Allen, *Paymaster.*
Geo. W. Brainerd, *Commissary.*

*Non-commissioned Staff.*

Robert C. Rathbone, *Sergt. Major.*
L. L. L. Clearman, *Quartermaster Sergt.*
Simon W. Scott, *Color Sergeant.*
Wm. H. Gibson, " "
Charles H. Winans, *Orderly.*
Wm. L. Watkins, *R. G. G.*
Marshall Lefferts, Jr., *L. G. G.*
Frederick S. Morrison, *Com Sergt.*
James W. Wilson, *Hospital Steward.*

*Band.*

David Graham, *Prin. Mus.*

| | | | | | |
|---|---|---|---|---|---|
| Claudio Graffulla, *Leader.* | | | Lindner, Charles, | *2d* | *C. Mus.* |
| Bader, Frederick, | *1st* | *C. Mus.* | Mosline, Fredoline, | " | " |
| Bader, Henry, | " | " | Menti, Frederick, | *3d* | *C. Mus.* |
| Corley, Thomas, | " | " | Menti, Adolph, | " | " |
| Diller, Francis, | " | " | Macchi, Ulias, | " | " |
| Duhy, Oliver, | " | " | Nichols, Adolph, | " | " |
| Fritz, Edward, | " | " | Quintana, Lucien, | " | " |
| Wernig, Charles, | " | " | Rogassi, Vito, | " | " |
| Gessner, Joseph, | *2d* | *C. Mus.* | Stobe, Henry, | " | " |
| Fielding, John, | " | " | Wernig, John, | " | " |
| Kendall, George, | " | " | Weckert, Adolphe, | " | " |
| Kappa, Carlo, | " | " | Anderson, John, | " | " |
| Kossack, William, | " | " | Brettell, Edward, | " | " |
| Eberhard, Nicholas, | " | " | O'Reilly, Michael, | " | " |

---

## FIRST COMPANY (A).

*Captain,* CHRISTIAN H. MEDAY.

*1st Lieutenant,* William H. Hume.

| *Sergeants.* | *Corporals.* |
|---|---|
| *Kitchen, George H. (*Orderly*). | Bensel, J. Warner. |
| *Murray, James. | Bergmann, August. |
| Buchanan, David. | Howe, Charles H. |
| Clough, Henry. | Hume, George W. |
| Archer, Anson I. | |

*Privates.*

| | |
|---|---|
| Akley, John M. | Belknap, Charles. |
| Ammerman, Albert. | Borden, Charles A. |
| Apelles, Charles H. | Bosworth, Charles P. |
| Apelles, Frederick. | Cooke, George T. |
| Baker, John T. | Corsa, William H. |
| Barr, Samuel C. | Crandall, Joseph W. H. |

* Those marked with a star were not mustered in.

Elliott, Archibald.
Foulke, William H.
Griffith, William.
*Grout, Thomas J.
Hamilton, Robert.
James, Benjamin A.
Jaques, Thomas.
Kingsland, Daniel C.
Kurtz, William.
Leach, Henry L.
Manning, William.
McKaye, James.
Meday, George K.
Mums, William M.
Munger, Calvin A.
Nichols, William A.
Pearsall, William, Jr.
Saunders, George F.
Scott, David.
Seaman, Charles H.
Sharp, Robert.
Sharp, William A.
Spring, Edward A.
Squire, Thomas P.
Stout, Burke C.
*Stranch, Oscar.
Swartz, John H.
Thompson, Allenby.
Thorne, William I.
*Trenor, Thomas F.
Van Ness, George.
Villeplait, Alfred B.
Walker, Nathan D.

## SECOND COMPANY (B).

*Captain*, Emmons Clark.

1st *Lieutenant*, Peter Palmer. 2d *Lieutenant*, George M. Smith.

*Sergeants.*

Allison, Richard (*Orderly*).
Ware, Richard F.
Van Norden, Charles S.
*Fonda, Richard D.
*Quilliard, Gulian V.

*Corporals.*

*Brower, Bloomfield.
See, William B.
Mix, Eugene.
Gould, Robert S., Jr.

*Drummers.*

Barker, William.
Brown, Charles.

*Privates.*

Agens, Frederic G.
Alden, James M.
Allison, William G.
Amerman, Jacob B.
Appleby, Charles.
Bacon, Benjamin.
Baker, John G.
Bernard, Walter.
Bostwick, Charles E.
Bird, John H.
*Bristow, Henry.
*Brumley, James L.
Buchan, Robert C.
*Burnet, Gilbert, Jr.
*Burtis, William A., Jr.
Cahill, Eugene C.
*Chase, Amos M., Jr.
Clark, Edward D.
Curtis, Albert A.
Davis, Alexander M.
Day, Martin N.
Debenham, George.

Dusenberry, Edwin.
Emerson, Charles.
Estwick, William.
Evans, Lemuel E.
Farnham, William T.
Findlay, Andrew, Jr.
Fishblatt, Solomon H.
Gregory, Frank.
Hill, Charles S.
Haddock, Washington M.
Hadley, Charles L.
*Harter, Frederic A.
Hatfield, Abraham, Jr
Jones, Matthias L.
Keep, Frederic E.
*Lane, R. Henry.
Lamibeer, William, Jr.
Leonard, Robert W.
Manuel, Richard.
Marsh, Joseph A.
Mather, Thomas D.
McKinley, Robert.
Miller, James W.
Mitchell, William A.
Moffatt, Bruce.
Montayne, William H.
Peixotto, Moses L. M.
Porter, Joseph T.
Postley, De Van.
Randal, James B.
Ray, Daniel G.
Robinson, Daniel.
Roome, James W.
Salisbury, Richard L.
Simpson, Irwin.
Smith, Daniel A.
Smith, James A.
Steele, Henry S.
Street, George W.
Struthers, Stephen R.
Sturges, Edward.
Taylor, Archibald.
*Taylor, John H.
Terret, Charles A.
Trimble, Samuel.
Vanderbilt, Isaac S.
Van Duyer, William.
*Walsh, William W.
Ward, Daniel T.
Ward, Egbert.
Webster, Edward B.
Whitfield, Edward A.
Williams, Edgar.
Williams, Roswell C.
Young, Albert M.

## THIRD COMPANY (C).

*Captain,* GEORGE T. HAWS.

1*st Lieutenant,* John W. Murray. 2*d Lieutenant,* Richard L. L

*Sergeants.*

Pollard, Don Alonzo (*Orderly*).
Dore, Jose.
Smith, Eugene B.
Burdett, Jacob, Jr.
Collins, George S.

*Corporals.*

Gulager, Philip D.
Reeve, Isaac T.
Burgoyne, Theodore.
Warren, Joseph C.

*Drummers.*

Barry, William.
Connor, Henry.

*Privates.*

Allen, William H.
Amory, John M.
Bonnett, Daniel B.
Broderick, Peter M.

*Broderick, William E.
Brower, John L.
*Bunce, Theodore D.
Butler, Edward M.
Clowes, Theodore F.
Collins, Thomas G.
Cook, Vincent L.
Crary, Charles F.
Edgar, Leroy.
Fuller, Charles W.
Gunn, Charles L.
Hart, Robert McD.
Hyde, Zebulon E.
Irving, Thomas R.
Jaffery, Frank C.
James, John F.
Kennedy, Charles S.
Langdon, Charles E.
Lobdell, William C.
Mangam, Franklin.
Marsh, Charles M.
Mattison, Lucius H.
Morris, William E.
Oakley, Alfred.
Oakley, Nelson H.
Peck, William H., Jr.
Platt, William C.
Robbins, Charles F.
Robinson, William G.
*Salter, George F.
*Samanos, Stephen A.
Scrymser, Walden P.
Sexton, Samuel J. M.
Smith, William H.
Spooner, Henry T.
Stanford, Joseph M.
Tracy, William W.
Van Cleet, James B.
Van Wyck, William E.
Warren, James R.
White, Oliver G.
Wheaton, George H.
*Worth, Thomas.
Yard, Welsey S.
Carr, William, *Hospital Cook.*
Griffin, Lemuel, *Hos. Wardmaster.*

## FOURTH COMPANY (D).

*Captain,* William H. Riblet.

1st *Lieutenant,* Henry Everdell.

*Sergeants.*

Fay, Logan (*Orderly*).
Earle, Edward.
Bunting, Robert S.
Manning, George F.
Smith, Frank K.

*Corporals.*

Dougherty, Horace F.
*Holly, Henry H.
Little, John L.
Kipp, William H.

*Privates.*

Aikman, Augustus H.
Balen, Peter, Jr.
Beard, Sylvester C.
*Bogert, Arthur W.
Boylston, Edgar C.
Breeden, Abner H.
Breeden, Charles E.
Cantrell, Joseph.
Cooper, Joseph G.
Cooper, Walter.
Crandall, Frank.
Day, Clarence S.
Dickerson, George A.
Dolbear, Thomas H.

Dubois, John S. L.
*Everdell, Frank.
*Ewen, Norman.
*Farnam, James.
Ferry, Edwin N.
Foster, Henry J.
Gautier, Samuel.
Gould, Beekman.
Halsted, Robert.
Hays, Benjamin J.
Hayward, Melville.
Holly, John E.
Hodgkinson, Thomas H.
Huntington, Charles P.
Jarvis, Edward A.
Ketchum, John B.
Lambert, William.
Lawrence, George A.
Magnus, Theodore.
Miller, William L.
*Nichols, William L.
Nugent, Henry.
Osborne, Elisha R.
Outcalt, Cornelius B.
Pendleton, Augustus F.
Scamoni, Andrew.
Sharp, Samuel C.
Steele, John H.
Stephenson, Joseph B.
Sturtevant, Chester.
Taylor, Joseph D., Jr.
Terhune, William H.
Watkins, Walter A.
Whitlock, Andrew M., Jr.
Woodhouse, Lorenzo G.
Yetman, James E.
Yetman, John V.

## FIFTH COMPANY (E).

*Captain*, Wm. A. Speaight.

1st *Lieutenant*, W. Seward, Jr. 2d *Lieutenant*, Stephen O. Ryder.

*Sergeants.*

Hyde, Albert W. (*Orderly*).
*Halstead, Elbert K.
*Kingsland, Edward W.
Braisted, Peter D.
Eckel, J. Lewis.

*Corporals.*

Barratt, George P.
Wyckoff, A. T.
Mapes, Daniel S.
Richards, Daniel W.

*Drummers.*

Flynn, Joseph.
Girard, Augustus.

*Privates.*

Bell, John A.
*Bell, Wm. G.
Cowles, Wm. G.
Dutton, Van Buren.
Fox, John W.
Fuller, Benjamin.
Gardiner, E. G.
Godley, John L.
Grosvinor, Levi.
Harward, Wm. E.
Hawkins, John M.
Haynes, C. O. F.
Jarvis, John F.
Jenkins, J. B.
Kingsland, Wm. H.
*Loud, John S.
Magary, Wm. W.
Murray, Robert.

Mazzetti, George W.
Nicholl, Augustus W.
Patterson, H. M.
Pease, Edward C.
Post, George W.
Quail, George.
Reid, Robert.
*Rogers, Charles.
Romaine, Wm. H.
Rust, John H.
Sadler, Thomas.
Schoonmaker, Henry P.
*Smith, Henry W.
*Stewart, William.
Tibbals, Lewis P.
Timolat, H. M.
*Vanderbilt, DeWitt C.
*Wall, William, Jr.
*Whitney, Thomas E.
Yeaton, Samuel C.
Young, Lewis L.
Fraser, John M., *Teamster.*

## SIXTH COMPANY (F).

*Captain,* Joseph B. Young.

1*st Lieutenant,* Edward O. Bird.
2*d Lieutenant,* Peyton Jaudon.

*Sergeants.*

Carnes, Lewis M. (*Orderly*).
Palmer, George H.
Thomas, George F., Jr.
Smedburg, Charles G.
Vance, W. Henry.

*Corporals.*

Vermilye, Washington P.
Gardiner, Charles C.
*Barbey, Henry J.
Middlebrook, George L.

*Drummers.*

Gerard, William.
Hancock, Thomas.

*Privates.*

Barney, Lewis T.
Bassett, Frederic B.
Birmingham, J. Erskine.
Bissell, Augustus H.
*Brady, Abner S.
*Brinkerhoff, Gordon G.
Bronson, Willett.
Burnham, Douglass.
Chambers, Samuel, Jr.
Clark, Washington J.
Congdon, Henry M.
Congdon, Walter.
Conger, William F.
Cozzens, Edward.
DeHart, William C.
Douglass, Archibald.
Dunne, James.
Elsworth, Asher M.
Fernald, William H.
Forgerson, Israel.
Foster, Augustus C.
Foster, James A.
Gallatin, Frederick.
Gordon, James.
Haight, Charles C.
Hardy, John F.
Harison, Francis.
Hart, Gifford R.
Hayne, Jacob W.
Hicks, Henry W.
Holly, Henry Hudson.
Hone, John.

Irwin, Frederick T.
James, Julian.
Jenkins, Elisha J.
Kip, William W.
*Lawrence, William B.
Little, Emlen T.
Livingston, Mortimer.
Long, John T.
Lyon, Amasa.
Lyon, Edward.
Mallaby, Theodore.
Marriner, Edward.
McCabe, James.
Middlebrook, Charles T.
Miller, John.
Miller, Lindley H.
Murray, Wisner.
Musgrave, Joseph.
Musgrave, Thomas B.
Norton, Charles L.
Pattison, William H.
*Pell, Alfred, Jr.
Pell, James B.
Pell, Robert T.
Potter, Horatio.
Potter, Robert.
Raynor, James W. (July 5).
Robson, John F.
*Smith, Edward S.
Sniffen, John A.
Stephenson, William W.
*Stoutenburgh, William A.
Taylor, Henry (July 7).
Teer, Henry T.
Thomas, Henry K.
*Timpson, John W.
Tomes, Charles H.
Turner, H. B. (June 30).
Van Benschoten, Edward W.
Van Rensselaer, Philip L.
Van Wagenen, Wm. M.
Vernon, George R.
*Walduck, David M.
Warren, Robert.
*Whiting, William T.
*Williamson, S. Abeel.
Wilson, George W.
Wood, Wilmer S.
*Woolsey, Theodorus B.
*Young, Mansfield.

## SEVENTH COMPANY (G).

*Captain*, GEORGE W. ELY.

*1st Lieutenant*, John H. U. Kemp. *2d Lieutenant*, Edwin M. Felt.

*Sergeants.*

Bidwell, Henry S. (*Orderly*).
Coger, John J.
Delano, Thomas E.
Meacham, George G.
McKesson, John, Jr.

*Corporals.*

Dunscomb, John H. A.
Sherman, Samuel J.
Chevalier, George.
Callender, William E

*Drummers.*

Lydecker, Albert.
Norwood, Richard.

*Privates.*

Anderson, John S.
Avery, John, Jr.
Bacon, Richard S.
Bancker, Gerard.

Banks, Joseph E.
Barreto, William H. H.
Beebe, William H.
Bennett, Augustus C. M.
Blunt, Edmund.
Bowne, Robert S.
Campbell, Allen S.
Cortelyon, James H.
Crane, Edward S.
Eddy, Clinton.
Fleming, Charles E.
Freeborn, James F., Jr.
Gardner, John W.
Geisse, William F.
Greene, Herbert G. C.
Hale, Edward D.
Harper, Condy.
*Hayden, James T.
Holdredge, David M.
*Hutchins, Robert A.
Ingersoll, James H.
Jackson, Charles A.
Kingsland, Phineas C.
Louderback, David, Jr.
McDonough, Louis R.
McGraw, Richard D.
McJimsey, Eugene.
Millie, Thomas H.
Perrin, Jared L.
Phipps, John M.
Pinkney, Frederick H.
Pomeroy, Edward G.
Pomeroy, Eugene H.
Pomeroy, George V., Jr.
Potts, William R.
Putnam, Edward T.
Putnam, Nathaniel W.
Rice, William F.
*Risley, Leander S.
Roberts, Eugene F.
*Schram, James E.
Schermerhorn, Charles H.
Schermerhorn, Edward E.
Schermerhorn, Louis.
Schermerhorn, William H.
Sherman, Albert G.
Shipman, Sylvester D.
Smith, Andrew J.
Stage, Thomas V.
Steers, Abram, Jr.
Stephens, Edward.
Stokely, Noah B.
*Stone, William H.
Taylor, William F.
Tiffany, George F.
Tiffany, Henry D.
Tiffany, Lyman.
Thorp, Richard A.
Trotter, Edgar A.
Van Loan, Benjamin F.
Wheelwright, William G.
Whittingham, Samuel H.
Woodward, Newton.
Yeoman, Anthony.

## EIGHTH COMPANY (H).

*Captain*, Henry C. Shumway.

1st *Lieutenant*, John W. Spicer. 2d *Lieutenant*, Gilbert L. Arrowsmith.

*Sergeants.*

Rogers, Edmund P. (*Orderly*).
*Marvine, William H.
Loder, Benjamin.
Ryder, Alfred V.
Mather, De Witt C.

*Corporals.*

Trowbridge, Joseph.
Easton, Alfred W.
Howell, William.

*Drummers.*

Peck, John.
Smith, Colville.

*Privates.*

Allen, Charles D.
*Arms, Charles E.
Barton, Charles A.
Bragaw, Elias T.
Burdett, Peter G.
Burkhalter, John H.
Casey, William C.
Champion, Charles P.
Coles, Edward O.
*Coles, William H. W.
Curtis, Benjamin L.
Dart, Edward.
Daskam, James W.
Dean, Lascallas.
Delano, Victor M.
Douglas, John A.
Dinsmore, William B.
Eager, Peter.
Easton, Frederick J.
*Eaton, Daniel C.
*Eno, Amos F.
Gifford, Sanford R.
Gillilen, John.
Gross, Francis, Jr.
*Hall, Robert L. S.
Hollister, Henry K.
Hurlbut, William H.
Jackson, Frank D.
Johnson, Ebenezer R.
Keeise, John.
Knight, Azariah.
*Lannery, William K
Mabie, Foster W.
Mann, Daniel S.
Mansfield, William D.
Morgan, William H.
Muller, Adrian H., Jr.
Murray, George W
Murray, Henry S.
Nielson, Edward W.
Owen, William H.
Pease, Walter A.
Polhemus, Henry A., Jr.
Richardson, George R.
Ross, William B.
Russell, Richard.
Satherwaite, John F.
Smith, Cyrus L.
Smith, Louis B.
Smith, William W.
Swift, Frederick B.
Talcott, Edward N. K.
Thomas, James R.
Van Woert, John.
Waldo, Howard.
Walz, Ernest.
Williams, George P.
Willis, John O.
*Woodman, Webster.

## NINTH COMPANY (I).

*Captain*, CHARLES A. EASTON.

1*st Lieutenant*, Henry A. Cragin.
2*d Lieutenant*, Charles C. White

*Sergeants.*

McBride, Irwin H. (*Orderly*).
Tyng, Thomas M.
Barnes, William H. L.
Moore, Lawrence, Jr.
Keeler, Edwin, Jr.

*Corporals.*

Avery, Henry N.
O'Brien, Oswin.
Corey, Robert P.
Ketchum, Edmund.

*Drummers.*

Terhune, Edward.
Van Raden, Augustus.

*Privates.*

Abecasis, Marco.
*Andrews, George D.
Arthur, Edward G.
Barney, Newcomb.
Bill, Avery.
Blackwell, Charles G.
Brock, Henry.
Bugel, Benedict.
Burdick, Samuel C.
Bush, Theodore H.
Caldwell, Elisha S.
*Calhoun, James.
*Carpenter, Samuel W.
Center, Alexander.
Church, Elihu D.
Clark, Robert N.
Clark, William M.
Davis, George T. M.
Dayton, George E.
Dunnell, George H.
Dunnell, John H
Edgar, Samuel P.
*Fordred, Drayson.
Huntington, Charles.
Kerr, Henry T.
King, Charles E.
Kinney, Charles N.
Knapp, Edgar S.
Lent, Whitman S.
Lewis, George W.
Lounsberry, James H.
Macfarlane, Victor W.
Marlor, George.
Martin, Peter H.
McCrea, John E.
Mingay, Elwood B.
Nandaine, George D.
Neilson, Charles E.
Oliver, Theodore.
Perkins, Frederick W.
Proper, Isaac.
Rockwell, Fenton.
Rodgers, John.
Rutherford, John H.
Ryan, William H.
Salisbury, Edward L.
Schermerhorn, Alfred.
Schermerhorn, William B.
*Seaman, Jamison C.
Seaman, William.
Shaw, Albert O.
Sprague, Charles G.
Stone, George H.
Sweet, Milton B.
Tufts, John M.
*Tyng, Charles R.
*Van Iderstine, Peter, Jr.
Van Nest, William L.
Wheeler, Thomas M.
Youle, George.

## TENTH COMPANY (K).

*Captain*, George C. Farrar (June 17).

1*st Lieutenant*, Thomas Lord, Jr.

*Sergeants.*

Lentilhon, Joseph (*Orderly*).
Lawrence, John.
Bleecker, James.
Bleecker, Theo. B., Jr.
Ray, James.

*Corporals.*

Clinton, Charles W.
McJimsey, Robert M.
Voorhees, Charles H.
Drake, Lawrence.

*Drummers.*

Field, John.
Corrie, Enice.

*Privates.*

Beebe, Edward.
Beyea, James L.
Boardman, Daniel F.
Bogert, Charles L.
*Bradshaw, William H.
Brown, Milnor.
Cannon, James (*Armorer*).
Churchill, John L. (June 5.)
Clark, Henry W.
Clarke, Frank (June 1).
Cox, Wittingham.
De Ruyter, Charles.
Du Bois, Cornelius I.
Edey, Henry.
Foote, Emerson.
*Freeborn, Thomas.
Gautry, Harrison J.
Guion, George G.
*Hart, Lucius, Jr.
Howes, Howard S.
Hyatt, Effingham T.
Jackson, Oliver P.
Kobbe, Wm. A., Jr. (June 5).
Lacombe, E. Henry.
Lawrence, Emlin N. (May 31).
Leggett, Francis W.
Livingston, Chas. (June 6).
Morris, James S. (June 6).
Morris, Stuyvesant F. (June 1).
Morse, N. B., Jr.
Milhall, Rene V.
Macy, Charles A., Jr.
McAllister, John.
Mortimer, Clarence A.
Moss, Nathan F.
Miller, George N.
Osborn, Charles H.
Pierson, Henry L., Jr.
Schenck, Charles S.
Schieffelin, Wm. H.
Scott, David J.
*Slosson, William.
Stewart, Albert P.
Tanitor, Frank L.
Taylor, James B.
Thorne, Jonathan.
*Tucker, John A.
Valentine, Albert E.
Van Cortlandt, Aug. (June 6).
Van Winkle, Edgar B. (June 3).
Welles, Ed. B.
White, John C.
Wotherspoon, Henry H.

The circumstances of muster-in just noted, and more especially the fact that the regiment had been forced to do duty at Baltimore instead of at the front, greatly increased the absenteeism, and the consequent difficulty of granting furloughs, even when the latter were really needed. The difficulties of maintaining the regiment effective were very great, and required much tact on the one hand and decision on the other. On the 4th of June, in reply to Colonel Lefferts's inquiries, Adjutant-General Hillhouse wrote, that, the muster not having yet been made, " there is no way of enforcing the attendance of absent officers." Two days after the Seventh took possession of Federal Hill, the War Department, in General Order No. 65, declared that "furloughs will not be granted by captains of companies or colonels of regiments on any pretext whatever. A furlough from such authority will not relieve a soldier from the charge of desertion." Colonel Lefferts at once reminded the Secretary of War of the peculiar circumstances under which the regiment had come on, as expressed in General Hillhouse's letter, and asked for the exercise of discretionary power. The Secretary promptly replied, in a letter to General Wool, making the case of the Seventh Regiment a special exception to the order just quoted. Mr. Stanton's letter closed as follows: "Colonel Lefferts will therefore be permitted to grant reasonable furloughs, with that discretion which he will be careful to exercise." This privilege was a great advantage gained to the regiment, and one for which they were very grateful.

The next step in the furlough matter was a notification, on the 3d of July, from Brigadier-General Morris, then commanding the forts, that "furloughs to enlisted men can be granted only in cases of extreme necessity, such as serious illness in the family, the evidence of which must accompany the applications." Finally, the War Department, in a fit of desperation over the absenteeism prevalent throughout the army, "revoked and absolutely annulled all furloughs by whomsoever given, unless by the War Department," and ordered all officers and men "capable of service" to forthwith join their regiments.*

Garrison life at Federal Hill was not vastly different (save for artillery drill) from camp life at Camp Cameron,

* General Orders No. 92 and No. 102. The Ninth Company of the Seventh Regiment expelled one of its members, on the 16th of June, for having failed to report on the expiration of his furlough, and to give reasons satisfactory for not reporting. This action was read at evening parade.

described earlier in this volume. What its general duties were may be learned from Standing Order No. 1, which still remained in force after the departure from Camp Wool, except that "inspection of quarters" was changed to five o'clock, P. M., and evening parade to six, P. M. It was a gay and pleasant life, with enough duty and service to make it enjoyable from reveille to tattoo. The morning gun at sunrise, followed by the rattlings of the reveille, startles every man from his bunk, or from his blanket spread under the trees or on the verandah. Roll-call and the morning's wash at the hydrant follow. Then comes a cup of coffee, by way of stimulus to the long company drill, which is terminated only by breakfast. This meal is attacked, after such an appetizer, with vigor, especially as the government rations have been eked out with milk, eggs, fruits, and vegetables bought from hucksters. Guard-mounting and company or battalion drill fill up the morning till dinner. Between that time and the inspection and parade of the evening there is time for leisure and camp sports, and for furloughs to visit the city or the other forts. The delicious hours of evening are passed first on the parapet, and then in front of company quarters, by officers and men in pleasant converse. Tattoo at ten breaks up these gatherings, and half an hour later come taps, when lights go out, and the day is done.

A few days after taking possession of the fort, Colonel Lefferts issued the following: —

### STANDING ORDER NO. 2.

Sentinels will not allow any one connected with the regiment to enter or leave the Fort, excepting officers, or such as may have a written pass.

The countersign will not be given to the Guard until Tattoo, after which time they will challenge all who approach.

Only officers are allowed the countersign; and when a soldier demands admittance to the Fort, upon giving the countersign he must be arrested and confined in the Guard-House.

Sentinels will not take orders, nor allow themselves to be relieved except by an officer or non-commissioned officer of the Guard, the Officer of the Day, or the Commanding Officer.

Sentinels will report every breach of orders or regulations which they are instructed to enforce. They must not quit their posts without being regularly relieved.

None but colored servants will be allowed to pass in and out at the rear sally port, except upon order of the officer of the Guard, who will, in such case, cause the order or the reasons for it to be registered in the Guard-Book.

The sally port will be closed at Retreat, and must not be opened again, under any pretext whatever, until eight o'clock, A. M, each day.

The Fort is not open to general visitors, but the friends and relatives of members of the regiment may be admitted. All such persons, however, must leave before twilight.

No one will be allowed on the parapet except the sentinels, Officer of the Guard, or such persons as may have official business there.

All persons arrested (officers excepted) must be *detained in the Guard-House* until guard-mounting, at which time they will be brought before the Commanding Officer. Soldiers who are late on passes, if not exceeding half an hour, may be allowed to go to their quarters on parole until guard-mounting.

At the suggestion of Surgeon Rogers, it was also made a standing order for the sentinel at the hospital post to permit no officer or non-commissioned officer (except the attendants) to enter or leave the hospital without a pass.

The battalion and company drills, which were rigid and thorough, were held in the fort, in the street, in the adjacent parade-ground, or in the open fields near Fort McHenry. The variety of *terrain* helped give the regiment the remarkable facility and proficiency in manœuvre which it acquired at Baltimore. The inspection of quarters, with the band playing, was always a soldierly and creditable performance ; but the most brilliant and attractive exercise was the evening dress-parade, held in the fort or the adjacent street, and usually followed by a drill in the manual of arms or battalion manœuvres. The number of visitors was always very large. Reviews were frequent. Artillery drill, with the heavy ordnance, was established by order of General Morris, and formed part of the day's duties. Police duty was performed with praiseworthy fidelity in all its details. Manning the fire-engine ought certainly to be introduced under the head of the sports, rather than the tasks, of garrison life, especially as no fires occurred during the Seventh's campaign. The guard duty was carefully attended to, as the importance of the station demanded.

"The guard," says one account, "is mounted with great care, and strictly according to regulation, so the soldier quietly submits to another inspection, stands steadily and composedly in the ranks while the band beats off, witnesses the wonderful evolutions of Drum-Major Graham, glances at the soldier critics who have for him no word or look of sympathy or pity, and is finally marched in review to the guard-house. If, on the first relief, he is immediately marched by the corporal to his post, and for the next twenty-four hours loses his name and personal identity, and is only known as No. 11, 17, or 24, he is fortunate if he escapes the dull posts at the magazines, or the horrors of the rear sally port, and secures a desirable position at the entrance or upon the parapet. The sentry upon the parapet has a fine field for observation and meditation. As he marches back and forth within his prescribed limits, he gazes philosophically upon the amphitheatre of house-tops, upon the beautiful river and bay, dotted with sails and alive with the pursuits of commerce, upon the green hills, or the blue waters of the Chesapeake in the distance, and it is not long before every object within his range of vision is as familiar as the scenes of home or childhood. Should the heat of the day or the brilliancy of the Southern sun be uncommonly oppressive, his movements become slow, listless, and languid, and he prays for his two hours to expire, and for the welcome relief. Rain sometimes visits the sentry upon his post, in which case he is seen, clad in rubber garments, facing the pitiless storm with arms secured, trudging through mud and water, an abject specimen of miserable humanity. Night shuts out the beautiful prospect, and brings silence and repose to the surrounding world, but no rest to the sentry. Through the long and dreary hours of the night his duty continues, and as there is nothing to divert the eye, he paces slowly up and down, rapt in meditation, dreaming of home, or friends, or of the bright events of the past, scanning leisurely the stirring events of the present, or conjuring up golden visions of the future. If it chance to be moonlight, then the guard duty at night is more pleasant than by day, for the scene is so brilliant in its calm repose, that many a soldier of artistic eye and poetic mind forgets his sleep, and enjoys its beauties with the sentry. Yet morning light and sunshine are always welcome, for they restore the garrison to life and activity, and announce the approaching end of the day's guard duty. When not upon post duty, the sentry must be at the guard-house, where he lounges through his few hours of leisure, ready at any moment at the cry, 'Turn out the guard!' to seize his musket, take his place in line, and salute the commandant of the post, the officer of the day, or any military visitor entitled to the honor. Nor is there any peace for the sentry, at the guard-house, at night. He must turn out to receive the 'grand rounds,' and if, by chance, he sleeps the corporal of the guard, in search of the members of his relief, wakes him every two hours by a sharp punch of the foot, by rolling him over, or by thrusting a lantern in his face." *

These routine duties, and a large class of special duties in detached service, which we shall next proceed to record, kept the regiment well occupied; and as there were few men to spare, no shirking or pretence of sickness was allowed by Surgeon Rogers. Work, drills, good rations, cleanliness, and abundance of high and pure air, kept the regiment in admirable health throughout the campaign.

On occupying Federal Hill, the Seventh Regiment found, that, in obedience to the orders of General Dix, repairs were making in its slopes, &c., by direction of Lieutenant-Colonel H. Brewerton, United States Corps of Engineers, under the immediate supervision of Assistant-Engineer N. H. Hutton. The Seventh arrived at a happy moment, since it had just previously been determined to use civilian laborers in place of enlisted men, as hitherto, in making these repairs, — anything but pleasant exercise in midsummer. Daily, therefore, Mr. Parkinson, the foreman, with a gang of laborers, entered the fort and ascended the ramparts to do this work, and, agreeably to request from Colonel Brewerton, was afforded "every facility of men and material for the repairs."

* History of Second Company.

On the 23d of June, Brevet Brigadier-General W. W. Morris, U. S. A., was placed by General Wool in command of all the forts in Baltimore and its vicinity, with directions to make an immediate inspection of them, to see that the guns, platform, and carriages were properly positioned and in working order. It was also ordered that "he will, as far as practicable, cause the garrisons to be instructed in the manual and manœuvres of the guns, and see that the magazines are properly supplied with ammunition." General Morris accordingly called upon Colonel Lefferts for an immediate report of the defensive condition of the post, and, after minutely inspecting the pieces mounted, to report the amount of repairs, if any, that may be necessary to make them fit for immediate use." A subsequent order called for reports of "how many days' fuel and forage you now have on hand at your post. What supply of water, for drinking and cooking purposes, have you within the works of your post? Also, what are the means of transportation at your post, namely, horses, wagons, boats, &c.?" Still another for information, "as soon as practicable, of the number of fire-engines, complete (and if the fixtures of the water-works at the post are adapted to the use of fire-engines), axes, pickaxes, shovels, spades, now at your post." And, in the course of his replies to these and many other inquiries showing an anxiety to put the fort into condition for an emergency, Colonel Lefferts said: —

"I would respectfully state that *three* of the eight-inch Columbiads require remounting, in consequence of the sinking of the parapets.

"A party of laborers, under a foreman, sent by the Engineer Department, is at work upon the fort, increasing the thickness of some of the parapets, and keeping the whole in order.

"I mentioned yesterday, that there are long galleries, or tunnels, running under the works. They are quite extensive; one on the north side passes under the barracks, and within twenty feet of the magazine; one running from the east side also passes under the barracks."

It should be noted, that, when the Seventh entered the

fort, it was discovered, that, ever since General Butler's entrance into it in 1861, it had been undermined, and people had been taking sand out from the hill. As to the remounting of the Columbiads, work was begun on them on the 7th of July, thirty men being detailed to mount and remount them, agreeably to the following order from head-quarters: —

"COLONEL, — The Brigadier-General Commanding having received a communication from the Engineer Office, stating that work would be commenced on the Columbiads platformed on the 3d inst., and asking for assistance, directs that thirty (30) men of your command be detailed and placed under the orders of the Assistant-Engineer, and in his absence under Ordnance-Sergeant Isaacs, who will receive instructions from the Assistant-Engineer."

This detail was chosen from the various companies, and, besides the work indicated, cleaned the guns, repaired the carriages, put the whole into working order, and arranged and distributed ammunition from the magazines. This work was performed under the superintendence of Ordnance-Sergeant Isaacs, who took his instructions from Assistant-Engineer Hutton.

The importance of Fort Federal Hill at this juncture was manifest by the strictness of the orders for its guidance. No sand or other material was suffered to be removed from the hill. Hucksters, laundresses, and camp followers in general, were excluded from the fort, unless they had proper vouchers for loyalty and good character. The troops were kept constantly supplied with forty rounds of ammunition and extra caps, and their pieces habitually loaded, in accordance with the following order from head-quarters: —

"I. The arms of the troops in garrison, at Forts Federal Hill and Marshall will be kept loaded habitually.

"II. Commanding officers of companies will see that their men are furnished with forty rounds of ball cartridges each, with extra caps in their pouches.

"III. Officers of the guard will be held responsible that the piece of every sentinel posted is in perfect firing order. The pieces will not be capped until it is necessary to fire."

The Columbiads and howitzers were also kept loaded with shot and shell; and Colonel Lefferts was particularly enjoined to have hand grenades ready, "with reference to the surrounding blocks of houses," in the following order: —

HEAD-QUARTERS, FORT MCHENRY, June 30, 1862.

COLONEL, — The Brigadier-General Commanding directs that the Columbiads and sea-coast howitzers at Fort Federal Hill be loaded with shell, the flank casemate twenty-four-pounder howitzers being loaded with grape-shot. This to continue until further orders.

The General leaves it to your discretion to keep any of the other pieces in your bastions loaded, and would recall to your mind his conversation with you concerning the importance of "hand grenades," in the peculiar position of your fort, with reference to the surrounding blocks of houses. The General takes it for granted that the muskets of your men are kept loaded, and in firing condition, at all times.

Very respectfully, your obedient servant,

AL. J. S. MOLINARD, *Capt. 2d Arty., A. A. A. G.*

While such were the daily duties within the fort, there were plenty of daily details for detached service without. One company was always on duty as before at Mount Clare Station, and the lightness of the task made it a coveted one, especially as there was more opportunity for passes and furloughs, with Baltimore and its beautiful environs for attractions, or a stroll to the old Carroll House (relic of Colonial grandeur turned to a tavern), or a bath in Spring Garden Creek. A guard of twelve men was always stationed at the storehouse of Brigade-Surgeon C. C. Cox, the medical purveyor of the department, on the corner of Eutaw and Conway Streets, for the protection of the public property at that depot. A guard of a sergeant, a corporal, and eight privates, was always on duty at the office of Quartermaster James Belger, having relieved the similar guard of the Third New York.

Guards, too, were constantly detailed on special detached service. Prisoners of war, arriving in the city in considerable bodies, were committed to the care of such details, and transported by boat to Fort Delaware, Fort Monroe, and other military prisons. The routine in such cases was commonly for a company, marching simply with drum and fife, to guard the prisoners from the city jail to the boat; a detachment of an officer and ten men usually transferred them from that point, being provided with one or two days' rations, as the case might require. The officer in command was furnished with a list of his prisoners, which he turned over to the commanding officer of the prison, taking a receipt therefor. Sometimes, in the march through Baltimore, it was the prisoners who got the demonstrations of sympathy, and the guard the demonstrations of hatred. These trips to Philadelphia and Fort Monroe were greatly coveted, as indeed was all special duty promising a little excitement. Guards, again, were detailed to accompany detachments of recruits, exchanged prisoners, convalescents, or deserters, to Harrison's Landing, Washington, and other points for delivery to the Army of the Potomac or the Army of Virginia. The order, in such cases, might be something like the following specimen: —

HEAD-QUARTERS MIDDLE DEPARTMENT,
BALTIMORE, MD., July 1, 1862.

COLONEL MARSHALL LEFFERTS, — You are hereby respectfully requested to detail one company of your command to report at the Baltimore City Jail, at one o'clock, P. M., of this day, for the purpose of escorting, as a guard, sixty-five prisoners of war to the boat at the corner of Pratt and Light Streets, for Fort Delaware One officer and ten men to proceed with said prisoners to Fort Delaware, and they to be delivered there to Captain A. A. Gibson, commanding at that post, and his receipt taken therefor. The residue of the escort may return to your quarters so soon as the prisoners are placed on board of the boat.

By command of Major-General Jno. E. Wool,
H. Z. HAYNES, *Major and A. D. C.*

(INDORSEMENT)

Received, Fort Delaware, Delaware, July 2, 1862, of Lieutenant Palmer, New York Militia, sixty-four prisoners of war.

A. A. GIBSON, *Captain Second Artillery, Commanding.*

Large details were often sent to remove the sick and wounded coming by steamer from Virginia or the hospitals. For example, three commissioned officers and seventy-five men removed the wounded from the Louisiana, July 21, and three officers and fifty men those of the Knickerbocker, July 25, reporting to Brigade-Surgeon C. M. Jones, Medical Director. The "History of the Second Company" says: "This unpleasant duty was performed with a care, kindness, and gentleness so remarkable, that it was noticed in general orders, and received the most flattering commendation from the surgeons."

Funeral escorts were furnished for a time to soldiers buried from the Camden Street General Hospital. A sad duty of this nature was that which a detachment had to perform in the escort of the remains of Lieutenant Baker, of Colonel Lefferts's staff, who died suddenly, on the 12th of June, of heart-disease. An escort was given to the remains of a member of the Sixty-Ninth Regiment of New York State Militia, then encamped at Cloud's Mills, Virginia, for which service hearty thanks were returned by his comrades in this Preamble and Resolution: —

"*Whereas,* Colonel Marshall Lefferts, of the Seventh Regiment New York State Militia, ordered and directed that said deceased should have a soldier's funeral, and paid the last tribute of respect, which, on account of the urgency of orders, we were prevented from doing; therefore

"*Resolved,* That Colonel Lefferts and the officers and men of his command are entitled to the lasting gratitude of the officers and members of not only this company but of the entire regiment; that while we, from the bottom of our hearts, deplore the loss of so brave a man as the deceased, the sorrow with which we are filled is alleviated by the prompt and noble impulse which sprung so spontaneously from the courageous bosoms of the Seventh; and that we tender to them our thanks, while we hope that not a soldier of them shall in like circumstances fail to receive similar honors."

At the funeral of Ex-President Van Buren (August 4, 1862), in obedience to orders from the War Department, a salute of thirteen guns was fired at dawn of day, and afterwards a single gun at intervals of thirty minutes between rising and setting sun, and at sundown thirty-four guns. The troops were paraded at 10 A. M., and the Department's order was read to them. The national flag was displayed at half-mast, officers wore crape on the left arm and on their swords, and the regimental colors were put in mourning for the rest of the campaign.

Besides these regular and frequent duties, there were many casual services to be performed, of which, in avoiding a laborious enumeration, one specimen may be given in the following order, sent June 24th from head-quarters to Colonel Lefferts, and acted upon instantly upon his reception, Company B furnishing the detail: —

COLONEL, — As some prisoners were being marched through the city to the jail this morning, a demonstration to rescue them was made from the house on Liberty Street, third door from Lexington.

Please send a guard of one N. C. Officer and twelve men to guard the premises until such time as the police can arrest the parties. There is a soldier of the Thirty-Seventh Massachusetts guarding the place.

By direction of Major-General Wool,

WM. D. WHIPPLE, *A. A. G.*

P. S. Please inform General Morris when you see him. There is not time to send the order through him. W. D. W.

There were details of officers for detached service. Lieutenant Murray, of Company C, temporarily acted as Acting Assistant Adjutant-General, or Post Adjutant, at Fort McHenry, and Assistant-Surgeon Rogers was assigned to duty at the same point. Captain Meday and Lieutenants Palmer and Jaudon were appointed by Department orders as a board "to examine a quantity of beef issued to the Seventh Regiment N. Y. S. M., and reported unfit for issue." Even the services of the band were called into requisition, on several occasions, for civic and patriotic purposes, by the people of Baltimore. One of these occasions, for example, was a flag-raising by the citizens of the Twelfth Ward in honor of the First Maryland Regiment, at the corner of Eutaw and Preston Streets, and another was the celebration of the Fourth of July under the auspices of the Union League Association. And, in addition to the band, a guard of the regiment was sometimes required. The Colonel of the Seventh himself was appointed by General Wool to inspect all the volunteers of the various States encamped at Martinsburgh, Williamsport, Hagerstown, and Frederick, besides the New York Volunteers at Harper's Ferry, with orders to make at each place "a rigid inspection of the troops, having reference to the appearance of the men, their clothing, arms, and equipments, and of the ammunition, including the number of cartridges in the possession of each man and also in store with the regiment, the tents and camp equipage, and the general police of the regiments, and whether the men are properly cared for and properly instructed in their drill." The following were his orders and instructions: —

Colonel Marshall Lefferts, of the Seventh Regiment New York State Militia is appointed to inspect the troops at Martinsburgh, Williamsport, Hagerstown, and Frederick. He will proceed to-morrow in this duty as far as Martinsburgh. After a rigid inspection of the troops of this command, having reference to the appearance of the men, their clothing, arms, and equipments, and of the ammunition, including the number of cartridges in the possession of each man, and also in store with the regiment, he will inspect the tents and camp equipage, and the general police of the regiment, and whether the men are properly cared for and properly instructed in their duties.

After performing the services above required, he will proceed to Williamsport, Frederick, and Hagerstown, and perform at each place similar services as required at Martinsburgh.

On returning, he will call at Harper's Ferry and report to Colonel Miles. After which he will inspect the several New York regiments of infantry at that post, where his inspections will be similar to those above required.

JOHN E. WOOL, *Major-General.*

HEAD-QUARTERS MIDDLE DEPARTMENT,
BALTIMORE, MD., August 7, 1862.

COLONEL, — In your inspections you will require a return of the troops you may inspect, and ascertain those present, sick, detailed, and on extra duty, and absent, the whole number of each regiment and company.

JOHN E. WOOL, *Major-General.*

COLONEL LEFFERTS, *Commanding Seventh Regiment.*

BALTIMORE, August 7, 1862.

COLONEL, — The bearer will hand you this note. He will be able to give you some important information. If you can aid him, you will make use of the company at Frederick, or any troops which may come under your inspection.

Very truly yours,

JOHN E. WOOL, *Major-General.*

TO COLONEL LEFFERTS, *Seventh Regiment, Frederick.*

This duty was performed, and an elaborate report of the condition of the various forces of the three armies, with suggestions of changes, was made by Colonel Lefferts to General Wool.

In fine, with such a multiplicity of duties and details, added to the necessities of granting furloughs to men who claimed them on grounds strongly appealing to justice and sympathy, and with the fact that the regiment was still further depleted, as during its first campaign, by members discharged to accept commissions in the volunteer army, it will be seen that its three months' campaign in Baltimore was a busy as well as a useful one, and to be remembered with pride and pleasure in its annals. "Detachments," says the "History of the Second Company," "were sent into the surrounding country to arrest notorious Secessionists, and one famous expedition was despatched to surprise a Rebel camp and capture their vessel, but failed to find the mythical conspirators or their phantom 'pungay.' . . . . On the 26th of June, a squad, under Sergeant Quilliard, was sent to take charge of a house from which a secession flag had been displayed, and to arrest its inmates."

There were also, of course, the customary inspections

and reviews, by Generals Wool and Morris, and many informal receptions of civil and military visitors, particularly of officers passing through Baltimore. General Burnside, returning from North Carolina to join the Army of the Potomac, and Colonel Corcoran, returning from his prison in Richmond, were received with the heartiest enthusiasm. After reviewing the regiment, the latter "addressed it with an earnestness and eloquence that electrified his hearers." As usual in the United States service, the fourth day of July was celebrated to order, with a national salute of thirty-four guns at meridian, fired by squads from the various companies, the rest of the regiment parading during the firing. The remainder of the day was devoted to amusement, and the regimental band helped dignify the somewhat primitive display of fireworks near the fort. However, General Morris took the precaution to order that "the bastions of the fort should not be used for any display of fireworks, as proposed by the Common Council." The news of the result of the Peninsular campaign had caused fears of an *émeute* in Baltimore during the day; all passes to the city were interdicted positively by orders from head-quarters, and the regiment was ordered to be ready within the fort, to march, at short notice, to any part of the city.

Camp sports, as in the campaign of 1861, were greatly resorted to, to offset camp duties; and aquatic sports, especially swimming, were of course favorites. The weather was exceedingly fine throughout the campaign, though sometimes very warm; but a gracious "General Order No. 5," from General Morris's head-quarters, on July 7th, formally declared that "until further orders the troops of this command will be allowed to wear 'straw hats' when not on dress duty, said hats to be procured at the expense of the officers and men of the command. Uniformity in shape and size will be observed in procuring said hats." For the rest, according to the "History of the Second Company," "pure air, cool breezes, refreshing showers, bright sunshine by day and charming moonlight by night, combined to make life pleasant, and to preserve the health and good spirits of the men. . . . . During the fine warm weather, swimming was a favorite amusement. The more expert and adventurous preferred the Patapsco, and from the docks or vessels plunged into its deep waters; others, less confident in their skill, sought the pure waters and sloping beach, and the shade and greensward of the more distant Spring Garden. The visits to Spring Garden were often extended beyond the Long Bridge to Ferry Bar, where lovers of aquatic sports could row or sail, and end the amusements of the afternoon with a splendid dinner upon fish, soft crabs, boiled chickens, and fresh fruit and vegetables, served in the best style of domestic and seaside cookery. Not a few patronized the bathing-accommodations within the fort; and in the evening, and at a late hour of the night, large numbers might be seen gathered around the hydrant, sporting in the large bathing-tub, or refreshing themselves with artificial showers from the inexhaustible fountain. The members of the Seventh Regiment will not soon forget the portly figure of Mrs. Robinson, the sutler of the post, and long may they continue to sympathize with her henpecked husband. The renowned Schillenger at length reigned in her stead." The same authority informs us touching the police or fatigue duty, of which the Seventh made something of a specialty: —

"From each company was detailed daily a sufficient number of men, in charge of a corporal, whose duty it was to sweep the quarters, keep them neat and clean, and collect and dispose of all the papers and rubbish that chanced to accumulate. It was a menial service, yet all in turn performed it; and, armed with broom, sprinkler, shovel, and wheelbarrow, the police squad was marshalled at least twice a day for this necessary duty. Its members endured patiently and cheerfully the bad jokes which were perpetuated at their expense, with the self-satisfying thought that others must endure the same to-morrow; and it was not uncommon for them to make their unpleasant duties a source of fun and amusement. The corporal of the police, if witty (as corporals often are), marshalled his men with all the pomp and ceremony of a military parade, drilled them in marching and in the manual of arms, addressed them upon the vast importance of their duties, and appealed to them as brave and patriotic soldiers to act well their part." A very fine theatrical company was also organized in the regiment, and gave successful performances.

As specimens of some of the other duties, beyond the limits of the fort, already spoken of, I take at random a few from very many official orders and documents of this date: —

FORT FEDERAL HILL, BALTIMORE, August 13, 1862.

LIEUTENANT-COLONEL WHIPPLE, *Assistant Adjutant-General.*

SIR, — In compliance with Special Orders No. 58, dated Head-quarters Eighth Army Corps, Baltimore, 9th August, 1862, I received from the Union Relief Rooms a detachment of enlisted men (fifty-eight in number) belonging to different regiments, and accompanied by my detail of fifteen men, as required by said order, proceeded to Harrison's Landing, and turned over the detachment of fifty-eight men to the Provost-Marshal-General, whose receipt is herewith enclosed. Which duty having been performed, I returned with my detail to this city, arriving this morning.

Very respectfully,

WM. H. RIBLET,

*Captain Company D, Seventh Regiment N. Y. N. G.*

HEAD-QUARTERS EIGHTH ARMY CORPS,
BALTIMORE, MD., August 24, 1862.

Colonel Marshall Lefferts, commanding the Seventh Regiment New York State Militia, will detail a non-commissioned officer and five men from his command to take charge of and conduct to Washington a detachment of convalescents now in the Camden Street Hospital, and in condition to be sent to their regiments. The non-commissioned officer in charge will ascertain whether the men belong to General McClellan's army or the Army of Virginia, before leaving, and upon his arrival in Washington will turn them over with the accompanying list to Brigadier-

General Wadsworth, commanding military district of Washington; having completed which duty, he will return to this city with his party. Colonel James Belger, A. D. C. and Quartermaster, will furnish the necessary transportation.

By command of Major-General Wool,

WM. D. WHIPPLE, *A. A. General.*

(INDORSEMENT.)

Captain Haws, of Company C, will cause the detail required by the written order to be made, and the instructions to be carried out.

M. LEFFERTS, *Colonel Commanding.*

To this summary of the duties and pastimes of the three months' garrison duty at Fort Federal Hill, it only remains to add a word regarding the regiment's return, and some events that preceded it. The result of the Peninsular campaign being such as to displease the military authorities at Washington, a change in command was made in Virginia and at Washington; and on the 22d of July the War Department issued a General Order confirming the designation of General Porter's corps as the Fifth Army Corps, and that of General Franklin as the Sixth, and constituting the forces of General Dix the Seventh, "those under Major-General Wool the Eighth," and those of General Burnside as the Ninth Army Corps, respectively. It was in this way that the Seventh Regiment became a part of the Eighth Army Corps. The losses of the army on the Peninsula, and the threatening aspect of the war, induced the President, on the 4th of August, 1862, to call three hundred thousand militia into the service of the United States, to serve for nine months, unless sooner discharged. So promptly was this call answered, that, when the time came for the three months' regiments to be mustered out, they were discharged, without any movement to retain them.

The Seventh, however, remained three days longer, at the special request of General Wool, who was unwilling that so important a post should be left by them until well provided for. Pursuant to the orders of the War Office, the regiments in the Eighth Corps were mustered on the morning of the 18th of August; on the 21st, an intimation that the service was drawing to a close came in Special Order No. 70, from the head-quarters of the Eighth Army Corps, directing "the commanders of all regiments enrolled for three months, serving in this army corps, and whose term of service has nearly expired," to "cause the necessary muster and pay rolls to be made out and forwarded." On the 24th, an order from General Wool instructed all the New York three months' regiments in his command to hold themselves in readiness to return to that city, "preparatory to their being mustered out of the service of the United States."

It so happened that the term of the Seventh expired that day, — the 24th. But at the special request of General Wool it remained in service, at his pleasure, till such time as it could be discharged without detriment to the needs of the Department. Accordingly, General Wool sent to Governor Morgan the following letter, in his own hand, which will best explain, in a few words, the importance of the position which the Seventh had occupied, the opinion entertained of its value as a regiment by the distinguished Corps Commander, and its conduct in volunteering to serve beyond its time: —

HEAD-QUARTERS EIGHTH ARMY CORPS,
BALTIMORE, August 24, 1862.

HIS EXCELLENCY E. D. MORGAN, *Albany*.

The Seventh Regiment New York State Militia will leave this Department on Thursday, the 28th, for New York, to be mustered out of service. Can you not send me a first-rate regiment to take its place in the fort on Federal Hill? It is an important position for the defence of Baltimore. The Seventh remains three days over its time of service at my request. Please answer.

JOHN E. WOOL, *Major-General.*

It is seen that now, as in 1861, the Seventh, after mustering in voluntarily for a longer time than they had agreed, willingly extended that longer time by three days, for the good of the service.

On the 26th, Colonel Lefferts received a notification from corps head-quarters that "the Major-General Commanding proposes to review your regiment to-morrow evening at five or half past five o'clock." This review took place in the presence of about three thousand persons, many of whom were distinguished officials, civil and military, and ladies; and, what with the salutes, the review, the elaborate battalion drill, the parade, the exceedingly complimentary comments of General Wool, and the pleasant entertainment given by the Colonel to the General and his staff, the occasion was made very enjoyable. The Press despatch, in describing this affair, says: —

"About five o'clock the visitors commenced arriving, and were courteously received by the officer of the day. They occupied seats in the balcony and along the porches of the barracks opening upon the parade. The companies, nine in number (the Tenth being necessarily absent), formed in line, and, soon after the colors were saluted, the rolling drum, the turn-out of the guard, and the discharge of cannon, announced the arrival of the General. A detachment of gunners manned the batteries and fired a salute of thirteen guns in honor of the head of the Department. At the same time the visitors, as well as the military, who were 'at rest' greeted the General with hearty cheers.

"The column, after going through the manual of arms, passed out of the work, and for an hour was drilled on Warren Street. All the movements (some by trumpet call) were most admirably executed, and were applauded by the visitors. After the review was over, General Wool addressed Colonel Lefferts, and spoke in the most commendable terms of the appearance and discipline of the men. He said that for many years he had been called upon to review columns some consisting of twenty thousand men, but he never saw a regiment which executed the various movements with so much regularity, and accompanied with so much animation and spirit. After the dismissal of the parade, the General and staff were entertained by Colonel Lefferts in the main building, during which time many pleasant things were said. The Colonel states that during their sojourn of three months in Baltimore they have made many friends, that not a single unpleasant circumstance has occurred, and that they will cherish many welcome reminiscences during their occupancy of the fort. It is also gratifying to state that the men leave in good health, only four of the entire command (about eight hundred in number) being reported unable to discharge duty."

On the 27th the order for relieving the Seventh was issued, the same day was rescinded, and on the day following was renewed. On the afternoon of Thursday the 28th of August, a New York regiment, one thousand strong, marched into the fort and relieved the Seventh, which was then about eight hundred strong. This regiment was commanded by the accomplished gentleman and devoted patriot, Colonel Peter Augustus Porter, who fell at Cold Harbor. It was the One Hundred and Twenty-Ninth New York, — a fine body of troops, who served no less than twenty months in the defences of Baltimore, on succeeding the Fifth and the Seventh New York, and then, under the name of the Eighth New York Heavy Artillery, over two thousand strong, rendered excellent service in Grant's Virginia campaign. Before evening the Seventh bade good by to Federal Hill, and was on its way, via Harrisburg, to Easton, Pennsylvania, which place was reached at 5 A. M. At noon of the 29th, after a twenty-four hours' journey, it reached New York, and was received, as before, with overwhelming enthusiasm by thousands of people assembled on the line of march from the pier to the armory. Their neat appearance, steady and soldierly march, and sunburnt faces, gave evidence of the work they had been doing, and the applause of the spectators was hearty and unrestrained. On the 5th of September the regiment was mustered out of the United States service by Captain Mott, after a term of one hundred and two days. On the 16th its members received pay for a service of three months and ten days.

It happened, that, during the last days of August, the country was again in excitement over the threatening movements of the enemy; and the National War Committee, meeting on the 2d of September in the Chamber of Commerce rooms, New York, earnestly urged the War Bureau to "recall the militia regiments from this city which have recently returned"; adding, "We believe they will go at a moment's notice." General Halleck curtly answered: "The New York militia regiments were requested to remain when the danger was more imminent than at present, but declined to do so. Under these circumstances they will not be recalled." A statement so utterly unfounded in fact, so unjust, and so ungrateful, brought out a sharp reply from Colonel Lefferts, published in the various newspapers of New York, and similar remonstrances from Lieutenant-Colonel Aspinwall of the Twenty-Second, Colonel Varian of the Eighth, and various officers of the Thirty-Seventh, Sixty-Ninth, Seventy-First, and the other regiments which had returned. These officers showed that their men would have gladly stayed, had their services been required, and some of them, like the Seventh, did stay several days beyond their term; but no such request as that alleged by General Halleck was ever made. The following was the letter from Colonel Lefferts, vindicating his regiment: —

"A telegraphic correspondence between the National War Committee and Major-General Halleck, published this morning, charges the regiments of the New York State Militia with refusing to remain in the field when asked to do so. General Halleck goes further, and states that the danger was then 'imminent, and, as they then refused, they will not now be recalled.'

"I feel that justice to the soldiers of my command requires that I should publicly deny the statement in so far as it relates to my regiment. The others will answer for themselves. I entertain a high regard and personal respect for the Commander-in-Chief, and feel that some blunder has been committed, causing him, perhaps quite innocently, to state what was not true, and what was ungenerous and unkind to those who have endeavored to do their duty. Many a soldier's honor will smart under the charge that they refused to remain when asked to do so, at a time when there was danger; and I most distinctly state that no such request was made, directly or indirectly, of me or of my regiment. Had it been made, I have no doubt it would have been promptly and willingly met. On two occasions when a dark cloud was hanging over our fair institutions, and the government called for troops, the Seventh Regiment marched at once, without regard to personal sacrifice, at the call. Let it be borne in mind that in both cases the service on the part of the regiment was voluntary, and it would not be likely to refuse its services under the circumstances stated. It will be seen from the following that the regiment was in no hurry to leave: —

EIGHTH ARMY CORPS, HEAD-QUARTERS MIDDLE DEPARTMENT,
BALTIMORE, August 24, 1862.

HIS EXCELLENCY E. D. MORGAN, *Albany*.

The Seventh Regiment, New York State Militia, will leave this on Thursday, 28th, for New York, to be mustered out of the service. Can you not send me a first-rate regiment to take its place in the fort on Federal Hill? It is an important position for the defence of Baltimore. The Seventh remains three days over its term of service, at my request.

JOHN E. WOOL, *Major-General.*

SPECIAL ORDERS No. 76.

HEAD-QUARTERS, MIDDLE DEPARTMENT,
BALTIMORE, August 27, 1862.

The Seventh Regiment, New York State Militia, will be relieved from duty in this department to-morrow morning, and, under the command of Colonel Lefferts, will proceed to the city of New York, when it will be mustered out of the service of the United States.

Colonel Porter, One Hundred and Twenty-Ninth Regiment New York Volunteers, now at Camp Belger, will march into and occupy Fort Federal Hill as the Seventh Regiment march out.

By command of Major-General Wool,
W. D. WHIPPLE, *Assistant Adjutant-General.*

I will now take occasion to state, that, when the regiment left for Washington, in May last, a letter from the Adjutant-General to the Honorable Secretary of War informed him that our term of service was only for thirty days. I saw Mr. Stanton before the thirty days were up, and he represented to me that the government was desirous that the regiment should be mustered into service for three months, giving his reasons for the request. I returned to Baltimore and represented to the members of the regiment what the Secretary had requested, and they immediately and without hesitation voted to remain three months. I appeal to those who have charge of the destiny of our country, whether this is the best way to secure soldiers or unite indissolubly the varied interests of our people.

MARSHALL LEFFERTS,
*Colonel Commanding Seventh Regiment.*

NEW YORK, September 4, 1862.

These remonstrances being brought to the notice of General Halleck, that officer sent an acknowledgment of the "error" into which he had fallen. "I now learn," he wrote on the 8th to Mr. W. H. Aspinwall, "that an order had been previously issued, without the knowledge of the Secretary of War or of myself, to send these troops back to New York at the end of their enlistment. When I telegraphed the New York committee, I supposed the regiments had, while here, declined to remain, but on their arrival in New York had offered to return. In this I was in error, and my telegram was calculated to do them injustice. Please explain this to them. H. W. HALLECK, General-in-Chief."

But though it did not return to the front, the service of the Seventh was not yet finished. A few days after the return, the Spinola Brigade, then recruiting for the war, broke out into a mutiny at its camp at East New York,—a mutiny partly due to the incompetency of many of its officers and the want of discipline among its men, but more immediately to the non-payment of a promised bounty. Drunk and disorderly, the dissatisfied soldiers defied and insulted their officers, who applied to have a trustworthy regiment sent them for guard, whom the rioters would fear. Brigadier-General Hall, commanding the First Division, on the 11th of September directed Colonel Lefferts to detail five companies of his command, with the necessary camp equipage, to report to General Spinola at his camp by noon of the 12th (Friday), for ten days' service, unless sooner relieved. Companies H, B, F, G, and I were accordingly detailed for this purpose, and were assembled at ten o'clock of Friday, the 12th, at the armory, armed and equipped, and were there supplied with twenty rounds per man. The battalion was put under command of Lieutenant-Colonel Price, and proceeded at noon to the camp, — the old familiar drill-ground at East New York. The day following, the other five companies were held in readiness to move in support.

The condition of the camp in which the mutiny occurred, at the time the Seventh Regiment was called upon, may be best pictured, probably, by quoting a small part of the account given by the New York Express, as follows: —

"Another Mutiny in the Spinola Brigade at East New York. — The Seventh Regiment, National Guard, ordered out, with Twenty Rounds of Ball Cartridges. — The Spinola Brigade has distinguished itself by another riot, and a sweeping skedaddle from camp. The last mutiny in which it engaged is still in the remembrance of the public, especially the residents of East New York, — the rendezvous of the troops, — where they have been a terror to peaceable citizens. Many of the prominent leaders in the recent riot had been removed from the camp, preparatory to being court-martialed, but several remained, and used every disadvantageous circumstance to demoralize the brigade.

"Yesterday, the second riot in the brigade occurred, the men having been previously prepared for it by intoxication. The cause of the mutiny is said to be the payment of bounty money only to recruits who have recently enlisted, thus shutting out others from the reward. The War Committee of Queen's County have awarded sixty dollars to all recruits who have enlisted within the last few days. This action resulted in hundreds of men joining the regiments composing the brigade. The bounty was paid them, and they secured, it is stated, leave of absence. They improved the indulgence by spending the money in the drinking-saloons in the neighborhood of the camp and throughout Williamsburgh and Brooklyn; and subsequently returned to the rendezvous drunk, disorderly, and insolent. Those in camp who were not so fortunate as to receive the bounty became disaffected, and in some instances the moneyed soldiers were challenged to fight. Encounters throughout the day were common, and the officers generally seemed to have lost all control of their men. The demoralization of the brigade will appear thorough and complete, when it is known, as stated by one of the men, that out of three thousand and eight men who took part in a dress-parade on Sunday last, not more than half that number were present in camp yesterday.

"At noon, on Thursday, the riot began to culminate. Some of the officers were hooted at by the men in the tents. At one time in the day the soldiers conspired to have a general skedaddle, and some of them escaped. They continued, however, to run in and out through the camp, and seemed to defy restraint. In this manner the men spent the day and night yesterday.

"In anticipation of a greater mutiny and a complete assault on the officers, it was determined to have a proper military force to guard the men, and, if necessary, shoot down a few to strike terror, if not discipline, in the rest. A requisition for troops was then made, and Colonel Lefferts, in obedience to an order of General Hall, ordered five companies of the Seventh Regiment, National Guard, to proceed to East New York. The companies arrived armed and equipped, with one day's rations, and were supplied with twenty rounds of ball cartridges. They proceeded to East New York, via the Grand Street (Williamsburgh) Ferry at noon.

"It is expected that they will meet with considerable opposition, but it will be perceived by the above arrangements that they are prepared for all emergencies."

Lieutenant-Colonel Price's detachment found, however, that the drenching rain-storm in which it marched over to East New York had apparently sobered the drunk and dampened the spirits of the disorderly. A disagreeable tour of guard duty, and sleep on the wet ground and in wet clothing and blankets, were the most unpromising features of the night. The week's hard guard duty which followed, though sometimes rendered exciting by attempts to desert, was mainly monotonous. For the rest, the following report of Colonel Price will sufficiently tell the story of the tour of duty at East New York: —

New York, October 7, 1862.

Colonel Marshall Lefferts, *Command'g Seventh Reg't N. Y. N. G.*

Colonel, — In accordance with your instructions, I proceeded, on the 12th ultimo, to East New York (for special guard duty at brigade encampment) with Companies B, F, G, H, and I of the Seventh Regiment, and reported to Brigadier-General F. B. Spinola, at half past five,

P. M., on that day, on the camp-ground; my total number being two hundred and twenty-two.

General Spinola was very anxious that I should furnish at least one hundred and twenty-five posts, and also desirous to withdraw his own guard (which he stated was not to be relied on); but upon my showing him it would be impossible to furnish more than fifty posts with the force under my command, he left the matter entirely to my discretion, and, as usual, returned to the city. Upon consultation with Adjutant Boker of the One Hundred and Thirty-Second New York Volunteers (one of the four regiments composing the brigade), I decided to post, as an exterior guard, fifteen men round the camp of the First Regiment, fifteen men round the camp of the Fourth, and twenty men round the barracks where the Second and Third Regiments were quartered. Our guard were furnished with a countersign, while their guard was not. The countersign for the night of the 12th was "Lefferts." During the evening, three detachments, under Lieutenants Spicer and Ryder and Sergeant ——, reported to me, — in all about fifty men.

On the morning of the 13th, under the direction of the Quartermaster and Adjutant, our camp was laid out, and tents for five companies pitched midway between the barracks and the camp of the Fourth Regiment. We spent the night of the 12th in the tents pitched for the Second Regiment, and vacated them about noon (before our own tents were all up), the Second Regiment having vacated the barracks ready to occupy their own camp.

A timely arrival of seventy-five rank and file under Lieutenant Lord, of Company K, at 6 o'clock on the afternoon of the 13th, enabled the Adjutant to turn off the guard without calling upon any of the previous guard for a second tour of duty. During the evening, Lieutenant Seward and Lieutenant Meday reported for duty.

I have to report, that Drum-Major Graham left the camp on the evening of the 13th, after having been refused permission to absent himself, and did not make his appearance during the time I was in command.

I have also to report, that liquor was openly sold inside our lines, as I believe, and was informed, by permission of the Commanding General. Upon my reporting to him the fact of liquor being sold within the line of sentries, he professed to be amazed, and said the practice must and should be abated. Finding that liquor was still openly sold, I directed the officer of the day (Captain Clark, Company B), by an order in writing, to notify the principal or the assistants of the main drinking-establishment (on one corner of the barracks) to close up said establishment within fifteen minutes after the receipt of the order, otherwise to arrest both principal and assistants, and have the guard close up said place. The principal immediately closed up the dram-shop (remarking that he had the permission of General Spinola to keep it open), and it remained closed, as I am informed, until the afternoon of said day (Sunday, 14th September), when General Spinola ordered and directed the establishment to be opened and remain open.

Upon inspection parade, at 9, A. M., on Sunday the 14th, there were present and on guard a grand total of three hundred and seventy-one rank and file, drummers, non-commissioned officers, and officers; but in this number were included very strong representations of Companies A, C, D, E, and K. At this parade I directed the officers in command of companies and detachments to report to me the names and residences of members absent without leave, and also the names and residences of members who had not up to that time made their appearance upon the ground. Before such reports could be received by the Adjutant, your order, directing Major Nevers to relieve me of the command of the detachment, was received. I immediately turned over the command to the Major, furnishing him with copies of all orders issued by me, as well as the original order from the acting Major-General, and such information as he desired. In response to my call upon the Adjutant for the returns I directed to be made to me, he informed me "that partial returns were made upon little slips of paper, and they had all been mislaid or lost." I at once called upon the captains of the first five companies for their reports in detail, and only yesterday received the last report. I append hereto said reports of Companies B, F, G, H, and I, which in substance are as follows: absent without leave, 14 (Company I, 12; Company F, 2). I have no doubt that others were absent from Companies B, G, and H, but they are not so reported. Not present at all at East New York, Company B, 15; Company F, 15; Company G, 36; Company H, 51; Company I, 17. Total, 134.

All of which is respectfully submitted,

JAMES PRICE,
*Lieut.-Colonel Commanding Detachment Seventh Reg't.*

The truth is, that, while it was undoubtedly an honor to the regiment to be the first called upon in an emergency of this kind, yet it was an honor somewhat familiar in its long historic experience with riots, and one that could not compensate for the disagreeable features of the duty. It was an ungracious task, and was so felt to be by the regiment, for militia to be employed in guarding volunteers; and the special circumstances of the case made the duty doubly disagreeable. Besides, following so close on the heels of a prolonged tour of duty at the South, it did not awaken that sort of interest it might otherwise have done. At best, it was felt to be a sorry afterpiece to the duty at Federal Hill; and hence, though it continued for a week, when the Seventh Regiment was relieved by the Twenty-Second, it is better to consider that the Seventh's campaign of 1862 ended with the 2d of September.

On the 6th of September, the Governor issued an order of thanks, through the Adjutant-General's office, to the returned militia of the State. "The Commander-in-Chief," it said, "avails himself of the occasion of the return of the Seventh, Eighth, Eleventh, Twelfth, Thirteenth, Nineteenth, Twenty-Second, Twenty-Fifth, Thirty-Seventh, Forty-Seventh, and Sixty-Ninth Regiments of the National Guard to the State of New York, to thank them for the services they have rendered to the country, and for the honor they have reflected on the State. Summoned the second time in thirteen months by a sudden and urgent call to the aid of the general government, they consented cheerfully to the sacrifice of private interests, and abandoned, at almost a moment's notice, all private occupations, to hasten to the defence of the national capital, then in danger. Habituated to the comforts and enjoyments of wealthy and peaceful communities, they have, during their prolonged absence from their homes, submitted without a murmur to the hardships, the privations, and to the labors of the life of a soldier, and they have discharged with fidelity and alacrity every duty they were called to perform, and have stood ready to encounter every danger they might be called upon to meet. Their conduct has entitled them to the thanks of the government they were summoned to defend, and has won for them the gratitude and confidence of the people. It gives assurance that, notwithstanding the vast army of volunteers the State of New York has sent to the defence of the Union, she has her National Guards always at her command, ready now, as heretofore, to respond to any call that may be made on it by the general government, and able at the same time to preserve the peace, maintain the rights, and defend the liberties of her own people, and from whatever form or whatever quarter they may be assailed."

The regiment had now, in the summer and autumn, reached its highest degree of discipline and soldierly excellence. Its brief campaign in 1861, its one hundred days' campaign in 1862, both in actual service, had given it an experience which nothing in its previous history had furnished. It was higher than ever in prestige, its ranks were full, its condition admirable, its enthusiasm very great. It was therefore with great confidence that Colonel Lefferts, on the occasion of the annual Washington's birthday parade, in 1863, invited, amongst other distinguished officers, Major-General George B. McClellan to review the regiment. "We should esteem it a high honor," he wrote to that officer, "if you would review the regiment on that day, at such hour and place, during the afternoon, as may be agreeable to you." To this invitation the General answered as follows: —

NEW YORK, February 19, 1863, 22 WEST 31ST STREET.

COLONEL MARSHALL LEFFERTS, *Command'g Seventh Reg't N. Y. S. N. G.*

COLONEL, — I have the honor to acknowledge the receipt of your very kind letter of the 18th.

I regret exceedingly that my engagements will not permit me to do myself the honor of reviewing your splendid regiment on the day in question.

While offering my thanks for the compliment you have paid me, permit me to express my great admiration for a regiment which has furnished so many excellent officers to our army, and which has so often shown itself ready to sacrifice everything in the service of the country.

I am, Colonel, very respectfully your obedient servant,

GEO. B. MCCLELLAN, *Major-General.*

# CHAPTER XVI.

## THE MARYLAND CAMPAIGN OF 1863.

SUMMER of 1863, which so gloriously culminated in the twin victories of Vicksburg and Gettysburg, dawned foreboding to the Union arms. The repeated checks experienced by General Grant before Vicksburg had begotten a distrust of his sixth attempt, now under way. In Virginia, five army commanders — McDowell, McClellan, Pope, Burnside, and Hooker — had in turn been overthrown. A great defeat had just been endured at Chancellorsville, — a defeat made the sorer by the hopes wherewith battle had been joined.

At this juncture a new terror loomed in the eastern horizon. Lee, inspired by his recent victory, and heading a numerous army, swept down the Shenandoah Valley, crossed the Potomac, and, before the stupefied North shook off its amaze, his vanguard bivouacked among the abandoned farms of Pennsylvania.

The wild cry that came from the latter State was hardly

needed to arouse the militia of New York and New Jersey. As audacious now as hitherto he had been wary, the Confederate commander had transferred the seat of war from Virginia to the North. His army, seventy thousand strong, was not only equal in effective numbers to the Army of the Potomac, but was at its highest mettle. On the other hand, the Union Army, which had lost thirty thousand men in two battles, was losing thousands more each day by expiration of service, and was now subjected to another change of commanders. It was clear at a glance, that, without instant check, the Confederate General would pass the Susquehanna, capture Washington, Baltimore, and Philadelphia, and dictate terms of peace on Northern soil. Or, at best, he would effect such a lodgement on that soil as would secure for his government the decisive advantage of foreign recognition.

Such was the crisis which summoned the militia of the North for the third time to the front, and such the crisis in which the Seventh marched, as ever, leading the van from New York.

To Milroy, who, with head-quarters at Winchester, commanded a force of ten thousand men, about two thirds effectives, had been committed the charge of the Shenandoah Valley. The initial step in Lee's scheme of invasion was to manœuvre Hooker from the Rappahannock by turning his right in the country lying east of the Blue Ridge. Milroy had just force enough to be despised as resistance and coveted in capture. The 14th of June, at nightfall, Ewell appeared in force before Winchester, and next day annihilated Milroy, taking four thousand prisoners, twenty-eight guns, and much spoil. Hooker was already rapidly retrograding from the Rappahannock; the Shenandoah avenue was clear for Lee's columns; the War Department had hurriedly divided Pennsylvania (to help matters) into two military departments; Governor Curtin had called — nay, shrieked — for the Pennsylvania militia to come forward, and his call had fallen mainly on deaf ears; when, on the 15th of June, the President, impressed with the magnitude of the crisis, summoned the nearest States, West Virginia, Maryland, Pennsylvania and Ohio, to furnish 100,000 militia forthwith, — West Virginia, 10,000; Maryland, 10,000; Pennsylvania, 50,000; Ohio, 30,000.

But, doubting (and with justice, as events proved) whether these 100,000 would be forthcoming in States like Pennsylvania and Ohio, where, at that time as now, the militia system was much neglected, Secretary Stanton simultaneously appealed to New York for 20,000 men, or less, to be hurried forward. This was a private appeal; but it received a response as prompt as an order; and it is a matter of history, that, in this dark hour before the dawn, New York furnished more troops upon her voluntary quota than any of her sister States appealed to in the President's original order.

On the 15th of June, simultaneously with the President's call, Secretary Stanton telegraphed as follows to Governor Seymour: —

WASHINGTON, June 15, 1863.

TO HIS EXCELLENCY GOVERNOR SEYMOUR, *Albany*.

The movements of the Rebel forces in Virginia are now sufficiently developed to show that General Lee, with his whole army, is moving forward to invade Maryland, Pennsylvania, and other States. The President, to repel this invasion promptly, has called upon Ohio, Pennsylvania, Maryland, and Western Virginia for one hundred thousand militia for six months unless sooner discharged. It is important to have the largest possible force in the least time; and if other States would furnish militia for a short term, to be credited on the draft, it would greatly advance the object. Will you please inform me immediately if in answer to a special call of the President you can raise and forward, say twenty thousand militia or volunteers, without bounty, to be credited in the draft of your State, or what number you can probably raise?

E. M. STANTON, *Secretary of War*.

Governor Seymour replied as follows: —

ALBANY, June 15.

HON. EDWIN M. STANTON, *Secretary of War.*

I will spare no effort to send you troops at once. I have sent orders to the militia officers of the State.

HORATIO SEYMOUR.

And, in fact, as the wires conveyed this despatch, they carried also stirring appeals and orders for immediate march from Governor Seymour to all the available regiments in the State. Here, for example, is the despatch sent to the Second Division head-quarters at Brooklyn: —

ALBANY, June 15.

MAJOR-GENERAL H. B. DURYEE, *Brooklyn.*

How many men from your division can be sent immediately for defence of Washington and vicinity, to serve for six months, they receiving the State bounty, and to apply on the draft? Answer at once. The Governor desires you will report here this evening in person.

J. B. STONEHOUSE, *A. A. A. G.*

The next day, Mr. H. H. Ward, manager of the telegraph office, telegraphed to Colonel Lefferts, then at Rye: "A reply from Stanton to Governor Seymour returns thanks, and thinks a strong movement of city regiments would be encouraging." And the following request, in fact, was sent to General Sanford for the use of the city regiments in Pennsylvania: —

WASHINGTON, June 16, 1863.

MAJOR-GENERAL SANFORD, *Albany.*

The government will be glad to have your city regiments hasten to Pennsylvania for a term of service. It is not possible to say how long they might be useful, but it is not expected that they would be detained more than three months, possibly not longer than twenty or thirty days. They would be accepted for three months, and discharged as soon as the present exigency is over. If aided at the present by your troops, the people of that State ought soon to be able to raise a sufficient force to relieve your city regiments.

EDWIN M. STANTON, *Secretary of War.*

The first telegram from Albany for help, meanwhile, had

come, as usual, to the Seventh Regiment. It was directed to Colonel Lefferts, and ran as follows: —

ALBANY, June 15, 1863, 7.15 P. M.

COLONEL MARSHALL LEFFERTS, *Seventh Regiment N. Y. S. G.*

The Governor desires to know immediately how soon the Seventh Regiment can be in readiness to move to Philadelphia. Cannot the Seventh be the first regiment?

J. B. STONEHOUSE,
*Acting Assistant Adjutant-General.*

Colonel Lefferts, who chanced to be absent from the city, at Rye, that evening, did not receive this despatch until the next morning at ten o'clock, when he answered at once, and directly to the point, "I can move with my regiment *this evening*"; adding a request to know definitely the length of service proposed, "in order to carry a full complement of men." Within an hour came the Governor's reply in the shape of a formal order to "proceed forthwith with your regiment, as full as possible, to Harrisburg, Pennsylvania, and report to Major-General Couch." The following is the text of the marching orders: —

ALBANY, June 16, 1863.

COLONEL MARSHALL LEFFERTS, *Seventh Regiment.*

The Governor directs that you proceed forthwith with your regiment as full as possible to Harrisburg, Pennsylvania, and report to Major-General Couch. They volunteer for a term not to exceed three months' service; most likely not more than thirty days' will be required. Requisition for transportation will be made upon Major Van Vliet, No. 6 State Street, and for subsistence upon Colonel A. B. Eaton, 7 State Street.

JNO. T. SPRAGUE, *Adjutant-General.*

These orders were not — such was the need of haste — sent through the regular and proper channels (for the regiment formed a part of the Third Brigade, Brigadier-General William Hall commanding), but directly from head-quarters at Albany. However, on receipt of the Governor's hurried order, Colonel Lefferts issued his own, requiring the departure of the regiment the same afternoon, and addressed forthwith to Major Van Vliet the following letter: —

NEW YORK, June 16.

MAJOR VAN VLIET, *Quartermaster U. S. A.*

SIR, — I am directed by his Excellency Governor Seymour to apply to you for transportation for my regiment to Harrisburg, Pennsylvania. I presume I shall have about eight hundred men, and can be ready late this afternoon. Will you please inform me at our armory, corner Third Avenue and Sixth Street, when and where such transportation will be ready.

M. LEFFERTS, *Colonel Seventh Regiment.*

The steamer Red Jacket, or the Kill Von Kull, was to have been, under this arrangement, at Pier No. 2, North River, at five o'clock, P. M., to convey the regiment on its way; but unfortunately General Hall, who, as we have seen, had heard nothing of Colonel Lefferts's order from Albany "to proceed *forthwith*," went to the armory that morning while the Colonel was absent, making the arrangements for transportation, and dismissed the officers and men already there assembled, until the following morning. On arriving at the armory, very soon after, Colonel Lefferts was greatly chagrined at finding he had lost by mere accident the benefit, as well as the *éclat*, of unusual promptness, and apprised the State authorities of the fact in the following despatch: —

June 16, 1863.

GENERAL JOHN T. SPRAGUE, *Adjutant-General, Albany.*

I had made my arrangements to leave this afternoon; but by some misunderstanding, General Hall, who did not know of my order to proceed, went to the armory and dismissed the men until to-morrow morning. This was done a short time before I reached the armory. Of course I could only follow the course indicated, and have made arrangements to leave to-morrow morning, at seven o'clock, A. M., if transportation is ready. The men understand that they go only for a short time, or, in other words, to meet the present emergency.

The reply from Adjutant-General Sprague was: "The Governor is gratified at your promptness, and hopes you will leave as you anticipate." The same message regarding the mistake at the armory was sent by Colonel Lefferts to General Van Vliet, who changed his arrangements for transportation. Orders were issued as follows for the assembly of the regiment at an early hour the next morning: —

"By order of his Excellency the Governor, the regiment will proceed to Harrisburg, Pennsylvania, and for this purpose will assemble at headquarters at seven o'clock, A. M., to-morrow, in full fatigue, with haversacks containing one day's rations, knapsacks, blanket, overcoat, and canteen. The commandant would suggest to the men to take but little baggage. Meeting of officers at five o'clock this afternoon "

At the officers' meeting, spoken of in this order, Colonel Lefferts was, by unanimous vote, requested to telegraph to the Governor that the regiment desired its services to be taken, as in 1861, "for the emergency," and not for continued campaigning. "Their honor," added the Colonel to his despatch, "to fulfil all duties during the time can be relied upon, and they do not ask any consideration from the government beyond the regular pay and transportation. Shall I go ahead on this understanding?" The Governor's reply was: "Go ahead on your proposition. Will see the regiment is not kept longer than thirty days."

Rain fell in torrents on the morning of the 17th, but the regiment marched with full ranks, in the finest spirits, and for the third time the streets were thronged with an enthusiastic multitude (this time armed with umbrellas) to cheer their departure. The alarm of the moment, on account of the nearness of the enemy on the one hand, and the spirit and promptness of the regiment on the other, gave fervor to this grand public ovation, even though the war was now an old story, and military pageants no longer attracted the popular gaze. A vast throng followed the regiment to the pier, and shouted hearty farewells as the steamer started for Amboy.

Delays on the road caused the regiment to reach Phildelphia late in the afternoon. There Colonel Lefferts was requested to report to Lieutenant-Colonel C. S. Ruff, Third Cavalry U. S. A., commanding at Philadelphia. That officer delivered him a written order from Major-General Halleck to proceed to Baltimore, as follows: —

"SIR, — You will proceed without delay to Baltimore, Maryland. Report on the arrival of your regiment to Major-General Robert Schenck, United States Volunteers, commanding that military department. Transportation is provided for your regiment via the Philadelphia, Wilmington, and Baltimore Railroad."

At 11 P. M., accordingly, the weary regiment was marched to the Baltimore depot, and packed in the cattle-cars provided for their transportation. At midnight, Colonel Lefferts telegraphed to General Sprague at Albany: "I have received orders from Major-General Halleck to proceed to Baltimore, and am now in the cars ready to leave for that city. I presume this will receive the sanction of the Governor." The answer was: "The Governor is much pleased with your promptness. Execute all your orders and report your strength."

And thus the campaign to Harrisburg, under the orders of Governor Seymour, became one to Baltimore, under the orders of General Halleck.

Baltimore at this time divided with Washington the anxiety of North and South. It was popularly believed to be Lee's primary objective. As its safety was certainly menaced, troops were poured into it, and the reinforcements originally directed upon Harrisburg were turned down to Baltimore. Fort Federal Hill dominates Baltimore; and Fort Federal Hill was once more intrusted to the keeping of the Seventh Regiment.

Major-General Robert E. Schenck commanded, at this epoch, the Middle Department and the Eighth Corps. To him, accordingly, on the 18th of June, Colonel Lefferts reported. A prospective disposition of the regiment had already been made at head-quarters; it had been attached to the Second Separate Brigade (Brevet Brigadier-General Morris commanding), of the Eighth Army Corps, and was under orders to proceed forthwith to Fort Marshall, and relieve the One Hundred and Fiftieth Regiment of New York Volunteers, then stationed there.

SPECIAL ORDERS No. 163.

HEAD-QUARTERS MIDDLE DEPARTMENT, EIGHTH ARMY CORPS,
BALTIMORE, MD., June 18, 1863.

4. The Seventh Regiment New York State Militia is temporarily attached to the Second Separate Brigade.

On their arrival, they will proceed without delay to Fort Marshall, and relieve the One Hundred and Fiftieth Regiment New York Volunteer Infantry, now stationed there.

The commanding officer will report to Brevet Brigadier-General Morris, commanding the Second Separate Brigade, for orders.

By command of Major-General Schenck,

WM. H. CHESEBROUGH,
*Assistant Adjutant-General.*

Colonel Lefferts marched his regiment to the barracks,— the old Continental Hotel,— which remained head-quarters until the afternoon of the following day. The members of the regiment were soon after dismissed from duty until half-past nine o'clock, P. M.

Orders for provost duty in the city came on the morning of the 19th. Lieutenant Lentilhon and twenty men were detailed from Company K to escort provisions to Fort McHenry; and the whole of the Second, Sixth, and Ninth Companies, under command of Captain Easton, guarded a body of prisoners, twelve hundred strong, taken by General Grant at Port Gibson, across the city from the Baltimore and Ohio Railroad depot, to the steamer plying to Fort Delaware. The filthy condition in which these troops had jealously preserved themselves made this duty particularly unsavory.

Meanwhile, the orders to proceed to Fort Marshall had

been revoked, and the destination of the regiment changed to Fort Federal Hill. The prospect of a protracted occupation of Baltimore was disheartening to the regiment, which had been hitherto in the highest spirits over the bright promise of a short campaign in the field. The dull round of garrison duty seemed doubly annoying at this crisis in the war; and the wish to escape its monotony was universal. However, at three o'clock, P. M., of the 19th, the regiment assembled and marched to the fort. A detachment of Colonel Peter A. Porter's regiment, now become the Eighth New York Heavy Artillery, still garrisoned it. The salutes of 1862 were now reversed; for, as the Tenth marched out, the Seventh marched in. But the fort was no longer the model of neatness and cleanliness they had left, and the quarters of the men had to undergo a thorough cleaning before becoming the comfortable apartments of the year before. Colonel Porter's command was then concentrated in Fort Marshall. The following were the orders of transfer: —

SPECIAL ORDERS No. 164.

HEAD-QUARTERS MIDDLE DEPARTMENT, EIGHTH ARMY CORPS,
BALTIMORE, MD., June 19, 1863.

4. So much of Paragraph 4, Special Orders No. 163, as directs the Seventh New York State Militia to proceed to Fort Marshall, is revoked. They will proceed forthwith to Fort Federal Hill, and relieve the detachment of the Eighth New York Volunteer Artillery, Colonel P. A. Porter commanding.

The Eighth New York Artillery, on being relieved, will proceed to Fort Marshall and relieve the One Hundred and Fiftieth Regiment New York Volunteer Infantry, now temporarily stationed there.

The One Hundred and Fiftieth Regiment New York Volunteer Infantry, on being relieved, will return to their former quarters at Belger Barracks.

By command of Major-General Schenck,
WM. H. CHESEBROUGH,
*Assistant Adjutant-General.*

Key-point, as it was, of the civic defences, the fort was

instantly put into the best possible condition, and soldierly vigilance and discipline were enforced. Artillery drill was begun at once, and unremittingly continued for several days, till its elements were made familiar, when the practice became more methodical. Assignments were made of the various companies to the principal defences, immediately on entering the fort, as follows: —

GENERAL ORDERS No. 14.

HEAD-QUARTERS SEVENTH REGIMENT, FORT FEDERAL HILL,
BALTIMORE, June 20, 1863.

The following assignment is made for the government of officers and men: —

| | |
|---|---|
| Bastion No. 1. | Lieut. Comdg. Waldo, Co. H.<br>Lieut. Comdg. Faunton, Co. A, guns 1, 2, 3, 4, 5, 6, 7. |
| Bastion No. 2. | Capt. Young, Co. F, guns 8, 9, 10, 11, 12, 13.<br>Lt. Comdg. Everdell, Co. D, guns 14, 15,* 16, 17, 18, 19. |
| Bastion No. 3. | Capt. Easton, Co. I, guns 20, 21, 22, 23, 24.<br>Capt. Dutton, Co. E, guns 25, 26, 27, 28.* |
| North Curtain. | Capt. Rogers, Co. K, guns 29, 30, 31, 32.*<br>Lieut. Comdg. Ryders, Co. C. |
| Bastion No. 4. | Capt. Clark, Co. B, guns 33, 34, 35,* 36, 37.<br>Lieut. Comdg. Felt, Co. G, guns 38, 39, 40, 41. |

The above-mentioned officers will be held responsible for the complete order, equipment, and state of efficiency of a requisite number of men for the respective localities mentioned. They will make themselves thoroughly acquainted with the different kinds of ammunition, where stored, &c.

By order,
COLONEL MARSHALL LEFFERTS.

Outside the forts, all was excitement. When would Lee come? *Would* he come? One party in the city feared, the other longed, for his approach; but preparations for a warm reception were made. "Extensive field works," says the "History of the Second Company," "were erected for the defence of the city; the streets leading into the country were barricaded, and all loyal men were organized, armed,

* Mortars. Captain Dutton and his Company were afterwards (June 30) transferred from Bastion No. 3 to Bastion No. 1.

and drilled. The excitement which prevailed on all sides was fearful, yet there seemed to be a firm determination not to yield the city without a desperate resistance; and Forts McHenry, Marshall, and Federal Hill were in perfect readiness, with shot and shell, to welcome the invaders." On the 20th of June, Colonel Lefferts was ordered from brigade head-quarters, "without delay, to send by his teamsters all the spades and pickaxes he can spare to the corner of Lansdale Street and Pennsylvania Avenue, Baltimore, and turn them over to Lieutenant Meigs, United States Engineers, at that place."

Within the forts, all was quiet but busy preparation. The brigade commander, General Morris, U. S. A., had been intrusted with the important command of the defences of Baltimore; and that officer, immediately on the Seventh's arrival, directed, by Special Orders No. 106, "that Colonel Marshall Lefferts, commanding Fort Federal Hill, shall drill his command twice each day in artillery and once in infantry until further orders. These instructions were strictly carried out. Rockets were, the same day, sent to the fort, to signal the enemy's approach, with the following instructions: —

HEAD-QUARTERS SECOND SEPARATE BRIGADE, EIGHTH ARMY CORPS, DEFENCES OF BALTIMORE, FORT MCHENRY, June 20, 1863.

COLONEL MARSHALL LEFFERTS, *Commanding Fort Federal Hill.*

COLONEL, — I am instructed by the general commanding to send you (30) thirty rockets, to be used as signals, if occasion should require. Should an approach of the enemy, or any other event, render it important, in your opinion, to summon the garrisons at Forts McHenry and Marshall to arms, *three rockets* will be sent up by you at intervals of two minutes. The sentinels at your post will be instructed accordingly. The same order is given at this post and at Fort Marshall, and the above signal from either of these forts will be duly observed and obeyed at your post.

By command of Brigadier-General Morris, U. S. A.,

E. W. ANDREWS,
*Captain and Acting Assistant Adjutant-General.*

Colonel Lefferts was further instructed to build an abattis entirely around the fort, procuring the brush and timber from Colonel Donaldson of the Quartermaster's Department. The original order read, "The work will be done by your own men"; but as no time could be lost, a subsequent order permitted him to employ citizens in laying it, if his own force was not sufficient to complete it as fast as the brush was supplied. These were the orders: —

HEAD-QUARTERS MIDDLE DEPARTMENT, EIGHTH ARMY CORPS,
BALTIMORE, June 27, 1863.

COLONEL MARSHALL LEFFERTS, *Commanding Fort Federal Hill.*

COLONEL, — The Quartermaster's Department has been ordered to furnish you with the necessary timber to construct an abattis around Fort Federal Hill. You will confer with Colonel Donaldson as to the amount you need, and push the work vigorously.

I am, very respectfully,

W. H. CHESEBROUGH,
*Lieutenant-Colonel and A. A. A. G.*

HEAD-QUARTERS SECOND SEPARATE BRIGADE, EIGHTH ARMY CORPS,
DEFENCES OF BALTIMORE, FORT MCHENRY, July 1, 1863.

COLONEL M. LEFFERTS, *Commanding Fort Federal Hill.*

COLONEL, — I am directed by the general commanding to state that you will build the abattis entirely around the fort. If the force you have is not sufficient to complete the work as fast as the abattis is supplied, citizens can be employed.

Your obedient servant,

A. VAN NESS, *Lieutenant and A. D. C.*

FORT CARROLL OFFICE, BALTIMORE, June 29, 1863.

COLONEL MARSHALL LEFFERTS, *Commanding Fort Federal Hill.*

SIR, — I have the honor to acknowledge the receipt of your communication of this date, concerning repairs, &c. required at Fort Federal Hill, and in reply would state that the present condition of the slopes, &c. is unavoidable. The only serious damage exists at the "northeast bastion on left face," where I am about constructing a retaining wall, which will be commenced to-morrow morning. Those portions of the east curtain yet unsodded are expected to be completed by the garrison of the fort. They were only abandoned on the removal of the Eighth New York Artillery, by whom all the recent repairs have been made.

Very respectfully, your obedient servant,

N. H. HUTTON.

Half a dozen other official orders and communications in reference to the abattis which the regiment threw down around their fort relate to the urgency of the work. All the bridges, roads, and other approaches to the city, were, of course, strongly picketed. To guard four important outposts became, in addition to its garrison duty, the charge of the Seventh. These were Locust Point, Mud Bridge, Long Bridge, and Sweitzer Bridge. A sergeant, two corporals, and thirteen privates of the Fifth Company were detailed as guard to Locust Point; a sergeant, two corporals, and ten privates of the Seventh Company to Mud Bridge; a sergeant, two corporals, and nine privates of the Ninth Company to Long Bridge; a sergeant, two corporals, and nine privates of the Sixth Company to Sweitzer Bridge. Their duties were those usually devolved on outpost guards, and the details were afterwards relieved in turn by others. On July 1st, a detail from Lieutenant Kitchen's company (A) relieved the guard at Sweitzer Bridge, and a detail from Lieutenant Ryder's company (C) relieved the guard at Mud Bridge.

Further to guard against surprise, a signal line was established on the turnpike from Baltimore to Hereford, twenty-one miles distant, by which route the enemy was expected. This signal line was put in charge of Captain James R. Hosmer, of the Quartermaster's Department, U. S. A., who had established about a dozen intermediate stations between the head-quarters in Monument Square and the cavalry picket at Hereford, in commanding positions upon hills, house-tops, and church-steeples. Three men, provided with the usual apparatus of flag, field-glass, and rockets, formed each station. Lieutenant Palmer and thirty-six men of the Second Company were detached for this service.

Within the city the Seventh Regiment was no less busy than at the fort and at the outposts. In addition to other duties, it acted as provost-guard, by Special Order No. 169, from corps head-quarters, as follows: —

"The commanding officer of the Seventh Regiment N. Y. S. M. will detail from his command one full company, to report every day until further orders, at nine o'clock, A. M., to Major William S. Fish, Provost-Marshal Eighth Army Corps, for patrol duty."

The Fourth Company (D), Lieutenant Commanding Everdell, and the Eighth Company (H), Lieutenant Commanding Waldo, were both detailed, in order that their joint strength might amount to about ninety men. On the 2d of July, the Sixth and Tenth Companies, under command of Captain Rogers, relieved the Fourth and Eighth in their duty.

Special provost duty was also required of the regiment. In one case, Colonel Chesebrough, of General Schenck's staff, came in person, an hour before midnight of June 27th, asking for a force of sixty or eighty men to go forthwith on an important expedition. In twenty minutes after Colonel Chesebrough's unexpected summons, the Second and Fifth Companies, roused from sleep, were tramping at double-quick along the pavements of the city. The "objective" proved to be the Maryland Club-House, suspected now, on the victorious approach of Lee's army, of being a trysting-place for disloyal citizens, who there brewed, not only pacific punch, but "treason, strategem, and spoils." The alarm had been taken and the Club-House shut, so that the expedition returned, foiled. The following memorandum is contained in the book of Regimental Records: —

HEAD-QUARTERS SEVENTH REGIMENT, FORT FEDERAL HILL.

At 11.10 P. M., June 27, 1863, a verbal order was received from General Schenck, through General Chesebrough in person, requiring a detail of from sixty to eighty men, which were promptly got together and left the fort in twenty minutes from the time the order was first received. The detail was from Companies B and E, and proceeded on the double-quick to Washington Monument, and, having performed the duty required, returned at one o'clock, A. M., June 28th, to the fort.

E. B. SCROOP, *Private Secretary.*

However, General Schenck was bent on preventing assemblies in the Club-House; and, soon after, the regimental patrol seized it and arrested the inmates.

Besides such new and lively experiences, there were also the old duties to perform of escorting prisoners and deserters to various points. On the 20th of June, Captain Rogers, with one non-commissioned officer and ten men, proceeded by transport to Fort Monroe, in charge of ninety-four Confederate paroled prisoners, and turned them over to the commanding officer at that point. On the 25th, Lieutenant Ryder, Company E, with one sergeant and ten men, proceeded to Annapolis to Camp Parole, in charge of forty-five paroled prisoners. On the 26th, Lieutenant Cragin, of Company I, with one sergeant and ten men, proceeded by Bay steamer to Fort Monroe, in charge of sixty-two Confederate prisoners, returning on the 28th. On the 29th, Lieutenant Smith, of Company B, with a sergeant, corporal, and ten privates of Company C, proceeded to Alexandria, Virginia, in charge of thirty-seven soldier prisoners, delivering them to the commanding officer of the camp of distribution. On the 4th of July, Lieutenant Palmer, with four non-commissioned officers and forty-five men of the Second Company, proceeded by steamer to Fort Delaware in charge of fifty-two captured Confederate officers.

Plenty of other work, too, was found for the regiment: it did not rust out. On the 23d of June, Captain Dutton, Company E, with sixteen men, proceeded to the Union Relief Saloon, Camden Station, for provost duty there under Lieutenant Titus. On the 29th, a sergeant, a corporal, and six men of Company A, Captain Bensel, reported for duty at Fort McHenry; and, on the same day, a permanent guard of two sergeants, four corporals, and twenty men, half each from Company I, Captain Easton, and Company K, Captain Rogers, was ordered to the same fort with fifteen days' rations. The Fort McHenry garrison was small, and it was not long, as we shall see, before two more calls for aid were made upon the Seventh Regiment and responded to. Even small loans of " a drummer and fifer " were effected by the " South Baltimore Union League " and kindred worthy organizations.

Such, in fine, were some of the multifold duties of garrison, of outpost, and picket, of signal station, of provost and patrol, of guarding and escorting prisoners and deserters, of caring for the sick and wounded, of eking out the numbers and duties of other regiments, and the like, which the Seventh was called upon to perform. It may well be believed that its life was not an idle one, and all fears of monotony in garrison life had proved groundless. One great source of annoyance, therefore, to Colonel Lefferts, was that he had not more men at command, in order to relieve the overworked, and to be able to render still more efficient service. Sometimes he had not men enough for guard at the fort.

Considering the suddenness of the call, considering also the large numbers of active members of the regiment who were serving at the front, and, moreover, the fact that the novelty of the war had worn off in 1863, the rally of the regiment in its third campaign had been very creditable. It had been joined, too, by several detachments, who had been unable to start with it. On the 18th of June a detachment of forty-seven non-commissioned officers and privates, Sergeant Van Norden, Company B, commanding, started from New York, forwarded by Captain Riblet. On the 20th the same officer forwarded a detachment of thirty-one men, under command of Orderly-Sergeant Pollard, of Company C. On the 22d he forwarded the regimental band, consisting of Grafulla and twenty-five men, besides nineteen non-commissioned officers and privates and two drummers, — Captain Bensel, Company A, commanding the whole party. On the 23d, Captain Haws left New York for the fort with ten or twelve men. On the 27th, Lieutenant Kitchen went forward with a small detachment. Colonel Lefferts even had an offer of one hundred men for the regiment from the returned veterans of the Fifth New York, but it was not accepted. It came in the following language: —

NEW YORK, No. 9 SECOND AVENUE, June 23, 1863.

COLONEL M. LEFFERTS.

SIR, — In behalf of a great number of the returned old men of the Fifth New York Volunteers, who built the fort you now occupy, which we fear is in some danger, I respectfully offer you one hundred veterans of this regiment, fully equipped in our uniform, to be attached to and under your command, in less than seven days from the receipt of your acceptance of the same. I refer you to Captain Easton, Private Schermerhorn, and numerous others of your regiment.

J. HENRY WHITNEY,
*Captain Fifth New York Volunteers.*

However, there were many who from good reasons, and many who from bad reasons, stayed behind in New York through the campaign. The unexpected and unwelcome detention of the regiment in Baltimore undoubtedly diverted some who would have gone on from doing so. "It is the old story of garrison life," they argued, "and there is really no need of us. As soon as we hear of the regiment's being in the field, we will join them." This was the solace they applied to their consciences, as well as the excuse they gave to their friends. In forwarding the first detachment of reinforcements, Captain Riblet wrote to Colonel Lefferts: "I think on Saturday or Monday as large or a larger detachment may be sent forward, unless the regiment should remain in Baltimore. In that case I am doubtful about it."

On the 25th of June, General Schenck sent a request to know the exact effective strength of the command. Colonel Lefferts, in response, reported a total of six hundred and fifty-two men; but from this was to be deducted the band (which did not march at the start, but arrived on the 23d), twenty-four strong, and the sick, numbering seventeen,—leaving an effective strength of six hundred and eleven, officers and men. To Colonel Lefferts, who, on the one hand, had been made aware of the real danger that menaced Baltimore, and the consequent importance of the post, and who, on the other, was constantly driven to new expedients to meet the large details daily made upon him, the backwardness of the young men in New York was very annoying. He telegraphed an urgent appeal for more men to Quartermaster Winchester:—

FORT FEDERAL HILL, BALTIMORE, June 27, 1863.

LOCKE W. WINCHESTER, *Fifth Avenue Hotel, New York.*

I wish you to see Riblet and tell him I want more men at once. There is a large number in the city who have professed to be waiting for the necessity to arrive. Now is their time. Let us see who will support their comrades.

MARSHALL LEFFERTS,
*Colonel Commanding Seventh Regiment.*

Two days later he telegraphed to Captain Riblet a still more pressing summons. This last telegram ran as follows:—

GENERAL ORDER No. 15.

SEVENTH REGIMENT NEW YORK NATIONAL GUARD,
FORT FEDERAL HILL, BALTIMORE, MD., June 29, 1863.

By order of the President of the United States and his Excellency the Governor of the State of New York, this regiment reported for duty in the field. As a number of the members did not come with the regiment, I feel it my duty, in obedience to the commands stated, to issue this order, and direct all officers and men to report at this post forthwith.

Captain William H. Riblet has been directed to furnish transportation, to whom application will be made.

We do not want substitutes or recruits; we have regular members enough of our own organization who have been drilled, and who should willingly share the dangers and work of their comrades. It has been represented to me that some members are prevented from joining their regiment because their employers refuse to allow them to leave their places of business. Can it be possible that those who are enjoying the benefits of our institutions, without the perpetuity of which their business would be worth but little, can refuse a few weeks' absence to a clerk or partner who is willing to do his mite toward the settlement of this great issue for a nationality, the benefits of which may bless his children, even if the father may look with cold blood upon the struggle which he does not care to participate in or assist?

MARSHALL LEFFERTS,
*Colonel Commanding Seventh Regiment N. Y. S. G.*

With this telegram Colonel Lefferts sent instructions to have a thousand copies printed, and every member in New York served with one. Sworn warrants of service were to be returned to him, and captains of companies were ordered to assist Captain Riblet in finding the probable whereabouts of the men. A copy was posted also on the armory bulletin board. The following call was also published in the New York newspapers: —

NEW YORK, June 29, 1863.

All officers and members of this regiment, remaining in the city, are requested to meet at the armory on Wednesday evening, July 1st, at eight o'clock. The object of the meeting is most important; and every member not already with the regiment in Baltimore is expected to be present.

B. M. NEVERS, *Major.*
H. C. SHUMWAY, *Captain Company H.*
W. H. RIBLET, *Captain Company D.*
GEO. W. ELY, *Captain Company G.*

In sending the telegram, Colonel Lefferts also hurriedly wrote a sharp letter desiring that its sentiments should be made public as far as publicity could do any good. We shall presently see the reason of this urgency. The letter was as follows: —

FORT FEDERAL HILL, BALIMORE, June 29, 1863.

CAPTAIN W. H. RIBLET.

MY DEAR SIR, — I have not been able, up to the present time, to find a few moments to write you. I have received your several detachments, and they have been much needed. I telegraphed you on Saturday evening, care of Winchester, that I wanted some men badly. We have not enough to defend the fort as it should be defended; and daily calls upon our force for details, with what we have out on picket and signal duty, make the work very hard indeed. I wish you would give my telegram publicity. Put a copy on the *armory bulletin board*, so that we can ascertain who will support their comrades.

Those young gentlemen who are so loud-mouthed about their willingness to rush on whenever there is danger can be informed that the time has come when such an exigency is more than probable. Should the Army of the Potomac be defeated, Baltimore will be attacked. It even may be before the general battle comes off; but shame to those men who will *wait to see* if there is to be a battle! By the time they find out, we shall not want them.

I never found the men so willing, obedient, and soldierly as they are this time, and I am proud of them, as I ought to be. They are supporting the honor of the regiment for those who hang about the streets of New York, and talk of their valiant INTENTIONS.

There are, in individual cases, good reasons to prevent men from coming, and no one is more willing than I to concede the existence of such cases, and to go out of his way to have such men relieved from duty. But I have neither respect nor patience for those who try to sneak out of their own duty by underrating the work of their companions, and slur their patriotism and sacrifices by saying *they*, too, are ready to come "when the regiment takes the field."

Pardon me if I write strongly, but I write as I feel. The future will justify all I say. I care not who knows just what I have written. I considered my verbal order sufficient for you to take charge, and push forward detachments, but I enclose you a written one for the purpose desired.

Yours truly,

M. LEFFERTS,
*Colonel Commanding Seventh Regiment.*

As June wore away, the crisis of that memorable battle-summer of 1864 drew on apace. Grand events occurred during the Seventh's sojourn in Baltimore. Lee, audacious and confident, gathering up to him from Fredericksburg the corps of A. P. Hill, had at length joined all his army of invasion in the Shenandoah Valley, whose seizure by Ewell, on the 13th of June, has been already recorded. On the 22d of June, Ewell's corps passed the Potomac, swept across Maryland, and entered Pennsylvania; two days later, Lee followed with his whole body. On the 27th the main Confederate Army encamped near Chambersburg, while to the north, along the Susquehanna, Early encircled York and Carlisle. General Lee addressed himself to join his whole force to Early.

At that juncture came Hooker's famous check to the Confederate campaign, — a move on which may have hung the fate of the Union. When, on the 13th of June, General Hooker heard that Lee's head of column was in the Shenandoah Valley, and was bearing down upon Winchester, he at once loosed his grasp on the Rappahannock, and, breaking camp, moved back to Fairfax and Manassas, in order to cover Washington, there remaining till Lee should develop his purpose. But instantly, on learning that Lee had crossed the Potomac, Hooker followed to the northern bank, yet not backward upon Washington, but, with martial inspiration, *forward* to Frederick.

The effect was instantaneous. Lee saw his communications to be menaced, and suspended his northward movement. Should Hooker continue to approach the South Mountains, and attain to Harper's Ferry, ruin would be in store. What, then, should be done?

To match Hooker's manœuvre with a move as imperious was the task imposed upon the Confederate chieftain. His resolve was prompt. Checking his northward march by the Cumberland Valley from Chambersburg, and turning easterly, he started across the mountain range, to *directly threaten Baltimore.* The orders to move on Harrisburg were revoked, and Baltimore became the objective. The design, of course, was to furnish Hooker a Roland for his Oliver, — to bring the Union forces to a halt in their menacing march, and to force them to retrace their steps, retrograding easterly towards Baltimore. This change of purpose was made on the night of the 28th of June; at dawn of the 29th, the columns were put in motion. This 29th of June was the date of Colonel Lefferts's homeward appeal, based on the ground that Baltimore was in peril;

for the rumor of its danger was already rife in the streets of the city. Let us again turn thither.

With Lee's march through Maryland and Pennsylvania, preparations to defend Baltimore were redoubled. Great vigilance was exacted. On the 24th of June, as has been said, a signal line was established to Hereford. Detachments of the Seventh Regiment were sent to supply the exigencies of Fort McHenry, and ammunition was sent to Fort Marshall, which latter point was commanded by the accomplished Colonel P. A. Porter, with his Eighth New York Artillery, after being relieved by Colonel Lefferts from the charge of Fort Federal Hill. The following was the correspondence: —

FORT MARSHALL, June 21, 1863.

COLONEL M. LEFFERTS.

DEAR SIR, — I send, by Lieutenant Swan of this regiment, General Morris's order for one of the howitzers of which we spoke. The howitzers and field pieces at Fort McHenry have been used for the barricades, so that we have had to call upon you. Will you be good enough to let me have, say fifty rounds of the canister and fifty rounds of the shell, for the piece. Yours truly,

P. A. PORTER,
*Colonel Eighth New York Volunteer Artillery, Commanding Fort Marshall.*

FORT MARSHALL, June 23, 1863.

DEAR COLONEL LEFFERTS, — I have written to General Morris about the six-pounder, at your fort, belonging to the United States. If he thinks it best for this fort to have it, he will give such an order. I have not asked for any more of the United States guns, thinking you would need them. I don't want you to think that I am trying to despoil you, but all I will have here will be one howitzer and one six-pounder (both from Federal Hill), and you will have left two howitzers and one good rifled piece, besides having a much better permanent armament than there is here. Yours truly,

P. A. PORTER,
*Colonel Eighth New York Volunteer Artillery, Commanding Fort Marshall.*

Messengers, meanwhile, brought news of the daily progress of Lee into Pennsylvania, and evidences that railroads and telegraphs were at the enemy's mercy. Now the news was that Carlisle had been evacuated; now that York had been surrendered to Early, who thereupon had levied $ 100,000 tribute and a plentiful supply of beef, bacon, bread, boots, and what not of food and clothing, upon the borough. How many days' marches was the enemy distant? This was the general inquiry. Here are some of the telegrams sent to the commanding officer of Federal Hill: —

BALTIMORE OFFICE.

COLONEL M. LEFFERTS, — Following just received. Special despatch to Philadelphia Bulletin: —

YORK, June 27, 1 P. M.

Nothing has been heard yet of Jennings's regiment. The attack on them commenced about three yesterday afternoon, by a large cavalry force, and continued to the last accounts. The loss is not known; but it is reported that a number were taken prisoners.

HANOVER JUNCTION, June 27, 1 P. M.

Telegraphic communication with Hanover Junction ceased a half-hour since; the inference is that the Rebels are there."

Respectfully,

A. WILSON, JR.

Following just received for Associated Press: —

HARRISBURG, June 28, 1 P. M.

A conflict is now going on in this vicinity, and the cannonading can be heard here. No particulars have yet been received.

Respectfully,

J. F. MATTINGLEY.

At length, on the night of the 29th of June, the climax of the excitement was reached. At sunrise of that day, Lee, calling back his cavalry advance from York and Carlisle, sent it sweeping along the roads leading to Baltimore. By nightfall, the rumor of this coming whirlwind had startled the people. It was even alleged that a body of Confederate horse had already made their appearance on the outskirts of the city, aiming to enter under cover of the night. Be this as it may, at midnight General Schenck sent word to the various forts that the enemy was upon them, and directing them to prepare for immediate attack.

HEAD-QUARTERS SECOND SEPARATE BRIGADE, EIGHTH ARMY CORPS,
DEFENCES OF BALTIMORE, FORT MCHENRY, MD., June 29, 1863.

COLONEL M. LEFFERTS, *Commanding Fort Federal Hill.*

SIR, — I am instructed by the Commanding General to inform you that there is evidence we are about to be attacked. You will immediately prepare.

Our information is direct from head-quarters Eighth Army Corps.

I am, Colonel, with much respect,
Your obedient servant,
E. W. ANDREWS,
*Captain and A. A. A. A. General.*

At the same moment, in that subtle, instinctive perception of gathering danger which is often to be observed among inhabitants of menaced places, the citizens rose in alarm. Neighbors aroused neighbors; the startling, ominous clang of heavy bells shook the church-steeples and vibrated in the midnight air; three rockets from McHenry, three from Marshall, three from Federal Hill, shot into the dark sky. And as bells rang, and signal-rockets streamed into the heavens, and the long roll of drums echoed from fort to fort, garrisons sprang to arms, artillerists stood in order to their guns, the citizens thronged to their barricades or lined the hasty breastworks on the highways, while within the forts sergeants were sharply calling the rolls of companies, and in the streets a half-subdued murmur of multitudes ran like a rumbling accompaniment. "The midnight brought the signal-sound of strife."

"The beat of the alarming drum
Roused up the soldier ere the morning star;
While thronged the citizens with terror dumb,
Or whispering, with white lips, 'The foe! they come! they come!'"

But fate had ordained another day and another field for the supreme arbitrament of arms. In that mysterious ordering of events, which, for want of better phrase to express our ignorance, we call the "chance of war," the two great armies of North and South were, without the precise determination of either commander, swiftly approaching on lines which made a collision inevitable at Gettysburg. Meade had succeeded Hooker in the command of the Army of the Potomac, and, in place of continuing his predecessor's policy of gaining Lee's rear, abandoned the westward march, and moved directly northward with his whole force, to throw down forthwith the gage of battle. Ignorant alike of the change of commanders and the change of policy, Lee continued his eastward march. So it fell out that on the same early morning, that of the 29th June, both armies started together, both towards each other, and yet each in the belief that the other was moving away. Lee moved eastward because he thought his adversary was moving westward, Meade moved northward because he believed Lee was likewise marching to the north. Thus the fortune of Baltimore, as it turned out, was not decided in its own streets, but its fate, the fate of Washington, nay, the fate of the Union, was put at hazard on the field of Gettysburg.

Not until the 4th of July, amidst their national festivities, did the little garrison at Fort Federal Hill receive the full tidings of what their comrades at the front had wrought at Gettysburg. Nevertheless, the afternoon before, they got, in the shape of a thousand prisoners from that three days' field, a sort of instalment of its fruits, — a token of the victory whereof the next morning brought assurance. These prisoners were sent to Fort McHenry, and, as its garrison was small, the Seventh, as usual, was called upon for help.

An hour before midnight of July 3d an order from General Morris was received, ordering the detail of a company to report forthwith at Fort McHenry with knapsacks and blankets. Captain Clark, of the Second Company, with a force of two sergeants, two corporals, and fifty privates, was detailed for this purpose, and reached the fort at midnight. The prisoners (except fifty-two officers confined within) slept on the greensward of the outer fort. Next morning Captain Dutton, of the Fifth Company, with the same complement, relieved the guard.

With more than ordinary enthusiasm, next day, was the national anniversary celebrated. There were extra luxuries at the company dinners, with patriotic songs, speeches, and toasts; and, under charge of Captain Easton, a national salute in honor of the day was fired at meridian in obedience to brigade orders. The good news from Gettysburg made all hearts rejoice; not so much that Baltimore was safe (though, with a Union defeat the Confederate flag must certainly have waved over it), as that the country was safe, and the whelming tide of invasion turned.

Suspension of all but unavoidable military duties had been the order for the holiday; but it happened that many extra services were required. The Fifth Company was on duty at Fort McHenry, guarding the prisoners. The Second, on being relieved, was ordered to furnish four non-commissioned officers and forty-five men to proceed to Fort Delaware, orders from corps head-quarters to "detail a company" for this purpose having just been received. This detachment, under Lieutenant Palmer, proceeded by steamer from Fort McHenry, in charge of the fifty-two captured officers, among whom was General Archer. Returning next day to Fort McHenry, it was again despatched to Fort Delaware with four hundred and fifty Confederate rank and file. Next, towards evening of the 4th, came an order for two companies to guard the Northern Central Railroad Depot in Calvert Street, and to man the litters of the Gettysburg wounded brought by the train from Westminster. A detachment for this purpose was made up from Company I, Captain Easton; Company D, Lieutenant Commanding Everdell; and the residue of Company B not detached, Captain Clark, — all under command of the latter officer. The long train reached the station after midnight. The Baltimore Union Relief Association supplied refreshments for the stout-hearted, suffering heroes, and the Seventh aided them from the cars to the ambulances which took them thence to the hospitals, or accompanied them to the Philadelphia train. It was dawn when the kindly work was done. The medical director, Surgeon Simpson, U. S. A., promptly requested of Colonel Lefferts that a like number of the regiment might be held for similar duty when called for.

On the 5th of July a company was called for from corps head-quarters to proceed to Fort McHenry with knapsacks, blankets, and a day's rations, to perform guard duty over one thousand prisoners of war just received at that post. Lieutenant Felt, commanding the Seventh Company, was ordered to proceed thither with his command, Quartermaster McClenachan furnishing transportation.

This was the last of the Seventh Regiment's duties at Baltimore. Its scene of action was to be suddenly shifted. As unexpectedly as it had been sent thither, it was now ordered away.

# CHAPTER XVII.

## AT FREDERICK.

GETTYSBURG had been fought and won. Lee was in flight, Meade pursuing. Such were the tidings of Sunday, the 5th; and all the church-bells of the North pealed with thanksgiving, and all the church-bells of the South tolled with lamentation.

Near midnight came a courier from corps head-quarters, with startling and peremptory orders. The regiment was detached from the Second Separate Brigade (General Morris), and assigned to the Provisional Brigade, General Briggs. It was ordered to march forthwith to Frederick, Maryland; and such was the urgency, that only blankets, overcoats, haversacks, and canteens were to be taken (light marching order), while baggage, camp equipage, and knapsacks were to be left at Fort Federal Hill. Each man was to carry three days' cooked rations, with sixty rounds of ammunition, the cartridge-boxes full, and twenty extra rounds on the person. The following was the order: —

AT FREDERICK.

*From the Original Painting by* GIFFORD, *owned by the Regiment.*

SPECIAL ORDER No. 180.

HEAD-QUARTERS MIDDLE DEPARTMENT, EIGHTH ARMY CORPS,
BALTIMORE, MD., July 5, 1863.

The Seventh Regiment New York State Militia is detached from the Second Separate Brigade, and is assigned to the command of Brigadier-General Briggs.

The regiment will proceed without delay to Frederick City, Maryland. They will go in light marching order, taking with them only their blankets, overcoats, haversacks, and canteens. They will be provided with three days' cooked rations and with sixty rounds of ammunition, forty in their cartridge-boxes and twenty on their person.

The baggage and camp equipage of the regiment will be collected together and left at Fort Federal Hill. The commanding officer of the Seventh Regiment New York State Militia will report forthwith to General Briggs for orders.

By order Major-General Schenck,

W. H. CHESEBROUGH,
*Lieutenant-Colonel, A. A. General.*

What did this surprise portend? The problem was soon solved. Pursuit was the new word of ambition with the victorious Army of the Potomac, and all available forces were to be turned into the path marked out by its commander. That path lay through Frederick.

At midnight, therefore, Colonel Lefferts issued his orders and despatched messengers to call in his outposts. Less than a third of the regiment was on duty in the fort, the residue scattered in half a dozen directions. There were detachments at Mud Bridge, Sweitzer Bridge, Locust Point, Long Bridge, Bush River, and Gunpowder River; special details in Baltimore and at Fort McHenry; a company absent guarding a thousand prisoners, and another on similar duty at Fort Monroe. But, although two of the regimental outposts were distant respectively nine and twelve miles, they were called in in season to move with the regiment at 8, A. M. The details of the Second and Seventh Companies, under Lieutenants Palmer and Felt, absent at Fort Monroe, rejoined the regiment, on the 7th, at Frederick.

Having reported to the new brigade commander, General

Briggs, Colonel Lefferts was directed by that officer to move forthwith to the Mount Clare station, in pursuance of the following order: —

HEAD-QUARTERS PROVISIONAL BRIGADE, EIGHTH ARMY CORPS,
July 6, 1863.

Colonel Lefferts, commanding Seventh Regiment, N. G., of the State of New York, having reported to these head-quarters for orders, will move with his command at once to the Mount Clare station of the Baltimore and Ohio Railroad, where he will await further orders.

H. S. BRIGGS,
*Brigadier-General Commanding.*

With these preparations the night was busy. All camp property was carefully stored, and a guard of invalids mounted over it. At 8, A. M., two fine regiments, the Fifty-Fifth and Sixty-Ninth New York State Militia, designated to relieve the Seventh, marched into Fort Federal Hill, and the Seventh marched out. In a drenching rain, it proceeded to Mount Clare station. There already were collected other regiments of the brigade, comprising both infantry and artillery. Aids were hurrying to and fro with orders; and soon came the turn of the Seventh to embark on the cars prepared for it. Then the train moved slowly, and with many delays, onward through a wild and picturesque region, to Monocacy Junction. "About noon," says one account, "the weather, which had been stormy and unpleasant, because clear and beautiful, and the men, from the tops of the cars, enjoyed the wild and romantic scenery for which that region is so famous; passing through handsome manufacturing villages, and greeted everywhere with great enthusiasm." At Monocacy Junction, General Briggs halted his brigade, and informed Colonel Lefferts that the regiment would bivouac for the night. A wheat-field lay in friendly and inviting neighborhood; and thence gathering straw for rude pallets, the tired regiment stretched out, some in the cars, some on the roadside, and sought to make up for many nights' rest broken in the past, and others apparently likely to be broken in the unknown future. Notwithstanding the orders to carry nothing but blankets and haversacks, Colonel Lefferts took the responsibility of instructing that knapsacks should be taken; and well he did, as their contents were greatly needed at Frederick.

During these two days, great military events had occurred. Let us briefly note how they came to pass. On the morning of the 4th of July, Lee, reading aright the moral of Gettysburg, drew in his flanks, threw up breastworks, and, under cover of his defensive position, dismissed his immense trains to the Potomac. The reconnoissances made by his adversary that day did not disclose his purpose; and accordingly, under cover of the night, he moved his main army down the Fairfield Road, and was gone. By the morning of the 7th of July, Lee's whole army was at Hagerstown.

Morning of the 7th of July found, also, the van of the Army of the Potomac at Frederick, and the main body hastening thither. For, the dilemma whether to hang directly upon the enemy's rear, or to make a flank movement east of the South Mountain by way of Frederick, had been resolved in the choice of the latter alternative. Thus it happened that, while Lee was retreating directly through the Cumberland Valley, Meade was sweeping around on the east side of the mountains.

What part in this chase the Seventh Regiment might take was an exciting speculation, as it lay on the night of the 6th July at Monocacy Junction. The troops then on the road and in the neighborhood of Frederick, under command of General French, generally expected an order to proceed again directly to Harper's Ferry, whence they had been recalled just before Gettysburg; and, indeed, a part of them were ordered thither. However, dawn of the 7th of July brought to Colonel Lefferts definite orders from General Briggs: —

HEAD-QUARTERS MONOCACY JUNCTION, July 7, 1863.

COLONEL LEFFERTS, *Commanding Seventh New York.*

COLONEL, — You will march without delay to Frederick City with your command, and report to General French for orders.

By order of Major-General H. S. Briggs,

BYRON PORTER, *Captain and A. A. G.*

Accordingly, at eight o'clock of a sultry July day, the regiment left the Junction, and moved along the broad turnpike to Frederick City, four miles distant.

Frederick and all the magnificent and picturesque region about it was, at this period, full of the signs of war. Corps and armies had again and again marched and countermarched through it, military hospitals had been established in its environs, and lately ten thousand men had encamped for many days there. As the regiment entered, it had the air of a permanent camp or of a garrison town. Now a party of prisoners was encountered, now a squad of convalescents; the huge army trains rumbled and ambulances rattled through the streets, foretelling the coming of the Army of the Potomac; aids and messengers spurred hither and thither; the yellow trimmings of the jaunty cavalry jacket mingled with infantry blue and artillery crimson: everywhere were soldiers. Here, of late, General French had held command. Withdrawn by Meade, with his eleven thousand men, from Maryland Heights, when that officer succeeded Hooker, he was left with seven thousand at Frederick, while the great armies fought at Gettysburg. To Frederick, also, came other reinforcements, reporting to General French, among which, as we have seen, was the Seventh Regiment. During the afternoon of the same day, July 7th, General Meade reached Frederick, and there established his head-quarters; and one of his first acts was to issue an order, declaring that "the troops at present under the orders of Major-General French are transferred to the Third Army Corps." This corps had, during the battle of Gettysburg, been under the command of General Sickles. It was now reinforced by French's large division, on being placed under the latter officer. The Seventh Regiment was attached to the Third Division of the Third Corps, — the "blue diamond" its corps and division badge. Such was the way in which the Seventh, at last, and most unexpectedly, became a part of the grand Army of the Potomac. The following was the official order : —

HEAD-QUARTERS ARMY OF THE POTOMAC,
FREDERICK, July 7, 1863.

I. The troops at present under the orders of Major-General French are transferred to the Third Army Corps, which will be commanded by General French. The detachment sent to Maryland Heights will not, however, join the corps until further orders.

By command of Major-General Meade,

S. WILLIAMS,
*Assistant Adjutant-General.*

On the morning of the 7th of July, then, as we have said, the Confederate Army was at Hagerstown, and the Union advance had appeared at Frederick. Colonel Lefferts reporting at 11, A. M., to General French, was immediately intrusted with the duty of picketing the road leading to Hagerstown and the turnpike leading to Emmetsburg. He at once detailed the Ninth Company to the former duty, and the Second Company to the latter ; with the rest of the regiment he then went into camp outside the city, half a mile to the southwest of it, on the Harper's Ferry Road.

The important command of Frederick City and Monocacy Junction, with their depots, storehouses, camps, hospitals, their important bridges, roads, and approaches, had hitherto, by order of General Meade, been vested in Major-General French, who also had command of the seven thousand or more troops in and around Frederick. But on his appointment to the command of the Third Corps, it became necessary to turn over that of Frederick, that he might put himself on the march with his corps. He selected as his successor Colonel Lefferts; and, the morning after his own new assignment to command, issued orders, turning over the post to him. As a force for his purposes. General French at the same time detached Colonel Lefferts's own regiment to remain on special duty, besides giving him command of the various regiments and parts of regiments to be left behind at Frederick, including infantry, cavalry, and several batteries of artillery.

Always an important post by reason of the military supplies in store, the camps, and the hospitals, as well as from the strategic importance of Monocacy Junction, Frederick had now temporarily a special importance by the concentration of the whole Union Army there. The picket companies of the Seventh, in marching out to their posts on Tuesday, had met the van of this great host, — its artillery reserve and immense trains of ammunition and supplies. From that time forward, for eight-and-forty hours, the mighty stream did not cease to flow. To properly police the city during the passage of friends, and to picket the outposts during the close proximity of foes, was the task assigned to Colonel Lefferts.

On the morning of the 8th of July, Colonel Lefferts assumed command of the city of Frederick, in the following order: —

GENERAL ORDER No. 1.

HEAD-QUARTERS FREDERICK CITY, MD., July 8, 1863.

By authority of Major-General French, commanding Third Army Corps, United States Volunteers, the undersigned assumes command of the city of Frederick, Maryland.

All instructions heretofore issued, having reference to the police regulations of the city, will continue to be observed until countermanded.

Major Cole, Maryland cavalry, will continue to act as Provost-Marshal.

MARSHALL LEFFERTS,
*Colonel Seventh Regiment N. Y. S. T., and Commanding Post.*

He proceeded to establish his head-quarters in the city, and to dispose his force at the points to be guarded. General French had taken nearly all his own troops, but some were still left at Frederick, and others were added.*

Of the outposts, the most important was Monocacy Junction, four miles south of the city. At this point the Monocacy, a considerable tributary of the Potomac, is crossed both by the Baltimore and Ohio Railroad and the turnpike leading to Washington and to Harper's Ferry. Monocacy was now also the main depot for the Army of the Potomac, with troops and supplies continually moving through it by rail and pike. The great railroad bridge had been once burnt by the enemy. The garrison of the post now consisted of one company of cavalry, one of infantry (afterwards increased to two), and a section of artillery. The cavalry picketed the region between the Monocacy and the Potomac, the infantry guarded both bridges, and the two pieces of artillery, planted on a commanding hill, swept the road and railroad crossings. The latter were very important to the communications of the Army of the Potomac, for even the crazy turnpike bridge was now in constant requisition, and crowded with wagons and men. Two large block-houses, one on either bank of the river, furnished additional protection to the bridges, and shelter to their garrison.

To this post Colonel Lefferts ordered the First Company of the Seventh Regiment, Captain Bensel commanding. To Captain Bensel, as commandant of the post, the cavalry and artillery detachments reported ; a section of Battery I,

* HEAD-QUARTERS ARTILLERY RESERVE, FREDERICK, MD., July 3, 1863.

Captain Sterling is hereby relieved from duty with the Artillery Reserve, and will report with his battery (Second Connecticut) to Colonel Lefferts, Seventh New York State Militia, for duty.

By direction of General Meade, the section of Captain Ranke's battery, with his command, is temporarily attached to Captain Sterling's command.

By command of Brigadier-General R. O. Tyler,

C. H. WHITTLESEY, *Captain and A. A. G.*

Fifth United States Artillery, Lieutenant McConnell commanding, was sent to Captain Bensel for the protection of the bridges.

HEAD-QUARTERS, FREDERICK CITY, July 8, 1863.

LIEUTENANT C. C. MCCONNELL, *Commanding Battery I, Fifth Artillery.*

SIR, — You will detail one section of your battery, with competent force, to report to Captain Bensel, in charge of picket at Monocacy Junction. Your guns will be so posted as to protect the railroad bridge at that point.

MARSHALL LEFFERTS, *Colonel Commanding.*

In addition to this obvious duty, the commanding officer at Monocacy was directed to place pickets on the approaches to the town (both the turnpike and a branch railroad connect Monocacy with Frederick), to keep a vigilant watch for spies and deserters, and to distinguish and give notice of the approach of expected friends as well as of enemies. For the rest, Captain Bensel took his instructions from Major Rolfe, who, with a battalion of the Fourteenth Massachusetts Heavy Artillery, had hitherto commanded the post, and whom he now relieved. The following orders in relation to the First Company's duty will be interesting: —

July 8, half past one, P. M.

CAPTAIN TORBETT, *A. A. A. G.*

CAPTAIN, — General Meade has ordered that the regiments from North Carolina yet to come up, viz. the One Hundred and Fifty-Eighth, One Hundred and Sixty-Eighth, One Hundred and Seventy-First Pennsylvania nine months' volunteers, and the Forty-Third Massachusetts, are to go forward to Harper's Ferry after they have provided themselves with three days' rations. Please direct my staff to follow at once to Harper's Ferry.

Very respectfully, &c.,

HENRY M. NAGLEE,
*Brigadier-General, Commanding Harper's Ferry.*

(INDORSEMENT.)

HEAD-QUARTERS, FREDERICK CITY, July 8, 1863.

Respectfully referred to Colonel Lefferts, Seventh New York Militia, commanding.

By order of Major-General French,

W. F. A. TORBETT,
*Lieutenant, A. D. C., and A. A. A. G.*

HEAD-QUARTERS, FREDERICK, July 8, 1863.

CAPTAIN W. P. BENSEL, *Monocacy Junction.*

SIR, — I enclose you copy of an order in reference to certain regiments. You will keep a vigilant lookout for these regiments, and show the enclosed to the commanding officer. You will also call upon Colonel Porter, Quartermaster, and inform him of the order, as these regiments are to be furnished with three days' rations.

I have ordered Lieutenant McConnell to report to you with one section of his battery. You are to take especial care of the railroad bridge, and place pickets on the approaches to the town.

MARSHALL LEFFERTS,
*Colonel Seventh Regiment N. Y. S. M., and Commanding Post.*

Soon after, Colonel Lefferts relieved Lieutenant McConnel at Monocacy in the following order: —

HEAD-QUARTERS, FREDERICK, July 9, 1863.

Captain Sterling, commanding Second Connecticut Battery, will direct Captain Ranke with his section of battery to relieve Lieutenant McConnell, to-morrow morning, at Monocacy Junction. Lieutenant McConnell will rejoin his command near Frederick City, and report to Captain Sterling.

By order of
COLONEL MARSHALL LEFFERTS, *Commanding Post.*

Meanwhile, Lieutenant-Colonel Price had succeeded temporarily to the command of the Seventh Regiment, and issued the following order: —

GENERAL ORDER No. 19.

HEAD-QUARTERS SEVENTH REGIMENT N. Y. S. M.,
IN CAMP, NEAR FREDERICK, MD., July 9, 1863.

By command of the Major-General commanding the Army of the Potomac, this regiment has been attached to the Third Army Corps, and by command of Major-General French of said Third Corps, Colonel Marshall Lefferts has been assigned to command of the defences in and around Frederick, with head-quarters at Frederick City.

Lieutenant-Colonel Price directs that all standing orders issued by Colonel Lefferts remain in full force and effect.

LIEUTENANT-COLONEL JAS. PRICE,
*Commanding Seventh Regiment.*

The main body of the regiment continued to occupy the

camp originally assigned to it by General French. The ground had been selected long before, for reasons of military convenience, being an open field about half a mile south-west of the city. Its long occupation, however, by other regiments, had cut up the ground, and the heavy storms had made it little better than a quagmire. Had the regiment possessed its tents, it might have been practicable to pitch them in another locality; but as all its camp equipage and baggage were at Fort Federal Hill, it only remained to put up with the local conveniences of the Frederick camping-ground. These consisted of a few fence-rails. And with these rails, together with straw made filthy by long service, rude tents were constructed, — the only shelter. The Colonel's head-quarters were distinguished by a few boards instead of rails. This delectable spot was styled in official documents "Camp near Frederick"; but unofficially it was known as "Camp Misery"; and only the consciousness that, under the circumstances, it was the best that could possibly be had, made it endurable. Storms made the leaky huts wet, and the whole camp was so much mire.

Fortunately, however, a large part of the regiment was always absent from camp on outpost duty, and this latter was neither monotonous nor disagreeable. Colonel Lefferts also made continual calls upon the regiment for various services of importance in his new command; we shall only need, henceforth, in this narrative, to refer to such of the Colonel's duties as were directly connected with the Seventh Regiment.

The First Company, as has been seen, had been assigned to Monocacy Junction. Here the duty was so agreeably exciting, the camp-life so pleasant, the scenery so magnificent, and all the surroundings of service so delightful, as to make it a coveted post. Captain Clark, whose company relieved the First, after some days, says: "Upon their arrival, on Saturday morning, the members of the Second Company pitched their tents about midway between the two bridges, upon a dry and elevated piece of ground, triangular in form, in the centre of which was the block-house, and the sides of which were the railroad, the turnpike, and the Monocacy River. Some preferred to locate within the block-house, and one eccentric party, in defiance of sun, wind, and storm, pitched their tent upon the top of it. One third of the company was detailed for twenty-four hours to guard the bridges and to watch the road beyond, and the remainder spent the day in fitting up their new quarters, or bathing in the river, or with the usual amusements and employments of camp-life. A more interesting and romantic location for a camp could not be found in many a league, and from the eminence occupied by the Second Company the eye rested upon a variety of scenery. There were mountains, hills, valleys, and plains; broad, fertile, and highly cultivated fields, rich in agricultural wealth and adorned with elegant farm-houses; and lands so rough and rugged that no husbandman would attempt to levy tribute upon the soil. The bright, clear waters of the Monocacy, almost concealed by luxuriant, overhanging trees, completed this diversified and charming scene; but lest the place might become dull and tedious from its rural quietness, the movements of army-trains by rail and pike gave life and animation to the picture.

"On Sunday, Monocacy was visited by a severe rain-storm, by which the river was suddenly swollen to a torrent, but the men were well sheltered, and in rain or in sunshine were contented and happy. In the evening, General Schriver rode out from Frederick to inspect the post, and while expressing himself pleased with its appearance and the correct performance of the required duty, he desired the officers to impress upon "the gentlemen of the Seventh" the military importance of Monocacy, and the necessity of constant vigilance. On the following day, the Tenth Company, Lieutenant Ray commanding, was ordered to Monocacy as a reinforcement to the Second. It was not unreasonable to expect a cavalry raid upon this important point, as the destruction of the Monocacy Bridge would seriously interrupt the communications of the Army of the Potomac, and Captain Clark ordered half of the entire force to be constantly on duty at the bridges. The rain continued, with intervals of sunshine, on Monday and Tuesday. When the weather was fair, the men amused themselves with target-firing, bathing, and unsuccessful attempts at fishing. Shooting snakes was also a favorite amusement; but Lieutenant Ray chanced to lodge a pistol-bullet in his own hand, and this circumstance rather dampened the ardor of the amateur sportsmen."

The Third Company was soon ordered to guard the U. S. A. General Hospital at Frederick. The guard previously stationed there by General French having been suddenly relieved without substitutes, Assistant-Surgeon R. J. Weir, the officer in charge, applied for a force of from fifty to seventy-five men. The Third Company, Captain Haws, was detailed for this purpose. Their duties were light, but, as Surgeon Weir's application urged, were "rendered the more necessary on account of the number of slightly wounded prisoners of war now here." There were eight posts to occupy, and quarters were provided for the guard on the grounds. The following were the orders for this company: —

HEAD-QUARTERS, FREDERICK CITY, July 9, 1863.

Lieutenant-Colonel Price, commanding Seventh Regiment New York State Militia, will direct the Third Company, Captain Haws, of his command, to report to Assistant-Surgeon Weir, Frederick Hospital, for guard duty, without unnecessary delay. They will draw their rations from the Regimental Quartermaster.

MARSHALL LEFFERTS,
*Colonel Seventh Regiment New York State Militia, Commanding Post.*

The next day, July 10th, the Eighth Company, Captain Shumway, was ordered to head-quarters. A press despatch says: "The large number of Union Army officers luxuriating around the hotels of Frederick has caused Colonel Marshall Lefferts, Military Governor, to establish a patrol guard to examine the passes of all officers found in the city, and those absent without authority from their commands are placed under arrest."

While the First, Third, and Eighth Companies were thus occupied, the Second and Ninth Companies continued their pleasant picket duties on the Emmettsburg and Hagerstown Roads. The main station of the Second Company was in a clover-field just north of the city, along the handsome and capacious Emmettsburg Turnpike, of which, with the fine fields and farm-houses adjoining, it commanded an extensive view. Comfortable huts were constructed forthwith from a pile of lumber lying in a neighboring yard. The guard relieved by the Second Company was a detachment of the Eighth Maryland Regiment. Lieutenant Smith, with a third of the company, was stationed at the advance picket post, half a mile out on the pike; a cavalry outpost was established a mile or two beyond.

"That part of the Army of the Potomac," says the "History of the Second Company," "which passed the picket station of the Second Company, and entered Frederick by the Emmettsburg Pike, consisted of the Second, Third, and Twelfth Corps. On account of the excellence and the superiority of this turnpike, the ammunition and quartermaster's trains of the entire army also passed this way. The head of the immense column reached Frederick on the forenoon of Tuesday, and for two days and nights a steady and uninterrupted stream flowed by of soldiers, artillery, and army wagons. The passage of this grand army, and its imposing appearance, can never be forgotten. Regiments of infantry, with their veterans of many battles, and their soiled and tattered banners, marched rapidly by; artillery in vast quantities, and of every variety, from the howitzer to the heavy siege gun, thundered along; and immense trains of wagons, with their teams of six mules and their negro drivers, moved noisily on, all hastening forward to intercept the retreating Rebel Army, which had been so severely punished at Gettysburg. The soldiers were in fine spirits, and, flushed with victory, were confident that they were about to deliver the death-blow to the Rebellion.

"As the picket duty of the Second Company was nominal during the passage of the Army of the Potomac, its members had ample time and a capital opportunity to witness the imposing pageant. Their neat gray uniforms and apparent leisure were constant subjects of amusement and badinage to the passing veterans. 'How are you, graybacks?' 'Where did you get your new clothes?' 'You'll be taken for Johnny Rebs,' and other amusing salutations greeted the idle spectators, all of which were good-humoredly given and as good-naturedly received. In nearly every regiment there were former members of the Seventh, now serving the country as officers of volunteers, all of whom were delighted to meet their old comrades, and halted to make inquiries after friends and acquaintances, in this and other companies of the regiment. General officers, all of whom seemed familiar with the name and history of the Seventh Regiment, and the services of its members, often paused to make some kind and complimentary remarks. Distinguished among them was the gallant General Geary, who halted his division to give 'three rousing cheers for the New York Seventh,' to which the Second Company responded with cheers for General Geary, for his division, for the Second Corps, and for the Army of the Potomac. The news had just been received of the fall of Vicksburg, and all joined in the shouts of joy, threw up their caps, and cheered for General Grant and his brave army.

"On Tuesday afternoon rain commenced falling, and the storm continued without much interruption during the passage of the Army of the Potomac. The fine turnpike resembled a river of mud and wăter, and the adjacent fields, which had bloomed with rural beauty, were fearfully devastated by the incessant movement of men, horses, and wagons. On Thursday the grand army had passed, the weather became clear and beautiful, and the Second Company, after the novel and exciting scenes of the last two days, settled quietly down to its military duties.

. . . . .

"The Union Army having left Frederick, it now became necessary for the Second Company to be watchful and vigilant, lest some roving band of Rebel cavalry should pass around to the rear, and dash into the town. It was ordered and expected to oppose any such attempt, and, if finally overpowered, to fall back upon the town and join the regiment. Upon the cavalry picket stationed a mile or two in advance, and upon the outpost in charge of Lieutenant Smith, was the chief responsibility; but the other members of the company were required to remain, during the day, in the immediate vicinity of their post, and at night to sleep in their clothes and upon their arms, and be ready for duty at a moment's notice. On one occasion, the company, having been warned of an expected cavalry raid, was alarmed at midnight by the approach of a large body of Union troopers, who were extremely fortunate in escaping a volley of musketry.

"During the passage of the army, provisions were at famine prices, and to purchase milk, bread, and eggs required a long purse and a forbearing temper. It was also difficult to procure the regular army rations, and the company fared roughly during its first two days of picket duty.

The army gone, provisions became more plenty; the members of the company proved capital foragers; and with the aid of a barrel of fine pork, which escaped from an army wagon and was forthwith confiscated, the commissary department was in a condition of comparative abundance. An adjacent field, in which army-trains had been parked, afforded rich foraging-ground after their departure. Tents sufficient to shelter the whole company were obtained; kettles, pans, axes, and other domestic utensils were found in abundance; and muskets, sabres, and pistols were secured as mementos of the events of the day, and of the wastefulness of a large army on the march. Horses and mules, disabled and abandoned by the army, were also abundant; and so many were captured that horseback-riding became a favorite amusement, and fears were expressed by some, that the Second Company would forget its light-infantry drill, and be captivated by the charms of the cavalry service. With the large supply of horses and mules, horse-racing grew into popularity, and dealings in horse-flesh were not uncommon. The price of these unfortunate quadrupeds, when sold to countrymen in search of good bargains, was from five to twenty dollars.

"While stationed on the Emmettsburg Pike, the company was visited by General Shaler, whose brigade passed through the South Mountain Valley, about ten miles west of Frederick. He was warmly welcomed by the members of his old command, who rejoiced to see him in such fine health and spirits, and wearing so gracefully his well-earned laurels. During Thursday and Friday, heavy firing was frequently and distinctly heard in the direction of Hagerstown, where Kilpatrick and Buford, with cavalry and light artillery, were constantly annoying the enemy."

A great spectacular attraction afforded to Camp Misery was the body of the spy Richardson, which swung from a bough near by three days and nights. This fellow had often visited Fort Federal Hill in 1862, while the Seventh was in garrison there, under a pretence of selling knick-knacks. Colonel Lefferts, conceiving that his carcass had long enough added to the natural beauties of Camp Misery, sent orders from head-quarters, on the 10th, to have it buried. This order was carried into effect as follows: —

SPECIAL ORDER No. 29.

IN CAMP NEAR FREDERICK, MD., July 10, 1863.

By order of Colonel Lefferts, commanding post Frederick City, the body of the spy Richardson is to be buried.

Captain Rogers, Company K, will detail one sergeant and ten men to proceed to the locust-tree in the rear of the camp under which the body now lies and execute the order promptly.

JAMES PRICE,
*Lieutenant-Colonel Commanding Seventh Regiment New York State Militia.*

(INDORSEMENT.)

This is to certify that the body of the spy Richardson was decently interred at the foot of the tree where he was hung.

SERGEANT JAS. BLEECKER,
*Tenth Company, Seventh Regiment.*

On the 10th of July, Captain Rogers, of the Tenth Company, was temporarily attached to Lieutenant McConnell's battery, by the following order: —

HEAD-QUARTERS, FREDERICK CITY, July 10, 1863.

Captain Rogers, Company K, Seventh Regiment New York State Militia, is temporarily attached to Battery I, Fifth United States Artillery. He will confer with Lieutenant McConnell, commanding battery, upon receipt of this order.

MARSHALL LEFFERTS, *Commanding Post.*

On the 11th, Lieutenant-Colonel Price, in pursuance of orders received from Colonel Lefferts, relieved the First Company at Monocacy with the Second, and relieved the latter from its picket duty on the pike with the Sixth Company, Captain Young. These changes were more acceptable naturally to the two latter companies than to the former, which returned to the regimental camp. "Packing its household goods in wagons and upon its mules and horses, the company marched cheerfully away through Frederick, and down the broad pike to its destination. The morning was charming; the march was enlivened by songs and jokes, all of which, irrespective of merit, were laughed at and applauded; and at ten o'clock, in the highest glee and good-humor, the company reached Monocacy. The only mishap of the morning was the running away of a vicious mule, that was made frantic by the rattle of pots and kettles upon his back, or by the shouts and blows of his young negro rider, and went dashing down the road, scattering his miscellaneous burden in every direction, and followed with rapid strides, amid shouts of laughter, by his disconsolate owners. The First Company having grumblingly departed for Camp Misery, the Second Company took possession of its new and delightful quarters at Monocacy."

But what now remains of the story of the Frederick campaign may be briefly told. The Army of the Potomac was already far beyond Frederick; it and its rival now faced each other on the Potomac at Williamsport. Frederick was restored to its normal condition; and Major-General Schriver (Inspector-General of the Army of the Potomac) arriving from Washington to take permanent command of the post, Colonel Lefferts was relieved by that officer, and resumed command of the Seventh Regiment. He forthwith, by General Schriver's direction, reinforced the garrison at Monocacy by another company, — the Tenth, Lieutenant Ray commanding. "Great vigilance" also was, by order of General Schriver, to be "enjoined on all the troops stationed there."

HEAD-QUARTERS, FREDERICK CITY, July 13, 1863.

COLONEL LEFFERTS, *Colonel Commanding Seventh N. Y. S. M.*

SIR, — You will please order forthwith another company of your regiment to Monocacy Junction, to be stationed there until further orders, to serve, with the company already at that place, as guards to the bridges and depot.

Consider the expediency of placing them under the command of a field officer, and enjoin great vigilance on all the troops stationed there.

Very respectfully, sir, your obedient servant,

ED. SCHRIVER,
*Major-General Commanding.*

The same day, the 13th of July, Lieutenant Felt, commanding the Seventh Company, relieved Captain Easton and the Ninth Company on the Hagerstown Road.

But the Frederick campaign, with its duties and pleasures, was now nearly over. A new and for the Seventh Regiment a final theatre of action during the war was already opened. The remarks made upon the two previous rolls apply to the roll now appended.

## MUSTER-ROLL FOR 1863.

*Colonel.*

MARSHALL LEFFERTS.

| *Lieutenant-Colonel.* | *Major.* |
|---|---|
| JAMES PRICE. | —— ——. |

*Staff.*

| | |
|---|---|
| William H. Hume, *Adjutant* | John C. Barron, 2*d Surgeon.* |
| Stephen Rogers, 1*st Surgeon.* | Gilbert T. Totten, 3*d* " |

Charles T. McClenachan, *Quartermaster.*

*Non-commissioned Staff.*

| | |
|---|---|
| Richard F. Ware, *Sergt. Major.* | Marshall Lefferts, Jr., *R. G. Guide.* |
| L. L. S. Clearman, *Quartermaster Sergt.* | John McKesson, *L. G. Guide.* |
| Wm. C. Platt, *Commissary Sergt.* | Edward Foote, *Sergt. of Guard.* |
| Charles H. Winans, *Ordnance Sergt.* | James W. Wilson, *Hospital Steward.* |
| Wm. H. Gibson, *Color Sergt.* | Charles W. Weinig, *Bugler.* |
| Peter D. Braisted, " " | David Graham, *Chief Musician.* |

*Band.*

Claudio S. Grafulla, *Band Master.*

| | | | |
|---|---|---|---|
| Fehz, Peter, | 1*st Class.* | Fielding, John, | 2*d Class.* |
| Diller, Francis K., | " " | Vroseck, William, | " " |
| Centerno, Lucien, | " " | Giblehausen, Henry, | " " |
| Bader, Frederick, | " " | Bader, Henry, | " " |
| Hente, Charles, | " " | Helfrich, Charles, | " " |
| Fritz, Edward, | " " | Gesner, Joseph, | " " |

| | | |
|---|---|---|
| Hoesline, Fredolino, | 3d | *Class.* |
| Dorty, Oliver, | " | " |
| Wahle, Frederick, | " | " |
| Worn, Louis, | " | " |
| Rosenberg, Sampson, | " | " |
| Salamon, Mitchell, | " | " |
| Anderson, John, | " | " |
| Centerno, Ottavio, | " | " |
| Corley, Thomas, | 3d | *Class.* |
| Conner, Claudio G., | " | " |
| Linhard, Andrew, | " | " |
| Girard, A., | " | " |
| Barry, William, | " | " |
| Denise, J., | " | " |
| Johnson, T., | " | " |
| Peck, J., | " | " |

---

## FIRST COMPANY (A).

*Captain,* William P. Bensel.

1st *Lieutenant,* Hugh M. Funston.

*Sergeants.*

Bogert, Peter J. (*Orderly*).
Murray, James.
Spelman, Wm. B.

*Corporals.*

Archer, Anson S.
Bensel, J. Warner.
Leach, Henry L.
Barr, Samuel C.
Pearsall, Wm.

*Privates.*

Apellas, Frederick A.
Apgar, Louis J.
Aston, Frederick S.
Baker, John T.
Barclay, James H.
Belknap, Augustus,
Belknap, Charles.
Bensel, Joseph.
Bornhoeft, John, Jr.
Boswell, William.
Bosworth, C. P. B.
Bull, William.
Byrne, Edward H.
Cowan, George W.
Dixon, Frederick B.
D'Orville, A.
Eagleson, James H.
Emory, Montlin.
Falconer, Robert S.
Flagg, James.
Giffing, Isaac.
Griffith, William.
Hall, Samuel B.
Hamilton, Robert.
Hewlett, A. C.
Kellock, William.
Lyon, Charles H.
Macfarlane, John A.
Maginn, John W.
Masterson, Joseph H.
McMurtry, Oscar
Morgan, Henry A., Jr.
Moulin, H.
Perry, D. A.
Saunders, George H.
Schefers, Jacob.
Schenck, Wilkins.
Sherman, Frederick.
Spelman, Boswell S.
Thorn, William J.
Vandeveer, J. R.
Vermilye, W. R., Jr.
West, Joseph C.
Winser, J. H.

## SECOND COMPANY (B).

*Captain*, EMMONS CLARK.

1*st Lieutenant*, Peter Palmer.
2*d Lieutenant*, George M. Smith.

*Sergeants.*

Gould, Robert S., Jr.
Van Norden, Charles S.
Buchan, Robert C.
Quilliard, Gulian V.
Brower, Bloomfield.

*Corporals.*

Mix, Eugene.
Agens, Frederick G.
Russell, James F.
Steele, Henry S.

*Privates.*

Alden, James M.
Amerman, Jacob B.
Bacon, Benjamin D.
Baldwin, A. De Witt.
Baptist, Francis A.
Bartholemew, James H.
Beekman, Benjamin F.
Bernard, Walter.
Bird, John H.
Blanck, Thomas, Jr.
Blauvelt, Robert B.
Brockner, Washington, Jr.
Brown, Wilbur F.
Chace, Oliver M.
Church, William P.
Clark, George C.
Clark, James W.
Corbiere, George F.
Cornwall, George J.
Curtis, Albert A.
Davis, Alexander M.
Dawes, Francis A.
Day, Martin N.
Debenham, George.
Decker, Reuben.
Dusenbery, Edwin.
Dusenbery, George E.
Eadie, William R.
Ferry, Theodore S.
Findlay, Andrew, Jr.
Fletcher, Walter.
Foster, Frederick.
Gano, Joseph J.
Gould, William R.
Gregory, Frank.
Gregory, Henry S.
Hadley, Charles L.
Haff, Stephen, Jr.
Hall, William S.
Havens, Jonathan N.
Isham, Henry P.
Kase, John, Jr.
King, Josiah N.
Kotman, Louis E.
Lowere, Charles H.
Lowere, Thomas H.
Mahoney, Daniel.
Mahoney, John H., Jr.
Mather, Thomas D.
McKinley, Robert.
Menzies, William, Jr.
Mitchell, William A.
Moore, William F.
Nash, Edward N.
Naudine, George.
Nodine, William.
Oakey, John.
Pearne, William D.
Pinckney, Isaac L.
Prankard, Francis T.
Robinson, James W.
Roome, Hugh R.
Roome, James W.
Russell, Lewis H.
Salisbury, Richard L.
Savage, John A.

Servoss, Elias B.
Sill, Frederick A.
Steele, Edward J.
Stevens, George D.
Stone, Foster.
Strang, John C.
Swift, Charles, Jr.
Taylor, John H.
Taylor, Joseph L.
Terrett, Charles W.
Thompson, Thomas.
Trimble, James D.
Trimble, Samuel.
Vanderbilt, George.
Van Duzer, William A.
Ward, Daniel T.
Ward, Samuel L. H., Jr.
Warner, Everardus.
Weeks, William F.
Whitfield, Edward A.
Wright, Charles S.
Wright, George H.
Young, Albert M.

## THIRD COMPANY (C).

*Captain*, George F. Haws.

*Sergeants.*

Pollard, Don Alonzo (*Orderly*).
Kennedy, Charles S.
Bend, William B.
Robbins, Charles F.

*Corporals.*

Allen, William H.
Conroy, Thomas L.
Burgoyne, Theodore.
Mattison, Lucius H.

*Privates.*

Abbott, Nelson.
Amory, John M.
Brower, John L.
Cammann, Jacob L.
Cammann, Oswald, Jr.
Cheesebrough, Maxwell W.
Conroy, William F.
Cornell, Thomas L.
Crary, Charles F.
Curran, Hugh McC.
DeGrort, Henry F.
Drinker, James S.
Edgar, Le Roy.
Geary, Horace P.
Gregory, George W.
Gunn, Charles L.
Haig, James B.
Hickcox, Thomas N.
Hyde, Zebulon E.
Jackson, William H.
Ketchum, Daniel P.
Mali, William W.
Mangam, Franklin.
Oakley, Alfred.
Pearce, Daniel B.
Robinson, William G.
Smith, Alexander M. C., Jr.
Steers, James.
Talbert, Benjamin G.
Tomkins, Henry.
White, John H.

## FOURTH COMPANY (D).

*1st Lieutenant,* Henry Everdell. *2d Lieutenant,* William H. Kipp.

*Sergeants.*

Dickenson, George A. (*Orderly*).
Taylor, Thomas S.
Balen, Peter, Jr.
Nugent, Henry.
Taylor, Joseph D., Jr.

*Corporals.*

Ferry, Edwin W.
Peterson, William T.
Breeden, Abner H.
Halstead, Robert.
Weyman, E. H.
Pendleton, Aug. F.
Sturtevant, C.
Ketcham, John B.

*Privates.*

Baily, Gardner.
Beard, Sylvester.
Bogart, Arthur W.
Bradford, James S.
Britz, Samuel.
Bulkley, E. O.
Bunting, Howard.
Bunting, R. S.
Crandall, Frank.
Devoe, Isaac W.
Dumont, John B.
Fairchild, Mort.
Geery, Samuel W.
Gillespie, S. F.
Groot, Willis.
Gulager, L. W.
Haas, Leonard.
Hays, Benjamin J.
Hill, Darwin E.
Holly, H. H.
Honeywell, Charles.
Houghtaling, Frank.
Hyatt, S. Burdett.
Jackson, Francis W.
Jarvis, D. M.
Jarvis, Edward A.
Jarvis, Jay.
Jones, William.
Kennedy, John E.
King, Joseph L.
King, R. J.
Kipp, Pearson H.
Kopper, Fred.
Lambert, Wm.
Mackenzie, John.
Miller, Wm. R.
Mixsell, Aaron.
Montgomery, Geo. W.
Nichols, Carmon.
Nichols, Henry.
Olssen, Edward J.
Osborne, Elbert J.
Outcalt, Cornelius.
Parr, Benjamin.
Peake, Wm.
Peters, Joshua.
Rosell, E. O., Jr.
Sanford, George H.
Schenck, D. D.
Schoonmaker, Hiram.
Smith, E. L.
Smith, Milton.
Terhune, Wm.
Thompson, J. J.

## FIFTH COMPANY (E).

*Captain*, Van Buren Dutton.

1*st Lieutenant*, Wm. Seward, Jr. 2*d Lieutenant*, S. Oscar Ryder.

*Sergeants.*

Wyckoff, Albert T. (*Orderly*).
Post, Geo. W.
Tibbals, Lewis P.

*Corporals.*

Miller, John P.
Hutchings, Edward W., Jr.
Murray, Robert, Jr.
Nicoll, Augustus W.
Colvin, William H.

*Privates.*

Abrams, Thomas D.
Baker, George W.
Beers, James E.
Bell, Wm. G.
Braisted, Francis M.
Canover, Gustavus W.
Coffin, George W.
Daily, Geo. H.
Dodworth, Allen R.
Donaldson, Thomas.
Edwards, John B.
Elliott, William P.
Goetz, J. William.
Grosvenor, Levi.
Hawkes, Thos. E.
Holbrook, Judson W.
Hopping, Augustus R.
Johnson, John.
Jones, George W.
King, Oliver.
Lockwood, Jesse C.
Losee, Augustus.
Losee, Edward M.
Mann, Charles W.
Matthews, Charles D.
McKibben, George.
McLean, Alexander W.
Meyers, Charles L.
Mix, Magellan F.
Moore, J. Spencer.
Moore, Thomas.
Noe, Augustus.
Palmer, George M.
Pease, Edward C.
Quail, George.
Quail, William.
Reid, Robert.
Reynolds, James E.
Rust, John H.
Searles, William B.
Shelley, Michael W.
Simpson, Joseph H.
Smith, Edward A.
Smith, Francis A.
Smith, Henry A.
Stegman, John H.
Talcott, Thomas H.
Thorn, John C.
Tibbals, Edward P.
White, Charles L.
Whitney, Joseph S.
Yeaton, Samuel C.

## SIXTH COMPANY (F).

*Captain*, Joseph B. Young.

*1st Lieutenant*, Edward O. Bird. *2d Lieutenant*, Peyton Jaudon.

*Sergeants.*

Brady, Abner S. (*Orderly*).
Erving, John.
Freeman, W. B.
Congdon, H. M.

*Corporals.*

Gardiner, Charles C.
Suydam, John F.
Middlebrook, C. T.
Hardy, J. F.
Pattison, William.
Nathan, H. H.

*Privates.*

Bull, William H.
Canfield, C. P.
Chambers, S. J.
Clearman, F. G.
Crocker, J. N.
Crow, A. T.
Daniel, William.
Forgerson, J. A.
Gaus, A.
Goodrich, W. R.
Harner, J. H.
Harrall, H. H.
Hendricks, E.
Hendricks, W. J.
Hone, John.
Hoy, Robert S.
Irwin, F. T.
Jennings, W. T.
Jones, W. P.
Kent, George A.
Little, W.
Livingston, M.
Macbeth, W.
Miller, John.
Mullaby, T.
Murray, W.
Musgrave, J. J.
Nathan, F.
Plestin, Charles F.
Powers, E. A.
Raynor, J. W.
Sibley, William H.
Simons, J. F.
Stillwell, R. H.
Storer, D. A.
Tallman, C. L.
Turner, H. B.
Vernam, A. H.
Wood, W. S.

## SEVENTH COMPANY (G).

*2d Lieutenant* (*commanding*), Edwin M. Felt.

*Sergeants.*

Delano, Thomas E. (*Orderly*).
Holdredge, David M.
Pomeroy, Eugene H.

*Corporals.*

Avery, John, Jr.
Dunscomb, John H. A.
Sherman, Samuel J.
Wheelwright, Wm. G.
De Lamater, Charles H.

*Privates.*

Anderson, Smith W.
Bacon, Richard L.
Banks, Joseph E.
Barretto, William H.
Beebe, Charles W.
Bennett, Charles F.
Bowne, Robert S.
Briggs, Benjamin C.
Burroughs, James S.
Callender, William E.
Clark, John G.
Cooper, George C.
Cortelyou, James H.
Crane, Edward I.
Crane, Frank G.
Drew, Thomas W.
Durant, George F.
Ely, Frederick W.
Freeborn, James F., Jr.
Gardner, John G.
Hale, Edward D.
Holdredge, Sterling M.
Ingersoll, James H.
Kingsland, Joseph T.
Louderbach, David, Jr.
Mackenzie, Mortimer L.
McJimsey, Eugene.
Millen, William.
Moore, George G.
Pomeroy, Edward G.
Putnam, Albert E.
Schermerhorn, Charles A.
Schermerhorn, Eugene E.
Schenck, William E.
Sherman, Albert G.
Sherman, Arthur W.
Simons, Henry C.
Simpson, William.
Steers, Abraham.
Trotter, Edgar A.
Turnbull, George R.
Van Loan, Benjamin A.
Van Sicklen, Henry K.
Voorhees, Frederick P.

## EIGHTH COMPANY (H).

1st *Lieutenant*, Howard Waldo.

2d *Lieutenant*, Gilbert L. Arrowsmith.

*Sergeants.*

Casey, Wm. C. (*Orderly*).
Howell, Wm. P.
Morrison, James, Jr.

*Corporals.*

Ryder, Alfred V.
Loder, Benjamin.
Mather, De Witt C.
Gifford, Sanford R.

*Privates.*

Abrams, James C.
Adams, William, Jr.
Allen, Charles D.
Bartlett, William E.
Benedict, James.
Berry, Samuel J., Jr.
Boyce, George A.
Burkhalter, John H.
Coles, Edward O.
Delano, Victor M.
Easton, Frederick J.
Forshay, George H.
Franklin, Peter B.
Garson, Thomas E., Jr.
Gillilan, John, Jr.
Gross, Frank, Jr.
Halsted, William H.
Hanford, William H.

Heiser, Frederick S.
Hoe, William A.
Hull, William R.
Jackson, F. D.
Knight, A. L.
McKune, James.
Mercein, James R.
Morrison, William A.
Murray, George W.
Oddie, John V. S.
Pease, Walter A.
Potter, Allen B.
Price, Charles A.
Richards, John S.
Sloane, William D.
Van Woert, J. V., Jr.
Williams, George P.

## NINTH COMPANY (I).

*Captain*, Charles A. Easton.

1st *Lieutenant*, Henry A. Cragin.

2d *Lieutenant*, Irvin H. MacBride.

*Sergeants.*

Keeler, Edwin, Jr. (*Orderly*).
Moore, Lawrence, Jr.
Burdick, J. C.
O'Brien, Oswin.
Corey, R. P.

*Corporals.*

Ketchum, Edmund.
Dummell, G. H.
Arthur, E. G.
Ryan, W. H.
Lounsberry, J. H.
Kingsland, D. C.
Sweet, M. B.
Edgar, S. P.

*Privates.*

Aclasson, De Lamater W.
Adams, Austin.
Albertson, Edwin.
Arthur, W. H.
Bill, Avery, Jr. (July 7).
Black, F. A.
Black, James.
Bogert, Jacob J.
Brink, H. P.
Burt, John (July 5).
Bush, Theo. H.
Church, J. A.
Church, E. D.
Churchill, F. A.
Coburn, J. W.
Crosby, H. L.
Cutter, H. M.
Dewitt, Peter.
Eames, G. H.
Fisher, H. C.
Franklin, Wm.
Germond, G. B.
Gilmour, M. J.
Glazo, G. J.
Hannah, George.
Haushe, J. B.
Hazeltine, J. M.
Howe, L. P.
Imlay, M.
King, C. E.
Knapp, E. S.
Lane, N. P.
Lent, D. W. C.
Lewis, George.
McCrea, J. E.
McDonald, Alex. (July 2).

Meeks, ——.
Merchant, A. T.
Merritt, A. B.
Miller, Anthony.
Mingay, E. B.
Mitchell, John.
Neilson, C. F.
Randall, ——.
Roberts, M. H.
Roberts, R. L.
Rutherford, J.
Salisbury, ——.
Schermerhorn, A.
Schermerhorn, W. B.
Schultry, Theodore.
Searle, H. A.
Smith, John W. (July 7).
Sprague, C. G.
Stine, George H. (July 7).
Sutherland, L. V.
Swan, H. C.
Taylor, James P.
Thistle, Boyd (July 7).
Van Iderstine, Peter.
Van Nest, G. G.
White, G. W.
Wilson, George.
Young, D. A.
Youle, George.

## TENTH COMPANY (K).

*Captain*, E. P. Rogers.

1*st Lieutenant*, James Ray. 2*d Lieutenant*, Jos. Lentilhon.

*Sergeants.*

Clinton, C. W. (*Orderly*).
Bleecker, James.
Gawtry, H. E.
Bleecker, T. B.

*Corporals.*

Drake, L.
Bogert, C. L.
Macy, Chas. A., Jr.

*Drummer*, Osborne, William.

*Privates.*

Bronson, O.
Bronson, W.
Burckle, I. J.
Churchill, J. L.
D'Hervilly, Ed.
Greene, R. H.
Hart, L., Jr.
Houghton, F. W.
Jones, E. R.
Kobbé, P. F.
Kobbé, W. A.
Lacombe, E. H.
Luqueer, F. S., Jr. (*Commissary*).
Macdonald, J. A.
Mann, S. V.
Milhan, R. P.
Mitchell, H. P.
Mitchell, R. G., Jr.
Moran, D. C.
Morris, Stuy't.
Mortimer, C. A.
Ostrander, R. W.
Paton, Jas., Jr.
Pell, A., Jr.
Pierson, E. F.
Reid, H. H.
Rogers, Phil.
Scott, D. J.
Taylor, J. B.
Thorne, J., Jr.
Van Ranst, S. T.
Warner, J. H.
Wetherspoon, H. H.
Wetmore, —— (*Engineer*).
White, J. C.

# CHAPTER XVIII.

## THE DRAFT RIOTS.

NO page of American civic history is blacker than that which records the "Draft Riots" of the midsummer of 1863,—an epoch alike terrible and disgraceful in the annals of the Republic. Of these riots the city of New York was the centre and source; and, though they forthwith spread to other large cities, in New York occurred their most terrible violence.

Saturday, the 11th of July, was the day appointed for the conscription under the Enrolment Act, in the city of New York. That a riot would come of it was expected, indeed, an incendiary hand-bill circulated on the eve of the 4th of July, had indicated an earlier outbreak; but the victory at Gettysburg seemed to have checked it. On the morning of Monday, the 13th, a mob collected around the enrolment office at the corner of Third Avenue and Forty-Sixth Street, drove out the enrolling officers, and set the building in flames. The police and a detachment of the Invalid Corps, who rallied to quell the *émeute*, were quickly repulsed.

Already a hydra-headed mob governed New York! The spark in an instant had burst into flame. Joined by thousands of frenzied workmen and idlers, the rioters soon found the city in their power. For three days they maintained a reign of terror. Enrolling-offices were burned; the Colored Orphan Asylum, a fine building devoted to a noble charity, was sacked and destroyed; the dwellings of citizens obnoxious to the mob were pillaged; black people of both sexes and all ages were shot at, chased through the streets, — each panting fugitive with a hundred miscreants at his heels. Here you might see a black man's little house in flames; there, the mangled body of its owner, clubbed or stoned to shapelessness; yonder, a negro hanging lifeless to a lamp-post. Mobs besieged alike obnoxious newspaper offices, great factories, — whose workmen they took by force to join them, — and the homes of eminent citizens. They tore down and trampled under foot the national flags, robbed stores in open day, and plundered and beat citizens in the street. Business was suspended, the street cars and stages did not dare to run, plate and property were concealed, houses were locked and fortified.

On Tuesday, the 14th of July, the news of the riot in New York reached the camp of the Seventh Regiment at Frederick and Monocacy, followed by instructions from General Halleck, at Washington, to proceed homeward forthwith and report to General Wool, then in command of the insurrectionary city. The order was transmitted to Colonel Lefferts through General Schriver, as follows: —

"SIR, — Major-General Halleck directs that the Seventh New York State Militia be sent to New York by railroad, to report to Major-General Wool. You will please to take immediate measures to carry out the order."

It was a welcome command. The work of the Seventh Regiment at the front was done. The exigency for which it had marched was happily ended. The victory at Gettysburg had settled the question of invasion, and both of the great armies, having crossed the Potomac, were now making their way into Virginia. The post of duty for the Seventh was no longer Maryland, but New York, — the protection of hearths and homes.

Colonel Lefferts, who had already received tidings of the riot, was prepared to act forthwith upon Halleck's instructions. He received the foregoing order in person at head-quarters in Frederick at four o'clock, P. M., of the 14th, and made all haste in its execution. With such celerity were his outposts and detachments called in and his camp broken, that, notwithstanding the roads were very heavy after a long storm, the whole regiment was gathered at Monocacy Junction in four and a half hours from the time the Colonel received marching orders at Frederick City. He had also sent one of his staff ahead to Monocacy to expedite the providing of transportation to Baltimore; but on arriving, at 8.30 o'clock, P. M., at the Junction, he found that the cars could not leave until 11.45, P. M. At that hour, the close, dirty, and comfortless trains started, and arrived in Baltimore at 5, A. M., of the 15th. At 8.30, A. M., the regiment left Baltimore by rail for Philadelphia, which it reached towards evening.

Meanwhile, Governor Seymour had sent to Colonel Lefferts an intimation that possibly the rails might be taken up at or near Newark, and the regiment there attacked, with a view to prevent or delay its arrival in New York. To foil this movement and to reach New York, where there was pressing necessity for the regiment's presence at the earliest hour, Colonel Lefferts arranged, with the assistance of Colonel E. S. Sanford, to transport the regiment from Philadelphia via Amboy, landing at Canal Street, — the latter point being suggested by Governor Seymour, who had so telegraphed: —

NEW YORK, July 15, 1863, 8.20 P. M.

COLONEL LEFFERTS, *Seventh Regiment N. Y. S. M.*

It will be best to land at Canal Street, unless you prefer a point lower down. Report to me at police head-quarters.

HORATIO SEYMOUR.

Accordingly, after supper at the Soldiers' Refreshment Saloon, Philadelphia, the regiment proceeded by rail to Amboy, which it reached at one o'clock in the morning, and there took steamer for New York. On the way, Private Schenck, of the Seventh Company, fell overboard and was drowned.

At dawn of Thursday, the 16th of July, the steamer touched the Canal Street pier, and the regiment promptly disembarked. Exaggerated accounts of atrocities which required no exaggeration, meeting the men on their journey, had prepared them to expect street-fighting, and it was supposed that every inch of their way would be contested. The silence and vacancy of the streets, usually so busy and noisy in the neighborhood, told at once the change that had come over the city. But through Canal Street and Broadway, without the slightest show of opposition, the regiment marched to the St. Nicholas Hotel, the head-quarters of General Wool, commanding the department. Reporting to that officer, Colonel Lefferts was by him directed to conduct the regiment to the armory, and there remain, ready for immediate service. The Veterans of the National Guard, "faithful guardians of the portal stood," having through the three days' menace of the mob there kept watch and ward.

The arrival of the Seventh Regiment in New York was hailed with satisfaction and delight by all peaceful and law-abiding citizens, and with execrations by the mob. We have described its welcome home after its earlier campaigns; a greeting far different was accorded now. No throngs so vast were assembled to greet its early coming;

but the welcome in the hearts of the citizens was more fervent than ever before. As the approach of the Seventh had been anxiously awaited, so its arrival gave general confidence to the distressed citizens, and diffused a grateful sense of tranquillity. The news was quickly telegraphed through the country, and was accepted everywhere as a pledge of the security of New York.*

Three days and nights the riot had raged; but it had reached its climax and was already subsiding. The police, who displayed admirable address and undaunted bravery against overwhelming numbers, a few detachments of Regulars from neighboring posts and of marines from the Navy-yard, and, at last, some volunteer and militia regiments returning home or going through the city to the front, made head against the mob. And many noble-hearted citizens, with a courage greater than that which a pitched battle usually requires, fought the savage mob in the streets. Nor was it a service without peril. Colonel O'Brien was brutally beaten to death by a legion of cruel assailants; and the gallant Jardine — a member of the Seventh, but then Colonel of the Eighty-Ninth New York Volunteers — was cruelly maimed by the rioters, suffering a compound fracture of the thigh, which disables him to this day. However, the police, the citizens, and the Regulars gave more wounds than they took, and killed and wounded some hundreds of the rioters in the various skirmishes. This slaughter had a good effect, insomuch that, after its first

* The Baltimore Daily Clipper of July 17 said: "The gallant New York Seventh, to whom our city and State is so much indebted, for its promptness on three several occasions flying to our aid, when we were endangered by Rebel forces coming over the Potomac, or by a worse foe in our midst, in the sympathizers with Rebellion on the 19th of April, 1861, were promptly recalled home to attend to the Copperheads of New York, and their agents, the mob of the Five Points; and as they are announced to have arrived there on the evening of Wednesday, we have strong reasons for believing that ere this the pestilent mob has been suppressed. With that regiment at home, and a man in command of the military district who understood his duty, this disgraceful riot would have been nipped in the bud."

fury was spent, and two millions' worth of property destroyed, the mob began to shrink from further responsibility.

The following order was issued by Colonel Lefferts on arriving in New York: —

"All members of this regiment are ordered to report at the armory, to their respective commandants, this afternoon at six o'clock, armed and equipped.

"No excuse, except that of sickness or other disability, will be received."

Those members who had remained in New York during the campaign had already performed efficient service during the riots. On the first day, Monday, all members of the regiment then at home were ordered to report at the armory, and were there on guard all night, ready to be called on. On Tuesday morning they were temporarily dismissed, under orders to report again for duty at half-past seven on Tuesday evening. At nine o'clock that night, a body of about seventy officers and men of the Seventh, and an equal force of the Twenty-Second Regiment, marched to Webb's ship-yard, to protect the iron-clad vessel there building. They were under arms all night, in a duty at once comfortless and perilous, as the mob often approached, yelling and threatening; it had forced the suspension of work on the vessel, that the workmen might join them, and menaced to destroy all the government property, valued at two million dollars. But their malignity vented itself only in threats. This detachment from the Seventh was re-enforced by a howitzer sent from the Navy-yard, whose presence had a good effect on the mob.

During Thursday morning the whole regiment remained in the armory. At 10, A. M., Colonel Lefferts reported to Governor Seymour. In consequence of the order (already recorded) directing him to leave all baggage at Fort Federal Hill, his men were entirely destitute of extra clothing, and they had not changed their underclothing for eleven days, during which time also they had not even had shelter-tents. Nevertheless, they were ready for instant duty.

However, there were signs of the waning of the riot. The street railroads had all recommenced running, and the workmen had mostly returned to the large factories and shops. The draft had been suspended, and thus the immediate cause for insurrection was taken away from the rioters. However, a residuum of rogues, thieves, drunken laborers, and others, still prolonged the carnival of crime from sheer love of it. The stronghold of this force was now on the east side of the city, in the upper wards,—in that neighborhood where Colonel O'Brien had been murdered. That part of the city, General Harvey Brown, United States Artillery, commanding in the city under General Wool, Department Commander, at once put under the charge of Colonel Lefferts.

During Thursday afternoon Colonel Lefferts received the following order:—

Colonel Lefferts of the Seventh Regiment, New York Militia, will proceed and take station with his regiment as follows. His head-quarters with one battalion at the Eighteenth Precinct, and one battalion under command of the senior field officer at the Twenty-First Precinct, the Colonel commanding both. He is charged with suppressing all mobs and riots, and will sternly use all means he has in doing so.

His district extends from Seventh Street to Sixty-Fifth Street, and he will make such further distribution of his regiment as he may think proper. He will continue in that district until he receives further orders, and will make frequent reports to these head-quarters.

By command of Brevet Brigadier-General Harvey Brown,

JOHN B. FROTHINGHAM, *Lieut.-Col., A. D. C., U. S. A.*

During the day, Colonel Lefferts also received an appeal for succor from General Sandford, who had been on duty at the Seventh Avenue Arsenal for several days, and from which point he now wrote as follows:—

COLONEL, — If not under orders from Major-General Wool, I wish you to report the number and disposition of your regiment. I am here with a very small force, entirely worn out with constant duty for three days, which I am anxious to relieve as soon as possible. Please to send a return as soon as possible of your present force, and upon what duty you are employed.

Yours, respectfully,

CHAS. W. SANDFORD, *Major-General.*

Upon the receipt of General Brown's order, Colonel Lefferts marched his command into the district there indicated. It comprised the part of the city lying between Seventh and Sixty-Fifth Streets, and between Third Avenue and East River. It included the hot-bed of the riot. Within this district occurred the sharp fight between the mob and the small body of Regulars, under Captain Putnam of the Twelfth Infantry (U. S. A.), with an insurgent loss, according to that officer, of thirty-three killed and wounded and twenty-four prisoners, while but a few of his men were wounded. Into this district Colonel Lefferts, towards evening, marched his regiment. An appeal being made to him for haste, on the ground that a street-fight was in progress in Twenty-Second Street, near Third Avenue, he hurried off two companies, — the Second, Captain Clark, and the Third, Lieutenant Murray, both under command of the former officer, — directing them to proceed through Second Avenue, to stop the fight if still going on, and thence proceed to the regimental station in Thirty-Fifth Street. With the main body of the regiment he proceeded soon after through Third Avenue to the same point.

In the neighborhood of Twenty-Second Street, the Second and Third Companies were assailed with missiles and with scattering shots from windows, doors, and house-tops. The fire was returned whenever practicable. Through this trying ordeal of the attack of a concealed foe, the men marched steadily and coolly to Thirty-Fifth Street, the rioters everywhere flying from the street to their houses and fences.

Fortunately, the only wound was that of Private Davis, who received a buckshot in the hand; the coats of Privates Curtis and King were torn by bullets. After dark, also, as Colonel Lefferts reports, his reconnoitring parties were "continually annoyed by shots from the houses and other places of concealment." One of the city papers next day said of this skirmish: —

"On the way, the mob fired on the soldiers from windows, house-tops, doors, and alley-ways. The soldiers returned the fire. None of the Seventh were injured. One of its members had a ball cut the back part of his uniform. The firing was of a straggling character. In the course of the march, taking both sides, perhaps some three hundred shots were fired. It is thought that many of the mob were wounded. Two are known to be killed and three to be injured."

The Second and Third Companies joined the rest of the regiment at Thirty-Fifth Street, where it was quartered for the night in a large rubber-factory. Colonel Lefferts's head-quarters were at the police station of the Twenty-First Precinct, two doors from Third Avenue, where also was posted the Eighth Company. While engaged in removing a wounded policeman to the Bellevue Hospital, the Eighth Company had an encounter with the mob. Other companies were properly disposed for guard duty. At 10, P. M., in obedience to instructions, Colonel Lefferts sent down to Fourteenth Street a battalion of four companies, together with howitzers (the latter under command of Captain Rogers, Company K), the whole under command of Lieutenant-Colonel Price; and this force thoroughly patrolled the district between Thirty-Fifth and Thirteenth Streets, and between Third Avenue and the river.

The night passed without further events of importance. Next morning, Colonel Lefferts made the following report: —

HEAD-QUARTERS SEVENTH REGIMENT, TWENTY-FIRST PRECINCT,
July 17, 1864.

GENERAL HARVEY BROWN.

SIR, — I have the honor to report the district under my charge as quiet after twelve o'clock, P. M. I was obliged to use harsh measures during the evening, but hope we shall have no further trouble.

In obedience to orders, a thorough patrol of the district between Thirty-Fifth Street and Fourteenth Street, Third Avenue and East River, was made last evening after ten o'clock, P. M. None of my men were injured.

MARSHALL LEFFERTS,
*Colonel Commanding Seventh Regiment.*

The morning papers contained stories of "severe engagements," with "losses in killed and wounded," on the part of the Seventh. But these were promptly contradicted.

While in command of his district, on the night of the 16th, Colonel Lefferts had been informed of several depots of arms in possession of the mob. One of the memoranda so received was accompanied by a rough plan of the premises to be seized, and the streets adjacent. It read as follows: —

"Opposite 145 East Twenty-First Street, four or five story house contains both a large number of men and a large quantity of carbines, ready to *use*. Their retreat can be headed off by a strong force placed in Twenty-Second Street, in the rear of opposite 145 East Twenty-First Street, and at the head of Twenty-First Street and Second Avenue."

Accordingly, on the morning of the 17th, he proceeded with his whole force to Thirty-Eighth Street, and there stretched a cordon of men around the block enclosed between Thirty-Eighth and Thirty-Seventh Streets, and Second and Third Avenues. This done, the houses in the block were entered and searched. He proceeded in like manner southerly, from block to block, toward Fourteenth Street, until about two hundred and fifty guns (many of them loaded and capped) had been collected and secured, beside a considerable quantity of clothing, which had been stolen from the store of Messrs. Brooks. In this work, Colonel Lefferts was aided by Acting Captain Brackett of the police, with a platoon of policemen. At two o'clock, P. M., he received orders from head-quarters to return to the regimental armory.

The riot, which began with the week, almost wholly died out with its close. Saturday, the sixth day, found the city nearly as tranquil as usual, save for the military forces moving hither and thither, and the remnants of the riotous population gathering in knots, and muttering the threats they had lately yelled in triumph. In the wake of the Seventh other militia regiments had hurried home from Maryland, and returning volunteer troops had been stopped and put on duty in the city. General Dix was put in command of the department, with General Canby in charge of the city. Cavalry, infantry, and artillery in abundance overawed the mob.

Colonel Lefferts, on the evening of the 18th, completely worn out and ill, left Lieutenant-Colonel Price in command. On the night of the 19th a part of the regiment was dismissed; but for two weeks thereafter the companies remained on duty by turns, one night each. August had well advanced before the elaborate precautions against riots were relaxed, and mob law had become a story of the past. The following was Colonel Price's order on this subject: —

GENERAL ORDER No. 2.

HEAD-QUARTERS SEVENTH REGIMENT, N. Y. S. N. G.,
NEW YORK, August 1, 1863.

In compliance with division order of this P. M., one full company consisting of one hundred men is hereby detailed for duty at the armory from day to day, together with two non-commissioned officers from each company not on duty, and two non-commissioned staff officers, until further orders. Captain Clark, with his command, will relieve the detachment of Company A at eight o'clock to-morrow morning. Captain Clark will be relieved in turn by the officer commanding company next in rank on Monday morning at the same hour, and the remaining companies will relieve in turn according to rank each twenty-four hours thereafter.

Morning reports will be made to the Adjutant in person before nine o'clock, A. M., together with a list of delinquents; absence from the city will not be considered an excuse for neglect of duty.

Officers will report in person to the commanding officer in case they desire to leave town.

By order of

JAMES PRICE,
*Lieutenant-Colonel Commanding.*

WM. H. HUME, *Adjutant.*

On the 17th of August, Colonel Lefferts received leave of absence, and Lieutenant-Colonel Price was directed by General Hall to assume command. This he did, and, in compliance with division and brigade orders of the same date, assembled the regiment on the following evening, in full fatigue dress, light marching order. The fact was that, on the 20th, the draft was to be resumed; and the entire regiment was thus again on duty for several days. At length, however, some respite came in the following order: —

GENERAL ORDER No. 5.

HEAD-QUARTERS SEVENTH REGIMENT, N. Y. S. N. G.,
NEW YORK, August 22, 1863.

Companies H, B, C, E, and A, composing the right wing, will remain on duty at the armory until Sunday, August 23, at eight o'clock, P. M., and then will be relieved by Companies G, I, K, F, and D, composing the left wing of the regiment, until August 24, at eight o'clock, P. M., and so alternate until further orders.

This arrangement will not change the tour of guard duty now in force, but the order is so far modified as to require but one energetic non-commissioned officer from each company to remain at the armory constantly.

Passes, not to exceed one sixth of the force on duty, may be given by the commissioned officers, in special cases, for short periods only, but every pass must be countersigned by the officer in command of the battalion.

Meals will be provided at seven, A. M., and two and seven, P. M., for three hundred and fifty men.

JAMES PRICE,
*Lieutenant-Colonel Commanding.*

Other reductions of force were subsequently made, and at length the guard duty was lightened by the two following orders: —

GENERAL ORDER No. 6.

HEAD-QUARTERS SEVENTH REGIMENT, N. Y. S. N. G.,
NEW YORK, August 28, 1863.

By permission of the Major-General commanding, the order of the 26th is so far modified as to reduce the number of men *constantly on duty at the armory to one hundred*, in addition to two non-commissioned officers from each company not on duty, and two non-commissioned staff officers.

Companies H and D, under the command of the senior officer, will commence the tour of guard duty to-morrow, Saturday morning, at eight o'clock, and be relieved on Sunday, the 30th instant, by Companies A and B, followed in succession, each twenty-four hours thereafter, by Companies I and C, F and G, and E and K, until further orders.

Reports will made to the Adjutant in person, at nine, A. M., each day.

By order of

JAMES PRICE,
*Lieutenant-Colonel Commanding.*

GENERAL ORDER No. 7.

HEAD-QUARTERS SEVENTH REGIMENT, N. Y. S. N. G.,
NEW YORK, September 1, 1863.

In compliance with brigade order of this date, the force on duty at the armory is reduced to twenty-seven men, viz. one sergeant, one corporal, fifteen men, together with one non-commissioned officer from each company not on duty, in charge of the company roster, and one non-commissioned staff officer.

Captain Dutton will detail one sergeant, one corporal, and fifteen men from Company E to report for duty to-morrow morning, at eight o'clock, to be relieved on Thursday, the 3d instant, by the same complement of men from Company K. The other companies, with like numbers, will relieve in turn according to rank, until further orders.

By order of

JAMES PRICE,
*Lieutenant-Colonel Commanding.*

W. H. HUME, *Adjutant.*

Thus this wearisome epilogue to the Maryland campaign lasted to the 10th of September, making the tour of duty for 1863 nearly a three months' tour after all.

Meanwhile, however, the " third campaign " proper had been formally ended on the 21st of July, 1863, when, for the third and last time during the war, the Seventh Regiment was mustered out of the United States service, after a campaign of six-and-thirty days.

In his order, three days later, expressive of thanks for this campaign, Governor Seymour said: —

"The Governor and Commander-in-Chief of the military forces of the State of New York, upon the return of those regiments of the National Guard who, upon his order, with a promptness and alacrity which excited the admiration of the whole country, went forth on a sudden call of danger to other States, expresses to them his thanks for their gallant and successful service, which has been alike honorable to them and to the State whose name and arms they are proud to bear.

"By the ready and vigorous assistance thus rendered, the soil of Pennsylvania was relieved from the presence of the invader, and aid was given to the national armies which helped to win the victories at Gettysburg.

"The people of the State of New York will remember with pride and honor with praise their fellow-citizens who had prepared themselves for this great work by a long period of drill and discipline at a time when general encouragement was withheld. It required no little moral courage to uphold our militia system when it had fallen into disrepute; but this has been done by the citizen soldiery of New York, who have nobly maintained their organization, and by their example and zeal revived a martial spirit throughout the State which we must regard as our surest protection in the hour of danger. It has shown the utility of that section of our national Constitution which declares that a 'well-regulated militia being necessary for the security of a free State, the right of the people to keep and bear arms shall not be infringed.' So careful were our fathers upon this point, that they exempted the musket from seizure and sale before they placed the tools of the mechanic and the implements of husbandry beyond the reach of the creditors' grasp. They confided the safety of the Republic to the hands of its citizens, and secured to them the musket as they did the ballot, for the defence of their rights and the protection of their interests. Time has demonstrated their wisdom.

"If our militia system is allowed to decay, all our institutions are weakened. The militia is the main strength of the executive to maintain the laws, put down insurrection, and to repel invasion.

"Within thirty days the uniformed militia of this State have gone forth to assist their brethren beyond our limits, and have returned to put down riot, arson, and robbery at home; they have aided in defending the national flag and honor upon the battle fields of other States, and, that done, their tread upon the pavements of this great city brought back a sense of security to its disturbed and endangered inhabitant.*

The arduous duties imposed upon Colonel Lefferts during the hot summer of 1863 had so impaired his health as to render it necessary for him to tender his resignation. Already, on the 9th of March, 1863, he had resigned his command, issuing this farewell order: —

Brother Officers and Soldiers of the Seventh Regiment, — I am about to issue my last order, and to bid you farewell. The older members of the regiment especially can understand what it costs me to sever my connection with those in whose company I have passed so many pleasant hours; but family cares and business relations, with constantly increasing demands upon my time, have long since warned me of the necessity of resigning my position as your commanding officer.

In the year 1851 I was elected from the ranks of the Eighth Company to a commission as Major, a few years later to that of Lieutenant-Colonel, and for nearly four years past I have served as Colonel commanding the regiment; and I have to thank you most sincerely for your unwavering support, and the cheerful confidence with which you have always obeyed my orders. How far we have been successful in maintaining the standard and *esprit de corps* of the regiment is shown, I think, by its numerical strength and complete equipment and organization as it stands today. Notwithstanding the large demands upon our ranks, since the war commenced, for officers, of whom we have furnished between three and four hundred of various grades, — most of them now serving in the army, — we have still upon our rolls more than eleven hundred rank and file who are ready for duty.

The services which you have performed during the past two years have been honorably acknowledged by the general government, as well as by your own State; and when impartial history shall record the events of the mighty struggle now going on, the Seventh Regiment will enjoy untarnished honor, in common with the noble spirits who have flocked to our country's standard to defend our nationality and republican liberty; and the names of your comrades, Winthrop, Farnham, Gadsden, O'Brien, and others, who have fallen in the field of battle, — now shrouded in mourning drapery on your walls, in touching tribute to their bravery and your loss, — will claim conspicuous places on the scroll which is to tell posterity of those who died in defence of the Constitution and the laws.

My proudest boast — the happiest of my recollections — is that I have never asked of you any service, or anything even out of the line of official duty, which has not been most readily and cheerfully granted. These are evidences of a friendship and mutual attachment which I trust will still continue when our official relations shall have ceased to exist.

Let the regiment only be true to itself, and no defence of its acts will ever be needed; its history will be recorded in the hearts of our citizens.

COLONEL MARSHALL LEFFERTS.

NEW YORK, March 9, 1863.

Two days later, the 11th of March, Colonel Lefferts transmitted his resignation to General Hall, commanding the Third Brigade, with an urgent request for its prompt acceptance at head-quarters. But with the resignation General Hall took the liberty of enclosing to Albany another document on the same subject, which had been quickly drawn up and put into his hands, namely, a petition signed by no less than twenty-four commissioned officers and seven hundred rank and file, urging Colonel Lefferts to remain in command, to which, also, he appended his own urgent official solicitation. The Adjutant-General responded, after recounting these facts: "I am instructed by his Excellency Governor Seymour to say, that with the foregoing expression of opinions, together with his own knowledge of your efficiency as a soldier, and added to these the appreciation, at the present time, of valuable officers in the State National Guard, induce him to ask you to reconsider the matter, and, if possible, withdraw your resignation."

Colonel Lefferts, upon these repeated solicitations, in a general order conveyed to his regiment his "thanks for their hearty expression of good-will, and desire that he should continue to command the regiment. The labor and responsibilities of the post," he added, "are made far lighter, when the commandant is generously supported, and mutual confidence is made the ground of success." And to General Sprague he wrote on June 10th: —

"I had tendered my resignation of the command of the Seventh Regiment only after mature consideration, and not without an effort to separate myself from honorable and agreeable associations which have always attended it, and not expecting the kind expressions of friendship and attachment from the members of the regiment which seem to have reached his Excellency the Governor to influence him in his decision.

"The desire expressed by my regiment, and the manner in which it was conveyed, were well calculated to shake my resolution, when I received the request of the Commander-in-Chief that I should reconsider my resignation. I sincerely thank his Excellency for his confidence, and the honor done me by your communication of the 25th ultimo.

"I leave my resignation as Colonel commanding the Seventh Regiment in your hands, to be taken up and accepted by his Excellency the Governor whenever he may see fit to do so. In the mean time I shall continue in the performance of my duty."

The Maryland campaign and the riots of 1863 followed close upon these events. The Colonel remained on duty through the summer; but the condition of his health made it imperative, in his view, after the duties of the campaign were over, to repeat positively the tender of his resignation, which he did on the 1st of August, after the riots, saying, in his letter: "Although the reasons for relinquishing my command last March were urgent, yet I did not feel that I could, with proper respect, insist upon its acceptance at that time; . . . . as my health is much impaired, I must add this to my former reasons, and respectfully beg that my resignation may now be accepted." To avoid, however, directly accepting this resignation, the Governor requested Colonel Lefferts "to continue the duties of his present grade," as it was intended that he should be placed in command of a brigade of infantry, to be raised in New York, with the Seventh Regiment as a nucleus. Colonel Lefferts's formal appointment as Brigadier-General was dated August 18, 1863, but the plan alluded to was, from various causes, not carried into effect.

Meanwhile, the authorities at Albany, as has been seen, granted Colonel Lefferts a two months' leave of absence from his regiment, for the restoration of his health.

On the 20th of October, Colonel Lefferts, upon the expiration of this furlough, again resumed command of the regiment, and in his general order for that purpose thanked Lieutenant-Colonel Price "for the care and fidelity with which he has performed his duties, and administered the affairs of the regiment during his temporary command." The same order announced the resignation of Captain and Brevet-Colonel H. C. Shumway, commanding the Eighth Company, — an accomplished and experienced officer, whose services as far back as the Astor Place Riots, and farther yet, are mentioned in the first chapter of the present volume, and whose services throughout the war have just been recorded. In accepting this resignation, Colonel Lefferts said: "The Commandant expresses his great regret at the resignation of Captain Shumway; his faithful services of *thirty-five years* have identified him with all the important movements of the regiment during that period of time, and it will always acknowledge his zeal and ability in promoting its growth and efficiency. He retires with the respect and good wishes of all the members of the regiment."

Some months later, a hostile invasion of the northern frontier of New York and Vermont from Canada was expected. Colonel Lefferts promptly addressed to General Dix the following offer of the services of his regiment, in the threatened emergency: —

NEW YORK, November 12, 1863.

MAJOR-GENERAL DIX, *Commanding Department of the East.*

SIR, — As circumstances may require a larger force of troops than you have at your immediate disposal to guard the frontier of our State against the threatened invasion from Canada by secession sympathizers, you can, in case of need, rely upon the support of the regiment under my command. They will require no official call of the President of the

United States, but stand ready to preserve inviolate their own State from the attempt herein referred to, or any other of a similar character. I am compelled to leave in the five-o'clock train for Troy. I can return at a moment's notice, and a few hours will suffice for the regiment to move. Inquiry at General Telegraph Office will find me.

I am, General, your obedient servant,

MARSHALL LEFFERTS.

This letter General Dix acknowledged in a warm letter of thanks, through Major Bolles, of his staff, who said: "The General directs me to express to you his hearty thanks for the offer of your regiment to guard the frontier of New York. He has returned from Buffalo, and thinks he will not need to avail himself of the services of that regiment which has so gallantly signalized itself heretofore by its prompt patriotism and great efficiency."

In February, 1864, Major Nevers resigned. Captains Emmons Clark and George T. Haws were successively elected to fill the vacancy, and successively declined. On the 31st of May, Captain Joseph B. Young was elected Major, and accepted.

Early in February, 1864, measures were adopted by Colonel Lefferts and his officers to secure the co-operation of the regiment in the famous Soldiers' Fair, held in New York soon after. A committee was appointed, of which the Colonel was made chairman, and a subscription raised, whose result was highly creditable to the liberality of the regiment. The following was the order announcing the result: —

GENERAL ORDER No. 9.

HEAD-QUARTERS SEVENTH REGIMENT, NATIONAL GUARDS,
NEW YORK, June 2, 1864.

The commandant of the regiment announces with great pleasure the following report of the Treasurer, in reference to the contributions of the members for the relief of the noble sick and wounded of our army: —

NEW YORK, May 1, 1864.

COLONEL MARSHALL LEFFERTS, *Chairman of Committee on Metropolitan Fair.*

SIR, — The following amounts were received by the Treasurer, in aid of the Metropolitan Fair, for the benefit of the United States Sanitary Commission: —

| | |
|---|---|
| Field and staff | $ 190.00 |
| First Company | 528.00 |
| Second Company | 1,850.00 |
| Third Company | 463 00 |
| Fourth Company | 570 50 |
| Fifth Company | 544.00 |
| Sixth Company | 1,816.00 |
| Seventh Company | 621.00 |
| Eighth Company | 630.00 |
| Ninth Company | 743.00 |
| Tenth Company | 573.00 |
| Non-commissioned staff | 55.00 |
| Total | $ 8,583.50 |

TREASURER'S OFFICE, METROPOLITAN FAIR,
April 22, 1864.

CAPTAIN EMMONS CLARK, *Treasurer of the Seventh Regiment.*

SIR, — The Treasurer of the Metropolitan Fair begs to acknowledge the receipt of $ 8,583.50 from the members of the Seventh Regiment, and to express the gratification with which the contribution has been received from a regiment so much respected at home, and who have done so much, through their officers and collectively, to vindicate the honor of the flag in the field.

ELLEN R. STRONG, *Treasurer.*

By order of Colonel Marshall Lefferts.

WM. H. HUME, *Adjutant.*

Early in June, 1864, General Lefferts, after fourteen years' service in the Seventh Regiment, procured the acceptance of his long-tendered resignation. Originally raised from his position as private in the ranks to the grade of field officer, — an honor without parallel in the regimental history, — he had served thirteen years successively as Major, Lieutenant-Colonel, and Colonel, commanding the regiment through the most trying, useful, and brilliant years which its annals record. Though retired from the active regiment, General Lefferts was chosen the Commandant of the Veteran Corps, on a vacancy occurring in that body, which position he holds at this present writing.

Emmons Clark
Col. Com. 7th Reg. N.G.S.N.Y.

On the 21st of June, Captain Emmons Clark was elected Colonel of the regiment. In July, Lieutenant-Colonel Price resigned his commission; and, on the 18th of August, Captain George T. Haws was elected Lieutenant-Colonel.

At a meeting of the board of officers held on the 1st of July, on motion of Lieutenant Ryder, a committee was appointed "to procure a site for a monument to the members of the Seventh Regiment who have been killed, or have died of disease or wounds, while in the service of the United States during the great Rebellion." This committee recommended that the monument should be erected in the Central Park, and was accordingly directed to make application to the Park Commissioners for a proper site. The application was not favorably received, the chief objections being that a monument of the character proposed would give a sepulchral appearance to the Park, and furnish a precedent for similar applications from other military organizations. We shall presently see what conclusions were afterwards reached on this subject.

On the 2d of May, 1864, a committee had been appointed, consisting of three officers and three non-commissioned officers and privates from each company, to consider a proposed change in the uniform. During the three campaigns of the regiment in 1861, 1862, and 1863, the uniforms of many members had been almost worn out, and the question for decision was, whether the old pattern should be followed or a new one selected, more adapted for use in field or camp. On the 3d of October, the board of officers voted to submit to the rank and file the following questions: —

"1. Are you willing to change the uniform, if the Quartermaster-General will allow to this regiment the same amount per man which is expended in uniforming other regiments of the National Guard?

"2. Do you desire that the new uniform shall be gray?

"3. Do you desire to change the style and adopt the French Chasseur?"

The vote resulted in favor of a change, but gray was to be retained as the distinctive color of the regimental uniform.

In the autumn of 1864, the regiment performed some annoying and monotonous guard duty at the armory. The exciting presidential contest and the renewal of the draft led the authorities to take various precautions against a repetition of the riots of 1863, and the guard at the armory was designed not only to protect, if required, the arms there stored, but to summon absent members promptly, and be ready at short notice to quell any disorder.

Besides the Fourth-of-July parade, and the October parade and review for inspection (when the number present was seven hundred and eighty-nine), the regiment paraded, by order of General Sandford, on the 19th of September, 1864, as funeral escort to Colonel W. T. C. Grower, Seventeenth New York Veteran Volunteers, killed at the battle of Jonesboro', Tennessee; and the same duty was performed on the 3d of November by the right wing, in honor of Lieutenant-Colonel Higginbotham, Sixty-Fifth New York Volunteers, killed at Cedar Creek on the 19th of October. On the 31st of December, 1864, the regiment paraded, by order of General Sandford, as escort to the remains of Hon. William L. Dayton, Minister to France.

On the 22d of February, 1865, the regiment paraded (to quote the language of the regimental order) "to celebrate the glorious success of General Sherman and his gallant army; the restoration of our national flag to Fort Sumter; and the capture of Charleston, the cradle of the Rebellion." On the 4th of March occurred the parade of the First Division, to celebrate the victories of the Union Army.

At a meeting of the board of officers, on the 1st of April, it was resolved to celebrate the anniversary of the departure of the regiment for Washington in 1861, and the following order was issued: —

GENERAL ORDER No. 8.

HEAD-QUARTERS SEVENTH REGIMENT NATIONAL GUARD, S. N. Y.,
NEW YORK, April 10, 1865.

To celebrate the anniversary of the departure of this regiment for Washington, on the 19th day of April, 1861, to defend the national capital, then in imminent danger, and in honor of the recent brilliant victories of the Union armies, resulting in the suppression of the great Rebellion, it is ordered that the regimental armory be illuminated on the evening of the 19th of April, and that a salute of one hundred guns be fired at eight o'clock, P. M.

The armory, finance, and music committees, and the board of officers, will act as a committee of arrangements for this celebration.

Captain Rogers and his command are detailed to fire the salute.

By order of Colonel Emmons Clark,
J. H. LIEBENAU, *Adjutant.*

Arrangements were already completed for a grand celebration, when the city and the whole country were startled and horrified by the news of the assassination of Abraham Lincoln, President of the United States. The following order was immediately issued: —

GENERAL ORDER No. 9.

HEAD-QUARTERS SEVENTH REGIMENT NATIONAL GUARD, S. N. Y.,
NEW YORK, April 15, 1865.

In view of the great calamity which has befallen the nation, in the death of its beloved Chief Magistrate, General Order No. 8 (for the illumination of the regimental armory, and the celebration of the recent victories of the Union armies) is hereby countermanded.

The armory committee will immediately drape the regimental armory and the council-room of the board of officers with mourning. and the committees of the several companies are directed to drape their respective rooms with the usual emblems of mourning.

By order of Colonel Emmons Clark,
J. H. LIEBENAU, *Adjutant.*

Major-General Sandford, commanding the First Division, honored the regiment by detailing it as especial escort and guard of honor to the remains of President Lincoln upon their arrival in New York, and while they remained in the city. The following is the regimental order: —

GENERAL ORDER No. 10.

HEAD-QUARTERS SEVENTH REGIMENT NATIONAL GUARD, S. N. Y.,
April 20, 1865.

I. In compliance with division and brigade orders, this regiment will parade as special escort to the remains of our late President, Abraham Lincoln, on Monday, 24th instant, fully uniformed and equipped (without overcoats or knapsacks) and with the usual badge of mourning upon the left arm. Roll-call of companies at half past seven o'clock, A. M.

II. This regiment will also parade, fully uniformed and equipped, (without overcoats or knapsacks), on Tuesday, 25th instant. Roll-call of companies at half past nine o'clock, A. M.

III. Companies D, B, and H, Captains Riblet, Palmer, and Smith, are detailed for special duty at the City Hall.

By order of Colonel Emmons Clark,
J. H. LIEBENAU, *Adjutant.*

The solemn pomp of the President's funeral in New York, the reception of the remains, their removal to the City Hall, the guard duty there performed by the Seventh Regiment, the division parade on the following day, when the Seventh acted as special escort to the remains as they moved in stately procession through the city to the Hudson River Railroad Depot, — these well-remembered incidents of that terrible epoch when a nation was bowed in sincere grief are sad but proud incidents in the regimental history. Colonel Clark and Lieutenant-Colonel Haws were selected from the regimental officers of the First Division, by Major-General Dix, to act with the officers of the army and navy as immediate attendants or guards to the remains of the President, while they lay in state in City Hall.

# CHAPTER XIX.

## SINCE THE WAR.

TO closing the regimental story which has occupied the pages of this volume brief space must be allotted. For, as it was fitting and necessary to preface that story with some account of the origin of the Seventh Regiment and its annals before the war, so those who have followed the narrative of the three campaigns to the end will naturally demand a few words touching the regiment's subsequent fortunes and its present condition. This brief account I now proceed to give, following as nearly as possible the chronological order of events.

The first noteworthy parade of the regiment after the war was in honor of the returning Sixty-Fifth New York Volunteers, whose close connection with the Seventh is expressed in the following General Order: —

GENERAL ORDER No. 15.

HEAD-QUARTERS SEVENTH REGIMENT NATIONAL GUARD, S. N. Y.,
NEW YORK, July 19, 1865.

This regiment will parade in full fatigue, gray trousers (without knapsacks), on Saturday, 22d instant, to receive and escort the Sixty-Fifth Regiment, New York Volunteers on its return from long and distinguished service in the field.

The nation owes a debt of gratitude to its gallant defenders which it can never repay, and every member of the Seventh should unite in this humble tribute of welcome to the brave and patriotic soldiers of the Republic. The Sixty-Fifth Regiment, New York Volunteers (United States Chasseurs), was, at its organization, almost entirely officered by members of the Seventh. Their brilliant career reflects honor on our organization, and the names of Generals Shaler, Hamblin, Gurney, and many others will live forever upon the pages of American history. Let them realize, by a warm and generous reception, that they have not been forgotten by their comrades, and that patriotism never fails to receive the affection and respect of the young men of New York.

By order of Colonel Emmons Clark,
J. H. LIEBENAU, *Adjutant.*

The several companies having approved the proposed changes in uniform, the board of officers sanctioned them in July. The new uniform consisted of gray chasseur jacket and trousers and fatigue-cap. Until the uniform coat, worn before the war, should be resumed, it was voted, that, for *full* uniform, epaulettes with black fringe should be worn with the jackets, and a uniform hat of modern pattern, with black plume. In this new uniform the regiment paraded at the annual inspection of October 20, 1865; but the change was not received with favor by the friends of the regiment or by the public generally. The new uniform was pronounced sombre and heavy in appearance, and the style of jacket and trousers, however well adapted to active service, was not sufficiently attractive in days of peace for a regiment of the National Guard. The subject of another change was constantly agitated from that time forward, until, in 1867, the members voted, by a considerable majority, to resume, without important change, the uniform as worn before the war.

On the 12th of August, 1865, the following order was issued, being a part of General Order No. 17 : —

> A committee of the board of officers has been appointed to select a site for a monument to those members of this regiment who have been killed, or have died from disease or wounds while in the service of their country, during the great Rebellion. The Fourth Company has inaugurated measures for a most liberal contribution to the Seventh Regiment Monumental Fund, and it is respectfully recommended that all the companies appoint committees to co-operate in securing the success of this most patriotic and noble object. No tribute is too great and no honor undeserved to the memory of our comrades who have shed their blood in the defence of free institutions, and who have bravely died that the country might live.
>
> By order of Colonel Emmons Clark,
>
> J. H. LIEBENAU, *Adjutant.*

During a visit of Lieutenant-General Grant to New York in November, 1865, the regiment was detailed to escort him, on the 21st, from the Fifth Avenue Hotel to the foot of Cortlandt Street, on his return to Washington; but the rain falling in torrents on that day, the General sent a despatch requesting that the parade might on that account be omitted. The regiment had previously, in July, serenaded General Grant at the Astor House, in presence of a large concourse of enthusiastic spectators; and about the same time the officers had given to General Sherman and staff a dinner at Delmonico's. At the annual (October) inspection in Washington Square, there were present a total of eight hundred and fifty-five.

The 31st of January, 1866, was made illustrious in the records of the regiment by its reception, at the Academy of Music, of those members who had served in the army and navy of the United States during the war, — the most brilliant levee of this character ever given in New York. The rapid *résumé* to which perforce this chapter is limited forbids any detailed description of this famous pageant, but I cannot forbear quoting a few paragraphs from the address of Major-General Dix on that occasion. In introducing General Dix, Colonel Clark said: —

"To the members who have served in the army and navy of the United States during the great Rebellion, the Seventh Regiment of New York extends a hearty welcome. The dangers of the battle-field are past; you have exchanged the hardships of the camp, the bivouac, and the march for the pleasures of your own happy homes, and now your former comrades, publicly recognizing your devotion to the flag of the Union, open wide the doors of hospitality. We have watched with pride your brilliant career during four long years of civil war; we have sympathized with you in defeat, and rejoiced with you in victory; and with peace smiling once more on our beloved land, we meet to-night to honor your patriotism and pay a tribute to your bravery. I have the honor of introducing to you, as the representative of the Seventh Regiment on this pleasant occasion, the distinguished statesman, soldier, and patriot, Major-General John A. Dix."

In the course of his address, General Dix said: —

"At the outbreak of the Rebellion, when the Sixth Massachusetts Regiment was attacked at Baltimore, and the deepest concern was felt for the safety of the capital, you were among the first to hurry to the scene of action. A gentleman high in position at Washington gave me, two or three years ago, an account of the condition of things there at the time of your arrival. Open communication with the North had been entirely suspended; railroad travel, and the transportation of the mails through the State of Maryland, had been broken up by force; and no intelligence could be obtained from the loyal portions of the Union, except through secret messengers and couriers, whose journeys were always performed with difficulty, and sometimes not without absolute danger. At this juncture, when all was uncertainty and doubt, when each revolving hour came freighted with some new burden of anxiety or peril, a column of armed men, with bayonets glittering in the sunlight, was seen entering the Pennsylvania Avenue, near the capitol; and the feeling of relief and security was unspeakable when the welcome intelligence spread throughout the city, as if by some magnetic influence, that the Seventh New York had come to oppose to the gathering cohorts of treason the ægis of its discipline and its name.

"In the early spring of 1862, when the Army of the Potomac was lying before Richmond, when Washington and Baltimore and the adjacent country were almost denuded of troops, and there were well-grounded apprehensions of a Rebel raid from the Valley of the Shenandoah, you volunteered your services a second time. I was in command at Baltimore when you arrived there with your gallant companions, the Twenty-Second, the Thirty-Seventh, the Sixty-Ninth, the Seventy-First, and, I believe, some other New York regiments, whose numbers I cannot at this moment recollect. You were detained at Baltimore by the government, at my special request, and during a large portion of this term of your service you occupied the post of honor, — Federal Hill, — that remarkable promontory rising up in the heart of the city, and seeming to be placed there by Nature as a site for a citadel. When you occupied it, it was crowned by a fort, as you see it before you (pointing to a painting representing it), built in the summer of 1861 to protect the city from external attack, and, if need be, to defend the city against itself. Happily, the unshaken loyalty of the Baltimoreans, through all trials and temptations, rendered the latter service unnecessary. In the summer of 1863, when General Lee invaded the State of Maryland with a powerful army, you volunteered your services a third time, and were assigned by the government to the defence of the city of Baltimore, on which an attack was considered imminent. During a portion of this third term of service you were again in the occupation of Fort Federal Hill, and during the residue on duty in the interior of Maryland, remaining in the field until after General Lee had retreated beyond the Potomac. You were then suddenly recalled here to assist in quelling the riot, and your reappearance had a powerful influence in restoring order and saving the city from further depredation.

"In the summer of 1864, when Rebel raiders from Canada were plundering our frontier, you tendered your services to me as commanding officer of this department; and they would have been accepted, had not some new regiments, which had never been in the field, claimed the privilege of serving the country. Most fortunate and enviable is the community in which the emulation of its citizens is, not to evade military duty, but to be received into the public service and to be assigned to posts of danger. Giving you all the praise which is most eminently your due for your promptitude, your patriotic spirit, and your alacrity on all occasions in accepting and courting military service, yet the crowning distinction of your regiment is in the large number of officers which you have furnished for other organizations.

"I hold in my hand a roll of five hundred and fifty-seven members of your regiment who received commissions in the army, the navy, or the volunteer service. Nine tenths of the number were serving with the regiment when the war broke out. Three rose to the rank of major-general, nineteen to the rank of brigadier-general, twenty-nine to the rank of colonel, and forty-six to the rank of lieutenant-colonel. Many whose names are on this roll of honor are sleeping in soldiers' graves. Others are moving about with mutilated limbs and with frames scarred by honorable wounds, the silent but expressive memorials of faithful and heroic service. For years before the war you devoted yourselves with an assiduity and a zeal worthy of all commendation to martial exercises, and I believe I may safely say that there was scarcely a man in your ranks who was not capable of leading other men, of commanding a platoon, a company, a battalion, or a regiment. And the gratifying result is, that under nearly every battle-flag which the State of New York unfurled you had an honored representative. The historian Justin, in his account of the preparations of Alexander the Great for his Asiatic expedition, says that some of the corps he organized were so well disciplined that one would have considered them not so much soldiers as the chosen leaders of soldiers. 'Non tam milites quam magistros militiæ electos putares.' You have fairly earned the same praise, and are justly entitled to the honorable appellation of *militiæ magistri*, — the leaders of soldiers."

The net receipts of this reception were about $4,000, — a sum appropriated, by vote of the board of officers, to the fund for the erection of a monument to the fallen heroes.

I must pass, with brief mention, the brigade field-day of June 13th; the annual parade of July 4th; the divisional parade of August 29th to receive President Johnson; the parade and drill of September 5th (with a review by Mayor Hoffman) at Tompkins Square, in honor of the completion, by the Street Department, of that new city parade-ground, set apart by act of the Legislature; the annual October inspection, at which seven hundred and eight were present; and the Evacuation-day parade.

In June the American citizens resident in Paris gave the regiment an invitation to visit that city during the Exposition of 1867. The proposed trip was for several months a topic of conversation and discussion among the active and exempt members, and attracted much attention in business and commercial circles. The subject was referred to a committee consisting of Captains George William Smith, Peter Palmer, and William H. Kipp; and these officers, after giving the subject a thorough and careful consideration, presented their views to the regiment, and the question was submitted to a vote of the members.

The vote of the members having been duly canvassed, the board of officers determined to decline the invitation. Although a very large number of the members were willing to incur the necessary expenditure of time and money, it was decided that the future welfare of the regiment might be endangered by so great a tax upon it. The decision of the regiment was received in Paris with many expressions of regret, and efforts were made to secure a further consideration of the subject. Arrangements had been substantially perfected for the reception and entertainment of the regiment, and there was every probability that the visit of the Seventh Regiment to France and England would have been the occasion of an interchange of memorable national courtesies. The following was the official correspondence between General Dix and Colonel Clark: —

PARIS, January 25, 1867.

COLONEL EMMONS CLARK, *Seventh Regiment New York National Guard.*

SIR, — I have received a letter from the Minister of Foreign Affairs, inquiring whether "a delegation from the militia of New York" was to be here during the Exposition. The Minister stated that the Emperor had received from Colonel Norton the intelligence that such a delegation would be sent, and thereupon orders were given to prepare for their reception. I answered that I had no official information on the subject; that I did not think the militia of New York had ever taken action with a view to send a delegation here; that a number of American gentlemen had proposed to the Seventh Regiment New York National Guard, a corps which had been greatly distinguished for many years, to visit Paris during the Exposition, but that I did not think the proposition had yet been favorably responded to by the regiment, and added that I would write and ascertain what probability there was that the proposition would be accepted; and I concluded by saying that in any event the militia of New York would be greatly honored by the Emperor's order, and by the attention given to the matter by his ministers. . . . .

I am very respectfully yours,

JOHN A. DIX.

NEW YORK, February 20, 1867.

GENERAL JOHN A. DIX, *Minister Plenipotentiary, Paris.*

SIR, — I have the honor to acknowledge the receipt of your communication of the 25th ultimo, and would respectfully reply: That during the summer of 1866 an invitation, signed by a large number of American citizens resident in Paris, was received by this regiment to visit that city during the Great Exposition in 1867; that upon due consideration of the subject the regiment decided for various reasons to decline the invitation, and such decision was communicated to Rev. Mr. Burlingame and others, under date of November 26, 1866; that the regiment has given the matter no further consideration; and that there is no probability or possibility that it will, under any circumstances whatsoever, visit Paris during the present year.

For the interest which Colonel Norton and many other distinguished American citizens resident in Paris have taken in this subject, and for their flattering assurances that a visit to Paris by this regiment would not be prejudicial to the good name of our country in Europe, I desire, in behalf of my command, to express the most grateful acknowledgments. To the Minister of Foreign Affairs, who has inquired of you as to the probability of a visit of this regiment to Paris in 1867, and has informed you of the orders of the Emperor to prepare for its reception, you will be so kind as to express our high appreciation of the distinguished honor.

I am, sir, very respectfully, your obedient servant,

EMMONS CLARK,

*Colonel Commanding Seventh Regiment National Guard, S. N. Y.*

Complimentary resolutions were adopted by the regiment, thanking Colonel Norton, American Commissioner in Paris, for the services just alluded to.

Early in 1867, the Central Park Commissioners adopted the following resolution: —

"*Resolved*, That the Comptroller of the Park be authorized to set apart the site hereafter mentioned, upon which the Seventh Regiment Monumental Association may erect a monumental structure, provided that neither such structure, nor any of its appendages, be of a sepulchral character, and that the design and plan of said structure shall be submitted to and approved by this board before any site be set apart; and provided, that, before any site be set apart, the Association shall give satisfactory evidence to the board of its pecuniary ability to complete the structure, according to such design and plan as shall be approved by the board; and provided, further, that said structure, when erected, shall be subject to the regulations made or to be hereafter established by the board, for the care and preservation of monuments, statuary, and such other structures within the Park. The site for said structure shall be either at a point just south of the Warriors' Gate, or such other point as may be approved by the board, upon the report and recommendation of the committee."

This offer was accepted by the Seventh Regiment Monumental Association on the 9th of March, and the companies were called on to pledge sums sufficient to guarantee the success of the enterprise. In response, each company pledged $ 2,500, — a total of $ 25,000 for the regiment. The design and execution of the monument were intrusted to the distinguished sculptor, J. Q. A. Ward. His work consists of a bronze statue, ten feet high, representing a private soldier of the Seventh Regiment, as he marched to the defence of the Union. A representation of this statue, from the pencil of Nast, will be found at the head of the "Roll of Honor" in the present volume. The cost of the figure was $ 23,000. Designs were also procured for the base of the monument, and the total cost is estimated at $ 60,000.

In April, Major Young resigned his commission, and on the 28th of May, Captain C. H. Meday was chosen to fill the vacancy. Early in the year, a new drum corps, thirty strong, was organized, which has been maintained with success to the present time. The usual parades occurred during the year. At the inspection in October, the number present was six hundred and eighty-two.

Mention has been made of the restoration of the old uniform, after the experiment with the chasseur style. The first parade in it (with a band of one hundred pieces) occurred May 28, 1868, and attracted great attention. The regiment was reviewed by Mayor Hoffman at City Hall, and by Mr. Burlingame and the Chinese Ambassadors at Union Square. A circular and order issued by Colonel Clark in October, 1867, had fully explained why these changes were made. The uniform was now the old style dress uniform and white belt, the old style fatigue with black belt, the old regimental button, with white pompon and epaulettes.

In July, 1868, the regiment had a very pleasant excursion to Norwich, Conn., which is too fresh in remembrance to require description in this place. The usual annual parades took place. The number present at the October inspection was six hundred and seventy-eight.

On the 19th of April, 1869, the regiment celebrated the eighth anniversary of that memorable "march to the war" which forms the proudest chapter in its history. A splendid floral display was made at the armory, and a stand of colors was presented to the regiment by Mayor Hall, in behalf of the city. Mayor Hall said: —

"COLONEL EMMONS CLARK, AND GENTLEMEN OF THIS VETERAN REGIMENT, — The mutual relations existing between you and the corporate authorities, as well as those between you and the nation, are comprehended by the occurrence that collects so brilliant an assemblage in this armory, which is at once your social club-room and your school of discipline. Eight years ago to-night you began your first march to the national capital in defence of the Union and Constitution, and across the very threshold of those gates of civil war which mad Rebellion then swung open. That occasion and its memories are still so vivid to us all, that this mere reference carries to every heart eulogy and honor. Many times afterward you aided in protecting the national capital; like as for half a century, parts, at least, of your present organization have protected this great metropolis during times of impulsive, riotous rebellion. And your fame has become national! Your relations toward the corporate authorities, whom I have the honor to-night to represent, have also been distinguished and are distinguishing. City records narrate many gifts of colors to your military organization or some of its component parts. Names as honored as those of DeWitt Clinton and Philip Hone have associated themselves with presentation of colors that you now own, as gifts from a grateful city. It may be your proud boast that like as the sturdy oak which breasts all storms can count its age by annular rings, so you can estimate your honorable years by the many stands of colors which you have during the past half-century received. To this metropolis its volunteer standing army is a necessity of security. Even its silent presence is ever a potent weapon in the hands of law and order, and a perpetual menace to the tumultuously disposed. In now presenting these colors, the corporate authorities do, therefore, simply but worthily symbol popular regard for representatives of that standing army. It is their municipal boast and pride to give you always the best quarters and the best civic welcome in return for your volunteer services. Less onerous is even large taxation for promoting the security that you and kindred organizations sacrificingly present to the city, than taxation sometimes imposed through the destructive voice of tumult. The corporate authorities trust soon to add to this gift of flags the gift of a site for a larger and more central armory. Receive, then, sir, this stand of colors, representing those of State, city, and regiment. Nor State nor city shall ever tremble for their safety or honor while in this regimental keeping."

In reply to Mayor Hall, Colonel Clark said:—

"To possess the respect and confidence of the constituted authorities, and to secure the favor and approbation of the public, are objects worthy the ambition of citizen soldiers. But objects so desirable are not won in a day, or without earnest, arduous labor. To this end, excellence in drill and discipline are absolutely indispensable, as well as the utmost promptness in responding to the calls of the proper authority whenever the peace of the city or the property of its citizens are in danger, or when foes, foreign or domestic, threaten the safety of the State or the nation. Nor is this all that is necessary to the permanent popularity and prosperity of a military organization. It must confine itself strictly to its legitimate military duties; it must abstain from all active interest in those affairs upon which good citizens differ, and it must impartially support the chief magistrates of the city and State, of whatsoever party or creed, in the enforcements of laws duly enacted, and in the preservation of the public peace. Last, but not least, its members must possess, and on all occasions exhibit, the attributes of the gentleman as well as the soldier. That the efforts of the officers and members of the Seventh Regiment, during the last half-century, to establish and maintain a military organization of this character have not been altogether in vain, must be inferred from your complimentary allusions to its past services, and to the place it now holds in the hearts of the people and in the estimation of the city authorities. This elegant stand of colors, the gift of the city of New York, which, as its honored chief magistrate, you have this night presented to the Seventh Regiment, is received by its officers and members with hearts overflowing with gratitude. To merit this munificent testimonial of public approbation shall be our earnest effort. In the future as in the past, may this regiment be found ever ready to defend the honor of our beloved city, and to protect the happy homes of its people."

An effort was made, during the legislative session of 1869, to secure a new site for a regimental armory in a more central location; but the bill for that purpose, after passing the Senate, failed by a small majority in the Assembly.

In July the regiment made a delightful visit to Troy, Albany, and Saratoga, and were received everywhere with hearty welcome both by the State authorities and private citizens. At the inspection in October there were present seven hundred and eighteen.

With this brief summary of the leading events in the regimental records since the war, we now turn to the list of members who served in the army or navy of the United States during the war, — a list fitly denominated the "Roll of Honor."

## FIRST COMPANY (A).

### 1. Captain Charles G. Bacon.

Entered the United States service, January 1, 1862, as Second Lieutenant in the Thirty-Ninth Regiment, New York Volunteers, being transferred from the Potomac Light Infantry of Georgetown, D. C.; was promoted to be First Lieutenant and Adjutant, April 1, 1862; was stationed, in April, 1862, at Harper's Ferry, with his regiment, and there appointed A. A. A. G., First Provisional Brigade; was captured and paroled with the garrison, September 15, 1862; was mentioned in brigade report for good conduct on the 14th September, 1862; at Annapolis was appointed A. A. D. C., on the staff of Brigadier-General Tyler, September 22, 1862; promoted to be Captain (Thirty-Ninth New York Volunteers), October 8, 1862, and served with his regiment till June, 1863, when he was authorized to raise the Thirty-Sixth New York Light Battery; in October, 1863, was made Adjutant of the Thirteenth New York Heavy Artillery; served with regiment till November 20, 1861, when he was appointed Acting Ordnance Officer for District East Virginia, on staff of Brigadier-General G. F. Shepley, and so continued till April, 1865.

### 2. Captain Robert Bailey.

Entered the United States service as First Lieutenant in the Sixth Regiment New York Volunteers; served with his regiment at Fort Pickens, and subsequently in Louisiana; was promoted to be Captain, Sixth New York Volunteers; was mustered out with his regiment.

3. Captain AUGUSTUS BELKNAP, JR.

Entered the United States service as First Lieutenant in the —— Regiment, New York Volunteers (First Long Island Regiment); promoted to be Captain; was wounded, and honorably discharged for disability resulting from wounds received in the service.

4. Midshipman CHARLES BELKNAP.

Entered the United States service as Midshipman in the United States Navy; served throughout the war, and is still in the naval service.

5. Ensign CHARLES WOLCOTT CHAUNCEY.

Entered the United States service, June 15, 1861, on board the United States steamer Susquehannah, Captain John S. Chauncey, United States Navy, as captain's clerk; promoted, July 1, 1861, to be aid to the commanding officer; served on the coast of North Carolina, on blockade duty, and took part in the naval battles at Forts Hatteras and Clark, August 29 and 30, 1861; was recommended for gallant conduct in action in official report to the Commander-in-Chief; was detached from the Susquehannah in October by reason of change of command.

6. Captain W. H. COOPER.

Entered the United States service as First Lieutenant of the —— Regiment, New York Volunteers; promoted to be Captain in same regiment; served in the Army of the Potomac in Virginia, and was mustered out with regiment. Died of disease contracted in the service.

7. Lieutenant G. F. COOKE.

8. Captain W. H. CORSA.

Entered the United States service as —— Lieutenant in one of the "Metropolitan" regiments, New York Volunteers; served in Louisiana; was promoted to be Captain, and was mustered out with regiment at expiration of term of service.

9. Surgeon J. C. DALTON.

Entered the United States service as Surgeon, upon staff of Brigadier-General E. L. Viele, commanding a brigade at Hilton Head, South Carolina, and served in the Army of the South until honorably discharged.

10. Captain B. F. DAVIS.

Entered the United States service as First Lieutenant —— Regiment, New York Volunteers; served in Louisiana, and took part in the various battles of the Red River campaign; was appointed Provost-Marshal under General Banks in this campaign; promoted to be Captain.

11. Lieutenant-Colonel W. J. DENSLOW, JR.

Entered the United States service as First Lieutenant in the Sixth New York Volunteers; served at Fort Pickens and in Louisiana; promoted to be

Captain, and served on the staff of Brigadier-General Dwight at Baton Rouge; was promoted to be Lieutenant-Colonel of —— Regiment, New York Volunteers.

12. Lieutenant A. D'ORVILLE.

13. Captain H. C. ELLIS.

Entered the United States service as Sergeant-Major of the Sixty-Fifth Regiment, New York Volunteers; served with the Army of the Potomac throughout the war, and took part with it in many important battles; was promoted to bo Captain.

14. Lieutenant R. D. EVANS.

Entered the United States service as —— Lieutenant in the Fourth Regiment, Excelsior Brigade, or Second Regiment of Fire Zouaves, New York Volunteers; served in the Army of the Potomac; was wounded, and honorably discharged for disability resulting from wounds received in the service.

15. Captain JAMES FAIRGRIEVE.

Entered the United States service as —— Lieutenant of First New York Mounted Rifles; was promoted to be Captain; served in Virginia.

16. Sergeant-Major GEORGE W. FREELAND.

17. Brigadier-General O. H. HART.

Entered the United States service as First Lieutenant in one of the regiments of General Sickles's (Excelsior) brigade, New York Volunteers; promoted to be Assistant Adjutant-General of the brigade; served with distinction in the Army of the Potomac, and in the armies of the West; promoted to be Colonel and Brevet Brigadier-General.

18. Captain C. E. HUBERER.

Entered the United States service as Captain in the Sixth Regiment, New York Volunteers; served at Fort Pickens and in Louisiana, and was mustered out with his regiment in 1863.

19. Lieutenant T. S. KIRKLAND.

20. Captain GEORGE LE FORT.

Entered the United States service, June, 1861, as Adjutant of the Fourth Regiment, Excelsior Brigade (Second Fire Zouaves), New York Volunteers. Served in the Army of the Potomac, Hooker's division, and was made aide-de-camp to General Sickles, and subsequently Captain of his company (D); was engaged in all the various battles of the Peninsula, with his brigade and division; in the battles under Pope, at Fredericksburg, at Chancellorsville, and at Gettysburg, acting at the latter as Inspector-General on the staff of Colonel W. R. Brewster, commanding the Second Brigade, Second Division, Third Army Corps. At Gettysburg he was severely wounded, but he sufficiently recovered to take part in the affair at Wapping Heights, where his conspicuous gallantry, shown on every field before, caused him to be honorably mentioned in official reports. He was engaged again in the Wilderness, and at Spottsylvania, and was killed May 20, 1864. His zeal, fidelity, and energy as a disciplinarian won him the highest praises of his superior officers. He was a participant in nearly forty larger or lesser engagements during his three years of active service. He was repeatedly offered promotion in other regiments, but preferred remaining simple Captain in the Fourth Excelsior. His patriotism was of the purest type, and he deserves a high place among his country's martyrs.

21. Adjutant C. H. Lyons.

Entered the United States service as Lieutenant in the —— Regiment, New York Volunteers. Was made Adjutant in the —— Regiment of New York Cavalry. Was wounded, and honorably discharged for disability, resulting from wounds received in the service.

22. Major Frederick J. Mears.

Entered the United States service in 1861, as Lieutenant in the —— Infantry (Regular Army). Was detailed to instruct volunteer officers at Arsenal, Washington. Appointed in 1861 Lieutenant-Colonel of Colonel Berdan's regiment of sharpshooters. Joined his own regiment in Oregon. Promoted to be Captain, and subsequently to be Major.

Is now on duty with his regiment.

23. Captain F. E. McIlvaine.

Entered the United States service as Captain in the Nineteenth Infantry (Regular Army).

24. Captain A. B. McGowan.

Entered the United States service in the Regular Army, and was stationed on the Pacific Coast. Is still in the regular service.

25. Sergeant-Major J. Morrow.

26. Lieutenant W. A. Nichols.

27. Lieutenant R. H. Plass.

Entered the United States service as Lieutenant in the —— Regiment of New York Cavalry.

28. Lieutenant C. L. Reynolds.

Entered the United States service as Lieutenant in the Fourth Regiment, Excelsior Brigade (Second Fire Zouaves), New York Volunteers.

29. Captain George W. Ring.

Entered the United States service as Captain in the —— Regiment of Michigan Volunteers.

30. Captain Theodore Russell.

Entered the United States service as Captain in the —— Regiment of New

York Volunteers, Colonel Cone commanding. Served in the Army of the Potomac, in its advance up the Peninsula, and was killed in battle at Fair Oaks, June, 1862.

31. Lieutenant J. W. SIBELL.

32. Major F. D. SLOCOMB.

Entered the United States service as First Lieutenant of the Forty-Third Regiment, New York Volunteers. Was promoted to be Captain in Ullman's Corps d'Afrique, and served in Louisiana. Was promoted to be Major.

33. Lieutenant BENEKE C. STOUT.

34. Lieutenant-Colonel CHARLES N. SWIFT.

Entered the United States service, August 18, 1862, as Private in Company F, Fifth New York Volunteers (Duryee's Zouaves). Was transferred, May 5, 1863, to Company C, One Hundred and Forty-Sixth New York Volunteers, at the battle of Chancellorsville. Was commissioned Captain, February 25, 1864 (after passing as Captain of first class, at an examination by General Casey's Board), of Company A, Thirtieth Regiment United States Cavalry Troops. Was brevetted Major, March 13, 1865, Lieutenant-Colonel March 13, 1865, "for gallant and meritorious service during the war."

Served in Maryland, Virginia, and North Carolina, in the Fifth, Eighth, Ninth, Tenth, Twenty-Third, and Twenty-Fifth Corps. Was engaged in the battles of second Bull Run, Wilderness, Antietam, Fredericksburg, Chancellorsville, Gettysburg, Germania Ford, Spottsylvania, Old Church, Petersburg, and Cox's Landing. Was in all of the campaigns of the Army of the Potomac, from the second Bull Run to the mine explosion, except during the interval after Gettysburg, till Grant took command. Was with Sherman in the march from Wilmington to Raleigh.

He was taken prisoner at Chancellorsville, and escaped by eluding the guard, and swimming the Potomac. Being detailed to recruit colored troops in Virginia and Maryland, he enlisted, unaided and alone, five hundred men in three months. He superintended the laying of a part of the abattis in front of the Ninth Corps at Petersburg, under a galling fire, in which he lost thirty men. He was brought down by typhoid fever, in front of Petersburg, June 10, 1864, and rejoined his regiment in the spring of 1865. He had charge of a convalescent camp at Wilmington, N. C., numbering two thousand five hundred men. He had not attained the age of twenty-one when discharged, in the spring of 1865.

35. Lieutenant CHARLES J. THERIOTT.

Entered the United States service, August 16, 1861, at San Francisco, as Commissary-Sergeant, First California Volunteers. Was promoted, June 4, 1862, to be Second Lieutenant, and June 1, 1864, to be First Lieutenant. Served in Arizona, New Mexico, under Generals Carleton and West, and in Missouri. Also held positions of A. A. Q. M., A. A. C. S., A. A. D. C.

Was engaged in skirmishes with the Apache and Navajo Indians. Resigned November, 1864. Was recommended by General Carleton as Captain and Commissary-Sergeant in the army.

36. Lieutenant E. C. TIFFANY.

37. Surgeon EUSTACE TRENOR.

Entered the United States service as Surgeon in the navy.

38. Surgeon JOHN TRENOR.

Entered the United States service as Surgeon in the —— Regiment of New York Cavalry. Served in the Department of the South and South Carolina. Died of disease contracted in the service while in the line of duty.

39. Captain J. J. TRENOR.

Entered the United States service as First Lieutenant in the —— Regiment of New York Volunteers, Colonel Cone commanding. Served in the Army of the Potomac, in front of Yorktown, and on the march up the Peninsula, in 1862. Was promoted to be Captain. Was killed in front of his company while leading it into action, at Fair Oaks, 1862.

40. Lieutenant S. C. THWAITE.

Entered the United States service as Lieutenant in the Sixty-Second Regiment of New York Volunteers (Anderson Zouaves). Was promoted to be Adjutant of the regiment. Served with his regiment in the Army of the Potomac.

41. Lieutenant A. B. VILLEPLAITE.

Entered the United States service as a Lieutenant in one of the regiments of Corcoran's Legion, New York Volunteers. Served in Virginia with his regiment.

42. Lieutenant M. P. WHITLOCK.

Entered the United States service as —— in the navy.

43. Lieutenant W. P. WHEELER.

Entered the United States service as Lieutenant in the —— Regiment of New Jersey Volunteers.

## SECOND COMPANY (B).

1. Captain HENRY H. ALDEN.

Entered the United States service as Second Lieutenant in the Forty-Second Regiment, New York Volunteers (Tammany Regiment). Was promoted to be First Lieutenant; and to be Captain, June, 1861. His company was among the first to cross the Potomac at Ball's Bluff, Va.; and he was killed at the battle at that place, October 16, 1861, while gallantly leading his command. He was buried upon the field, but his remains were recovered under a flag of truce, and his funeral was attended in New York at the armory of the Seventh

Regiment, the Second Company escorting the remains till their departure for the home of his family in Massachusetts.

2. Colonel WILLIAM H. ALLEN.

Entered the United States service as Colonel of the First Regiment, New York Volunteers, May 8, 1861. Served at Fortress Monroe under General Butler, and was at the battle of Big Bethel. Was cashiered and dismissed from the service September 10, 1861, the principal charge against him being the burning, without orders, of a field of wheat owned by Major Thompson of the Rebel Army. In June, 1862, was authorized, by a special order of President Lincoln, to raise a regiment, the One Hundred and Forty-Fifth Regiment, New York Volunteers, which was mustered into the United States service on the 11th September, 1862. Commanded this regiment in the Army of the Potomac until November, 1862. While at Washington, by order of the Secretary of War, to revise pay-rolls, a new Colonel was commissioned by Governor Morgan and detailed to the command of the One Hundred and Forty-Fifth Regiment. Served as Aid to General Wool during the riots in New York in 1863.

3. Captain RICHARD ALLISON.

Entered the United States service, August 30, 1862, as Captain of Company I, One Hundred and Twenty-Seventh Regiment, New York Volunteers. Served at Washington, under Heintzelman, from September 12, 1862, to April 18, 1863; at Suffolk (Va.), under Peck, from April 18 to May 5, 1863, during the siege of Suffolk; in Southeastern Virginia, under Dix and Keyes, to July 10th; in the Eleventh Corps, until August 7th; in the Department of the South, under Gillmore and Foster, from August 13, 1863, to July 1, 1865. Was present at a skirmish at Diascund Bridge (June 11, 1863); a severe skirmish at Baltimore Cross-Roads (June 30, 1863); at the attack on Forts Johnson and Simpkins, by small boats (July 2, 1864); and in many raids and reconnoissances around Charleston Harbor. Was in command of the "Boat Infantry" at Morris Island, composed of Companies D, E, I, and K, of his regiment, his duty being to patrol and picket the water between Morris and James Islands and Charleston Harbor. August 2, 1864, he commanded the reconnoissance which made a complete circuit of Fort Sumter, with three small row-boats. Though often attempted, this is the only time the feat was ever accomplished. General Foster, in an official letter, forwarded to Captain Allison by the district commander, General Schimmelpfening, thanked "the officers and men who made this reconnoissance of Fort Sumter," and expressed himself as "much pleased with their energy in the enterprise."

September 7, 1864, was detailed as A. A. Inspector-General of the department. Took part in the movement from Beaufort against the Savannah and Charleston Railroad, in November, in co-operation with Sherman's march through Georgia. Was engaged severely at Grahamsville (November 30th), Devaux Neck (December 6th), and frequently again (7th, 9th, and 29th December) during the movement, his regiment losing very heavily. Was Provost-

Marshal of the city of Charleston from March 28, 1865, to July 1, 1865, when he was mustered out of service with his regiment.

4. Major CHARLES APPLEBY.

Entered the United States service, March, 1863, as First Lieutenant in Ullman's brigade (colored troops). Was promoted, January, 1864, to be Captain in the Eightieth United States Colored Troops. While Lieutenant, he took command of one hundred men from the brigade, on an expedition to Jackson, La., and had a skirmish with Logan's command. Took an active part, with his regiment, in the siege and capture of Port Hudson, June, 1863. Was engaged in picket and provost duty in Louisiana and Texas through 1863, 1864, and 1865. Was detailed as Judge Advocate by General Andrews at Port Hudson, March 16, 1864. At Marshall (Texas) he was Provost-Marshal.

He was wounded in the arm, in the skirmish near Jackson. He was brevetted Major, May 21, 1866, and still remains in the United States service.

5. Hospital Steward EVERT S. BEDFORD.

Entered the United States service in July, 1861, as Hospital Steward of the Sixty-Fifth Regiment, New York Volunteers (United States Chasseurs). Served in the regiment with the Army of the Potomac through the Peninsular campaign, and afterwards in Northern Virginia and Maryland. Was discharged for disability in 1863.

6. Captain EDWARD BERNARD.

Entered the United States service, June 4, 1861, as First Lieutenant in the Eleventh New York Volunteers (Ellsworth's Zouaves), and took part in the battle of Bull Run, July, 1861. October 1, 1861, resigned to be commissioned as Captain in the Sixty-Fifth Regiment, New York Volunteers (United States Chasseurs). Took part, with his regiment, in the siege of Yorktown, and the battles of Williamsburg, Fair Oaks, Seven Pines, and the Seven Days' Battles. In the last of these, Malvern Hill, he was wounded, late in the afternoon of July 1, 1862, by a gunshot wound in the left leg, the bullet passing through the leg half an inch below the knee-joint and taking out both bones. Being permanently disabled, he resigned, December, 1862, and the resignation was accepted in March, 1863. Was mentioned in official orders.

7. Lieutenant-Colonel GEORGE A. BERNARD.

Entered the United States service in June, 1861, as First Lieutenant of the Sixty-Fifth New York Volunteers (United States Chasseurs). Was promoted to be Captain, December, 1861. Was appointed Aide-de-Camp upon the staff of General H. D. Terry, commanding the Third Division, Sixth Corps, and was afterwards transferred to the staff of General D. A. Russell, remaining with that officer till his death at Winchester. Was retained on the staff by General Frank Wheaton, who took command of the division after Russell's death, and so remained till the end of the war.

He was engaged in the various battles of the Peninsular campaign, at the second Bull Run, Antietam, Fredericksburg under Burnside and Fredericksburg under Hooker, Gettysburg, the Wilderness, Spottsylvania, Cold Harbor, the battles before Petersburg, and nearly all the battles of the Army of the Potomac. He was with the Sixth Corps in the Valley under Sheridan, in all its battles there. He was present at the capture of General Lee, and, with his corps, was stationed at Danville until July, 1865. Was mustered out with his regiment, August 18, 1865.

He was brevetted Major, June 10, 1864, for gallant and meritorious conduct at Cold Harbor. April 2, 1865, he was brevetted Lieutenant-Colonel upon the recommendation of General Frank Wheaton.

8. Captain J. F. Bisbee.

Entered the United States service, May 31, 1861, as First Lieutenant, Company B, Sixty-Second Regiment, New York Volunteers (Anderson Zouaves). Was promoted to be Captain, July 31, 1862. Took part in the battles at Yorktown, Williamsburg, Seven Pines, Fair Oaks, Malvern Hill, Turkey Bend, second Bull Run, Antietam, and first Fredericksburg; and in skirmishes at Warwick Court-House, Bottom's Bridge, Golding Farm, and Williamsport. In all these engagements he had command of his company. Resigned, March 27, 1868, from disease contracted in the service.

9. Lieutenant Richard R. Browner.

Entered the United States service in April, 1861, as First Sergeant in Fifth Regiment, New York Volunteers (Duryee's Zouaves). Commissioned Second Lieutenant in May, 1861, and First Lieutenant, August 16, 1861, and appointed Adjutant in January, 1862. Served at Fortress Monroe, Fort Federal Hill, and in the Peninsular campaign. Resigned in June, 1862.

10. Brigadier-General William Henry Browne.

Entered the United States service, May 24, 1861, as Lieutenant-Colonel Thirty-First New York Volunteers. Was promoted July 6th to be Colonel of the Thirty-Sixth New York Volunteers. Brevetted Brigadier-General, as of March 13, 1865, "for gallant and meritorious services during the war." Commanded his regiment at Blackburn Ford and Bull Run, at West Point, Golding's Farm, and through all the Seven Days' battles. At Antietam he commanded a mixed brigade at the fords. At Fredericksburg and at Marye's Heights he commanded a brigade, composed of the Seventh, Tenth, and Thirty-Seventh Massachusetts, Thirty-Sixth New York, and Second Rhode Island. At Salem Heights, May 3, 1863, he was shot through the left knee by a minie bullet, which shattered the thigh-bone, and was carried from the field. General Sedgwick especially mentions him in his official report of this battle as among those whose "skill and gallantry displayed in the management of their respective brigades deserves the special notice of the commanding general." Before he had recovered from his wound his regiment had, July 15, 1863, been mustered out of service.

Not long after he was appointed Colonel of the Veteran Reserve Corps, passing the highest examination among twenty-four candidates. He was made member of examining boards, and served in various other capacities, finally being assigned to the command of the Second Brigade, Veteran Reserve Corps, consisting of six regiments, stationed in Virginia. In August, 1864, he was made Provost-Marshal-General and Chief Mustering and Disbursing Officer and Superintendent of Recruiting for Maryland and Delaware, and so continued until July, 1866, when he was honorably mustered out. Besides the regular actions already noted, he was engaged in many skirmishes. General Scott wrote of him as "my gallant brother-soldier in the campaign of Mexico." Major-Generals Hooker, Franklin, Newton, and Slocum strongly recommended him for promotion. General Sedgwick wrote: "I add my testimony to, and express my admiration for, the ability as an officer, the high attainments, and the soldierly qualities which have marked your career from your entrance into the service. . . . . Of your gallantry and undaunted bravery on the occasion of the storming of the Heights of Fredericksburg, while at the head of your brigade, and subsequently on the hotly contested field of Salem Heights, where you received your agonizing wound, I cannot speak with too much praise. The bravery of the soldier, the skill of the officer, and the courage of the gentleman were so happily blended, that your conduct on that day afforded a noble example, the memory of which must long live in the hearts of all your friends and comrades."

11. Captain John C. Broomfield.

Entered the United States service as Captain in Sixth Regiment, New York Volunteers, in December, 1861, and joined his regiment at Fort Pickens, January 18, 1862. After a few months' service at Fort Pickens and vicinity, resigned his commission.

12. Lieutenant A. Martin Burtis.

Entered the United States service, August 31, 1861, as 1st Lieutenant of Company K, Ninth Regiment, New York State Militia, or Eighty-Third Regiment, New York Volunteers; was made Quartermaster, June 21, 1862, and so remained till mustered out. Was in Abercrombie's brigade, Banks's corps, during 1861 and 1862, in the Shenandoah Valley, and, from March, 1862, in Hartsuff's brigade, McDowell's corps. Took part in all the campaigns of the Army of the Potomac, after McDowell joined Pope, under McClellan, Burnside, Hooker, and Meade, till he was mustered out with his regiment, June 8, 1864.

13. Lieutenant-Colonel William Chalmers.

Entered the United States service as Captain in the One Hundred and Thirty-Second Regiment, New York Volunteers. Took part in the battle of Bull Run, and was mentioned with praise in brigade reports. Went through the whole Peninsular campaign, taking part in the battle at West Point and the Seven Days' Battles. Resigned commission at Harrison's Landing, August 8, 1862, on account of disease contracted in the service. Commissioned Lieutenant-Colonel of Eighty-Third Regiment, New York Volunteers (Ninth Regiment, New York State Militia), October 13, 1863. Crossed the Rapidan with General Meade, and was at the battle of Mine Run. Commanded his regiment at the battle of the Wilderness and in subsequent actions. Mustered out with his regiment in July, 1864.

14. Lieutenant WILLIAM O. CHAPMAN.

Entered the United States service in February, 1862, as a private in the Ninety-Fifth New York Volunteers. Soon after was promoted to be Sergeant and detailed as Commissary Sergeant. Was made Second Lieutenant, June 13, 1862, and First Lieutenant and Quartermaster, January 27, 1863. Served with his regiment, throughout its three years of service in Virginia, in the Army of the Potomac, in the First Division of the First Corps, McDowell's, (afterwards Reynolds's,) and then in the Third (Wadsworth's) Division of Warren's Fifth Corps. Served as Regimental Quartermaster (and from time to time as Brigade Commissary and Quartermaster) from August 12, 1862, till the muster out of the regiment on March 6, 1865, by reason of expiration of service.

15. Major JOSEPH J. COMSTOCK, JR.

Entered the United States service as Second Lieutenant, Third Rhode Island Volunteers, in July, 1861, First Lieutenant and Adjutant, August 18, 1861. Went with General Sherman's expedition to Port Royal, South Carolina, in 1861, and was commissioned Captain of artillery, in March, 1862. Was at the battle of James Island, and with General Mitchell at the engagement on the Charleston and Savannah Railroad, in October, 1862. Commanded a mortar battery in the attack on Morris Island, in July, 1863, and a battery of one-hundred-pound Parrott guns at the capture of Forts Gregg and Wagner. Commissioned as Major of the Eleventh United States Colored Heavy Artillery in November, 1863, and was placed in command of Fort Esperanza, Texas. Assigned to the command of Forts Jackson and St. Philip, near New Orleans, in 1864, and Camp Parapet, on the Mississippi River, in 1865. Resigned in September, 1865.

16. Captain JAMES C. COOLEY.

Entered the United States service as First Sergeant in Company D, One Hundred and Thirty-Third Regiment, New York Volunteers, August 15, 1862. Commissioned Second Lieutenant, August 29, 1862; First Lieutenant, December 3, 1862; Captain, May 28, 1864. Was in the Banks Expedition to New Orleans, in both campaigns against Port Hudson, in the Red River campaign, in the expedition to Sabine Pass, and the second expedition to Western Louisiana, serving as Aide-de-Camp to General Paine, and as Acting Assistant Adjutant-General to General Emory. He took part in the engagements at Bisland and Vermilion Bayou. In July, 1864, accompanied General Emory, commanding Nineteenth Army Corps, to the Shenandoah Valley, and was in all the battles under General Sheridan, especially Winchester, Fisher's Hill, and Cedar Creek. In February, 1865, served as Aide-de-Camp to General Merritt, in the great cavalry raid of General Sheridan to the James River and Petersburg. Was with the Army of the Potomac until the surrender of General Lee. In May, 1865, commissioned Second Lieutenant in the Fifth Cavalry (Regular Army), and brevetted First Lieutenant and Captain, "for gallant and meritorious services during the war." Was promoted to be First Lieutenant, Fifth Cavalry, July 28, 1866.

17. Lieutenant-Colonel Robert Cottier.

Entered the United States service as Lieutenant-Colonel of One Hundred and Sixteenth Regiment, New York Volunteers, September 5, 1862. Was in the Banks Expedition to New Orleans. Commanded his regiment in the first advance and assault on Port Hudson, and in the engagement at Plain Store, Louisiana. His regiment lost, in the assault at Port Hudson, nearly half its men. Resigned May 29, 1863.

18. Major-General Abram Duryee.

Entered the United States service, May 9, 1861, as Colonel of the Fifth Regiment, New York Volunteers, (Duryee's Zouaves). Was promoted to be Brigadier-General, August 31, 1861, and Major-General by brevet, March 13, 1865. Was at the battle of Big Bethel, Virginia. Commanded the district of Baltimore, Maryland, and erected Fort Federal Hill. Commanded a brigade under General McDowell, in Northern and Central Virginia, in the spring of 1862; and served under General Pope, being actively engaged in the battles at Cedar Mountain, Rappahannock Station, Thoroughfare Gap, Groveton, Bull Run, Chantilly, South Mountain, and Antietam. At Antietam he was slightly wounded, — the third wound he had received in the service. During the temporary absence of General Duryee, on leave, the command of the division was conferred on an officer of inferior rank. General Duryee demanded his rank and command, on the ground that he was identified with the division from its organization, and was its senior general officer, as well as for his past services; but the command was withheld from him, without the assignment of cause, whereupon, in 1863, General Duryee resigned.

General Pope, in his official report, says: "General Duryee commanded his brigade in the various operations of this campaign with ability and zeal." General McDowell refers to the "gallantry of Generals Duryee and Tower at Thoroughfare Gap, and the battle of the 30th, in which the former was slightly and the latter severely wounded." General Ricketts, in his official report of second Bull Run, says: "General Duryee's brigade advanced into the woods, driving the enemy along the old railroad excavation, until directly under their guns. While occupying this ground, General Duryee was subjected to a heavy fire of artillery and infantry, in which he received a slight wound and a severe contusion from a shell, but remained at his post animating his men, who behaved admirably.

" . . . . In recapitulating the services of brigade commanders, I would make particular mention of Brigadier-General Duryee for his noble conduct at Thoroughfare Gap, and his indomitable courage displayed at Bull Run, while holding a trying position." General Meade's report of the battle of South Mountain speaks highly of the promptness of General Duryee in ascending the mountain in support of the Pennsylvania Reserves, which resulted in the defeat of the enemy. General Rickett's report of Antietam says: " I commend the general good conduct of the division, and would mention, particularly, Brigadier-General Duryee, Colonels Coulter and Lyle, and Captains Matthews and Thompson of the artillery. Indeed, both officers and men displayed courage under a severe fire." Governor Fenton, in forwarding the brevet of Major-General, "conferred," as he said, "by the President, in recognition of your faithful and distinguished services in the late war," added: " In behalf of the State, allow me to thank you for the gallantry and devotion which induced this conspicuous mention by the general government."

19. Lieutenant-Colonel ALEXANDER DOUGLAS.

Entered the United States service in August, 1862, as Captain in the Twenty-Second Regiment, New Jersey Volunteers. Was promoted to be Lieutenant-Colonel, September 22, 1862. Served with the Army of the Potomac in the winter of 1862 – 63, at Fredericksburg and Aquia Creek. Commanded his regiment from its organization until his resignation in March, 1863.

20. Paymaster WILLIAM LEE DARLING.

Entered the United States service, December 18, 1861, under an appointment as Acting Assistant Paymaster. Was commissioned as an Assistant Paymaster in the Regular Navy, June 30, 1864, and promoted to be Paymaster, May 4, 1866. He was in the South Atlantic Squadron, under Dupont; in the West Gulf Squadron, under Farragut; and in the North Atlantic Squadron, under Porter. He took part in several engagements on the Red and Mississippi Rivers, including the battle ending in the capture of the ram Queen of the West, on Grand Lake, Louisiana, the attack on Sabine Pass, Texas, and both naval engagements at Fort Fisher. At Fort Fisher he was mentioned by the commanding officer in his report to the Secretary of the Navy. He was attached, after the war, to the United States practice ship Macedonian, at the Naval Academy, Annapolis.

21. Captain JAMES J. DE BARRY.

Entered the United States service, September 24, 1862, as Captain of Company D, One Hundred and Seventieth New York Volunteers, and served in Corcoran's brigade, Hancock's corps. Served in Virginia, and took part in the engagements at Suffolk, and those on the Blackwater and Nansemond Rivers in April and May, 1863. Served throughout Grant's Virginia campaign, in the Second Corps, taking part particularly in the battles of the Wilderness, May 5 and 6, 1864; Spottsylvania, May 18th; North Anna, May 24th and 26th; Cold Harbor, June 2d and 10th; Petersburg, June 16th, 17th, 18th, 22d, and 23d; Deep Bottom, July 25th and August 15th; Ream's Station, August 25th. He was present at Lee's surrender, and was mustered out, with his regiment, July 15, 1865. He was three times wounded, once while skirmishing, May 1, 1863; again at Blackwater River; again at Deep Bottom.

22. Lieutenant LEWIS G. DUDLEY.

Entered the United States service in July, 1861, as First Sergeant in Sixty-Fifth Regiment, New York Volunteers (United States Chasseurs). Commissioned Second Lieutenant in January, 1862. Was in the battles of the Peninsular campaign, in Northern Virginia, and at South Mountain and Antietam in 1862, and in the battle at Fredericksburg under General Burnside. Resigned in February, 1863. Commissioned Second Lieutenant in First Regiment Veteran Cavalry, New York Volunteers, October 17, 1863, and served until the end of the war under General Sheridan, in the Valley of the Shenandoah, and in the great raid to the James River and Petersburg.

23. Lieutenant HENRY B. DYER.

Entered the United States service, July 20, 1861, as First Lieutenant of the Sixty-Fifth Regiment, New York Volunteers (United States Chasseurs). Served with his regiment at Washington, D. C., during the winter of 1861 – 62, and resigned his commission in the following spring on account of sickness.

24. Captain WILLIAM EDWARDS.

Entered the United States service, October 3, 1861, as First Lieutenant Sixth Regiment, New York Cavalry. Was promoted to be Captain, October 5, 1862. Served in Northern Virginia, and was mustered out with his regiment at the expiration of its term of service.

25. Captain CHARLES EMERSON.

Entered the United States service as Second Lieutenant One Hundred and Seventy-Fourth Regiment, New York Volunteers, May 28, 1862; First Lieutenant One Hundred and Sixty-Second Regiment, New York Volunteers, July 2, 1864; Captain, February 10, 1865; honorably discharged May 21, 1865. Served, in 1863, in Department of the Gulf, as Acting Assistant Adjutant-General on the staff of General Banks. Was in the Têche campaign, and at the siege of Port Hudson in 1863. In July, 1864, joined his regiment in the Shenandoah Valley, and served through the whole campaign under General Sheridan. In October, 1864, assigned to duty as Acting Assistant Adjutant-General upon the staff of General Emory, and in April, 1865, as Provost-Marshal on the staff of General Dwight.

26. Colonel NOAH L. FARNHAM.

Entered the United States service in May, 1861, as Lieutenant-Colonel of Eleventh Regiment, New York Volunteers (Fire Zouaves). Was at the capture of Alexandria, Virginia, and, upon the death of Colonel Ellsworth, succeeded him as Colonel of the regiment. Superintended the erection, by his regiment, of Fort Ellsworth, at Schuters' Hill, Virginia. Although suffering from severe illness, he was actively engaged at the battle of Bull Run, Virginia, July 18, 1861, and, while leading his regiment in the most gallant manner, was struck by a musket-ball upon the side of the head. He died in the hospital at Washington on the 14th of August, 1861, from abscess of the brain, resulting from the wound received at Bull Run.

27. Lieutenant Benjamin Gregory.

Entered the United States service, July 22, 1861, as Second Lieutenant of Seventh Regiment (Harris Light), New York Cavalry; was promoted to be First Lieutenant, August 1, 1861, and Adjutant, February 1, 1862. Served in Northern Virginia, and was under General Kilpatrick in various engagements and skirmishes, until August, 1862. Was wounded August 9, 1862, while covering the retreat from Cedar Mountain, Virginia. Appointed Paymaster, United States Army, September 1, 1862, and served in the armies of General Sherman and General Thomas. Resigned July 1, 1864. Was mentioned by General George D. Bayard, in report of advance on Fredericksburg in April, 1862, and by General King, in report of skirmish near Hanover Junction, July 22, 1862. Lieutenant-Colonel Judson Kilpatrick, in the latter affair, mentions "Adjutant Gregory, who fearlessly carried orders on the field," with high praise for "his untiring exertions during the entire expeditions."

28. Paymaster Henry S. Gregory.

Entered the United States service, October, 1863, as Acting Assistant Paymaster in the navy, and was ordered to the United States steamer Nyanza. Served in the West Gulf Squadron, and was stationed at Brashier City and Mississippi Sound. Took part at the capture of Mobile. Was honorably discharged November, 1865.

29. Paymaster Oscar Hall.

Entered the United States service, November, 1861, as Assistant Storekeeper of store-ship Vermont, and was on board during the dangerous voyage of that vessel to Hilton Head, South Carolina, in February, 1862. Served in the Department of the South until July, 1863. Appointed Acting Assistant Paymaster in the United States Navy in 1863, and stationed at Mound City, Illinois. Resigned in 1864.

30. Lieutenant Norwood A. Halsey.

Entered the United States service, August 20, 1861, as Second Lieutenant in the Tenth Regiment, New York Volunteers. Was engaged in all the battles of the Peninsular campaign in 1862, and was promoted to be First Lieutenant, July 9, 1862, for "meritorious conduct" during the seven days, which order was read to the whole brigade. Was also in the battles under General Pope in Northern Virginia, and at South Mountain and Antietam. Was appointed Assistant Provost-Marshal on the staff of General French, and served in that capacity until mustered out with the regiment, May 7, 1863.

31. Engineer R. F. Hatfield.

Assistant Engineer in United States Navy in September, 1861, and ordered to gunboat Winona. Was actively engaged at the capture of Forts Jackson and St. Philip, and was at the surrender of New Orleans. Resigned, on account of sickness, in July, 1862.

32. Captain Townsend L. Hatfield.

ntered the United States service, September 10, 1861, as Second Lieutenant of Company C, Forty-Eighth Regiment, New York Volunteers; First Lieutenant, December 29, 1862; Captain, August 28, 1863; transferred to Signal Corps, January, 1862; was at the capture of Port Royal Ferry, in General T. W. Sherman's expedition, January 1, 1862, and that of Fort Pulaski, April, 1862; was with the army during Admiral Dupont's attack on Charleston Harbor, July 9th; was one of the storming party that took Morris Island, and was present at the storming of Fort Wagner; was present and wounded at the second attack on Fort Wagner; January, 1864, was ordered to Florida with Seymour, and was at the battle of Olustee; remained in Florida until honorably discharged, July 1, 1865.

33. Lieutenant-Colonel Henry G. Healy.

Entered the United States service, July 17, 1861, as Captain in Sixty-Fifth Regiment, New York Volunteers (United States Chasseurs); was promoted to be Major, July 20, 1862, and Lieutenant-Colonel, May 26, 1863. Was in all the battles of the Peninsular campaign and those in Northern Virginia, and at South Mountain and Antietam, in 1862. Was at the battle of Fredericksburg under General Burnside, and was wounded at the storming of Marye's Heights, at Fredericksburg, under General Sedgwick in 1863, receiving a gunshot wound through the body. Resigned, in 1864, on account of disability from wounds received in the service.

34. Captain Henry H. Harrall.

Entered the United States service, June, 1862, as Lieutenant in the Twenty-Third Connecticut Volunteers, and served at New Orleans until his regiment was mustered out, in 1863. In April, 1864, enlisted as a private in Twenty-Second Regiment, New York Volunteers, and was engaged in the battles in the Shenandoah Valley, under General Sheridan. Detached, and commissioned Captain in the Thirty-Seventh Regiment, colored troops. Served in South Carolina, and mustered out August, 1865. Was present also at Bull Run as a private in the Seventy-First New York.

35. Major William W. Harral.

Entered the United States service, August, 1861, as Lieutenant and Quartermaster of the Ninth Connecticut Volunteers. Promoted to be Captain and Division Quartermaster on the staff of General Butler, March 8, 1862. Was with Butler in the expedition to New Orleans, and some time after its capture was appointed Major and Aide-de-Camp on the staff of that officer, with whom he remained till Butler was relieved by Banks. Subsequently served as Chief of Staff to General Strong, in the operations of Gillmore against Charleston. Was present in the operations that resulted in the capture of Morris Island, and participated in the attacks on Fort Wagner and the bombardment of Fort Sumter. Resigned his commission on the death of General Strong, in the summer of 1863. Was complimented in general orders by General Strong for trying to recover the body of Colonel Shaw, of the Fifty-Fourth Massachusetts Colored Volunteers, and by General Gillmore for crossing Light-house Inlet for reinforcements in an open boat and under a heavy fire.

36. Purser THOMAS W. K. HOLDEN.

Entered the United States service, December 28, 1861, as Purser of the United States ship Boston, and participated in the capture of Fort Pulaski, the bombardment of Fort McAllister, the capture of Fernandina, the destruction of the Nashville, the bombardment of Charleston, the two captures of Jacksonville, the two expeditions against Pocotaligo Bridge, and the capture of James Island. Resigned July 22, 1863.

37. Brigadier-General EDWARD JARDINE.

Entered the service in April, 1861, as Captain of Company G, Ninth New York Volunteers. Promoted to be Major, February 8, 1862, Lieutenant-Colonel, 1863, Colonel, 1863; and brevetted Brigadier-General in May, 1865.

Served in 1861, in Virginia, under Butler, taking part in the engagement at Big Bethel and the expedition to Hatteras Inlet; and in North Carolina in 1862, under Burnside, taking part in the battles at Roanoke Island (for which he was promoted), and Camden, where he was slightly wounded. Returned with Burnside and the Ninth Corps to Virginia, in 1862, and took part in the battles of South Mountain and Antietam, in command of the Eighty-Ninth New York Volunteers, and in the battle of Fredericksburg. In April, 1863, he was mustered out with his regiment, by reason of expiration of term (two years) of service, but reorganized it as Colonel, July 15, 1863; took part, with his command, in suppressing the New York Draft Riots, and was severely wounded, being beaten by the mob, and suffering a compound fracture of the thigh, which disabled him for life. Resigned in May, 1865, on account of his wounds, and received for services at "Hatteras, Roanoke, Camden, South Mountain, Antietam, and Fredericksburg" the brevet rank of Brigadier-General.

38. Captain EUGENE KELTY.

Entered the United States service, July, 1861, as First Lieutenant, Nineteenth Regiment, Massachusetts Volunteers. Subsequently commissioned Captain in Thirtieth Regiment, Massachusetts Volunteers, and accompanied the expedition of General Butler to New Orleans. Was killed at the battle of Baton Rouge, Louisiana, in July, 1862. In General Butler's official report he is mentioned as "that gallant officer and admirable soldier, Captain Eugene Kelty, of Company I, Thirtieth Massachusetts, who was ordered to deploy his brave and active company of Zouaves as skirmishers on the right, and, in the performance of that duty, fell bravely at their head."

39. Major JAMES S. KING.

Entered the United States service, July 2, 1861, as Second Lieutenant in Sixty-Fifth Regiment, New York Volunteers (United States Chasseurs). Was promoted to be First Lieutenant in January, 1862. Resigned, on account of ill health, in July, 1862. Commissioned Captain in the One Hundred and Sixty-Second Regiment, New York Volunteers, in September, 1862, and resigned, on account of ill health, in July, 1863. Commissioned First Lieutenant in Seventy-Ninth Regiment, New York Volunteers, in October, 1864, and Captain in June, 1865. Brevetted Major for gallant and meritorious conduct. Commissioned Second Lieutenant, Thirteenth Infantry (Regular Army), May 11, 1866, and is still in the United States service. Served in all the battles of the Peninsular campaign in 1862, and under General Banks in Louisiana. Was Provost-Marshal for several months of the Parish of St. John the Baptist. Served in the Army of the Potomac, on the staff of General Parke, as Provost-Marshal, and throughout the siege and capture of Petersburg, where he was wounded, and had his horse killed under him. Was present at the final battles and at Lee's surrender.

40. Major JOHN LAWRENCE.

Entered the United States service, August 20, 1861, as First Lieutenant, Seventy-Third Regiment, New York Volunteers (Second Fire Zouaves); Adjutant, November 19, 1861, Captain, January 2, 1863, and Major, January 16, 1863. Served through the Peninsular campaign, in Northern Virginia, under General Pope, and was at South Mountain, Antietam, Fredericksburg, Chancellorsville, and Gettysburg. Resigned in 1863.

41. Major ROBERT W. LEONARD.

Entered the United States service, September 15, 1862, as First Lieutenant and Adjutant in One Hundred and Sixty-Second Regiment, New York Volunteers; Major, June 14, 1863. Served in the Department of the Gulf, under General Banks. Was with the expedition to Sabine Pass, at the battle of Bayou Têche, in the Red River Expedition, and at the capture of Port Hudson. Volunteered in the forlorn hope organized for the assault on Port Hudson. Resigned in 1864, on account of disease contracted in the service.

42. Captain J. HENRY LIEBENAU.

Entered the United States service in December, 1861, as Captain and Assistant Adjutant-General, and was assigned to the staff of General Viele; served in the Department of the South, and was frequently mentioned in general orders; superintended the erection of batteries on the Savannah River, and was at the capture of Fort Pulaski; served at Norfolk in 1862 - 63, as Assistant Adjutant-General and Provost-Marshal. Resigned in October, 1863.

43. Master's Mate J. WALTER MACKIE.

Entered the United States service, October, 1861, as Master's Mate in United States Navy, and was ordered to bark Restless; was in the blockade service at Charleston, South Carolina, and vicinity in 1862, and upon the coast of South Carolina and Florida in 1863; resigned, on account of sickness, in 1864; was honorably mentioned for services.

44. Lieutenant-Colonel DAVID W. MARSHALL.

Entered the United States service as First Lieutenant, Sixteenth Regiment, Ohio Volunteers, May 4, 1861, and appointed Adjutant, May 18, 1861; commissioned Captain in Fifty-First Ohio Volunteers, October 3, 1861, Major, May 31, 1863, and Lieutenant-Colonel, January 18, 1865; mustered out at Victoria, Texas, October 1, 1865; was in the battles of Philippi and Carrick's Ford, in Western Virginia, in June, 1861; at Stamford, Dobson's Ford, Perryville, and Stone River in 1862; and at Ringgold, Chickamauga, Lookout Mountain, and Mission Ridge in 1863; was in all the battles during General Sherman's advance on Atlanta, in 1864, and at the battles at Franklin and Nashville, Tennessee, under General Thomas; was wounded at Jonesboro', Georgia; served at various periods and places as Judge-Advocate, Assistant Adjutant-General, and Assistant Inspector-General; was actively engaged in twenty important battles, and very many skirmishes.

45. Lieutenant-Colonel JOSEPH E. McFARLAND.

Entered the United States service, June 1, 1861, as First Lieutenant of the Eleventh Regiment, New York Volunteers (Fire Zouaves); Captain, August 4, 1861, and Lieutenant-Colonel, March 4, 1862; was at the battle of Bull Run in July, 1861; served with the regiment at Fortress Monroe and Newport News in 1861, 1862, and was mustered out with the regiment in May, 1862.

46. Captain JAMES A. McMICKIN.

Entered the United States service August 21, 1861, as Second Lieutenant, Forty-Third Regiment, New York Volunteers; First Lieutenant, October 1, 1861; Captain, July 17, 1862; served with his regiment through the Peninsular campaign (1862), and under General Pope in Northern Virginia; was at the battles of South Mountain and Antietam, and at Fredericksburg, under General Burnside; resigned, on account of ill health, December 30, 1862; his company, at Antietam, was in the sharply contested cornfield, and General Hancock, riding up to him, ordered him to "clear out" a house full of sharpshooters who were picking off our artillerists; it was done, and Hancock visited the company during the day, and complimented it on the performance.

47. Captain DAVID MILLER.

Entered the United States service, August 3, 1861, as Captain in Sixty-Fifth Regiment, New York Volunteers (United States Chasseurs); was engaged in the battles of the Peninsular campaign in 1862; appointed Lieutenant-Colonel of the Fifth Metropolitan Regiment in September, 1862, but declined; resigned in November, 1862, on account of disease contracted in the service, his resignation being accepted by Colonel Shaler with "deep regret and great reluctance"; has been mentioned in general orders.

48. Lieutenant JAMES MILLER.

Entered the United States service, April 20, 1861, as private in the Fifth Regiment, New York State Volunteers (Duryee Zouaves); commissioned as Second Lieutenant of Company H, May 9, 1861; served under Butler at and near Fort Monroe, and was detailed by that officer, July 15, as drill-master to the "Union Coast Guard," from which duty he was relieved August 13, and rejoined his regiment at Baltimore; he carried to General Dix a letter signed by General Butler, which said: "I desire to bear testimony to his faithful and efficient service on that duty, for which I hope he may have consideration." Resigned September 6, 1861, in consequence of disease contracted in the line of duty.

49. Lieutenant SILAS A. MILLER.

Entered the United States service in August, 1861, as a private in the Twelfth Infantry (Regular Army), and was shortly afterwards appointed Sergeant; was appointed Sergeant-Major December 23, 1862, and promoted to be Second Lieutenant 19th February, 1863; served under General Banks in the Shenandoah Valley, and was taken prisoner at the battle of Cedar Mountain, Virginia, and confined six weeks at Belleisle; was at the battle of Fredericksburg under General Burnside, and at Chancellorsville under General Hooker; commanded his company at the battle of Gettysburg, and was killed in the engagement of the second day. At the time of his death, he was acting as colonel of a volunteer regiment, and had given an order for his men to lie down, but himself remained standing, when he was shot through the heart by a sharpshooter. He had already been promoted to a first lieutenantcy, but never knew it. He was buried on the field, and afterwards his remains were removed to the National Cemetery at Gettysburg.

50. Lieutenant-Colonel DAVID I. MILN.

Entered the United States service, August 20, 1861, as Second Lieutenant in the Sixty-Fifth Regiment, New York Volunteers (having previously served from July 4 to August 8 as a volunteer officer of the Eleventh New York Volunteers, being present at Bull Run); was promoted to be First Lieutenant, January 1, 1862; Captain, August 1, 1862; Major, December 2, 1864; and Lieutenant-Colonel, June 20, 1865; served in the line, and in the Army of the Potomac, from the beginning to the end of the war; was in all the battles of the Peninsular campaign, — at Chantilly, at Marye's Heights, at Gettysburg, and in the battles of Grant's campaign from the Wilderness to Petersburg; was at the capture of General Lee, and was stationed at Danville, Virginia, until June 1, 1865; was detached from the Army of the Potomac from August to December, 1864, and was then in the several engagements under General Sheridan in the Shenandoah Valley; at the battle of Spottsylvania was wounded in the head by a musket-ball, in the assault on the angle, May 12, 1864; was brevetted Lieutenant-Colonel, "for services during the campaign closing with the surrender of Lee"; mustered out July 27, 1865.

51. Captain James B. Mix.

Entered the United States service, November 27, 1861, as First Lieutenant and Adjutant of the Eleventh New York Cavalry (" Scott Nine Hundred ") ; was promoted to the captaincy of Company D, September 27, 1862 ; served as commanding officer of President Lincoln's body-guard during the summer and fall of 1862; was injured, and for a time disabled, while escorting the President on one occasion from the Soldiers' Home to the White House, in assisting the President, who had lost control of his horse ; was placed in command of the Old Capitol Prison, May 11, 1863 ; April 17, 1864, rejoined his regiment at New Orleans, and, with his company, was placed in command of St. James's Parish, Louisiana ; was honorably discharged September 12, 1864. Received the following autograph letter from President Lincoln : " I take pleasure in certifying that Captain James B. Mix commanded a troop of cavalry escorting me between the White House and the Soldiers' Home, and that I became a great deal attached to him. I have not had any reason to change my estimation of him. A. Lincoln."

52. Brigadier-General Edward L. Molineux.

Entered the United States service, September 27, 1862, as Lieutenant-Colonel, One Hundred and Fifty-Ninth Regiment, New York Volunteers ; was promoted to be Colonel, November 25, 1862; was with the Banks Expedition to New Orleans, and in the first movement against Port Hudson. In April, 1863, was severely wounded in the face, at the battle of Irish Bend, La, where his regiment lost nearly one third its numbers. In August, 1863, was appointed on staff of Major-General Franklin, as Inspector-General and Provost-Marshal of the Thirteenth and Nineteenth Army Corps. Was in the battles of Vermilion Bayou and Carrion Crow, and in the Red River campaign. In January, 1864, placed in command of the La Fourche District. Transferred with Nineteenth Army Corps to Virginia, and was at the siege of Petersburg. Commanded a brigade under General Sheridan in the battles in the Shenandoah Valley. Upon the recommendation of General Sheridan, he was breveted Brigadier-General for gallantry at Cedar Creek, to date from that battle. In December, 1864, was sent with a brigade to General Sherman, and placed in command of the defences of Savannah. In May, 1865, took possession of Augusta, and commanded the district of Northern Georgia and South Carolina until August, 1865. Was honorably mentioned in several department orders, and in various official reports, for the good order maintained in that region. In the battles of Winchester, Fisher's Hill, and Cedar Creek his regiment lost heavily, and he was specially mentioned in the corps reports of each of the fights for promotion for gallantry. At Augusta he had charge of one hundred thousand bales of cotton captured, and ten million dollars' worth of military stores and bullion. On being mustered out, the merchants and Common Council of the city gave him a complimentary address, and various county meetings voted thanks.

53. Engineer Isaac Newton.

Entered the United States service, June 14, 1861, as First Assistant Engineer, United States Navy. Ordered to the frigate Roanoke, and was in the blockading service until December 1, 1861. Detached and ordered to New York "for duty in connection with Ericsson's battery," afterwards known as the Monitor. February 7, 1862, was ordered to report to Lieutenant-Commander Worden, United States Navy, as Chief Engineer of United States iron-clad Monitor. Was the Chief Engineer during the engagement with the Rebel ram Merrimac, and the attack upon Fort Darling, August 14, 1862. Detached and ordered to report to Rear-Admiral Gregory at New York as "superintendent of iron-clad vessels at that place." Performed that duty until resignation, February 8, 1865. During this period accompanied many iron-clads to their destination on the Southern coast; superintended the preparation of the large torpedoes called "devils," intended for use against Charleston; and was constantly engaged in the preparation of plans for the new iron-clads. Was an original and constant advocate of the Monitor system, and during the war defended it in the principal journals and reviews of this country. The officers of the United States iron-clad Monitor received a vote of thanks from Congress for their gallantry and success in the engagement with the Rebel ram Merrimac. Captain Worden says: "In the emergency which arose on the passage to Hampton Roads he showed great readiness in resources, and quickness in the application of them. In the action with the Merrimac he did his duty with coolness, skill, and energy."

54. Colonel Theodore W. Parmelee.

Entered the United States service, October 31, 1862, as Colonel One Hundred and Seventy-Fourth Regiment, New York Volunteers. Served in the Department of the Gulf under General Banks in 1863, and commanded the brigade sent on a forced reconnoissance, to open communication with Admiral Farragut, after he had passed the batteries of Port Hudson. Was injured on the expedition by the fall of his horse, and was discharged January 8, 1864, in consequence of injuries received in the service.

55. Captain W. D. Pearne.

Entered the United States service August, 1861, in the Fourth New York Cavalry, and served, "without rank or pay," through Fremont's campaign in the Shenandoah, in 1862, and through Pope's campaign in Virginia, until after the second battle of Manassas. Was commissioned First Lieutenant Fifteenth New York Cavalry, August 19, 1863, and served thenceforth in the Shenandoah Valley. Commanded his company at the battle of New Market, covering the retreat to Cedar Creek, and took part in the engagements at Piedmont, Waynesboro', and Lynchburg, under Hunter, and, as Aide-de-Camp to Colonel Tibbitts, commanding brigade, in those at Winchester, Snicker's Gap, Ashby's Gap, and in the Maryland campaign against Early. In December, 1864, under Sheridan, took part in the fights at Lacy Springs, Waynesboro', and Ashland Station, and in the battle of Five Forks.

At the second Bull Run he was slightly wounded; at Piedmont he acted as special Aid to General Hunter. December 25, 1865, he was brevetted Captain.

56. Captain MOSES L. M. PEIZOTTO.

Entered the United States service, July, 1862, as Captain One Hundred and Third Regiment, Ohio Volunteers. Was at the battle of Perryville, Ky., and, after the retreat of General Bragg, was actively employed in Southern Kentucky. Resigned his commission in January, 1863, on account of disease contracted in the service.

57. Sergeant GURDON S. PHIPPS.

Entered the United States service in June, 1861, as Sergeant in Sickles's brigade, with the promise of a commission upon taking the field. Acted as the instructor of his company, and served in General Hooker's division in Maryland, during the winter of 1861 - 62. Was in the battles of the Peninsular campaign, in 1862, and in Northern Virginia, under General Pope, numbering ten severe engagements. Was mortally wounded at Bristow Station, Va., September, 1862, and was left upon the battle-field. After suffering from hunger, thirst, and a painful wound for three days, was removed to a hospital in Washington, where he died.

58. Colonel HENRY M. PORTER.

Entered the United States service, January 15, 1862, as Captain Seventh Regiment, Vermont Volunteers; Major, August, 1862; Lieutenant-Colonel, August 26, 1865; and Colonel, October 13, 1865. Served in the Department of the Gulf, and was at the battles at Baton Rouge and Donaldsonville, La. Was Provost-Marshal of New Orleans from November, 1863, to August, 1864, and was mustered out April 6, 1866.

59. Lieutenant DE VAN POSTLEY.

Entered the United States service, October 15, 1862, as Second Lieutenant in One Hundred and Seventy-Fourth Regiment, New York Volunteers. Was in the campaign of General Banks in Western Louisiana, and against Port Hudson, in 1863. Was killed at the battle of Donaldsonville, La., in July, 1863. His funeral was attended in New York by the Second Company.

60. Captain JAMES W. POWELL.

Entered the United States service, June 20, 1861, as First Lieutenant of the Seventy-First Regiment, New York Volunteers (Sickles's brigade), and was made Adjutant, July 18. Promoted to be Captain, July 31, 1862. Was promoted to be Major of the One Hundred and Twenty-Sixth New York Volunteers, but declined. Was transferred, June, 1863, to Veteran Reserve Corps. Participated in thirteen engagements, namely, Yorktown, Peninsular campaign, Fair Oaks, Seven Pines, Seven Days' Battles, second Malvern Hill, Bristow Station, Fredericksburg, 1862, and subsequent campaign. He received a gunshot wound in the thigh at Bristow Station, August, 1862, and a scalp wound at Altoona, in May, 1864. Colonel H. L. Porter said: "No officer was more brave, gallant, or efficient." Resigned from the volunteer service, June, 1866, after over five years' continuous service. Was appointed July, 1866, Captain in the Forty-Second Infantry, and is still in the Regular service.

61. Lieutenant GLENN PUTNAM.

Entered the United States service in December, 1861, as Second Lieutenant in Sixth Regiment, New York Volunteers, and joined his regiment at Fort Pickens, in January, 1862. Was with the expedition of General Banks through Western Louisiana to Alexandria, and to Port Hudson, and participated in the battles and skirmishes of the campaign. Mustered out, July, 1863.

62. Lieutenant CHARLES R. REED.

Entered the United States service, February 10, 1862, as Second Lieutenant in the Marine Artillery Corps, New York Volunteers, and served in North Carolina in 1862 and 1863.

63. Lieutenant-Colonel HENRY FRANKLIN SAVAGE.

Entered the United States service in June, 1861, as First Lieutenant and Adjutant of the Twenty-Fifth Regiment, New York Volunteers. He was made Major July 20, 1861, and was present in the reserve at Bull Run. He was in the Peninsular campaign of 1862, and at Hanover Court-House he led the left wing of his regiment. He was severely wounded in the right arm, but refused to quit the field, until, exhausted and weak, he was thrown from his horse, and at first left for dead. He was mustered out of the service for disability; first, however, having been promoted to be Lieutenant-Colonel, June, 1862. He never recovered from his wound, dying, after a short and severe illness, October 17, 1862. "Colonel Savage," writes one who knew him well, "was a brave, faithful, and patriotic soldier and a conscientious gentleman. In the discharge of his duties in the Seventh he was attentive and exact even to punctiliousness. He was known in the regiment as the Model Sentinel. Anxious to learn, and ready in acquiring a knowledge of the duties of his position, no one could surpass him in correct and soldierly habits and demeanor; ardently devoted to his adopted country, no one chafed more restlessly than he at the few days' delay which intervened between the muster out of the Seventh and his muster in as Adjutant of the Twenty-Fifth.

"Privately and socially, he was a universal favorite. His presence was always welcome. Physically, he was erect, well formed, and well proportioned; warm-hearted and genial, he was only known to be loved. Had it been his fortune to have lived and fought through the war, he would have won, and honorably worn, the stars of a general."

64. Major-General ALEXANDER SHALER.

Entered the United States service, June 11, 1861, as Lieutenant-Colonel Sixty-Fifth Regiment, New York Volunteers (United States Chasseurs), and

Colonel, July 17, 1862. Served with great distinction in the Army of the Potomac, upon the Peninsula, in 1862, and was actively engaged at Williamsburg, Fair Oaks, Malvern Hill, and other important battles of the campaign. Served under General Pope in Northern Virginia, and under General McClellan in Maryland. Was at the battle of Fredericksburg, under General Burnside, December, 1862. Commanded a brigade, and led the advance at the capture of Fredericksburg, and the storming of Marye's Heights in May, 1863. Was commissioned Brigadier-General of Volunteers, for gallantry and meritorious conduct, May 26, 1863. In May, 1863, General Abercrombie recommended the government to give Colonel Shaler a high position in the Regular Army, declaring that he had always found him, "whether in battle or in camp, cool, collected, and capable," and no officer in his command more deserving in every respect. General Hooker testified to the "fine character and eminent soldiership of Colonel Shaler." General Sedgwick "urged his promotion for his services and gallantry." General Newton said: "He is distinguished for his exact discipline in camp and coolness in an emergency. In our last campaign on the Rappahannock, his gallantry and soldierly qualities were fully tested." His conspicuous gallantry at Marye's Heights, and the capacity he had shown for command, caused many of the leading citizens of New York to unite in a request to the President for promotion, which, as has been said, was promptly conferred. Served with the Army of the Potomac in the campaigns of 1863, and was at the battle of Gettysburg. In the brilliant affair of Rappahannock Station General Shaler played a chief part, General Sedgwick's order saying (November 8, 1863): "The taking of the heights on the right by Neil's and Shaler's brigades was admirably accomplished." During the winter of 1863-64 was stationed at Sandusky, Ohio, in charge of the prison for Rebel officers, at Johnson's Island. Was taken prisoner at the battle of the Wilderness, in May, 1864, and was confined at Charleston, S. C., within range of the United States batteries on Morris Island. Was exchanged in August, 1864, and ordered to report to General Canby, at New Orleans. Commanded the post of Columbus, Ky., and in January, 1865, assumed command of the Second Division, Seventh Army Corps, and the post of Du Vall's Bluff, Ark. Was brevetted Major-General, July 27, 1865, for "continuous, faithful, and meritorious services throughout the war, and especially for gallantry in the assault upon Marye's Heights, Fredericksburg, Va., and the battle of Gettysburg and the Wilderness." Mustered out of the service, August 24, 1865.

On the 23d of January, 1867, General Shaler was appointed Major-General of the First Division National Guard, S. N. Y., by Governor Fenton, and still commands the division.

### 65. Captain Simon W. Scott.

Entered the United States service, September 9, 1862, as Quartermaster of the One Hundred and Seventy-Fourth Regiment, New York Volunteers. Was in the campaigns of General Banks in Louisiana, in 1863, and was commissioned Captain and Assistant Quartermaster. Resigned in 1864.

### 66. Captain George W. Selover.

Entered the United States service, August 20, 1861, as First Lieutenant, Sixty-Fifth Regiment, New York Volunteers (United States Chasseurs), and as Captain, November 1, 1862. Was in the principal battles of the Peninsular campaign, and at South Mountain and Antietam. Was at the battle of Fredericksburg, under General Burnside. Resigned January, 1863.

### 67. Colonel George W. Stilwell.

Entered the United States service, June 20, 1861, as Captain, Sixty-Seventh Regiment, New York Volunteers; brevetted Major for "gallant and meritorious services," July 23, 1866; Lieutenant-Colonel, September 13, 1866; and Colonel, October 16, 1866. Served through the battles of the Peninsular campaign of 1862, and commanded his Regiment at the battles of Williamsport, South Mountain, and Antietam. Was at the battle of Fredericksburg, under General Burnside. Resigned on account of disease contracted in the service, January 1, 1863. Colonel Stilwell began raising his company April 17, 1861, and enlisted one hundred and two men.

### 68. Captain Charles H. Stirling.

Entered the United States service, June 30, 1861, as private in the Sixty-Second Regiment, New York Volunteers (Anderson Zouaves). Was promoted successively to be Quartermaster, Sergeant, and Second Lieutenant. Was mustered in as First Lieutenant, August 31, 1861, at Washington. November 15, 1861, was appointed Aide-de-Camp on General Peck's staff; October, 1863, was appointed Acting Assistant Inspector-General upon General Peck's staff; June 4, 1864, was commissioned as Captain.

Was in all the battles of the Peninsular campaign, and at the siege of Suffolk in 1863, and in several skirmishes and battles in Virginia and North Carolina in 1863 and 1864. He was twice wounded at Williamsburg, and again at Fair Oaks, where also he had two horses shot under him. General Peck mentioned him for "gallant conduct" in his report of Fair Oaks, and also in his report of Williamsburg. Later, he declared that Captain Stirling "had always acquitted himself with distinction." Received many recommendations for promotion. Resigned November, 1864.

### 69. Lieutenant Eliphalet W. Stratton.

Entered the United States service, August 15, 1862, as First Lieutenant in Twenty-Eighth Regiment, Connecticut Volunteers. Went with the Banks Expedition to New Orleans, and was in the movements against Port Hudson in 1863, his regiment losing heavily. Mustered out with his regiment in September, 1863.

### 70. Lieutenant-Colonel Charles H. Tay.

Entered the United States service in May, 1861, as Captain of Second Regiment, New Jersey Volunteers. Was at the battle of Bull Run in 1861, and in the battles of the Peninsular campaign. Was commissioned Major for gallantry and meritorious conduct at the battle of Gaines's Mills, and commanded his regiment in all the battles of Northern Virginia, under General Pope, and at South Mountain and Antietam. In October, 1862, commissioned Lieutenant-Colonel of Tenth Regiment, New Jersey Volunteers. Served at Norfolk, Va., and in Pennsylvania, in 1863. Commanded his regiment in all the battles of the campaign of 1864, from the Wilderness to Petersburg, Va. Was taken prisoner at the battle of Spottsylvania, and was recaptured on the following day by General Sheridan, and accompanied him in his raid upon Richmond. Was in the various battles under General Sheridan in the Shenandoah Valley, and was taken prisoner at Winchester, and confined at Lynchburg, Danville, and Libby. Exchanged February 22, 1865, and resigned March 7, 1865, on account of disability for active service, contracted by reason of his hardships and long imprisonment. At this time he had had nearly four years of continuous service, and had taken part in about thirty battles and heavy skirmishes.

Captain Tay was appointed Brigade Engineer by General Kearney, and his services during the erection of Fort Worth were highly complimented in orders by that officer.

71. Captain LUCIAN M. THAYER.

Entered the United States service, October 2, 1861, as First Lieutenant in the Fifty-Third New York Volunteers (D'Epineul Zouaves). Took part in the Burnside Expedition to North Carolina; but at Hatteras the transport containing his regiment was blown out to sea, and was picked up by the steamer Ericsson, after a cruise of forty-two days. The regiment was mustered out in May, 1862.

Re-entered the service, August 19, 1862, as Captain in the Fifty-First Massachusetts Volunteers, and served under General Foster in North Carolina, taking part in the battles at Kinston, Whitehall, and Goldsboro'. Was mustered out, with his regiment, in July, 1863.

72. Lieutenant HENRY J. TIEMANN.

Entered the United States service, September 5, 1862, as Second Lieutenant in One Hundred and Fifty-Ninth Regiment, New York Volunteers. Was with the Banks Expedition to New Orleans, in the Red River Expedition, at the siege of Port Hudson, and in other engagements in Louisiana. Appointed Aide-de-Camp to General Birgh, February 5, 1863. Resigned January 1, 1864.

73. Captain GEORGE F. E. TYBRING.

Entered the United States service, August 24, 1861, as Second Lieutenant Seventy-Third Regiment, New York Volunteers; First Lieutenant, May 4, 1862. Was engaged in the battles of the Peninsular campaign, in 1862. Appointed Captain and Assistant Quartermaster, in 1863, and served in the campaigns of the Army of the Potomac in that year, in the campaign of General Grant from the Wilderness to Petersburg, and under General Sheridan in the Shenandoah Valley. Mustered out August 27, 1865.

74. Captain Charles S. Van Norden.

Entered the United States service in 1861. Served in Western Virginia under General Rosecrans, in the summer and autumn of 1861, as military instructor of the Second Regiment, Virginia Volunteers, with the rank of Captain.

75. Lieutenant A. H. Vroom.

Entered the United States service, September 9, 1862, as First Lieutenant, Twenty-First Regiment, New Jersey Volunteers. Served with the Army of the Potomac in Virginia, and was at the battle of Fredericksburg, and storming of Marye's Heights, under General Sedgwick. Mustered out with his regiment, June 19, 1863.

76. Captain Almar P. Webster.

Entered the United States service May, 1861, as First Lieutenant in Ninth Regiment, New York Volunteers (Hawkins's Zouaves). Was promoted to be Captain, September 3, 1862. Was at the battle of Big Bethel, and with the Burnside Expedition to North Carolina, his company being the first to land at Hatteras Inlet. Wounded at the battle of Roanoke Island. Transferred with his regiment to the Army of the Potomac, and was in the battles in Northern Virginia under General Pope, and the battles of South Mountain and Antietam under General McClellan, and at Fredericksburg under General Burnside. At Antietam his company carried in sixty-three men, and lost forty-one killed and wounded. Was at the siege of Suffolk by Longstreet in April, 1863. Mustered out, with his regiment, in June, 1863.

77. Captain E. B. Webster.

Entered the United States service in August, 1862, as Second Lieutenant, One Hundred and Sixty-Fifth Regiment, New York Volunteers (Second Duryee's Zouaves). Was promoted to be First Lieutenant, September 6, 1863; Captain, August, 1865. Served in the Red River campaign, under General Banks, in the Shenandoah Valley under General Sheridan, and in Georgia under General Sherman. Was Aide-de-Camp to General Grover, from August, 1864, to the close of the war. Mustered out October, 1865.

78. Captain G. V. Weir.

Entered the United States service, June 18, 1861, as Second Lieutenant in the Fifth United States Artillery. Was promoted to be First Lieutenant in 1863. Served in Virginia successively in McDowell's army before the battle of Bull Run, in the First Corps, under McCall, Meade, Reynolds, and Seymour, in the Artillery Reserve under Tyler during the Gettysburg campaign, in the draft riots, in the Second Corps under Warren, and in the Shenandoah Valley under Crook, Averill, and Sheridan.

He was with the Army of the Potomac throughout the Peninsular campaign of 1862, Pope's Virginia campaign, McClellan's Maryland campaign, and the campaigns of Burnside, Hooker, and Meade, and afterwards in the campaigns of Sheridan and others in the Shenandoah in 1864. He took part in the battles of Mechanicsville, Gaines's Mills, Charles City Cross-Roads, Malvern Hill, Groveton, second Bull Run, South Mountain, Antietam, first and second Fredericksburg, Gettysburg, Snicker's Gap, Winchester, July 24, 1864, Moorefield, Winchester, September 19, 1864, Fisher's Hill, and Cedar Creek, besides many other engagements. Was brevetted Captain, and in 1867 was in service with his regiment at Fort Monroe, being Adjutant of the post.

79. Captain William H. Williams.

Entered the United States service, November 14, 1861, as Second Lieutenant in Fifth Regiment, New York Cavalry (Ira Harris Guard); First Lieutenant, May 2, 1862; and Captain, May 28, 1862. Was with General Banks in the Shenandoah Valley, in 1862, and with General Pope in his campaign in Northern Virginia. Resigned February, 1863.

80. Lieutenant James Wood.

Entered the United States service, August 1, 1862, as First Lieutenant, One Hundred and Seventy-Fourth Regiment, New York Volunteers. Was with the Banks Expedition to New Orleans, and was actively engaged in various engagements in Louisiana, including the attack upon Port Hudson, and the battle of Donaldsonville. Resigned August, 1863, on account of disease contracted in the service.

## THIRD COMPANY (C).

1. Captain George W. Bacon.

Entered the United States service, November 10, 1861, as First Lieutenant, Company I, Ninety-First Regiment, New York Volunteers. Was promoted to be Captain, October, 1862. March 7, 1862, A. D. C. on the staff of General Brannan, and so continued till honorably discharged, March 17, 1863. Served in Department of the South, at Key West, Port Royal, &c. Took part in the capture of Jacksonville (Florida), and the St. John's River Expedition in October, 1862, and Mitchell's expedition towards Pocotaligo soon after. Was engaged in several other skirmishes in the Department.

2. Colonel William P. Baily.

Entered the United States service, May 16, 1861, as Lieutenant-Colonel of the Second Regiment, Delaware Volunteers. Promoted, August 22, 1862, to be Colonel. Served in the First Division, Second Corps, under Generals Sumner, Richardson, and Hancock. Took part in the Eastern Shore Expedition, under General Lockwood, and was engaged at Gaines's Mills, Peach Orchard, Savage Station, Nelson's Farm, White-Oak Swamp, Malvern Hill, Malvern Hill second, Charlestown, Snicker's Gap, Falmouth, Fredericksburg, Chancellorsville, Gettysburg, Falling Waters, Manassas Gap, Mine Run, Wilderness, and Spottsylvania Court-House. Was wounded in the left breast by a fragment of shell at the battle of Fredericksburg, disabling the left arm so that at this time it is of little use. Was mustered out, with his regiment, May 16, 1864.

At Fredericksburg, where Colonel Baily was severely wounded, he, with his regiment, led the charge of Zook's brigade; at Chancellorsville the regiment was highly complimented by General Hancock; at Gettysburg it lost half its men; and there Colonel Baily commanded the Fourth Brigade, after the wounding of Colonel Brook. At different times he commanded every brigade in the division.

3. Captain Eugene F. Benedict.

4. Captain W. G. Bomford.

Entered the United States service in 1861, as First Lieutenant in the First Infantry (Regular Army). Served in the Army of the Potomac through the war, and is still in the Regular service.

5. Lieutenant-Colonel Jacob L. Brower.

Captain, United States Colored Troops, serving in Department of the South.

6. Lieutenant Charles L. Brown.

Sergeant, Fifty-Seventh New York State Volunteers, served during war.

7. Captain W. C. Burton.

Entered the United States service in 1861, in the —— Regiment. Was appointed on the staff of General Brennan, and served in the Department of the South, at Key West, at Hilton Head, and in Florida.

8. Lieutenant George B. Butler, Jr.

Entered the United States service, July 1, 1861, as private in the Second Artillery (Regular Army). Was promoted in August, 1861, to be Second Lieutenant in the Third Infantry. Promoted to be First Lieutenant, 1862. Was engaged with his regiment in the campaigns of the Army of the Potomac, especially in the battles at Chancellorsville and Gettysburg, with the Fifth Corps, under General Sykes. Was noticed for gallant conduct in the second day's battle of Gettysburg; in the third day's battle he was severely wounded, losing his right arm. Resigned from the service in October, 1863, having no desire to remain in it after being disqualified for active duty.

9. Captain A. S. Bush.

10. Lieutenant-Colonel W. H. Chesebrough.

Entered the United States service, May 14, 1861, as First Lieutenant, Eleventh Infantry (Regular Army), and was assigned as Aid to General Schenck, commanding Ohio brigade, of Tyler's division. Served at Bull Run through the whole of Rosecrans's West Virginia campaign, in its various actions in 1861; in the Shenandoah Valley, under Fremont and Milroy and Sigel, in 1862, being present at the battles at McDowell and Cross Keys; served also the same year as A. A. A. G., and as mustering officer of the First Corps, and was present at the actions at Cedar Mountain, Rappahannock (August 23d), Freeman's Ford, Sulphur Springs, Waterloo Bridge, Centreville, Groveton, and second Bull Run. January 27, 1863, was appointed Lieutenant-Colonel and A. A. G., Eighth Corps, and remained on the staffs of Generals Schenck, Lockwood, and Lew Wallace, who successively commanded the Middle Department and the Eighth Corps. Resigned April 26, 1864. At the first Bull Run Colonel Chesebrough had his horse killed by a solid shot, and at the second Bull Run had a horse killed by a bullet.

11. Colonel Clinton G. Colgate.

Entered the United States service, June 19, 1861, as Major Fifteenth Regiment, New York Volunteers. Was promoted to be Lieutenant-Colonel in August, 1861, and Colonel, November, 1862. Served as Lieutenant-Colonel throughout the Peninsular campaign in the Engineer Corps (General Woodbury), participating in all its battles. Joined Burnside at Falmouth, and laid the pontoon bridge across the Rappahannock at the first battle of Fredericksburg, for which he was specially noticed in general orders. Was with Hooker at Chancellorsville, and laid the pontoons across the Rappahannock at Fredericksburg, Banks's Ford, and United States Ford. Mustered out, with his regiment, June 20, 1863. While under orders to proceed to New York for this service, he volunteered his command to cover the dismantling of the works at the evacuation of Aquia Creek; and for this service he received a letter of thanks, designed for publication, from General G. K. Warren, commanding, in which he says that by this volunteer service "much public property and many lives were saved."

12. Paymaster Cyrus R. Crane.

Entered the United States service as —— Paymaster. Served in the Department of the East.

13. Lieutenant Gardner K. Doughty.

Enlisted in Forty-Eighth New York Volunteers; was wounded at Olustee; promoted to be a Lieutenant, and discharged at close of war.

Entered the United States service, December 2, 1861, as private in the Forty-Eighth Regiment, New York State Volunteers (Colonel Perry). Was promoted to be First Lieutenant, June 1, 1863. Served in South Carolina, Georgia, Florida, and Virginia, under Gillmore and Seymour, in the Tenth Corps. Was engaged at Port Royal Ferry, Coosahatchie, Savannah River, Fort Pulaski, Olustee, Chester Station, and Drury's Bluff (Virginia), at which last place he was shot in both shoulders. Was mustered out, with his regiment, December 1, 1864.

14. Lieutenant-Colonel Thomas Elliot.

Captain, Bemis Heights Regiment, —— New York State Volunteers; served in Army of Potomac, and under Hooker in Western Army. Promoted to Lieutenant-Colonel.

15. Captain L. A. Fish.

Entered the United States service, July 25, 1861, as private in Company C, Ninth Regiment, New York Volunteers (Hawkins's Zouaves). Promoted to be Corporal, October 1, 1861; to be Sergeant, August 20, 1862. Commissioned Second Lieutenant, Company E, One Hundred and Seventy-Fourth New York Volunteers (Fifth Metropolitan Guards), October 21, 1862. Promoted to be Captain, Company E, July 13, 1863. Was present at the capture of Hatteras, August 29, 1861, at the battles of Roanoke Island and Camden, North Carolina, at South Mountain and Antietam; in the Banks Expedition to Louisiana, and the Port Hudson campaign, including the battle at Donaldsonville, the fight at Port Hudson Plains, and the various assaults and the siege of Port Hudson, and the Sabine Pass Expedition. Volunteered in the forlorn hope at Port Hudson. Honorably discharged January 25, 1864.

16. Adjutant Philip D. Gulager.

Entered the United States service as Assistant Adjutant-General. Served on the staff of General Ulmann, in Louisiana.

17. Captain Moses C. Hagadorn.

18. Major-General Joseph E. Hamblin.

Entered the United Stated service, April 22, 1861, as Adjutant of Duryee's Zouaves (Fifth New York Volunteers), and was commissioned May 10, 1861. Promoted to be Captain, August 10, 1861. Commissioned Major of First United States Chasseurs (Sixty-Fifth New York Volunteers), November 4, 1861. Promoted to be Lieutenant-Colonel, July 20, 1862; Colonel, May 26, 1863; Brigadier-General by brevet, "for gallant and meritorious services at Cedar Creek, Virginia," October 19, 1864; Brigadier-General, May 19, 1865; Major-General by brevet, for conspicuous gallantry at the battle of Sailors' Creek, Virginia, April 5, 1865.

Served in all the campaigns of the Army of the Potomac, and also in the Washington and Shenandoah Valley campaign, under Phil Sheridan. Was at the battles of Big Bethel, Yorktown, Williamsburg, Fair Oaks, Glendale, Malvern Hill, Antietam, Fredericksburg, Marye's Heights, Salem Heights, Gettysburg, Rappahannock Station, Mine Run, Wilderness, Spottsylvania Court-House (two battles), Cold Harbor, Winchester, Fisher's Hill, Cedar Creek (or Middletown), Hatcher's Run, in front of Fort Fisher on the Petersburg Line, Petersburg (the final charge), and Sailors' Creek, Virginia. Was wounded by a rifle-ball at the battle of Cedar Creek, through the right thigh, and confined three months; but, with this exception, was constantly on duty from the beginning to the end of the war, and his brigade and regiment were the last ones mustered out of the Army of the Potomac.

19. Lieutenant-Colonel Robert McD. Hart.

Entered the United States service in 1862, and rose, through various grades, to be Lieutenant-Colonel and Inspector-General, in the Sixth Army Corps. Was killed at Cedar Creek, Virginia.

20. Captain William Howland.

Entered the United States service as Captain in the One Hundred and Twenty-Seventh Regiment, New York Volunteers. Served in Virginia and in South Carolina. Was wounded and honorably discharged with his regiment.

21. Captain Frederick Hurst.

Entered the United States service as Captain in the Forty-Seventh Regiment, New York Volunteers. Served in the Department of the South, in South Carolina. Was wounded at the assault on Fort Wagner, and was taken prisoner and carried to Charleston, where he died of his wounds.

22. Major Frank Jeffrey.

Major Sixth Connecticut Volunteers.

23. Lieutenant Edgar Ketchum, Jr.

Entered the United States service in 1863, as Second Lieutenant in the Signal Corps, United States Army. Was on duty, in 1864, at New Market, Virginia, and Georgetown, District Columbia. At the former point was engaged in the repulse of Longstreet's forces, December 10, 1864. Took part in Terry's capture of Fort Fisher, where the signal flags and torches were a mark for sharpshooters. Had his signal-station on the parapet next day, when the magazine exploded. Took an active part in the operations of Schofield and Cox against Wilmington, and was with Terry from Wilmington to Raleigh. Was honorably discharged August 12, 1865.

24. Lieutenant Lewis M. Johnson.

Lieutenant New York State Volunteers; served in Army of Potomac.

25. Captain J. M. Lewis, Jr.

26. Sergeant David O. Logan.

Entered the United States service in 1861, as a private in the Ninth Regiment, New York Volunteers (Hawkins's Zouaves). Was promoted to be Sergeant. Served in North Carolina, and in the Army of the Potomac, in the various campaigns of the regiment, and was mustered out with it at the expiration of its term of service.

27. Captain Henry W. T. Mali.

Entered the United States service as Second Lieutenant, Twentieth Massachusetts Volunteers. Was wounded at battle of the Wilderness, promoted to be Captain, and discharged at close of the war.

28. Paymaster J. W. Mangam.

Entered the United States service, June 5, 1863, and was attached to the Potomac flotilla. Served in blockade duty on the Potomac flotilla, under Commodore Parker, on the United States steamer Eureka, and the mortar schooner Matthew Vassar. Resigned, December 1, 1863, in consequence of fever contracted in the service.

29. Lieutenant CHARLES F. MARSH.

Lieutenant Twenty-Fifth New Jersey.

30. Brigadier-General GILBERT H. MCKIBBEN.

Entered the United States service, October 9, 1861, as Second Lieutenant in the Fifty-First Regiment, New York Volunteers. Promoted to be First Lieutenant, May 16, 1862; Captain, and Assistant Adjutant-General United States Volunteers, October 14, 1862. Brevetted Major, Lieutenant-Colonel, Colonel, and Brigadier-General, "for long and distinguished services during the war," December 2, 1864; and in January, 1865, was assigned to duty according to his brevet rank as Brigader-General. December 9, 1864, appointed Colonel of his regiment, but declined. Served with the Army of the Potomac, and in North Carolina, Kentucky, and Tennessee Was present at the following battles: Roanoke Island, Newbern, second Bull Run, Chantilly, South Mountain, Antietam, Fredericksburg, Vicksburg, Jackson, Knoxville, Campbell's Station, Tennessee, Strawberry Plains, Tennessee, Loudon, Tennessee, Wilderness, Spottsylvania, Cold Harbor, Tolapotamoy, and six of the battles around Petersburg and Richmond. Was shot through the face before Petersburg, 18th June, 1864, and thereby incapacitated for duty eighty days. Mustered out of the service September 19, 1865.

31. Captain SAMUEL G. MILLIGAN.

Entered the United States service as Captain, in Kilpatrick's regiment cavalry (New York Harris Light). Served in Virginia. Died from disease contracted in service on the Rapidan, in the line of duty.

32. Captain HENRY H. MOTT.

Entered the United States service, September 1, 1861, as First Lieutenant, Company A, Fifty-Seventh Regiment, New York Volunteers. Promoted to be Captain, February 8, 1862. Served in Virginia, with the Army of the Potomac, Second Corps, and took active part in the battles at Yorktown, Williamsburg, Fair Oaks, Gaines's Mills, Peach Orchard, Savage Station, White-Oak Swamp, Malven Hill, Antietam, Fredericksburg, second Bull Run, Auburn, Bristow Station, and numerous skirmishes. Was also in the defences of Washington during Early's raid in 1864. Was afterwards detailed, commanding Kendall Green Barracks, at Washington; and Acting Assistant Adjutant-General at Fort Bunker Hill, District Columbia, and of Post Elmira, New York; and at New Orleans, in 1866. Was wounded in the hip, in the lung, and in the right arm, the latter wound being a compound fracture, rendering the arm nearly useless. Was honorably discharged September 8, 1866.

33. Lieutenant GEORGE H. PACKWOOD.

Second Lieutenant, Twentieth Massachusetts Volunteers. Served in front of Petersburg, and discharged at close of war.

34. Lieutenant WILLIAM H. PECK.

Entered the United States service as Lieutenant. Served in Quartermaster's Department, Army of the Potomac.

35. Lieutenant AMBROSE H. PURDY.

Quartermaster.

36. Captain HERMAN G. RADCLIFF.

Entered the United States service in July, 1861, as First Lieutenant, Eighteenth Infantry (Regular Army). Was with General Buell in his Kentucky and Tennessee campaign, and afterwards with General Rosecrans. Took part in the battle of Perryville, and commanded his company throughout the four days' battle of Stone River, or Murfreesboro'. He was already, at this time, suffering from disease contracted in the service, in the line of duty, and his devotion and activity during the battle so accelerated it, that he died at Murfreesboro', a few days after the battle.

37. Sergeant LOUIS L. ROBBINS.

Enlisted private, Twenty-Third Massachusetts Volunteers. Served in Ninth Army Corps till April, 1863; transferred to Eighteenth Army Corps; served till October, 1864, when he was discharged.

38. Lieutenant ALEXANDER M. C. SMITH, JR.

Lieutenant Second New York Cavalry, and transferred to Sixteenth New York Artillery.

39. Lieutenant JOSEPH M. STAMFORD.

Entered the United States service in 1863, as Lieutenant Company H, Thirty-Eighth Regiment, New Jersey Volunteers, Colonel Sewell. Served on the James River at Fort Powhatan, and was soon after made Post Adjutant of Fort Pocahontas, so remaining until the close of the war. Was chiefly engaged in garrison and outpost duty.

40. Captain WALDO SPRAGUE.

Entered the United States service, May 24, 1861, as Ensign in the Seventeenth Regiment, New York Volunteers. Was promoted to be First Lieutenant and Adjutant, July 14, 1862; was promoted to be Captain, January, 1863. He served throughout the Peninsular campaign under McClellan, at second Bull Run under Pope, at Fredericksburg under Burnside, at Chancellorsville under Hooker, and on the White House raid under Stoneman. He was shot through the body, and had his left arm broken at Bull Run. Was honorably mentioned. Was mustered out of the service with his regiment, June 6, 1863.

41. Captain THEODORE STAGG.

42. Brigadier-General HENRY EDWIN TREMAIN.

Entered the United States service, July 13, 1861, as First Lieutenant, Second New York Fire Zouaves. Served as Aide-de-Camp, on brigade staff of the Excelsior Brigade, under General Sickles and Nelson Taylor on the Peninsula, throughout all the battles of that campaign; was specially mentioned in brigade reports at Williamsburg for "ability"; at Fair Oaks for "courage, zeal, and ability"; at Malvern Hill, for "zeal and gallantry"; was transferred with the corps to Pope's army, and was engaged at Bristow Station and second Bull Run, and captured at the latter battle. General Nelson Taylor's report says, "His bravery and gallantry excited my admiration, and have my warmest thanks"; and "he was taken prisoner while endeavoring to check the panic and the rapid advance of the enemy." He had previously been commended in official reports of "The Orchards," June 25, of Glendale, and of Bristow, for "courage, devotion to duty under all circumstances, intelligence, and usefulness."

Was confined in Libby Prison, among the "hostages" of 1862; was exchanged and returned to Sickles's division staff, October, 1862, as Assistant Inspector-General; was present at Fredericksburg and Chancellorsville, being mentioned for gallantry in latter battle. Served as Aide-de-Camp on Hooker's staff, at the latter's request, until his relief by Meade. Took part in the battle of Gettysburg, on the staff of General Sickles, who there lost a leg. In 1864 volunteered on General Butterfield's staff, at Chattanooga, and took part in the battles at Dalton and Resaca, being specially mentioned in orders for great gallantry and efficiency. Was then ordered to rejoin Sickles. In November, 1864, requesting field duty of the Secretary of War, he was ordered first to General Mott's staff (Third Division, Second Corps), and then to General Gregg's (cavalry) staff, afterwards General Crook's. Took part at the battles of Hatcher's Run, Dinwiddie Court-House, Jetersville, Sailors' Creek, &c., to Lee's surrender.

On recommendation of many officers, was brevetted Major and Aide-de-Camp during the Chancellorsville campaign; Lieutenant-Colonel (March 13, 1865), and Colonel (June 12, 1865), for "gallant and meritorious services"; Brigadier-General (November 29, 1865), "for faithful and meritorious services during the war." Remained on duty in South Carolina and elsewhere after the war, and was honorably discharged April 29, 1866.

### 43. Lieutenant Walter Ruthven Tremain.

Entered the United States service, July, 1861, as Second Lieutenant, Second New York Fire Zouaves, Seventy-Third Regiment, New York Volunteers. Was commissioned afterwards First Lieutenant of the Fifty-Third Regiment New York Volunteers, and was subsequently transferred to the One Hundred and Thirty-Second New York Volunteers (Colonel Classen), and acted for a time as Adjutant. Served at Suffolk and on the Blackwater under General Peck, in 1862. His unremitting devotion to his duties on severe picket and expeditionary duty was followed by a fever, which resulted in his death, December 25, 1862. Almost his last thoughts were for his country, and his only regret was that he had "done so little for her." His service was thoroughly patriotic. A strict disciplinarian, and soldierly and dignified in courage, his great amiability endeared him to his brother-officers and men. His regiment passed resolutions of respect to this "most efficient, prompt, and promising young officer," "endeared to us by his kind, generous nature," and "of the country a brave and noble defender." One who knew him well writes: "Although but nineteen when he died, he was generally thought to be much older. He was handsome in feature and form, graceful in manner, but without affectation, sincere and true in all his relations, an obedient son, a loving brother, a true patriot, and a youthful martyr to his love of country and the cause of republican government." He was the second son of Edwin R. Tremain of New York, and brother of General H. E. Tremain.

### 44. Captain William W. Tracy.

Entered the United States service, December 17, 1862, as Second Lieutenant of the Thirty-First New York Volunteers, was promoted to be First Lieutenant, January 14, 1863, and served as Adjutant from June 15 to October 14, 1863. Served in the Sixth Corps in the Chancellorsville campaign, where his regiment lost half its numbers. February 4, 1864, was commissioned as Captain in the Twenty-Sixth United States Colored Troops, and served in South Carolina, part of the time on the staffs of Generals Saxton and E. E. Potter. Was engaged in the battle at Pocotaligo, and in numerous skirmishes around Charleston Harbor. Was mustered out, with his regiment, August 31, 1865.

### 45. Lieutenant-Colonel Thomas R. Turnbull.

Entered the United States service as Lieutenant-Colonel of one of the New York Metropolitan Regiments. Served in the Department of the Gulf, Louisiana.

### 46. Captain George Tuthill.

Entered the United States service, May 27, 1861, as Captain in the Ninth Regiment, New York State Militia, afterwards the Eighty-Third Regiment of New York Volunteers. Served in June and July, 1861, on the Upper Potomac and in Virginia under Generals C. P. Stone, Patterson, and Banks. July 5 was detached by General Stone to a command at Harper's Ferry, with headquarters at Sandy Hook. While there he received and transmitted the famous disputed order of General Scott to General Patterson, to prevent the junction of Johnston with Beauregard at Manassas. This order was put into the hands of a courier by Captain Tuthill, and sent to General Patterson, then at Martinsburg, and there delivered to his Adjutant-General. The order was, as nearly as I can remember, in these words: "General Patterson, General. Push on with all despatch. Admit of no delay. Prevent a junction of the enemy at all hazards. (Signed) Winfield Scott." July 24, was relieved by Colonel Gordon with the Second Massachusetts. Left the service from sickness contracted in the line of duty.

### 47. Surgeon Thomas Barnett Tuthill.

Entered the United States service as Surgeon in the Navy. Served throughout the war, mostly in the North Atlantic Squadron.

### 48. Sergeant Lewis C. Updike.

Private, One Hundred and Seventy-Sixth New York Volunteers; served in Nineteenth Army Corps, Department of the Gulf.

49. JAMES B. VAN CLEEF, U. S. N.

Entered the United States service as sailor; served with Farragut.

50. Lieutenant WILLIAM A. VERPLANCK.

Entered the United States service as First Lieutenant, in the Orange County Regiment, New York Volunteers (Colonel Ellis). Served in the Army of the Potomac.

51. Adjutant WILLIAM S. WATKINS.

Entered the United States service, November, 1861, as Lieutenant of Company K, Eleventh Regiment, New York Volunteers. Served at Newport News, Va., until July, 1862, when his regiment was mustered out of the service. September 9, 1862, was commissioned as First Lieutenant and Adjutant of the One Hundred and Seventy-Fourth Regiment, New York Volunteers. Served in the Department of the Gulf, and was at the engagements at Plains Store, Donaldsonville, Port Hudson, &c., during the campaign under Banks. Resigned, on the consolidation of his regiment, March 11, 1864.

52. Captain GEORGE R. WHEATON.

Entered the United States service as a Captain in one of the New York Metropolitan Regiments. Served in the Department of the Gulf, Louisiana, and was discharged with his regiment.

53. Surgeon JAMES M. WILSON.

Entered the United States service as Acting Assistant Surgeon in the navy. Served under Admiral Porter. Was at the attack on Fort Fisher. Is now Assistant Surgeon in the United States Navy.

54. Major ALBERT H. WINSLOW.

Entered the United States service, June 4, 1861, as Captain of Company A, Eighth Ohio Volunteers (mustered June 22). Was promoted November 25, 1861. Served in 1861 in West Virginia and the Shenandoah Valley. October 26, took part in the assault and capture of Romney, and on the 6th and 7th January in the affair at Blur's Gap. Served in the Shenandoah Valley in the spring of 1862; was at the battle of Winchester, May 23, and in the subsequent skirmishes; was transferred to the Peninsula, and took part in the repulse of the enemy on the 3d, 4th, and 5th of July. Was in all the subsequent battles and skirmishes of the Army of the Potomac, in the Second Corps, till mustered out, July 13, 1864, — amongst the more important being Winchester, Antietam, Fredericksburg, Chancellorsville, Gettysburg, Mine Run, Cedar Run, Bristow Station, Wilderness, Brock's Cross-Roads, The Po, North Anna, Spottsylvania, Cold Harbor, and several of the battles before Petersburg. Was constantly with his regiment in the above-mentioned battles and campaigns; had command of it much of the time, and was in entire command of it from the battle of Spottsylvania to the close of its term. Was frequently honorably mentioned.

55. Captain David T. Wright.

Entered the United States service as First Lieutenant in the Fifty-Seventh New York Volunteers. Served with his regiment in the Army of the Potomac, and in the West (Ninth Army Corps). Was promoted to be Captain.

56. Brigadier-General John C. Wright.

Entered the United States service, October 8, 1861, as Captain of Company A, Fifty-First New York (Veteran) Volunteers. Promoted to be Major, March 14, 1863; to be Lieutenant-Colonel, December 30, 1864; to be Colonel, March, 1865, and brevetted Brigadier-General of Volunteers, March, 1865. Took part in the Burnside Expedition to North Carolina, and participated in the battles of Roanoke Island and Newbern. With his division, (Reno's) joined Pope in Virginia, and was present in the action of Kelly's Ford, Rappahannock Station, White Sulphur Springs, Bristow Station, second Manassas, and Chantilly. Under McClellan, took part in the battles of South Mountain and Antietam; and under Burnside, in the battle of Fredericksburg. Afterwards, with Burnside, proceeded to Kentucky, and thence, under Parke, to reinforce General Grant at Vicksburg. After the surrender of Vicksburg, took part in the Jackson campaign under Sherman. Subsequently returned with Parke's command to Kentucky, where his regiment re-enlisted. With the Ninth Corps joined the Army of the Potomac, in May, 1864, and participated in all the battles of Grant's campaign, viz.: Wilderness, Spottsylvania, Cold Harbor, Jones's Farm, Bethesda Church, Tolopotomy Creek, and the engagements in front of Petersburg, up to the battle of Poplar Grove Spring Church. At the latter action (September 30, 1864) was taken prisoner. After six months' imprisonment at Richmond (Libby Prison), Salisbury, and Danville, was exchanged, and rejoined his command two days after Lee's surrender. Upon the arrival of the Ninth Corps at Alexandria, was assigned to the command of Camp Anger, where he remained until his muster out, August 4, 1865. Was slightly wounded at Antietam, Fredericksburg, and Petersburg. At various times performed the duties of Assistant Adjutant-General, Assistant Inspector-General, Provost-Marshal, and Assistant Engineer on General Burnside's staff, and superintended the erection of the earthworks on the Ninth Corps front at Petersburg.

57. Captain William E. Van Wyck.

Entered the United States service, August 29, 1862, as Captain Company F, One Hundred and Thirty-First Regiment, New York Volunteers. Joined the Banks Expedition to Louisiana. Took part in the first attempt on Port Hudson, March, 1862, and in the battle at Irish Bend, Louisiana, April 14, 1863. Was on provost duty in Brashear City, on election duty in New York (November, 1864), and received honorable mention by General Butler, and was with Sherman at Goldsboro'. Was acting Aid on brigade staff, June, 1865. Commanded the regiment for a short time. Mustered out, with his regiment, August 2, 1865.

## FOURTH COMPANY (D).

1. Brigadier-General William B. Barton.

Entered the United States service in 1861 as Major in the Forty-Seventh Regiment, New York Volunteers, and was promoted through all the grades to be Brigadier-General. Served in the Department of the South.

2. Lieutenant Henry C. Belden.

3. Lieutenant Albert C. Burdick.

4. Lieutenant Joseph Cantrell.

Entered the United States service, February 26, 1863, as Second Lieutenant in the Third Regiment, United States Volunteers. Was promoted to be First Lieutenant in the Eighth Regiment, Corps d'Afrique, December 15, 1863. Was stationed at Port Hudson and Baton Rouge, Louisiana, and was on duty at Port Hudson for a short time during the siege. Was honorably discharged February 15, 1864.

5. Colonel Alford B. Chapman.

Entered the United States service in 1861 as Captain in the Fifty-Seventh Regiment, New York Volunteers. Served in the Army of the Potomac. Was in all the battles of the Peninsular campaign, and those in Northern Virginia and Maryland, in 1862. Was severely wounded at Fredericksburg, under Burnside, while in command of his regiment, and protecting the pontoon bridge on the Rappahannock. Promoted to be Colonel, and served continuously in the Army of the Potomac, through all its marches and battles, until the battle of the Wilderness in May, 1864, where he was killed, while in command of the division skirmish line.

6. Ensign Walter Cooper.

Entered the United States service in 1862 as Captain's Clerk on gunboat Mandilla. Was promoted to be Ensign for gallantry in an engagement on the Mississippi River. Was captured and confined in Libby Prison. Was detailed as Secretary to Admiral Dahlgren at Charleston. Remained in the service until the close of the war.

7. Captain George A. Crocker.

Entered the United States service, September 7, 1861, as Second Lieutenant in Company E, Fifth Cavalry (Regular Army). September 11, 1861, was promoted to be First Lieutenant. October 11, 1861, was made Adjutant of the Sixth Cavalry. June 27, 1862, was promoted to be Captain of Company A. Served as Aid on the staff of General Keyes, in the Fourth Army Corps. Served also on the staff of General Sickles, and that of General Pleasanton. Served as Aid to General Buford, and was A. I. G. of First Cavalry Division, Army of the Potomac. Was captured at Brandy Station, October 11, 1863, and exchanged at Wilmington, North Carolina, March 1, 1865. Was honorably discharged May 15, 1865, at the expiration of the war.

8. Lieutenant-Colonel William H. Crocker.

Entered the United States service, October 12, 1861, as Captain in the Sixth Regiment, New York Cavalry. Was successively promoted to be Third, Second, and Senior Major, and Lieutenant-Colonel. Served one year on the staff of Major-General Pleasanton, commanding the cavalry of the Army of the Potomac, as Assistant Inspector-General. He was relieved from this duty at his own request, to take command of his regiment, which he retained until January 1, 1865, when he resigned, having commanded his regiment in several engagements, and been honorably mentioned.

9. Lieutenant William E. Fiske.

10. Captain Henry J. Foster.

Entered the United States service in September, 1862, as Adjutant of the One Hundred and Thirty-Third Regiment, New York Volunteers. Served throughout the Têche and Port Hudson campaigns, and was wounded at the fight before Port Hudson, May 27, 1863. Served on the staffs of Generals Banks and Bowen. Was appointed by General Banks Provost-Marshal of the Parish of La Fourche, Louisiana, the largest and wealthiest in the State, except Orleans. Was promoted to be Captain, and resigned in September, 1864.

11. Lieutenant S. F. B. Gillespie.

Entered the United States service, September 5, 1864, as a private in Company B, Eightieth Regiment, New York Volunteers (Colonel Hardenburgh). Promoted to be Second Lieutenant, Company I, December 1, 1864, and detailed as Assistant Provost-Marshal of prisoners at City Point, under General Patrick. April 15, 1865, was put in command of the prisoners confined in Castle Thunder at Richmond. In June, 1865, was detailed as Assistant Commandant of City Prisons at Richmond, and Assistant Provost-Marshal on the staff of General Ordway. Was mustered out with his regiment, February 12, 1866.

12. Sergeant Louis Gulager.

Entered the United States service as private in the Seventeenth Infantry (Regular Army). Served in the Army of the Potomac and in Texas till the close of the war. Was promoted to be Sergeant.

13. Brigadier-General William Gurney.

Entered the United States service in 1861 as Captain in the Sixty-Fifth Regiment, New York Volunteers. Served with the Army of the Potomac through the Peninsular campaign of 1862. In September, 1862, was promoted to be Colonel of the One Hundred and Twenty-Seventh Regiment, New York Volunteers. Served at Norfolk; served with the Army of the Potomac in 1863, after Gettysburg, and in the Department of the South, at Charleston Harbor. Was wounded at Pocotaligo Bridge. Was put in command of the city of Charleston after its capture, and was promoted to be Brigadier-General.

14. Captain EDWARD A. HARRISON.

Entered the United States service in May, 1861, as First Lieutenant in the Seventy-Fourth Regiment, New York Volunteers (Fifth Excelsior). Was promoted, March, 1862, to be Captain of Company H. Served with the Excelsior Brigade in Lower Maryland, participating in Graham's Aquia Creek raid and Sickles's Dumfries raid. Took part in the Peninsular campaign, was at the siege of Yorktown, and thereafter in all the battles in which Hooker's division was engaged, from Williamsburg to Bristow Station. At Williamsburg he behaved with great gallantry, and narrowly escaped, being shot through his forage-cap, the bullet grazing the skull, and severing the hair in its course. At Bristow Station, in August, 1862, he lost his life, being shot dead at the head of his company. A brother-officer writes of him: "He was regarded by his comrades as one of the bravest of the brave. His company loved him as a father. He was courteous, he was generous to a fault, and would divide his last dollar with a comrade. He was a true friend. May his memory be ever green in the records of the Fourth Company, for the Seventh Regiment lost in him one of its noblest sons."

15. Lieutenant CHARLES R. HICKOX.

Entered the United States service in the Fifth Artillery (Regular Army), and served two years as First Lieutenant in the Fifth Artillery, with the Army of the Potomac.

16. Adjutant LEONARD HAY.

Entered the United States service as Second Lieutenant in the Ninth Infantry (Regular Army). Was stationed in California, with his regiment, during the war. Was promoted to be First Lieutenant and Adjutant. Is still in the Regular Army.

17. Sergeant-Major WILLIAM A. JACKSON.

Entered the United States service as Sergeant in the howitzer battery attached to the Ninth Regiment, New York Militia, afterwards the Sixth New York Battery. Served during the war in Army of the Potomac. Was promoted to be Sergeant-Major.

18. Sergeant JOHN JARVIS.

19. Lieutenant-Colonel EDWARD H. LITTLE.

Entered the United States service, June 18, 1861, as First Lieutenant in the Sixty-Fifth Regiment, New York Volunteers (United States Chasseurs). Promoted to be Captain, June 1, 1862, at Fair Oaks. Promoted to be Major, September 20, 1862. Promoted to be Lieutenant-Colonel, March, 1865. Was on duty with his regiment throughout the war in the Peninsular campaign (taking part in the siege of Yorktown and the battles of Seven Pines, Fair Oaks, Charles City Cross-Roads, and Malvern Hill), and in the Maryland campaign of 1862. Served at Suffolk and on the Peninsula in 1863, under Generals Peck, Dix, and Keyes, and in August, 1863, in the Department of the South, under Gillmore. Was mustered out, with his regiment, July 17, 1865.

20. Captain John L. Little.

Entered the United States service as First Lieutenant and Adjutant in the One Hundred and Twenty-Seventh, New York Volunteers. Served with that regiment in the Army of the Potomac and in the Department of the South. Was promoted to be Captain.

21. Lieutenant A. V. B. Lockrow.

Entered the United States service as Lieutenant in the Fourteenth Regiment, New York Heavy Artillery. Stationed in the fortifications near Washington.

22. Colonel James E. Mallon.

Entered the United States service as First Lieutenant and Adjutant of the Fortieth Regiment, New York Volunteers. Served in the Army of the Potomac. Acted as Provost-Marshal successively on the staffs of Generals Hamilton, Kearny, and Sedgwick. Was promoted to be Colonel of the Forty-Second Regiment, New York Volunteers, and was killed at Bristow Station, while in command of the brigade of which his regiment formed part, on the 11th of October, 1863.

23. Lieutenant-Colonel Alexander S. Marshall.

Entered the United States service in June, 1861, as First Lieutenant and Adjutant in the —— Regiment of West Virginia Volunteers. Served through Rosecrans's campaign in West Virginia, and afterwards with Lander and Shields in the Shenandoah Valley. Served through the Peninsular campaign, through Pope's campaign in Northern Virginia, at South Mountain, Antietam, and the first Fredericksburg. In 1863 and 1864 served at the West, under Sherman, and was mustered out in July, 1865, at Washington, with Sherman's army. Was promoted through the successive grades to be Lieutenant-Colonel.

24. Lieutenant A. C. Merritt.

Entered the United States service as Lieutenant, and served in the Signal Corps of the Army of the Potomac.

25. Lieutenant Aaron J. Mixsell.

26. Lieutenant John E. Moies.

Entered the United States service as Sergeant in —— Regiment of Rhode Island Volunteers. Was promoted to be Lieutenant in Corps d'Afrique. Served in Louisiana, and died at New Orleans of disease contracted in the service.

27. Lieutenant-Colonel Samuel W. McPherson.

Entered the United States service in May, 1862, as First Lieutenant of the Fifty-Third New York Volunteers. In September, 1862, he was mustered out, regiment being consolidated. Commissioned First Lieutenant of One

Hundred and Seventy-Fourth New York Volunteers, in October, 1862. Went in the Banks Expedition to Louisiana, and took part in the engagement at Bayou Saras and the siege of Port Hudson. Resigned in consequence of disease contracted in the service. In September, 1863, was commissioned First Lieutenant and Adjutant of the Twenty-Fifth New York Cavalry; Captain, March, 1864; Major, July, 1864; and was brevetted Lieutenant-Colonel in 1865, for gallant and meritorious service during the war.

Served in Virginia, under Sheridan, in 1864 and 1865, until the close of the war. Took part in the cavalry engagements at Ashland, Hanover Court-House Landing, June 3, 1864; Jones Bridge, Charles City Cross-Roads, and White-House Landing; Halltown and Smithfield during Early's raid; and in the action in front of Washington, July 11, 1864. His regiment charged the buildings occupied by Early's sharpshooters, and cleared and burned them, to give range to Fort Stevens. Was mustered out with his regiment in July, 1865.

### 28. Lieutenant Charles J. Murphy.

Entered the United States service in June, 1861, as First Lieutenant and Quartermaster of the Thirty-Eighth New York Volunteers. Took part in the first battle of Bull Run, serving in the ranks with a musket, and was specially noticed for gallantry by his superior officers. When the army retreated, he refused to leave, and remained, dressing the wounds of the wounded in his own and other regiments, and was captured, sent to Richmond, and thrust into prison. He devoted his whole time to caring for the wounded there, until September, 1861, when he, with Colonels Raynor and Hurd, effected the daring escape famous at that time and since, and crossed Virginia alone to our lines. All the commissioned and non-commissioned officers of his regiment unite in a document, praising, in the highest terms, his "courage, humanity, and self-sacrifice." Six of the surgeons at Sudley Church Hospital, in a public letter, pronounced his devotion and activity at Bull Run "greater than that of any other five men." General Shields sent word to the President that Lieutenant Murphy had, "by his noble-hearted conduct as a prisoner, in aid of the wounded troops, earned the praise of the whole army." Whereupon the President wrote: "If there be any vacancy of a captaincy in the Regular Army not already promised, let it be given to Charles J. Murphy." With this prospect, Lieutenant Murphy resigned his commission in his regiment. While awaiting the commission so indicated he went as a volunteer to the Peninsula, and cared for hundreds of wounded, at his own expense, through the severe and trying campaign. He did service to the wounded on many fields thereafter, without rank or pay, and was mentioned in public documents in the highest terms, by many officers and men of the Union Army. Surgeon Dunster wrote: "His services so freely rendered, in a time of the direst confusion and distress, were of great value, and have received the grateful thanks of both the men he helped to care for and the officers he so nobly assisted." A soldier communicates a brief memorandum, as follows: "We were strangers, and he took us in; naked, and he clothed us; an hungered, and he gave us food."

29. Lieutenant JOSEPH NEUSTAEDTER.

Entered the United States service October, 1862, as First Lieutenant and Quartermaster of the Eighth New York Volunteers. His regiment was mostly on picket duty during the winter. In January, 1863, he was surprised and captured, while riding with an orderly, by a body of Stuart's cavalry, and sent to Libby Prison, where he was confined till May. Was then sent to Salisbury, and remained till August, when he was exchanged. Resigned, November, 1863, his health being impaired by prison hardships. "This was the second time I had enjoyed Richmond hospitality; the first was as a member of the Seventh Regiment in the Monroe Excursion of 1858."

30. Brigadier-General ROBERT NUGENT.

Entered the United States service in 1861 as Lieutenant-Colonel of the Sixty-Ninth Regiment, New York Militia, for three months' service; was commissioned Captain in the Sixteenth Infantry (Regular Army); served with distinction through the war, and was brevetted Brigadier-General.

31. Sergeant-Major EDWARD J. OLSSEN.

Entered the United States service, 8th November, 1863, as private in the Seventeenth Infantry (Regular Army), and was promoted to be Sergeant-Major of the regiment, April 7, 1864; served in Ayres's division of the Fifth Corps; took part in the battles of June 17 and 18 before Petersburg, and was in the breastworks with his regiment thereafter till June 29, supporting Battery D of the Fifth Artillery, constantly under fire; on the 18th, 19th, and 21st of August took part in the battles on the Weldon Road, his brigade (Hayes's) opening the battle and remaining till the close, on the 21st; at Peeble's Farm (or Poplar Grove Church) his regiment was so badly cut up that General Warren ordered it, at the close of the battle, into the Corps Provost Guard) there being but thirty-three men left of the ninety-nine (to which the regiment had previously been reduced) that went into action. Is still on duty with his regiment, at last accounts, in Texas.

32. Major MORTIMER B. OWEN.

Entered the United States service, September 4, 1861, as Second Lieutenant, Company G, Fifty-Seventh Pennsylvania Volunteers; was promoted to be Captain, December 4, 1861; served in the Army of the Potomac under Generals McClellan, Hooker, Burnside, and Meade; participated in the siege of Yorktown, the battles of West Point, Fair Oaks, Savage Station, Charles City Cross-Roads, Malvern Hill, Harrison's Landing, and second Bull Run; was twice wounded; was taken prisoner at second Bull Run; was brevetted Major, March 17, 1863; was mustered out with his regiment, October 9, 1863.

33. Lieutenant WILLIAM H. ROOME.

Entered the United States service as Lieutenant; served in the Department of the South.

34. Lieutenant-Colonel GEORGE SANGSTER.

35. Captain J. Daniel Schuller.

Entered the United States service November 15, 1861, as Second Lieutenant in the Eighty-Seventh Regiment, New York Volunteers; promoted to be First Lieutenant, April 19, 1862; served in the Third Corps under Kearny, and took part in all the battles of the Peninsular campaign; was wounded in the hand in one of the Seven Days' Battles; was engaged at the second Bull Run, and was there captured and sent to Libby Prison; was recommended for promotion after the Seven Days' Battles, and was brevetted Captain, May 18, 1866; was honorably discharged at end of service.

36. Major Frank K. Smith.

Entered the United States service as Captain in the One Hundred and Twenty-Seventh Regiment, New York Volunteers; served in the Army of the Potomac and in Department of the South; was wounded at Pocotaligo Bridge; was promoted to be Major, and mustered out with his regiment at the close of the war; served on the staffs of Generals Hatch and Schemmelpfennig, commanding in Charleston Harbor.

37. Lieutenant Samuel J. Smith.

Entered the United States service as Lieutenant in one of the New York Metropolitan Regiments; was wounded at Port Hudson.

38. Sergeant Archibald A. Snodgrass.

Entered the United States service as Sergeant in the Sixth New York Battery; discharged on account of disability, from disease contracted in the Peninsular campaign, in 1862.

39. Colonel Z. L. Spaulding.

Entered the United States service, in 1861, as Major in the Twenty-Seventh Regiment, Ohio Volunteers; served under Generals Grant, Rosecrans, and Sherman in the armies of the West; was promoted to be Lieutenant-Colonel and Colonel, and commanded a regiment at Vicksburg.

40. Captain Samuel H. Starr.

Entered the United States service as Captain in the Fourth Company, Third Regiment, Missouri Volunteers; served in the Army of the West; died from disease contracted at the siege of Vicksburg.

41. Captain Peter B. Steel.

Entered the United States service as First Lieutenant in —— Regiment New York Volunteers (Van Wyck Legion); promoted to be Captain; served in the Army of the Potomac and Department of the South.

42. Captain Joseph B. Stevenson.

Entered the United States service in one of the New York Metropolitan Regiments; served also in the navy.

## FIFTH COMPANY (E).

1. Lieutenant-Colonel THOMAS J. ADDIS.

Was wounded, and died in the service.

2. Captain JAMES BELL.

Entered the United States service, in 1861, as a private in the First Regiment, New York Volunteers (Colonel Allen); was promoted through all the grades, and was mustered out with the regiment, in 1863, as Captain; served in the Army of the Potomac, and was in its various engagements previous to June, 1863; rendered distinguished service, also, as a scout.

3. Captain E. D. BENEDICT.

Entered the United States service as Captain of cavalry; served in Texas.

4. Captain GEORGE W. BISSELL.

Entered the United States service as Captain in the Ninetieth Regiment, New York Volunteers; served in the Department of the South; died in 1864, from disease contracted in the service.

5. Sergeant JOHN BOLTON.

Entered the United States service, May, 1861, as private in the Seventy-Ninth Regiment (Highlanders), New York Volunteers; was promoted to be First Sergeant in 1863; served with his regiment in Virginia, South Carolina, Kentucky, Mississippi, East Tennessee, and Maryland, and took part in the battles of first Bull Run, Lewinsville, Port Royal, Port Royal Ferry (January 1, 1862), Secessionville, James Island, Cedar Mountain, Kelly's Ford, Bull Run number two, Chantilly, South Mountain, Antietam, Fredericksburg, Vicksburg, Jackson, Blue Springs (Tennessee), Fort Sanders, Knoxville, Wilderness, and Spottsylvania; was mustered out with his regiment, May, 1864.

6. Captain WILLIAM A. BRUSLE, JR.

Entered the United States service, June 18, 1863, as Captain, Company C, Thirteenth New York Cavalry; transferred, as Adjutant, to Twenty-Fifth New York Cavalry, March 23, 1864; promoted to be Captain, Company H, Twenty-Fifth New York Cavalry, December 21, 1864; served in Virginia and Maryland under Sheridan; was present at the engagements of White House Landing, Fort Stevens, Halltown, Opequan Creek, Winchester, Luray, Fort Republic, Woodstock, New Town, Cedar Creek, Madison Court-House, Waynesboro', and capture of Richmond; mustered out with his regiment, July 7, 1865.

7. Purser HENRY C. BRAISTED.

Entered the United States service as Purser in the United States Navy, and was attached to the United States steamer Cossack, plying around Jacksonville, Fernandina, Beaufort, St. Helena, Fort Pulaski, Fort Monroe, &c.; length of service, fourteen months.

8. Captain C. R. Cargill.

9. Captain William Coles.

10. Lieutenant F. H. Corrie.

Entered the United States service, August 28, 1861, as Second Lieutenant in the United States Marine Corps; promoted to be First Lieutenant, November 25, 1861; served in the marine battalion at Port Royal in 1861 and 1862, and took part in the naval assault on Fernandina, Florida, March, 1862. At Fort Fisher, in December, 1864, and January, 1865, commanded the marine guard of the Powhatan, flag-ship of the Third Division, the marines in both engagements manning a battery of nine-inch guns; landed on the beach below Fort Fisher, January 16, 1865, and commanded a company of marines in the assault of that date; was favorably mentioned by Commodore Schenck, division commander, in his report of the engagement. In March, 1865, while the Powhatan was "repairing damages" sustained at Fort Fisher, he obtained a short leave of absence, went to the front at Petersburg and Richmond, and volunteered as Aide-de-Camp to General Miles, commanding First Division, Second Corps. For his services in the severe battle of the 25th March he was publicly thanked on the field by General Miles, who next day wrote as follows: "Sir, permit me to acknowledge the service rendered by you in the battle of the 25th. Acting entirely in a volunteer capacity upon my staff, your coolness and gallant bearing under the severest fire were calculated to give encouragement to the troops, while your prompt transmittal of orders proved you to be a most efficient aide-de-camp. Please accept my thanks for the valuable assistance you afforded me yesterday in an engagement which, being in an entirely different arm of the service from your own, was marked by unusual spirit and severity."

11. Lieutenant Frederick Creighton, Jr.

12. Lieutenant Robert Eagan.

13. Captain Edward S. Earle.

14. Major Francis S. Earle.

Entered the United States service June 20, 1861, as First Lieutenant and Adjutant of the Fourth Regiment, Michigan Volunteers. Promoted to be Major and Assistant Adjutant-General on General Morell's staff, September 10, 1862. Took part, as Adjutant, in all the campaigns of the Army of the Potomac, from the first Bull Run to Antietam, being present at the following battles: First Bull Run, Yorktown, New Bridge (on the Chickahominy), Hanover Court-House, Mechanicsville, Gaines's Mills, Malvern Hill, second Bull Run, and Antietam. Was wounded in the knee at Malvern. In the memorable "Seven Days," in the Second Brigade, First Division, Sixth Corps, to which he belonged, every regimental commanding officer was killed (two at Gaines's Mills and two at Malvern), and the rank and file suffered proportionately. After Antietam, General Morell was assigned to the Upper Potomac, where Major Earle served till honorably discharged, May 18, 1863.

15. Engineer FREDERICK ECKEL.

Entered the United States service, July, 1861, as an Acting Second Assistant Engineer on board the United States steamer Saranac. Served in the Pacific Squadron under Admiral Bell. Resigned at San Francisco, after two years' service.

16. Adjutant FRANK C. FILLEY.

17. Lieutenant-Colonel LOUIS FITZGERALD.

Entered the United States service, June 1, 1861, as First Lieutenant, Company C, Eleventh Regiment, New York Volunteers (Ellsworth Zouaves). Promoted to be Captain August 1, 1861, for gallantry at the first battle of Bull Run, as stated in orders. After disbandment of the Eleventh New York Volunteers, was commissioned First Lieutenant, Company K, Fortieth Regiment, New York Volunteers (Mozart), January 24, 1862. March, 1862, "officer of the trenches," under Major-General Hamilton, at siege of Yorktown. Also served, on the Peninsula, as Provost-Marshal, First Division, Third Corps, and as Aide-de Camp to General Kearny. June 25, 1862, promoted to be Captain, Fortieth New York Volunteers, to rank from May 26, 1862, "for gallantry in the battle of Fair Oaks," as stated in orders; December 4, 1862, Aide-de-Camp to General D. B. Birney; December 22, 1862, Aide-de-Camp to General Foster, commanding in North Carolina; October 26, 1864, Major, First Regiment, Missouri Volunteers; February 17, 1866, promoted to be Lieutenant-Colonel; August 11, 1866, brevetted Lieutenant-Colonel (National Guard State New York) "for faithful and meritorious services" during the war. Served in Third Corps; in Eighteenth Corps (North Carolina and at Fort Monroe); in Tenth Corps (at head-quarters in South Carolina); in the Army of the Ohio as Aide-de-Camp successively to the major-generals commanding the Ninth Corps, the Twenty-Third Corps, the Fourth Corps, and the Cavalry Corps; in Eastern Tennessee with above command and in Vicksburg, Mississippi, under General Dana. Was actively engaged in the battles of first Bull Run, Yorktown, Peach Orchard, Williamsburg, Seven Pines, Fair Oaks, Monocacy, Fredericksburg, Little Washington, North Carolina; second Newbern, Knoxville, Dandridge; last attack on Charleston and Stono Inlet; was wounded in ankle at first Bull Run; in knee at Williamsburg, and in hip at Fair Oaks; was blown up by torpedoes in gunboat Hiram Barney on James River, Virginia. Honorably discharged February 27, 1865.

18. Sergeant AUGUSTUS FLEET.

Entered the United States service in 1861 as First Sergeant in —— Regiment, New York Volunteers. Took part in the Peninsular campaign with the Army of the Potomac, and was killed at Fair Oaks, and buried on the field.

19. Major ALFRED FOOTE.

Entered the United States States service, May 14, 1861, as First Lieutenant in the Fourteenth Infantry (Regular Army). Promoted to be Captain

January 18, 1865; Brevet Captain, August 18, 1865; Brevet Major, November 5, 1865. Served in the Fifth Corps, Army of the Potomac, under Generals Meade, Sykes, Ayres, Hayes, Winthrop. Took part in the battles at Falmouth, Chancellorsville, those of the Burnside Expedition, the Gettysburg campaign, Petersburg and Weldon Railroad; on the 18th of June, 1864, before Petersburg, was wounded in the left leg; on the 18th of August, 1864, on the Weldon Railroad, was wounded through the right shoulder, with resection of five inches of the bone from the shoulder down. Was retired (November 5, 1866) from active service (first-class), having partially lost the use of his left leg and almost entirely the use of his right arm. Has mustered in and out, in the States of New York and Louisiana, about eighty thousand men.

20. Adjutant CHARLES J. FROTHINGHAM.

Entered the United States service as First Lieutenant and Adjutant in Connecticut Artillery.

21. Captain F. GRAIN, JR.

Entered the United States service as Captain. Served in the Army of the Potomac.

22. Lieutenant LEVI GROSVENOR.

Entered the United States service, February 27, 1864, as private in the Tenth Regiment, New York Volunteers. Was promoted to be Sergeant in April, 1864, and to be Lieutenant, January 1, 1865. Served through Grant's Virginia campaign of 1864 and 1865, in the Second Corps (Hancock), Carr's brigade, Gibbon's (Second) division. Took part in all the battles from the Wilderness to Appomattox Court-House. Was shot in the hand at Spottsylvania Court-House. Was mustered out with his regiment, at the end of the war, June 31, 1865.

23. Captain WILLIAM P. HALSTED.

Entered the United States service July 20, 1861, as Captain in the Sixty-Fifth Regiment, New York Volunteers. Became Senior Captain, and at times was in command of the regiment. Served in the Sixth Corps, in Virginia and Maryland, and took part in the battles of Williamsburg, Seven Pines, Fair Oaks, White-Oak Swamp, Malvern Hill, and Burnside's Fredericksburg. Previous to the battle of Malvern Hill he had been placed under arrest, in consequence of not taking command of his company when so ordered, his ground being that he was at the time on the sick-list, and unable to perform duty. When the battle commenced, feeling better, he succeeded, with three other officers, in rallying about four hundred men belonging to different regiments. These were formed in a regimental line, the right company being placed under his command; and the regiment under that of Lieutenant-Colonel Colburn, of the staff of Major-General McClellan. The day after the battle the following order came from the head-quarters of the Army: "Captain William P. Halsted is released from arrest, and will report for duty with his company. Whatever his conduct may have been heretofore, his behavior yesterday entitles him to not only release from arrest, but to great credit for gallantry and efficiency. By command of Major-General McClellan, A. V. Colburn, Assistant Adjutant-General." Was honorably discharged, March 8, 1863.

24. Captain J. M. Hawkins.

Entered the United States service as ——; was Captain on Major-General Augur's staff.

25. Lieutenant C. O. F. Haynes.

Entered the United States service as Captain in the One Hundred and Thirty-First Regiment, New York Volunteers. Was wounded at Port Hudson, and discharged for disability.

26. Captain G. M. Husted.

Entered the United States service as Captain in the Forty-Seventh Regiment, New York Volunteers. Served in the Department of the South. Afterwards appointed Quartermaster and stationed in New Orleans.

27. Captain B. R. Keefler.

Entered the United States service, December 30, 1861, as Captain Company A, Seventy-Eighth Regiment, New York Volunteers. Served in Virginia; was present at the skirmishes at Bolivar Heights and Camp Hill (May, 1862), and the battles of Cedar Mountain, Rappahannock, White Sulphur Springs, Bristow Station; was acting as a field officer much of the time. Was honorably discharged May 28, 1863, on account of disease contracted in the service while in the line of duty.

28. Lieutenant-Colonel J. G. Kappner.

Entered the United States service in 1861. Served on General Fremont's staff in Missouri.

29. Lieutenant S. M. Kellinger.

Entered the United States service, August 1, 1861, as Second Lieutenant, Company G, Sixty-Fifth Regiment, New York Volunteers (United States Chasseurs). Served with the regiment throughout the Peninsular campaign, in all its battles from Yorktown to Malvern. Had command of his company at Fair Oaks. Resigned at Harrison's Landing, on account of severe sickness contracted during the campaign. In 1864 went to the Western Army, and went through the campaign from Chattanooga to Atlanta, being commissioned as Aid at Twentieth Corps head-quarters, commanded by General Hooker. Was at the battles of Buzzards' Roost, Altoona, Kenesaw Mountain, and the siege of Atlanta, entering the latter city with General Slocum and escort. On the evacuation of Atlanta by General Sherman he returned to Nashville.

30. Colonel W. E. Kidder.

Entered the United States service, July 16, 1861, as First Lieutenant, Thirteenth Regiment, Massachusetts Volunteers. Was brevetted Colonel, January 21, 1863. Served in the Army of the Potomac, Sixth Corps, General Sedgwick. Acted on the staff of Colonel Leonard, commanding the brigade

July 1, 1862, was wounded in the left arm and hip, but did not quit the field. July 3, 1862, was captured. January 12, 1863, was exchanged. Resigned, January 30, 1863, on account of sickness, contracted by long and close confinement in Libby Prison.

31. Lieutenant William H. Kingsland.

Entered the United States service, October 2, 1862, as Lieutenant in the One Hundred and Twenty-First Pennsylvania Volunteers. Was captured by Mosby near Fairfax Court-House. Was a prisoner eight months, being confined first in Libby and then at Andersonville, where he died of starvation.

32. Captain George W. Lewis.

Entered the United States service as Captain in the Sixty-First Regiment, New York Volunteers. Died at Harrison's Landing, Virginia, from wounds received in the battles before Richmond in 1862.

33. Captain John S. Loud.

Entered the United States service, January 3, 1863, as First Lieutenant in the Twelfth New York Cavalry. Promoted to be Captain, November 20, 1863. Served in North Carolina and Virginia, under Generals Foster, Ord, Schofield, Cox, Kilpatrick. Took part in the battles and expeditions in the former State in 1864, at Newbern, Kingston, Plymouth, Little Washington, Tarboro' raid (1863), Greenville, Jacksonville, and, in 1865, under Schofield and Cox, at Kingston, Wise's Forks, Mosely Hall, and Goldsboro'. Was detached in command of a squadron as escort to Generals Schofield and Cox, February, 1865. Mustered out in July, 1865.

34. Lieutenant Benjamin T. Martin.

Entered the United States service, July, 1861, as Second Lieutenant, Company E, Forty-Ninth Regiment, New York Volunteers. Went with Sherman's Expedition to Port Royal, and was engaged at Port Royal Ferry, January 1, 1862. Was promoted to be First Lieutenant for good conduct in that affair. In March, 1862, was detached as A. D. C., on General Doubleday's staff, and served in Virginia. Was at the battles of Gainesville, second Bull Run (where his horse was shot), South Mountain, Antietam, Fredericksburg, Chancellorsville, and Gettysburg. Was mentioned in orders and in the report of every battle in which the First Corps took part, up to and including Gettysburg. Thence proceeded with Doubleday to Washington, and was temporarily detailed as A. D. C. on Augur's staff.

35. Lieutenant S. E. L. Mitchell.

36. Brigadier-General Joseph J. Morrison.

Entered the United States service, May 27, 1861, as Captain of Company A, Ninth Regiment, New York State Militia, and in December, 1861, as Captain of Battery B, Third Regiment, New York Artillery. Promoted to be Colonel of the Sixteenth New York Heavy Artillery, December 18, 1863. Brevetted Brigadier-General, United States Volunteers, March 13, 1865, "for faithful and meritorious services during the war." Participated in the Burnside Expedition to North Carolina, in the battles at Kingston, Whitehall, and Goldsboro'; in the reduction of Fort Sumter, and the captures of Fort Fisher, Petersburg, and Richmond. Was mentioned in general orders by General Foster, for gallantry at the battle of Goldsboro' in repulsing with his battery the desperate attack of Pettigrew's brigade. The Sixteenth New York Heavy Artillery, raised through his exertions, was the largest ever recruited in the United States, numbering three thousand and thirty-three men, of whom twelve hundred were transferred to other regiments. Mustered out August 30, 1865, at the close of the war.

37. Lieutenant George W. Murray.

38. Colonel James R. O'Beirne.

39. Ensign H. M. Patterson.

Served in the United States Navy during the war.

40. Lieutenant W. A. Prentiss, Jr.

41. Lieutenant George A. Price.

42. Captain Thomas J. Roberts.

43. Captain William H. Romaine.

Entered the United States service as Captain in the One Hundred and Thirty-First Regiment, New York Volunteers. Served with General Banks in Louisiana, and was at Port Hudson and in the Red River Expedition.

44. Captain Frank A. Silva.

Entered the United States service in 1861. Was Captain in the First New York Volunteers. Was at Big Bethel, and served on the Peninsula until 1862.

45. Major M. A. Stearns.

Entered the United States service in April, 1861, as Second Lieutenant, Company A, Third Regiment, New York Volunteers. Was promoted to be First Lieutenant and Adjutant of the Sixty-Fifth Regiment, New York Volunteers, August, 1861. October, 1861, promoted to be Major of the Second Missouri Cavalry. Resigned, from disability, January, 1862. Appointed Adjutant, Second New York Veteran Cavalry, October, 1863. Promoted to be Captain in the Twenty-Fifth New York Cavalry, December, 1864. Appointed Second Lieutenant, Eighteenth Infantry (Regular Army), April, 1865. Promoted to be First Lieutenant, July, 1866. Was engaged in the battles of Big Bethel, Winchester, and Leesburg (Virginia), Mill Spring (Kentucky), Lexington, Pierce's Mill, and Kirksville (Missouri), and Red River campaign (Louisiana). Was wounded at Kirksville and Pierce's Mill. Still in the Regular Army.

46. Lieutenant Noah B. Stokely.

Entered the United States service as Lieutenant in Corps d'Afrique, and served with General Uhlmann, in Louisiana.

### 47. Lieutenant HENRY M. TIMOLAT.

Entered the United States service, August 30, 1862, as First Lieutenant in the One Hundred and Thirty-First Regiment, New York Volunteers. Served in Maryland, Virginia, and Louisiana. Took part in numerous skirmishes in Louisiana, the storming of Port Hudson, the battle of Vicksburg, and the second battle of Winchester (September 19, 1864), where he was mortally wounded. receiving a bullet in his breast, during a most gallant charge at the head of his company, of which he had command at that time. But five survived out of the eighteen men whom he took into the charge.

On the eve of battle he was suffering intensely with rheumatism, and was urged to remain behind, but he would not. The last that was seen of him he was limping along, urging his men forward. During two years' service he never asked for or accepted a furlough. He was son of an officer who had served under Napoleon, and left a wife and three children. The Fifth Company escorted his remains to Greenwood.

### 48. Lieutenant-Colonel GEORGE TUCKER.

Entered the United States service, December 30, 1861, as Second Lieutenant, Company A, Seventy-Eighth New York Volunteers. Promoted to be Major and Lieutenant-Colonel, Corps d'Afrique, February and March, 1863. Served in Virginia, and was present at the battles of Bolivar Heights, Camp Hill, Cedar Mountain, Rappahannock, White Sulphur Springs, Bristow Station. His service in the Shenandoah Valley was under Banks, Sigel, and Pope, and that in Eastern Virginia under Geary. Afterwards he served in Louisiana, during the Red River campaign, under General Banks. He died of disease contracted in the latter campaign, at New Orleans, in the summer of 1865.

### 49. Captain WILLIAM H. UNDERHILL.

Entered the United States service, April 23, 1861, as Captain of Company G, in the First Regiment, New York Volunteers. Served near Fort Monroe, and took part in the battle at Big Bethel, under Butler, June 10, 1861. In August received an honorable discharge, on the ground of the return, by active service, of physical disability, arising from an injury received in the Astor Place Riots, in 1849, while on duty there with his regiment, and from severe varicose veins, which rendered him unfit for duty in the field.

### 50. Major PHILO VOSBURGH.

Entered the United States service November 22, 1861, as Second Lieutenant in the Thirty-Sixth Regiment, New York Volunteers, and was promoted to be First Lieutenant, August 2, 1862. Served with the Army of the Potomac through all the battles of the Peninsular campaign, including Lee's Mills, South Mills, Bolton's Bridge, Seven Pines, Fair Oaks, Gaines's Mills, White-Oak Swamp, and Malvern; also at Chantilly, Fairfax Court-House, Fredericksburg, Marye's Heights, Salem Heights, and also through the battles of the Red River campaign under Banks. Was promoted for gallant conduct on the Peninsula, and especially for capturing the colors of the Fourteenth North Carolina Regiment, at Malvern, July 1, 1862, and was complimented on the field the same day by Generals Couch and Abercrombie. Was mustered out with his regiment, July 15, 1863. Was commissioned Captain of the Eighty-Fourth United States Colored Troops, October 10, 1863, and served in Louisiana (frequently commanding the regiment) till mustered out, August 31, 1865. Received a brevet (N. Y. S. N. G.) of Major for meritorious services during the war.

51. Captain F. E. WALDRON.

Entered the United States service as Captain in Thirty-First New York Volunteers. Served two years in the Army of the Potomac, and was in all the principal engagements during that period.

52. Captain JAMES L. WAUGH.

Entered the United States service, May 1, 1861, as Captain in Fifth Regiment, New York Volunteers (Duryee's Zouaves). Served at Fort Monroe, Baltimore, and Alexandria. Was at Big Bethel. Mustered out with his regiment, January 2, 1862.

53. Captain ROBERT WHEATON.

54. Lieutenant L. L. YOUNG.

Entered the United States service as Lieutenant of artillery. Served in the Army of the Potomac. Was wounded and disabled.

## SIXTH COMPANY (F).

1. Colonel ALEXANDER ANNAN.

Lieutenant and Quartermaster One Hundred and Third and One Hundred and Twenty-Eighth Regiments, New York Volunteers. Captain Third Rhode Island Volunteers.

2. Captain HENRY ARNOLD.

Captain, Forty-Seventh Regiment New York Volunteers, Company K. Killed at the battle of Olustee, Florida, February 20, 1863. He was a brave and efficient officer.

3. Major-General LEWIS T. BARNEY.

Entered the United States service in January, 1862 (at the age of seventeen years) as a voluntary Aid to General T. W. Sherman, Department of the South. Took part in the various reconnoissances in South Carolina and Georgia, and in the Florida Expedition of Dupont and Wright. October 11, 1862, was commissioned First Lieutenant Sixty-Eighth New York Volunteers. Acted as Aid to General Saxton and Assistant Inspector-General in the Tenth Corps, Department of the South. Was present at the battles at James and Morris Islands and Fort Wagner. Was made Captain and Assistant Adjutant-General, and, March 24, 1864, was commissioned Colonel of the One Hundred and Eightieth New York Volunteers. Took part in the fight at Bloody Bridge

(South Carolina), and was there wounded. In July, the One Hundred and Eightieth was consolidated, and he was commissioned Colonel of the One Hundred and Sixth Regiment, New York Volunteers. On duty under Butler in the New York elections, and took part in the battle of Cedar Creek. In January, 1865, resigned in consequence of his injuries received at Bloody Bridge. Was made Brigadier-General by brevet, March 13, 1865, for gallant and meritorious services during the war. At this time he was twenty years of age. Was breveted Major-General. Was frequently mentioned and thanked in orders.

4. Colonel CHARLES G. BARTLETT.

Captain, Twelfth Regiment, United States Infantry, Brevet Lieutenant-Colonel United States Army, Colonel United States Colored Troops.

5. Lieutenant JAMES W. BENKARD, JR.

Lieutenant, United States Volunteers. Aide-de-Camp to Generals King and Augur.

6. Captain JABEZ H. BRADBURY.

Captain, Fourth Regiment, Missouri Cavalry. Chief of staff of General Asboth.

7. Major CLARENCE S. BROWN.

Major, United States Volunteers. Aide-de-Camp to General McDowell.

8. Lieutenant GEORGE L. BROWNING.

Lieutenant, Fourteenth Regiment, United States Infantry.

9. Captain CHURCHILL J. CAMBRELING.

Entered the United States service, April, 1861, as Lieutenant in the Fifth New York Volunteers, Duryee's Zouaves. Was engaged in a skirmish at New County Bridge, and afterwards led the assault with a small detachment at Big Bethel. Was recommended for "bravery and good conduct at the battle of Great Bethel," in Colonel Duryee's report, and also "for gallant conduct in action," in Captain Kilpatrick's report. Promoted to be Captain, September 3, 1861. At Yorktown, in 1862, was assigned to the command of Battery No. 13, his company serving as siege artillerists. Served during the Peninsular campaign, under General McClellan. Was present and in command of his company in all the battles of the Chickahominy, from Hanover Court-House to Harrison's Landing, including the Seven Days' Battles, Mechanicsville, Gaines's Mills, Malvern Hill, &c., &c. Was recommended by Colonel Duryee for gallantry and good conduct at the battle of Gaines's Mills, 17th June, 1862, and was recommended for promotion by Major-Generals G. K. Warren and Fitz-John Porter. Elected Major of Tenth Senatorial District Regiment, New York Volunteers, but owing to prolonged sickness, the result of exposure and hardship, was prevented from qualifying in the regiment. Resigned commission in consequence of continued ill health in the fall of 1862.

10. Captain SAMUEL CAREY.

Lieutenant United States Volunteers. Aide-de-Camp to General W. F. Smith.

11. Lieutenant-Colonel Lynde Catlin.

Captain Fifteenth Regiment, United States Infantry; Brevet Major, United States Artillery; Lieutenant-Colonel, United States Volunteers; Assistant Inspector-General to General Lew Wallace.

12. Captain P. R. Chadwick.

Entered the United States service, in 1861, as Adjutant of the One Hundredth Regiment, New York Volunteers. Took part in the Peninsular campaign in 1862, and was present in all the battles. December 31, 1862, was commissioned Captain and Assistant Adjutant-General, and was assigned to duty in the Department of the South, serving on the staffs successively of Generals Seymour, Gillmore, and Hatch, and taking part in the operations thereof, 1863 and 1864, until his resignation, April 2, 1864.

13. Lieutenant-Colonel Floyd Clarkson.

Entered the United States service, November 11, 1861, as Major, in the Sixth New York Cavalry. Served in Virginia, in the Peninsula, at Peach Orchard (or Allen's Farm), Savage Station, White-Oak Swamp, and Malvern Hill. Resigned October, 1862. April 7, 1863, was commissioned Major of the Twelfth New York Cavalry. Served in North Carolina, and took part in Foster's raids to Warsaw, Kenansville, Rocky Mount, Tarboro', &c. In June, 1864, was Inspector-General of Newbern. In the spring of 1865 took a conspicuous and gallant part in the series of battles in the movement of Schofield and Cox upon Wilmington. Was brevetted Lieutenant-Colonel for services.

14. Captain Poinsett Cooper.

Entered the United States service, September 1, 1861, as Second Lieutenant in the Second Regiment, New York State Militia, or the Eighty-Second Regiment, New York Volunteers. Was appointed and mustered in as First Lieutenant, in the Forty-Second Regiment, New York Volunteers, March 17, 1862; promoted to be Captain, September 17, 1862; appointed Assistant Inspector-General, June 1, 1863, First Brigade, Second Division, Second Army Corps. Served under Generals Stone, Sedgwick, Sumner, Howard, Couch, Gibbon, Hancock, Webb. Was always with the Second Army Corps, from the time General McClellan took command. He was engaged at Ball's Bluff, siege of Yorktown, Fair Oaks, Savage Station, Glendale, Malvern Hill, and the skirmishes during the seven days' retreat from front of Richmond to Harrison's Landing, second Bull Run, Antietam, Fredericksburg, Bristow Station, Mine Run, Gettysburg, and Wilderness. Was wounded in the foot at Antietam. Was wounded in the thigh at Bristow Station. Was wounded in the leg at the Wilderness, and, on being carried to the rear, was shot by guerillas in the breast. Was mustered out of service, July, 1864, with his regiment, at the expiration of its term of service, and being unfit for duty from the wounds received at the Wilderness.

15. Captain EDWARD A. COWDREY.

Captain Ninety-Fifth Regiment, New York Volunteers. Mortally wounded at Five Forks, Va.

16. Major FRANK H. COWDREY.

Captain and Brevet Major, United States Volunteers. Assistant Adjutant-General to General Hayes.

17. Captain EDWARD COZZENS.

Left Leavenworth, June 20, 1861, with the brigade of Regulars under command of Major S. D. Sturgis, and was appointed by General Nathaniel Lyon Acting Assistant Quartermaster, and Acting Assistant Commissary-Sergeant, July 31, 1861, with rank of Captain. Acted as Aid to Major Sturgis at the battle of Wilson's Creek, Mo., and was complimented in his official report of the battle. Afterwards served on the staff of General J. McKinsty as Acting Assistant Commissary-Sergeant of his division in Fremont's campaign in Missouri. Resigned, and entered the First United States Chasseurs (Sixty-Fifth New York Volunteers) as Second Lieutenant, March 12, 1862. Promoted to be First Lieutenant, August 1, 1862 ; Captain, December 1, 1862. Participated in the battles of Yorktown, Williamsburg, Fair Oaks, Gaines's Mills, Turkey Bend, Malvern Hill (where he had command of the color company), Antietam, Fredericksburg, Marye's Heights, Salem Church, Gettysburg, Rappahannock Station, and Wilderness. Was wounded while on the skirmish line at the Wilderness battle. Was discharged, with his regiment, September, 1864.

18. Captain JAMES D. W. CUTTING.

Captain, United States Volunteers. Aide-de-Camp to General McDowell.

19. Lieutenant-Colonel LOUIS L. CUVILLIER.

Captain, Fifty-Fifth Regiment, New York Volunteers. Brevet Lieutenant-Colonel, United States Volunteers.

20. Captain ARCHIBALD DOUGLAS.

21. Lieutenant CHARLES N. DUBOIS.

Lieutenant, One Hundred and Thirty-First Regiment, New York Volunteers.

22. Captain ROBERT S. DUMONT.

Entered the United States service, April 19, 1861, in the Fifth Regiment, New York Volunteers (Duryee's Zouaves). Raised the first company for that regiment, and was mustered in as Captain, April 25, 1861. Went to the Peninsula with the regiment. Was stationed at Camp Hamilton, Hampton, Va., in Butler's department, and was thanked by General Butler in general orders, for a reconnoissance made by a part of the company under his command, immediately previous to the battle of Big Bethel. Was prostrated by sunstroke, and obliged to resign on account of his health, October 1, 1861. Received the appointment of secretary to Rear-Admiral C. H. Bell, commanding

United States naval forces in the Pacific Ocean, December 11, 1861, with the rank of Lieutenant in the navy. Was appointed Judge-Advocate-General of the Pacific Squadron, May 9, 1863. Resigned, on account of continued ill health, March 1, 1864.

23. Brigadier-General JACOB E. DURYEE.

Entered the United States service in 1861, as First Lieutenant in the Fifth Regiment, New York Volunteers (Duryee's Zouaves), and distinguished himself at Big Bethel, being shortly afterwards made Captain. In 1862 he was promoted to be Lieutenant-Colonel of the Second Maryland Volunteers, and he commanded this regiment through Burnside's campaign in North Carolina, and Pope's in Northern Virginia, and was at South Mountain and Antietam. He was brevetted Colonel and Brigadier-General for gallant and meritorious services.

24. Captain GEORGE P. EDGAR.

Entered the United States service August 1, 1861, on the staff of General Fremont, in Missouri, as Assistant Adjutant-General, with the rank of Captain; as such served at the battle of Fredericktown, Mo., and at the post of Cape Girardeau, Mo., until the General was relieved of his command. From December 1, 1861, to July 10, 1862, was Captain and Aide-de-Camp on the staff of Major-General John A. McClernand, of Illinois, at Fort Donelson, and thereafter until compelled to retire by an attack of the typhoid. After recovering, he received, July 10, 1862, a commission as Captain and Additional Aide-de-Camp on General Wool's staff, and was assigned to Major-General Lew Wallace for duty, with whom he served until April 21, 1863, when he was mustered out of the service by the Secretary of War. January 6, 1864, he was reinstated and ordered to report to Major-General Butler for duty. During that interim was volunteer Aide-de-Camp to General Judah, at the battle of Buffington Bar, Ohio, with John Morgan, in July, 1863.

April 29, 1864, his resignation as Captain and Additional Aide-de-Camp was accepted. Was highly recommended for gallantry and efficiency by Generals McClernand, Plummer, N. B. Buford, Lew Wallace, Judah, and others.

25. Captain JOSEPH S. EDSALL.

Captain, Eleventh Regiment, Missouri Cavalry.

26. Lieutenant C. H. ELLINGWOOD.

Lieutenant, First Regiment, New York Volunteers.

27. Lieutenant ASHER M. ELLSWORTH.

Lieutenant, One Hundred and Sixty-Fifth New York Volunteers. Quartermaster. Died in front of Port Hudson, at the siege in 1863.

28. Captain JOEL B. ERHARDT.

Captain, Vermont Cavalry. Captain and Provost-Marshal, Fourth District, New York.

29. Lieutenant JAMES F. EVANS.

Lieutenant, Fifth Regiment, New York Volunteers (Duryee Zouaves).

30. Lieutenant-Colonel GEORGE W. FORD.

Major, Fiftieth Regiment, New York Volunteers, Engineers; Brevet Lieutenant-Colonel, United States Volunteers.

31. Lieutenant JAMES W. FORD.

Lieutenant, One Hundred and Thirty-Second Regiment, New York Volunteers.

32. Lieutenant G. W. FORNEY.

33. Brigadier-General JOHN A. FOSTER.

Colonel, One Hundred and Seventy-Fifth Regiment, New York Volunteers; Brevet Brigadier-General, United States Volunteers.

34. Captain JOHN W. FRENCH.

Entered the United States service, October 24, 1861, as Second Lieutenant in the Eighth United States Infantry. Was on mustering and recruiting service till June 1, 1863. Served with regiment in the field and in New York till December 18, 1863. Was Aide-de-Camp to Brigadier-General Stannard, and Pass Officer of the city and harbor of New York till May 1, 1864. Served with regiment in the field till June 1, 1864. Commissary of Musters, Second Division, Ninth Army Corps, till January 13, 1865. Aide-de-Camp to Brigadier-General R. Ingalls, Chief Quartermaster, armies of the United States, till October 1, 1865. Served with regiment till November 20, 1866. Appointed Adjutant, Eighth Infantry, January 31, 1866. Promoted First Lieutenant, January 13, 1866. Adjutant-General, military command of North Carolina, from October 1, 1866, till November 20, 1866. Appointed Captain, Fortieth Infantry, November 20, 1866, to date from July 28, 1866. Brevetted First Lieutenant and Captain, for gallant and meritorious service, in the battles of Weldon Railroad and Hatcher's Run. Engaged in all the battles of the campaign of 1864. Was with General Grant's staff on duty, as Aid to General Ingalls during the last campaign, and at Lee's surrender. In January, 1865, volunteered to sink, with the assistance of a navy officer, two schooners in Trent's Reach, James River, under Howlett House Battery, to prevent the Rebel iron-clads from descending the river. This was successfully accomplished, General Ingalls, speaking of the latter exploit, says : " Captain French served on my staff with great credit and gallantry. I had sent him, by order of the Lieutenant-General, up the river with vessels laden with coal, to sink two on the night of the 25th to fill up the gap made in the obstructions. He performed the service under the enemy's guns with great gallantry. This service was of the highest importance, and was performed under many hardships and perils, at the time the Rebel iron-clads attempted to descend the James."

35. Lieutenant JAMES GORDON, JR.

Lieutenant, Fourth Regiment, United States Colored Troops.

36. Captain S. Augustus Gould.

Aide-de-Camp to General Steele.

37. Captain Charles C. Haight.

Captain, Thirty-Ninth Regiment, New York Volunteers.

38. Lieutenant Edward L. Halsted.

Entered the United States service, November 15, 1861, as Second Lieutenant in the Fortieth Regiment, New York Volunteers. Was detailed to the signal corps, and served with Banks in the Shenandoah Valley on staffs of Generals Crawford, Hatch, and Sullivan. Served also at Loudon Heights; on the Potomac flotilla; on Pony Mountain, near Culpepper Court-House; and afterwards successively on staffs of Generals Merritt, Sedgwick, Wright, Sheridan, and Torbert. Resigned January 5, 1865.

39. Lieutenant-Colonel Richard F. Halsted.

Entered the United States service, June 14, 1861, as Major of the Fortieth Regiment, New York Volunteers. April 26, 1863, was appointed Captain and Aide-de-Camp to General Sedgwick. Served always with the Army of the Potomac until its dissolution; then went to Department of Texas. Served, as staff officer, with Major-Generals John Sedgwick and H. G. Wright; and under division commanders Heintzelman, C. S. Hamilton, and Kearny, and, before organization of Army of Potomac, under Franklin. Served in the Sixth Corps, temporarily in the Second and Ninth, General Sedgwick having been assigned to those before taking command of the Sixth. With this corps made the Shenandoah Valley campaign. Was engaged at Williamsburg, Fair Oaks, the Seven Days, Fredericksburg second (Sixth Corps alone, — rest of army at Chancellorsville), Marye's Heights, Salem Heights, Gettysburg, Rappahannock Station, Wilderness, and following days till death of Sedgwick, May 9. Came home with his remains. Returned June 1. Cold Harbor (two engagements), Winchester or Opequan, Fisher's Hill, Cedar Creek, assault on Petersburg, Sailors' Creek, besides skirmishes such as Mine Run, Locust Grove, movement against Early at Washington, crossing of Shenandoah River by Sixth Corps, etc. Was brevetted Major and Lieutenant-Colonel of Volunteers, and resigned July 1, 1866.

40. Captain William P. Halsted.

Captain in the Sixty-Fifth Regiment, New York Volunteers.

41. Major-General Charles Schuyler Hamilton.

Major-General, United States Volunteers.

42. Lieutenant John F. Hardy.

Lieutenant, Thirty-Fourth Regiment, New Jersey Volunteers.

43. Captain Henry W. Hicks, Jr.

Captain, One Hundred and Sixty-Fifth Regiment, New York Volunteers. Mortally wounded in front of Port Hudson, La.

44. Lieutenant-Colonel SAMUEL J. HOPKINS.

Entered the United States service, August 29, 1862, as Captain in the Seventh Regiment, New Jersey Volunteers. Served until April, 1864, in Mott's (Third) Brigade, Second Division, Third Army Corps, and afterwards, till end of war, in Second Brigade (Mott's), Third Division, Second Corps. Mustered out with regiment October 7, 1864. Commissioned Captain and Lieutenant-Colonel, Fortieth Regiment, New Jersey Volunteers, early in 1865. Was in the battles of Fredericksburg, Chancellorsville, McLean's Ford, Kelly's Ford, Wilderness, Spottsylvania, North Anna, Tolopotomy, Cold Harbor, Petersburg, Deep Bottom, Strawberry Plains, and other actions around Petersburg. Was slightly wounded at Chancellorsville, and again at Spottsylvania. His regiment captured five stands of colors at Andersonville.

45. Captain FRANCIS A. HOWELL.

Captain, One Hundred and Thirty-First Regiment, New York Volunteers.

46. Colonel HARMON D. HULL.

Entered the United States service, May 9, 1861, as Captain in the Fifth Regiment, New York Volunteers (Duryee's Zouaves). Was promoted to be Major, September 7, 1861, and Lieutenant-Colonel, October 29, 1862. Was appointed Colonel to raise the One Hundred and Sixty-Fifth Regiment, New York Volunteers, in October, 1862. Commanded his company at Big Bethel, and served throughout the Peninsular campaign. Resigned on account of ill health, January 22, 1863.

47. Lieutenant JOHN L. HYDE.

48. Captain JULIAN JAMES.

Captain, United States Volunteers; Aide-de-Camp to General G. K. Warren.

49. Major RUFUS KING, JR.

Entered the United States service, August 5, 1861, as Second Lieutenant in the Fourth Artillery (Regular Army), and was promoted to be First Lieutenant. Served in West Virginia with Rosecrans, and throughout the Peninsular campaign, in all its battles. At White-Oak Swamp, the Captain of his battery (Hazard) having been mortally wounded soon after the battle began, he took command of it (an eight-gun battery), and prevented the enemy from building a bridge over the swamp until the retreat of our forces had been secured to Harrison's Landing. The battery (A) lost nearly half its number in killed and wounded, under a concentrated fire from twenty pieces massed by the enemy. He was brevetted Captain "for gallant and meritorious conduct at White-Oak Swamp." Took part, with his crippled battery, at Malvern Hill. Took part in the battles of Bull Run, South Mountain, and Antietam, the battery being attached to the Second Corps, and in every battle of the Army of the Potomac, except Gettysburg, he being furloughed for sickness at that time, but arriving, at the end, having crossed the enemy's lines with despatches from W. F. Smith, at Harrisburg, to General Meade. Operated with the cavalry after Gettysburg, commanding his battery, which had been selected as one of the "Horse Batteries." Thereafter, engagements were daily during campaigning seasons, and he participated in all the engagements. Also participated in General Sheridan's raid, which was a succession of battles from the Wilderness to Cold Harbor, just before the army crossed the James, when his battery being crippled from severe service, it was sent to Washington to recuperate, where he remained with it until the end of the war. Has been recommended for brevets by Generals Sumner, Hancock, Pleasanton, and Gregg. Was brevetted Major for gallant and meritorious services during the war.

50. Lieutenant-Colonel Samuel B. Lawrence.

Entered the United States service (to rank May 14, 1861) as First Lieutenant, Sixteenth Regiment, United States Infantry, filling vacancy caused by death of Theodore Winthrop, killed in battle at Big Bethel. Promoted to be Captain, May 3, 1862. Served in the Army of the Cumberland under Generals Buell and Rosecrans during their campaigns in 1861, 1862, and 1863. From March to August, 1863, was assigned to duty as Commissary of Musters for the Twentieth Army Corps, and attached to the staff of General McCook, also temporarily assigned as Chief Commissary of Musters for the Army of the Cumberland, under Rosecrans. August, 1863, assigned to duty at the War Department, Washington, as assistant to Colonel Fry, Provost-Marshal-General. March, 1864, assigned to duty as Assistant Adjutant-General of the Eighth Army Corps, and appointed Chief of Staff to General Lew Wallace, commanding the Middle Department and Eighth Army Corps, and continued as such until the corps was disbanded and the Middle Department abolished, after the surrender of the Rebel armies, when he resigned his commission in the Regular Army, which was accepted to date August 14, 1865. He received brevet commissions as Captain, United States Army, "for gallant and meritorious service at the battle of Shiloh, Tennessee, 1862"; Major and Lieutenant-Colonel, United States Army, "for faithful and meritorious services during the war."

51. Brigadier-General William Hudson Lawrence.

Entered the United States service May 14, 1861, as First Lieutenant, Fourteenth United States Infantry. Promoted to be Captain, Fourteenth Infantry, November, 1861; to be Colonel, Thirty-Fourth New Jersey Volunteers, September, 1863. Brevet Major and Brevet Lieutenant-Colonel, United States Army, June, 1865. Brevet Brigadier-General, United States Volunteers, August, 1865. Served on the Peninsula under Fitz John Porter, Fifth Army Corps; remained in this corps, under Generals Meade and Sykes, until June, 1863. Served in Mississippi, Kentucky, Tennessee, and Alabama in Sixteenth Army Corps, under General A. J. Smith, from November, 1863, until the end of the war. Took part in the battles of second Bull Run, Antietam, Fredericksburg, Chancellorsville. Accompanied A. J. Smith on his expedition after

Forrest to Jackson (Tennessee). Commanded Columbus, Kentucky, when it was summond to surrender by part of Forrest's command, under General A. Buford, April 13, 1864. At the siege of Mobile, taking part in the attack of Spanish Fort and Fort Blakely, was engaged in numerous skirmishes-Captured the notorious guerilla "Jim Kersterson," of Tennessee, killing and destroying his band. Was slightly wounded at second Bull Run, and sun-struck on the march to Gettysburg, Virginia.

Was mentioned in General Grant's report of the operations of the army for the last year of the war, for his refusal to surrender Columbus, Kentucky; and for the same, by all the public journals about April 14, 1864; mentioned by the Committee on the Conduct of the War for same, and for refusing to receive Rebel flags of truce at Columbus, Kentucky, after the Fort Pillow massacre. The garrison of Columbus, Kentucky, on the morning of the demand for its surrender, was under one thousand effective men, when the minimum garrison required for the two forts was three thousand. He was reinforced shortly after. wards by about five thousand of the ninety days' troops, mostly from Illinois. Was ordered to the command of Maryfield, Kentucky, in September, 1864, when that post was threatened. "During his whole service continually met members of the Seventh Regiment, New York National Guard, holding high positions, doing honor to themselves and country." Resigned in August, 1865, the war having ended.

52. Captain Mortimer Livingston.

Captain, One Hundred and Third Regiment, New York Volunteers.

53. Captain Theodore Mallaby, Jr.

Examined and passed as Second Lieutenant for Signal Corps, United States Army, October, 1863. Commissioned, July 15, 1864. Served in Tennessee during the war, in Texas after the war. Distinguished himself in operations with Stoneman and Wilson in their extended cavalry expeditions of 1865, and received warm commendations in the report of the chief signal officer, Department of Cumberland. He carried the War Department despatches from Washington to Macon, to General Wilson, ordering the capture of Jefferson Davis. Served as Aide-de-Camp to General Gibbs in Texas. Honorably discharged February 7, 1866.

54. Major Edward Marrenner.

Major, United States Volunteers, Assistant Adjutant-General to Major-General Hancock.

55. Colonel Thomas B. Marsh.

Entered the United States service, August 18, 1861, as Second Lieutenant, First United States Voltigeurs, afterwards Fifty-First New York Volunteers. Promoted First Lieutenant, Fifty-First New York Volunteers, March 14, 1862. Captain, September 30, 1862. Major, December 31, 1864. Lieutenant-Colonel, April 29, 1865. Brevet-Colonel, United States Volunteers, "for gallant and meritorious services during the war," March 13, 1865. Served in North Carolina, Virginia, Maryland, Kentucky, Tennessee, and Mississippi, and was on the staffs of Major-Generals Reno, Parke, Burnside, Wilcox, Potter, Sedgwick, and Smith. Was in the battles of Ronoake Island, Newbern, Fort Macon, Clark Mountain, Kelly's Ford, second Manassas, Chantilly, Frederick, South Mountain, Fredericksburg, siege of Vicksburg and Jackson, Loudon, Campbell Station, siege of Knoxville and Fort Sanders, Wilderness, Spottsylvania, first and second North Anna, Tolopotomy Creek, Bethesda Church, Cold Harbor, First Petersburg, Petersburg mine explosion, Petersburg final attack. Mustered out August 5, 1865.

56. Sergeant George L. Middlebrook.

Entered the United States service, October 7, 1864, in the Forty-Eighth Regiment, New York Volunteers. Promoted to be First Sergeant Company I, June 4, 1865. Served in Second Brigade, Second Division, Tenth Corps, first under Butler at Chapin's Farm, Virginia, and then under Terry in the North Carolina campaign. Mustered out September 1, 1865.

57. Major Lindley M. H. Miller.

Major, United States Colored Troops. Died in the service, June, 1864.

58. Colonel Charles L. Norton.

Colonel, Seventh Regiment, United States Colored Troops.

59. Captain George H. Palmer.

Captain, United States Volunteers, Aide-de-Camp to General Rosecrans.

60. Lieutenant-Colonel Tattnall Paulding.

Captain, Sixth Regiment, United States Cavalry; Brevet Lieutenant-Colonel, United States Army.

61. Paymaster Charles B. Perry.

Assistant Paymaster, United States Navy.

62. Major Horatio Potter, Jr.

Captain, Seventh Regiment, New York Artillery; Brevet Major, United States Volunteers.

63. Captain James P. Raymond.

Entered the United States service, October 10, 1861, as First Lieutenant, Ninetieth New York Volunteers. Adjutant, December 13, 1861; Captain, August 16, 1861. Post Adjutant and Acting Assistant Adjutant-General eight months. Served in South Carolina and Florida under Generals Brannan, Hunter, and Mitchell. Resigned April 13, 1863. Commissioned Captain in One Hundred and Thirty-First New York Volunteers, September 12, 1863. Served in Louisiana and in Shenandoah Valley, Nineteenth Corps. Was mentioned for gallantry at Winchester and Fisher's Hill. Mustered out July 26, 1865.

64. Lieutenant S. H. Robbins.

Lieutenant. Aide-de-Camp to General Butterfield.

65. Lieutenant-Colonel William H. Roome.

Entered the United States service, June 17, 1861, as Second Lieutenant, Sixty-Fifth New York Volunteers. December 14, 1861, was promoted to be First Lieutenant and Adjutant. On April 11, 1863, was commissioned by the President Captain and Assistant Adjutant-General. On the 19th September, 1864, for services at the battle of Winchester, was brevetted Major and Assistant Adjutant-General; and for general services was brevetted Lieutenant-Colonel and Assistant Adjutant-General from November 19, 1864. Was in all the battles of the Army of the Potomac from Yorktown to Petersburg, missing no skirmish or battle in which his regiment was engaged, until, January 18, 1865, he resigned on account of severe wounds. Was also in the Shenandoah campaigns, with the Sixth Corps. General Upton, in his report of Winchester, says (September 19, 1864): "Captain William P. Roome, Assistant Adjutant-General, Second Brigade, distinguished himself by repeated acts of gallantry. Without hint or suggestion he hastened wherever danger was the most threatening, and by his personal example contributed greatly to the success of the day. I have never known in battle an officer to do his duty more nobly or efficiently." General McKenzie said (October 11, 1864): "I have the honor to transmit the following names of officers for brevet rank for gallant service in the action and at the date set opposite their names. . . . . Captain William P. Roome, Assistant Adjutant-General, to be Brevet Major and Assistant Adjutant-General, for gallant and meritorious conduct at the battles of Opequan or Winchester, and Fisher's Hill, September 19 and 21, 1864. . . . . If any of these mentioned deserve promotion more than the others, I would especially call attention to the name of Captain William P. Roome, Assistant Adjutant-General." General Upton wrote, October 30, 1864, to the Secretary of War: "He served in the Sixth Corps in nearly all of its battles up to July, 1864, when he was assigned to my brigade, joining it with a high reputation for zeal, gallantry, and integrity. At the battle of Winchester, when, by the disaster of the Nineteenth Corps, the fate of the day seemed to hang upon the conduct of the last reserve thrown into action, so conspicuous was his gallantry and so marked were his services, that on the field, and in the presence of his brother-officers, I promised to do all in my power to secure his promotion. Later in the day, when the successful attack was made, he was again wherever the presence of a staff officer was most necessary, and bore important orders with a zeal that I have never seen surpassed. In every official report, as division commander, I made special mention of him, and recommended his immediate promotion. On all occasions, whether in his office, in camp, or campaign, or in battle, Captain Roome has proven himself a brave, efficient, and patriotic officer." The same officer wrote to Captain Roome: "I will state as a simple fact, that not only were you the best Adjutant-General I ever had, but that I saw little, if any, space for improvement. Your habitual promptness and zeal, the alacrity with which you performed every duty, and, above all, the coolness and intrepidity you displayed in battle, won my highest admiration and regard." General Shaler wrote to President Lincoln: "In fitness for the rank of Major and Assistant Adjutant-General, I know of no superior in the service." General Hamblin wrote: "On the field he has ever acted with distinguished gallantry, particularly at Malvern Hill, Gettysburg, battles of the Wilderness, Spottsylvania, and Cold Harbor." He was severely wounded at the battle of Cedar Creek in the valley of the Shenandoah, on the 19th of October, 1864. The ball entered about one half inch from the hip-joint, and passed through the lower part of abdomen, — a dangerous wound, causing long suffering.

66. Major PHILIP SCHUYLER, JR.

Entered the United States service, May 14, 1861, as First Lieutenant. United States Infantry (Regular Army). Appointed Regimental Adjutant, November 5, 1861, and so remained till appointed Captain, July, 1863, Brevetted Major, United States Army, to date from April 9, 1865. Served in the Army of the Potomac, in the early part of the campaign of 1862, the latter part of campaign of 1863, and through the campaigns of 1864 and 1865; was present at the battles of Rappahannock Station, Mine Run, Wilderness, Spottsylvania, North Anna, Cold Harbor, Petersburg (June 16 and 17, 1864), Burnside's Mine, Weldon Railroad, second Hatcher's Run, Fort Stedman, Boydton Plank-Road, Five Forks, Petersburg (April 2, 1865), Amelia Court-House, and surrender of General Lee. Acted during 1863, 1864, and 1865 as Acting Assistant Adjutant-General and Chief of Staff to Provost-Marshal-General, Army of Potomac and Department of Virginia, and was Acting Provost-Marshal-General, Army of Potomac, from November 24, 1864, to March 16, 1865. Resigned June 30, 1865, at close of war. Was brevetted Major, United States Army, "for gallant and meritorious services during the recent operations resulting in the fall of Richmond, Virginia, and the surrender of the insurgent army under General Robert E. Lee, to date from April 9, 1865.

67. Colonel ROBERT G. SHAW.

Entered the United States service, May, 1861, as Second Lieutenant in the Second Regiment, Massachusetts Volunteers. Served with his regiment in Virginia. At Cedar Mountain was Aid to General Gordon. In the charge of his regiment on that field twenty-two young officers went in, of whom thirteen were killed or wounded, five left dead on the field. He was engaged at Antietam, and was commissioned, January, 1863, Colonel of the Fifth-Fourth Regiment, Massachusetts Volunteers, raised by Governor Andrew, and the first colored regiment ever recruited under State authority. Served in South Carolina, and took part with his regiment in the battle of James Island. On the 19th of July, 1863, he headed with his regiment the famous storming column at the assault of Fort Wagner. When about one hundred yards from the fort the Rebel musketry opened with such terrible effect, that for an instant the first battalion hesitated, but only for an instant; for Colonel Shaw, springing to the front and waving his sword, shouted, "Forward, Fifty-Fourth!" and with another cheer and a shout, they rushed through the ditch, and gained the parapet on the right. Colonel Shaw was one of the first to scale the walls. He stood erect to urge forward his men, and while shouting for them to press on was shot dead on the parapet. A stalwart negro-man had fallen near him. The Rebels said the negro was a color-sergeant. The Colonel had been killed by a rifle-shot through the chest, though he had received other wounds. Brigadier-General Haygood, commanding the Rebel forces, said: "I knew Colonel Shaw before the war, and then esteemed him; had he been in command of white troops, I should have given him an honorable burial. As it is, I shall bury him in the common trench, with the negroes that fell with him."

68. Lieutenant W. M. G. Shaw.

Lieutenant, Forty-Second Regiment, New York Volunteers.

69. Captain Alexander E. Sheldon.

Captain, Fourth United States Infantry, Regular Army.

70. Captain Augustus Shimmel.

Entered the United States service, June 18, 1861, as Lieutenant and Quartermaster, Eighth Regiment, New York Volunteers. Promoted to be Captain and Acting Quartermaster, United States Volunteers, February 19, 1862. Served nearly four years in Virginia and Georgia, and resigned, April 22, 1865, in consequence of physical disability contracted in the field. Was present at the battles of Bull Run, Cross Keys, Strasburg, Culpepper, (Slaughter Mountain), Waterloo Bridge, White Sulphur Springs, Warrenton, Manassas, Fredericksburg, Chancellorsville, Chattanooga, Kingston, Resaca, Big Shanty, Kenesaw Mountain, Chattahoochee River, Atlanta, Savannah. Was mentioned by Generals Ingalls and Steinwehr, for "valor and energy in protecting our property," the occasion being an attack by Stuart's cavalry on the field-train of the Eleventh Corps, then (August 23 1862) under his care at Catlett's Station. He formed his train in hollow square, and with a guard of twenty men of the Forty-Fifth New York Volunteers repulsed the attack.

71. Lieutenant Charles G. Smedberg.

Lieutenant, Fourteenth Regiment, United States Infantry. Died in camp, near Falmouth, Virginia.

72. Lieutenant-Colonel William R. Smedberg.

Captain, Fourteenth Regiment, United States Infantry. Brevet Lieutenant-Colonel, United States Army.

73. Chaplain J. Tuttle Smith.

Entered the United States service as Chaplain in the Regular Army, and was assigned to the "Ladies' Home United States Army General Hospital," where he remained until its close in June, 1865. Resigned, Surgeon P. A. O'Connell indorsing the resignation as follows: "Reverend J. Tuttle Smith has been on duty at this hospital since May, 1862. During the first year his services were wholly gratuitous, and he has been constant and industrious in the discharge of his duties since. During the whole period of his connection with the hospital he has devoted both time and money to the benefit of the soldiers."

74. Lieutenant-Colonel William W. Stephenson.

Entered the United States service, September 22, 1862, as Captain, Company C, One Hundred and Sixty-Fifth Regiment, New York Volunteers. Served in the Nineteenth Corps, Virginia and Louisiana. Promoted to be Major, July 26, 1865; brevetted Lieutenant-Colonel, May 9, 1866, for gallant and meritorious services during the war. Served in various engagements in Louisiana, and under Sheridan, and on the staffs of various general officers as Aide-de-Camp.

75. Lieutenant Henry A. Still.

Lieutenant, Fifty-Sixth Regiment, New York Volunteers.

76. Captain Edward C. Sturgis.

Captain, One Hundred and First Regiment, New York Volunteers. Aide-de-Camp to General Heintzelman.

77. Adjutant Charles T. Sutton.

Entered the United States service, May 22, 1861, as Adjutant of the Thirty-Third Regiment, New York Volunteers. Was elected Lieutenant-Colonel, but not appointed Served through the Peninsular campaign, and was specially engaged at Williamsburg, Mechanicsville, and Golden Farm. Was also engaged at Drainesville and Crampton Pass, and at Antietam commanded his regiment for a time. Resigned, from disease contracted on the Peninsula, October 29, 1862.

78. Captain Deforest H. Thomae.

Captain, One Hundred and Sixty-Fifth Regiment, New York Volunteers.

79. Captain Gould H. Thorp.

Entered the United States service, September 6, 1862, as First Lieutenant, One Hundred Sixty-Fifth Regiment, New York Volunteers; September 18, 1862, promoted to be Captain. Served in Louisiana, under General Banks (Nineteenth Corps), at battle of Pentachoula (or Clinton Cross-Roads), Baton Rouge, Port Hudson, and "New Iberia campaign," Louisiana. Mentioned in orders for gallant conduct while commanding skirmishes at Pentachoula, Louisiana. Wounded three times while charging on Port Hudson, May 27, 1863, and was in hospital ten months from his wounds. Resigned March 14, 1864, in consequence of ill health.

80. Lieutenant FREDERIC A. TRACY.

Lieutenant, Twelfth Regiment, United States Infantry. Died in the United States service June 3, 1862.

81. Captain FANNING C. TUCKER.

Entered the United States service as First Lieutenant, Company D, One Hundred and Third Regiment, New York State Volunteers, February 18, 1862. Promoted to captaincy of Company H, April 4, 1862. Served under Generals Burnside in North Carolina, Pope in Virginia, and McClellan in the Maryland campaign. Was wounded at the battle of Antietam, September 17, 1862, and left the service soon after, in consequence of disability from wounds.

82. Captain WILLIAM GRACIE ULSHOEFFER.

Entered the United States service, July 4, 1861, as First Lieutenant and Adjutant, Thirty-Sixth New York State Volunteers. Promoted to be Captain, November 12, 1861. Detached as A. A. A. G., on the staff of General Devens, September 10, 1861, and A. D. C. to General John Newton, commanding Third Division, Sixth Corps, from October, 1862, till mustered out with his regiment, June 30, 1863. Took part in all the engagements in which his division participated, with the exception of Malvern Hill.

83. Lieutenant WILLIAM HENRY VANCE.

Entered the United States service, September 15, 1862, as First Lieutenant, One Hundred and Sixty-Fifth New York Volunteers (Second Duryee Zouaves). Acted as Adjutant of regiment, and commanded color company at assault on Port Hudson, May 27, 1863, where he was wounded by grape-shot in the left breast. Relieved from sentence of court-martial (disobedience of orders), by special order of President Lincoln, for "gallantry in action." Was A. I. G. and A. D. C. to General Nickerson, at Port Hudson. Served in various other engagements in Louisiana. Honorably discharged, February, 1864.

84. Lieutenant CHARLES F. VAN DUSER.

Lieutenant, Twelfth Regiment, United States Infantry. Killed at Gaines's Mills, on the Peninsula.

85. Lieutenant JAMES H. VAN NOSTRAND.

Lieutenant, Third Regiment, New Jersey Cavalry. Died a prisoner of war at Lynchburg, Virginia.

86. Major PHILIP L. VAN RENSSELAER.

Entered the United States service, July 7, 1862, as Second Lieutenant, Company F, Second New Jersey Cavalry. Promoted to be Captain, September 8, 1862, and to be Major of same regiment, September 8, 1863. Served in all the States in rebellion except two, viz. North and South Carolina, but principally in the Southwest and in the Department of the Gulf and Military Division of West Mississippi, under Grierson, A. J. Smith, Banks, Canby,

Mower, and Sheridan, principally employed in raiding through the country, destroying railroads, crops, and military stores, fighting guerillas, and skirmishing with detachments. Was at one time on duty on Canby's staff as Assistant Provost-Marshal-General of the division. Resigned June 27, 1864.

87. Captain George R. Vernon.

Entered the United States service, in 1861, and served as A. D. C. at battles of Big Bethel and Bull Run, Virginia. Joined Fourteenth United States Infantry, September 29, 1862. Promoted to be Second Lieutenant, February 27, 1863; First Lieutenant, June 18, 1864; Quartermaster and A. C. S., First Battalion, Fourteenth Infantry, October 7, 1865; Brevet Captain, October 27, 1864; Captain, May 24, 1867. Engaged in battles of Big Bethel, Bull Run, Chancellorsville, Mine Run, Gettysburg, Wapping Heights, Beverly Ford, Rappahannock Station, defences of Washington, 1864. Chapel House, sieges of Yorktown, Fredericksburg, Petersburg, and Richmond. Brevetted Captain, "for gallant and meritorious conduct at Poplar Grove Church and Hatcher's Run." In the field at the surrender of General Lee's army, April, 1865. Is still in the Regular Army.

88. Lieutenant James B. Vose.

Lieutenant, One Hundred and Sixty-Fifth Regiment, New York Volunteers.

89. Captain Robert Warren.

Lieutenant, One Hundred and Sixty-Fifth Regiment, New York Volunteers; Captain, One Hundred and Forty-Sixth Regiment, New York Volunteers; Aide-de-Camp to General Warren.

90. Master Benjamin S. Weeks.

Entered the United States Navy, September 2, 1861, as Master's Mate. Promoted to be Acting Master, December 21, 1861. Took part in the battles below New Orleans, and those at Vicksburg and Fort Fisher. Was captured at Sabine Pass, September 8, 1863, and held as prisoner of war eleven months. Resigned April, 1865, at close of war.

91. Lieutenant Edward W. West.

Lieutenant, First Regiment, United States Artillery; Aide-de-Camp to General Hooker.

92. Lieutenant Roswell Weston.

Lieutenant, First Regiment, United States Sharpshooters.

93. Paymaster F. A. Wheeler.

Assistant Paymaster, United States Navy.

94. Engineer George H. White.

Assistant Engineer, United States Navy.

95. Colonel William W. Winthrop.

Major and Judge Advocate, United States Volunteers; Brevet Colonel, U. S. A.

96. Surgeon WILMER S. WOOD.

Assistant Surgeon, United States Volunteers.

97. Lieutenant GEORGE W. YOUNG.

## SEVENTH COMPANY (G).

1. Captain R. S. ALCOKE.

Entered the United States service, November 20, 1861, as Fifth Sergeant, Company K, Fifty-Seventh Regiment, New York Volunteers. Promoted to be First Sergeant, September 8, 1862; First Lieutenant, September 17, 1862; and Captain, January 1, 1864. Served in the Third Brigade (French, Zook, McDougall), First Division (Richardson, Hancock, Caldwell, Barlow, Miles), Second Corps (Sumner, Couch, Hancock), and took part in the battles of Fair Oaks, Gaines's Mills, Peach Orchard, Savage Station, White-Oak Swamp, Malvern Hill, Antietam, Pontoon Bridge at Fredericksburg, Chancellorsville, Gettysburg, Wilderness, Cold Harbor, Petersburg. Lost his left arm at the elbow, at Fredericksburg. Was shot through the right breast and lung with a minie-ball at Petersburg, and was mustered out October 17, 1864, for disability.

2. Captain C. A. ALVORD, JR.

Served in the Army of the Potomac.

3. Lieutenant-Colonel SMITH W. ANDERSON.

Entered the United States service, March 3, 1864, as Lieutenant-Colonel, Ninety-Third Regiment, United States Colored Infantry. Served under General Franklin in the Nineteenth Army Corps, chiefly in Louisiana and in guerilla fighting. Was wounded in the neck in a skirmish in the Têche country. Mustered out at end of war, July 5, 1865.

4. Captain T. H. ANNABLE.

Entered the United States service, September 18, 1861, as Captain, Twenty-Sixth Regiment, Massachusetts Volunteers. Served in the Department of the Gulf, under Generals Butler, Banks, and Franklin. Was engaged at La Fourche Crossing, Lafayette, Pleasant Hill, Sabine Cross-Roads. Served on staff of Generals Franklin, Sherman, and Emory. Honorably discharged, February 18, 1864, in consequence of disease contracted in service, while in line of duty.

5. Captain EDWIN BISHOP.

6. Lieutenant-Colonel GEORGE BISHOP.

7. Captain EDWIN BLUNT.

8. Lieutenant A. SCHUYLER BOGART.

Entered the United States service, September, 1861, as Second Lieutenant in the First United States Chasseurs, Sixty-Fifth Regiment, New York Volunteers. Served under General McClellan on the Peninsula, and was mortally wounded in the knee at Fair Oaks. He was sent to New York, June 7, and died June 23, 1862, in the 23d year of his age. His commission as First Lieutenant, a promotion for gallant conduct, reached his friends at the time of his death. "*Note.* — He was a gallant fellow, and, had he been spared, would undoubtedly have made his mark. J. H. Kemp, for Committee of Seventh Company."

9. Brigadier-General R. N. Bowerman.

Entered the United States service, June 27, 1861, as First Lieutenant, Eleventh Regiment, New York Volunteers. Promoted to be Captain, October 4, 1861; Lieutenant-Colonel, Fourth Regiment, Maryland Volunteers, August 1, 1862; Colonel, March 27, 1863. Was brevetted Brigadier-General, United States Volunteers, April 1, 1865. Served throughout the war, from Bull Run to Five Forks, and took part in the battles of first Bull Run, Savage Station, Wilderness, Spottsylvania, Tolopotomy Creek, Cold Harbor, Weldon Railroad, White-Oak Ridge, Newport News, White-Oak Swamp, Laurel Hill, North Anna River, Bethesda Church, Norfolk Railroad, Dabney Mills, Five Forks. Was wounded by a minie-ball through right arm at the capture of the Weldon Railroad, August 21, 1864. Again wounded through the left arm at the battle of Five Forks, April 1, 1865, while in command of the Second Brigade, Second Division, Fifth Corps. Commanded the Maryland brigade in General Warren's Fifth Corps, Army of the Potomac, as follows: battles around Spottsylvania Court-House in May, 1864; after the first day at Laurel Hill; at the battle of Dabney Mills (second Hatcher's Run), February 6, 1865; and again at the battle of Five Forks, Virginia, April 1, 1865. Was brevetted Brigadier-General for this battle, upon recommendation of General R. B. Ayres, Division Commander. Was mustered out, May 31, 1865, and commissioned Lieutenant-Colonel, Thirty-First Infantry, United States Army, October 10, 1866. Is still in the army.

10. Paymaster C. J. Breck.

Entered the United States service as secretary to Commodore Baldwin, United States ship Vermont, which position he occupied for about two years.

11. Captain A. H. Britton.

Entered the United States service, August, 1862, as First Lieutenant, Company K, One Hundred and Forty-Fifth Regiment, New York Volunteers. Promoted Captain in 1863, and was honorably discharged in January, 1865.

12. Colonel H. S. Chatfield.

Entered the United States service, August 30, 1861, as Captain Forty-Third Regiment, New York State Volunteers. Transferred to Seventy-Eighth Regiment, New York Volunteers, as Captain, August 23, 1863. Promoted to be Lieutenant-Colonel, November 23, 1863; Lieutenant-Colonel (by consolidation) of One Hundred and Second Regiment, New York Veteran Volunteers, July 12, 1864; Colonel, June 5, 1865. Served in Virginia (Keyes's corps) and at the

West (Twelfth Corps). Took part in the Peninsular campaign, and in campaigns from Chattanooga to Atlanta, from Atlanta to Savannah, from Savannah to Raleigh. Took part in the battles of Lee's Mills, Yorktown, Williamsburg, Golden Farm, Savage Station, White-Oak Swamp (McClellan's seven days' change of base), Wauhatchie, Lookout Mountain, Mill Creek Gap, Resaca, Pine Knob and Lost Mountain, New Hope Church (or Dallas), Culp's Farm, Kenesaw Mountain, Peach-Tree Creek, Savannah, Bentonville, N. C. His regiment was the first to enter Savannah, 3 A. M., December 21, 1864. Was mustered out with regiment, July 21, 1865.

13. Major J. N. COYNE.

Entered the United States service, December, 1861, as Second Lieutenant in the Eighty-Seventh New York Volunteers. Soon resigned (the regiment delaying its organization) and made his way to the Excelsior Brigade, then at Lower Potomac, and was mustered in as a private of Company B, of the First Excelsior Regiment, July 22, 1862 (having previously declined a commission offered in the Fourth Regiment). Served through the Peninsular campaign, Was Fourth Sergeant at Williamsburg, and commanded company. Next day, was promoted to be Second Lieutenant, and was mentioned by Colonel Dwight for gallant and conspicuous conduct. At Fair Oaks, commanded company, and received flesh-wound in right arm. Was mentioned "for bravery and meritorious conduct." Was captured at Savage Station, but exchanged before the second Malvern. At Bristow Station was mentioned in Hooker's report. At second Bull Run received flesh-wound in the hip. December 27, 1862, was made Second Lieutenant. Was at Fredericksburg and at Chancellorsville. Was promoted to be Adjutant at Gettysburg. Received a scalp-wound there, and was mentioned as follows: "Adjutant J. N. Coyne, First Regiment Excelsior Brigade, particularly distinguished himself for coolness and bravery during the most trying moments, and fully sustained the high character won in previous actions." At Wapping Heights had a horse shot under him, and was promoted to be Captain. Took part in the actions at Cold Harbor and those around Petersburg, until June 24, 1864. Was mustered out with regiment, July 1, as Captain of color company. Was appointed Captain in Hancock's new (First Veteran) corps, and resigned June 12, 1865. Was brevetted Major.

14. Lieutenant-Colonel ABRAHAM DENIKE.

Joined Company G, Fifth New York Volunteers (Duryee's Zouaves), and was commissioned Captain, April 20, 1861. Served with the regiment under Butler, and was at Big Bethel, being senior Captain. Resigned September 6, 1861. Was commissioned Lieutenant-Colonel of the Fifty-Third Regiment, June 6, 1862, and recruited and organized the same. The regiment was consolidated with others, and he resigned October 12, 1862.

15. Major E. DONALDSON.

Entered the United States service, September 26, 1861, as Second Lieutenant, Eleventh New York Volunteers (Ellsworth's Zouaves); First Lieutenant February 15, 1862. Mustered out with regiment, June 2, 1862. November 20, 1862, commissioned Second Lieutenant, Sixth New York Heavy Artillery; First Lieutenant, June 1, 1863; Captain, April 25, 1864; Brevet Major, New York Volunteers, January, 1865. Served in the Second, Third, Fifth, Sixth, and Twenty-Second Corps. Was engaged in the battles of Wapping Heights, Laurel Hill, Todd's Tavern, Po River, Salient, Harris's Farm, North Anna, Bethesda Church, Petersburg, Cedar Creek, and served in the Shenandoah campaign also from September, 1864 to January, 1865. Was A. A. G. of "Kitching's brigade," honorably mentioned by Meade, and served in other staff capacities. Mustered out August 24, 1865.

16. Sergeant H. DUNCAN.

17. Captain JAMES DURYEE.

18. Lieutenant-Colonel WILLIAM B. C. DURYEE.

Entered the United States service as First Lieutenant, Third Maryland Volunteers, and detailed as Aid to General Duryee, June 11, 1862; was made Captain and Assistant Adjutant-General, United States Volunteers; was at battles of Rappahannock, Thoroughfare Gap, second Bull Run, South Mountain, and Antietam, at which last he received a severe gunshot wound; served afterwards on staff of General Webb; at Bristow Station received special mention for "coolness and bravery." At Mine Run his horse was shot under him; here he was mentioned for "prompt efficiency." Resigned from the effects of his wounds, December 24, 1863.

19. Major EDWARD EDDY, JR.

Entered the United States service, August 6, 1861, as First Lieutenant, Company A, Forty-Seventh Regiment, New York State Volunteers; was promoted Captain, April 29, 1862, and Major, September 29, 1863; was in Sherman's expedition to Port Royal, November, 1861; present at battle of Port Royal Ferry, January 1, 1862; General Benham's operations on James Island, South Carolina; battle of Secessionville, June 16, 1862; captured by the enemy near Warsaw Sound, Georgia, March 23, 1863; exchanged, May 10, 1863; present at Gillmore's operations on Morris Island, South Carolina, and assaults on Fort Wagner; then appointed Acting Assistant Inspector-General to General Seymour's expedition to Florida; present at battle of Olustee, February 20, 1864; then appointed Acting Assistant Inspector-General, Second Division, Tenth Army Corps, forming part of the Army of the James; was present at all the engagements of that corps during campaign of 1864, including battles of Swift's Creek, Drury's Bluff, Petersburg, explosion of the mine in front of Petersburg, battles at Deep Run, Appomattox Creek, Fort Harrison, Cold Harbor, Chapin's Farm, &c.; was mentioned in official reports; resigned October 20, 1864.

20. Lieutenant John H. Gardner, Jr.

Entered the United States service in September, 1862, as Commissary, with the rank of First Lieutenant, in the Third New York Cavalry; he joined the regiment at Newbern, North Carolina, and remained with it at and in the vicinity of Newbern for eight months, when he resigned.

21. Lieutenant J. Graham Gardner.

Entered the United States service in 1864, as Adjutant in the Fourth United States Colored Troops, and served as Assistant Aide-de-Camp on the staff of General Duncan, in Army of the James. Was at battle of New Market. Resigned October 13, 1864.

22. Lieutenant W. F. Geisse.

23. Captain Lewis B. Goodnow.

24. Colonel E. R. Goodrich.

25. Brigadier-General Charles A. Hartwell.

Entered the United States service, August 5, 1861, as First Lieutenant, Eleventh Infantry, United States Army. Appointed Battalion Adjutant, Eleventh Infantry, October 16, 1861; brevetted Captain, United States Army, June 27, 1862, for battle of Gaines's Mills, Virginia; brevetted Major, United States Army, June 14, 1863, for battle of Port Hudson, Louisiana; brevetted Lieutenant-Colonel, United States Army, March 13, 1865, for services during the war; appointed Colonel, Seventy-Seventh United States Colored Infantry, afterwards Tenth United States Colored Artillery (heavy), December 1, 1863; brevetted Brigadier-General, United States Volunteers, March 13, 1865, for services during the war. Mustered out of volunteer service February 22, 1867, and promoted Captain, Eleventh Infantry, United States Army, October 4, 1866. Served with the Eleventh Infantry in the Army of the Potomac, from the beginning of the war until taken prisoner, while wounded, at Savage Station, Virginia, June 30, 1863. After having been released from Richmond, was assigned to duty as Aide-de-Camp to General Banks, and accompanied him to Louisiana. Remained with Banks until the capture of Port Hudson; served as Aide-de-Camp on staff of General Ayres for short time; was twice mentioned in orders for official services; participated in the battles of Mechanicsville, Gaines's Mills (wounded in the thigh), Savage Station (taken prisoner), Rappahannock Station, Bristow Station, Port Hudson, Louisiana, 27th of May and 14th of June; Red River campaigns of 1863 and 1864. Is still in Regular Army. The company committee add: "The following indorsement is written upon Colonel Hartwell's discharge from volunteer service, dated February 22, 1867: 'Character without blemish as a gallant soldier and honorable gentleman.' Philip H. Sheridan, Major-General, United States Army."

26. Captain E. J. Henry.

Entered the United States service, September, 1861, as First Lieutenant, Eleventh New York Volunteers; Captain, February, 1862; honorably discharged, June, 1862; Captain, One Hundred and Twenty-Seventh New York Volunteers, August, 1862; served in Virginia and North Carolina (see Captain Allison's record, in Second Company), in all the engagements of his regiment. At Devaux Neck was wounded in right foot, permanently disabling it; was mentioned in general orders for services at the attack on James Island batteries; served also at Suffolk, Virginia, during the siege, in Dix's movement on the Peninsula, and at Diascund Bridge; also at Honey Hill, Salkahatchie, and Coosahatchie; commanded a battery on Morris Island. Mustered out, July 17, 1865.

27. Lieutenant T. W. B. Hughes.

Entered the United States service in 1861 as Second Lieutenant, "Union Coast Guard," afterwards Ninty-Ninth Regiment, New York Volunteers; was in the Burnside Expedition to North Carolina, and was at battles of Roanoke Island, and was complimented for his service with his naval battery. After the capture of Winton, Lieutenant Hughes was engaged at Newbern, and was severely wounded in that action, his naval battery suffering severely. He was mentioned with praise in General Foster's report of the action, and (an unusual thing) in the official report of Secretary Welles. Resigned, on account of wounds and sickness, August, 1862. Was offered a commission as Major, and one as Lieutenant-Colonel, but was incapacitated by his wounds from service.

28. Quartermaster William D. Hale.

Entered the United States service in 1861 in Quartermaster Department. Served under Colonel Herman Biggs, Chief Quartermaster of the Burnside Expedition, and was on duty in North Carolina under Generals Burnside and Foster; was transferred to Department of the Gulf under General Banks, and was stationed at Baton Rouge until he resigned his position in July, 1864.

29. Major Robert A. Hutchins.

Entered the United States service, September, 1862, as Captain and Assistant Adjutant-General, First Division, Ninth Corps. Was brevetted Major for gallant and meritorious conduct at the battle of the Wilderness, December 4, 1864. Served in all the campaigns and battles of the Ninth Corps, East and West, particularly at South Mountain, Fredericksburg, Blue Spring (Tennessee), Strawberry Plains (Tennessee), Weldon Road, Antietam, second Fredericksburg, Walker's Ford, Wilderness, Peeble's Farm, and battles in front of Petersburg, besides a large number of skirmishes. In the battle of the Wilderness he was severely wounded in the groin by a minie-ball, while gallantly rallying the broken troops of a division of the Ninth Army Corps. He submitted to three painful operations for this wound. Was mustered out, August, 1865. Was mentioned for distinguished gallantry, for coolness and presence of mind in every general engagement in which he participated, by the commanders under whom he served, and was particularly mentioned for distinguished gallantry by General Willcox, in his report of the battle of the Wilderness.

30. Lieutenant James H. Ingersoll.

31. Brigadier-General Samuel B. Jones.

32. Major P. C. Kingsland.

33. Captain Louis H. Lent.

Entered the United States service, September 5, 1861, as Captain of Company A, Forty-Eighth Regiment, New York Volunteers. Served in Department of the South, South Carolina and Georgia, under Generals T. W. Sherman, Hunter, O. M. Mitchell, and Gillmore, in Tenth Army Corps. Was engaged in taking of Port Royal, Fort Pulaski, and Morris Island. Fell, shot through the heart, at Morris Island, July 10, 1863, while acting as Major, and leading a forlorn hope on a charge of Rebel rifle-pits. Buried on the field. [" A gallant soldier and gentleman." — *Com.*]

34. Colonel John P. Leverich.

35. Captain James H. Lounsberry.

Entered the United States service, April 23, 1861, as a private in the Fifth Regiment (Duryee Zouaves), New York State Volunteers. Promoted to be First Sergeant, May 9, 1861 ; First Lieutenant, September, 1861 (General Orders Number 102, Head-quarters Army) ; Captain, August 30, 1862. Was present at Big Bethel, and the whole of the Peninsular campaign ; was taken down with the fever in the swamps of the Chickahominy. Rejoined the regiment, after Antietam, serving in all its campaigns until mustered out, at expiration of service, May 14, 1863.

36. Sergeant Thomas H. Millen.

37. Captain L. R. McDonough.

38. Captain George A. Morey.

Entered the United States service in 1861, as Lieutenant Company E, Seventy-Fourth Regiment, New York Volunteers (Fifth Excelsior). Was promoted to be Captain. Served with the Excelsior Brigade on the Lower Potomac, in command of river picket-boats, opposite enemy's positions at Shipping Point and Aquia Creek, and was in all expeditions sent out from that point. Joined McClellan's army at Cheesman's Landing, in 1862 : fought in battle of Williamsburg, and part of time commanded the regiment during that battle The brigade and regiment were both highly complimented in orders for their behavior in that action. Fought through Fair Oaks and Seven Pines, and was then employed in engineer duty in the swamps until stricken down with malarial fever, of which he died about 23d June, 1862. His last words were, " O, my poor boys ! " His last thought was of his company.

39. Major John D. Moriarty.

Entered the United States service, June 2, 1861, as Major of the Seventy-Third Regiment, New York State Volunteers. Served in Virginia through the Peninsular campaign, at Yorktown, Williamsburg, Stafford Court-House,

Baltimore Cross-Roads, Seven Pines, Fair Oaks, and the Seven Days' Battles, and at South Mountain and Cedar Creek. Captured at Piedmont, October 19, 1864, and paroled February 10, 1865.

### 40. Colonel EDWARD MURRAY.

### 41. Adjutant ALBERT A. NEAL.

### 42. Colonel WILLIAM NORTHRIDGE.

### 43 Captain FITZ-JAMES O'BRIEN.

Entered the United States service, in the winter of 1861, as Captain and Aide-de-Camp on the staff of General Lander commanding in West Virginia. He was engaged in action soon after reaching his new command. In the brilliant skirmish at Bloomery Gap, Lander, O'Brien, and two soldiers dashed upon an ambuscade, and captured three officers and eight men. O'Brien retained the sword and accoutrements of the Rebel captain as trophies, — trophies soon to be borne upon his own coffin. Two days later, February 16, O'Brien headed a body of cavalry which encountered a superior force of the enemy. He met the Rebel leader, face to face, and two simultaneous shots were heard: the one fired by O'Brien carried instant death; that which he received pierced his shoulder; but he still rallied his men, and brought off all save himself unharmed. His wound was a terrible one, and after great suffering a critical surgical operation was suggested by the surgeon. O'Brien writes: "I gave up the ghost, and told him to go ahead. There were about twelve surgeons to witness the operation. All my shoulder-bone and a portion of my upper arm have been taken away. I nearly died. My breath ceased, heart ceased to beat, pulse stopped. However, I got through. I am not yet out of danger from the operation, but a worse disease has set in. I have got tetanus, or lockjaw. There is a chance of my getting out of it, that 's all. In case I don't, good by, old fellow, with all my love! I don't want to make any legal document, but I desire that you and Frank Wood should be my literary executors, because after I 'm dead I may turn out a bigger man than when living." He died April 6th, from the results of the operation, — died at the threshold of a grand career, — a great poet and a brave soldier.

### 44. Captain JOHN OLDERSHAW

Entered the United States service, July 18, 1862, as First Lieutenant, Company K, Eleventh New Jersey Volunteers. Promoted to be Captain, October 11, 1863. Served in the Second and Third Corps in Virginia, and took part in the following battles, namely, Fredericksburg, Chancellorsville, Gettysburg, Wapping Heights, Kelly's Ford, Locust Grove, Mine Run, Grant's campaign from the Rapidan to Petersburg, and all the subsequent movements and battles in front of that city, in which the Second Corps was engaged, to the surrender of Lee and the Army of Northern Virginia at Appomattox Court-House Served for a time as Inspector-General of First Brigade, Second Division, Third Corps. At the battle of

Chancellorsville was detailed on General Berry's staff, commanding the Second Division, Third Corps. Was complimented on the field by the General, who said, "I shall not forget your services, sir." General Berry was killed the next morning. Was appointed to the command of the Division Pioneer Corps on General Mott's staff. November 15, 1864, was ordered to the Irish Brigade as Inspector under Colonel Nugent. Was with the brigade in the battle of the 29th March, 1865, outside the works, when it repulsed several severe attacks of the enemy, the men standing in line of battle for three hours without shelter, expending in that time about one hundred rounds of ammunition per man. He opened boxes and distributed ammunition along the line, under a galling fire. Was recommended for brevet rank and mentioned honorably in report of operations. Mustered out, June, 1865.

45. Lieutenant-Colonel WILLIAM PATTEN.

46. Captain JAMES PLANT.

47. Lieutenant-Colonel EUGENE F. ROBERTS.

Entered the United States service, April 23, 1861, as private in the Tenth New York Zouaves, and served under Butler near Fort Monroe. Resigned December 23, 1861. February 28, 1863, was commissioned senior Captain in Ulmann's brigade (colored troops), and served in the Department of the Gulf under Banks, Andrews, Ulmann. Served at siege of Port Hudson; was at battle of Plain Store and fight at Redwood Bridge under General Grierson. Served in the Department of Florida under General Asboth, and on 21st July captured Fort Hodson and Rebel flag with two companies of colored troops. Served in expedition to Pollard, Alabama. Commanded right wing in the battles of Escambia Bridge, Mitchell Creek, and Pine Barren Creek. Served in the Mobile campaign under Generals Steele, Hawkins, and Pyle. Was in the nine days' fighting and assault and capture of Fort Blakely and Mobile. Served at Apalachicola and Dry Tortugas. Was honorably discharged March 5, 1866, by expiration of term. Was brevetted Major and Lieutenant-Colonel, "for gallant and meritorious services during the war."

48. Lieutenant J. F. ROBINSON.

49. Brigadier-General ALLEN RUTHERFORD.

Entered the United States service as a Captain in the Ninth Regiment, New York State Militia (Eighty-Third Regiment, New York Volunteers), on the 27th of May, 1861; was promoted to be Major, 7th January, 1862, and Lieutenant-Colonel, 30th September, 1862. Was appointed a Lieutenant-Colonel in the Veteran Reserve Corps, 4th December, 1863. Served under Generals Banks, Pope, McClellan, Hooker, Burnside, and Grant. Belonged to the First Army Corps of the Army of the Potomac. Was brevetted Colonel and Brigadier-General of Volunteers "for gallant, faithful, and meritorious services," and remains in the army as First Lieutenant, Forty-Fourth United States Infantry (Regular Army).

50. Private William E. Schenck.

Entered the United States service as private in the Seventh Regiment, New York State National Guard. Served in the Maryland campaign in 1863, and was lost overboard in the steamer conveying his regiment home to New York, about 2, A. M., July 19, 1863.

51. Captain F. J. Steers.

Entered the United States service, December 24, 1861, as First Lieutenant, Company C, Ninetieth Regiment, New York State Volunteers. Promoted to be Captain, April 9, 1864. Mustered out, with regiment, at the end of three years' service. Served in Nineteenth Army Corps in the Têche country, at Port Hudson, Donaldsonville, in the Shenandoah Valley, and in garrison at Key West, Florida, Fort Jefferson, Tortugas, and Beaufort, South Carolina, and was on detached service at Ricker's and Hart's Islands, New York Harbor. While on Ricker's and Hart's Islands, acted as judge advocate to two general courts martial. Served also as Aide-de-Camp, First Brigade, First Division, Nineteenth Corps.

52. Lieutenant-Colonel George H. Stevens.

Entered the United States service, April 7, 1861, as Captain in the Second Regiment, Wisconsin Volunteers. Was promoted to be Major, August 30, 1862, and to be Lieutenant-Colonel, January 26, 1863. He served in Virginia, beginning at the skirmish of Blackburn's Ford, and then at Bull Run, where he exhibited the greatest coolness, bravery, and soldierly qualities, in the midst of the confusion. At Gainesville and second Bull Run he was also conspicuous, commanding his regiment after the three field-officers were wounded. Was engaged also at South Mountain, Antietam, Fredericksburg, Gettysburg, and in many skirmishes and reconnoissances. At Gettysburg, though so unwell as to be counselled by the Colonel and Surgeon to go to an ambulance, he led the left wing into action, and received a mortal wound in the abdomen, from which he died July 5. The late Colonel of his regiment, Governor Fairchild (who lost an arm at Gettysburg), says: "He was a faithful, hard-working officer, and brave as a lion, never flinching from duty or danger, and accomplished in all that went to make up a first-class field-officer. He died as a soldier would wish to die, with the harness on, and face to the foe. You cannot speak too highly of his soldierly qualities." His remains are buried in the National Cemetery at Gettysburg.

53. Major Robert K. Stewart.

Entered the United States service in July, 1861, as Lieutenant, Second Regiment Artillery, New York Volunteers. Promoted to be First Lieutenant, September 25, 1861. His regiment did garrison duty in the forts on south side of the Potomac for about eighteen months. Served under General Pope in his campaign, and was slightly wounded at second battle of Bull Run. Served with Grant on his march to Richmond, at Spottsylvania Court-House; was twice wounded, once in the body and once in right ankle. Was captured in same battle, and was prisoner for over ten months at Richmond, Andersonville, Macon, Charleston, and Columbia, South Carolina. Was honorably discharged from the service April 5, 1865.

54. Captain R. BURNETT SMITH.

Entered the United States service, May 14, 1861, as First Lieutenant, Eleventh United States Infantry. Was brevetted Captain for gallantry at the battle of Chapel House, Va., October 1, 1864. Resigned, January 1, 1866. Was present and took part in the following battles and engagements: siege of Yorktown, Gaines's Mills, Malvern Hill, Petersburg, Mine Explosion, Weldon Railroad, Poplar Grove Church, Chapel House, W. W. Davis's house, Virginia.

55. Lieutenant-Colonel HENRY STREET.

56. Brigadier-General F. E. TROTTER.

Entered the United States service, November 14, 1861, as Captain, Company I, One Hundred and Second Regiment, New York State Volunteers. Promoted to be Major, July 15, 1862, Veteran Reserve Corps; as Captain, June 15, 1863; Major, October 15, 1863, Lieutenant-Colonel, March 30, 1864; Brevet Colonel and Brevet Brigadier-General, for gallant and meritorious services, March 13, 1865. Served in the battles at Harper's Ferry, Cedar Mountain, siege of Washington, and Banks's campaign, Shenandoah Valley. Received a musket-ball through left arm, near shoulder, and a shell-wound of right foot, and a glance shot on left knee, at Cedar Mountain, August 9, 1862. Contracted fever and ague twice, typhoid fever three times, and small-pox in line of duty. Was appointed and confirmed as Captain, Forty-Fifth Infantry, Regular Army.

57. Lieutenant-Colonel SAMUEL TRUESDELL.

Entered the United States service, July 1, 1861, in the Sixty-Fifth Regiment, New York Volunteers (First United States Chasseurs), as First Lieutenant. Promoted "on the field," at Fair Oaks, to be Captain, for gallantry, June 1, 1862. Brevetted by Governor Fenton, Major and Lieutenant-Colonel, "for gallant and meritorious services in the late war." Took part in all the battles of the Peninsular campaign and all the battles and skirmishes of the Sixth Corps, subsequently, including those in the Shenandoah Valley, except the Wilderness and Spottsylvania. March 30, 1863, Acting Assistant Inspector-General, First Brigade, Third Division, Sixth Corps. While his brigade was temporarily guarding prisoners at Johnson's Island, Ohio, he was appointed, by the general commanding United States forces at Sandusky and Johnson's Island, "Treasurer of the Funds of Prisoners of War" on Johnson's Island. March 5, was appointed Treasurer of the Post Fund. During his service in Johnson's Island performed the duties of Post Quartermaster and Post Commissary of Subsistence, during the absence of those officers. Was mustered out, with his regiment, September 12, 1864.

58. Colonel CHARLES TURNBULL.

Entered the United States service, in September, 1862, as Colonel of the First Metropolitan (One Hundred and Thirty-First) Regiment, New York Volunteers. Was on duty at Parole Camp, Annapolis, and afterwards with Banks, in Louisiana, his regiment being the first to land at Baton Rouge.

59. Captain WILLIAM H. UNDERHILL.

60. Major HENRY VANDER WEYDE.

Entered the United States service, June 20, 1861, as Second Sergeant, Sixty-Fifth Regiment, New York Volunteers. Was promoted to be First Sergeant, January 1, 1862; Sergeant-Major, November, 1862; Second Lieutenant, December 1, 1862, Captain, February, 1865. Was brevetted Major, for gallant and meritorious services. Took part in the battles of Lewinsville, Yorktown, Williamsburg, Fair Oaks, Seven Pines, Malvern Hill, second Bull Run, Antietam, Williamsport, Fredericksburg, Marye's Heights, Salem Heights, Wilderness (where he was captured, but escaped), Spottsylvania, North Anna, Cold Harbor, Petersburg, Winchester, Fisher's Hill, Cedar Creek, where, his horse being shot under him, he was thrown down and captured, imprisoned at Libby and Danville; exchanged February 22, 1865. Mustered out August 1, 1865. Served on staffs of Generals Wheaton, Russell, and Jackson. Was honorably mentioned. General Hamlin wrote: "He has greatly distinguished himself by his exceeding gallantry in every action; I know few men whom I can so conscientiously recommend." General Wheaton says: "A brave and accomplished soldier, having served upon my staff, in battle and in camp, with great credit."

61. Adjutant E. VAN NESS.

Entered the United States service, November 21, 1861, as Adjutant, Eighty-Seventh Regiment, New York Volunteers. Took part in the Peninsular campaign, in Kearny's corps, his regiment being in the advance going up and in the rear-guard on the retreat. Participated in the skirmish in front of Yorktown, the battles of Williamsburg and Fair Oaks, and the skirmish on the extreme left on the 25th June, in which his regiment lost very severely. Supported DeRussay battery at the battle of Malvern Hill. At Harrison's Landing was detailed as Regimental Quartermaster. Mustered out by consolidation, September 6, 1862.

62. Captain THEODORE C. VIDAL.

Entered the United States service, September 5, 1861, as Second Lieutenant Forty-Eighth Regiment, New York Volunteers. Was promoted to First Lieutenant, December 24, 1862, and Captain, September 30, 1863. Detailed to Signal Corps, April 6, 1862. Took part in the occupation of Hilton Head, Port Royal Ferry, Fort Pulaski, battle of Coosahatchie, capture of Morris Island, bombardment and assault of Fort Wagner, assault on Fort Sumter, capture of Wagner and Gregg, fight at St. Mary's Ford, battle of Olustee,

Birney's raid and occupation of Baldwin, battle of Honey Hill, Devaux Neck, and Combahee; occupation of Charleston. Was mentioned in general orders by Major Beard at the capture of Fort Pulaski; in general orders by General Seymour at battle of Olustee; by Captain Town, Chief Signal Officer, V. S., in the following terms: "I take great pleasure in mentioning the following-named officer for gallant and meritorious service, Lieutenant Vidal, for efficiency under fire before Fort Wagner, and in the batteries on the 18th of July, and upon several other days." He also accompanied the expedition under Colonel Osborn to assault Sumter. Also mentioned in general orders from Bureau of Signal Corps, for capture of Rebel signal-flags at Baldwin; mentioned by Captain G. S. Dana at Olustee, and by Captain Merrill, for "zeal and energy in discharge of duty." Mustered out August 21, 1865.

63. Captain William J. Williams.

Entered the United States service, September 1, 1861, as Captain of Company E, Fifty-Sixth Regiment, New York Volunteers. Served in Virginia, in Keyes's corps, and moved up the Peninsula. He was killed by a shell at the battle of Fair Oaks, May 31, 1862, at the head of his command. "The universal testimony of his fellow-officers and of his men," writes one of the former, "is that he was a good officer and a brave man. His untimely death was mourned throughout the command." S. Truesdell adds: "A true gentleman, an accomplished officer, and a gallant soldier."

64. Lieutenant H. J. Winters.

Entered the United States service, June 4, 1861, as Sergeant, Third Regiment, Excelsior Brigade. Was promoted to be First Lieutenant, and served till June 5, 1862, when he was permanently disabled by being thrown from a horse, and in consequence was mustered out of the service. Was commended as a disciplinarian by regimental and brigade officers.

## EIGHTH COMPANY (H).

1. Captain James T. Baker.

Entered the United States service as Captain, Sixty-Fifth Regiment, New York Volunteers.

2. Paymaster John M. Baker.

Entered the United States service as Paymaster in the navy. Was promoted to be Ensign. Served till close of war.

3. Major Robert P. Barry.

Entered the United States service, May 14, 1861, as Captain of the Sixteenth Regular Infantry, and served with his regiment in the Army of the Ohio in the campaigns of 1862, under Buell and Rosecrans. Commanded his company (F, First Battalion) in the battle of Shiloh, April 7, 1862; in all the subsequent operations under Buell, and in the battle of Murfreesboro', under Rosecrans. In the latter action his company lost two officers and thirty-five out of forty-six men killed and wounded. In this battle (December 31, 1862) was wounded in the jaw and arm, and was captured and paroled. Was on invalid duty during 1863 in the Provost-Marshal-General's department as Inspector of the State of Iowa. Commanded his regiment during most of the Atlanta campaign under Sherman, and took part in the battles at Buzzards' Roost, New Hope Church, Kenesaw, Neal Dow Station, the Chattahoochee, Utoy Creek, and the assault on the defences of Jonesboro' (September 1, 1864). Resigned his commission on account of ill health contracted during the Atlanta campaign, and was brevetted Major after his resignation.

4. Sergeant-Major Charles Augustus Barton.

Entered the United States service as Sergeant-Major of the —— California Regiment.

5. Captain Clarence A. Blake.

Entered the United States service in March, 1862, as First Lieutenant, Company A, One Hundred and Third New York Volunteers. Served in North Carolina with his regiment on picket duty, and April 24th was appointed Acting Aide-de-Camp on Nagle's staff (First Brigade, Reno's division). Served in Virginia in 1862, taking part in the battles of Kelly's Ford, Chantilly, second Bull Run, South Mountain, Antietam, and Fredericksburg. Resigned after Fredericksburg, from rheumatism and sickness contracted in the campaign. Was mentioned favorably in brigade reports.

6. Lieutenant N. H. Baylis.

Lieutenant in the Signal Corps.

7. Major Hollis W. Buckley.

Entered the United States service, August 8, 1861, as First Lieutenant, Battery C, First Rhode Island Artillery. Promoted to be Captain, Battery D, October 22, 1864. Brevetted Major, United States Volunteers, March 5, 1865, "for faithful and meritorious services." Served in Virginia and at the West. Took part in the Peninsular campaign in 1862, Groveton, Manassas, Antietam, Fredericksburg, Morgan's raid in Kentucky and Ohio in 1863, Burnside's campaign in Kentucky and East Tennessee, including siege of Knoxville, and battles of Lewins, Campbell's Station, Blue Spring, and Fort Sanders; Wilderness campaign, with Ninth Army Corps in Army of the Potomac in May, 1864; Shenandoah Valley campaign of General Sheridan in summer and fall of 1864, including battles of Charlestown, Winchester, Fisher's Hill, and Cedar Creek, until October 22, 1864, when discharged by reason of the expiration of term of service.

8. Ensign H. D. Burdett.

Served in the United States Navy.

9. Lieutenant-Colonel William L. M. Burger.

Entered the United States service in 1861, as Adjutant, First Regiment,

New York Engineers. Served during the war, and was Acting Adjutant-General on General Sickles's staff when mustered out of service.

10. Lieutenant-Colonel Charles H. Burtis.

Lieutenant-Colonel, Seventh Regiment, New York Volunteers.

11. Paymaster Frank Cargill.

Assistant Paymaster, United States Navy. Served about two years.

12. Captain W. J. Carleton.

Entered the United States service, August 21, 1861, in the Forty-Eighth New York Volunteers, and appointed Third Sergeant. Promoted to be Second Lieutenant, December 19, 1861; to be First Lieutenant, February 21, 1863; to be Captain, November 1, 1863. Served in Virginia, South Carolina, Georgia, and Florida, in the Tenth Corps, under Generals T. W. Sherman, Mitchell, Hunter, and Gillmore. Participated in the reduction of Fort Pulaski, in the sieges of Forts Wagner and Sumter and of the city of Charleston, and in the battle of Olustee. During about one half his term served in the ordnance corps. Mustered out November 13, 1864, at the expiration of his term of service.

13. Major James S. Casey.

Entered United States service in 1861, as Second Lieutenant, Fifth Regiment, United States Infantry (Regular). Was Post Adjutant on Governor's Island for some time. Transferred to Fort Warren (Boston Harbor), having charge of Rebel prisoners, including Mason and Slidell. Transferred to General Parke's staff, Ninth Army Corps. Assisted in the operations before Petersburg and Richmond until close of war. Stationed at present at Fort Sumner, New Mexico.

14. Major Oliver Cotter.

Entered the United States service in May, 1861, as First Lieutenant in the Thirteenth Regiment, New York State Militia. Served three months at Annapolis. January 20, 1862, commissioned Captain in the Fifth Regiment, New York Heavy Artillery. Was on garrison duty in New York Harbor, Baltimore, Fort Monroe, and Maryland Heights. Took part in Hunter's movement up the Shenandoah Valley in 1864, and took active part in the battles at Piedmont and Lynchburg. Was honorably discharged, February 3, 1865, for disease contracted in the service. Brevetted Major, 1866.

15. Lieutenant Thomas W. Dick.

Lieutenant, Eighth Regiment Heavy Artillery.

16. Surgeon William B. Eager, Jr.

Entered the United States service, September 2, 1862, as Surgeon, One Hundred and Sixty-Second Regiment, New York Volunteers. Served in the defences of Washington and in the Banks Expedition. December 21, 1862, appointed Medical Director on staff of General T. W. Sherman. Was in Red

River campaign and at Port Hudson, and at latter, in charge of Division Hospital; also in charge of United States General Hospital at Franklin, Louisiana. Mustered out by consolidation, February 17, 1864.

17. Captain HENRY C. ELLIS.

Sergeant-Major, Sixty-Fifth Regiment, New York Volunteers.

18. Captain WILLIAM IRVING ELLIS.

Entered the United States service in 1861, as Lieutenant, Second Regiment, Rhode Island Volunteers. Was transferred to Subsistence Department, and promoted Captain.

19. Captain AMOS F. ENO.

Entered the United States service, July 28, 1862, as Aide-de-Camp on staff of John S. Phelps, Military Governor of Arkansas. November 10, 1862, was appointed and commissioned Adjutant-General of Arkansas, with rank of Colonel. As volunteer aid to General Osterhaus, took part in battles of Champion Hills, Edward's Station, and the Big Black, Mississippi, and had charge of raising three Arkansas regiments of white troops. His office as Adjutant-General was abolished by General Orders 211, A. G. O., dated July 9, 1863.

20. Lieutenant ROBERT O. N. FORD.

Lieutenant in Marine Corps from 1862. Is still in the service.

21. Captain S. J. FOSTER.

Captain, Forty-Eighth Regiment, New York Volunteers.

22. Brigadier-General H. S. GANSEVOORT.

Entered the United States service, May 14, 1861, as Second Lieutenant in the Fifth Regular Artillery. Promoted to be First Lieutenant, Fifth Artillery, March 1, 1862; to be Lieutenant-Colonel, Thirteenth New York Cavalry, June 20, 1863; to be Colonel of the same regiment, March 28, 1863 (?); to be Brigadier-General in 1865. Was mustering officer at Harrisburg in September, 1861; and as such mustered in several thousand volunteers. After serving at the Camp of Artillery Instruction, near Harrisburg, was stationed at Fort Monroe, in March, 1862. Served with Battery C, Third Artillery, for several months during the Peninsula campaign, and in Keyes's corps during the "Seven Days." At Harrison's Landing was promoted to be First Lieutenant, Fifth Artillery, and served in Battery C of that regiment, attached to Meade's brigade of Reynolds's division, Army of the Potomac, during the operations in the autumn of 1862. Participated in the battles of Groveton, second Bull Run, South Mountain, and Antietam. Remained with the Army of the Potomac till 1863, when he was granted leave of absence to accept appointment as Lieutenant-Colonel of the Thirteenth New York Cavalry. Served in command of that regiment (in Lowell's brigade), operating, in the region southwest of Washington and east of the Blue Ridge, against guerillas, and in scouting, raiding, &c., until the close of the war. The command was mostly independent.

23. Captain James B. Grant.

Captain, First Regiment, New York Engineers.

24. Captain F. H. Grant.

25 Adjutant William Henderson.

26. Brigadier-General John Hendrickson.

Entered the United States service as Captain, Ninth Regiment, New York Volunteers. Promoted to be Brigadier-General, Veteran Reserve Corps.

27. Lieutenant Henry W. Hubbell, Jr.

Joined Brigadier-General H. G. Wright as volunteer Aide-de-Camp at Annapolis, October 12, 1861, and sailed with the expeditionary corps under Dupont and Sherman, participating in the operations which resulted in the reduction of Port Royal. Soon after returned to New York, and was commissioned Second Lieutenant in the Fortieth New York Volunteers. Detailed from his regiment to report to General Wright, on whose staff he was placed in December, 1861. Participated in the reduction of Fort Pulaski, in the operations against Fernandina and Jacksonville, and in the operations against Charleston, under General Bonham, terminating in the battle of Secessionville. Received honorable mention in the report of that action. In July, 1862, accompanied General Wright to the Department of the Ohio, remaining there on the staff of that officer till April, 1863, when Wright was assigned to the First Division, Sixth Corps, Army of the Potomac. Served with this corps at the battle of Gettysburg, and in the operations preceding and following it till November, 1863, when, owing to consolidation of his regiment, he was mustered out of service. Appointed Second Lieutenant, First United States Artillery, December, 1866.

28. Captain John H. Hull.

Entered the United States service, October 30, 1862, as Captain in the One Hundred and Seventy-Fourth Regiment, New York Volunteers. Served in the Banks Expedition, and in the siege of Port Hudson, and the various battles connected with the latter. Resigned, August 27, 1863, in consequence of paralysis resulting from rheumatism.

29. Captain James C. Hyatt.

Entered the United States service, May, 1861, as First Lieutenant in the Thirty-Second Regiment, New York Volunteers, and took part in the battle of Bull Run. Was Provost-Marshal of Alexandria until November, 1861. Promoted to be Captain, Eleventh Regiment, New York Cavalry, June 7, 1862, and served along the Potomac on patrol duty. June 30, was engaged in battle at Shepherdstown. Was in the reserve at Gettysburg. Ordered to Department of the Gulf, and was engaged at Doyle's plantation in July, 1864, and in the raids to Clinton and West Pascagoula. Served also in Arkansas. Mustered out, with regiment, June 7, 1865.

30. Paymaster T. GRANVILLE HOYT.

Paymaster in the United States Navy.

31. Lieutenant WILLIAM C. JACOBSON.

Entered the United States service in 1862, as Second Lieutenant in Fifth Regiment, New York Heavy Artillery.

32. Lieutenant E. R. JOHNSON.

Lieutenant, Third Regiment, New York Volunteers.

33. Private J. LAWRENCE KEESE.

Accidentally killed while with Seventh Regiment at Washington in 1861. The circumstances are related in Chapter X. of the present volume.

34. Captain EDWARD C. KITTLE.

Entered the United States service in June, 1861, as Captain in the Sixty-Fifth Regiment, New York Volunteers. Resigned May 2, 1862, to accept a captaincy in the Sixty-First Regiment, New York Volunteers. Joined the latter regiment at Fair Oaks, and served throughout the Peninsula campaign, the regiment losing all but five officers and eighty men in the battles. Was at Fredericksburg, in Caldwell's brigade, Hancock's division, Second Corps, and, Colonel Nelson A. Miles being wounded, took command of his own regiment and that of the Sixty-Fourth New York Volunteers, and was among those ordered to hold the town until the army had crossed the river. In this battle he was struck twice, — once with a canister-shot on the left arm, partially paralyzing it, and once by a spent musket-ball. Was mentioned in reports, and recommended to promotion for this battle. At Chancellorsville, led the left of the skirmish line, and took part in the general engagement, though he had been under the surgeon's care up to the time of the battle. Took part in the battle of Gettysburg, and the subsequent engagements till August 24, 1863, when he was honorably discharged from the service. In 1866 received and declined an appointment as Captain in the Fortieth United States Infantry. Was recommended by General Miles for the brevet of Major.

35. Lieutenant E. KIRBY.

Entered the United States service, September 19, 1862, as private in Company H, Fifth Regiment, New York Artillery. Soon after promoted to be Corporal; Commissary Sergeant in May, 1863; Second Lieutenant, June, 1863. Served in garrison at Baltimore and Harper's Ferry, and took part in the battles of July 4 and 5, 1864, at Maryland Heights. Served through Sheridan's Shenandoah campaign, his regiment losing heavily at Winchester. Resigned, from physical disability, in November, 1864.

36. Captain J. N. T. LEVICK.

Entered the United States service, June 11, 1861, as Second Lieutenant, First Regiment, Excelsior Brigade, New York Volunteers. Promoted to be First Lieutenant, May 6, 1862; promoted to be Captain on the battle-field,

April 30, 1862. Served in the battles of Williamsburg, Seven Pines, all the Seven Days' Battles, including second Malvern Hill, at second Bull Run, Bristow Station, Fredericksburg, and Chancellorsville. Was honorably discharged April 30, 1863.

37. Captain WALTER LLOYD.

Captain, One Hundred and Seventy-Fourth New York Volunteers.

38. Captain E. S. MANN.

Captain on General Ulmann's staff in 1862.

39. Captain WILLIAM D. MANSFIELD.

Captain in One Hundred and Seventy-Fourth Regiment, New York Volunteers. Served at Port Hudson.

40. Major-General JOHN M. MCNEIL.

Entered the United States service as Colonel of a Missouri regiment. Promoted to be Major-General.

41. Major CHARLES E. MEARS.

Entered the United States service in August, 1861, as Captain in the Fourth Regiment, West Virginia Volunteers. Served on the Kanawha River, and resigned in December, 1861. In March, 1862, was appointed Major of the Marine Artillery Corps raised from the State of New York; the regiment served in North Carolina under General Burnside, and afterwards General Foster. Was stationed part of the time at Newbern, and for some months commanded the post at Roanoke Island. Participated in the march to Tarboro', North Carolina, and in the battles at Kingston and Goldsboro', in the fall and winter of 1862.

42. Captain ALBERT V. MEEKS.

Entered the United States service August 31, 1861, as Captain in the Sixty-Second Regiment, New York Volunteers. Served in the Peninsular campaign, and took part in the battles of Williamsburg and Fair Oaks. Was wounded in the latter battle. Resigned at the close of campaign, from disability resulting from wounds.

43. Captain S. A. MELLICK.

Captain of First Regiment, New York Mounted Rifles. Died at Fortress Monroe in 1862.

44. Captain E. R. MERRIMAN.

45. Captain THEODORE W. MORGAN.

Captain, Ninety-Third Regiment, New York Volunteers.

46. Colonel ALBERT P. MOULTON.

Entered the United States service, June 1, 1862, as Captain, Company F, Third Regiment, Pennsylvania Reserve Corps, and as such served three years.

Took part in the battles of Drainesville, Mechanicsville, Gaines's Mills, Charles City Cross-Roads, and Malvern Hill; also at Chantilly, second Bull Run, South Mountain, Antietam, and Fredericksburg. In West Virginia, in 1864, took part in the affairs of Moorfield and New Creek, and the battles at Cloyd Mountain, New River Bridge, Piedmont, Lexington, Lynchburg, Snicker's Gap, Winchester (July 25, 1864). His regiment now being mustered out of service, he was re-mustered with the veteran troops as Colonel of the Fifty-Fourth Regiment, Pennsylvania Volunteers, and took part under Sheridan in the battles of Winchester, September 17, 1864, Fisher's Hill, Strasburg, and Cedar Creek. Was then transferred to the Twenty-Fourth Corps, under Gibbons, in the various battles around Petersburg, and the general assault of April 2, 1865. Took part in the pursuit of Lee, and was engaged at High Bridge, or Farmville, April 6, 1865. Mustered out June 1, 1865. Was wounded at Fisher's Hill, and made prisoner at High Bridge, but released three days later, at Lee's surrender.

47. Lieutenant-Colonel H. S. Murray.

Entered the United States service, August 14, 1862, as Captain, Company B, One Hundred and Twenty-Fourth Regiment, New York Volunteers. Was promoted to be Major, July 2, 1863, and to be Lieutenant Colonel, September 19, 1864. Served in the Army of the Potomac in Third Division, Third Corps, under Generals Stoneman, Sickles, and French, and in Third Division, Second Corps, under Hancock and Birney. Participated in the battles of first Fredericksburg, Chancellorsville, Wilderness, Spottsylvania, Cold Harbor, and all the continuous fighting in which the Second Corps was engaged, from May 5, 1864, to October 27, 1864. Was wounded May 3, 1863, at Chancellorsville, Virginia, by a minie-ball, which entered full in the mouth, taking out four upper and four lower front teeth, and lodging in the back of the neck. Was left on the field for dead, and was so reported in the official lists of casualties, Was a prisoner two weeks, and arrived home to find his family in mourning for his death, and his obituary notices published in the newspapers. Was again wounded by a shell, and taken prisoner at Hatcher's Run, before Petersburg, Virginia, October 27, 1864, and enjoyed the hospitality of the celebrated Libby for four months. Was exchanged early in April, 1865, and resigned, the war being over.

48. Captain E. B. Norton.

Captain, Subsistence Department.

49. Brigadier-General John H. Oley.

Entered the United States service.

50. Paymaster William H. Owen.

Entered the United States Navy as Assistant Paymaster, September 30, 1862. Assigned to duty in the "mortar flotilla," October 15, 1862. Served under Admiral Lee, in the North Atlantic Squadron, blockading Wilmington, North Carolina, and other inlets on that coast; also served under Admiral Dahlgren, in the South Atlantic Squadron, on duty off Charleston, South Carolina. Resigned from the service, October 8, 1863.

51. Adjutant LEWIS O. PARMLEE.

Entered the United States service in 1862, as Adjutant, First Regiment Berdan Sharpshooters. Killed at Antietam in 1862.

52. Lieutenant FREDERICK T. PEET.

Entered the United States service, June, 1861, as Second Lieutenant, Company H, First United States Sharpshooters (Berdan). Served at Washington and on the Peninsula. Took part in the battles at Yorktown, Chickahominy, Hanover Court-House, Savage Station, White-Oak Swamp, and Nelson's Farm. Was wounded in the chest at Nelson's Farm at eight, P. M., June 30, 1862, and as the surgeons pronounced him dying, no effort was made to probe his wound. Was taken prisoner and sent to Libby. Was exchanged under a special flag from General McClellan, after a few weeks' imprisonment. Still carries the bullet in his chest, and is in good health. When shot, was from seventy-five to one hundred feet from the enemy. Was mentioned by General Barlow or General Caldwell, commanding brigade in Sumner's corps. Was officially killed, or so reported; read his obituary with interest in the Brooklyn "Eagle." Transferred to the United States Marine Corps, in July, 1862. Served at Morris and Folly Island, and was one of the first men to enter Fort Wagner. Is now First Lieutenant in the Marine Corps.

53. Lieutenant-Colonel CHARLES EDWIN PRESCOTT.

Entered the United States service, June 8, 1861, as Captain of Company C, Eighty-Third Regiment, New York Volunteers. June 16, 1862, resigned to organize the One Hundred and Thirty-Second Regiment, New York Volunteers, of which he was commissioned Lieutenant-Colonel, September 11, 1862. Served at Suffolk, Virginia, and in the Shenandoah Valley. Resigned December 12, 1862.

54. Lieutenant EDWARD L. POSTLEY.

Lieutenant, One Hundred and Seventy-Sixth Regiment, New York Volunteers.

55. Captain PHILIP C. ROGERS.

Entered the United States service as Lieutenant, Fifty-Fifth Regiment, New York Volunteers. Served with honor, and was mentioned in orders.

56. Adjutant J. F. SATHERWAITE.

Adjutant, Twenty-Second Regiment, New Jersey Volunteers.

57. Colonel CHARLES E. SMITH.

Colonel, Eleventh Regiment, Michigan Infantry.

58. Lieutenant CHARLES L. SMITH.

Lieutenant, Ninth Regiment, United States Infantry.

59. Captain ADRIAN SPEAR.

Entered the United States service as private in Twentieth Regiment, Massachusetts Volunteers. Was promoted to be Captain.

60. Colonel PERCY B. SPEAR.

Entered the United States service, November 30, 1861 as Captain and Commissary of Subsistence, United States Volunteers, and was assigned to Martindale's brigade, Porter's division. Served in the Fifth Corps from its organization to the end of the Rebellion, and acted as Aid in almost all its engagements. At second Bull Run had his horse killed under him by a shell, and was severely wounded in falling. Served as brigade, division, and (after October 24, 1862) as chief commissary of the corps. Was complimented by McClellan at Hanover Court-House for being the only commissary who had his supplies up, ready for issue, the night after the battle. The chief commissary acknowledged in his report his indebtedness to the fine administrative abilities of Captain Spear. Major-Generals Meade, A. B. Eaton (Commissary-General), Butterfield, Crawford, Martindale, and Barnes gave the highest public testimony to his conspicuous services. He was mustered out, November 22, 1865, and received the brevets of Lieutenant-Colonel and Colonel for meritorious services.

61. Captain E. N. K. TALCOTT.

Entered the United States service, August 20, 1862, as Second Lieutenant, Company E, First Regiment, New York Engineers. Promoted to be First Lieutenant, February 6, 1863; to be Captain, January 9, 1865. Served in the Tenth Corps in South Carolina and in Army of the James, and after March, 1865, as Aide-de-Camp to General Gillmore. Was present as engineer officer at the various corps operations, — the siege of Charleston, siege of Petersburg, and the movements on both banks of the James. Was on duty as Depot Engineer at Bermuda Hundreds and at Fort Monroe. Was mentioned favorably in report of siege of Charleston. Was in Florida Expedition, 1865. Mustered out, with his regiment, August 1, 1865.

62. Lieutenant J. J. WEBBER.

Lieutenant, Fifty-Seventh Regiment, New York Volunteers.

63. Captain J. HOWARD WELLS.

64. Lieutenant J. D. WICKHAM.

Entered the United States service as Lieutenant, Ninth Regiment, New York Volunteers. Resigned on account of ill health. Died soon after.

65. Captain GEORGE C. WILLIAMS.

Captain, Fifty-Fifth Regiment, New York Volunteers.

## NINTH COMPANY (I).

1. Captain C. J. C. BALL.

2. Sergeant J. BARRETT.

3. Lieutenant L. W. BRAINARD.

4. Lieutenant Wm. L. Bramhall.

5. Captain Theodore H. Bush.

6. Lieutenant-Colonel W. B. Coan.

7. Engineer A. M. Cummings.

Served in the United States Navy.

8. Lieutenant Barry Davies.

9. Lieutenant G. D. Davis.

10. Lieutenant George E. Dayton.

11. Sergeant Fordred Drayson.

Served in Virginia with the Army of the Potomac, and was killed in the battle of Cold Harbor in the summer of 1864.

12. Lieutenant Clinton Eddy.

13. Captain Franklin Ellis.

14. Lieutenant D. R. Franklin.

15. Captain Samuel Giberson.

16. Captain L. O. Goodridge.

17. Brigadier-General E. E. Graves.

18. Sergeant R. M. Harmstead.

19. Major Nathaniel P. Lane.

Entered the United States service, March 17, 1864, as Second-Lieutenant, Sixty-Sixth Regiment New York (Veteran) Volunteers. Promoted to be First Lieutenant, June 15, 1864; Captain, December 15, 1864. Served in the battles around Petersburg, Deep Bottom, New Market Heights, blowing up of the mine, Reams's Station, August 28, 1864, where he was wounded in the left hip by a piece of shell; Hatcher's Run, Strawberry Creek, Armstrong's Mills, Five Forks, Southside Railroad. Was mentioned by General Ramsey (Fourth Brigade, First Division, Second Corps) in brigade orders. Mustered out May 29, 1865. Brevetted Major.

20. Lieutenant J. P. Manning.

21. Captain Henry Matthews.

22. Sergeant T. A. McCrossen.

23. Brigadier-General N. B. McLaughlin.

Entered the United States service, March 27, 1861, as Second Lieutenant, United States Cavalry (Regular Army), and was ordered to Fort Monroe. Promoted to be First Lieutenant, May 3, 1861, and to be Captain, July 17, 1862, Assistant Inspector-General, Army of Kentucky (Q. A. Gillmore) in 1862.

Commanded Tenth Kentucky Cavalry in pursuit of Morgan same year. October 1, 1862, was commissioned Colonel First Massachusetts Volunteers, and took part in the battles of Fredericksburg and Chancellorsville. At the latter battle believes that Stonewall Jackson was killed by the First Massachusetts, whose skirmish lines were so advanced that they captured during the same night many officers and men of the enemy who advanced carelessly, singly or in groups, believing they were in their own lines. Was brevetted Major in the Regular Army, May 3, 1863, "for gallant and meritorious services at the battle of Chancellorsville." Took part in all the subsequent battles of the Army of the Potomac, in the Second and Third Corps, till after Spottsylvania, when the term of his volunteer regiment expired, and they were mustered out. Joined his own regiment (Regular) before Atlanta, and was eight days in the trenches there. Ordered again to Army of the Potomac as Colonel of the Fifty-Seventh Regiment, Massachusetts Veteran Volunteers. Was appointed September 30, 1864, Brigadier-General of Volunteers by brevet for gallant and distinguished services at the battle of Poplar Grove Church, and thereafter commanded brigade in the Ninth Corps, at Pegram's Farm, Weldon Road, before Petersburg and Southside Railroad. At the assault on Fort Steadman, March 25, 1864, after recapturing one battery and in attempting to recapture the fort, he was taken prisoner and sent to Libby, there remaining till Lee's surrender. Was brevetted Colonel in the Regular Army for gallant and meritorious services during the assault upon Fort Steadman. Was mustered out of his volunteer rank, September 1, 1865, and joined his command in the Regular Army. During the last year of the war, always commanded a brigade or division. Was brevetted Brigadier-General in the Regular Army, March 13, 1865, for gallant and meritorious services in the field during the war.

24. Major B. B. MILLER.

25. Engineer EDWARD B. MINGAY.

26. Colonel R. T. MITCHELL.

Entered the United States service, August 8, 1861, as Captain of an "unassigned company," afterwards in the Fifty-First Regiment, New York Volunteers. Took part in the Burnside Expedition to North Carolina, and in the battles of Roanoke Island and Newbern. Was for a time in command of the regiment in North Carolina. Joined Pope (in Ninth Corps) at Slaughter's Mountain, and served as rear-guard thence to Manassas, involving a fortnight's constant marching and skirmishing. Acted as Lieutenant-Colonel in the battles of second Manassas, Chantilly, South Mountain, Antietam, Sulphur Springs, and Fredericksburg. After a campaign in Kentucky, joined Grant, with Ninth Corps, at Vicksburg, and took part in the siege and surrender of Vicksburg and Jackson. At Jackson temporarily commanded the Thirty Fifth Massachusetts, which regiment was the first to enter the city, capturing two hundred and fifty prisoners, and hauling down the enemy's flag from the Capitol. In January, 1864, marched in command of the regiment to East

Tennessee, thence to Kentucky and Maryland, and was there appointed Inspector-General on General Parke's staff, and, August 14, 1864, of the Ninth Corps. Took part in the battles of the Wilderness, Spottsylvania, North Anna, Tolopotomy Creek, Bethesda Church, Cold Harbor, first attack on Petersburg, Weldon Road, Pegram House. Resigned and honorably discharged October 18, 1864. Was promoted to be Major, September, 1862; Lieutenant-Colonel, 1863; and brevetted Colonel, 1865.

27. Lieutenant G. C. Moore.

28. Lieutenant Theodore Oliver.

29. Captain Nelson Plato.

30. Captain Fenton Rockwell.

31. Captain John Rodgers.

Entered the United States service, August 7, 1862, as Second Lieutenant in the One Hundred and Thirty-First Regiment, New York Volunteers. Took part in the Banks Expedition to Louisiana, in the two attacks on Port Hudson, and the movement into the Têche country. Was wounded slightly in the leg at the battle of Irish Bend. Was promoted, February 9, 1864, to be Captain of Company G, Eighty-Seventh Regiment, Corps d'Afrique Engineers, and was stationed at Brazos de Santiago. Had a skirmish at Clarksville. Mustered out, by consolidation, November 2, 1864.

32. Surgeon A. Orimel Shaw.

Entered the United States service, July 13, 1863, as Assistant Surgeon of the Twentieth Regiment, Maine Volunteers, and joined the regiment in the field. Was promoted to be Surgeon, November 10, 1863. Served in the Fifth Corps, Army of the Potomac, and was on duty in the following battles: Rappahannock Station, Mine Run, Wilderness, Spottsylvania, Tolopotomy Creek, North Anna, Cold Harbor, Petersburg, Weldon Railroad, Peeble's Farm, Hatcher's Run first and Hatcher's Run second. Was appointed Acting Brigade Surgeon, December 1, 1864. Resigned February 22, 1865, on account of disability from malarial disease.

33. Lieutenant A. B. Spier.

34. Captain T. B. Stout.

35. Major Ivan Tailof.

Entered the United States service in 1861, as Sergeant in the Sixty-Fifth Regiment, New York Volunteers (First United States Chasseurs), and participated in all the campaigns of that regiment, being promoted through various grades to be Captain. Mustered out, with his regiment, in 1864, and re-entered the service as Inspector-General on General Hancock's staff.

36. Lieutenant George F. Van Brunt.

37. Lieutenant GEORGE M. WELLES.

38. Captain WILLIAM WHEELER.

Killed at the battle of Culp's Farm, Virginia.

39. Lieutenant D. W. WHITE.

40. Lieutenant JAMES G. WHITE.

41. Major W. H. WILEY.

Entered the United States service, June 3, 1862, as First Lieutenant Company I, Independent Battalion, New York Volunteers. Promoted to be Captain, June 4, 1863. Served in South Carolina. At the siege of Fort Wagner he was detached as commandant of Companies E and B, and assigned to a battery of heavy artillery in the trenches. Finally commanded the first battery from the fort, consisting of Cohorn mortars, planted one hundred and fifty yards from Wagner. After the capture his command was assigned to the fort as artillerists. Mustered out, by consolidation, February 6, 1864. Was favorably mentioned by general officers. Brevetted Major "for gallant and meritorious services during the war."

42. Major THEODORE WINTHROP.

Entered the United States service in May, 1861, as Captain in the Fourteenth Regiment, United States Infantry (Regular Army), and reported as A. D. C. to General Butler. Took part in the battle of Big Bethel, June 10, 1861, and while gallantly leading a detachment of troops into action was shot dead by a North Carolina rifleman. He was buried where he fell, before the ramparts; but his body was recovered under a flag of truce, and even the enemy praised his conspicuous gallantry. His remains were brought to New York, and Colonel Lefferts ordered that, "as a tribute of respect to the memory of Major Theodore Winthrop, late of Company I, National Guard, who lost his life in a gallant charge at Bethel, Virginia, while serving on the staff of Major-General Butler, an escort is hereby detailed, consisting of the First, Sixth, Seventh, and Ninth Companies." The Ninth Company passed the following resolutions:—

"*Resolved*, That in the death of Major Winthrop the United States service has lost a valuable and energetic officer, whose place cannot quickly be filled; one who, while acting with this corps, was ever most forward to perform every duty, however arduous; one whose refinement of manner and dignity of bearing, combined with great amiability, endeared him to all his associates.

"*Resolved*, That it be entered on the minutes and indicated in orders that the members of the company will wear the usual badge of mourning while on duty, for thirty days."

The remains of the gallant officer lay, on their arrival, in a metallic coffin, in the officers' room at the Seventh Regiment armory, until escorted by his old comrades through the city for conveyance to New Haven and the family burying-place. At the time of his death Major Winthrop wore the undress uniform of the National Guard.

## TENTH COMPANY (K).

1. Captain HOFFMAN ATKINSON.

Acting Adjutant-General on General Smith's staff.

2. Lieutenant HENRY BRADSHAW.

First Lieutenant on General Seymour's staff.

3. Lieutenant MILNOR BROWN.

Entered the United States service in August, 1862, as Lieutenant of Major Willard's battalion of light artillery. The battalion was stationed at Governor's Island, and subsequently at Fort Schuyler. He aided in recruiting this organization, acting as Second Lieutenant, but did not obtain a commission until December, 1862, when, weary of the delay which he had experienced in the artillery, he applied for and obtained the commission of Second Lieutenant in the One Hundred and Twenty-Fourth Regiment, New York Volunteers (Infantry), commanded by Colonel Ellis. At the same time he accepted the position of Aide-de-Camp on the staff of Brigadier-General James Bowen, and with that officer sailed for New Orleans on the 6th January, 1863. There he remained without seeing active service until the early part of the following summer, when he returned to the North, and, just before the battle of Gettysburg, joined his regiment, then connected with the Army of the Potomac. On the 2d of July he fell while commanding his company in the midst of the battle, having received a ball in his forehead. His remains were escorted to Greenwood Cemetery by the Tenth Company, Seventh Regiment, on the 10th October, 1863.

4. Captain THOMAS B. BUNTING.

Entered the United States service in June, 1861, as Captain of a "Light Company" (known as "Bunting's Battery"), recruited by him and attached to the Ninth Regiment, New York State Militia. Subsequently the company became the Sixth New York Independent Battery. Served in the Shenandoah Valley, under Patterson and Banks, and then all along the Potomac, guarding posts, fords, &c., by piece and section, with head-quarters at Poolesville, under General Stone. In November, 1861, reported, with his battery, to General Hooker on the Lower Potomac, there being put in command of the artillery of Hooker's division, and so continuing till his resignation, January 30, 1862. On resigning, General Hooker wrote to him as follows: "Captain, I am sorry to learn that your connection with the Sixth New York Battery is severed, and that I am to lose you as its commander. Since you have been in command of your battery you have given me no cause to complain, as you have devoted your whole time in promoting its efficiency and character, and when off duty your relations with me have been no less agreeable and satisfactory. Again I regret that you are to leave the service, and my best wishes will follow you wherever you go."

5. Major John H. Coster.

Entered the United States service, September 12, 1861, as Captain of Company F, First New York Volunteers. Took part in the Peninsular campaign, in Berry's brigade of Kearny's division. Was severely wounded at Glendale, and left behind in the field hospital, on the retreat. Was captured and confined in Libby Prison. Exchanged July, 1862, and discharged from disability, arising from wounds, March 3, 1862. Appointed Colonel of New York Volunteers by Governor Seymour, and gave up appointment 1863. Commissioned by Governor Low as First Lieutenant, Seventh California Volunteers. Served as Aide-de-Camp to General McDowell, commanding Department of California, from November 10, 1865, to March 31, 1866, his regiment being then mustered out. Commissioned Captain, First Arizona Volunteers, by Governor McCormick. Served as Aide-de-Camp to General McDowell from April 1, 1866, to June 13, 1866, having then resigned. Commissioned First Lieutenant, Thirtieth United States Infantry, May 14, 1867. Appointed as Aide-de-Camp to General McDowell. Commissioned Major of Volunteers by brevet, "for gallant and meritorious services during the war." Commissioned Captain, United States Army by brevet, for gallant and meritorious services during the action of Glendale.

6. Lieutenant Jeremiah W. Costar.

Second Lieutenant, Second Regiment, New York Cavalry.

7. Colonel Charles Coster.

Colonel One Hundred and Thirty-Fourth Regiment, New York Volunteers, commanding brigade.

8. Lieutenant Whittingham Cox.

First Lieutenant, Fourth Regiment, United States Infantry.

9. Lieutenant John L. Churchill.

First Lieutenant, Third Regiment, United States Infantry.

10. Paymaster Frank Clark.

Paymaster United States Navy.

11. Major Samuel Dana.

Entered the United States service, August 5, 1861, in the Seventeenth Regiment, United States Infantry, and was engaged in garrison and recruiting service until April, 1863, when he joined his regiment at Potomac Creek, Va., and served through the battles of Chancellorsville and Gettysburg, receiving in the latter battle a wound through the leg at the knee-joint, from which he has never recovered. Was laid up several months in consequence of this wound, and was then assigned duty in recruiting and provost-marshal service. Was transferred on the 23d of September, 1866, as ranking Captain of the Twenty-Sixth Infantry. Was brevetted Major, United States Army, "for gallant and meritorious services at Gettysburg, to date from July 2, 1863."

12. Lieutenant-Colonel J. LIVINGSTON DE PEYSTER.

Captain and Brevet Lieutenant-Colonel, Ninety-Sixth Regiment, New York Volunteers. On General Crawford's staff.

13. Captain EDWARD D'HERVILLY.

Captain First Regiment, New York Volunteers. For list of campaigns and battles of his regiment, see records of Colonel Leland and General Pierson, below.

14. Lieutenant WILLIAM DIMMOCK.

Lieutenant, Eighty-Second Regiment, New York Volunteers.

15. Lieutenant DAVID DRAKE.

Entered the United States service, August, 1861, as Second Lieutenant, Seventeenth New York Volunteers. Adjutant and mustering officer of the One Hundred and Seventy-Sixth Regiment, New York Volunteers, August, 1862, and of the Thirteenth New York Heavy Artillery, May, 1863. First Sergeant, Seventeenth United States Infantry, January, 1864. Discharged June 30, 1865. Served thirty-six months, of which twenty-three were in the field, taking part in the battles at Spottsylvania, North Anna, Cold Harbor, Weldon Road, Peeble's Farm, front of Petersburg, &c.

16. Major C. J. DUBOIS.

Captain, Connecticut Volunteers. Brevet Major. Wounded at Gettysburg.

17. Captain THOMAS FREEBORN.

Entered the United States service, September 11, 1862, as Second Lieutenant, First Regiment, New York Mounted Rifles. Was promoted to be First Lieutenant, November 24, 1862, and Captain, May 11, 1863; was at Suffolk during the siege by Longstreet; was shut up in Bermuda Hundreds under Butler in 1864; was at the cavalry attack on Petersburg under Kurtz and Gillmore; was present at the various engagements on the Richmond Railroad, the attack on Drury's Bluff, and the engagements at Deep Bottom and the north bank of the James, by Hancock's command, including that at Fort Harrison, where the regiment was dismounted and held an advanced position, receiving commendation for its gallantry. Served on Weldon Railroad, and was mustered out with regiment, May 16, 1865.

18. Adjutant CHARLES A. GADSDEN.

Adjutant, Ninth New York Volunteers (Militia). Killed at Camden, North Carolina, April 19, 1862.

19. Major THEODORE K. GIBBS.

Field service as an officer, commenced December, 1861, as Lieutenant in the First United States Artillery, at Fort Pickens. Was in all the engagements at that fort till the capture of Pensacola, when he commanded Battery A. Served through the campaign at Port Hudson, in command of First Indiana Battery, and for a time commanded all the artillery. Served with his battery at Morris Island and in Florida at Ten-Mile Station, Baldwin, Saint Mary's Ford, Lake City, and Olustee, at which battle he was wounded. Served also at Drury's Bluff, and Proctor's Creek, and in command of Battery A. Fifth Artillery, at Cold Harbor, where he was severely wounded in the head, not recovering for four months. Then served at the siege of Petersburg, at Hatcher's Run, and throughout the pursuit of Lee. Was brevetted Captain, United States Army, for gallant and meritorious services at Olustee and as Major, United States Army, for gallant and meritorious services at Cold Harbor. Major Elder says: "At Folly Island I found his battery in splendid condition, the men well disciplined and drilled, and the horses and material giving evidence of the best care directed by judgment and skill."

20. Lieutenant RICHARD B. HALL.

First Lieutenant, Second Massachusetts Battery.

21. Lieutenant HERBERT H. HALL.

22. Lieutenant JOHN G. HECKSHER.

First Lieutenant, Twelfth United States Infantry.

23. Captain H. H. HOLBROOK.

Captain, Fifty-First Regiment, New York Volunteers. Senior Aid, Ninth Corps.

24. Lieutenant-Colonel EDWARD P. HOLLISTER.

Lieutenant-Colonel, Fifty-Seventh Regiment, Massachusetts Volunteers.

25. Adjutant EFFINGHAM T. HYATT.

Adjutant, Thirty-Fifth Regiment, Missouri Volunteers.

26. Lieutenant-Colonel WILLIAM A. KOBBE.

Entered the United States service, May, 1861, as private, One Hundred and Seventy-Eighth Regiment, New York Volunteers. Was promoted to be Corporal; to be Sergeant; to be Second Lieutenant; and, October 17, 1863, to be First Lieutenant. Served in Sixteenth Army Corps throughout the Mississippi Valley, took part in Meridian Expedition under Sherman, and in the battle at Clinton. In A. J. Smith's division, stormed Fort De Rassy and took conspicuous part in the battle of Pleasant Hill. Marched in A. J. Smith's corps (styled Smith's guerillas, from their rapid raids), famous for its rapid and long, forced marches, all over the West. Took part in the battles of Tuppello, and Hurricane Creek, Mississippi, and then drove Price through Missouri into Kansas by a seven-hundred-mile march, engaging him at Franklin. Aide-de-Camp on brigade staff at the battle of Nashville, thence proceeded to the siege of Mobile and assaulted Fort Blakely. Promoted in 1865 to be Captain and Assistant Adjutant-General on Davies's staff. Mustered out March 1, 1866. Brevetted, at recommendation of General Thomas, as Major and Lieutenant-Colonel; March 17, 1866, Second Lieutenant, Nineteenth Infantry; in 1867, First Lieutenant in Thirty-Seventh Infantry.

27. Captain F. W. LEGGETT.

Entered the United States service, November 3, 1862, as Captain of a company raised at his own expense for the Ninth Michigan Cavalry. Served in Kentucky in constant skirmishing with John Morgan, Everett, and other guerillas. Served in Tennessee around Knoxville, fighting General Jones, at Carter's Station and Zollicoffer. Served at Knoxville under Burnside. Was in battles of Clinch Mountain, Morristown, Bean Station, Blains Cross-Roads and other engagements, for which he received commendation of his superior officers.

28. Lieutenant-Colonel FRANCIS L. LELAND.

Entered the First New York Volunteers in 1861, as a line officer, and was promoted to be Major and to be Lieutenant-Colonel. Served with the Army of the Potomac on the Peninsula, and through the Maryland campaign. On the Peninsula, the First New York Volunteers was on picket in the rear of the retreating army through the 29th of June, and, on the 30th, being engaged at Glendale or Charles City Cross-Roads, lost, in killed and wounded (including all its color-guard, comprising four sergeants and eleven corporals), two hundred and eighty men. For other facts, see record of General Pierson, below.

29. Major THOMAS LORD, JR.

Entered the United States service, October 8, 1862, as Aide-de-Camp and Assistant Adjutant-General on the staff of General Dix, in Virginia and Department of the East, until July, 1865. Was then ordered to staff of General Hooker, as Assistant Adjutant-General. Mustered out November, 1865. Brevetted Major, United States Volunteers, for meritorious services, to date July 7, 1864.

30. Captain HENRY W. MILLER.

Captain, One Hundred and First Regiment, New York Volunteers.

31. Captain GEORGE M. MILLER.

Captain, on General Meagher's staff.

32. Major R. L. MORRIS.

Entered the United States service in July, 1861, as First Lieutenant, Eighteenth Infantry. Took the field December, 1861. Served at the siege of Corinth, the battles of Perryville, Stone River, Buzzards' Roost, Resaca, New Hope Church, Kenesaw Mountain, and at many skirmishes during Buell's and Sherman's campaigns. Served for a short time on the staffs of Generals Townsend and L. Thomas. Promoted to be Captain, December 31, 1862; brevetted Major, United States Army. Is still in the army.

33. Captain ROBERT MORRIS.

Captain, First Regiment, New York Volunteers.

34. Major NATHAN F. MOSS.

Major, Eleventh Regiment, Rhode Island Volunteers.

35. Lieutenant J. Delancey Neill.

Captain on General Duryea's staff.

36. Brigadier-General J. Frederick Pierson.

Entered the United States service, May 27, 1861, in the First Regiment, New York Volunteers. Was promoted to be Major, July 29, 1861; Lieutenant-Colonel, September 10, 1861; Colonel, October 9, 1862. Was made Brigadier-General by brevet, March 13, 1865. Fought the regiment in the following engagements: Big Bethel, Hampton Roads, Fair Oaks, Peach Orchard, Glendale or Charles City Cross-Roads, Malvern Hill, second Bull Run, Chantilly, Fredericksburg, second Fredericksburg, Chancellorsville, besides many smaller affairs. Part of the time commanded the Third Brigade, First Division, Third Corps. Was wounded at Glendale (where his horse was killed under him), and was shot through the shoulder and chest at Chancellorsville, while leading a charge. Mustered out, with his regiment, May, 1863. Again sworn in, in June, 1863, as Aid to General Hall, who was sent into Maryland with New York militia, and served three months.

37. Lieutenant-Colonel Henry L. Pierson.

Entered the United States service, September 6, 1862, as Adjutant, One Hundred and Forty-First Regiment, New York Volunteers. November 1, 1862, was appointed Captain and Assistant Adjutant-General, United States Volunteers. December 13, 1863, Lieutenant-Colonel, Second New Orleans Volunteers. Resigned July 1, 1864. Served in Department of Gulf.

38. Colonel Clifton K. Prentiss.

Entered the United States service, March 30, 1862, as private, Company I, Fifth Regiment, Maryland Volunteers. July 30, 1862, Second Lieutenant, Sixth Maryland Volunteers. August 27, 1862, Captain. December 2, 1862, Major. Served at Winchester, August 13, 1863, and at Opequan Creek; also at Locust Grove, November 27, 1863. Was in battles of Wilderness and Grant's campaign, including Cold Harbor and Petersburg. Then sent to Shenandoah Valley, serving with great distinction at Fisher's Hill, Cedar Creek, and Fort Stedman. On the 1st of April was in the grand charge at Petersburg, where he was mortally wounded, the ball striking him in the chest; but he lingered several months. Was recommended for gallantry and for a "position in the Regular Army," by Generals Wright, Ricketts, Seymour, and Keifer. Brevetted Lieutenant-Colonel and Colonel of Volunteers, April 2, 1865, for gallant and meritorious services at Petersburg.

39. Captain J. Henry Plume.

Captain, Assistant Adjutant-General, New Jersey Volunteers. Killed at Manassas, August 29, 1862.

40. Adjutant Fritz Robert.

Adjutant, Fourth Regiment, New York Cavalry.

41. Paymaster WILLIAM H. REID.

Acting Assistant Paymaster, United States Navy.

42. Captain HENRY A. SAND.

Entered the United States service, October, 1861, as Captain in the One Hundred and Third Regiment, New York Volunteers. Joined Burnside in North Carolina, and served with distinction in several expeditions. Went with Burnside to Virginia, and served for a time as Provost-Marshal at Falmouth. Was in the reserve at South Mountain. At Antietam charged in front of his regiment, and, the color-bearer falling under a terrific fire, he took the flag and planted it far ahead, calling, "Come on, boys! come on, come up to that!" he fell, his thigh shattered by a cannon-ball, in the moment of victory; and, after enduring his sufferings with great fortitude, died on the night of the 30th of October, 1862. His old comrades of Company K followed his remains to their resting-place in Greenwood.

43. Captain ROBERT S. SEABURY.

Captain on General Owen's staff. Killed at Spottsylvania, May 6, 1864.

44. Major WILLIAM H. SCHIEFFELIN.

Entered the United States service in August, 1862, as Major in the First Regiment, New York Mounted Rifles. Served at Suffolk during Longstreet's siege, and was constantly on scouting and skirmishing duty for a year in Virginia and North Carolina. Served also as volunteer Aid on General C. C. Dodge's staff.

45. Captain F. A. SCHERMERHORN.

First Lieutenant and Brevet Captain on General Griffin's staff.

46. Lieutenant DAVID J. SCOTT.

First Lieutenant, Tenth Regiment, United States Infantry, on General Corse's staff.

47. Adjutant W. H. M. SISTARE.

Adjutant, New York Volunteers.

48. Captain J. STEWART SLASSON.

Captain, on General Augur's staff.

49. Lieutenant WRIGHT STAPLES.

Entered the United States service as Lieutenant, in the Eleventh United States Infantry. Killed at the battle of the Wilderness. Against the urgent remonstrances of the surgeon and of his brother-officers, he rose from a sick-bed in the field hospital to join his comrades in action, and fell, while rallying his men in face of the enemy. His commanding officer declared that the regiment — and its record is equal to any — possessed no braver man or better officer. His comrades all testify to his personal courage, his high sense of honor, and his manly disposition. His Company, K, Seventh Regiment, passed resolutions of respect to his memory.

50. Adjutant J. BRAINERD TAYLOR.

Entered the United States service, May 24, 1861, as Adjutant, Seventeenth Regiment, New York Volunteers. Served in garrison at Washington. Resigned in spring of 1862. Enlisted in Twenty-Fifth Regiment, New York Cavalry, was made First Sergeant, and served at Washington, in Early's raid, and in Shenandoah Valley, in 1864, at Cedar Creek, Salem, Newtown, Halltown, Charlestown, and Winchester.

51. Sergeant-Major ED. F. THOMPSON.

Sergeant-Major, Eighteenth Regiment, United States Infantry.

52. Lieutenant W. W. TOMPKINS.

First Lieutenant, Third Regiment, United States Artillery.

53. Surgeon A. VAN CORTLANDT.

Surgeon, United States Army.

54. Major STEPHEN VAN RENSSELAER.

Major, Seventeenth Regiment, United States Infantry.

55. Captain E. B. VAN WINKLE.

Entered the United States service, December 27, 1862, as First Lieutenant, One Hundred and Third New York Volunteers, and was detailed as Aide-de-Camp to General Viele. Served also with regiment at Folly Island, and on staffs of Generals Gibbon, Gillmore, and Hatch. Was engaged at Bloody Bridge, Honey Hill, and Combahee. February 2, 1865, was commissioned Captain of the One Hundred and Third Regiment, United States Colored troops. Resigned July 11, 1865.

56. Brigadier-General EGBERT L. VIELE.

Entered the United States service in 1861 as Brigadier-General, United States Volunteers. Proceeded with his brigade on the Dupont Expedition, which captured Port Royal. Took prominent part in constructing the batteries which reduced Fort Pulaski. Was engaged in the occupation of Norfolk, under Wool, and was made Military Governor of the city. Resigned in 1863.

57. Adjutant W. S. WALLACE.

Adjutant, First Regiment, New York Volunteers. For list of campaigns and battles of First Regiment, New York Volunteers, see records of General Pierson and Colonel Leland, above.

58. Major O. WETMORE, JR.

Major, Thirteenth Regiment, New York Artillery.

59. Private EDWARD B. WELLES.

60. Adjutant JOHN C. WHITE.

Adjutant, First Regiment, New York Volunteers. For list of campaigns and battles of First Regiment, New York Volunteers, see records of General Pierson and Colonel Leland, above.

61. Captain JOHN B. WINSLOW.

Entered the United States service as Corporal in Battery K (Bunting's Battery), Ninth New York State Militia, afterwards the Sixth New York Independent Battery, and served with it till in front of Yorktown; was then commissioned Captain and Assistant-Quartermaster, United States Volunteers, to date from April 14, 1861, and as such received, issued, and paid for all the forage used by McClellan's army on the Peninsula. Served afterwards in the Fifth Corps, successively as Brigade or Division Quartermaster on the staffs of General Barnes, General Humphries, Captain A. P. Martin, of Third Massachusetts Battery, commanding the Artillery Brigade of the Fifth Corps, General J. J. Bartlett, and General Griffin. Was then, in December, 1864, ordered to Sherman's army, and reported successively to the staffs of Generals Easton, Howard, and Logan. Thereafter served at Louisville, Ky., and Columbus, Ga. Was honorably discharged, January 8, 1867. Was present at the battles of Ball's Bluff, Fredericksburg, Chancellorsville (in which his horse was killed), Gettysburg, and most of the battles from the Wilderness to Petersburg.

62. Engineer CHARLES WINTER.

Served in the United States navy during the war.

# NAMES AND RANK

OF THE MEMBERS OF THE

# SEVENTH REGIMENT, NATIONAL GUARD,

WHO WERE KILLED OR DIED OF DISEASE OR WOUNDS IN THE UNITED STATES SERVICE.

---

*First Company (A.)*

1. Captain George B. Le Fort, killed at the Wilderness, Va.
2. Captain Theodore Russell, killed at Fair Oaks, Va.
3. Captain J. J. Trenor, killed at Fair Oaks, Va.

*Second Company (B).*

4. Captain Henry H. Alden, killed at Ball's Bluff, Va.
5. Colonel Noah L. Farnham, died from wounds, Bull Run, Va. (1861).
6. Captain Eugene Kelty, killed at Baton Rouge, La.
7. Lieutenant Silas A. Miller, killed at Gettysburg, Pa.
8. Sergeant Gordon S. Phipps, killed at Bristow Station, Va.
9. Lieutenant D. Van Postley, killed at Donaldsonville, La.

*Third Company (C).*

10. Lieutenant-Colonel Robert McD. Hart, killed at Cedar Creek, Va.
11. Lieutenant John A. Baker, died in the United States service, Fort Federal Hill, Md.
12. Captain Frederick Hurst, died from wounds, Charleston, S. C.
13. Captain H. G. Radcliffe, killed at Murfreesboro', Tenn.
14. Captain Samuel G. Mulligan, died in the United States service, Elizabeth, N. J.
15. Lieutenant W. R. Tremaine, died in the United States service, New York.

*Fourth Company (D).*

16. Colonel Alford B. Chapman, killed at the Wilderness, Va.
17. Captain Edward A. Harrison, killed at Bull Run, Va. (1862).
18. Colonel James E. Mallow, killed at Bristow Station, Va.
19. Lieutenant James E. Moies, died in the United States service, New Orleans, La.
20. Captain Samuel H. Starr, died in the United States service, Vicksburg, Miss.

*Fifth Company (E).*

21. Lieutenant-Colonel Thomas J. Addis, died from wounds in the United States service.
22. Captain George W. Bissell, died in the United States service.
23. Sergeant Augustus Fleet, killed at Fair Oaks, Va.
24. Lieutenant William H. Kingsland, died at Andersonville, Ga.
25. Captain George W. Lewis, died from wounds, Harrison's Landing, Va.
26. Lieutenant Henry N. Timolat, killed in the Shenandoah Valley, Va.
27. Lieutenant-Colonel George Tucker, died in the United States service, New Orleans, La.

*Sixth Company (F).*

28. Captain Henry Arnold, killed at Olustee, Fla.
29. Captain Edward A. Cowdrey, mortally wounded at Five Forks, Va.
30. Captain Asher M. Ellsworth, died in the United States service, Port Hudson, La.
31. Captain Henry W. Hicks, mortally wounded at Port Hudson, La.
32. Major Lindley M. H. Miller, died in the United States service, New York, June, 1864.
33. Colonel Robert G. Shaw, killed at Fort Wagner, S. C.
34. Lieutenant Charles J. Smedberg, died in camp, near Falmouth, Va.
35. Lieutenant Frederick A. Tracy, died in the United States service, New York, June 3, 1862.
36. Lieutenant Charles F. Van Duser, killed at Gaines's Mills, Va.
37. Lieutenaut James H. Van Nostrand, died a prisoner of war at Lynchburg, Va.

*Seventh Company (G).*

38. Lieutenant A. S. Bogert, died from wounds, Fair Oaks, Va.
39. Captain Louis C. Lent, killed at Fort Wagner, S. C.
40. Captain Fitz-James O'Brien, died from wounds, Blooming Gap, Va.
41. Captain George A. Morey, died in United States service, Harrison's Landing, Va.
42. Lieutenant-Colonel George H. Stevens, killed at Gettysburg, Pa.
43. Captain William J. Williams, killed at Fair Oaks, Va.
44. Private William E. Schenck, drowned in United States service, New York Harbor.

*Eighth Company (H).*

45. Private J. Lawrence Keese, killed in United States service, Washington, D. C.
46. Captain S. A. Mellick, died in the United States service, Fortress Monroe, Va.
47. Adjutant Lewis O. Parmelee, killed at Antietam, Md.

*Ninth Company (I).*

48. Major Theodore Winthrop, killed at Great Bethel, Va.
49. Captain William Wheeler, killed at Culp's Farm, Va.
50. Sergeant Fordred Draysen, killed at Cold Harbor, Va.

*Tenth Company (K).*

51. Lieutenant Milnor Brown, killed at Gettysburg, Pa.
52. Adjutant Charles A. Gadsen, killed at Camden, N. C.
53. Captain J. Henry Plume, killed at Manassas, Va.
54. Major Clifton K. Prentiss, died from wounds, Petersburg, Va.
55. Captain Henry A. Sand, killed at Antietam, Md.
56. Captain Robert Seabury, killed at Spottsylvania, Va.
57. Captain Wright Staples, killed in the Wilderness, Va.
58. Private Edward B. Welles, died in United States service, Baltimore, Md.

---

Total number of members of the Seventh Regiment, N. G. S. N. Y., who served as officers in the Regular and Volunteer Army and Navy of the United States during the Great Rebellion: —

| | |
|---|---|
| Company A | 43 |
| " B | 80 |
| " C | 57 |
| " D | 42 |
| " E | 54 |
| " F | 97 |
| " G | 64 |
| " H | 65 |
| " I | 42 |
| " K | 62 |
| Total | 606 |

Number of members of the Seventh Regiment, N. G. S. N. Y., who were killed or died of disease or wounds in the United States service during the Great Rebellion, 58.

# APPENDIX.

## I. THE MARCH TO WASHINGTON.

*Report of Colonel Lefferts to the Adjutant-General's Office, in accordance with General Order Number* 10, *May* 13, 1861.

SIR, — In compliance with General Order Number 10, I have the honor to submit the following report: —

The regiment under my command forms part of the First Division of New York State troops, of New York City. We left New York April 19th, at six o'clock, P. M., by cars, provided by the United States Quartermaster's Department, and arrived in Philadelphia about 3.30 o'clock, A. M., 20th April, when I was informed we could not go farther by rail. At 5.20 o'clock, A. M., I telegraphed the Honorable Secretary of War.

I received no answer to the despatch, and the information given me having been confirmed, that no transportation could be had south of Havre de Grace, or certainly not south of Baltimore, I chartered the steamer Boston, at twelve o'clock, M., which was about ready to sail for New York. I had her cargo taken out, coaled, provisioned, &c., embarked my command and sailed at four o'clock, P. M., same day. Not finding any government vessel at the mouth of the Potomac, and without any information as to the state of affairs in Virginia, I deemed it prudent and best to go to Annapolis, where I could take position and assist in making, by the way of Perrysville, a military base line connecting the North and East with the capital.

We arrived at Annapolis Monday morning, April 22d, about daylight. We did not land until five o'clock, P. M., having been a part of the day endeavoring to hail the steamer, with General Butler and command on board, off the sand-bar.

We landed under protest of the Mayor and committee of citizens of the city.

We remained at Annapolis until daylight, 24th April. The cause of this detention was the want of food for the march; also ammunition, of which we had but ten rounds, and especially the want of one or two wagons to accompany the march, for sick and wounded and which could not be procured even at an exorbitant price. I marched with my command for nineteen hours, mending railroad track as we progressed, carrying rails, spikes, &c., &c., for the purpose, on one platform-car pushed by hand. We also had two other platform-cars, — one for sick and wounded, the other mounted with twelve-pound howitzer, ammunition, grape and canister. These were also pushed by hand. We arrived within one and a half miles of the Junction at daylight of the 25th, where we halted, sending two detachments forward to secure the depot and keep open the communication with the main body. From the Junction we were brought on by cars, arriving in Washington on the 25th April, twelve, noon, and were quartered in the Capitol in the Hall of Representatives, where we remained until the afternoon of the 2d May, when we pitched our tents, by directions from head-quarters, at this place, Mount Pleasant, and named our camp Camp Cameron.

By report this morning, our aggregate is eleven hundred and fifty-six men.

We have eight infantry and two flank companies.

We have rifle muskets for the eight companies and sword-bayonet rifles for the two flank companies.

We have about thirty rounds of ammunition per man. I consider the command in a good state of drill, and the evolutions are according to Hardee, excepting the manual, which is Scott's, or Infantry of the Line.

Some of my companies have been drilled as skirmishers.

The whole regiment commenced target-practice on Saturday, May 11th, at seventy-five yards, and the result of the first day's practice was fifty-five hundredths hits, target twenty-two and seventy-two inches.

The bayonet-exercise has not been taught generally. The regiment have camp equipage for one thousand men.

The organization of the Quartermaster's, Commissary, and Medical Departments are efficient.

---

## II. THE MARYLAND CAMPAIGN.

### *Colonel Lefferts's Official Report.*

New York, January 4, 1863.

General Wm. Hall, *Commanding Third Brigade.*

Sir, — In compliance with your instructions to report in reference to the last campaign of my regiment, I would state that my orders having come direct from head-quarters at Albany, and upon and subsequently to my arrival at Philadelphia having been entirely detached from your brigade and attached to the Third Army Corps of the Army of the Potomac, — Major-General French commanding, — I made my report in November last to the Adjutant-General at Albany; but hereto append a copy, which I suppose will meet your wishes.

I am, sir, your obedient servant,

Marshall Lefferts, *Colonel Commanding.*

NEW YORK, November 1, 1863.

J. T. SPRAGUE, *Adjutant-General.*

SIR, — I have the honor to report that on the morning of the 16th June I received the following telegram : —

ALBANY, June 15, 7.15 o'clock, P. M.

TO COLONEL MARSHALL LEFFERTS, *Seventh Regiment N. Y. S. N. G.*

The Governor desires to know, immediately, how soon the Seventh Regiment can be in readiness to move to Philadelphia.

Cannot the Seventh be the first regiment?

J. B. STONEHOUSE, *A. A. Adjutant-General.*

As I was absent from the city I did not receive this despatch until the next morning at ten o'clock, when I answered as follows :—

NEW YORK, June 16, 10 o'clock, A. M.

J. B. STONEHOUSE, *A. A. General, Albany.*

Have just arrived in this city, and have your telegram. I presume I can move with my regiment this evening. In order to carry full complement of men, it is necessary that I should be able to state to them definitely the time they will be required to be absent; and it will be difficult for them to remain any length of time, leaving on such short notice. Can they volunteer without being mustered into the service of the United States?

M. LEFFERTS, *Col. commanding Seventh Regiment.*

To which I received the following answer : —

ALBANY, June 16, 10.55 o'clock, A. M.

TO COLONEL M. LEFFERTS.

The Governor directs that you proceed forthwith with your regiment as full as possible to Harrisburg, Pennsylvania, and report to Major-General Couch.

They volunteer for not to exceed three (3) months' service, most likely not more than thirty (30) days will be required.

Requisition for transportation will be made upon Major Van Vleit, No. 6 State Street, and for subsistence upon Colonel A. B. Eaton, 7 State Street.

JOHN T. SPRAGUE, *Adjutant-General.*

Upon receipt of this telegram, my orders for assembly of the officers and men was promulgated, and requisition made for transportation to be in readiness, and should have taken our departure; but General Hall, who did not know of my order to move immediately, went to the armory and detained the men until the following morning, — of which I promptly advised you by telegraph.

At an early hour on the morning of the 17th June, we left the city, *via* Amboy, with a total of men, but in consequence of delays on the road did not reach Philadelphia until late in the afternoon.

At this point I was requested to report to Colonel Ruff, U. S. A., commanding at Philadelphia, who informed me that I should proceed to Baltimore, in conformity to the following order :—

HEAD-QUARTERS, PHILADELPHIA, PA., June 17, 1863.

TO COMMANDING OFFICER, *Seventh Regiment N. Y. S. M.*

SIR, — You will proceed without delay to Baltimore, Md. Report on the arrival of your regiment to Major-General Robert Schenck, U. S. V., commanding that military department. Transportation is provided for your regiment *via* the Philadelphia, Wilmington, and Baltimore Railroad.

By command of

MAJOR-GENERAL HALLECK, *General-in-Chief.*

C. S. RUFF, *Lieutenant-Colonel, Third Cavalry, U. S. A., commanding Philadelphia.*

Although I held your order to proceed to Harrisburg, I could not doubt you would desire me to go where there was the most need of my services, and at once marched my regiment forward, sending you the following notification of the change : —

PHILADELPHIA, Midnight, June 17, 1863.

J. T. SPRAGUE, *Adjutant-General.*

I have received orders from Major-General Halleck to proceed to Baltimore, and am now in the cars ready to leave for that city. I presume this will receive the sanction of the Governor.

M. LEFFERTS, *Colonel commanding Seventh Regiment.*

Upon arrival at Baltimore, I reported to Major-General Schenck, and was ordered on duty in the city for that night and following day, when we were directed to relieve the One Hundred and Twenty-Ninth Regiment N. Y. S. V., Colonel Porter, at Fort Federal Hill. We remained at that post until the 3d July, during which time we were actively engaged on outpost and other duty, being frequently reduced to one hundred and fifty men in the fort.

On the 5th July we were ordered to report to General Briggs, and proceed to Frederick, Md., in light marching order, leaving tents, knapsacks, and baggage behind. This order was received during the night, and although two of our outposts were distant nine and twelve miles respectively, they were called in, and the regiment moved from the fort at eight o'clock, A. M., in a drenching rain.

At Monocacy Junction we were detained some time, awaiting the decision of, I believe, Major-General Meade, whether the troops then on the road should go to Harper's Ferry; finally, we received orders to march to Frederick City. By order leaving two detachments for duty near that city, the regiment went into camp on the road to Harper's Ferry. We were here assigned to duty in the Third Army Corps, Army of the Potomac. On the 9th July, by the following order, I assumed command of Frederick, relieving General French, who was ordered to the command of the Third Army Corps : —

## SPECIAL ORDER No. 24.

HEAD-QUARTERS, FREDERICK CITY, July 8, 1863.

II. Colonel Lefferts, Seventh Regiment N. Y. S. M., is detailed on special duty in Frederick City. Colonel Lefferts will make such arrangements for guarding the depots, and for the police required for the city, as he may deem necessary.

III. Major H. A. Cole, Maryland Cavalry, will report to Colonel Lefferts for instruction.

IV. The battalion, Fourteenth Massachusetts Heavy Artillery, under Major Rolfe, now on duty at Monocacy Junction, will be relieved by a detachment from the Seventh Regiment, New York; after which, Major Rolfe will report to these head-quarters in person.

By order of MAJOR-GENERAL FRENCH.

Monocacy Junction was made the grand depot for the Army of the Potomac, and a large portion of the army was then moving through Frederick to South Mountain, Hagerstown, and pressing the Rebel Army to Williamsport. Our duties were active, and, I trust, faithfully performed. On July 14 I received the following order, at four o'clock, P. M. Called in the various detachments, and marched to Monocacy Junction.

HEAD-QUARTERS, FREDERICK, July 14, 1863.

COLONEL LEFFERTS, *Commanding Seventh Regiment, N. Y. S. N.*

SIR, — Major-General Halleck directs that the Seventh Regiment, N. Y. S. M., be sent to New York by railroad, to report to Major-General Wool. You will please to take immediate measures to carry out the order.

EDWARD SCHRIVER, *General Commanding.*

I had already been notified by telegraph of the disgraceful riot in New York city, and upon receipt of the foregoing order made all haste in its execution. Detachments were called in, and. notwithstanding the roads were very heavy from a three days' storm, we reached Monocacy Junction in four and a half hours from the time I received the order at Frederick City. I had sent one of my staff to the Junction to explain the necessity of the transportation being ready, but I regret to say we did not leave the Junction until 11.45 o'clock, P. M., and from this hour until daylight of the 16th July we were on the road.

Receiving from his Excellency the Governor an intimation that the rails would be taken up at or near Newark, and my regiment probably attacked, which circumstance might delay my arrival in New York City, and the pressing necessity for our presence, I succeeded, with the assistance of Colonel E. S. Sandford, in arranging with the authorities to transport the regiment *via* Amboy, landing at Canal Street. I marched up Broadway to the head-quarters of Major-General Wool, at St. Nicholas Hotel, and reported for duty. I was directed by the General to proceed to the regimental armory and remain in readiness for immediate service. At ten o'clock, A. M., I reported to his Excellency the Governor that, in consequence of the order directing us to leave all baggage behind upon our departure from Baltimore, to join the Army of the Potomac, — then moving upon Hagerstown, Md., — my men were entirely destitute of extra clothing; and had not at the time of their arrival in New York changed their underclothing for a period of eleven days, — during which time they had also been without even shelter-tents.

At three o'clock, P. M. of the same day I received the following order: —

## ORDERS.

NEW YORK, 16th July, 1863.

Colonel Lefferts, of the Seventh Regiment, New York State Militia, will proceed and take station with his regiment as follows: —

His head-quarters with one battalion at the Eighteenth Precinct, and one battalion under command of the senior field officers at the Twenty-First Precinct, — the Colonel commanding both. He is charged with suppressing all mobs and riots, and will sternly use all means he has in doing so.

His district extends from Seventh Street to Sixty-Fifth Street, and he will make such further distribution of his regiment as he may think proper. He will continue in that district until he receives further orders, and will make frequent reports to these head-quarters.

By command of

Brev. Brig.-Gen. HARVEY BROWN.

JOHN B. FROTHINGHAM, *Lieut.-Col. A. D. C. U. S. A.*

Upon its receipt I at once marched my command into the district indicated, making my head-quarters at the Police Station, Thirty-Fifth Street, two doors from the Third Avenue.

Although we were fired upon during the march, and in some cases shots returned, yet I knew of no casualties. After dark my detachments of observation were continually annoyed by shots from the houses and other places of concealment. At ten o'clock, P. M., I directed a detachment of four companies, and a battery of two pieces under command of Captain Rogers, Company I, to pass through the district under command of Lieutenant-Colonel Price, as low down as Fourteenth Street. This was promptly executed.

I herewith subjoin my report of the following morning.

HEAD-QUARTERS, TWENTY-FIRST POLICE PRECINCT, 17th July.

GENERAL HARVEY BROWN, *Police Head-quarters.*

SIR, — I have the honor to report the district under my charge as quiet after 12 o'clock, P. M. I was obliged to use harsh measures during the evening, but hope we shall have no further trouble.

In obedience to orders, a thorough patrol of the district between Thirty-

Fifth Street and Fourteenth Street, Third Avenue, and East River, was made last evening after 10 o'clock, P. M.

None of my men were injured.

MARSHALL LEFFERTS, *Colonel commanding Seventh Regiment.*

During the night of the 16th I was informed of several depositories of arms in the custody of the mob, and accordingly, on the morning of the 17th, I proceeded with my whole force to Thirty-Eighth Street and Second Avenue, and by surrounding the block, the houses were searched. This I continued from square to square, toward Fourteenth Street, aided by a platoon of police under charge of Acting Captain Blacket, who rendered efficient service.

Some two hundred and fifty arms (many of them loaded and capped) were secured, and considerable clothing, which had been stolen from the store of Messrs. Brooks.

At 2 o'clock, P. M., of this day, I received orders from head-quarters to return to the armory.

On the afternoon of the 18th I was obliged, by indisposition. to give the command to Lieutenant-Colonel Price.

From this period the regiment remained on duty without anything material to note.

I have the honor to be, sir, your obedient servant,

MARSHALL LEFFERTS, *Colonel Commanding.*

THE END.

Cambridge : Stereotyped and Printed by Welch, Bigelow, & Co.

www.ingramcontent.com/pod-product-compliance
Lightning Source LLC
LaVergne TN
LVHW010523100826
845148LV00001B/79

* 9 7 8 1 4 2 5 5 7 6 3 8 7 *